STUDIES
OF
CHILD LANGUAGE
DEVELOPMENT

edited by **Charles A. Ferguson**
Committee on Linguistics
Stanford University

and

Dan Isaac Slobin
Department of Psychology
University of California
Berkeley

Studies
of
Child Language
Development

HOLT, RINEHART AND WINSTON, INC.
New York   Chicago   San Francisco   Atlanta
Dallas   Montreal   Toronto   London   Sydney

Copyright © 1973 by Holt, Rinehart and Winston, Inc.
All rights reserved
Library of Congress Catalog Card Number: 72-85904
ISBN: 0-03-077450-0
Printed in the United States of America
   4 5 6   0 3 8   9 8 7 6 5 4 3 2

To the memory of the children of our times who have been prevented from learning to speak by bombs, bullets, gas, and napalm.

PREFACE

Adults have been interested in how children learn to speak since ancient times. In fact, the first recorded psycholinguistic experiment is reported by Herodotus, and dates back to about 600 B.C. At that time, the Egyptian king Psammetichus attempted to solve the problem of innate factors in language acquisition by having two children raised in a speechless environment. According to Herodotus, the children's first word was *bekos*, the Phrygian word for 'bread,' and accordingly the Egyptians conceded to the Phrygians in antiquity of ancestry. Modern theorists, however, lacking such unequivocal evidence, keep the ancient debate alive. It has been our intention, in preparing this collection of readings, to provide the reader with a compendium of the sorts of empirical evidence available today on the child's acquisition of language. The readings have, accordingly, been selected on the basis of the data which they provide. We have explicitly avoided papers which are primarily theoretical in content. The data available to us are suggestive—by no means as conclusive as the data of King Psammetichus. We hope that many readers will be stimulated by the reports of these findings to develop their own theoretical notions and to go on to enrich the data base for further theorizing.

The first serious investigators of child language were parents, listening to the miracle of language development in their own homes, and we present some of the classic accounts of those observant parents in this volume. Other investigators have developed controlled means of elicitation and observation, and some of their studies are also included here. A number of the studies appear here for the first time in English. An understanding of the universal and particular aspects of language acquisition requires comparative data from many languages. Investigators at Berkeley, Stanford, Harvard, and elsewhere have begun to apply modern techniques of study to children in a variety of cultures (see Slobin, 1967, and references in this volume). We are beginning to read dissertations on the acquisition of such disparate languages as Samoan (Kernan), Tzeltal (Stross), Japanese (Sanches), Arabic (Omar), Luo (Blount), Finnish (Bowerman, Argoff), Serbo-Croatian (Radulović), Hungarian (MacWhinney), German (Roeper), and, of course, English. Thus the narrow range of languages reflected in the studies printed here (12 languages from four major language families) is being considerably expanded. (Studies of the acquisition of 40 different native languages, belonging to 14 major language families, are listed on page 177; and studies of at least 13 additional languages are currently in progress.)

The reader who wishes to explore the theoretical issues underlying the study of child language is referred to a volume edited by Slobin, *The ontogenesis of grammar* (1971b). There he can find the range of heated debate on questions of nativism and empiricism in the child's development of language, in a symposium including Martin Braine, Susan Ervin-Tripp, David McNeill, David Palermo, I. M. Schlesinger, Dan I. Slobin, and Arthur Staats. Important theoretical issues are also raised in papers published in two recent conference volumes, *Cognition and the development of language* (Hayes, 1970) and *Advances in psycholinguistics* (d'Arcais and Levelt, 1970). Recent reviews of the field also serve to guide the interested reader through the theoretical thickets (see Braine, 1971b; Ervin-Tripp, forthcoming; McNeill, 1970; Menyuk, 1971). Roger Brown's *A first language* (in press) explores the early stages of language development in depth. Slobin's *Psycholinguistics* (1971c) may help orient the beginning reader to the general context of theory and research in psycholinguistics.

A full bibliography of writing on child language, from the years 1250 to 1967, can be found in Slobin's revised and augmented edition of *Leopold's bibliography of child language* (1972). Continuing coverage of the field is now available in the quarterly *Language and Language Behavior Abstracts*. We have provided editorial comments at numerous places throughout the volume, and the bibliographical references to all of these comments are gathered together in a single bibliography at the end of the book.

In editing this volume we have not tried to be completely up-to-date in theory or comprehensive in bibliography. Nor have we limited ourselves to the reprinting of only careful studies with "clean data." Rather, we hope to have selected papers which present *provocative* data, even if scanty. We have been aided by many good colleagues and friends in our selection—among them, David McNeill, Susan Ervin-Tripp, Martin Braine, and numerous others. We owe special thanks to Carolyn Wardrip for bibliographic assistance, to Caroline Stoel and Elinor Yeates, who worked long and hard on the technical aspects of the volume, and to our translators. If this volume stimulates the reader to improve upon the understanding of child language development presented here, it will have served its purpose.

Stanford University   C. A. F.
University of California, Berkeley   D. I. S.
September 1972

CONTENTS

PART TWO
GRAMMAR

STUDIES
OF
CHILD LANGUAGE
DEVELOPMENT

Part One

PHONOLOGY

In the course of acquiring full competence in his native language, the child must acquire a competence in its sound system: he must become able to hear and produce sounds in the way the fully competent users of the language hear and produce them. This phonological competence includes at least five different but interrelated matters.

1. Obviously the child must learn to use the distinctive sound differences of his language. The speaker of English, for example, is able to use the difference between *Tom* and *Tim*. If someone asks *Who's coming tonight?* and one of these names is the answer, he is able to hear in terms of the difference and make the correct identification even in the absence of any other contextual clue, and he is able to produce the difference so that other speakers can hear it correctly. The particular ranges of sound and the differences between them differ from language to language and must be acquired. Sound segments or "phonemes" like the /t/, /i/, and /m/ of *Tim* represent the opposing terms of the sound differences or "oppositions" used in a language: $Tom \neq Tim \neq Kim \neq Kip$. Every language has its own system of phonemes and oppositions for the child to acquire (see Gleason, 1961, pp. 257–270).

2. Every phoneme may be viewed as a simultaneous bundle of phonetic characteristics, "distinctive features," and it is clear that the speaker of English is able in some sense to use these features directly as such in the language. For example, some sounds are unvoiced and others voiced, differing by the absence or presence of the feature of voicing; thus /s/ and /f/ are [−vce] and /z/ and /v/ are [+vce], and the speaker of English makes direct use of this in pronouncing *house*, the noun, with /s/ but *house*, the verb, with /z/, and similarly *grief*:

1

grieve and all the other instances where English makes a noun into a verb by adding the feature of voicing. Some distinctive features like the [±vce] of English occur in other languages in quite similar forms, and new attempts are being made to arrive at a universal framework of phonetic features (for example, see Chomsky and Halle, 1968, pp. 293–329), but every language has its own arrangements and its own uses of distinctive features for the child to acquire (see Jakobson and Halle, 1956, pp. 20–36).

3. Strings of phonemes are pronounced and heard in different patterns of prominence; that is, some sequences are louder than others or change in pitch or differ in other special ways, and the speaker of a language is able to use this "prosodic" or "accentual" machinery in the way his language requires. In English, syllables are pronounced with different degrees of stress, and this variation is important in the grammar of the language; thus the speaker of English in using words with the suffix *-tion* always produces and expects to hear the highest stress on the syllable immediately before the *-tion*, regardless of where the highest stress is on the simple word from which the suffixed one is derived (for example, prevént : prevéntion, demólish : demolítion, élevate : elevátion). Every language has its own prosodic system for the child to acquire. (See Kingdon, 1958, for English; Hockett, 1955, pp. 65–72, attempted a survey of the possibilities in general.)

4. Some strings of phonemes are more "pronounceable" than others in a language; that is, some combinations of sounds are more likely to occur in actual words in the language and are easier for the speakers to hear and reproduce in newly coined words or foreign words. In English, consonant combinations like /st/ or /pl/ are more pronounceable at the beginning of words than one like /ft/ or /ml/. There are many English words like *stack*, *stain*, *sty* or *plaque*, *plain*, *ply*, but only very rare or marginal words would begin with /ft/ or /ml/. The inventor of a name for a new product or a new technical concept might possibly invent a word like *stike* or *plang* but hardly *ftack* or *mlish*. Some preferences are widespread among languages, some even universal, but every language has its own patterns of restrictions on pronounceability which the child must acquire (see Scholes, 1966).

5. Sentences may be said with different intonations in such a way that they have different meaning even though all the words are the same, and every sentence actually spoken has some kind of contour of the fundamental pitch and related phenomena as part of its total auditory content. In English a sentence like *What does he want?* may be said with a number of different intonation contours, and an adult speaker can readily distinguish, for example, a contour which simply asks for the information from one which means *Did you ask "What does he want?"*, the latter having a characteristic high pitch and final rise. Some features of intonation, voice quality, and the like, may be universal, and others may be so different in function from the sentence itself as to constitute a more or less autonomous channel of communication. But every language has its own system of sentence contours which the child has to

acquire. Lieberman (1967, pp. 171–195) reviews linguistic studies of intonation, chiefly of English. Two recent books offer full technical descriptions of intonation and related phenomena: Crystal, 1969, and Lehiste, 1970.

At the very least, investigations of the child's phonological competence and theories accounting for it must deal with the child's ability to perceive and discriminate among the sounds and sound differences of these five kinds; in addition, they must deal with the child's ability to produce the sounds correctly and appropriately both in imitation of someone else's utterances and in the spontaneous production of natural communication. The three dimensions of perception, imitation, and spontaneous production *are probably not related* in a simple, direct way, and presumably the theories ultimately should account for the relations among them.

So far, the major attempt at a theory of phonological development in the child is that presented in Jakobson's *Child language, aphasia and phonological universals* (usually referred to as *Kindersprache*, the first word of the title of the original work published in German in 1941) and in a somewhat different version in Jakobson and Halle (1956). Jakobson's theory makes essentially three claims: (1) the sound system of a child has "structure" in the same senses that adult phonology has structure (for example, similar entities, similar patterns of variation and distribution) and in addition shows regular patterns of substitution for adult phonemes/features; (2) the development of phonology in the child can best be described in terms of the successive acquisition of increasingly differentiated oppositions of distinctive features; and (3) there is a universal pattern of development which is reflected also in the distribution of feature oppositions among the world's languages and in the pattern of dissolution of phonology in aphasic patients. Other explicit theorizing about the processes of phonological development is in terms of the selective reinforcement of sounds by the behavior of the surrounding users of the language (Mowrer, 1960, chapter 3) and in terms of universal physical/physiological constraints on human perception of speech sounds (Olmsted, 1966). The most recent approaches to phonological analysis typified by Chomsky and Halle (1968), Harms (1968), and Kiparsky (1968) raise new questions for child language development which are only beginning to be explored (see Chomsky and Halle, 1968, pp. 50, 296–297, 330–331).

The phonological studies included in this volume range from anecdotal accounts to reports of laboratory experiments, but most are based on careful observation of a single child under natural conditions, and most use methods of linguistic analysis that focus on one or more of the aspects of phonological competence identified above.

—C.A.F.

EARLY STAGES

Playing with Distinctive Features in the Babbling of Infants

—— *Jeffrey S. Gruber*

Gruber's report is based on the babbling of one child on one day; it makes no attempt at a full description or analysis and suggests no generalization to other children's behavior. Its value lies in the attempt to find regularities in the subject's babbling behavior which can be expressed in formal rules employing distinctive features. The rule structure Gruber presents may not be completely convincing, but it is certainly suggestive of a line of research which might be valuable. Other studies, such as Menyuk's "The role of distinctive features in children's acquisition of phonology" (reprinted in this volume), Anisfeld and Gordon (1968), and Messer (1967), are concerned with distinctive features in language acquisition, but there have been no further published studies of distinctive features in babbling.   —C.A.F.

In this report I shall describe the data obtained all on one day, consisting of the utterances of an infant, aged 403 days.[1] We shall discuss the utterances in an attempt to discover what if any patterns exist among them. It will be seen that significant patterns do exist when distinctive features are referred to,[2] and further theoretical implications of these patterns will be touched upon.

The following sequences of more than one syllable were found in the babbling of Mackie at the age of 403 days. This corresponds to an advanced stage of babbling. Approximately six weeks later the babbling has greatly

From *Quarterly Progress Report No. 81* (1966, pp. 181–186) of the Research Laboratory of Electronics, Massachusetts Institute of Technology. Reprinted with the permission of the author and the Research Laboratory of Electronics, Massachusetts Institute of Technology.
[1] Material for this study comes from the longitudinal investigations headed by Margaret Bullowa, M.D., entitled "Development from Vocal to Verbal Behavior in Children," NIH Grant MH 04300–01–04.
[2] These are the distinctive features postulated in R. Jakobson, M. Halle, and C. G. M. Fant, "Preliminaries to Speech Analysis," Technical Report No. 13, Acoustics Laboratory, M. I. T., 1952.

4

decreased, and the child makes much simpler and much less frequent sequences of sound. It appears that the child at this later stage is speaking language, as opposed to babbling which is intentional, but not meant to be intelligible, sequences of sound. Utterances at this later stage, if and when produced, for the most part correspond to morphemes of English.

The largest number of sequences of more than one syllable consisted of any number of syllables beginning with a nonGrave segment, followed by any number of syllables beginning with a Grave segment. Here, a syllable is defined rather loosely, because of possible great complexity in the initial nonVocalic segment, and because of the difficulty in ascertaining the presence of a vowel between nonVocalic segments at times. In general, however, a syllable is a sequence consisting of a nonVocalic segment followed by a Vocalic segment, possibly augmented by one or more glides. When a particular segment is colored, either at the onset or the offset, by the features of some other type of segment, the symbol indicating the coloring segment is raised from the line.

Such sequences of nonGrave syllables followed by Grave ones are exhaustively listed below:

1.   NONGRAVE   GRAVE

ye	dew	tæ	gə	wᵛə				
	dey	dæ	gə	wᵛə				
		dæ	gi	vʷəy				
		yi	p					
		ye	mp					
		ye	ge	vʷi				
	yeh	yo	wey					
		də	we	gi	we	gi	we	gi
		yə	gə	m:				
ye	ye	gi	vʷih					
		də	we	gi	gi	wi	wi	ge
de	yə	wa						
	nə	mᵛ						
dəʳ	tə	m	ᵛgəʳ					

Next we see that there were sequences consisting only of nonGrave syllables, which are listed below:

2.   NONGRAVE

yəˡ	do	dəh	
	do:	yo:	
əʳ	dey	day	ti
də	do		

In addition there are sequences of syllables beginning with only Grave segments:

3.   GRAVE

	ge	vʷiy	
	ge	vʷi	
	ge	v	
m	ngi	vʷeh	
m	ngo		
	bə	wˠə	
m	ba	wə	
way	be	b	
way	w:		
mə	mə	wə	

No sequences of syllables beginning with a Grave segment followed by a sequence of syllables beginning with a nonGrave segment occur. (There are two exceptional cases: *e wi na* and *go we dæ*. These two cases are exceptional in that they have the segments /n/ and /d/, the voiced fricative, both of which occur very seldom in sequence. After our analysis we shall be able to handle these two cases.)

Consequently we see that we have the generality up to this point that every babbling sequence consists in any number of nonGrave syllables followed by any number of Grave syllables, including zero as a possible number of syllables. We also get sequences of all sorts consisting of only one syllable, which will also follow from the generalization above.

We have also on this day sequences consisting of syllables beginning with /h/, followed by any number of syllables beginning with a nonGrave segment, as below:

4.   /h/   NONGRAVE

hə		yə	
hə		yə	
heʷ	hə	yo	
he		dyo	dyəy
he		yˠaʷ	

There is a couple of sequences consisting of an /h/ followed by a non-Grave syllable, followed by a Grave syllable:

5.   /h/   NONGRAVE   GRAVE

ha	ye	gə
hə	y:	w:

Although there were no sequences consisting of /h/ followed by a Grave syllable, we shall have evidence to include that as a possibility later. Consequently we can elaborate our generalization to say that a babbling sequence consists of any number of /h/-initial syllables, followed by any number of non-Grave-initial syllables, followed by any number of Grave-initial syllables. In other words, we have a set of sequences corresponding to a finite-state language, expressed by the formula:

f-1.   [h]* [nonGrave]* [Grave]*

There were only four sequences in the data which appeared to be real exceptions to f-1. These are

6. Exceptions

wə	heh
næ	hæ
da:	ho:
ga	he fˡʷo

Apparent exceptions only, however, are the very long sequences:

7. Apparent Exceptions

hey	də	bˠə	də	bˠə			
hə		bʷi	de	wi		de	wə
h	wi	bʷe	də	bi		de	bi	we
ha	yə	go	ha	yə	wə		
	yə	vʷə	yə	vʷə		yə	
	de	wa	də	gɔ	ge		

It seems that these sequences may be treated as repetitions of the formula f-1. In favor of this is the length of these sequences and some very apparent iterative characteristics about them.

If we allow f-1 to be repeated, however, and since single syllables do occur, we in fact allow anything at all to occur. What will save this from being vacuous would be some evidence, such as intonation or pause, which would necessitate the postulation of a sequence boundary. This will be investigated. Even without this, however, we could predict that the utterances that follow the rule given above are far more numerous than those that do not.

Note in the repetitions of 7, we have two instances of an /h/ followed by a Grave sequence, so that we are corroborated in including this possibility in the generalization above.

If rule f-1 represents a reality of the infant's babbling, it is reasonable to ask what in fact the infant is doing on a more explanatory level. What we can say is that the initial segments of syllables increase in markedness from beginning to end in the sequence. A segment unmarked (u) for some feature is said to take the simplest or least effort value for that feature; a segment marked (m) for some feature takes the more complex value for that feature. Which is the marked and which is the unmarked value of a given feature is a question of universal grammar.

It has been postulated that /h/ represents a segment marked only for the feature Vocalic, being unmarked in all others. /y/ is marked for Sonorant and /d/ is marked for Consonantal, both being marked for Vocalic. Hence /y/ and /d/ have two marks, Vocalic and Consonantal or Sonorant. In a parallel fashion, /w/, /g/, and /b/ have three marks, differing from the others in being marked for the feature Grave. Thus /h/ is less marked than /y/ or /d/; and /y/ or /d/ is less marked than any of /w/, /g/, or /b/.[3]

The universal rules for interpreting markedness (m's and u's) in terms of feature values (+'s and −'s) for the features indicated here are:

r-1.   [m Vocalic] → [− Vocalic]
            [u Vocalic] → [+ Vocalic]

            [m Sonorant] → [+ Sonorant]
            [u Sonorant] → [− Sonorant]

            [m Consonantal] → [+ Consonantal]
            [u Consonantal] → [− Consonantal]

            [m Grave] → [+ Grave]
            [u Grave] → [− Grave]

In particular, we have the following:

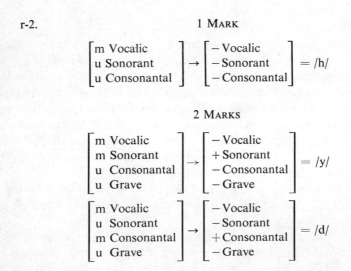

r-2.   1 MARK

$$\begin{bmatrix} \text{m Vocalic} \\ \text{u Sonorant} \\ \text{u Consonantal} \end{bmatrix} \rightarrow \begin{bmatrix} -\text{Vocalic} \\ -\text{Sonorant} \\ -\text{Consonantal} \end{bmatrix} = \text{/h/}$$

2 MARKS

$$\begin{bmatrix} \text{m Vocalic} \\ \text{m Sonorant} \\ \text{u Consonantal} \\ \text{u Grave} \end{bmatrix} \rightarrow \begin{bmatrix} -\text{Vocalic} \\ +\text{Sonorant} \\ -\text{Consonantal} \\ -\text{Grave} \end{bmatrix} = \text{/y/}$$

$$\begin{bmatrix} \text{m Vocalic} \\ \text{u Sonorant} \\ \text{m Consonantal} \\ \text{u Grave} \end{bmatrix} \rightarrow \begin{bmatrix} -\text{Vocalic} \\ -\text{Sonorant} \\ +\text{Consonantal} \\ -\text{Grave} \end{bmatrix} = \text{/d/}$$

[3] I am indebted to Richard Carter for having pointed this out to me. The revitalization and reinterpretation of the Prague School notion of markedness is due to Morris Halle.

3 Marks

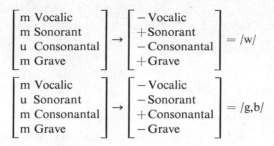

$$\begin{bmatrix} \text{m Vocalic} \\ \text{m Sonorant} \\ \text{u Consonantal} \\ \text{m Grave} \end{bmatrix} \rightarrow \begin{bmatrix} -\text{Vocalic} \\ +\text{Sonorant} \\ -\text{Consonantal} \\ +\text{Grave} \end{bmatrix} = /w/$$

$$\begin{bmatrix} \text{m Vocalic} \\ \text{u Sonorant} \\ \text{m Consonantal} \\ \text{m Grave} \end{bmatrix} \rightarrow \begin{bmatrix} -\text{Vocalic} \\ -\text{Sonorant} \\ +\text{Consonantal} \\ -\text{Grave} \end{bmatrix} = /g,b/$$

Intuitively, then, what this seems to mean is that the child begins an utterance with a certain degree of markedness, which he may increase in subsequent syllables of the sequence. The child may be thought of as playing a game, which consists of adding more commands to the syllable, producing more complex initial segments, for syllables toward the end of the sequence.

Several of the exceptions, such as *e wi na* and *go we dæ*, can now be seen not to be exceptions at all, since nasality, when it appears, must be marked, as must continuancy. Thus markedness still increases from left to right.

The Development from Sound to Phoneme in Child Language

—— *Walburga von Raffler Engel*

This very condensed summary of Professor Engel's paper provides no information on the procedures of obtaining the data, it is unclear at several important points, and it seems to generalize widely on very limited evidence. It is, however, of value because it offers reliable documentation for at least one case where a child had contrasting intonation contours before he had productive control of any vocalic or consonantal contrasts. A somewhat similar case is reported in Leopold's *Speech development* (1939, Vol. 1, p. 82): Hildegard had an interjection ʔə (later replaced by *da*) which had a deictic, attention-calling meaning when said in an abrupt fashion with high pitch, but had a requesting or desiderative meaning ('give me' or 'I want') when said with a rising, questionlike intonation. Engel regards it as a general phenomenon that a child starts with a *suono base* of very general meaning (for example, *m, ə, bu*), used with contrasting intonation contours; see Engel, *Il prelinguaggio infantile* (1964, ch. 9, pp. 79–96) for additional references. Lewis (1951) and Lieberman (1967, pp. 44–47) have further discussion. C.A.F.

Die Entwicklung vom Laut zum Phonem in der Kindersprache. In E. Zwirner and W. Bethge (eds.), *Proceedings of the Fifth International Congress of Phonetic Sciences, Munster 1964*. Basel/New York: Karger, 1965, pp. 482–485. Translated from German by Catherine Houghton and edited by Charles A. Ferguson. Reprinted with the permission of the author and S. Karger AG (Basel, Switzerland).

Observations of various small children and then a specific study of my son, who is now three years and two months old, with almost daily written annotations since his first cry, yield data that substantiate well-known facts and bring to light new things, particularly the importance of humming sounds [*Summlaute*].

Screaming and crying are probably expression, but they are not language. They continue even after language is completely perfect. Nor are gurgling sounds precursors of language. They are continued by sounds of pleasure.

Babbling sounds by contrast seem to be true attempts at language. They disappear when language has been mastered and reappear only with speech difficulties such as stuttering or the acquisition of a foreign language. Furthermore, babbling sounds occur at a time when the child already understands some spoken things. Active speech begins very quickly after passive speech, but the latter takes significantly longer to develop.

Even though the first *m* or *b* sound after the period of humming probably still does not stand for a precise word, it nevertheless seems to me to be a conscious attempt at linguistic expression or at least at imitation of language. The first word-like sound formation of my small son was *am*, when he was hungry. Just one week later, at nine months, he said his first real word *pappa*, the Italian word for food (Italian is my child's first language). He sat in a corner of his playpen and said the word over, more and more clearly. Then he drew himself up, beaming, and said *la páppa*, the same word with an article, the way he usually heard it from us. When he was babbling he had had the same concentrated facial expression of trying out a word, and the same crafty smile, as he had when I approached him at these moments. When one speaks to a four-month-old baby, one gets to hear babbling, too, as an answer.

I consider the first words of a child to be merely an imitation of what is heard; but two months after my son had uttered his first word I was already able to ascertain how he observed my lip movements. Shortly thereafter he combined auditory and visual attentiveness and tried with conscious effort to pronounce his "words" more correctly. So first we have sound without meaning and then the full word. The word is at first determined purely by ear, and then by the eye as well (lip imitation), and then it depends simultaneously on the ear and the eye.

With the first word, or the second, depending on whether semantic considerations are included or excluded in the definition of the phoneme, we are already in the field of phonemics, in fact, the total field of phonemics, segmental as well as suprasegmental, which were certainly not perceived as different by my son. After the youngster had already been able to say Mama (*mámà*) for a while, he came out with *mamá*, to call for his father. Not until afterwards did he gradually correct the *m* until it became *p*. Here, the first phonetophonemic difference was not in the articulation but in the intonation. *The melodic factors, then, appeared before the articulatory ones.* When I had noted this, I recalled that every word uttered up to that point had had its own melodic character. The name of our dog, Achilles, had come out as a trisyllabic *a*.

Then I thought back to the time before the onset of babbling sounds. In the period between gurgling and babbling sounds, one can observe cooing, a kind of labial humming. This humming, which has nothing to do with singing, very quickly assumed sentence-like intonation. In my opinion, up to now not enough importance has been attributed to these humming sounds. (I might note briefly here that although my son obviously possesses an excellent feeling for language, he is unfortunately abundantly unmusical.) The youngster—like all children his age—carried on, humming, whole monologues with questions and answers:

Not long after this humming period my son used the nasal bilabial as a definite, conscious means of expression. He pointed with his finger at things that he wanted to show me and said *m*; when he asked if he could have them, the pitch rose:

After nursing, when the lip nerves are able to articulate phonetically and to form the bilabial *m* or *b* (as vocalized consonant *m*, *b*, or together with shwa, *əm*, and so on, or fricativized as *bw*, and so on), *sentence intonation* appears as the first phenomenon of language; thereafter *word intonation*. Then comes the variable *sound*, which is worked over into the word. The word has at the same time its own accent. Pitch and stress, which are to be sure very intertwined, appear simultaneously. Throughout all its stages of development, the difficult word *Papà* always had the stress on the last syllable, which also always had the right pitch. At eleven months, for example, it was *da:dá*. The words *Papà* and *pappa* were never confused. The word *pappa* was pronounced perfectly at nine months, while the youngster was thirteen months old before he could say *Papà* correctly. In my opinion, then, the segmental phoneme does not appear until after the suprasegmental phoneme.

In a more advanced speech period, then, we gradually have a larger and larger inventory of segmental phonemes, possibly without allophones at first. We are still dealing with a phonemics *sui generis*. The child has command over only a few sounds, and these may be phonetically wrong; but his sounds are organized in such a way as to be semantically distinct from one another. This statement, by the way, shows again that one cannot really ignore meaning after all, when one studies linguistic problems.

To sum up, the stages of development are as follows: the first, still non-expressive, purely phonetic attempt at language is the bilabial. Next comes sentence intonation, the meaning of which is difficult to make out. This is followed by the melodic-phonemic bilabial (saying *m* and pointing to things) and then the melodic-articulatory word, or "sentence word."

As at the beginning of comprehension ability, so also in speech the way seems to lead from the large and general to the specific: the imitation of the word occurs before that of the sound.

DEVELOPMENT OF THE PHONEMIC SYSTEM

CHINESE •

The Cantian Idiolect: An Analysis of the
Chinese Spoken by a Twenty-eight-month-old Child

—— *Yuen Ren Chao*

Many investigators are either fully convinced or at least heavily influenced by Jakobson's claim (1968) that the phonology of a child at any given time has a phonemic structure of its own, but most structural studies of child phonology are diachronic, covering a considerable period of time. Chao's article of 1951 is a brilliant exception, in which he provides a full structural analysis of the child's phonology during a particular one-month period, with only incidental references to preceding or following stages.

Chao bases his analysis of Chinese phonology on the traditional Chinese unit, the spoken syllable corresponding to a single Chinese character. Although in the modern spoken language two or three syllables may be combined into a single unit with a consistent meaning, Chinese speakers still feel that the character-syllable is the Chinese equivalent of the word in other languages.

The syllable has a maximum of three parts: an initial consonant, a nuclear vowel, and a final glide; the syllable as a whole also carries a distinctive tone. The initial consonant may be any one of eighteen phonemes or may be absent. The vowel may be one of three phonemes: a high vowel, sometimes omitted in transcription, which ranges in sound all the way from /i/ to /u/ depending on the preceding consonant; a midvowel transcribed /e/ and /o/ which also varies in pronunciation; and a low vowel /a/. The syllable may end here or the nuclear vowel may be followed by one of five final phonemes: a nasal (*n* or *ng*), a vowel glide (*i* or *u*), or a kind of *r*. The tone of a syllable may be one of four: first tone which is high and level(-), second tone which is midrising to high ('), third tone which is midlow, dipping and rising to midhigh (ˇ), and fourth tone which is high falling to low (`). The third tone varies in value depending on the following tone, and some syllables are without tone. The whole system, greatly oversimplified in this summary, is variously analyzed by linguists (see Hartman, 1944; Hockett, 1947; Chao, 1948; Martin, 1958; and Cheng, 1968 for details and references).

The transcription used here by Chao is based on National Romanization,

From W. J. Fischel (ed.), *Semitic and Oriental Studies . . . to William Popper*. Berkeley: University of California Press, 1951, pp. 27–44. Reprinted with the permission of the author and the Regents of the University of California.

which among its other conventions marks the tones by ingenious use of letters: doubling certain consonants and vowels, insertion of *h*, *r*, and *q*, and changing *i* and *u* to *y* and *w*. National Romanization is said to be easy for Chinese speakers to learn to use, but in an article of this kind it seems to complicate the presentation, especially for readers more interested in child language acquisition than in orthographies for Chinese. The system is summarized by Chao in footnote 3.   —C.A.F.

With all the increase of interest and the amount of work done in the descriptive treatment of the Chinese language and languages in China, little attention has yet been given to the language of the Chinese-speaking child. Dr. H. C. Chen (Ch'ên Ho-ch'in), the well-known child psychologist of Shanghai, has made some study of children's speech,[1] and the present writer has recorded the phonologies of three nonstandard dialects, of which two were children's speech.[2] In the present study an attempt will be made to give a fairly all-round description of the speech of a Mandarin-speaking child, to include the phonology, grammar, and vocabulary, as well as to give indications, where it is relevant, of the situations in which the words or sentences were actually used.

The subject of this study is one of the writer's grandchildren, whose name, for present purposes, shall be "Canta," and whose form of idiolect at this recording may be called "Cantian 49," or "Cantian" for short.

Although born and reared in America, Canta has had an almost entirely Chinese language environment. More than half the people around her are speakers of Standard Mandarin, and the others are also speakers of Mandarin of sorts. Canta's speech is therefore also a form of Mandarin—or Mandarin in the making. Some contact with English, as well as borrowings from English in the Chinese she hears, has resulted in a few English words in her speech, but she adapts them into her own phonological system much more than do the bilingual speakers around her.

Since a child's language changes more rapidly than that of an adult, it might seem possible here to make a diachronic study in the history of one person's language. For example, an early record of about one year ago shows that there was only one general fricative, no semivowel in any position, and one instead of two rising tones, so that [hε] high-rising was either *shye* 'shoe' or *shoei* 'water,' which are now distinguished in her speech. Unfortunately the early records were rather incomplete. Pressure of work and a period of absence, during a time when there were rapid changes in Canta's speech, resulted in a

[1] *Êrh-t'ung hsin-li chih yen-chiu* [*Studies in Child Psychology*] (Shanghai, 1947), Vol. II, pp. 203–281. The point of view here is, however, more psychological than linguistic.
[2] "Three Examples of the Dialectal Nature of Abnormal Pronunciation" (in Chinese, with English summary), *Bulletin, National Research Institute of History and Philology, Academia Sinica*, V (1935), 241–253.

very unsatisfactory state of the early records. The present study is therefore only a synchronic one over a "specious present" of about one month, and earlier materials are mentioned only for incidental comparison.

I. PHONOLOGY

For typographical convenience and for easy reference to the grammatical and lexical sections, National Romanization[3] will be used for citing forms in the environmental language, and an adapted form of the system will be used for the subject's language. Only a minimum of phonetic symbols (in square brackets) will be used, and for finer phonetic details more use will be made of descriptions than of the "narrow" forms of symbols.

A familiar feature of children's language is underarticulation and consequent reduction of many distinctions. In interpreting the values of the sounds described below, it should be borne in mind that sounds represented by the same symbol, say *t*, are considerably less clearly and less strongly articulated in the subject's speech than in the environmental adult language.

In our citations of Cantian forms, a semiphonemic notation will be used, which will give some idea of the actual allophones under one phoneme if they differ considerably in value or, as with respect to the mid vowels, if the phonemic instability is too great to permit a synchronic snapshot to be in sharp focus.

The initial consonants of Cantian are as shown in the accompanying tabulation.

	Unaspirated Voiceless Plosives	Aspirated Voiceless Plosives	Nasals	Fricatives
Labials	*b*	*p*	*m*	*f*
Dentals or palatals	*d*	*t*	*n*	*s*
Velars or glottals	*g*	*k*		*h*

The initial *b* is practically the same in value and distribution (i.e., occurrence in words learned from adult language) as in Standard Mandarin ("S.M."),

[3] An easily accessible exposition of the system can be found in the author's *Mandarin Primer* (1948; Cambridge, Mass.), esp. chap. ii. The system of tonal spelling, from a reader's point of view, can be summarized as follows: (4) Syllables ending in -*h*, -*ay*, -*ey*, -*w*, -*nn*, -*nq* (pronounced with -*ng*), -*ll* (pron. with vocalic *r*) are in 4th Tone (falling). (3) Syllables with doubled vowels or with the combinations *ae*, *ao*, *oe*, *ea*, *oa*, *eo* are in 3d Tone (low-dipping). (2) Syllables not in 3d or 4th Tone are in 2d Tone (high-rising) (*a*) if they have initial or medial *y* or *w*, or (*b*) if they have -*r* after a vowel, or (*c*) if they have *m*-, *n*-, *l*-, *r*- but not *mh*-, *nh*-, *lh*-, *rh*-. (1) Syllables not in 4th, 3d, 2d Tones are in 1st Tone (high-level). Atonic or neutral tone syllables are marked by a dot placed *before* the syllable.

with the usual voicing in unstressed intervocalic position, as *bah.ba* ['pàba]:[4] *bah.ba* 'papa.' Initials *p* and *m* have also the same values and similar distribution as in S.M., as *pah* : *pah* 'afraid'; *mae* : *mae* 'buy.'

The phoneme /f/ varies between a labiodental value [f] and a bilabial value [φ], a difference which will be recorded in our citations. The variation is partly conditioned in that the bilabial value is more likely to go with *u* and the other value with other sounds, but there is a slight amount of free variation. In distribution the phoneme occurs in words derived from S.M. *sh* (i.e., [ʂ]), *h*, as well as from *f*, as *φu* : *shu* 'book'; *φua* : *hual* 'flower'; *faandji* : *farng.tzy* 'house.''

The unaspirated voiceless initial /d/ (apart from becoming voiced under the same conditions as *b*) has three values, a dental value *d* [t], a palatal plosive [t'] (not simply dental palatalized),[5] and a palatal affricate [tś], the last two to be romanized as *dj* in our citations. These three values are either phonetically conditioned or in free variation and are allophones of the same phoneme /d/. The dental value occurs after back vowels, the two palatal values (plosive and affricate) in free variation with each other occurring after other vowels, with more use of the affricate when the entire final is *i*. As several S.M. initials are rendered by this one phoneme, its allophones cut across the S.M. initials in a somewhat complicated fashion. The following examples will exhibit the type of relations referred to.

	/d/	Dental, *d* [t]	Palatal, *dj* [t']	[tś]
		CANTIAN		
S.M. dental plosive	*d*[t]	*dah* [ta]: *dah* 'big'	*djiaw* [t'iau]: *diaw* 'dropped'	*djih* [tśi] or [ti]: *dih* 'floor'
S.M. dental affricate	*tz*[ts]	*doh* [tə]: *tzuoh* 'sit'		*djih* [tśi] or [t'i]: *tzyh* 'writing'
S.M. retroflex affricate	*jᵣ*[tʂ]	*da* [ta]: *ja* 'prick'		
S.M. palatal affricate	*jᵢ*[tś]		*djiaw* [t'iau]: *jiaw* 'shout'	*dji* [tśi] or [t'i]: *ji* 'chicken'

---

[4] When there is a colon between cited forms, the form or forms before the colon are in Cantian and those after it are in S.M.

[5] Front palatal plosives are so rare in languages that there are no symbols for them in IPA. I only know of their existence in Tibetan (Lhasa dialect), in some of the dialects of Shantung, such as of Lintzŭ, and in Karlgren's reconstruction of Ancient Chinese. On the other hand, they are fairly common in children's speech. Why? There is perhaps a physiological reason for this. As soon as the tongue takes a *front* palatal position, the area of contact is so large that it would be very difficult to release the closure cleanly enough to avoid friction, and any friction there would result in an affricative sound, as when French palatalized dental *Tiens, tiens!* [tjɛ̃ tjɛ̃] becomes palatal affricative [tśɛ̃ tśɛ̃]. On the other hand, since a child's tongue is smaller than an adult's (even though its jawbones, as Jespersen showed, are not much smaller), there is less chance that friction will develop, and during the period when dentals are not clearly formed, palatal plosives are likely to result.

The pure dentals were attained only recently. Before that, all front stops had been palatal, so that [hi't'ău] served both for S.M. *shii-jeau* 'wash the feet' and *shii-tzao* 'take a bath.'

The initial /t/ behaves quite similarly to /d/. Examples are, dentals in *tan* [t'an] : *tang* 'soup'; *ta.ta* : *tsa.tsa* 'wipe a little'; *tar* : *char* 'tea'; palatal plosives in *tjyɛn* : *tyan* 'sweet' or *chyan* 'money'; *daatjih.ie* : *daatih.le* 'sneeze'; *tjihte* : *chihche* 'automobile.' A noticeable difference in the treatment of the aspirated palatal initial is the greater use of the affricative value, due no doubt to the greater likelihood of friction when there is aspiration. Thus, not only words with *i* as complete final have affricative initials, as when *dj* occurs, but also words with *i* as medial. In other words, not only the syllable *tjih*, but also words like *tjyɛn* cited above, often begin with [tś'] as well as with [t''].

The nasal initial /n/ has a palatal value and will be written *ń* in the citations as a reminder orthography. It has not yet acquired a completely dental articulation before nonpalatal sounds, as *d* and *t* have done. Thus, *ńa* : *na* 'take'; *ńaw* : *naw* 'to be fussy' or *niaw* 'urine.'

At the end of a syllable /n/ has also a palatal value, *ń*, before a pause but assimilates to the articulation of the following sound, *m* before *p*, *ng* before *k*, etc. We shall write final *n* without modification in our orthography except that a few occurrences of final *m* are so written when it is part of the point under discussion. Final *n* is usually quite weak, even weaker than in S.M.; in fact, it sometimes amounts to no more than a final nasalization of the preceding vowel.

The phoneme /s/, orthographically *ś*, is very weakly articulated, with wide passage and little friction. Consequently the point of articulation is less sharply defined, but distributed over a palato-alveolar region similar to the *esh* sounds in languages, like English, in which palatal and retroflex fricatives are not distinguished. Examples are: *śaa.iė* : *saa.le* 'spilt.'

Words with S.M. *shu* or *shu-* are normally rendered by *φu*, as *φu* : *shu* 'book'; *φuai* : *shuai* 'stumble'; *φuo* : *shuo* 'say.'[6] But the word for water is so frequent that it begins to break the general pattern and forms a vanguard syllable *śoei*, which is quite out of step with the other forms. (Originally it had been *hɛ* and later *φoei*, now discarded.)

The velar plosives *g* [k] and *k* [k'] became normalized to standard values very early. There was no noticeable tendency to substitute *dau* ('knife') for *gau* 'cake,' so common among Chinese children, though not so nearly universal as generally supposed. There was some substitution of *k* for *h* for a brief period, but it passed long before this recording.

The fricative initial /h/ before open vowels is a glottal [h], as *hao* : *hao* 'good,' as against the velar or pharyngeal fricative [χ] in S.M. Before medial *u*, there is stronger articulation in the lips than at the back of the tongue or at the glottis, so that S.M. *hual* 'flower' becomes *φua* and S.M. *huay* 'bad'

---

[6] In this connection it may be noted that along a region from about central Anhwei to central Shensi there are many dialects in which S.M. *shu* or *shu-* is rendered by *φu* or *fu*, for example, Sian *fu* 'book,' *fei* 'water.'

becomes φuay in Cantian. Consequently, words with hu- in S.M. are transferred to Cantian φ, which is an allophone of /f/. When, however, u is the whole final and not a medial, S.M. h is kept as [h] and therefore also Cantian /h/, as huudji : hwu.tzy 'mustache.'

The medials have developed in a way typical of children's speech, namely, omitted at first (baw for biaw), added as part of the consonant (ńaw for niaw), and finally fully admitted. At the stage recorded, the status of the medials is as follows.

For i after labials it tends to be present when stressed, but absent in proclitic position. There is, however, some free variation in stressed position. Thus, beau : beau 'watch'; baw or biaw : bu yaw 'don't want'; but .be donn : bye donq 'don't move.'

For the medial u the final uo usually loses the medial and has the value o [ɔ], as doh : tzuoh 'sit,' though in φuo it is kept. The initials g, k, h generally retain the medial u, as huoo : huoo 'fire.' In proclitic position, however, the u is usually lost, as .hotjoei : huootoei 'ham.' With other finals the medial u after dentals takes a somewhat palatal value, as tjoei [t''üěi] : toei 'leg'; after other initials its value is [u], as guai : [kuāi] : guai 'good.'

The medial iu or ü occurs only in the word yueh.iàn : yueh.liang 'moon,' where it has the same (front) value as in nuclear position, as in yu : yu 'fish.'

Of semivowels occurring initially, i is more underarticulated and less clearly palatal or dental, just as ś is underarticulated and not clearly dental or retroflex or palatal. In distribution Cantian initial i includes S.M. l- and r- as well as original i-, as yai : lai 'come'; yèh : reh 'hot'; yaw : yaw 'want.' A nasal ending sometimes results in a substitution of a nasal initial in place of S.M. l-, as ńeen : leeng 'cold'; ńiindah : liingdall 'necktie.'

There are fewer endings in Cantian than in S.M. The endings -i and -u are extremely open, so that the resulting diphthongs are very close to monophthongs. In proclitic position, they are quite lost, as haakann or .hakann : haokann 'pretty.' There is only one nasal ending, which is usually palatal in articulation, as tjwan : either chwan 'ship' or chwang 'bed';[7] don : jong 'clock.'

The retroflex ending -l in S.M. (i.e., [-r]) is simply dropped and only the vowel is retained, as wa : wal 'to play.' A middle central vowel in S.M. is given the low vowel value, as .daydah : tzayjell 'it's here'; ahyi : ellyi 'second aunt.' Note also that, in dropping the ending, it is from the form heard that the ending is dropped and not from the morpheme alternant that would be used in S.M. if there were no suffix. For example, S.M. yihdeal 'a little' is Cantian .idjea and not *.idjean, such as occurs in djean.śin : dean.shin 'refreshment.'

The vowel system is less amenable than S.M. to reduction to three phonemes: high, mid, and low.

---

[7] The mid-lower Yangtze Mandarin in Grandma's speech equates chwan 'ship' with chwan 'bed,' but, this being part of the Cantian system, Grandma's equating was probably not the main cause of this coalescence.

The apical high vowel *y* has in S.M. a dental value in *tzy*, *tsy*, *sy* (Wade-Giles *ŭ*) and a retroflex value in *jy*, *chy*, *shy*, *ry* (Wade-Giles, *ih*). The first type is combined in Cantian with the high front vowel *i*, as *wah.dji* : *wah.tzy* 'stocking.'[8] The second type is kept distinct and has a value intermediate between a retroflex apical vowel and a palatal *i*, just as the Cantian consonant *ś* is intermediate between retroflex [ṣ] and palatal [ś]. Examples are *tjy* : *chy* 'eat'; *śy* : *shy* 'wet.'

For some reason this vowel did not for a long time combine with the *un*aspirated initial *dj*, thus *tjyy* (with aspirated initial) both for S.M. *jyy* 'paper' and for S.M. *chyy* 'ruler.' In proclitic position, *tjy* becomes *tu* or *tji*, as *.tufann* or *.tjifann* : *chy-fann* 'eat dinner.'

The other high vowels *i*, *u*, *iu* have the same values [i, u, ü] as in S.M. and approximately the same distribution, apart from changes into *i* and *u* from the apical vowel, as just noted.

As for the low vowel or low vowels, *a* usually has a central or slightly fronted value. In this connection, note that the palatal or semipalatal articulation of *ń* and *ś* has had serious effects on the vowel system. While the separation of pure dentals, retroflexes, and palatals in S.M. makes it possible to deal with vowels in an extremely simple fashion, the absorption of the medial in Cantian *ń* and *ś*, and to a less degree in *dj* and *tj*, has made it necessary to set up more vowels. Thus, S.M. *shian* and *san* can be phonemicized as /sian/ and /san/, where the medial will take care of the difference in vowel qualities [ɛ] and [a]. But in Cantian it will be necessary to recognize *śɛn* and *śan* as having different vowel phonemes. Again, in the contrast between *tjyàn* : *chyang* 'wall,' where the Cantian *a* remains a low vowel, and *tjyɛn* : *chyan* 'money' where Cantian ɛ and S.M. *a* are both the same half-low vowel, we find an additional situation where an extra vowel phoneme is needed.

The mid vowel or vowels are also more complicated in Cantian than in S.M. Simple stressed *e* has the same back unrounded value as in S.M., but with less tendency to become an ascending diphthong. For S.M. *uo* and *ou*, diphthongs of smaller range are used. After dentals, and in unstressed positions for all initials, *uo* becomes *o*, as already noted, and *ou* becomes *e*. After initial semi-vowel *i-* there are two vowels [e] and [ɛ], according to the allophone in S.M. Thus, there is contrast between *yėh* [jə] : *reh* 'hot' and *yee* [jɛ] : *yee* 'also.' The problem of two kinds of mid vowels, one central and one back, has plagued phonemicists of the Peiping dialect,[9] who have used somewhat drastic solutions. There the problem has to do with such contrasts as are found in *ge'l* 'song' versus *gel* 'root,' where words with retroflex suffixes derived from

---

[8] In this particular suffix, an earlier form, after the -.*dji* form was begun, was an ejected '*t*, with closed glottis and dental oral explosion, resulting in a high-pitched expiratory click. This was used for about two months and abandoned about four months ago.

[9] See Lawton M. Hartman 3d, "The Segmental Phonemes of the Peiping Dialect," *Language*, XX (1944), 35–36; Charles F. Hockett, "Peiping Phonology," *Journal of the American Oriental Society*, LXVII (1947), 259–267.

stems ending in *e* and those ending in *e* plus *-i* or *-n* are involved. Here the same problem comes up even in root words.

When the mid vowel *e* is followed by endings *-i* and *-n* it has a rather more fronted value than S.M., as *men* : *men* 'door.' The change from S.M. mid vowel in *-el* to the low vowel *a* (with dropping of the retroflex ending) has already been noted in our discussion of endings.

Another special vowel quality in Cantian is in what in National Romanization is written *ong*, the actual S.M. vowel in it being an open *u*. But the Cantian forms for the *ong* words have a fairly open—medium—*o* sound. After velar initials it tends to be a nasalized vowel. After other initials it is followed by the usual palatal nasal ending (unless assimilated). The treatment of S.M. *ong* is therefore another reason for using an "allograph" *o*, if not a phoneme.

The difficulty with the vowel system is that it is in a state of extreme flux, where the various changes from one stage to the next in the approach to adult language are not going on all in step, thus resulting in internal inconsistencies. Some of this is true of historical change in adult language, as seen in various phonemic anomalies, such as, for example, the lone word d'*i* 'earth' in Ancient Chinese, the only instance of a dental stop with that type of final. But in adult language there is usually time for some stabilization to set in, so as to allow the phonemician to catch his breath, whereas here the vowels float about and will not stay put until they attain adult S.M. status.

The tones of Cantian are much more regular and stable, though distinctly different from S.M. in several respects. Canta acquired tones very early, as most Chinese children do. Isolated tones of stressed syllables are practically the same as in S.M. In terms of the four-interval, five-point system of tonal notation,[10] starting from 1 up to 5, the tones of S.M. are: 1st Tone, high-level, "55:"; 2d Tone, high-rising, "35:"; 3d Tone, low-dipping, "214:"; and 4th Tone, high-falling-to-low, "55:".

Like that of most Mandarin-speaking children, Canta's modification of 3d Tone into "half 3d," that is, low-falling "21:," comes sooner than the modification of 3d Tone into 2d Tone before another 3d Tone. This is also true of other Cantian tones. Some of the half 3d-Tone words were of course learned as fixed combinations and never heard as full 3d Tones, as in *yiidji* ("21: 55:") : *yii.tzy* 'chair.' But even in made-up combinations in which the first syllable is known in full 3d-Tone form, the change into half 3d Tone seems already to have been acquired, as *yeou* ("214:") 'have' in end position, versus *yeou tarn* ("21: 35:") 'have candy.' There are occasional slips, as *Dah yeou* ("214:") *tjwan* 'There is a ship here,' followed immediately by *Dah yeou*

---

[10] See Y. R. Chao, "A System of Tone-letters," *Le Maître phonétique* (1930), p. 24. A rough approximation to the tone values can be obtained by humming the numerals in quotes as *do, re, mi, fa, sol,* e.g., "35:" as *mi-sol* (on a sliding scale, of course).

("21:") *yu* 'There is a fish here,' where the 3d-Tone word *yeou* before a 2d Tone was given the full 3d Tone the first time and then a half 3d Tone right afterward.

The raising of a 3d-Tone word before another 3d Tone is, however, only beginning to be learned. Thus, *Beau yeou* ("21: 214:") 'The watch is there,' instead of normal S.M. "35: 214:". On one occasion she said *Bii yeou* 'The pencil is there' first in the tones "21: 214:"; then, after a few seconds, she corrected herself and gave the S.M. form "35: 214:".

The shifting tones of *i* 'one' and *bu* 'not,' which in S.M. are in the 4th Tone before 1st, 2d, and 3d Tones, and 2d before the 4th Tone, are usually generalized into the 4th Tone by most Mandarin-speaking children before they learn the shift. There is not enough material on *i* to judge by. The tone of *bu* is still 4th before all tones, as *buh day djii.śa* : *bwu tzay dii.shia* 'is not below.'

A feature of Canta's stress system that is of great phonological importance is the existence of true proclitic syllables, that is, weak and atonic syllables before a tonic stress. In S.M., weak and atonic ("neutral tone") syllables occur mostly in enclitic positions. Cantian has such forms too, as *poh.de* : *poh.le* 'has broken.' But while S.M. has no true iambs[11] but only quasi-iambs with half stress in initial position and full stress in end position in a polysyllabic group, the same combination in Cantian is often a true iamb, with neutral tone and quite weak stress for the first syllable, as *.be'ńa* : ͵*bye'na* 'Don't take it!'

When this initial weakening does occur, there is great reduction in medial, ending, and even the vowel. Thus, *śoei* : *shoei* 'water,' but *.śi'djiaw* : ͵*shuey 'jiaw* 'to sleep'; *śao* : *sheau* 'small,' but *.śa'yi* : ͵*sheau yi* 'little aunt.'

The pitch of neutral tone in proclitic position is middle or half-high. The pitch for enclitic position is approximately as in S.M. After the 1st Tone, if it is not a sentence particle, it is half-low, as in S.M., as *ɸua.dji* ("55: .2:"): *shua.tzy* 'brush.' If, however, it is a sentence particle, it stays up, as *Dańńhe* ("55: 55:") : *Tzang.le* 'It's got dirty.' This gives a peculiarly Cantian intonation.

After a 2d-Tone word, which ends at pitch "5:," a neutral tone in S.M. comes down to the middle "3:". But the Cantian syllable in such a position stays up at "5:" and is usually not weak, that is, it is actually a 1st Tone. Moreover, the original 2d Tone usually changes into a half 3d Tone,[12] as *biitji* ("21: 55:") : *byi.ti* ("35: .3:") 'mucus from the nose.'

---

[11] This view is not generally accepted. For present purposes it would be sufficient to say that for many of those forms in S.M. which are only quasi-iambs, Cantian has true iambs.
[12] This is an instance of the lack of synchronism between tone and segmental elements, where an intrasyllabic rise (for the 2d Tone) is delayed and becomes an intersyllabic rise. The same phenomenon has been observed in the early speech of Canta's third aunt (who was one of the subjects of the study referred to in note 2 above), though she could not, of course, have influenced her.

In *aadotjeandji* ("21: 55: 21: 55: "): *eel(.dou)chyan.tzy* ("21: .2: 35: .3:") 'earring,' the last two syllables *tjeandji* have the same tonal pattern as in *djeandji*: *jean.tzy* 'scissors.' Moreover, *yiidji* serves both for *yi.tzy* 'soap' and *yii.tzy* 'chair,' a point tested by showing Canta alternately a piece of soap and a chair in quick succession and asking what they were. She made no effort to distinguish them and seemed mildly amused that they had the same name. That she had heard the 2d Tone plus neutral at least sometimes is shown in her self-correction when she echoed someone's mentioning *shyebar.tzy* 'shoe-horn,' first as *śɛrbaadji* ("35: 21: 55:"), and then corrected herself by saying with S.M. tones *śɛrbar.dji* ("35: 35: .3"). The tonal pattern of the last two syllables is, however, still rare with her.

After the 3d Tone, as seen in the example just given, a neutral in S.M. is given a high pitch "55:" (instead of the usual "4:"). It is not weak and should also be considered as being in the 1st Tone. After the 4th Tone, the pitch of a neutral tone is low, as in S.M.

The initial of a neutral-tone syllable in enclitic position undergoes certain changes. Some of these changes are as in S.M., such as the voicing of *b*, *d*, *g*, etc., as already noted. If the preceding syllable ends in a nasal, a following unstressed plosive (occasionally stressed ones, too), whether aspirated or un-aspirated, becomes a nasal. Thus, the names of the colors with the subordinative particle *.de* attached take the following forms: *horn.ñe*: *horng.de* 'red'; *hoanñhe*: *hwang.de* 'yellow'; *ñaanñhe*: *lan.de* 'blue'; but *yuh.de*: *liuh.de* 'green.' For *pyngguoo* 'apple,' which she spoonerizes into what would be **kwenpoo*, she actually says *.kemmoo* (".4: 214:").

This assimilatory feature has resulted in a peculiar difficulty in her terms of address. People in the family have the publicly used terms: *bah.ba* 'papa' and adapted English forms *mha.mhi* 'mommy,' *guam.pa* 'grandpa,' *guam.ma* 'grandma.' She had difficulty in saying the last two and started to use spooner-ized forms *pan.ngua* and *mam.ma*. She was laughed into correcting herself, but because of this law of nasal assimilation the only phonologically possible form in the Cantian system is *guam.ma* for both *guam.pa* and *guam.ma*. Under cor-rection by people in the house, with displaced contrasting stress on '*pa* and '*ma*, she could force herself to say *.gem'pa*, *.gem'ma* (with English intonation on the contrasting syllables). But the term she naturally uses for either grand-parent at latest recording is still *gam.ma* and *.gem'pa* in free variation, with a slight preponderance of the former for 'grandpa' and the latter for 'grandma.' She also fails to respond distinctively if told by a third person to give something to *guam.pa* (or *guam.ma*), and she would act according as one or the other grandparent is likely to be the person concerned, irrespective of the form spoken.

Canta's speech, like that of many other children, includes spoonerisms, sometimes resulting in permanent forms which replace the originals entirely. The following instances have been recorded:

CANTIAN ACTUAL	CANTIAN PROTOTYPE	S.M.	MEANING
.kemmoo	*.penguoo	pyngguoo	'apple'
.kem.moodjy	*.penguoodjy	pyngguoojy	'apple cider'
djinn.hite	djih.hinte	tzyhshyngche	'bicycle'
pan.ngua	*guam.pa	"guam.pa"	'grandpa'
śayii	iaśyy	lhashyy	'go to stool'
śenntja	tjennśa	chennshal	'shirt'
Tarn biau, dann.ńe.	Tarn dan, biaw.de.	Tarng tzang, bu yaw .le.	'The candy is dirty, I don't want it any more'
twen.huen	hwen.tuen	hwen.tuen	'One Ton' (stuffed dumplings)
tjy.śe	śy.de	shy.de	'wet'

Once, when a recording machine was used to record her speech and she heard the sentence *Yi.geh kuohren tzoou .de puh.tzy.lii .chiu .le* 'A rich man has gone into a store,' she repeated it as *Pohyèn dǫou kuh.dji .iè* 'Broken man gone into the pants.' Since then she has called phonographs or disk records "pohkuh.dji."

II. GRAMMAR

Just as the sounds are underarticulated in Cantian, so are the sentences underconstructed. It is true that the topic-comment relation in standard Chinese subject-predicate relation is already a looser relation than that of actor-action, and that the direction of action of verbs can be outward or inward according to (linguistic or situational) context; hence there is nothing specially Cantian in construction in sentences like: *Bey bii .bu nonndu*: *Woo bii bwu nonq-diou* 'I, pencil don't cause to lose,—I won't lose my pencil.' But since the verb-object order is not used in Cantian except in fixed combinations, the preceding construction bears a larger share of syntactical burden than it does in S.M. For example, *Yi jidaa wey* 'Aunt egg feed': *Yi wey (woo) jitzeel* 'Aunt feed (me) eggs.' *Bey hairyaw dey.geh day* 'Baby still want this wear.' Since *hairyaw* is used for *yaw* 'want' in general, and *dey.geh* is used for both S.M. *jey.geh* and *ney.geh*, and the thing referred to was a brooch at some distance, it should be translated as *Woo yaw day ney.geh* 'I want to wear that.' But it would be midleading to leave the analysis there and regard 'wear that' as simply verb-object transposed. The real construction, in view of other parallel forms, is that of a subject-predicate clause serving as object of *hairyaw*. The constructional translation, with idiomatic equating of syntactic words, is, therefore, 'I wish that that be worn.'

There is a predominance of a few typical beginnings and endings (other than particles) of sentences over all other forms. Typical beginnings are:

Bey . . . 'I, the Baby . . .'
Śennday . . . : *Shianntzay* . . . 'Now . . .'
Ah, . . ., *ah*! for example, *Ah, deh* φ*u, ah*! 'Look, this is a book, look!' This form was later abandoned in favor of the next.
Tjin! : *Ting*! 'Listen,' but actually used for either looking at something or listening to something. This was also abandoned and replaced by the currently used form below.
Ńeekann or *.ńekann* or *.ńekan* : *Nii kann* '(You) look!' or, less frequently, *Ń-ńau*! : *Nii chyau*! '(You) look!'
Deh or *Deh.hy* or *Deh.śy* : *Jeh.shy* 'This is.'
Hairyaw : *hairyaw* 'still want,' 'want more,' but actually used as *yaw* in asking for things even for the first time. It is often used before a sentence in the sense of 'I wish that . . .' as: *Hairyaw Bey tarntjyn wan.ńe* '(I) wish (that) I (be helped down from the piano stool because my) playing the piano is finished.'
Buh 'not' is also often used to negate whole sentences, as *Buh śoei ge dah* : *Shoei buh* (or *bye*) *ge .de jell* 'Don't put the water here.'

Common predicates are:

. . . *baw* or *biaw* : . . . *bu yaw* 'don't want,' 'not wanted' (name of thing not wanted in subject position and less frequently in object position).
. . . *ńaa.tji.de*? : . . . *naal .chiu .le*? 'Where is . . . gone to?'
. . . .*daydah* or . . . .*daydah .ńe* : *tzay*[13] *jell* (*.ne*) '. . . is here.'
. . . *fanndah* : . . . *fanq .de jell* 'Put the . . . here.' (*Fanq*, used by half the people in the house, is not the usual S.M. word for 'put,' as the next is.)
. . . *gedah* : . . . *ge .de jell* 'Put the . . . here.'
. . . *wan.ńe* : . . . *wan.le* 'finished . . .' is used as a complete predicate rather than as a complement as in S.M. Thus, *tjyfann wan.ńe* in normal S.M. construction would be *chy-wan.le fann .le* or *chy-fan chy-wan.le* 'have finished eating.' Once in a while the S.M. repetitive construction is used, as *Bey tjifann tjibaa.ue* : *Bey chy-fann chy-bao.le* 'I have finished eating dinner.'

Subordination is mostly in the same word order as in S.M., but the subordinative particle *.de* is not used except in fixed combinations. Examples are *Bey wah.dji* : *Bey* (*.de*) *wah.tzy* 'My stocking'; *Mhamhi geei śer djiaw .de* (i.e., . . . *.le*) 'The shoe Mommy gave me has come off'; *Deh.hy gam.ma mae* ("21:") *bii* ("214:") : *Jeh.shy guam.pa mae .de bii* 'This is the pencil grandpa bought.' But at least once, clearly enough from the situation, a restrictive modifier followed: *Deh.hy Bey śɛr baw* : *Nah.shy Bey bu yaw .de shye* 'Those are my discarded shoes.'

It is not common for Chinese children to make up compounds other than

---

[13] S.M. does have a form *day* 'to be at,' but it is not frequently heard around the house.

transient compounds such as numerals plus classifiers. This is also true of Cantian, with two or three interesting exceptions. One is *djihśoei*:*dihshoei* 'ground-water,' which she applies to 'sea, river, lake, pond, inlet.' The first time she made this up was when she saw a pond. The other is *huooden*:*huoodeng* 'fire-light' a term she invented when she saw lit candles at a house she was visiting. On most previous occasions, when the word *deng* was heard, it referred to electric lights. Rice soup is called *fannhetan*, where *hetan*:*he-tang* 'drink soup' is used as a noun for 'soup.'

Parts of speech and form classes in general are greatly underdifferentiated, and one instance of use in agreement with S.M. syntax should not be taken as conclusive evidence that certain words are being used in the same function as in S.M. We have just noted that, in the compound *fannhetan*, *hetan* is not verb-object, but a noun. The sentence *Bey hairyaw gaybey.uo* seems to mean 'I want to cover myself with the quilt,' an interpretation apparently confirmed when she is satisfied when so covered. But on another occasion she said *Bry taandji, deh gaybey.uo—bry gaybey.uo, gaybe.ou śannyou.ue*:*Bwu.shy taan.tzy, jeh (shyh) (gay)bey.uo—bwu.shy (gay)bey.uo, (gay)bey.uo shanq-lou .le* 'It's not a blanket, it's a quilt—it's not a quilt, the quilt is gone upstairs.' The obvious conclusion is that *gaybey.uo* 'to cover with a quilt' in S.M. is in Cantian a noun 'quilt.' But the obvious is not necessarily true. To attribute a noun or a verb category to the Cantian syntax is to read too much adult grammar into it. Actually, both verbal expressions in S.M. like *gay-bey.uo*, and substantive expressions like *shoei* when occurring in Cantian, are still undifferentiated in her language. *Śoei*:*shoei* in *Deh.hy śoei* 'This is water' seems to be a substantive, but most of the time it means 'I want to have a drink of water.' *Śoou*:*shoou* 'hand,' but in *Bey śoou deng* it means '(I) touch the (the lamp).' *Kannbaw* 'to read a newspaper' in S.M. is either 'to read a newspaper' or 'newspaper.' *Biitji*:*byi.ti* 'mucus from the nose' in S.M. also means in Cantian 'wipe my nose' and 'tissue paper.' When *tayyèh. ue*:*tay reh.le* was spoken for taking off a bib in order to put a pin on the dress below, it was not a wrong statement about her sensation of warmth, but a real request.

Like most other children, Canta finds personal pronouns, or "shifters," difficult to acquire. The only personal pronoun that Canta uses is *ńii*, and mostly in special combinations. *Ńeekann*:*Nii kann* 'Look' has already been noted. The form *gī*, from *geei nii* 'for you' (i.e., for Canta herself), is often used. The active independent use of *ńii* is established by a sentence *Gam.ma day ńii* (stressed) *tu.tjiu*:*Guam.ma day nii chu.chiu* 'Grandma will take you (i.e., me) to go out.' Previous to this utterance the word *nii* had not been heard for at least half an hour. The pronouns *woo* and *ta* and their compounds are not in the Cantian vocabulary.

Numerals do not form a significant part of the vocabulary. She recites the numerals for fun in random order, but not to use them as numbers. The form *i.geh* is used, but more frequently for several things than for one thing, the reason being that when there are several things other people often count *yi.geh*, *leang.geh*, *san.geh*, etc., and the first word gets better remembered. Plurality of things is expressed by repeating the name of the thing, as *tjihte*, *tjihte*, *tjihte* 'many automobiles.' At one stage, when Little Aunt had been correcting her *geng* for *deng* 'light' by making her say "*de-de-deng*," she began to call a light *dededen*. Then, passing the Bay Bridge one night, with its many lights along the way, she said, "De-de-de-de-de-de-...-den!"

The perfective particle .*le*, often with the 'new-situation' meaning, had been acquired for some time, with the phonetic substitution .*ie*, but recently she was dissatisfied with the palatal articulation and so changed it to .*de*, which is dental enough, like .*le*, though not so good with respect to manner of articulation. But it continues to be .*iè* after words ending in -*i*, .*ue* after words ending in -*u*, and .*ńe* after nasal endings. Thus, *yai.iè* : *lai.le* 'has come'; *hao* .*ue* : *hao* .*le* 'all right now'; *ńeen.ńe* : *leeng* .*le* '(I'm) getting cold.' That this particle has been learned as an active and independent lexical unit is shown by the following examples. .*Ńekann Bey doh.śa* (1-second pause) .*de* : *Nii kann Bey tzuoh* .*shia* .*le* 'Look, I've sat down'; *daatjih.iè* .*de* : *daa-tih* .*le* '(I have) sneezed,' where the .*iè* in *daatjih.iè* is from the fixed form *daa-tih* .*le*, while the .*de* was added as the particle meaning 'here is something happening.'

Questions understood and asked are mostly limited to the form ... *shyh sheir* 'Who is ...?' ... *tzay naal* .*ne?* 'Where is ...?' and *Jeh.shy sherm.me?* 'What is this?' The form *Nah.shy sherm.me?* 'what's that?' is understood but not used. There is an abbreviated Cantian form .*De.me?* often used in asking the names of things (near or distant). When not so abbreviated, a rising-tone interrogative interjection (not a particle) is often added after a comma-length pause: *Deh.hy śe.me*, ɜ̃?

The active use of *śe.me* : *sherm.me* 'what' in attributive position was a very recent acquisition. The first recorded use was *Deh śe.me te?* : *Nah.shy sherm.me che?* 'What (sort of) vehicle is that?' *Deh ée.me ha?* : *Nah.shy sherm.me hual?* 'What (sort of) flower is that?'

Other forms of questions, such as questions involving *yaw.bu.yaw*, *yeou. mei.yeau*, etc., questions ending in .*ma* and involving interrogative words other than those mentioned above, are not in active use. The sentence *Deh.hy bu.hy yaφa* : *Jeh.shy bwu.shy yashua* was apparently a question of the A-not-A form. But the actual stress and intonation and the situation showed that it was not a question, but a statement: 'This is a not-toothbrush.' Real questions in the A-not-A form or .*ma* form are not even understood unless helped out by the situation, in which case an apparent answer is not really an answer to the question, but rather an utterance made in response to the situation. Thus, no answer could be elicited from the question *Shianqpyi tzay naal jao.jaur* .*de?* 'Where did you find the eraser?' In her active use of the form ... .*daynaa* .*de?* apparently meaning 'where is ...?' it is as much a command to look for something as a question about the location. Now that the eraser is found, there is no point in asking where it was found. As usual, I think it is more accurate to regard this as evidence, not for the primacy of the pragmatic function of language, but for the lack of differentiation of the early functions of language. In fact, for months after Canta began to say *hɛ* at the sight of water or while drinking water, it never occurred to her that the same sound could be used as a means of obtaining water to drink.

There is a larger proportion of foreign loans in interjections than in other words. There is *Ouch*! for minor hurts, *Oh-oh*! ("5: 22:") for minor mishaps, *Hi*! for greeting other children, *'bye*! (with Chinese voiceless initial but English intonation "423:") for parting. These are used along with the usual Chinese interjections *Oio! Aio! Aiio! Ah*! etc. A voiced *h* with a prolonged neutral vowel *ə* is used for expressing impatience or exasperation, which can shade into actual crying in extreme cases. A very constant stylistic feature of Canta's speech is the changing of speaking to singing at the moment when there is evidence that a repeated request is acceded to, even though no overt action is taken. Thus, if *Bey yaw he śoei* 'I want a drink of water' is repeated several times, and the tone becomes more and more impatient, the moment someone acknowledges the request and says, say, 'I'll get you some water as soon as I am through with this,' then the same words *Bey yaw he śoei* will be sung to various improvised tunes (not in adult scales). If the initial request is repeated four or five times, a promise to grant it will invariably be followed by singing of the words.

In more complicated organization of words into sentences there is some experimentation in putting building blocks together, whether they form any building she has seen before or not. Some of these turn out to be quite normal S.M. constructions, as:

> *Bey śannpyi daynah .ée* : *Bey shianqpyi tzaynall .ne* 'I, eraser is there.'
> *Gam.ma i.śan dah yeou .ue, ńiindah dah yeou .ue* : *Guam.pa i.shang jell yeou .le, liingdall jell yeou .le* 'Grandpa clothes here are, necktie here is.'

But some sentences are difficult to understand without the help of the situational context. Examples are:

> *Kaiden nah* : *kai-deng nall,—kai nall .de deng* 'Turn on the light over there.'
> *Hetan soou* : *he tang shoou,—na shoou he tang* 'drink soup with the hand.'
> *Ńeekann Bey yee tjy djidaa wan.ńe* : *Nii kann Bey yee chy-wan.le jitzeel .le* 'Look, I've also finished eating my eggs.'
> *Bey hairyaw tjoei danńha* : *Bey hairyaw toei tzang .le, —Woo yaw tsa.tsa toei, woo toei tzang .le* 'I want to have my leg wiped, my leg is dirty.'
> *Gam.ma yeou* ("214:") *bii* ("21:") *śannpyi* : *Guam.pa yeou bii shianqpyi* 'Grandpa has pencil eraser.' In view of the full 3d Tone on *yeou*, the true analysis should probably be 'Grandpa (does) have (when it is a question of) pencil eraser.'
> *Bey hairyaw kannbaw day naa.tji .de?* : *Bey hairyaw kannbaw daw naal .chiu .le, —Woo yaw kann (.de) baw naal .chiu .le?* 'Where is the newspaper I want to read?'
> *Bey yeandjin me'oou.ue djinn.dji Canta* : *Bey yean.jing meiyeou.le jinq.tzy Canta* 'My eyes have no glasses (to) mirror Canta.' The translation of *djinn.dji* by the

verb 'to mirror' is not so far-fetched as it might seem, since Cantian nouns and verbs are not such distinct things as in S.M.

(At top of her voice, *ff*:) *Dahdjinn*! : *dahjinq.tzy* 'big mirror.'

(Someone says: *Bye jiaw*! 'Don't shout!')

(Then, after 2 min., *p*:) *Bey śεnnday .budjiaw* (*mf*:) *Dahdjinn* (*pp*:) *wan.ńe*. Here, the specially greater loudness on repeating the word *dahdjinn* was obviously to quote her own previous shouting, but the construction is quite a mixed one, consisting of *Bey shianntzay bwu jiaw* "*Dahjinq*" *.le* 'I am no longer shouting "Big mirror"' and *Jiaw* "*Dahjinq*" *jiaw-woan.le* 'I am through shouting "Big mirror."'

Cantian 49 has just emerged from the prattling stage. But under emotion, especially of exciting interest, such as trying to narrate a scene of a recent past, there are still long and rapid strings of unphonemicizable sounds, mixed here and there with real words. Such passages are difficult to transcribe, even from the phonograph recordings.

There is occasional intentional playing with language. Words and phrases are often sung to improvised tunes, as has been noted above. Sometimes a syllable would be put through the four tones, although Canta has not heard the order of the tones more than ten times. In playing with the tones on more than one syllable, there is often substitution of intersyllabic change for intra-syllabic change, as has already been noted in her speech pattern. Thus, the four tones played on her own name "Canta" take the form "5: 55:," "5: 35:," "21: 5," "55: 1:".

In playing with tones, the resulting syllables are usually not expected to make sense. Once, when she said the word *.śidjao* : *shii-tzao* 'take bath' in four tones ".5: 55:," ".5: 35:," ".5: 214:," ".5: 51:," she was surprised and amused that the last one made sense, since in proclitic position *śuey* normally becomes *śi* and the result is *.sidjiaw*: *shuey-jiaw* 'go to sleep,' which is what she does after taking her bath.

There is often intentional misnaming of things. Thus, after having learned that a cushion is called *djεnn.dji* : *diann.tzy* and not *taandji* : *taan.tzy*, the word for 'blanket,' she often answers uniformly "taandji" when asked what various other things are. Since the word *taandji* was once used as the wrong name for something, a more subtle interpretation for it, when it continues to be used for everything, might be 'wrong name for that thing.'

III. VOCABULARY

Only active vocabulary spoken on her own initiative and not by immediate echoing is included here. Items which are obsolete at this stage are so marked. Needless to say, bound forms are not taken out of context and given what would be the S.M. meaning. Thus, while both *ńaw* : *naw* 'fussy, make noise' and *.beńaw* : *bye naw* 'don't make such a noise' are included, only *.bedonn* : *bye donq* 'don't move' is entered, since **donn* : *donq* 'move' is not known to have occurred in any other context. As in S.M., the main stress in a group is always on the last syllable not preceded by a dot, which is a sign for weak stress, or "neutral tone."

On the orthography used here see page 15, esp. footnote 3.

A!: *A*! (with initial glottal stop, in both Cantian and S.M. after a proposal, with an 'all is well' intonation) 'shall we?' 'let's'

aadoutjɛɛndji : *eelchyan.tzy* 'earring'

aadou : *eel.dou* 'ear'

ah.dji : *wah.tzy* 'stocking,' obsolete, superseded by *wah.dji*

Ahyi : *Ellyi* 'Second Aunt,' term of address

Ahyiah.ɸu : *Ellyi.fu* 'Second Uncle,' term of address

Aio! or *Aiio*! : (same) 'Goodness!'

au.djin : *iodine* '(tincture) of iodine'

audjyn : *iodine* 'soy bean sauce'; 'dark gravy' (second syllable given a 2d Tone, apparently to distinguish it from real iodine)

baw : *baw* 'newspaper'

baw, biaw : *bu yaw* 'don't want'; 'I don't want it'

baede : *bair.de* 'white'

beau : *beau* 'a watch'

.beda : *byejel* '(safety) pin'

.bedonn : *bye donq* 'don't move'

.bena : *bye na* 'don't take it'; 'something not to be taken,' as *Deh.hy .bena* 'this is. . .'

.benaw : *bye naw* 'don't make such a noise'

.benga : *biinggal* 'crackers'

.benonn : *bye nonq* 'don't play with that'; 'something not to play with'

.betuu : *bye tuu* 'don't spit it'; 'to eat down,' as *Bey .betuu wan.ñe* 'I have finished not-spitting it (i.e., swallowing it)'

bey : *baby* 'doll'; also applied to children of the same age as herself or older

Bey or *Bey.bei* : *Baby* 'I, the Baby'

biaw, baw : *buyaw* 'don't want'; I don't want it'

bi.bi : *pipi* (Fr) = *śañaw*

biidji : *byi.tzy* 'nose'

biitji : *byi.ti* 'mucus from nose'; 'wipe my nose'; 'tissue paper'

bindjyn : *bingchiling* 'ice cream'

bo.bo : *bor.bo* 'Uncle,' addressing men of father's generation

bu, bu.hy, bry : *bwu.shy* 'is not'

.budjiaw : *buhjydaw* 'I wonder' (not used as direct reply 'I don't know,' which is expressed by mere silence)

.budjuey : *bwuduey* 'that's wrong'

buhśaa : *buh saa* 'will not spill'

buhtern.ñe : *buh terng .le* 'doesn't hurt any more'

'bye [*ḫai*] : 'Goodbye!'; 'leave, go away'

da : *ja* 'prick'

daa : *daa* 'beat, strike'

daambann.ñe : *tzeem bann .ne?* 'what shall we do?' (spoken in fun, apparently without knowing what this expression is used for)

daatjih.iė : *daa-tih.le* 'sneeze'

dah : *dah* 'big'

dahdjinn : *dah-jinq.tzy* 'big mirror'

dahkoou : *dahkoou* 'with wide-open mouth'

dahtaan : *dahchaang* 'overcoat'

dan : *tzang* 'dirty'

danñhe : *tzang .le* 'dirty, soiled'

.danaa.tji.de : *daw naal .chiu .le* 'where is . . . gone to?'

dannge : *dah.muge* 'thumb'

dao : *jao* 'look for'

daśann : *jawshianqjinq.tzy* 'camera'

dau : *dau* 'knife'

day : *day* 'take along'

day : *day* 'put on'; 'wear'

daydah, .daidah : *tzayjell* 'it's here'

.day ñaa.ñe : *tzay naal .ne* 'where is . . .?'

daynah, .dainah : *tzaynall* 'is there'

dededen : *deng* 'lamp, light' (obsolete)

.de.me : *Jeh sherm.me* 'what is this?'

deh, deh.hy : *jeh.sh* 'this is'

den : *deng* 'lamp, light'

denn.dji : *denq.tzy* 'a stool'

dey.geh : *jey.geh* 'this, that'

djeandji : *jean.tzy* 'scissors'

djean.śin : *dean.shin* 'refreshment'

djeau : *jeau* 'foot'

djeou, djeou-pas-bon : *jeou*   'wine'; 'wine, which is no good (for children)'

djeudji : *jyu.tzy* 'orange.' (This is the family usage. In S.M., *jyu.tzy* is 'tangerine' and *chern.tzy* is 'orange.')

dji : *ji* 'chicken'

-.dji (or *dji* after 3d Tone) : *.tzy* noun suffix

djiandjeou : *deanjeou* 'tincture of iodine'

djiannh(u)ah : *diannhuah* 'telephone'

djiannte : *diannche* 'streetcar'

djiaw : *jiaw* 'shout'

djiaw.iė : *diaw .le* 'come off'; 'dropped'

djidaa : *jitzeel* 'egg'

djieedji : *dye.tzy* 'plate, saucer'

.djigaa : *tzyhgeel* 'myself'

djih : *dih* 'floor, ground'

djih.hinte, djinn.hite : *tzyhshyngche* 'bicycle'

djih.śa : *dih.shia* 'floor, ground'

djihśɛrdah : *jih shyedall* 'tie the shoestring'; 'shoestring'

djihśoei : *dihshoei* 'ground-water,' applied to pond, sea, etc.

djii.śa : *dii.shia* 'below'

djio : *ding* 'nail, screw'

djinn.dji : *jinq.tzy* 'mirror'

djiuśoei : *jyu.tzyshoei* 'orange juice'; 'orange'

djoadji : *joa.tzy* 'paw'

djoei : *tzoei* 'mouth'

djudju : *dudu*   'train' (obsolete, too childish for her)

djyy = (second) *tjyy*

doh.śa : *tzuoh.shia.lai* 'sit down'

don : *jong* 'clock'

doou : *tzoou* 'walk'; 'go, leave'

do.śan : *juo.shanq* 'is on the desk'

duh.dji : *duh.tzy* 'belly'

ɔ̃— : ɔ̃— 'uh—'; 'er—'

ɔ̃? (long rising tone) : *ar?* 'huh?'

ein (sic!) : *ian* 'cigarette'

faandji, hoandji : *farng.tzy* 'house'

fann : *fanq* 'put'

fanndah djinn.dji : *fanqdah-jinq* 'magnifying glass'

fannhetan : *fanntang* 'rice soup'

feidji : *feiji* 'airplane'

φoei : *shoei* 'water' (obsolete, replaced by *śoei*)

φu.dji : *shu.tzy* 'comb'

φuh : *shuh* 'tree'

φu : *shu* 'book'

φua.dji : *shua.tzy* 'brush'

φuai : *shuai* 'fall, stumble'

φuaya, yaφua : used for both *shuaya* 'brush the teeth' and *yashua* 'toothbrush'

φuo : *shuo* 'say'

φu-tour : *shu-tour* 'comb the hair'

ga : *gal* 'liver'

ga.ga : *caca* (Fr.) = *iaśyy*

gan ńhe : *gan .le* 'dry'

gau : *gau* 'cake'

gaybey.ue : *(gay)bey.uo* 'quilt'

ge : *ge* 'put'

ge.bey : *ge.bey* 'arm'

geei : *geei* 'give'

.gī : *geei .nii* 'for you' (i.e., me)

gon, gon.gon : *gong.gong* term of address for men who are of grandfather's generation, or who look so

gon.bo : *gongbor*   'greatuncle-uncle,' Cantian term of address for an intermediate generation

gongonntjihte : *gonggonqchihche* 'bus'

goou : *goou* 'dog'

guai : *guai* 'good' (of children)

guanmen : *guanmen* 'shut the door'

gunae : *goodnight* 'good night'; 'to kiss'

gwu.tu : *gwu.tou* 'bone'

haakann, .hakann : *haokann* 'pretty'

haatji, haatjy : *haochy* 'good to eat'; 'to eat'

.ha.duduh : —   'How do you do?'

hairyaw, hairyaw yaw : yaw 'want'; 'want some more'

hao : hao 'good'; 'not dirty'; 'not wet'

hao .ue : hao .le 'all right now'

.hayou : hwangyou 'butter'

he : he 'drink'

.hei.djidjia, hweidjia : hwei-jia 'home'

hetan : he tang 'soup'

Hi! [hai] : — 'Hi!'

hoanńhe : hwang.de 'yellow'

horn.ńe : horng.de 'red,' any bright color

.hotjoei : huootoei 'ham'

h(u)a : hual 'flower'

h(u)ah : huah 'draw'; 'write'

huoo : huoo 'fire'

·huooden : — 'candle'

h(u)oote : huooche 'train'

huudji : hwu.tzy 'mustache'

hwen.tuen, twen.tuen, twen.huen : hwen .tuen 'one ton' (stuffed dumplings)

.hy, .śy, śyh : .shy, shyh 'is'

ia.dji : ia.tzy 'duck'

iaia, ia.ia : — 'to rock' (as rocking chair); 'to sway' (as tree) (a made-up (word)

iaśyy, śayii : lha-shyy 'go to stool'

i.djea : yihdeal 'a little'

i.ge : yi.ge 'several' (sic!)

i.śan : i.shang 'dress'

kafei, kafei-pas-bon : kafei 'coffee'; 'coffee, which is no good (for children)'

kaiden : kai-deng 'turn on the light'; 'the light'

kaimen : kai-men 'open the door'

kannbaw : kann-baw 'read the newspaper'; 'newspaper'

kei.śi : — 'kiss'

.kemmoo : pyngguoo 'apple'

.kenmoodjy : pyngguoojy 'apple cider'

koh.dji, obsolete form for both *kow.dji* and *kuh.dji*, q.v.

kow.dji : kow.tzy 'button'

ku : ku 'cry'

kuay.dji : kuay.tzy 'chopstick'

kuhdah : kuhdall 'belt' (not necessarily for *kuh.dji* 'pants')

kuh.dji : kuh.tzy 'pants'

maa : maa 'horse,' also applied to 'sea-horse' when seen in a picture for the first time

maedon.śi : mae dong.shi 'buy things'

mam.ma : guan.ma 'grandma' (obsolete)

maw.dji : maw.tzy 'hat'

meeimhau : mei.mau 'eyebrows'

meiyeou.ue : meiyeou .le 'have not'; 'there is not'; 'not there'

men, mhein : men 'door' (second form made up for fun)

me'oou.ue : meiyeou .le 'have not'; 'there is not'; 'not there'

mey.mei : mey.mei 'younger sister,' applied to girls (sometimes boys) of the same age as herself or younger

mha.mhi ("55: 22:") : — 'mommy,' term applied to her own mother only

mhamhi ("5: 5:") : — 'Look!' term used for introducing a remark to anyone

mhau (with very fronted and long *a*) : *mhau* 'cat'

.mɛnbau : miannbau 'bread'

mɛnn : miann 'noodles'

mhein, see *men*

ńaanńhe : lan.de 'blue'

naa.tji.de : naal .chiuh .le 'where is . . . gone to?'

ńaeńhai : nae.nai term of address for women of grandparents' generation, usually prefixed by surname

ńao : neaul 'bird'

ńaw : naw 'be fussy'; 'make noise'

ńaw : niaw 'urine'

ńean = yean

ńeen : leeng 'cold'; 'to be stripped to the waist'

ńeekann, ńekann, .ńekan : nii kann 'look' (directing attention)

ńii : nii 'you' (Canta herself only)

ńiindah : liingdall 'necktie'

ńiou : niou 'ox, cow'

ńiounae : niounae '(cow's) milk'

ń-nau : nii chyau '(you) look!'

ńoan.φu : *noan.huo* 'warm'

nonndu : *nonq-diou* 'cause to be lost'

nònnφuay : *nonq-huay* 'to spoil by play-ing with'

oh-oh ("5: 22:") : — 'oh oh' used as in English

oio! ("5: 5:") : *oio!* interjection for a sudden (but not too important) turn of events. Cf. preceding item

ouch! : — 'ouch!'

pah : *pah* 'afraid,' used principally when in danger of falling

pair : *pair* '(playing) card'

pam.ma, pam.pa, pan.ngua : *guam.pa* 'grandpa' (obsolete)

par : *par* 'crawl'

parn.hɛ : *parng.shie* 'crab'

pas bon : — (with voiceless initial in both words) 'tastes bad'; also used as suffixes to *kafei, djeou,* and *tar,* q.v.

penntour .ue : *penq.le tour .le* 'I bumped my head'

pih.bu, pih.u : *pih.gu* 'buttocks'

poh kuh.dji : *poh kuh.tzy* 'broken trou-sers,' term applied to phonographs or records

śaabiah : *sheaubiall* 'small pigtail'

śaa.iè : *saa.le* 'spilt'

śaańhuńhu : *sheaunhiounhiou* 'little fin-ger'

śaanńhe : *saan.le* 'come loose'

Śaayi = *.Śayi*

.śabɛnn.dji = *śaabiah*

.śag(u)ah.dji : *sheauguah.tzy* 'under-shirt'

śahyeu : *shiah-yeu* 'rain'

śahyou : *shiah-lou* 'go downstairs'; 'downstairs'

śan : *suan* 'sour'

śańaw : *sa-niaw* 'urinate'

śandjiau : *shiangjiau* 'banana'

śanntjwan : *shanq-chwang* 'go up the bed' 'on the bed'; 'bed'

śannyou : *shanq-lou* 'go upstairs'; 'up-stairs'

.śanpyi, śannpyi : *shianqpyi* 'rubber (band)'; 'eraser'

śao : *sheau* 'small'

śaur : *shaurl* 'spoon'

śaw : *shiaw* 'laugh'

.Śayi, Śaayi : *Sheauyi* 'Little Aunt,' term of address

Śayi : *Sanyi* 'Third Aunt,' term of ad-dress (for a different person from above)

.śɛbaadji, śɛrbar.dji : *shyebar.tzy* 'shoe-horn'

śɛbon (with voiceless *b*) : — 'c'est bon,' i.e., 'tastes good'

.śɛdah : *shyedall* 'shoestring'

.śɛdjih : *shiee-tzyh* 'to write'

śɛɛ : *shiee* 'to write'

śɛh.śɛ, hɛh.hɛ : *shieh.shie* 'Thank you' (in response to something given)

śɛnnday : *shianntzay* 'now'

śerm.me, .śe.ńe : *sherm.me* 'what'; 'what kind of'

śɛr, śeir : *shye* 'shoe'

.śibuh : *sueibuh* 'diaper'

.śidao, .śidjeau : *shii-tzao* 'take bath'

.śidjeau : *shii-jeau* 'wash the feet'

.śi.djia-i : *shueyjiaw-i* 'nightshirt'; 'bath-robe'

.śidjiaw : *shuey-jiaw* 'go to bed'; 'sleep'

Śihyi 'Fourth Aunt' = *.Śayi*

sinn : *shinn* 'letter'

śinn.sin : meaning unknown, occurring in *Gam.ma buhyeou śinn.śin.*

śiou.śi : — 'Susie' (formerly *hiou.hi*)

śiow.dji : *shiow.tzy* 'sleeve'; term also applied to undershirt the sleeve of which is sucked

śoei : *shoei* 'water'

śoo.iś : *suoo.le* 'locked'

śoou : *shoou* 'hand'; 'touch with hand'

śooudjiah : *shooujiuall* 'handkerchief'

śooudjin : *shoou.jin* 'towel'

śy.de : *shy.de* 'wet'

śyh = *.hy*

śy.iś : *shy.le* 'it's (got) wet'

śyi.śi : *shii.shi* 'just wash'; 'give it a washing'

śyy : *shyy* 'excrement'

't (glottalized *t* with oral explosion) : *.tzy,* noun suffix, now replaced by *.dji,* q.v.

ta : *cha* 'fork'

taandji : *taan.tzy* 'blanket'

ta.mi : — 'Tommy'

tan : *chuan* 'put on'; 'wear'

tann : *tanq* 'hot'

Tan.ta : *Kan.ta* 'Canta'

tao.ue : *chaur.le* 'it's (got) wet'

tar, *tar-pas-bon* : *char*   'tea'; 'tea, which is no good (for children)'

tarn : *tarng* 'candy'; 'sugar'

tarntjyn : *tarn-chyn* 'play the piano'

ta.ta : *tsa.tsa* 'wipe a little'

tay : *tsay* 'vegetable'

.tayėh.ue : *tay reh .le* 'too hot'; 'take off' (a sweater, a bib, etc.)

tay djonn.ńe : *tay jonq .le* 'it's too heavy'

tay.iang : *tay.iang*   'sun,' sometimes also applied to the moon

tayśɛrn : *tay shyan* 'too salty'

tern : *terng* 'it hurts'

tjɛnbii : *chianbii* 'pencil'

tjibaa.ue : *chy-bao.le*   'have eaten enough'; 'I want to leave the table'

tjeai.de : *chii.lai.le* 'have got up'

tjennśa : *chennshal* 'shirt'

tjih : *tsyh* '(small) fishbone'

tjihte : *chihche* 'automobile'

tjihtjyou : *chihchyou* 'balloon'

tjin : *ting* 'listen!' previously also used for 'look!'

tjoei : *toei* 'leg'

tjuan.hu : *chuang.hu* 'window'

tjuei.tjuei : *chuei.chuei*   'blow' (hot food, etc.)

tjwan : *chwan* 'ship'; 'bed'

tjy, *tji* : *chy* 'eat'

tjyän : *chyang* 'wall'

tjyɛn : *chyan* 'money, coin'

tjyɛn : *tyan* 'sweet'

tjyfann, *tjifann* : *chy-fann* 'eat dinner'

tjyy : *chyy* 'ruler'

tjyy, *djyy* : *jyy* 'paper' (can say *djyy* with effort)

to : *tuo* 'take off'

tośɛr : *tuoshye* 'slipper'

tośɛr : *tuo shye* 'take off shoes'

tooufa : *tour.fa* 'hair' (of the head)

tu.chiu : *chu.chiu* 'go out'

tufann = *tjyfann*

tuh.dji : *tuh.tzy* 'rabbit'

twen.tuen = *hwen.tuen*

wa : *wal* 'play with'

wan.ńe, *woanńhe* 'finished,' applied to many things, as *Kaiden wan.ńe* 'Turn on the lights finished,' i.e., 'The lights are out'

wey : *wey* 'to feed'; also used for 'help' in general, such as taking her by the hand in going downstairs

woan : *woan* 'bowl'

yaφua = *φuaya*

yah : *lah* 'hot' (of taste)

yai : *lai* 'come'

yai.e : *lai.le* 'has come'; 'here is . . .'

yàn : *yang* 'sheep'

yeaba : *laa.ba* '(toy) horn'

yean, *ńean* : *lean* 'face, check'

yeandah : *yeanjienql* 'eyeglasses'

yeandjin : *yean.jing* 'eye'

yee : *yee* 'also'

yeh : *reh* 'warm, hot'

yɛnn.dji : *yuann.tzy* 'garden'

yi : *yi* 'aunt'

yiidji : *yi.tzy* 'soap'

yiidji : *yii.tzy* 'chair'

.yobo (pause) *śibiin* : *luo.bosybiing* 'hot biscuits stuffed with radish shreds'

yoobo : *luo.bo* 'radish'; 'turnip'

you : *you*   'grease' (on fingers or clothes)

yow : *row* 'meat'

yu : *yu* 'fish'

yu : *liu* 'donkey' (pronounced *yæ* when trying to distinguish from above)

yueh.iàn : *yueh.liang* 'moon'

yuh.de : *liuh.de* · 'green'; 'blue'

yun.tai : *yun.tsai* 'cloud'

ENGLISH •

A number of developmental studies of English phonology have been published, ranging from brief notes in journals to substantial monograph-length descriptions. Some of these studies are based on observation of the author's own children and interpretation of the data in relation to the theory of Jakobson's *Kindersprache* (1968). Studies by Velten (1943) and Weir (1962, pp. 28–68) are good examples of this tradition. The most detailed and informative study of this kind is Leopold's volume *Sound-learning in the first two years* (1939–1949, Vol. 2), which presents a full description of his daughter's sounds from the first month to the beginning of the third year, including analysis of substitutions for adult sounds as well as structural interpretation of her phonology in its own terms. Summaries and reworkings of this material appear in Leopold (1953–1954), Ferguson (1968), and in the Moskowitz paper in this volume. The Moskowitz paper extends the tradition, combining data from previous studies with fresh data and discussing the issues from a somewhat broader perspective of linguistic theory.

A very different line of research is represented here by the Winitz and Irwin article. Studies of this kind exploit intensively a body of data secured by controlled procedures from a selected population of children. The studies published by Irwin and his associates typically are based on longitudinal records of some 90 children and are concerned with frequency of occurrence of sound types, making no distinction between babbling and speech and no reference to distinctiveness in function. A line of phonological research not represented here is the large-scale statistical analysis of children's ability to pronounce speech sounds, which provides different kinds of data (see, for example, Templin, 1957).

A quite new line of research uses the strategy of eliciting data by experimental techniques in order to check a specific linguistic or psycholinguistic hypothesis. The Menyuk studies such as the one reprinted here, and Menyuk and Anderson (1969), are examples of this approach, which provides still different kinds of data.

All the papers included here presuppose a phonemic analysis of English; convenient presentations of English phonology for nonspecialists are Bronstein (1960) and Gimson (1962), which provide further references; the most modern treatment is Chomsky and Halle (1968), which is very technical and difficult to relate directly to child phonology, but highly suggestive on a number of points.   —C.A.F.

Syllabic and Phonetic Structure of Infants' Early Words
—— *Harris Winitz and Orvis C. Irwin*

The purpose of this article is to report an analysis of three aspects of infant speech, namely, the syllabic structure, the phonetic structure and the

From *Journal of Speech and Hearing Research*, 1958, **1**, 250–256. Reprinted·with the permission of the authors and the American Speech and Hearing Association.

vowel and consonant composition of early words. The data were selected from files of the Iowa Child Welfare Research Station. A complete account of the subjects and of the methodology employed in the original collection and analysis of the data has been described by Winitz and Irwin (*13*). With regard to this present investigation an additional fact should be mentioned: phonetic utterances interpreted as words were recorded both in the International Phonetic Alphabet and in the English alphabet.

PROCEDURE

Definition of a Word

In this study an utterance was counted as a *word* if it could be categorized as: (1) a word approximation, (2) a standard word or (3) a self-language word.

Word Approximation.   In a recent study McCurry and Irwin (*11*) called attention to the fact that the infant's early words may not be of the same phonetic structure as those of adults but may be approximations of words in which some of the phonemes are the same. They have defined a *word approximation* as "a phonetic pattern which is interpreted by the observers at the time of the transcription as an attempt by the infant to pronounce a standard word. The word approximation is further delimited as a phonetic pattern in which one or more of the phonetic elements of the standard word, either vowel or consonantal elements, are present. This means that some elements of the standard word are omitted, and other elements are substituted or added."

Standard Word.   McCurry and Irwin (*11*) have defined a *standard word* in terms of its phonetic listing in Kenyon and Knott's *Pronouncing Dictionary of American English* (*5*). The present investigators felt that several exceptions to the definition of a standard word were justified because many words used in the home by parents and learned by children are not of the exact phonetic structure listed by Kenyon and Knott. The following gives examples of such exceptions:

> The following form of 'daddy' was accepted: [dædi]. The following forms of 'mother' were accepted: [mɑmi], [mɑmu], [mɑmʌ], [mɑ], [mɑm], and [mɑmə]. The following forms of 'baby' were accepted. [beɪbi] and [bebi]. Words such as 'doggy,' 'choo-choo,' 'bow wow,' 'tick-tock,' 'moo moo,' etc., were considered as standard words when they were of the correct phonetic structure. If these words were not of the correct phonetic structure, they were considered word approximations.

Self-Language Word.   Another category has been added to include some of the infant's first words which do not meet the criteria of standard word or word approximation. This category, *self-language word*, may be defined as a phonetic pattern which is interpreted by the observers at the time of transcription as an attempt by the infant to pronounce a standard word, although not one of the phonetic elements of the standard word is present. An instance of this is [bʌ] for 'dog.'

Selection of Data

The data, as described by Winitz and Irwin (*13*), were grouped and reported in 15 two-month intervals or age levels, beginning with age level one (months one and two) and ending with age level 15 (months 29 and 30). Age levels seven (months 13 and 14), eight (months 15 and 16) and nine (months 17 and 18) were selected for analysis in this study because they represent, according to previous investigations (*10*), the period of infancy during which infants are reported to utter their first words. The records selected for this study were those for children who, according to the available records, uttered at least one word at one of the above age levels.

Table 1 indicates the distribution of subjects, records and words at each

TABLE 1   NUMBER OF SUBJECTS, RECORDS AND WORDS AT AGE LEVELS SEVEN (MONTHS 13 AND 14), EIGHT (MONTHS 15 AND 16) AND NINE (MONTHS 17 AND 18).

AGE LEVEL	SUBJECTS	RECORDS	WORDS
7	23	38	137
8	35	62	224
9	35	58	268

age level. Table 2 shows the number and percentage of standard words, word approximations, and self-language words that were subject to analysis at each age level.

TABLE 2   NUMBER AND PERCENTAGE OF STANDARD WORDS, WORD APPROXIMATIONS, AND SELF-LANGUAGE WORDS IN THE SPEECH OF INFANTS AT AGE LEVELS SEVEN (MONTHS 13 AND 14), EIGHT (MONTHS 15 AND 16) AND NINE (MONTHS 17 AND 18).

AGE LEVEL	STANDARD WORDS		WORD APPROXIMATIONS		SELF-LANGUAGE	
	N	%	N	%	N	%
7	22	16.06	114	83.21	11	.73
8	53	23.66	170	75.89	1	.45
9	103	38.43	151	56.35	14	5.22

Method of Analysis

In line with the specific purposes of this paper the data were analyzed for each of the following categories: (1) syllabic structure, (2) phonetic structure and (3) vowel and consonant composition.

Syllabic Structure. In order to analyze the syllabic structure of the infant's early words, a modification of the categories employed by Chen (2), in a study of the repetitious patterns of the phonemes of infants, was used and the following categories were employed: (1) monosyllabic words with two phonemes, such as [bi]; (2) monosyllabic words with three phonemes, such as [bim]; (3) words consisting of a repeated syllable, such as [bibi]; (4) words consisting of a repeated syllable with an added phoneme on the final syllable, such as [bibim]; (5) words consisting of two syllables in which one sound is common and one sound varies, such as [bibɪ]; (6) words consisting of two syllables in which one sound is common and one sound varies and a phoneme is added to the second syllable, such as [bibɪm]. In the above analysis, diphthongs, blends, and affricates were considered single units or "phonemes" since these combinations of sounds tend to be heard as elemental units.

Phonetic Structure. To investigate the phonetic structure of the infant's early words, the elemental sounds or phonemes were tallied and presented in terms of percentages. Additional analyses included several vowel (front, middle and back) and consonantal (by place and manner of articulation) categories.

Consonant and Vowel Composition. To investigate the consonant-vowel composition of infants' early words, the words were analyzed to determine

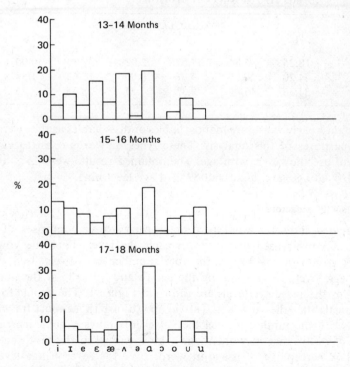

Figure 1. Profiles of vowel phoneme percentages in the words of infants at age levels seven (months 13 and 14), eight (months 15 and 16) and nine (months 17 and 18).

whether they were constituted only of vowels, only of consonants, or of both vowels and consonants.

RESULTS

Syllabic Structure

The results of the analysis of the syllabic structure of the words are shown in Table 3. An examination of the last column in this table indicates that most

TABLE 3   PERCENTAGES OF WORD TYPES IN THE SPEECH OF INFANTS AT AGE LEVELS SEVEN (MONTHS 13 AND 14), EIGHT (MONTHS 15 AND 16) AND NINE (MONTHS 17 AND 18) . WORDS WERE CLASSIFIED AS (1) MONO-SYLLABIC WORDS WITH TWO PHONEMES; (2) MONOSYLLABIC WORDS WITH THREE PHONEMES; (3) WORDS CONSISTING OF A REPEATED SYLLABLE; (4) WORDS CONSISTING OF A REPEATED SYLLABLE WITH AN ADDED PHONEME ON THE FINAL SYLLABLE; (5) WORDS CONSISTING OF TWO SYLLABLES IN WHICH ONE SOUND IS COMMON AND ONE SOUND VARIES; AND (6) WORDS CONSISTING OF TWO SYLLABLES IN WHICH ONE SOUND IS COMMON AND ONE SOUND VARIES AND A PHONEME IS ADDED TO THE SECOND SYLLABLE .

AGE LEVEL	WORD CLASSIFICATION						TOTAL
	1	2	3	4	5	6	
7	18.25	5.84	17.52	2.92	31.39	0.00	75.92
8	44.20	20.09	5.36	0.00	15.63	1.34	86.62
9	34.33	15.67	9.33	.37	28.36	.75	88.81

of the infant's early words are monosyllables or dissyllables as they were classified for the purposes of this analysis. These types of words seem to vary in percentage of use, however, with age. The obtained results were 76% at age level seven, 87% at age level eight and 89% at age level nine.

Phonetic Structure

Table 4 indicates what percentage each vowel comprises of the total number of vowels used in words for each age level. Thus the vowel [i], for example, comprises 5.49% of the total number of vowels used during the seventh age level, 13.57% during the eighth and 13.79% at the ninth. Vowel profiles for the three age levels are shown in Figure 1. The profile for age level seven reveals that the vowels [ɪ], [ɛ], [ʌ] and [ɑ] are those most frequently used in words. By the ninth age level the vowel [ɑ] shows a great increase in percentage of occurrence in word usage. The sound [ɪ] in the ninth age level has doubled in percentage of usage in words over the seventh age level. The [ɛ] and [ʌ] vowels show some decrease in percentage of usage with increased age.

Table 5 indicates the percentages of vowel categories, classified according

TABLE 4   VOWEL PHONEME PERCENTAGES IN THE WORDS OF INFANTS
AT AGE LEVELS SEVEN (MONTHS 13 AND 14), EIGHT (MONTHS 15 AND 16)
AND NINE (MONTHS 17 AND 18).

VOWEL	AGE LEVEL		
	7	8	9
[i]	5.49	13.57	13.79
[ɪ]	11.76	10.80	7.14
[e]	5.49	8.03	5.81
[ɛ]	15.69	4.43	4.49
[æ]	7.06	7.48	5.81
[ʌ]	18.04	10.52	8.80
[ə]	1.18	.83	.17
[ɑ]	19.22	18.28	31.89
[ɔ]	.78	1.66	1.10
[o]	2.75	6.88	6.31
[ʊ]	8.63	7.20	9.30
[u]	3.92	10.53	5.15

to Fairbanks (3), used in the words of infants at age levels seven through nine.
This table shows that the percentage of front vowel usage in words is greater
at age level seven than the percentage of back vowel usage. At age level eight
the percentages are the same, but at age level nine the percentage of back
vowels is considerably higher than that of the front vowels. The use of the
middle vowels relative to other vowels decreases from age level seven to age
level nine.

The percentages of consonantal phonemes are listed in Table 6. Consonant
profiles appear in Figure 2. An examination of the table and the profiles indicates that labials are used in words more frequently than are other consonants.
Among the labials the [b] sound is dominant. The post-dentals as a group are
next in order of usage in words. Here the consonant [d] is the outstanding
phoneme. The profiles show that back consonants at the seventh age level
comprise a small percentage of the total consonants used in words. The percentage of back consonants becomes slightly higher at age levels eight and nine.
This finding indicates that when words appear in the vocalization of infants a

TABLE 5   PERCENTAGE OF VOWEL CATEGORIES, CLASSIFIED ACCORD-
ING TO FAIRBANKS (3), USED IN THE WORDS OF INFANTS AT AGE LEVELS
SEVEN (MONTHS 13 AND 14), EIGHT (MONTHS 15 AND 16) AND NINE
(MONTHS 17 AND 18).

AGE LEVEL	FRONT	MIDDLE	BACK
7	45.49	19.21	35.30
8	44.31	11.63	44.32
9	36.87	9.30	53.82

TABLE 6 CONSONANT PHONEME PERCENTAGES IN THE WORDS OF
INFANTS AT AGE LEVELS SEVEN (MONTHS 13 AND 14), EIGHT (MONTHS
15 AND 16) AND NINE (MONTHS 17 AND 18).

CONSONANT	AGE LEVEL		
	7	8	9
[p]	.42	2.44	1.15
[b]	33.90	27.74	37.61
[m]	17.80	7.93	5.28
[w]	12.29	4.88	4.13
[ʌ]	.00	.00	.00
[f]	.00	.30	3.21
[v]	.00	.00	.00
[θ]	.00	.00	.00
[ð]	.42	.00	.46
[t]	2.12	7.62	4.13
[d]	23.31	19.82	19.27
[n]	.85	4.57	7.11
[s]	.85	2.44	2.06
[z]	.00	1.52	.92
[ʃ]	.00	.61	1.83
[ʒ]	.00	.00	.00
[l]	1.27	.30	1.37
[r]	.00	2.44	.97
[j]	.00	1.83	.00
[ç]	.00	.00	.00
[ŋ]	.00	.00	.23
[k]	2.54	8.23	4.36
[g]	2.12	3.36	4.36
[x]	.00	.00	.00
[h]	2.12	3.96	1.61
[ʔ]	.00	.00	.00

reversal has occurred in the situation which Irwin (4, 5) found concerning the status of back consonants during the first months of life. During early infancy velars and glottals are relatively frequent, but with the appearance of words during the second year of infancy there is a decrement in the relative frequency of their usage.

Tables 7 and 8 indicate the percentages of consonants, classified according to Fairbanks (3) by place and manner of articulation, used at the three age levels. With regard to place of articulation the labial and post-dental sounds constitute more than 80% of the consonantal sounds at each age level. With regard to manner of articulation the plosive consonants greatly predominate over nasal, semivowel, fricative and glide consonants at all three age levels.

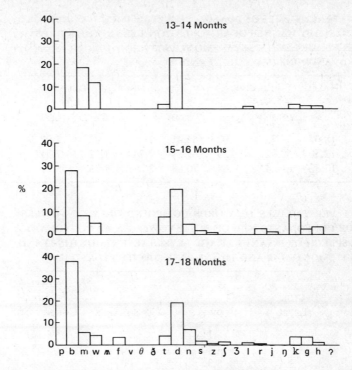

Figure 2. Profiles of consonant phoneme percentages in the words of infants at age levels seven (months 13 and 14), eight (months 15 and 16) and nine (months 17 and 18).

Vowel and Consonant Composition

Table 9 shows that about 95% of the early words of infants contain both vowels and consonants. At age level seven only a small percentage of words composed only of consonants were recorded. At all age levels words composed only of vowels constitute about five per cent or less of the total words spoken.

TABLE 7   PERCENTAGES OF CONSONANTS, CLASSIFIED ACCORDING TO FAIRBANKS (3) BY PLACE OF ARTICULATION, USED IN THE WORDS OF INFANTS AT AGE LEVELS SEVEN (MONTHS 13 AND 14), EIGHT (MONTHS 15 AND 16) AND NINE (MONTHS 17 AND 18).

AGE LEVEL	LABIAL	LABIO-DENTAL	LINGUA-DENTAL	POST-DENTAL	VELAR	GLOTTAL
7	64.41	.00	.42	28.40	4.66	2.12
8	42.99	.30	.00	41.15	11.59	3.96
9	48.17	3.21	.46	37.61	8.95	1.61

TABLE 8   PERCENTAGES OF CONSONANTS, CLASSIFIED ACCORDING TO
FAIRBANKS (3) BY MANNER OF ARTICULATION, USED IN THE WORDS OF
INFANTS AT AGE LEVELS SEVEN (MONTHS 13 AND 14), EIGHT (MONTHS
15 AND 16) AND NINE (MONTHS 17 AND 18).

AGE LEVEL	NASAL	PLOSIVE VOICE-			SEMI- VOWEL	FRICATIVE VOICE-			GLIDE
		VOICED	LESS	TOTAL		VOICED	LESS	TOTAL	
7	18.65	59.33	5.08	64.41	1.27	.42	2.97	3.39	12.29
8	12.50	50.92	18.29	69.21	2.74	1.52	7.31	8.83	6.71
9	12.62	61.24	9.64	70.88	2.29	1.38	8.71	10.09	4.13

TABLE 9   PERCENTAGES OF WORDS COMPOSED ONLY OF VOWELS,
ONLY OF CONSONANTS, OR OF BOTH VOWELS AND CONSONANTS
IN THE SPEECH OF INFANTS AT AGE LEVELS SEVEN (MONTHS 13 AND
14), EIGHT (MONTHS 15 AND 16) AND NINE (MONTHS 17 AND 18).

AGE LEVEL	VOWELS	CONSONANTS	VOWELS AND CONSONANTS
7	5.11	.73	94.16
8	4.45	.00	95.55
9	3.36	.00	96.64

DISCUSSION

Syllabic Structure

The findings of this study appear to be in agreement with reports found
in the literature. Berry and Eisenson (1) have suggested that the syllabic structure
of the first words are either dissyllables, such as *baba*, or monosyllables, such
as *ba*. Similarly, McCarthy (10) has stated, "Children's babbling often consists
of repetition of identical or similar syllables so that the first vocal utterances
to acquire meaning are usually reduplicated monosyllables such as *mama*, *dada*,
nana, *bye-bye*, *tick-tick*, *choo-choo*, and the like." Lewis (8) has reported that
85% of early words are either monosyllabic or reduplicated monosyllables
(39% of the former and 46% of the latter).

Phonetic Structure

This study has some bearing on the controversy concerning which consonants are first mastered by the infant, namely, whether they are labials or
back consonants. The statement is made in the literature that labials are the
earliest sounds (6, 9, 12). The Iowa studies (4, 5) have shown that in the early
months of life the first consonants uttered are back consonants and that labials
are relatively infrequent. The present study has shown that during the second

year of life labial consonants are most frequent as elements in word structure. The inference seems reasonable, then, that some of the observations reported previously in the literature were not made on infants in the early months of life, but were made on infants who were beginning to say their first words.

SUMMARY

The syllabic structure, phonetic structure and vowel and consonant composition of the infant's early words were studied at three age levels: the seventh (months 13 and 14), the eighth (months 15 and 16), and the ninth (months 17 and 18).

A high percentage of the words were either monosyllables or dissyllables. The vowel sounds varied in relative use at the different age levels with the exception of the vowel [ɑ], which was outstanding at each age level. The labial and post-dental sounds constituted more than 80% of the consonant sounds at each age level. A higher percentage of front and back vowels than of middle vowels were used. Approximately 95% of the words were composed of both vowels and consonants.

REFERENCES

1. Berry, M. F., and J. Eisenson, *Speech Disorders: Principles and Practices of Therapy*. New York: Appleton-Century-Crofts, Inc., 1956.
2. Chen, H. P., Speech development during the first year of life, a quantitative study. Ph.D. dissertation, University of Iowa, 1946.
3. Fairbanks, G., *Voice and Articulation Drillbook*. New York: Harpers, 1940.
4. Irwin, O. C., Infant speech: consonant sounds according to place of articulation. *Journal of Speech Disorders*, **12**, 1947, 397–401.
5. Irwin, O. C., Infant speech: consonant sounds according to manner of articulation. *Journal of Speech Disorders*, **12**, 1947, 402–404.
6. Jespersen, J. O. H., *Language: Its Nature, Development and Origin*. New York: Holt, 1928.
7. Kenyon, J. S., and T. A. Knott, *A Pronouncing Dictionary of American English*. Springfield, Mass.: Merriam Co., 1949.
8. Lewis, M. M., *Infant Speech: A Study of the Beginnings of Language* (2nd ed.). London: Routledge and Paul, 1951.
9. Löbisch, J. E. L., *Entwickelungsgeschichte der Seele des Kindes*. Wien: C. Haas, 1851.
10 McCarthy, D., Language development in children, in *Manual of Child Psychology*, L. Carmichael, ed. (2nd ed.). New York: John Wiley & Sons, Inc., 1954.
11. McCurry, W. H., and O. C. Irwin, A study of word approximations in the spontaneous speech of infants. *Journal of Speech and Hearing Disorders*, **18**, 1953, 133–139.

12. Tracy, F., *The Psychology of Childhood* (3rd ed.). Boston: Heath, 1896.
13. Winitz, H., and O. C. Irwin, Infant speech: consistency with age. *Journal of Speech and Hearing Research*, **1**, 1958, pp. 245–249.

The Role of Distinctive Features in Children's Acquisition of Phonology[1]

—— *Paula Menyuk*

It has been postulated that the speech sounds of all languages are composed of bundles of features whose parameters are both articulatory and acoustic in nature (Jakobson, Fant, and Halle, 1963). It is the matrix of features which differentiates speech sounds from one another by certain attributes. For example, some sounds are differentiated from other sounds in terms of the presence or absence of voicing (/p/ vs. /b/), and then others in terms of the presence or absence of continuancy (/ʃ/ vs. /tʃ/). Some sounds are differentiated from others by a number of attributes involving, for example, nasality, voicing, place, etc. (/m/ vs. /k/). If a comparatively small set of features or attributes can describe the speech sounds in all languages, then, it is hypothesized, these attributes are related to the physiological capacities of man to produce and perceive sounds.

It has also been proposed that in the child's acquisition of the phonological classes and phonological rules of his language a regular and valid sequence in the developmental course can be observed (Jakobson, 1962). This sequence is presumably based on the child's increasing capacity to further differentiate speech sounds by the distinctive features of the sounds in a language. For example, at some stage of development, he may distinguish sounds into ± nasal (/b/ vs. /m/ or /d/ vs. /n/) but be unable to distinguish between sounds in terms of place of articulation (/b/ vs. /d/ or /m/ vs. /n/). The actual facts of this developmental course have yet to be obtained although several models of this development have been proposed based on the hypothesis that the direction is from the least marked segments in terms of features to progressively more marked segments. However, we do not have the data to posit a specific order of acquisition of feature distinctions.

Despite the fact that this developmental course has not been carefully analyzed and that there is, in fact, very little research reported on the perceptual distinctions children can make between speech sounds during early childhood

From *Journal of Speech and Hearing Research*, 1968, **11**, 138–146. Reprinted by permission of the author and the American Speech and Hearing Association.

[1] This work was supported in part by the National Institutes of Health (Grant 5 RO1 NB–04332–05) and by the U.S. Air Force Cambridge Research Laboratories, Office of Aerospace Research, Contract No. AF19 (628)–5661. Grateful acknowledgment is given to Allan C. Goodman and his staff at the Children's Hospital Medical Center, Boston, Massachusetts, for making available the data on the results of the Templin-Darley tests of articulation.

(from birth to 3 years), there has been some data collected on the mastery of speech sounds by American children aged 2 to 6 (Powers, 1957) and the correct usage of consonants in syllables by Japanese children aged 1 to 3 (Nakazima, 1961). Some data have been collected on the sound substitutions made by children, roughly 3 to 7 years, during the developmental period (Menyuk, 1964a), and the substitutions made by children, age 3 to 12, with articulation problems. In addition, there is some data on the perceptual confusions of adults (Wicklegren, 1966).

The purpose of this paper is to analyze, in terms of its distinctive feature content, available data concerning correct usage of consonants during the morpheme construction period, the data obtained on the consonant substitutions made by children during the developmental period and those made by children with articulation problems, and the available data on the confusions of adults. It might then be possible to define the order of the acquisition of the attributes of speech sounds and, thus, derive some information about possible cues used in the perception and production of consonants by children during the developmental period rather than merely labeling the process. Further, it might be feasible to derive possible explanations for the order observed in terms of the capacities of the human organism to produce and distinguish speech sounds.

METHOD AND RESULTS

The features investigated in this analysis were gravity, diffuseness, stridency, nasality, continuancy, and voicing. The data on adult consonant substitutions were obtained from the results of an experiment in which subjects were asked to recall a list of syllables composed of consonant plus /a/. The developmental data were obtained by transcribing the consonant substitutions produced by children while spontaneously generating sentences. The data on children with articulation problems were obtained by transcribing the consonant substitutions produced by children while spontaneously generating sentences (Menyuk, 1964b), and an analysis of the results of the Templin-Darley articulation test (Templin and Darley, 1960) which had been administered to a group of children diagnosed as having articulation problems.

The data on the mastery of consonantal speech sounds was analyzed by determining the percentage of sounds containing a feature which was used correctly at various ages during the developmental period observed. For example, if 3 out of the 10 speech sounds marked + grave in the grammar were correctly used or mastered at age X, then it was noted that there was 30% usage of this feature at this age. This same calculation was done for all the features.

Figure 1 shows the rise in percentage of usage of features by American children over an age range of 2 and a half to 5 years, and indicates the order of mastery of speech sounds containing these features during this period. According to this data complete mastery of the consonant sounds occurs after 6+ years. Consonant clusters were not included in this analysis.

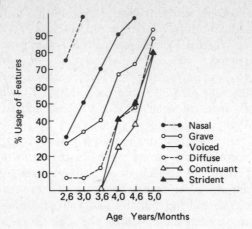

Figure 1. Percentage of usage of features in consonants used correctly from age 2 and a half to 5 years by American children.

Figure 2 shows the percentage of usage of features in correct use of consonants in syllables by Japanese children over an age range of 1 to 3 years, and indicates the order of correct use of consonants containing these features during this period. It should be noted that the Japanese population was younger than the American population, but that correct production in a syllable rather than mastery in words was being examined.

If we examine the rank order both in terms of time of mastery or correct usage, and percentage of mastery or correct usage at the oldest age sampled,

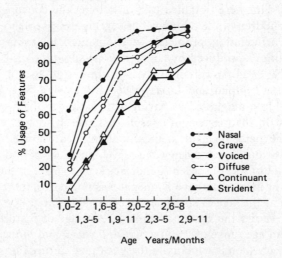

Figure 2. Percentage of usage of features in consonants used correctly from age 1 to 3 years by Japanese children.

**TABLE 1   RANK ORDER OF USE OF FEATURES AS SHOWN IN THE
CORRECT USE OR MASTERY OF CONSONANTS.**

RANK ORDER	JAPANESE AGE 1–3	AMERICAN AGE 2.5–5 YEARS
1	nasal	nasal
2	grave	grave
3	voice	voice
4	diffuse	diffuse
5	continuant	continuant
6	strident	strident

we can observe a striking similarity between Japanese and American children in the order of feature acquisition during the developmental periods observed. This is shown in Table 1. Both groups of children were proportionately using consonants which contained the features + nasal, + grave, and + voice more correctly and mastering them sooner than those which contain the features + diffuse, + continuant, and + strident.

In the case of American children, where we do have statistics on frequency of consonant usage by adults (Irwin, 1947), these results are largely a contradiction of what is presumably heard in the primary linguistic data. An analysis of the rank order of feature usage as shown in the proportional usage of consonants by English speaking adults is: diffuse, nasal, voiced, continuant, strident, and grave.

To examine the role of the distinctive features in the consonant substitutions of children acquiring the sound system of their language, and in those acquiring this system in a sufficiently deviant manner to be labeled "articulation problems," and to examine the role of these features in the perceptual confusions of adults, the following procedure was used. All of the substitutions observed were analyzed by noting which features were maintained in the substitution. If, for example, /t/ was substituted for /θ/ as in "tank" for "thank", the following is the analysis that resulted:

	t	θ		t	θ		t	θ
Nasal	–	–	Voice	–	–	Continuant	–	+
Grave	–	–	Diffuse	+	+	Strident	–	–

It could then be noted that all the features were maintained in this substitution except continuancy. The percentage of maintenance of features for all the substitutions in the three groups was then calculated and a rank order of maintenance of features obtained. This rank order for the three groups is given in Table 2.

As can be seen in Table 2, there are differences between groups in rank order of maintenance of features in substitutions. Stridency is the feature best

**TABLE 2   RANK ORDER OF MAINTENANCE OF FEATURES IN
CONSONANT SUBSTITUTION.**

RANK ORDER	ADULT RECALL	CHILDREN'S PRODUCTION DEVELOPMENTAL	CHILDREN'S PRODUCTION ARTICULATION PROBLEM
1	strident	voice	nasal
2	voice	nasal	voice
3	nasal	strident	grave
4	continuant	continuant	continuant
5	grave	grave	diffuse
6	diffuse	diffuse	strident

maintained by adults in their recall of CV syllables, while it is the feature least maintained by the children in the "articulation problem" group in their production of consonants. Voicing and nasality continue to rank high in all groups. In the adult group and the developmental group, gravity and diffuseness rank lowest in feature maintenance while gravity ranks high in the "articulation problem" group.

A chi-square evaluation was used to compare the percentage of maintenance of each feature in the consonant substitutions of the three groups. There are no significant differences between the adults and the children developing language normally in the percentage of maintenance of each feature in substitutions. The children with articulation problems maintain all features significantly less in their consonant substitutions than do children who are developing language normally. The only exceptions are the features ± nasal. In these cases there is no significant difference between the groups. Also the difference is less marked with the features ± grave. These results are shown in Table 3.

**TABLE 3   PERCENTAGE OF MAINTENANCE OF FEATURES IN
CONSONANT SUBSTITUTION.**

FEATURE	PERCENTAGE OF ADULT RECALL	PERCENTAGE OF CHILDREN'S PRODUCTION DEVELOPMENTAL	P* VALUE	PERCENTAGE OF CHILDREN'S PRODUCTION ARTICULATION PROBLEM
Voice	85	100	0.01	58
Nasal	85	100		88
Grave	69	50	0.05	29
Strident	88	75	0.01	9
Continuant	75	67	0.01	17
Diffuse	56	50	0.01	13

* P value obtained by chi square evaluation.

DISCUSSION

The results of the above analysis indicate that the distinctive features of the speech sounds of the language that were examined play a differing role in the perception and production of these sounds. One can observe the same order in acquisition and relative degree of mastery or correct usage of sounds containing the various features by groups of children from two differing linguistic environments, indicating that a hierarchy of feature distinction may be a linguistic universal, probably dependent on the developing perceptive and productive capacities of the child. The features which dominate these children's correct usage of consonants at the beginning stages of morpheme construction are + nasal, + grave, and + voice. When we observe the substitutions of adults in recall of consonants, and the consonant substitutions in the productions of children who are developing language normally and those who are not, we observe that the features of voicing and nasality are among the best maintained in these substitutions. One might then postulate that the features ± nasal and ± voice are easiest to perceive, recall, and produce.

± Strident and ± continuant features seem to play a differing role depending on the task, the age of the subject, and his status in the acquisition of the sound system of his language. In recall of consonants by adults, ± strident features are best maintained. Consonants containing + strident and + continuant features are correctly used or mastered last by both Japanese and American children. In the production of consonants by normal speaking children, ± strident features are those best maintained after ± voice and ± nasal features. However, for the children with articulation problems, ± strident features are those least maintained. + Strident, + continuant, and − grave features are very bound up together by virtue of the fact that most consonants marked + strident in grammar are also marked + continuant (the only exceptions are the stops /tʃ/ and /dʒ/) and − grave (the only exceptions are the labio-dentals /f/ and /v/), (Halle, 1961). The sounds /f/ and /v/ are mastered earlier than the other stridents, and the stops /tʃ/ and /dʒ/ are less frequently substituted in the development of the phonological system than their continuant complements, /ʃ/ and /ʒ/. Further, the sounds which are mastered last and most frequently substituted are not − strident but + continuant and − grave (/θ/ and /ð/). It may be that it is not, as has been traditionally assumed, the articulatory gestures used to produce the + strident aspect of a consonant per se (at least for normal speaking children) that makes these consonants late in the developmental scale and difficult to master, but, rather the + continuant and − grave aspects of these sounds.

A possible explanation for this conclusion may be that the other features of consonants which are maintained better and acquired and mastered sooner seem to represent articulatory gestures which have on-off characteristics or a maximal degree of difference. The vocal cords vibrate or they do not (± voice); the sound is emitted through the nasal passages or it is not (± nasal). The attributes + continuant and − grave seem to represent a varying degree of difference. It is on for a somewhat longer time than a burst (+ continuant) and it is produced somewhere other than the periphery of the vocal mechanism (− grave). These statements are merely hypothetical explanatory notions. Much further exploration is needed to isolate the specific parameters of speech stimuli which are easier or more difficult to distinguish and produce.

A feature which also seems to represent a maximal degree of difference is the feature + grave. If a consonant is marked + grave, it is produced at the periphery of the vocal mechanism (i.e., /b/ and /g/). This may account for the fact that consonants marked + grave are used relatively earlier and mastered sooner by both Japanese and American children and that children with articulation problems more frequently maintain the features ± grave in their substitutions than do the other two groups. The features of place, ± grave, and ± diffuse, are least maintained in the recall of consonants by adults and in the production substitutions of children acquiring the phonological rules of their language. In this instance we may be observing the results of the statistical occurrences in the language. According to Denes (1963), the most frequent occurrence of minimal pairs in English is from plosives to fricatives (± continuant or ± strident), then from nasals to semi-vowels and liquids (± nasal), and then a change in voicing. The most frequent errors in consonant substitution by adults takes place among the plosives and the fricatives (an error of place) but not between them. The most frequent errors in consonant substitution by children developing normal language normally takes place among the plosives, fricatives, and semi-vowels and liquids (an error of place) and, in addition, in fewer instances, errors in continuancy occur. The most frequent substitutions in these instances occur between the following sounds: ð/d, θ/t.

One might hypothesize that errors are not usually made between plosives and fricatives, in most instances, because this is a distinction important in the language since it differentiates minimal pairs, whereas errors in place frequently occur since this distinction is not important. In this case knowledge of the language in terms of its minimal-pairs content would be necessary. On the other hand, one might also hypothesize that it is easier to perceive differences between plosives and fricatives than among them and, therefore, the language evolved so that the most frequent occurrence of minimal pairs reflects this greater ease in distinction. Again, this hypothesis needs further exploration through an analysis of the minimal pairs content of other languages and the consonant substitutions of children acquiring these languages.

One further factor should be discussed in terms of the role of distinctive features in children's acquisition of phonology. As was stated, the speech sounds of the language are composed of a bundle of features. They are not only ± a feature. The child, therefore, must in most instances observe several distinctions between speech sounds. As we have noted, distinction between sounds which differ from each other only in one feature (place of articulation) seems to cause the greatest difficulty both in recall by adults and production by children. The one other feature distinction that is frequently not observed is continuancy. The tendency, then, seems to be nonobservation of a single feature differentiation in the most frequent consonant substitutions of the child who is developing language normally. For example, we find substitutions such as "tar" for "car," "dis" for "this," or "fink" for "think." In each of these substitutions all the attributes are maintained except for one in each instance (i.e., place, continuancy, stridency).

In the case of children with articulation problems there are several features which may be nondistinct simultaneously. If we take as an example the case of an 11-year-old boy with no known physiological factor causing his persistent articulation problem we observe the following rules in his grammar:

1. All stops which are + grave or − grave become − grave
                         − diffuse   + diffuse   + diffuse
                                                    + voice
2. All final stops become − voice.

From rule 1 the following morphemes are produced: "dar" for "car." "dirl" for "girl," "die" for "tie," "bidder" for "bigger," "walding" for "walking," and "midden" for "mitten." However, morphemes such as "baby" and "paper" are correctly produced. From rule 1 and 2 the following morphemes are produced: "Bop" for "Bob," "dit" for "did," "doot" for "good," "wat" for "wage," and "date" for "cake." Because of the nonobservation of both place and voicing distinctions in his construction of morphemes, this child's speech becomes almost incomprehensible. This was not the result when only one attribute was not being observed as in the consonant substitutions of normal-speaking children. This difference leads us to the question of memory for the various features which distinguish speech sounds, and memory for the use of these features in phonological rules. Comparative studies of substitutions in speech sound components and the use of these components in sequences may elicit information about the effect of possible differences in basic memory capacity to acquire the phonology of the language. Further, they may allow us to more clearly define incomprehensibility in terms of the features that are not observed and in what context.

An attempt has been made to examine several pieces of evidence to determine the role that distinctive features play in the child's acquisition of the sound system of his language, and to relate the results of this examination to some hypotheses about the child's developing perceptual and productive capacities. Through this kind of analysis, possible explanations of the correlations between the primary linguistic data the child hears and how he deals with it at various stages of development may be derived. In this analysis different kinds of data, which have bearing on the processes of phonological acquisition and development, have been lumped together. Further, the role of the distinctive features has been analyzed in a very gross manner in that the use of these features in the phonological rules of children was not examined but only their role in sound acquisition. Therefore, the analysis presented in this paper is quite preliminary. However, the evidence for a more thorough and meaningful analysis is still to be obtained. The major lack, at present, is that no data is available on the perceptual distinctions children make during the developmental period of morpheme construction and on their use of phonological rules during this same period.

REFERENCES

Denes, P. B., On the statistics of spoken English. *Journal of the Acoustical Society of America*, **35**, 1963, 892–904.

Halle, M., On the role of simplicity in linguistic descriptions. American Mathematical Society, Proceedings of Symposia in Applied Mathematics, Structure of language and its mathematical aspects, **12**, 1961, 89–94.

Irwin, O. C., Infant speech: consonant sounds according to manner of articulation. *Journal of Speech Disorders*, **12**, 1947, 397–401.

Jakobson, R., *Selected Writings I*: The Netherlands: Mouton, 1962, pp. 317–402, 491–503, 538–546.

Jakobson, R., C. G. Fant, and M. Halle, *Preliminaries to Speech Analysis*. Cambridge: M.I.T. Press, 1963.

Menyuk, P., Syntactic rules used by children from pre-school through first grade. *Journal of Child Development*, **35**, 1964a, 533–546.

Menyuk, P., Comparison of grammar of children with normal and deviant speech. *Journal of Speech and Hearing Research*, **7**, 1964b, 109–121.

Nakzima, S., N. Okamoto, J. Murai, M. Tanaka, S. Okuno, T. Maeda, and M. Shimizu. The phoneme systematization and the verbalization process of voices in childhood, *Shinrigan-Hyoron*, **6**, 1962, 1–48.

Powers, M. H., Functional disorders of articulation-symptomatology and etiology, in L. E. Travis, ed., *Handbook of Speech Pathology*. New York: Appleton-Century-Crofts, 1957.

Templin, M. C., and F. L. Darley, *The Templin-Darley Tests of Articulation*. Iowa City, Iowa: Bureau of Educational Research and Service, Extension Division, State University of Iowa, 1960.

Wicklegren, W. A., Distinctive features and errors in short-term memory for English consonants. *Journal of the Acoustical Society of America*, **39**, 1966, 388–398.

The Two-Year-Old Stage in the Acquisition of English Phonology

—— *Arlene I. Moskowitz*

It is a widely held view among linguists and psycholinguists that the phonology of a child's speech at any stage during the acquisition process is structured

From *Language*, 1970, **46**, 426–441. Reprinted with the permission of the author and the Linguistic Society of America.

(cf. Jakobson, 1941). Such structure, however, has not been well documented in the past. This paper is an attempt to find and present the phonological structure of three children at age two.

One possible approach, used in §1 below, is an analysis of substitutions, or sets of correspondences between the child's renditions and the utterances of the adult model. Such an approach reveals much information about phonetic structure, distribution, and particular problems which the child is encountering and overcoming at the moment. Another approach, used in §2 below, is a phonological analysis, potentially more revealing of structure, but encompassing many more theoretical problems. To be most useful, the resultant phonology should fit into a series of phonologies, each of which describes an independent stage with segmental and rule structure, and the totality of which presents a unified picture of the development of segmental and rule structure from the post-babbling stage to the full mastery of English phonology.[1] But such a developmental sequence may not be uni-dimensional in detail, since the child may attempt to work with incorrect hypotheses which are later rejected, or may regress at times.

The first of these two approaches is parallel to the linguistic study of borrowing. The types of changes a child makes in "borrowing" words from the language of the environment are as revealing of the borrower's phonological structure as are the changes which language X imposes on the borrowed words of language Y. Likewise, a series of phonologies covering a period of several years in the life of a particular child can be treated as a special case of the study of internal diachronic phonology.

The writing of a phonology for a child's speech is especially problematic because there are no existent theories which can be directly applied. It is not at all obvious that we would want to attribute to the very young child the complicated rule structure which generative phonology (cf. Chomsky and Halle, 1968) employs to describe mature speech. There is reason to believe that, from the beginnings of speech, the child incorporates phonological rules into his system, although his rules may bear no resemblance whatever to those of the adult phonology. But the vocabulary of a two-year-old presents little if any of the morphological evidence which would justify postulating for him underlying representations which are in any way more "abstract" than those of a traditional phonemic level. Likewise, bi-unique autonomous phonology (e.g., Bloch, 1948, esp. §54.3) is not only inadequate for the description of data of this type (which is highly variant and is produced under a linguistically unusual set of articulatory constraints), but may obscure much of the structure we are trying to reveal. Consider the typical requirement of such a theory that no two phonemes may share a single allophone. Such a requirement apparently led Weir 1962 to the conclusion that her son had no $/\theta/$ in his structure, because every word in which $[\theta]$ occurred had a variant pronunciation with either [f]

---

[1] See Ferguson, 1968, for an example of this longitudinal approach, as well as one of model-and-replica (= analysis of substitutions).

or [t]; therefore the phonemicization of such words had to include either /f/ or /t/. This solution is only a partial satisfaction of the requirement anyway, as the dental spirant is an allophone of two phonemes; and it obscures the fact that those (and only those) words in which the child has such alternations happen to have as their model from the adult language words with /θ/, not with /f/ or /t/.[2] But even the more satisfying solution of postulating a /θ/ phoneme for Anthony Weir's speech would still violate the bi-uniqueness requirement, and this indicates the unreasonableness of placing such a restriction on the two-year-old's speech patterns. Ten renditions by a two-year-old of the same word during the course of two hours may be as phonetically different as are ten words of the adult vocabulary.

Since the value of phonologies of children's speech lies in their display of the progression of structure, new methods of phonological analysis and new evaluation criteria will have to be developed. The procedures of the present study are somewhat ad hoc and atheoretical; work during the coming years should produce more information about the required methods and criteria.

1. Mackie. The data for the first child are taken from the corpus in Albright and Albright, 1956. The corpus consists of 232 utterances transcribed in a notation which seems to be a hybrid of Trager-Smith phonemics and IPA. The child, whom we will call Mackie, was 26 months old at the time of recording, and was the older of two male children. Parents and child are native speakers of English.

1.1. Although the form of transcription chosen obscures much relevant information about Mackie's vowel system, it reveals enough information about the consonants to allow a substitution analysis, which Table 1 provides. Its statistics include the data for every token of every word occurring in the corpus.[3] About 200 different words appeared in the corpus; the most frequent occurred 25 times. Most words occurred in a variety of phonetic guises, although vowels were more variable than consonants. For example, the word *taxi* occurs as [tæksiy], [ta·siy], [tæsiy], [taksi], [taxtiy], and [taksiy]; *look at* occurs as [wukət], [ləkz], [lukə], and [lowgu]. No junctures or word boundaries were provided in the phonetic corpus, but since the two-year-old child's breathing capacities simply are not well enough developed to permit such long strings to occur without breaks, it would be arbitrary and misleading to count all consonant occurrences which are not sentence-initial or sentence-final as "medial." I therefore chose the only slightly arbitrary path of assuming the existence of word boundaries in all expected positions. (Word boundaries were not assumed to

---

[2] For other relevant arguments, see Braine, Ms, esp. §1.1.

[3] One utterance was omitted from the substitution analysis because no gloss was provided for it. In addition, both the situational context of the corpus and the phonological material led me to believe that the gloss 'flower are (or want) to drink' which had been provided for [flâwəətətríŋk] was incorrect, and I took the liberty of substituting the gloss 'flower water drink.' Two other utterances were re-glossed similarly.

separate those phrases which are usually learned as a unit by the child, e.g., *look at*.)

In general, consonants are less stable in final positions than either initially or medially. Omissions occur in final position comparatively often, while in initial and medial positions substitutions are made frequently and omissions are rare. For example, Table 2 shows the percentages of correct correspondences, incorrect substitutions, and omissions totaled over all stop consonants.[4]

If we think of the English consonant system as consisting of 24 phonemes, then Mackie has substantially acquired 19 of them, is in the process of acquiring three (/v z ð/), and is missing two (/ž θ/). The absence of /θ/ from the inventory is real; there are three potential examples, and Mackie substitutes other consonants in two of these instances. On the other hand, the absence of /ž/ is an accidental gap in the corpus; it is not clear whether Mackie is able to pronounce [ž] correctly, or whether he would omit it or substitute other phones for it.

According to the data compiled by Wang and Crawford 1960, /θ/ and /ž/ are by far the least frequent consonant phonemes in English. This fact may account for the relative infrequency of opportunity for Mackie to display his competence in the pronunciation of either phoneme; but relative frequency of occurrence in adult speech plays no more than a minor role, if any at all, in predicting the order in which a child will acquire phonemes. Such a conclusion is obvious if we examine the relative frequencies of adult spirantal phonemes. The average data for the ten studies discussed by Wang and Crawford are: /s/ 7.02, /ð/ 4.76, /z/ 3.57, /v/ 2.88, /f/ 2.75, /š/ 2.03, /θ/ 0.88, and /ž/ 0.87. (It should be noted that affricates were counted as clusters in that study, and so the figures for the sibilants are somewhat higher than they might otherwise be.) When we compare Mackie's ability to pronounce spirants, which will be discussed subsequently, we have a totally different picture: he has learned /s f š/,

---

[4] Victoria Fromkin (personal communication) has pointed out that this "instability" of consonants in final position could be handled by assuming that Mackie has an optional deletion rule. Such a deletion rule would be even more powerful if we attach to it a Labov-type variable. Note that all consonants occur correctly in final position 63.8% of the time, while stop consonants—as can be seen from Table 2—occur correctly 64.5% of the time in final position. In comparison, however, stop consonants are deleted in final position 30.4% of the time, while non-stop consonants are deleted only 19.5% of the time—a very significant difference. The fact that stop consonants are deleted one-and-a-half times as frequently as non-stop consonants in final position is very striking when we consider that stop consonants are far more frequent in their occurrence than any other consonants, that they were probably introduced into the phonetic-phonemic repertory earlier than most other consonants, and that they occur correctly in initial and medial positions with very high frequency (88.8% and 83.4% respectively). This important difference is highlighted by the assumption that Mackie does have a rule $C \rightarrow \emptyset \mid -\#$, to which is attached the variables 30.4% for stop consonants and 19.5% for all other consonants. William Wang (personal communication) has suggested that this seemingly strange situation may be in part due to the fact that relatively fewer acoustic cues accompany final stop consonants than other final consonants, and that the cues are even further reduced if the stop consonant is unreleased.

TABLE 1   MACKIE: CONSONANT SUBSTITUTIONS.
Phones in parentheses are less significant because of their small number of occurrences.

MODEL	INITIAL	SUBSTITUTIONS INTERVOCALIC	FINAL
/p/	p 16	p 5 (β 1)	p 5 (∅ 2)
/t/	t 43 (h 1, k 1)	t 14 (∅ 2, y 1, x 1, k 1)	t 55, ∅ 33 (k 1, d 1)
/k/	k 23 (t 2, g 1, st 1)	k 39 (θ 2, g 1, kx 1, t 1, ʔ 1)	k 13 (∅ 3)
/b/	b 60 (t 1, p 3, d 1, β 1)	b 4	(b 2, bp 1, t 1)
/d/	d 32 (t 5, ǰ 4)	∅ 22, d 14 (t 3)	d 10 (∅ 4, t 3)
/g/	g 24 (b 2, d 1, k 1)	—	g 4
/s/	s 14	s 15	s 22 (∅ 2)
/š/	(š 2)	(š 1)	—
/z/	—	z 4, s 3 (∅ 1)	z 14 (š 1, ∅ 3, s 7)
/ž/	—	—	—
/f/	f 17 (t 1)	(f 2, φ 1)	(φ 1, ∅ 1)
/v/	—	(v 1, β 1, vf 1, b 1)	(d 1, b 2, p 1)
/θ/	(t 1, s 1)	—	(θ 1)
/ð/	d 96, ð 10 (∅ 11, t 5, y 1, s 1)	(ð 1)	—
/m/	m 31	m 21	m 7 (n 1)
/n/	n 16	n 14 (t 1)	n 46 (ŋ 1, d 1, [Ṽ] ∅ 2)
/ŋ/	—	(ŋ 2)	ŋ 22, n 3 (∅ 2)
/l/	l 8 (w 2)	l 6 (∅ 3)	∅ 14, w 5 (l 3, d 1)
/r/	r 12 (w 2, y 1, ∅ 1)	r 3, w 3 (y 1, t 1, ∅ 1)	r 19, ∅ 15 (w 1)
/č/	č 4	(č 2)	(č 1)
/ǰ/	ǰ 14 (d 1)	—	—
/h/	h 23 (∅ 2, ʔ 1)	h 6	—
/y/	y 3 (∅ 1)	(y 1)	—
/w/	w 19 (∅ 3, β 1, y 1)	w 6	—

is in the process of acquiring /z v ð/, and has not learned /θ/. (As mentioned above, the status of /ž/ is questionable.) The fact that Mackie has learned /f/ and /š/ but not the higher-frequency /ð z v/ indicates that relative frequency in adult speech bears little relation to the order of acquisition of consonant phonemes.

Of the 19 consonants which have been acquired, only three are distributionally defective. In final position there are no occurrences of /ǰ/ or /š/, and medially none of /ǰ/ or /g/. That is to say, there are no potential examples in the corpus to illustrate what would happen to these phonemes in the missing positions.

1.2. The child's stop consonants are fairly regular in their correspondence to those of the adult model. Almost all of the very few fluctuations which do occur involve the substitution of another stop consonant for the appropriate

TABLE 2   MACKIE: CONSONANT SUBSTITUTIONS.

Position	Correct	Incorrect	Omissions	Number of Tokens
initial	88.8%	11.2%	0.0%	223
medial	83.4%	12.1%	4.4%	91*
final	64.5%	5.1%	30.4%	138

* There were actually 26 omissions in medial position. Only four are considered in these data, as the other 22 occurred in pronunciations of the word *daddy*. Of those 22, 21 are one-syllable renditions (typically transcribed as [day]) which probably represent a residue pronunciation from an earlier stage. The one additional occurrence is probably two syllables long ([da : iy]); and there are three occurrences which do show a dental stop in medial position. Mackie is probably just beginning to "correct" his pronunciation of this residue word to fit into his system.

one. In initial positions, however, there are several substitutions of either [t] or [ǰ] for adult /d/. These are primarily assimilations of voicelessness or manner of articulation to the initial consonant of the preceding syllable: e.g., [hwətsǰuwiŋ ǰoyǰadi] 'What's doing Joy, Daddy?' Such assimilations of initial consonants occur across (and including) up to four syllables. The large number of omissions of intervocalic /d/ is accounted for primarily by instances of the word *daddy*, the pronunciation of which is probably a residue of an earlier stage (see Table 2, note). All of the stop consonants are established in final position except for /b/, which seems still to be in flux.

Nasals are quite stable in all positions: in the entire corpus, only four fluctuations involve loss of nasality, and only five involve incorrect place of articulation. Pre-vocalic /h w y/, as well as the affricates—/č ǰ/—are also stable. /l/ and /r/ are fairly stable; both are omitted quite often in final position. The phone [w] is the most frequent incorrect substitution for both of them.

1.3. Mackie is still, apparently, in the process of mastering the spirantal consonants, and they are therefore the most interesting aspect of this corpus. /s/ is the only spirant for which there is evidence of complete mastery; it occurs frequently in all positions, and there are no substitutions for it in any of those positions. In comparison, /z/ is not yet stable: its articulation is the same as that of /s/, but only about half of its total number of occurrences are correctly voiced.

The consonant pair /θ ð/ presents.a considerably different picture. The voiceless dental spirant has not yet entered the inventory; out of three possible occurrences, the record shows one [t], one [s], and one [θ]. /ð/, on the other hand, has entered, although marginally: it is recorded 11 times, but [d] substitutes for it an additional 96 times. The lack of phonetic data precludes any definitive explanation of what is happening, but I would hypothesize that both [d] and [ð] are articulated with the flat front of the blade of the tongue, rather than with the tongue-tip, and thus the two consonants have identical place of articulation. Thus Mackie's problem with /ð/ is that he has not yet acquired the feature of continuance for this consonant.[5]

Labiodental /f/ is fairly stable, being pronounced correctly a total of 19 times of a potential 23; but /v/ is still certainly marginal. Of eight potential occurrences, only one is recorded as [v]. Of the others, five substitutions are stop consonants, indicating that manner of articulation is problematic here; two are voiceless; and six locate the place of articulation incorrectly. Although there are few occurrences of /š/, they are all produced correctly; /ž/ never occurs.

1.4. Mackie has mastered the distinctive features [±high] and [±anterior] (as used in Chomsky and Halle) which distinguish the velar stops ([+high, −ant]) from the labials and dentals ([−high, +ant]). Insofar as these features extend into his spirant system, they are utilized: [s] ([−high, +ant]) is never confused with [š] ([+high, −ant]). The feature [±coronal] has also been mastered—since, with only one exception ([-d] substituting for [-v]), [αcor] is never confused with [−αcor]. At this stage, then, place of articulation is a problem for Mackie only with respect to [v], not with respect to [f] or any other spirant.

The feature [±voice] is handled correctly for all stop consonants; thus we might conclude that Mackie has learned this feature. He never substitutes a voiced constant for any of the four voiceless spirants; he very rarely substitutes a voiceless consonant for /v/ or /ð/; but he frequently substitutes [s] for /z/.

For the pairs [p:f], [t:s], and [d:z], the feature [±cont] has been learned; for the pairs [b:v], [t:θ], and [d:ð], the feature is "coming in" in the following skewed way: the spirants never substitute for the stops, but the stops often substitute for spirants.

Thus we see that for the three consonants which Mackie is acquiring (/v z ð/), the acquisition process is approached in entirely different ways. Mackie has essentially learned all of the distinctive features relevant to the correct production of /f v s z θ ð/. Yet only two of these six phonemes are integrated into his system well enough to be specified as "learned." The situation suggests that *the learning of distinctive features per se is not a primary goal of Mackie's linguistic practice at this time*. Once learned, then, a feature does not necessarily spread rapidly throughout the system to all relevant segments.[6]

1.5. There are only a few generalizations which can be made about sub-

---

[5] It should especially be noted that this seems to be the only voiced-voiceless spirant pair of which the voiced phoneme is learned first.

[6] Victoria Fromkin (personal communication) has pointed out that these facts directly contradict the motor theory of speech perception: "It seems quite obvious that in terms of production, at least, what is being learned is feature combinations, i.e., segments, which makes a lot more sense when you consider the articulatory process. This does not mean that distinctive features are not learned, but they must be learned in combination after they are perceived. . . . There is no question but that children perceive differences before they articulate them."

stitution behavior in consonant clusters. Stop consonants are often preserved in clusters, except in the medial or final cluster /ts/, where usually only /s/ is preserved. /f/ and /s/ are also retained, and [z] and [s] occur equally for /z/. When /l/ and /r/ are not preserved, [w] is frequently substituted for both. In clusters where /w/ should occur, however, it is often dropped, except after /h/.

2. Hildegard. The second set of data is a complete vocabulary of about 200 words in phonetic form for Hildegard Leopold at age 2, reported in Leopold 1939 (vol. 1). Hildegard heard both English and German spoken at home, but her phonetic development seems to be only very slightly affected by the latter language, possibly because it was her mother who spoke English. The mother's dialect is a Midwestern variety of American English.

2.1. Hildegard's vowel system consists of 12 phonemes. One (/æ/) is marginal, as it occurs in only one word ([ŋæŋæ] 'grandpa');[7] the other 11 are stable, and occur in simple nuclei as well as in combination to form long vowels, diphthongs, or both. Table 3 shows the distribution of Hildegard's vowels, and

TABLE 3   HILDEGARD: VOWEL DISTRIBUTION.

alone	i ι e a (æ)	a ɔ o ʊ u ə
first element	i e ɛ a	a ɔ o ʊ u
second element	i ι a	ɔ o ʊ u ə

Table 4 gives examples from her vocabulary. Although Hildegard certainly does not have examples in her speech of diphthongs and long vowels which would fill all cubicles of an 11-by-11 matrix, she is obviously experimenting beyond the model which English provides. For example, although English makes no use of vowel length, Hildegard does: compare [wɔk] 'walk' and [wɔ:k] 'fork'; [bu] 'balloon, spoon,' [nu] 'new,' and [mu:] 'moo.'[8] In addition, there are several diphthongs in Table 4 which do not occur in the adult model; especially note [ʊι], [ɛa], [oi], and [oι]. In other words, *Hildegard is using her ability to combine two vowel qualities into a diphthong as a productive process by which she may construct new words with complex vowel nuclei not present in standard English.*

2.2 Hildegard has 15 consonant phonemes, including marginal /ŋ/ (see Table 5). In initial position, 14 phonemes are needed to account for the 14 phones which occur. In medial position, there are 15 phonetic "contrasts," but only 9 of the phonemes are needed to describe the situation. In other words, *medial position is the location of maximal phonetic experimentation, while initial position is the location of maximal contrast and stability.*

---

[7] This is also the only word in which /ŋ/ occurs, but the decision to label one and not the other of the two phones [ŋ] and [æ] a phoneme would have to be arbitrary.

[8] In a few words, Hildegard would seem to have "triple" vowels. These are considered here to consist phonetically of a long vowel and a short one separated by a syllable boundary of some sort. The relevant examples are [ʔa·i] 'alley,' [da·i] 'candy,' [da·ι] 'dolly,' [do·i] 'Joey,' [nɔ·i] 'naughty.'

TABLE 4   HILDEGARD: VOWEL NUCLEI.

Simple vowels		Diphthongs		Long vowels	
/i/	[mi] 'me', [bi] 'peas'	/iə/	[biə] 'pillow'	/aa/	[ha:] 'Haar'
/ɩ/	[hɩ] 'here', [bɩ] 'big'	/ea/	[bea] 'pail'	/ɔɔ/	[wɔ:k] 'fork'
/e/	[he] 'hang', [we] 'way'	/eə/	[meə] 'mehr'	/oo/	[do·i] 'Joey'
/a/	[ma] 'come on', [na] 'now'	/ɛɩ/	[ʔɛɩ pi] 'airplane'	/uu/	[mu:] 'moo'
/ɑ/	[ma] 'man', [jɑbɑk] 'sandbox'	/ɛa/	[bɛa] 'bear'		
/ɔ/	[dɔ] 'gone', [nɔ] 'no'	/aɩ/	[ʔaɩ] 'eye'		
/o/	[do] 'cold', [bo] 'blow'	/aʋ/	[ʔaʋ] 'au!'		
/ʋ/	[bʋ] 'put', [nʋk] 'coat'	/aʋ/	[ʔɑʋx] 'out'		
/u/	[du] 'do', [bu] 'spoon'	/ɔɩ/	[bɔɩ] 'boy'		
/ə/	[dɩkə] 'chicken', [ʔəwe] 'away'	/oi/	[noiš] 'noise'		
		/oɩ/	[doɩš] 'stone'		
		/ʋɩ/	[bʋɩ] 'pudding'		

Almost all of the rules which describe the variation occurring in medial position actually describe a situation of syllable reduplication. Despite the complexity of such rules, they seem to be significant in Hildegard's speech development at the moment, for a variety of reasons: (1) Hildegard does not reduplicate syllables of necessity, as the majority of her two-syllable words are not reduplications. (2) At least one rule, that for /j/, does not apply strictly to reduplicated forms but is rather more general (and perhaps newer). Thus it applies to such words as [haja] 'Helen' and [nɔjə·k] 'New York' as well as to [jojo] 'hello.'

TABLE 5   HILDEGARD: CONSONANT PHONOLOGY.

Phoneme	Initial	Medial	Final
/p/	p-	-b- / [bVᵢ < Vⱼ > __Vᵢ < Vⱼ >]; -p- / [ʔV__]; -b-	-p
/b/	b-		
/t/	t-	-t-	-tʻ
/d/	d-	-d-	-t
/k/	g-	-g- / [gVᵢ__Vᵢ]; -k-	-kʻ
/g/			-k
/m/	m-		
/n/	n-	-m- / [mVᵢ—Vᵢ]; -ŋ- / [ŋVᵢ— Vᵢ]; -n-	-n
(/ŋ/)	ŋ-		
/š/	ž-	-š-	-š
/h/	h-		-x
/č/	č-	-č- / [čVᵢ—Vᵢ]; -j-	-č
/w/	w-	-w-	
/l/	j- ~ l-		
/j/	j-	-j- / [Vᵢ—Vᵢ]; -l-	

(3) The occurrence of the phonemes /t/ and /d/ suggests that they may have once occurred in the distribution

$$-d- \, / \, [dV_i\!\!-\!\!V_i]; \, -t-$$

but have since expanded. (And indeed the dental stop phonemes would not be an unreasonable place for innovation to begin.) Thus we do find [dɔdə] 'Dodo,' [dada] 'thank you, danke,' [doti] 'doggie,' [dita] 'there's a . . . " and [titi] 'sticky,' none of which violate the above rule, but also [dadi] 'stocking,' which does. And there are no forms [kV$_i$kV$_i$] or [pV$_i$pV$_i$] parallel to [titi].

In final position, only voiceless phones occur. (Final /n/ is simply a notational way of accounting for Hildegard's final nasal vowels.) Where Hildegard has a voicing contrast phonemically in final position, it is manifested as a phonetic contrast of aspiration vs. non-aspiration.

Hildegard's speech also requires the following low-level phonetic rule:

$$\emptyset \rightarrow \text{?} \begin{Bmatrix} \#\!\!-\!\!V \\ V_1\!\!-\!\!V_2V_3 \end{Bmatrix} \quad \text{where } V_1 \neq V_2.$$

Thus, in all words which begin with a vowel, glottal stop is automatically inserted. ([aɪta] 'highchair' must be marked as an exception). There are four items in the vocabulary which apparently contain medial [ʔ]: [meʔa] 'Mary Alice,' [miʔaʊ] 'meow,' [ʔaʔa] a German nursery word, and [wek ʔap] 'wake up.' The last is apparently a two-word phrase, and is accounted for by the first part of the rule; the first might be similarly considered. It is not unreasonable to assume that the nursery word also contains an internal boundary, and that the first part of the rule therefore accounts for both instances of glottal stop in it. [miʔaʊ] is in contrast with the other five lexical items (cf. fn. 8) which have $V_1V_2V_3$ sequences in that it is the only one in which $V_1 \neq V_2$. Thus it can be accounted for by placing the appropriate restriction on the second part of the rule.

Because of the unattainability of the Leopold volumes, Table 6 contains the complete vocabulary with my phonemic and Leopold's phonetic transcription.

3. **Erica.** The third analysis is based on a corpus which I collected on 5 August 1968. The longest utterance of the 526 in the sample is nine morphemes; the average sentence length is three morphemes. The child, Erica, was two years and 12 days old. Her parents speak standard General American English, but she hears additional dialects (and several other languages) spoken by other adults in the neighborhood.

3.1. Many adults who have considerable contact with Erica have independently reported to me the fact that her speech sounds amazingly correct to them. It is difficult to completely reconcile such impressions with the fact that Erica's speech falls short of being "correct" in a great many respects. Two contributing factors may be her mastery of the English vowel system and her control over intonation contours. Although in a few tokens her vowels are

TABLE 6 HILDEGARD: VOCABULARY.

Phonetic	Phonemic	Gloss	Phonetic	Phonemic	Gloss
ʔa	a	all	biə	biə	pillow;
ʔā	an	on			spiel(en)
ʔaʔa	a a	(German	biš	biš	piece; please
		nursery	bɩt	bɩd	pick
		word)	bɩtə	bɩtə	bitte
ʔa·i	aai	alley	bitš	bič	beads; beach;
ʔaɩ	aɩ	ei!; egg; eye; I			Brief
ʔaɩni	aɩni	ironing	bo	bo	blow
ʔaɩ ~ ʔaɩš	aɩ ~ aɩš	eins	bɔɩ	bɔɩ	boy
aɩta	aɩta	highchair	bok	bog	bug
ʔalə	alə	alle	bokʻ	bok	broken; book
ʔap	ap	up	botʻ	bot	boot; boat;
ʔapa	apa	apple			Brot
ʔapu	apu	open	bu	bu	balloon;
ʔati	ati	ice-cream			spoon
ʔatobiə	atopiə	automobile	bʋ	bʋ	put
ʔaʋ	aʋ	au!	bubu	bupu	paper
ʔaʋx	aʋh	auf; aus; out	bʋɩ	bʋɩ	pudding
ʔaʋto	aʋto	auto	bʋš	bʋš	push
ʔawaɩ	awaɩ	all right	bʋtʻ	bʋt	kaputt
ba	ba	piano	da	da	cover; da;
baba	bapa	papa			down;
babi	bapi	bobby-pin			trag(en)
baɩ	baɩ	buggy	dada	dada	thank you;
baɩbaɩ	baɩpaɩ	bye-bye			danke
baɩk	baɩg	bike	dadi	dadi	stocking;
baɩtʻ	baɩt	bite			Nackedei
bak	bag	block; box	da·i	daai	candy
bakə	bakə	back	da·ɩ	daaɩ	dolly
balu	baju	bottle	daɩ	daɩ	cry; drei; dry
bati	bati	button	dak	dag	duck
baš	baš	brush	daš	daš	crash; dress
baʋ	baʋ	ball; bauen;	dɑš	dɑš	Katz; scratch
		bell; Baum	datʻ	dat	forgot
baʋkʻ	baʋk	Bauch	daʋ	daʋ	towel
bea	bea	pail	diə	diə	dear
bɛa	bɛa	Bär; bear	dɩk	dɩg	drink; stick
bebi	bepi	baby	dɩkə	dɩkə	chicken
bek	beg	bake	dɩš	dɩš	kiss
bekə	bekə	bacon	dɩt	dɩd	this
beš	beš	bathe	dita	dita	there's a . . .
betʻ	bet	Bett	do	do	cold; comb;
bi	bi	peas			door; go;
bɩ	bɩ	big			throw

TABLE 6   HILDEGARD: VOCABULARY—*continued*

Phonetic	Phonemic	Gloss	Phonetic	Phonemic	Gloss
dɔ	dɔ	gone	jojo	jojo	hello
dɔdɔ	dɔdɔ	Dodo	jok' ~ lok	lok	Loch
do·i	dooi	Joey	ma	ma	come on
doɪš	doɪš	stone	mɑ	mɑ	man
dok	dog	toast	maɪ	maɪ	mine; money
dot	dod	coat; don't	mama	mana	mama
doti	doti	doggie	maš	maš	much
du	du	do; too	mɑʋš	mɑʋš	mouse; mouth
dukɔ	dukɔ	dunkel	me?a	me a	Mary Alice
duš	duš	juice	meə	meə	mehr
?ɛɪpi	ɛɪpi	airplane	mek	meg	make
?ɛk	ɛg	egg	meme	mene	Marion
?ɛt'	ɛt	in	mi	mi	me
?əwe	əwe	away	mi?aʋ	ɱiaʋ	meow (for cat)
gaga	kaka	cracker	mik	mig	milk
gek	keg	cake	mit'	mit	meat
ha:	haa	Haar	mu:	muu	moo (for cow)
hã	han	hand	na	na	now
haɪ	haɪ	high; ride	naɪš	naɪš	nice
haɪš	haɪš	heiss	naɪt'	naɪt	night
haɪt'	haɪt	light	naš	naš	nass
haɪta	haɪta	Hildegard	nɑt	nɑd	not
haja	haja	Helen	ni	ni	knee
hat	had	hot	nɪk	nɪg	neck
hat'	hat	hat	nɔ	nɔ	no
haʋdžu	haʋču	Handschuh;	nɔ·i	nɔɔi	naughty
		Taschen-	noiš	noiš	noise
		tuch	nɔjɔ·k	nɔjɔɔk	New York
haʋx	haʋh	soap	noš	noš	nose
haʋš	haʋš	house	nu	nu	new
he	he	hang(en)	nʋk	nʋg	coat
hea	hea	hair	ŋæŋæ	ŋæŋæ	Grandpa
hɪ	hɪ	here; hier	?ɔɪlo	ɔɪlo	oil
hɔ	hɔ	home	?ɔɪno	ɔɪno	Onkel
hoti	hoti	hottey	pik	pik	pieks!
		(horsey)	pikəbu ~	pikəpu ~	peek-a-boo
hu	hu	room	pikbu	pikpu	
?iə	iə	ear	pɪti	pɪti	pretty
?it'	it	eat	pu	ɲʋ	poor; pooh
ja	ja	ja	žu	šu	shoe
jabak	japak	sandbox	žuš	šuš	zu
jaɪ	jaɪ	lie; slide;	te	te	train
		write	tɪ-ta	tɪta	tick-tock
jašut	jašud	sun-suit	titi	titi	sticky

TABLE 6 HILDEGARD: VOCABULARY—*continued*

PHONETIC	PHONEMIC	GLOSS	PHONETIC	PHONEMIC	GLOSS
tšutšu	čuču	choo-choo	wek ʔap	weg ap	wake up
tu	tu	through; two	wet	wed	wet
tušbaš	tušbaš	toothbrush	wetʻ	wet	wait
tutiš	tutiš	cookie(s)	wewe	wewe	(German nurs-
ʔutš	uč	Fuss			ery word)
waι	waι	fly; zwei	wi	wi	feed; read;
waιtʻ	waιt	right			three
walu	walu	water	wι	wι	rug
waš	waš	wash; watch	wiə	wiə	wheel
wa·ti	waati	Milwaukee	witʻ	wit	feet
waʋ	waʋ	flower	wιtʻ	wιt	fix
waʋ	waʋ	Frau	wιti	wιti	Fritzchen
waʋwaʋ	waʋwaʋ	Wauwau (Ger-	wiwi	wiwi	Rita
		man nursery	wə	wə	fall; roll
		word)	wɔ:k	wɔɔk	fork
waʋwi	waʋwi	Milwaukee	wɔk	wɔk	walk
[phonetic and semantic interference			wɔkəbebi	wɔkəpepi	rock-a-bye
from *way, away, far away*]					baby
we	we	way; where	woš	woš	Florence

different phonemically from the expected, she has learned the complete vowel system, including glides, and uses it correctly a large percentage of the time, even in new words. Her sentence contours are those of the adult language; in imitation situations she is able to produce fundamental frequency contours which look very much like those of her mother, although her pitch peaks are consistently higher. In free speech, Erica's average syllable duration is considerably longer than that of her mother, but when she imitates (2-, 3-, and 4-syllable phrases), her total syllable duration is quite close to that of her mother, and in one sample differed only by two milliseconds.

A phonological analysis of Erica's speech reveals a system very close to the adult model in structure but different in small details: there are slightly different restrictions on co-occurrence and allophonic distribution. Almost all of her pronunciation problems remain within the consonant system.

A phonological rule which seems to be typical of many children is also shared by Erica, although it seems to be an optional rule in her speech: that of dropping an initial zero-stress syllable before a subsequent primary stress syllable. This rule is utilized for ten tokens and ignored for another eight, so that we have side by side such examples as [tʰɛ́tʰu·] 'potato,' [tʰá·mis] 'pajamas,' [mɛ́ĕdʒotš] 'tomatoes,' [mǎntʰə] 'banana'; and [hól bĭnànə] 'whole banana,' [əβéï] 'away,' [ɛlf·á·səo] 'El Paso.' As further evidence that this situation reflects a stress rule, and is not due to word length alone, it should be noted that none of the words which occur without the first syllable of the model are more than three syllables in length, while Erica has other words in her own speech of up to five syllables.

3.2. Erica has almost completely mastered the stop consonants and nasals: e.g., [máĭk⁼əl] 'Michael,' [ɑn ðə pʰɔ́dǯo] 'on (in?) the puddle,' [ni· fíəl ɔ bɛ́t⁼əɹ] 'knee feel all better,' [k⁼ós·iĭdɔɹ] 'grocery store.' (Vowels are redundantly, and correctly, nasalized between nasalized consonants.) Voicing is incompletely learned for the stop consonants; however, where a voiceless consonant is substituted for the corresponding voiced one, it is often not of quite the same quality as the usual voiceless counterpart. There seems, in fact, to be some range of "quality" which she uses more consistently than voicing to distinguish in her own speech the voiced and voiceless stops of the adult model. It is difficult to describe the exact physical nature of this contrast, although it might be labeled subjectively a tense-lax distinction. Aspiration is a freely occurring feature with all stop consonants, although it occurs most frequently by far with the voiceless "tense" stops. There seems to be only one environment, in fact, in which Erica consistently does not aspirate stops: where the adult model would have a cluster of /s/ plus stop, she always has simply an unaspirated stop without an /s/.⁹ For example, [k⁼ɛ́ɹ] 'square,' [dɔ́di] 'study,' [dɔɹ] 'store,' [t⁼akʰ] 'stack.'

Place of articulation has been learned for stops also; but there are a few words, apparently a residue from an earlier stage, in which stops occur with incorrect place of articulation. For example, *dog* and *duck* are imitated correctly, but in free speech both words begin with [g]: *gog* and *guck*.

3.3. Like Mackie, Erica is having difficulty with fricatives. The problem seems to be one of motor control. Except for the bilabials, all fricatives suffer from her inability to maintain her articulators in as finely adjusted position as is required. As a result, fricatives are either too open or too closed—in the latter case, becoming affricated. It is the same process that converts many of her /l/'s to a [j]-like quality.

/s/ and /š/ are rarely affricated, and are almost always too open. Both are "blade," not "groove," spirants. The place of articulation for /š/ is always correct, but /s/ varies along a continuum from dental to palato-alveolar. Thus it seems that the blade articulation and the more central position of contact are more neutral in some sense.

[ž] occurs initially as a substitute for adult [š] in a few tokens, e.g., [džuz ɔ·ɔ̃f ... žuz ɔ·f] 'shoes off ... shoes off'; and Erica is able to imitate [ž] in nonsense syllables. But there are no examples in her free speech where the adult phoneme /ž/ would be expected. Erica has exactly the same articulatory problems with /z/ as with /s/, but also the additional problem of voicing, which is a freely variant feature for this consonant, e.g., [p⁼i·ẓ·] 'please,' [ɛ́·sə ɔ́ˇn ðɛ́k⁼əs bɛ́·d] 'he's on Erica's bed.'

/f/ is well established, but /v/ is not. Initially, /v/ is a voiced bilabial stop;

---

⁹ This phenomenon was first noticed by W. W. Gage, and is reported in Braine, MS.

finally, it is a voiceless fricative. Medially, it covers a larger range, although it is always characterized by voicing and the participation of at least one lip in the articulation. The manner of articulation covers the range from pure stop to pure fricative, encompassing some intermediate positions; e.g., [bériy] 'very,' [hi· havɩŋ tʰəŏũtʰ] 'he having toast,' [junɩbɔ́ɹsijeǐ] 'university.'

But the most interesting aspect of Erica's acquisition of fricatives is that of /θ/ and /ð/. Where /ð/ should occur initially, [d] occurs about half of the time, and the consonant is omitted completely the other half of the time. Medially, the same situation obtains, except in the following environments: after any nasal consonant (including both velars and dentals), after a nasalized vowel, and after a dental stop consonant. In these positions, /ð/ is pronounced correctly as [ð]; e.g., [ĩn ðɔ́· báθ tʰɔ́bʰ] 'in the bathtub,' [hɪǐ gɔ̃ówɩŋ ðɛ́jɔ̃] 'he going there,' [hi gówɩŋ tʰu ɹáǐd ðəbɔ́s] 'he going to ride the bus,' [izĩ ði í·jə] 'this is the E.' In fact, in one word which is not nasalized in the adult model, Erica added nasalization to the vowel preceding the correctly-pronounced /ð/. This particular sub-system is an instance of a child's employing phonological structure which is quite unusual by the standards of the adult model. This fact suggests that the study of child phonology may be able to contribute to the theory of phonological universals by calling our attention to unusual phonological situations which may not occur at all in natural languages, but which the human mind seems to be programmed to cope with.

In this corpus Erica has only one example of [θ], in the word [báθ təbʰ]; and she manages (probably unintentionally) to avoid *three* in her random counting: 1, 2, 7, 4, 6. (In subsequent sessions, however, it becomes obvious that Erica substitutes [f] for /θ/ with great regularity. Only the words *bath* and *bathtub* occur with [θ] as well as with [f].)

3.4. Erica pronounces /r/ correctly in all positions and even in clusters. The lateral /l/, however, usually occurs in its "opener" form as [j], although sometimes clearly as [l], and it is omitted frequently in some clusters; [r] never substitutes for /l/. These facts are especially surprising in light of the fact that almost all published studies of children learning English indicate that the mastery of /l/ precedes that of /r/. Yet Erica's speech is striking in that she is able to correctly pronounce all of the allophones of /r/—as exemplified in such words as *more*, *very*, and *run*—while /l/ is often mispronounced as [j], and never as [w][10]; e.g., [də lĩ̌f] 'the leaf'; [ɩš jéǐo] [i· jélǐo] 'it's yellow'; [pʰɔ́dəl], [pʰɔ́dǐo] 'puddle'; [bəjún] 'balloon'; [i·jévɩ̌n] 'eleven'; [fa·ǐ] [flɔ˅·ǐ], [f·aǐ] 'fly'; [fɹɑ˄·g⁻] 'frog'; [pʰé·ǐgɹɑɔ̃nd] 'playground'; [aɹjí·n] 'Arlene'; [pʰɔɹ éšjǐi] 'poor Leslie'; [kʰaɹs·] 'cars'; [bíəɹ] 'beer.' (By age 2:6, Erica seems to have given up her attempts to produce /l/ in a cluster, although it is pretty stable intervocalically. At that time, [r] is the usual substitute, producing some interesting interactions

---

[10] Erica has, as far as I can tell, only one residue word left from an earlier stage when /r/ had not yet been mastered: her own name is usually pronounced as [a·kɑ], although sometimes as [ɛɹkkʰɑ].

with the adults who hear her speech as "correct": at the dinner table one night, Erica's exclamation /kráp/ was greeted with consternation rather than with the response she had anticipated, until she expanded it into /kráp jɔr héə̃ndz/).

4. Summary. For many decades, those interested in the acquisition of phonology have collected data about the order in which different children acquired phones or phonemes. The comparison of such data has caused despair, as almost no two children acquired such units in the same order, and no patterns could be found.

In 1941 the study of child phonology took a great leap forward as Jakobson's highly significant work integrating the studies of phonology acquisition, sound change, and aphasia switched the emphasis from units of sound to distinctive features. Although subsequent workers have found that some of Jakobson's proposals concerning the order of acquisition of distinctive features are inaccurate, and others are not explicit enough to be tested, the framework has become available for many of the regularities of phonology acquisition to be discussed. It is interesting and significant that, despite the considerable changes and advances in the theory of distinctive features, and the long-standing knowledge that Jakobson's theory is not completely accurate, no advances in the theory of phonology acquisition have been made.

Just as a theory based only on segmental units cannot explain what happens when a child learns to pronounce his language correctly, so also a theory based only on distinctive features cannot in isolation explain this process adequately. The data given in this paper exemplify some instances of the learning of features: e.g., within the stop consonant system, those features which distinguish places of articulation have been learned. This same small set of data also exemplifies the learning of individual phonemes as just that; examples are easily found among the discussions of fricatives. In addition, we find that the child learns some phonemic or feature contrasts in a differential way which may be related to the universal constraints described by marking conventions like those of Chomsky and Halle. For example, we may refer to Mackie's skewed learning of the contrast described by the feature of continuance; he has clearly learned the unmarked value of the feature, but is still acquiring the marked value. The same situation cannot be explained logically with a theory which describes the acquisition process as one of successive splits, implying that the minus and plus values of a feature are learned concurrently.

Even with a vocabulary of fewer than 200 words, Hildegard already has an incipient rule structure; and even though that rule structure bears little resemblance to the one which she will develop during the ensuing five or so years, it may be viewed as a reflection of the child's ability to handle rules in phonology, and perhaps even the pre-determined capacity to process phonological information in a rule-structured way. Erica's unique rule determining the distribution of /ð/ indicates that we may find very little uniformity among children along their respective paths from babbling (with no rule structure) to mastery of their languages (with almost-complete rule structures). Further research may show that there is a finite, although large, set of possible rule forms which the child may attempt to incorporate into sound systems, and such knowledge will contribute greatly to our notion of "possible phonological rule."

I have tried to show in this paper that the child does not adopt one integrated strategy for coping with several unique facets of the same situation. Despite the stability of a relevant feature in other parts of his vocal system, the child may encounter considerable difficulty in transferring that feature to a new segment. The roots of this problem may lie in articulation, as the motor control necessary for speech is far more exacting than that required for any other activity the two-year-old child encounters or attempts. Returning to the example of Anthony Weir's speech given in the introduction, the distributional evidence leaves no doubt that the consonant segment $/\theta/$ is part of his competence; performance is being inhibited by articulatory interference.

As Jakobson has emphasized, the learning of phonology is an extremely creative process; thus a theory describing the process must allow for creativity. A theory relegating all learning to one particular aspect, such as features, or oppositions, or phonemes, or rules, is therefore doomed to failure in some measure. An adequate theory must at least incorporate the contributions of segmental, distinctive problems, and of universal phonological phenomena, which may "emerge" at various pre-determined times, in comparison with language-idiosyncratic phenomena, which are learned at specific times. It must be able to account for such diverse facts as the early acquisition of the nasal consonants vs. the late acquisition of most voiced fricatives, the early production of [s] and [f] vs. the late production of $[\theta]$, and the relatively early stability of the incredibly complex system of vocalic segments which English presents to the learning child. And it must account for the diversity of creative extensions which the child may apply to a phonological system, such as Hildegard's extension of the vowel system.

A new theory of phonology acquisition must go even farther than this, into realms which have not been discussed here at all. Underlying all of the data which have been discussed is the extremely significant fact that the child is faced with two different tasks which have previously been lumped under the title of "phonology acquisition." The major cause for our long history of failure to find the "patterns" in the child's learning of phonology is that we have been looking only at a rather over-simplified form of phonetic acquisition as reflected in corpus data. But while the child is learning pronunciation, or phonetic representation, he is also learning the system, or phonological representation. The assumption that the phonetic level is acquired in a uniform way by all children has been disproved over and over again. There must, however, be a set of necessary and sufficient constraints on the order of acquisition with respect to the level of phonological representation; this is obscured by the interference of phonetics. With our current techniques for the study of child phonology, inquiry breaks down where total phonetic identity dissolves the surface representation of phonological oppositions which the child may, in fact, possess.

Thus future investigations must find ways of differentiating these two types of learning.[11]

REFERENCES

Albright, Robert W., and Joy Buck Albright, The phonology of a two-year-old child. *Word*, **12**, 1956, 382–390.

Bloch, Bernard, A set of postulates for phonemic analysis. *Language*, **24**, 1948, 3–46.

Braine, Martin D. S., The acquisition of language in infant and child, in *The learning of language*, Carroll Reed, ed., New York: Appleton-Century-Crofts, 1971.

Chomsky, Noam, and Morris Halle, *The sound pattern of English*. New York: Harper & Row, 1968.

Ferguson, Charles A., Contrastive analysis and language development. *Georgetown monograph series on languages and linguistics*, **21**, 1968, 101–112.

Jakobson, Roman, *Child language, aphasia, and phonological universals*. Translated by A. R. Keiler. The Hague: Mouton, 1968. [Originally published in 1941.]

Leopold, Werner F., *Speech development of a bilingual child*. 4 vols. Evanston: Northwestern University Press, 1939–1949.

Wang, William S.-Y., and John Crawford, Frequency studies of English consonants. *Language and Speech*, **3**, 1960, 131–139.

Weir, Ruth H., *Language in the crib*. The Hague: Mouton, 1962.

[11] This paper was supported in part by the American Council of Learned Societies and the Social Science Research Council. I am indebted to Charles A. Ferguson and William S-Y. Wang for helpful discussions of the ideas contained in this paper, which is an expanded version of a paper presented at the Linguistic Society of America, 29 December 1968.

GARO •

Language Development of a Garo and English-Speaking Child
—— *Robbins Burling*

Psycholinguistically oriented developmental studies of children acquiring non-European languages have, until the last few years, been quite rare (except for Japanese), and Burling's study of his son learning Garo is valuable on this ground alone. In addition, however, his clear handling of the bilingual aspects of the language development and his thoughtful references to Jakobson, Leopold, and Velten make his study one of the most interesting in the tradition of the linguist-parent observing his own child and attempting

From *Word*, 1959, **15**, 45–68. Reprinted with the permission of the author and the International Linguistic Association.

structural analysis. Some of the points made in passing deserve attention in any attempt to formulate a general theory of phonological development. Examples: the use of whispering throughout the word, corresponding to voiceless consonants in the model (p. 71; see also Leopold, 1939–1949, Vol. 2, pp. 359–360); ephemeral use of a phonemic distinction not present in the model (p. 78); see also Velten, 1943); vowel contrasts as the first stable distinctions in the second-language phonology (p. 78; see also Shvachkin, p. 105).   —C.A.F.

Toward the end of October, 1954, I arrived with my wife and small son Stephen in the Garo Hills district of Assam, India, where we were to spend most of the next two years making a social anthropological study of the Garo.[1] These people, one of India's tribal populations, number a quarter of a million and speak a language belonging to the Bodo group of Tibeto-Burman.[2] When we arrived, Stephen (who was born on the last day of May, 1953), was one year and four months old and was just beginning to attach meanings consistently to some of the vocal activity that he had been emitting in profusion for many months. His first few words were English, but he immediately came into regular contact with Garo speakers and soon added Garo words to his vocabulary; in fact, for the greater part of the time we were there, his Garo was significantly more fluent than his English. Since there have been few studies of child language in non-Indo-European languages, I kept a record of my son's linguistic development and have assembled the results here.

The study of a child's speech is a delightful one, not the least satisfying aspect being the frequent enjoyment that one's informant shows in having so much attention paid to him by his father. Nevertheless, it is beset with difficulties that never arise in the study of adult language. Children won't repeat themselves the way good adult informants can be persuaded to do. It is next to impossible to try to compare minimal pairs directly, both because of the poverty of the children's vocabulary and because of the difficulty in getting them to repeat forms. Moreover, children speak with less precision and much less consistency than adults. With wide variation within the limits of a phoneme and with the difficulty of comparing minimal pairs it is frequently impossible to specify precisely the time when the child first makes a new contrast within the range of speech sounds that had formerly been a single phoneme. Nevertheless the ideal for which I have striven is an analysis of the successive additions of the distinctive features rather than a detailed description of the ever changing phonetic minutiae of his speech.

[1] This paper is an expanded and revised version of one read at the 1958 summer meeting of the Linguistic Society of America. The opportunity to work in the Garo Hills was provided by a fellowship from the Board of Overseas Training and Research of the Ford Foundation.
[2] I have assembled a descriptive grammar of the Garo language which is to be published shortly.

Stephen began to use Garo words within a few weeks of our arrival, but his English vocabulary grew steadily and it was several months before Garo became clearly predominant. The eventual triumph of Garo was aided by a protracted hospitalization of his mother which, except for short visits, removed him from close contact with his most important single English model. She was hospitalized through most of March and April, 1955, when he was one year and nine and ten months old. At this time, I spoke to him frequently in Garo, which diluted the effectiveness of the second major English source. Even after this the continued illness of his mother forced him into greater contact with Garos than might otherwise have been the case. The result was steady progress in the Garo language, which I believe he learned in much the same way as any Garo child.

PHONEMES AT ONE YEAR AND FOUR MONTHS

When we arrived in the Garo Hills, Stephen was one year and four months old and had a total vocabulary of a mere dozen words, but even those required a considerable phonemic inventory. He seemed to distinguish three vowel positions; a low unrounded vowel, generally central, though sometimes varying toward the front, as in *papa* 'papa'; a high front unrounded vowel as in *kiki* 'kitty'; and a mid or high mid back and strongly rounded vowel, as in *tu* 'door.'

As these examples also show, he clearly distinguished three stops in roughly the positions of *p*, *t* and *k*. Usually the stops were unaspirated and somewhat varyingly or mildly voiced, and in this case they were used with voiced vowels. Occasionally, however, the stops were strongly aspirated and without voicing, and in such cases they were invariably accompanied by unvoiced vowels, resulting in an explosive whisper: [k'aₐk'aₐ] 'custard,' [p'aₐ] 'up.' He interpreted all English voiced stops as unaspirated, but voiceless stops were sometimes interpreted in one way and sometimes in another, although he was generally consistent for any one word. For instance, 'papa' and 'kitty' never had aspiration, while 'custard' and 'up' always did. He also confidently used two nasals, *m* and *n*, as in *ma* 'more' and *nana* 'banana.' I never heard the nasals used except with fully voiced vowels. He had then three vowels, five consonants, and a distinction of voice and aspiration that cut across both the vowels and stops.

At this time all of his words were of the form CV or CVCV; if the latter, the two syllables were always identical. The first progress after our arrival came at one year and five months when he learned suddenly and decisively to use two different syllables in the same word, including either different vowels or different consonants. 'Kitty' was then pronounced as *kiti* rather than as the earlier *kiki* and one of his first Garo words was *babi* (standard Garo *ba-bir-si*) 'cook,' his name for our cook.

If this appears to be an extensive phonemic repertory, it should be emphasized that it was available to Stephen at the very threshold of his use of meaningful speech. Though I did not keep careful records of the preceding period, my impression is strong that most if not all of the distinctions which I have described were present in the babbling which preceded his real speech.

Though these phonemes were first used for English words, he soon began using them in Garo words as well. For a considerable time he formed words from both languages with what amounted to a single phonemic system, and so for the first part of the record it is largely possible to ignore the existence of two languages. For the remainder of the paper, rather than adhering to a strictly chronological account, I will discuss in turn the development of various aspects of his speech, and in the final section I will make a few general observations and some comparisons with other children whose speech development has been described.

CONSONANTS

About a month after our arrival, at one year and five months, he began to use a lateral in *lala* 'Emula,' the name of his Garo "ayah" (nurse). Soon afterward he began experimenting with affricates and spirants. The affricate was established first in *ci* 'cheese,' but by the age of one year and seven months, he had both this affricate and a spirant in *sosa* (Garo *so-si-a*) 'wet.' Both *s* and *c* were pronounced intermediate to the position of the nearest English sounds (*s* and *š*; *ts* and *č*) and from the beginning were very similar to the Garo phonemes.

At about the same time he began to use a labiodental approximating English *f* and with refinement in the voiced/voiceless opposition that was achieved just shortly afterwards, he briefly used *v* as well. Garo does not have phonemes near to this position, and presumably as a result, *f* and *v* failed to become established. In fact they disappeared completely for a period and were replaced in English words by the bilabial stops.

The disappearance of *f* and *v* can be taken as marking his real transition to the Garo language. Everything earlier might be considered to be just as much English as Garo, but only Garo influence can explain the loss of these phonemes. He began to use *f* and *v* once more at two years and four months, but even at 2:7 (years and months), a full year after they first appeared, these consonants were inconsistently articulated.

By 1:7, the rather ephemeral distinction between voiced and unvoiced vowels, and the associated distinction between unaspirated and aspirated consonants, had disappeared, being replaced by a consistent distinction between voiced and unvoiced stops. At that time *p t k* and *b d g* became consistently distinct in the prevocalic position, and the associated vowels were invariably voiced. Stephen's pattern then came considerably closer to both that of Garo and of English, since the languages share the voiced/voiceless contrast. In

Garo the contrast is made only for syllable initials, and this is the only position in which Stephen made it for most of our stay.

At just about the same age (1:7), he began to use *w* and *h* both for the English phonemes, and for the Garo phonemes, which are phonetically similar to those in English, as in *hai* which in Garo means 'let's go' and the English word *wet*.

At 1:9, he added *ŋ* to his roster of phonemes. This does not occur initially in either Garo or English and so its appearance had to await the development of more complex syllables than he had had when the other nasals were first used. An example is *doʔoŋ* (Garo *joʔ-oŋ*) 'bug.' This example also shows that at this same age the intervocalic glottal stop appeared. It was several months before he could use the glottal stop in the other positions in which it occurs in Garo.

With the addition of these phonemes, there was only one other Garo consonant outstanding: *j*, a voiced affricate which is intermediate as to position between English *dz* and *j* and is thus the voiced counterpart of the Garo *c*. A *j* first appeared at one year and ten months, but for several months thereafter, Stephen used it only irregularly, frequently substituting *d* both for the *j* phoneme of Garo and for its nearest equivalents in English. As soon as *j* was well established (by two years and three months), Stephen had all of the basic phonemic distinctions of the Garo consonants.

Correct pronunciation involves more than simply keeping the phonemes distinct from each other, however, and further refinement in his consonants consisted of increased precision and vigor in articulation, wider distribution of some consonants, growing sensitivity to allophonic distinctions, and better mastery of clusters.

An example of the way in which he gradually gained precision in his articulation is provided by his velar stops. He had had these since we arrived in the Garo Hills, but at first it was impossible to describe them more precisely than simply velar stops. Possibly because of the sheer small size of the mouth, but also because of imprecision and variation, one could not hope to specify the exact point of articulation. By one year and three months, however, his *k* and *g* had settled into the far back post-velar position which is characteristic of Garo, and he interpreted English *k* and *g* the same way, giving a distinctively foreign quality to English words with these phonemes.

At 1:6 his syllable pattern was expanded to include the CVC pattern when he was able to use a final *t* in *dut* 'milk.'[3] Final *n* followed at 1:7 in *mun* 'moon,' *ŋ* appeared finally (its only position) only at 1:9 and final *m* and *l* appear in my records at 1.10. The *k* sound was used finally by 2:0 but *p* was not regularly used in that position until 2:4. Until then, he substituted either

---

[3] Those acquainted with the Indic languages may recognize some familiar items in my examples. Garo has borrowed heavily from Bengali, including the word for "cow's milk" as opposed to "mother's milk." Stephen learned these as Garo words, which indeed they are, and I do not distinguish between them and older Garo words.

k or *t* in place of final *p*, as in *jit* 'jeep,' and *cik-a* (Garo *cip-a*) 'shut.' The *s* sound was used finally as early as it was used in any other position and in this Stephen surpassed the Garo pattern, which has final *s* only in a small number of imperfectly assimilated loanwords.

From the beginning his word-final stops were unreleased and therefore corresponded to the Garo allophonic pattern. This was carried over into English so that the final consonants of such words as *bed* were consistently unreleased. Medially he was at first inconsistent. Stops might be aspirated once and unaspirated the next time, so that at 1:10 he pronounced 'papa' either as [p'ap'a] or as [p'apa]. At 2:0 he learned to make the consistent distinction between syllable initial and syllable final allophones of the stops which contrast with each other medially, syllable initials being aspirated like word initials, and syllable finals being unaspirated. Garo has no true medial consonants since every one must be associated with either the preceding or following vowel, and the difference can be summarized by specifying the position of syllable juncture. At two years, then, with the establishment of some of the consonantal allophones, syllable juncture was also becoming established.

There is a single phoneme in Garo which if syllable initial is a flap, but if syllable final varies from a lateral much like the English *l* to a sound intermediate between a lateral and a flap, with considerable free variation. At first, Stephen pronounced every instance of this phoneme as [l], which amounted in some cases to the use of the wrong allophone of the correct phoneme. Thus in place of Garo *ra-ma* 'road,' he would say [lama]. This is a substitution which I heard small Garo children make, and in fact Garos recognize it as typical childish speech. At two years and three months, Stephen began to shift his initial examples of this phoneme in the direction of a flap and by 2:5 he could execute an expert flap. However, even at 2:7 he occasionally continued to replace the flap with [l] in words that he had known for a long time. New words were pronounced correctly, but some that had become firmly fixed before he was able to articulate correctly were slow to shift.

At two years and five months, also, he was suddenly able to use the glottal stop in clusters (phonetically these are glottalized consonants, though I find it easier to analyze them as clusters), and also in the phonetically distinct situation of preceding a consonant in the following syllable. He was then able to produce beautifully such Garo words as *naʔŋ-ni* 'your'; *maʔn-a* 'to be able'; and *aʔ-kor* 'hole,' and also said /jʌʔm-bo/ with a glottalized *m* substituting for the *mp* cluster of the English 'jump,' together with the Garo imperative suffix *-bo*, so this word expressed the command 'jump!', an example of the phonetic and morphological assimilation of English words into Garo that was typical of his speech.

Garo is not rich in consonant clusters, but my data are not complete even for those which it has. An isolated initial *st* cluster appeared as early as 1:10 in *stas* (English 'stars'), but these were not regularly used for many months. Initial combinations of a stop with *r*, which are the commonest Garo clusters, apparently first began about 2:5. At 2:8 he could make the initial *hw* in English, and could consistently add English plural *s* after other consonants, but other English clusters were still regularly simplified.

The result of this progressive development was a steady approach to the Garo consonantal pattern. He used more consonants pre-vocalically than post-vocalically, which is in accordance with the Garo pattern, and his allophones were settling down to the Garo pattern.

At 2:8 Stephen's English consonantal system still had several lacunae. The single Garo *s* was used in place of the four English phonemes /z, ž, s, š/. Though he eventually learned to make a voiced spirant in imitation, he never did so spontaneously. English *r* was replaced by *w*; post-vocalically it was sometimes omitted all together. He never substituted the phonetically very different Garo *r*. The spirants θ and δ were replaced by various other phones: *den* 'then,' *ti* 'three,' *ala* 'other,' *samsiŋ* 'something,' *bæfwum* 'bathroom.' The labiodentals *f* and *v* were fairly distinct by 2:8. Occasionally they were pronounced as good labiodental fricatives, but more often were bilabial fricatives. Even this latter position kept them distinct from any other phoneme. He did not keep voiced and voiceless consonants distinct in the final position.

VOWELS

I have pointed out that at the time of our arrival Stephen had three distinct vowels. At 1:6 several new vowels appeared with great rapidity, and for some time his vowels were in such a state of flux that it was difficult to analyze them systematically. His vowels were always much less well defined than the consonants, and more variable in successive utterances. He sometimes experimented with various vowels, used one briefly and then abandoned it. I once heard him pronounce the word 'moon' with high front rounded and unrounded vowels, a mid central vowel, and a high back rounded vowel in rapid succession, giving every appearance of groping for a sound that suited him. At 1:6 vowel clusters first appeared with *ai* in *kai* 'Karen.' The two vowels were quite distinct and most easily considered as separate syllables. Other vowel sequences soon appeared: *i* following a front rounded vowel toward the end of the month, and *oi, au, ui,* and *ia* occurred occasionally at 1:7, all of them being bisyllabic. Most of these were relatively rare at this time, but by then *ai* was well established and frequently used. It is the commonest vowel sequence in Garo. By the end of 1:7 I felt that mid front and back vowels were fairly well established, as in *we* 'wet' and *po* 'Paul,' though 'teddy' was still pronounced occasionally as *tidi* rather than as *tedi*.

Various other vowels were heard occasionally. He used a mid central unrounded vowel in [vʌvʌvʌ] for a noise that a dog makes, with the vowel more emphasized than most examples of the mid central English vowel. A mid front rounded vowel was recorded first in conjunction with a following *i*, but later also alone in [tö] 'toy,' which was also sometimes [töi]. This even appeared briefly in an unvoiced form in [kʻöₐk,ʻₐ] 'cookie.' This and a higher front rounded vowel occurred occasionally through 1:7, but by the end of that month, I was inclined to feel that they were non-distinctive variants of the back rounded vowels. The use of [ʌ] was occasional, but not consistent until later. By the end of 1:7, then, he seemed to be settling into a five-vowel system much like the Garo one.

For some time after this, however, *e* gave him trouble and it was only six months later, when he was just two years old, that it was unambiguously distinct from both *a* and *i*. In fact, for a while the *e* disappeared, and once when he was one year and ten months old, I was unable even to get him to imitate it successfully, though he would imitate many other vowels easily. When trying to imitate *e* he would substitute either [i] or [ai]. The failure of the *e* to become well established until later seems surprising both since *o*, which first appeared at about the same time, was by 1:10 thoroughly established, and because both Garo and English have unrounded vowels in the mid front position, so there would seem to have been ample chance for him to hear these vowels, and model his own speech upon them.

At 1:10 the mid central [ʌ] was reasonably well established in English words, and by his second birthday, the mid front *e* was again secure. At two years and one month, he seemed to be differentiating a separate and lower vowel from *e* toward the *æ* position of English, although Garo has no comparable vowel. The addition of [ʌ] and *æ* represented his first enduring progress beyond Garo.

By 2:1 Stephen's vowel system was well enough defined and his articulation precise enough to make possible a more conventional synchronic description:

/e/ was a front mid, unrounded vowel. It was close to the correct position of Garo but was used also for the English /e/ of 'bed,' which is similar.

/æ/ had become distinct from /e/ and was used in English words only, even though these were generally incorporated into Garo sentences.

/a/ remained a low central vowel, used for both the Garo and the English vowels which are similar to each other.

/o/ was a back rounded vowel, intermediate to the cardinal positions of [o] and [ɔ], and therefore close to the proper position for the Garo vowel. It was also used for English words with similar vowels.

/u/ was settling down to the position of conventional Garo; high, usually central and not quite so sharply rounded as the early high back vowel from which it has been derived. This vowel appeared also in such English words as 'turn.'

/ʌ/ remained rarer than the other vowels. It was phonetically not too different from the non-final allophone of the Garo /i/ (for a discussion of which see just below), but as his speech developed /ʌ/, which was used only in English words, seemed clearly to become separated from /a/ while the non-final allophone of Garo /i/ was derived from the more extreme high front [i]. That is, if there was uncertainty about an English word containing /ʌ/, the uncertainty always was whether or not it was distinct from /a/.

/i/ was a high front and unrounded vowel, something like the English vowel in 'beat' but with no glide. The Garo /i/ has several striking allophones, but for the most part at this time, Stephen used a high front unrounded vowel in all positions.

He used vowel sequences of all sorts easily. He did not tend to diphthong-ize them, but maintained the syllabic division between them which is appropriate to Garo.

The most serious imperfection in his Garo vowel system at 2:1 was the absence of some of the allophones of /i/. Improvement came at 2:3 when he began to make a consistent allophonic distinction between the /i/ of open and closed syllables. Non-final Garo /i/ was then pronounced somewhat lower than final /i/ in just about the position of English vowel [ɪ] in 'hit.' This was not yet exactly the proper position of the Garo allophone, which in adult speech is pronounced considerably to the rear of the English [ɪ], but at least some allo-phonic distinction was being made. The same phone [ɪ] was used in English words such as 'hit' while [i] was used for the English nucleus [iy]. In his speech the contrast between the high [i] and the slightly lower [ɪ] was actually phonemic, since the higher one could be used in English words where it appeared non-finally (such as 'feet'), though this is an impossible position for the similar allophone of the Garo vowel. What in Garo were allophones were actually separate phonemes in Stephen's speech of the time, since he used them in English words, in positions not found in Garo. The next step in the development of his high front vowels was not clearly established until 2:8, when the non-final allophone of the Garo vowel shifted securely to the rear to its proper position [ɨ]. This meant that [ɪ] was used only in English words and [ɨ] only in Garo words. But by this time, as is described below, several other developments had brought about a systematic separation of the vowel systems of English and Garo.

At 2:7 Stephen had still not acquired any further distinctively English vowels. For the complex vowel nuclei of English he either used non-fused sequences of Garo-like vowels, or simple Garo vowels. Thus for /ey/ of 'make' he generally substituted the Garo sequence /e-i/ without the fusing of the English nucleus. Similarly for /ay/ of 'pie' and /aw/ of 'out' he substituted /a-i/ and /a-u/ respectively. For /iy/ of 'heat' he substituted the simple high Garo /i/, for /ow/ of 'boat' the Garo /o/, and for /uw/ of 'food' the Garo /u/.

I have described Stephen as having phonemes that are distinctively Garo ([ʔ]) and others that are distinctively English ([ʌ, æ]), as well as many that were used in words of both languages. At least until early in his third year, however, his speech was most efficiently described as a single phonemic system. It was an approximation to Garo, with the addition of a few phonemic distinctions which are not found in that language. Even at the age of 2:7 his Garo was clearly better than his English, and he could still be described as speaking a variety of Garo that happened to have a great many English loanwords. Some of the phonemes of his speech were found only in these loanwords, but there was no indication that he recognized these words, or these phonemes, as having any special status. Other English phonemes were interpreted by him according to Garo speech patterns.

By 2:8 and 2:9 I felt that Garo and English were becoming differentiated as phonemic systems. Many English vowels now seemed to be becoming fixed in positions slightly different from the nearest Garo vowels, although since the differences were often small and since there was so much free variation in his speech, it was not easy to specify exactly the moment of separation.

At this time [ɪ] was used exclusively for the English phoneme and the non-final allophone of the Garo high front vowel had moved away to the rear. English /e/ also seemed to be consistently pronounced slightly lower than the Garo /e/ and English /ɔ/ of 'dog' was now lower than Garo /o/. The high back vowels seemed less stable but again English /u/ of 'put' was at least sometimes pronounced further to the rear than the high mid Garo /u/. I could detect no distinction between Garo and English /a/, which are virtually identical in adult speech.

Most of the complex nuclei were becoming more thoroughly united as diphthongs in the manner appropriate to English rather than to Garo. This was true of /ey, aw, ay, ɔy, ɔw/ and /uw/. For /iy/ he continued to use the high front Garo /i/ which lacked any glide.

In other words, in the two months from 2:7 to 2:9 a systematic separation of the two vowel systems took place, and it was impossible to continue to describe them as one system. This is in contrast to the consonants, where— except for the addition of *f* and *v*—Stephen never went beyond the Garo system, and for as long as we were in India, he simply used the closest available Garo phones as replacements for the English phonemes.

SUPRASEGMENTALS

Garo, although a Tibeto-Burman language, does not have phonemic tone, and so the history of Stephen's speech cannot include the development of recognized tones. However, he fleetingly used a distinction which, even if idiosyncratic, was based partly upon tone. At the age of 1:6, I noticed that he made a fairly clear and consistent distinction between the words 'papa' and 'bye-bye' on the basis of length and tone. Both had unaspirated consonants and voiced vowels, but the word 'papa' was pronounced with a higher tone and very rapidly, while the word 'bye-bye' was pronounced with a lower tone and more slowly. Some other words seemed to have similar characteristics, though none were as clear as this pair, and the distinction did not last for long.

A month later, at 1:7, length was clearly used as a distinctive feature of certain words which represented noises, such as [di:di::] to represent the noise of an automobile horn, and [ʔoʔoʔo::] for the sound of a crowing rooster.

DEVELOPMENT OF LANGUAGE SKILLS BY STEPHEN BURLING.

AGE (YEARS AND MONTHS)	CONSONANTS	VOWELS	OTHER LINGUISTIC PROGRESS	IMPORTANT NON-LINGUISTIC EVENTS
1:4	p t k m n	i u a		Arrival in Garo Hills
1:5	l			
1:6	c	Vowels rapidly shifting		
1:7	s w h (f) (v) voiced/voiceless contrast	i u (e) o a		
1:9	ŋ intervocalic ʔ			Mother in hospital
1:10	(j)	ʌ		„ „ „
1:11			First unambiguous morpheme substitution	
2:0		e	Syllable and word juncture in Garo	
2:1		æ		
2:2			Recognizes the existence of two languages	Living away from Garo Hills, but contact with Garo continues
2:3	j [r] allophone of l	ɪ		Return to Garo Hills
2:5	Clusters with glottal stops			
2:6			English developing rapidly	
2:8		Systematic differentiation of Garo and English vowel systems		

(This rather marginal use of the glottal stop actually preceded its use in non-onomatopoetic words by at least a month.)

At 1:7 he used the exaggeratedly high and then falling intonation which is used by Garos to emphasize great distance. Even by two years, however, his speech was not connected enough to do more than begin to catch incipient intonational patterns. At two years he sometimes used the slightly rising intonation which terminates Garo words, and I heard the typical low and falling English intonation with the word 'there' to convey the sense of 'there, that's done.' Stress does not have an important role in Garo, and I heard no significant stress variations, except for the emphasis of shouting.

MORPHOLOGY AND SYNTAX

At one year and seven months, I began to notice a few utterances which, from an adult point of view consisted of more than one morpheme. He would say *cabo* (< Garo, *ca?-* 'eat' and *-bo*, the imperative suffix); *galaha* (< Garo *gar-* 'fall' and *-a-ha* 'past'); kukigisa (Garo *cookie ge-sa*) 'one cookie'; *guboi* 'good boy.' At 1:10 he was occasionally attaching the form *-gipa* to strings of speech or to nonsense, but only occasionally in positions where this suffix (which makes modifiers out of verbs) could have made any sense. I also recorded different inflectional forms of the Garo first person singular pronoun, *aŋa aŋasa*, and *aŋnisa*, which have somewhat diverse meanings, though presumably he learned these individually and did not construct them himself. His closest approach to substitutability was in phrases with the word *ba-o* 'where' as in *po bao* 'where's Paul?'. I heard this word used once or twice with nouns other than 'Paul,' but was still doubtful that these were formed by him. It seemed more likely that all were learned as entire phrases. His speech could thus not be described as having utterances of more than one morpheme, since the constituents were not substitutable. Gradually he acquired more such forms, particularly combinations of verb bases with one or another of the principal verb suffixes which indicate such things as tense. He regularly used the suffix which he heard most often with the verb, as the imperative forms of 'eat' and 'get dressed' and the past of 'fall,' since 'falling' was most often discussed after it happened.

Then on the first day of May, at one year and 11 months, I was sure for the first time that he could use suffixes freely and add any one of several suffixes to any verb. This was a decisive step and after that, he constantly produced new forms. On virtually the same day, he also was able to form syntactical constructions with a noun subject and a verb. Both morphological and syntactical constructions came at the same time and once the initial ability to make substitutions was gained, he went forward rapidly with more and more complex constructions.

From his first use of the constructions of verb with a principal suffix, he used the suffixes *-gen* 'future,' *-bo* 'imperative,' *-a-ha* 'past,' and *-a* 'present or habitual,' which are probably the ones most commonly used by adults. Shortly there followed -gi-nok 'immediate' or 'intentional future' and -jok 'recent past,' but even a month later at two years these were not used so readily as the others.

Soon after his second birthday he was beginning to use some of the adverbial affixes, which form a characteristic feature of Garo. These affixes are placed directly after the verb base but before the principal verb suffix, and modify the meaning of the verb base in various ways. Early in his third year it was difficult to know how freely he was using these, but the ability to form new constructions with them seemed to be beginning. By then I had recorded the following: -ja- 'negative,' -eŋ- 'continuous,' -at- 'causative,' -ba- 'progression toward the speaker,' -aŋ- 'progression away from the speaker,' and -be- 'very.'

Shortly after his second birthday I had also recorded a few constructions with another class of verb suffixes, a class which follows the principal verb suffixes, and which can be called terminators. He did not use these frequently but I recorded -ma 'neutral interrogative,' -mo 'interrogative anticipating agreement,' and -de 'emphatic.'

He also used a few noun suffixes, though none of them as freely as the principal verb suffixes. The most frequently used was -ci 'in the direction of,' while its more emphatic and precise near synonym -ci-na was somewhat less frequent. At various times -ba 'also,' -ni 'possessive,' and -na 'dative' were used, most commonly with the pronoun for 'I.'

The third and last inflected class of Garo is that of numerals, which are formed from numeral classifiers and the quantifiers. Just before his second birthday Stephen began to experiment with combinations of classifiers and quantifiers, putting them together in the correct way, but with no apparent understanding of their meaning. A few days after his birthday, however, he saw a small bug, and said joʔoŋmaŋsa 'one bug,' including quite correctly the classifier used for all animals, maŋ-. A few days later I recorded him saying gegini in referring to two pieces of a cookie, correctly joining the classifier ge- to the word for 'two,' -gin-i.

The only English morphological construction which he had even incipiently used was the plural, which I recorded in isolated instances such as ais 'eyes' and stas 'stars.' But the plural marker was not freely used and could not be substituted. Although this English plural marker appeared very shortly after he first started using Garo affixes, it had not become substitutable or elaborated the way the Garo affixes had. At the same time he gradually acquired a few English phrases such as 'get down,' 'come in,' and 'good night.' all of which were of course learned as units, and their parts were not substitutable in any way.

Stephen's first freely formed constructions involving more than one word were those whicn combined a noun as a subject and a verb as a predicate. The construction in Garo is much like that in English, but his first sentences were clearly Garo. For one thing, they almost at once included a Garo principal suffix on the verb, so the sentences included three morphemes. Examples are: *ba-bi on-a-ha* 'Babi (the cook) gave (it to me)' and *doʔo bilaŋaha* 'bird flew away.' He continued often to use verbs alone without a subject, but since this conforms to adult Garo, where the subject need not be expressed if no ambiguity arises, this was not a babyish trait on his part.

Soon after his use of subject-verb sentences, he started to use verbs with nouns in other cases. My first recorded example is on May 17, two and one half weeks after his first construction: *papaci reaŋna* 'go to Papa.' On June 4 I recorded two three-word sentences (four and five morphemes respectively): *aŋa tolet naŋa*, 'I need toilet,' and *lala bi taleŋa* 'Emula is preparing the bed.' In both these examples one word was derived from English, though the word order, morphology and phonology were all completely Garo. This assimilation of English words into Garo was characteristic of his speech for as long as we were in the Garo Hills.

By 2:0 he was also using possessives correctly, attaching the possessive suffix to one noun, most frequently *aŋa* 'I,' and then following it by a name of the thing possessed. At that time also there were the first constructions of a noun with a numeral, examples of which have already been given. By early June, then, just after his second birthday and a bit over a month after he first clearly used morpheme substitution, he had used the following constructions (those marked with * were used most freely and frequently, while those in parenthesis were only incipient, and those left unmarked were well established, though not among the commonest):

> Morphological constructions
> verb base plus adverbial affix
> * verb base (with or without an adverbial affix) plus principal verb suffix
> complete verb plus terminator
> noun plus principal noun (case) suffix
> (numeral classifier plus quantifier to form a numeral)
> Syntactical constructions
> * noun (in various cases) plus verb to form sentence
> * possessive noun plus noun
> (noun plus numeral)

Even at this early stage I had never noticed him using obviously incorrect morpheme order. He spoke in a simplified way, of course, and sometimes left things out, but he did not reverse the proper position of morphemes or words. This is perhaps not remarkable since given the freedom of word order (not morpheme order within the words), incorrect word order is not easy to achieve in Garo. In learning these constructions, he apparently always used the construction first in certain specific examples which he learned as a whole and by rote. After using several of these for a while, he would learn to generalize on the construction, and to substitute different morphemes or words in the same construction.

For the next few months, until 2:3, his grammatical development was largely a matter of consolidating and improving the steps that had already been begun in May at 1:11. By September he was freely and correctly using many adverbial affixes and principal verb suffixes. Both these classes had been considerably expanded. At 2:1 I recorded his use of the general suffix *-kon* 'probably,' and by 2:2 he was using it in such a way as to show that he understood its meaning. At 2:2, I recorded the suffix *-ode* 'if,' but could not tell whether he understood its meaning or could use it freely. These innovations are significant in that they involve members of still another class of suffixes that had not been represented earlier and which are inserted after the principal suffix but before the terminator if there is one. He also used several of the principal noun suffixes (case markers) correctly and readily. Of the noun suffixes, the possessive marker continued to be used most regularly. His syntax included the simple form of the Garo sentence with nouns in various cases, followed by the verb. However, he sometimes put one noun, often a pronoun, after the verb, which is a correct Garo way of giving emphasis to the noun. More elaborate constructions, with phrases, clauses, conjunctions, and the like, were still absent from his speech.

The only English construction which he could freely use at 2:3 was that with 'more,' such as *mo ci* 'more water.' Here *ci* is the Garo for water, but the construction is quite foreign to Garo, and is clearly English. The few other English phrases which he used, including even such complex ones as 'what are you doing,' had been memorized as units and the parts were not separable.

By the age of two and a half, he had the system of verb inflection essentially complete, including the use of at least some of the members of every class of verb suffix, and all of the common ones. He used many adverbial affixes easily. I heard examples of as many as three adverbial affixes in one word, which is as many as adults commonly use, though it is not a formal limit. He had also begun to use members of a group of verb suffixes which can convert verbs to a substantive function. At 2:6 he was able to use the important verb suffix *-gi-pa*, by which Garo verbs are put into a form which can be used to modify nouns. He had used *-gi-pa* much earlier, appending it to strings of nonsense, but such "babbling" had stopped by 2:1, and now the suffix was used correctly and with understanding. A few weeks after this appeared, he added the somewhat similar suffix *-a-ni*, which is used to make abstracts from verbs, such as 'heat' from 'hot' or 'walking' from 'walk.'

He also used members of every class of noun suffix, though he did not use every single suffix. He used most of the principal noun suffixes and a good many of the secondary noun suffixes which follow the principal suffixes, and he frequently and easily used the terminating noun suffixes *-san* 'only,' *-dake* 'like, in the manner of,' *-ba* 'also,' and *-de* 'indeed.' Personal pronouns, which in Garo act grammatically like nouns, were added slowly. He had used *aŋa* 'I' since 1:11, but *naʔa* 'you sg.' was recorded only at 2:4, *ciŋ-a* 'we exclusive' at 2:5, and *bi-a* 'he, she' at 2:6. Others were even later.

At 2:6 he could use numbers incompletely and tried to count, but frequently got the order reversed. Two months later he was able to count to ten with occasional mistakes in Garo, and more consistently correctly in English, and he understood the numbers at least to three. He used several numeral classifiers in Garo quite readily, though except for -sak (for people) and -maŋ (for animals) it was doubtful whether he really understood their meaning.

He was weaker in the use of particles. He used few adverbial particles except bak-bak 'quickly,' and only a few of the conjunctions. Lacking most of the conjunctions, he was able to form few complex sentences, though by 2:6 he was making the balanced type of Garo sentence in which two similar verbs, one generally positive and the other negative, are paired together with their associated nouns, without an intervening conjunction.

Reduplication is used grammatically in a number of ways in Garo, but by this time I had not yet detected Stephen using any reduplicated forms. The slow acquisition would seem to indicate that the grammatical reduplication of adult speech has little to do with the reduplicated forms of infantile speech which occur so ubiquitously and which Stephen had used from the beginning of his speech.

SEMANTICS

Besides making steady progress in phonology and grammar, Stephen spoke about a continually widening range of subjects. In some cases he learned a new word in either Garo or English, and for some time used that word in all circumstances, without ever using an equivalent in the other language. In other cases, however, he simultaneously learned English and Garo words with approximately the same meanings, as though once his understanding reached the point of being able to grasp a concept he was able to use the appropriate words in both languages. I first recorded the English word swallow and the Garo min-ok-a 'swallow' on the same day. He learned to count in the two languages in parallel fashion, and could recite numbers in either one and keep the two sets generally distinct even before he became confident and consistent in reciting them in the right order. It was clear that in both languages he could recite numbers before he had any real ability to count or to understand the meaning.

By one year and ten months he was beginning to use color terms in both English and Garo, with great interest, but with little understanding. He would point to something and mention a color term in either language that had no relationship to the color of the object. When later at 2:9 he suddenly grasped the meaning of color terms, and was able to consistently call a red thing red, he was able to do so in both English and in Garo simultaneously. At about the same time he started to use various indicators of time, such as last night, yesterday morning, and corresponding Garo terms, again with little understanding except that he kept terms for past time separated from those for the future. This imprecise use of time markers was in striking contrast to his correct use of spatial terms such as *here*, *there*, and various Garo equivalents, which he had started to use correctly much earlier.

At 2:9 Stephen began for the first time to ask explicitly about words. He would occasionally start to speak, pause, point to something, and ask *wats dis;* receiving an answer, he would proceed to use the word in his sentence. He asked such questions equally well in both English and Garo. He also talked about words, though it was difficult to know how well he grasped the sense of the sentences he used. For instance, he would point to his nose and say *in English it is nose*, or *in Garo it is giŋ-tiŋ*, but he would sometimes get these reversed and call a Garo word English or vice versa. When he was two years and ten months old, I was able to interest him in playing a game with me. I would ask him a question such as "What does hand mean," and he would promptly supply the Garo equivalent; or, if I supplied him with a Garo word, he would return the English. He gave no indication that he noticed which language I presented him with, but consistently gave the opposite one. When I asked for the meaning of the word "table," however, for which the Garos use a word borrowed from English which is phonetically similar to the original, Stephen paused only briefly and then supplied the translation "dining room table." At 2:9 also, he started using the word *said* and its Garo equivalent *a-gan-a* correctly and with understanding in direct speech—another indication of his growing awareness of speech as a phenomenon that can be talked about. In either Garo or English he was able to say such things as *I said "sit down!"*.

BILINGUALISM

As early as the age of 1:6, not quite two months after our arrival, I recorded what then seemed to me like translation. If we asked him if he wanted milk, he would unhesitatingly indicate the affirmative with the Garo equivalent *dut* 'milk.' However, six months later I could still find no evidence that he was really aware of the existence of two different languages in his environment. As in the case of *milk* and *dut* he did recognize that there were two words for certain things and sometimes he would say them together, one after the other, clearly recognizing that they were equivalents. But all his constructions at that time were completely Garo, the only significant English influence being lexical.

We spent about two months from the middle of July to the middle of September (2:1 to 2:3) in Gauhati, Assam, away from the Garo Hills, where Stephen came into contact with several English speakers, as well as numerous Assamese speakers. He continued to be cared for to a great extent by his Garo "ayah," who even sought out the companionship of other Garos, so his contact with that language was never broken. But while we were in Gauhati, I began to feel that he really recognized the existence of the separate languages. He quickly learned who did not speak Garo and rarely attempted to speak to them. He was always more shy with them than with Garo speakers. By 2:3 he could understand a considerable amount of English, but spoke little. He then showed a facility for translating exactly what was said in English into idiomatic Garo. If I asked him a question in English, he was likely to give an immediate and unhesitating reply in Garo.

After returning to the Garo Hills, life was somewhat more normal. He had more continuous and intimate contact with his mother than he had had for some months. This finally resulted at the end of 1955, when he was two and one half years old, in an explosive expansion of his ability in English. Though his English never caught up with his Garo as long as we stayed in the Garo Hills, he developed a taste for speaking English with native English speakers and to my chagrin he came to prefer to speak English with me. Occasionally, when I failed to understand his still very foreign English, he would with obvious condescension translate into Garo, which, being said more correctly, was easier to understand. He translated without hesitation and with no apparent difficulty in switching from one language to the other. He frequently spoke to me in idiomatic English and immediately repeated it in just as idiomatic Garo for someone else's benefit.

We remained in the Garo Hills until October, 1956, but the pressure of other work prevented me from keeping detailed records of Stephen's speech after April (2:10), while his increasing tendency to speak English with me and the increasing skill with which he spoke in both languages made it both more difficult and less rewarding to do so. When we left the district, there was still no doubt that Garo was his first language (when he spoke in his sleep, it was in Garo) but English had become a flexible means of expression as well. We spent about a month traveling across India. At first he attempted to speak Garo with every Indian he met, but by the end of the month was learning that this was futile. I tried to speak Garo with him from time to time, but he rarely used full Garo sentences even then.

The last time he ever used an extensive amount of Garo was on the plane leaving Bombay. He sat next to a Malayan youth who was racially of a generalized southern mongoloid type, so similar to many Garos that he could easily have passed for one. Stephen apparently took him for a Garo, recognizing the difference between him and the Indians that had failed to understand his language in the past weeks. A torrent of Garo tumbled forth as if all the pent-up speech of those weeks had been suddenly let loose. I was never again able to persuade him to use more than a sentence or two at a time. For a couple of months he would respond to Garo when I spoke to him, but he refused to use more than an occasional word. After this, he began failing even to understand my speech, though it was frequently difficult to know just how much was really lack of understanding and how much was deliberate refusal to cooperate. Certainly at times he would inadvertently give some sign that he understood more than he meant to, but increasingly he seemed genuinely not to understand, and within six months of our departure, he was even having trouble with the simplest Garo words, such as those for the body parts, which he had known so intimately.

CONCLUSIONS

In the preceding sections I have described the manner in which one child acquired speech. A few general observations about his linguistic development and a comparison of it with that of some of the other children whose language learning has been previously described remain to be made.

The earliest stage recorded here, with three stop positions, three widely spaced vowels, and two nasals, corresponds closely to the pattern which Jakobson suggests to be characteristic of an early stage of speech, except that to these Stephen added temporarily the cross-cutting distinction of aspiration in the consonants and unvoicing of the vowels.[4] Stephen was not slower to articulate velar stops than the others, unlike some children that have been studied.[5] Some advances, notably the acquisition of the voiced/voiceless contrast, were systematic and added several new phonemes together, though even this was not carried so far as to add a voiced spirant, which Garo lacks, or (until later) a voiced affricate, which Garo does have. Other phonemes seemed to be added individually and it is difficult to see any consistent pattern in their order of appearance.

Viewing his speech as developing by the successive addition of distinctions, or minimal contrasts, provides for the most part an efficient means for analyzing his progress. However, progress was not without its interruptions. Some new steps, such as the acquisition of the contrast between voiced and unvoiced stops or the ability to make glottalized consonants, appeared so rapidly as to be almost datable to the day. In most other cases, however, months elapsed between his first tentative efforts to use a new sound, and its final unambiguous incorporation into his phonemic system. This meant that his language was progressing on several fronts simultaneously and later developments were often beginning before earlier ones were completed.

Apparently Stephen developed phonemic contrasts more rapidly than some children in comparison with the speed of expansion of his vocabulary. Velten, for instance, notes the large number of homonyms in his daughter's speech which appeared as her vocabulary outstripped her ability to produce phonemic contrasts adequate to keep all the items distinct from one another.[6] This was never the case with Stephen, and from a linguist's point of view the problem was more often finding minimal pairs for comparison. Homonyms arising from failure to make the proper contrasts were not common.

It was notable that in the earliest stages of his speech, he briefly used several distinctions (voiceless vs. voiced vowels, tone, length) that are found in neither of

[4] Roman Jakobson and Morris Halle, *Fundamentals of Language* (The Hague, 1956), pp. 37–42.
[5] Werner F. Leopold, *Speech Development of a Bilingual Child* (Evanston, Illinois, 1939–1949), Vol. 2, p. 417.
[6] H. V. Velten, "The Growth of Phonemic and Lexical Patterns in Infant Speech," *Language*, **19**, (1943), p. 287.

the languages that he was learning. One presumes that if these features had been present in his environment he would have started learning them from that time. It might be suggested then that learning a language is not only a matter of learning not to make certain phones, but also of learning not to make certain contrasts which arise apparently spontaneously as a child first tries to speak.

Two and a half years seems remarkably early to have acquired all of the phonemes and all of the important allophones of the language. However, the fact that at the age of four years and four months, almost a year after returning to the United States, he had not yet completed his English phonemic inventory ($/\theta/$ and $/\eth/$ were inconsistently articulated) would seem to deny any extraordinary precociousness, although in general he did seem to be an early talker. Perhaps this provides some objective measure of one's intuitive feeling that Garo does have a simpler phonemic system than English.

Most studies of child language have put heavy stress on the number of words used in a sentence. This is true of much of the psychological literature, but it is also true of Leopold's work. My feeling as I observed Stephen's language, and my conclusion now, is that the number of words or morphemes is perhaps the least important criterion of grammatical progress. What from an adult point of view are multi-morphemic words, or multi-word sentences, were used before their complex nature was recognized by Stephen. The most significant single advance in his ability came when he learned to make substitutions, and once this was achieved, he was soon able to make sentences with not just two morphemes but with three and more. One simply cannot reasonably speak of a two-morpheme stage of his speech development. (Since Garo has such complex word formation, it is more significant to consider the number of morphemes in a sentence than the number of words.)

It has generally been assumed that syntactical constructions precede morphological ones. Leopold states baldly, "In the field of grammar, syntax comes before morphology. The student of child language becomes very conscious of the fact that the morphological devices are a luxury of fully developed languages. The small child gets along quite well without them, for a short or long time."[7] It is difficult and perhaps arbitrary in many languages to draw the line between morphology and syntax, but it is extremely convenient to make such a distinction for Garo, since there are stretches of several syllables set off by characteristic junctures which can be called words, and the grammatical devices used to form these words are very different from those used to join words together. If the distinction is made, Stephen defied the generalization that syntax comes first by learning to make both types of constructions simultaneously. Some reasons for this are obvious: What I am calling morphology in Garo is much more essential than the morphological process of English, or even of the

---

[7] Werner F. Leopold, "Patterning in Children's Language Learning," *Language Learning*, **5** (1953–1954), p. 10.

other European languages. Morphology is not a "luxury" of the fully developed language. Moreover, it is far more regular, and therefore no doubt easier to learn than the morphology of European languages. What I am calling Garo morphology, then, has somewhat the character of syntax in the European languages, but Stephen's method of learning this morphology was not comparable to that by which other children have been observed to learn English syntax. Most histories of child speech have reported a period in which many words are used together with minimal regard for the standard order. Children have been described as using ill-connected sequences of words, and only gradually learning to join them closely together with proper order, juncture and intonational pattern.

One of the striking features of Stephen's speech was the rarity with which he reversed the order of morphemes or words. This was true of his earliest Garo sentences and also was true of his English when it finally began. This was in marked contrast to my own daughter who learned English as her first language two years later, and to other children such as Velten's daughter.[8] My daughter regularly produced such garbled masterpieces as *reading a mommy a book Nono* 'Mommy is reading a book to Nono (her nickname)' or *Nono falling Nono jammies pant* 'Nono's pajama pants are falling down.' Stephen never distorted normal order in this way. I do not know whether this is due to peculiarities of the Garo language or to Stephen. It is true that word order is freer in Garo than in English, but he was consistent in phrases where word order is not optional (such as that formed from a possessor and possessed noun) and he was entirely consistent from the very beginning in the order of morphemes within words, which is as rigid in Garo as word order in English, even though these morphological constructions were as early as syntactical constructions. I could readily observe the gradual acquisition of new grammatical constructions and repeatedly the same pattern was followed. He would first learn a number of examples of the construction by rote and at this stage it was generally difficult to tell whether he understood the meaning of the construction or not, though for the most part this seemed unlikely. He would then generalize the construction and learn to substitute other appropriate forms in the same construction. Even after this, one could not always be sure whether the meaning was grasped or whether he was simply generating sentences mechanically and for the pleasure of it. Whatever the case, however, these constructions were rarely grammatically incorrect, and sooner or later it would become clear that he was using them under semantically appropriate conditions. Considering the progressive acquisition of new constructions brought the same clarification to his grammatical development as considering the successive acquisition of phonemes brought to the analysis of the phonetic record.

As soon as Stephen began to form constructions of his own, he incorporated English morphemes and words into Garo sentences. He appended Garo

[8] Velten, p. 290.

suffixes to English words without the least hesitation, but there was never any doubt that his early sentences were Garo, since the morphology and syntax were Garo even if the lexical items came from English. I once heard the sentence *mami laitko tunonaha* 'mommy turned on the light' where the roots of every word were English, but the suffixes (*-ko* 'direct object marker' and *-aha* 'past tense'), word order, and phonology were Garo and there was no doubt that the sentence should be considered a Garo one. When he finally began to form English sentences, he just as readily adopted Garo words into English. This mutual borrowing was made easy partly because his models did the same. All the English speaking adults around him constantly used Garo words in their speech, and Garos borrow readily from English. However many morphemes might be borrowed, there was seldom any question as to which language he was using since affix morphology and syntax were either all Garo or all English. After his vowel systems became differentiated at 2:8, the phonology was also appropriate to the choice of grammatical system. It was only shortly before the systematic separation of the vowels that he used many English sentences. Before that, he spoke with a single linguistic instrument, forged largely from Garo, but with the addition of English vocabulary and a few extra English phones. Later, when he did have two linguistic systems, the two never appeared to interfere with each other. He spoke one language or the other, never a mixture of the two.

One final comparison with Leopold's daughter is worth making. Leopold insists that a striking effect of bilingualism was the looseness of the link between the phonetic word and its meaning.[9] His daughter never insisted on stereotyped wording of stories. Leopold believed that this was due to the fact that she heard the same thing constantly designated by two different phonetic forms, so that form and meaning were not rigidly identified with each other. There can never have been a child more obsessional in this respect than Stephen. When we read to him, he instantly protested the slightest alteration in any familiar text. This was true even though we read to him in his second language, English, where one would suppose the form and meaning to be least rigidly identified. It must have been an idiosyncratic trait rather than bilingualism that freed Leopold's daughter from insistence upon stereotyped wording.

In the fall of 1958, at the age of five and a half, Stephen is attending kindergarten in the United States. He speaks English perhaps a bit more fluently and certainly more continuously than most of his contemporaries. The only Garo words he now uses are the few that have become family property, but I hope that some day it will be possible to take him back to the Garo Hills and to discover whether hidden deep in his unconscious he may not still retain a remnant of his former fluency in Garo that might be re-awakened if he again came in contact with the language.

[9] Leopold, *Language Learning*, **5**, p. 13.

RUSSIAN •

The Development of Phonemic Speech Perception in Early Childhood

—— *N. Kh. Shvachkin*

The Shvachkin study of Russian children published in 1948 remains the most informative single experimental investigation of child phonology development. The author, who apparently carried out his study without reference to Jakobson's *Kindersprache*, was concerned with the way Russian children learn to discriminate the vowel and consonant phonemes of their language, and his conclusions are in general agreement with Jakobson's. Some details of Shvachkin's procedures are unclear, and he depends heavily on his own subjective judgment, but one must be impressed by the step-by-step progress of his thinking and his patient search for explanation in articulatory, perceptual, and semantic factors. In general, his methods, criteria, and conclusions are clear and convincing within the limits of his goal, and one could wish for equally informative studies of other languages.

Shvachkin recognized that some of his conclusions might be limited by the nature of the Russian phonological system, but he repeatedly suggested generalization to other languages. His passing references to language universals and phylogenesis of language are not reliable, but they show the same concern that Jakobson expressed in *Kindersprache* and are indications of how investigation of child phonology development in one language may be related to a general theory of language.

The Russian sound system, as customarily analyzed, has a dozen voiced–voiceless pairs of consonants (*p–b, s–z,* and so on), plus four sonorants /m n l r/, a *ts*–type affricate /c/, and a voiceless velar *kh* fricative /x/. Almost all of these have palatalized counterparts (*p–p', m–m',* and so on) pronounced with a kind of *y* off-glide, and in addition there are *ch* and *y*. There is a simple five-vowel system /a e i o u /, but the pronunciation of the vowels varies considerably depending on the nature of the surrounding consonants. Stress is used distinctively and some vowels are "reduced" when unstressed for example, *o* becomes *a*). The writing system generally represents the palatalized consonants by using special "soft vowel" letters for the following vowel, but Shvachkin avoids this complication in his transcription. (Appendix A provides the transliteration system from Cyrillic used in the following translation.) For a convenient description of Russian phonology see Boyanus (1955); modern treatments are Halle (1959) and Lightner (1965).   — C.Λ.F.

Razvitiye fonematicheskogo vospriyatiya rechi v rannem vozraste. *Izvestiya Akademii Pedagogicheskikh Nauk RSFSR*, 1948, **13**, 101–132. Translated from Russian by Elena Dernbach and edited by Dan I. Slobin.

I. FORMULATION OF THE PROBLEM

No other problem in the psychology of child language has been as thoroughly investigated and as unsatisfactorily solved as the problem of phonetics. There is not a single research study in the field of child language in which the researcher has not touched on the subject of speech sounds and has not expressed his own views on that subject.

In particular, the question of the role played by articulation and hearing in the phonetic development of the child has raised heated discussions. Some investigators have stressed the exclusive role of articulation in the formation of speech sounds, placing no importance on the role of hearing. On the other hand, others have attributed the development of sounds in child language totally to the perfection of hearing. Investigators who were not satisfied with the one-sided explanations of the articulation and the hearing theories of sound development in child language attempted to find a solution in combining the two. They proposed that both articulation and hearing jointly determine the formation of speech sounds.

It is absolutely certain that the appearance of sensory-motor connnections at age four months is the most important requirement for the development of speech and, in particular, speech sounds. Likewise, one cannot deny the importance of articulation and hearing in the development of speech. Articulation and hearing are both fundamental for the formation of speech.

However, as we will see later, the development of sounds in child language does not depend on these factors alone. There is experimental evidence that the basic determining factor underlying the phonemic development of child language, as well as the development of articulation and hearing, is the semantics of the language. The semantic development of child language determines the phonemic development.

Investigation of the semantics of child language is usually connected with the appearance of the first words acquired by the child from adult speech, although rhythmic and intonational patterns of child speech also bear a definite semantic load. These patterns do hold some meaning, even if their semantic features are very different from the semantic structure of adult speech.

These features are clearly seen when the child begins to use words acquired from adult speech. The child's initial usage of a word is still unchanged. For a long time the acquired word appears in his consciousness as the same kind of expression as the rhythmic and intonational signals. The semantics of these words bear a clear stamp of the peculiar semantic structure of child language.

Indeed, knowledge of the semantics of the child's "first words" astounds the investigator by its extraordinary structure.

One boy designated with a sound combination "*dany*" not only the sound of a bell, but the clock, telephone, and little bell as well. One girl used the sound combination "*mu*" to designate a cow and a big bird, while calling a calf "*au*." Another girl called a dog "*va-va*," but a big dog and a cow "*mu*."

For one child the sound combination "*ki-ki*" means not only a cat, but cotton, and in general, anything soft. For another child "*va*" is a white plush dog, a muffler, a live cat, or father's fur coat; "*s'apa*"[1] for another boy is not only a hat but also the sky.

Sometimes opposite phenomena are designated with one sound combination: "*bu*" means both to put out and to light a candle; "*l'a*" means both to come and go.

One more example. Walking by the river with a two-year-old girl, I found a small twig. I asked her, "Inna, what's this?" Her answer was "*paka*" [*palka* = stick]. Then I threw the twig into the air. "What's this?" I asked. "*T'ipka*" [*ptichka* = bird], she answered. The twig drawing a peculiar trajectory fell into the river. The girl, crying, asked: "*Day ypka*" [*day rybku* = give (me the) fish]. At first I did not understand what she wanted. She led me to the river and pointing with her hand to the floating twig demanded: "*Day ypka.*"

It is evident that the object, during those two minutes, acquired three different names. The explanation is that in the consciousness of the child the name of the object has not become constant in the way it is for us. It changed in the consciousness of the child according to the function it was performing at the time. From the function of the object the child designates a name for the object. This is the way a child that age thinks. Thus, a twig that appeared in the hand, air, or water could be respectively called "stick," "bird," and "fish." A child is inclined to give the same name for everything in the air, and another name for everything in water. What gives rise to such peculiar polysemy of the first words of the child?

First of all they are not yet words in the true sense. The "first words" of a child express his experiences with the perception of an object; they do not yet have any constant meaning. These "first words" are not words which conceptualize the essential features of the object. They are semantic complexes, embracing things with similar meaning to the child. This union, in turn, is conditioned by three factors: denotative, affective, and functional similarity experienced by the child in the process of perception and expression. However, these three factors are not experienced by the child separately but together. For example, with a sound combination "*uuu*" the child expresses his experience upon seeing a train and cars not only because these objects have a similar denotative meaning but also because for the child these objects have affective and functional similarity.

Thus, "the meaning" represented by the complex experience of denotative, affective, and functional similarity of perceived objects is a semantic unit of the earliest child speech. This "meaning," by its undifferentiation and diffuseness, leads the child, for example, to express by a semantic complex "*fu-u*" anything that is associated with "warmth." This "meaning" directs the

---

[1] [*Editor's note*: The apostrophe indicates palatalization (softening) of consonants. *S'apa* is the child's pronunciation of *shlyapa* 'hat.']

perception of the child when he combines "*shlyapa*" [hat] and "*nebo*" [sky] into one semantic complex "*s'apa*." The "first words" of the child, in their peculiar semantic originality, remind us of the "primordial words" of human speech, which Marr compared to fairy tale transformations. These words are characterized by their semantic diffusion and lability.

The unique phonetic features of the initial period in child speech development correspond to the unique semantic features. As we shall see later, it is not the phoneme (a phonetic unit of oral speech) but the intonation, the rhythm, and later a general sound picture of words which bear a semantic load at this stage.

The semantic function of intonation in the initial stage of child speech has been observed by many parents. Shilova states: "The most interesting phenomena are the voice inflections of my son, especially when he is dissatisfied or hungry" (1923). Shilova first noticed the appearance of the new voice intonations when her son was age 5,11.[2] "Hearing the intonations I now can guess what he wants, whether it is to eat, sleep or whether he is, in general, dissatisfied with something. He has voice inflections for everything" (1923). Shmidt says: "Everything is based on intonations" (n.d.). Menchinskaya notes that her son at five months had different inflections for pleasant and unpleasant experiences (n.d.). In Goyer's (1927) observations of his son's babbling one can find the most interesting facts about the semantic function of intonation. Goyer stresses the semantic significance of intonation. "Voice intonation still plays a decisive role in pronunciation of vowel sounds" during the babbling period (p. 44). "All the sound differentiations are evidently conditioned by differentiations in voice intonations" (p. 15).

At this early stage intonation plays a semantic role not only in expressing the child's experiences but also in the perception of adult speech by the child.

Thus, intonation plays a leading semantic role in the child's comprehension and expression. This stage of speech development occurs when the child is about six months old. In the sixth month, rhythm takes on a special semantic function. Kitterman (1913), Rau (1930), and other investigators have noted the early perception of speech rhythms.

I was able to trace the semantic role of rhythm in one casual game with a group of children at the crawling stage in a day nursery school. Usually when I clapped my hands the children clapped after me. At the same time I pronounced the sound combination "*stuk-stuk*." Then I stopped clapping and only pronounced "*stuk-stuk*." The children resumed clapping. This prompted me to complicate the game. I began to change the sound combination, keeping the same rhythm. I said: "*stuk-stuk, tuk-tuk, uk-uk, u-u*." After different variations the children still continued clapping in time to my words. But when, after pro-

---

[2] In the generally accepted age notation, 5,11 designates 5 months and 11 days; that is, figures to the right of the comma indicate days, those to the left, months. Years are indicated to the left of the month, separated by a semicolon (;). Thus, for example, 1;5,20 means 1 year, 5 months, and 20 days.

nouncing "*u-u*," I said only "*u*," the children made no specific movement. There was lack of coordination in their movements and some children did not clap at all. Then after pronouncing "*u-u*" I said "*o-o*," keeping the same rhythm. The children clapped, not noticing the sound change. Then I tried to pronounce sound combinations in reverse order: "*u-u, uk-uk, tuk-tuk, stuk-stuk.*" The children clapped every time. Then I suddenly said "*stuk.*" The children still clapped. It is evident that, by preserving the full sound picture of the initial sound combination, rhythm was not the only factor involved in the children's sound perception.

Experimental evidence shows that after intonation and rhythm are established the sound picture of the word begins to acquire a semantic importance. This occurs when the child is almost one year old. The initial stage of semantic diffuseness in child speech corresponds to *phonetic diffuseness*. This is the *first* feature of the phonetic form of speech at this stage.

The *second* feature of speech at this level lies in the fact that intonation, rhythm, and the general sound picture of a word *directly express* the child's thoughts and feelings. They are the immediate carriers of speech content.

What determines the transition from prephonetic speech to phonetic speech? How does a child, who can semantically distinguish intonation, rhythm, and combinations of sounds in a word, begin to perceive speech sounds and use them as the only means of differentiating the meanings of words?

The surrounding speech, heard by the child, presents a fluctuating and changeable process, very complex in sound structure. In order not to lose oneself in this stream of sounds, it is not enough to be able to perceive the sound variations. Not all differences between sounds are equally important. Some sound relations which are relatively less marked acoustically are more important in a given language than other sound differences which are acoustically sharper. Thus, for example, the distinction in the Russian language between the prelingual and postlingual *r* can be clearly perceived by ear, but it does not serve to distinguish word meanings. At the same time, the much finer acoustic distinction between palatalized and unpalatalized *r* does serve this function.

Thus, a child is faced with the very complex task of choosing from among all the sound variations in spoken language those sound relations which play the role of differentiating meanings in the language.

The child has to perform a very complex operation not only in isolating the differences between sounds but also in generalizing of the articulatory-auditory features of speech sounds. This generalization reflects the relations of sounds in a given language.

Formal-acoustical similarity, or similarity of articulation, that is, physical and physiological features of speech sounds, definitely cannot form the basis for this generalization. The *semantics* of the language can be the only basis. Owing to the fact that the child communicates through words, he gradually masters the meaning of the word; he begins to generalize the sounds which make up words. The child passes through words to the phonemic perception of speech.

With the transition of child speech to a verbal-semantic structure, the phonetic structure of speech changes as well. Sound, which before was the direct carrier of meaning, acquires the function of differentiating meanings. The phoneme and phonemic speech come into existence.

Two periods are thus marked in the development of child language. I will call, conditionally, the language of the first period *prephonemic* and *prosodic* speech and that of the second period *phonemic* speech.

Thus, under the influence of semantic change the child moves toward the phonemic perception of speech, which is connected with a radical reconstruction of both articulation and speech perception. The elements of this transformation are seen in the beginning of the second year of life.

In the prephonemic period of speech, sound accompanies articulation and follows the movements of the speech organs. Goyer accurately caught this in his son at the moment when the child was pronouncing the sound combination *aiaiai*[3] as an expression of tenderness and the sound combination *ooiooiooi* as an expression of strong agitation. The different phonetic structure of these sound combinations is determined, as Goyer points out, by the fact that the above mentioned "shades of feeling correspond to completely different relations of the positions of all the muscles participating in the two expressions" (1927, p. 46).

Subsequently, in the phonemic period of speech, the correspondence between sound and articulation radically changes. Articulation becomes voluntary, corresponding to the sound to be expressed. Voluntary control is the basic characteristic of the articulation of phonemes. This is the reason why the sounds of prephonemic speech and the sounds of phonemic speech, regardless of a certain acoustical similarity, are essentially different from one another.

In addition, the very acoustics of prephonemic speech sounds is in some degree different from the acoustics of phonemic speech sounds. Many prephonemic speech sounds cannot be introduced into any human language. Thus it was not without cause that the mother of Borya Sokolov referred to the sounds he made when he was two months old as "turkey" sounds, since they were similar to the cry of the turkey (Teplov, 1947, p. 11).

With the transition to voluntary articulation all such sounds disappear, and with them also disappear some sounds which are phonetically similar to the sounds of phonemic speech. This often amazes the observer. "The sounds *r* or *l* which are pronounced by the 6 to 7 month old child cannot be pronounced by him when he is 2 to 3 years old." How can one explain such a phenomenon?

The conditions cited above solve this problem very simply. A child in the prephonemic period of speech, in reality, does not pronounce the sounds

---

[3] [*Editor's note*: In all quotations which represent a child's pronunciation the author's transcription is preserved (see Appendix A). All other transliterations from Cyrillic follow the standard system used in this anthology.]

expressed by him; they, accompanying articulation, "pronounce themselves"; these are involuntarily pronounced sounds. At the time when the child moves on to voluntary pronunciation, it turns out that he cannot pronounce all sounds and that he cannot immediately master the articulation of all sounds of speech.

A. N. Gvozdev (1927, p. 66) notes the formation of constant phonemic hearing in his son Zhenya. At age 1,9, Zhenya did not yet distinguish between *kartinka* and *karzinka; pechka* and *spichka,* and so on. But after some time Zhenya suddenly began to treat pedantically the accuracy of pronunciation of the words perceived by him. Gvozdev reports: "Zhenya repeatedly corrected the guttural pronunciation of Volodya, especially when the latter said š instead of s" (1927, p. 106).

The phonemic formation of child speech essentially depends on the psychological features of the phonemes. Investigation of the basic elements of phonemes reveals four basic features, as outlined below.

Phonemes appear in connection with the formation of words. The phoneme, serving to differentiate word meanings, includes a set of phonetic representations. As defined concretely in the speech process, the phoneme is a *representation,* or *image.* At the same time, the phoneme is a *generalization* of phonetic representations which are similar in regard to their function of differentiation of meanings. This is why the phoneme is a peculiar unit, being both general and unique. This is the essence of the dual nature of the phoneme. There lies the essence of the psychological contradictions embodied in the phoneme.

This contradictory nature has been a stumbling block for the majority of phonologists. Baudoin de Courtenay (1895) and Shcherba (1912) stressed the concreteness of the phoneme and talked about the phoneme as a representation. Others, on the other hand, stress the abstractness of the phoneme and speak of the phoneme as a concept. S. I. Bernshteyn tried to define the contradictory essence of the phoneme in Wundtian terms: "The phoneme is an aggregate of representations," or a "representational idea" (1927, p. 22). In addition, in a later work, Bernshteyn defines the phoneme, as a "general concept of a complex of articulatory-auditory signs which possess well-known functional properties" (1937, p. 28).

The main deficiency of these definitions consists in that those phonologists who speak about the phoneme as a representation have in mind the function of the phoneme in the process of a single concrete utterance, while those phonologists who define the phoneme as a concept understand it only as a product of the scientific thought of the linguistic phonologist. Experimental research on the formation of phonemes in child speech reveals that the phoneme emerges as a generalization based on representations (ideas). Each act of phonemic expression by a child is a concretization of this generalization, without whose existence the speech process would be impossible.

Therefore, the *generality* of the phoneme, *based on the facts of representation,* is the first and basic psychological feature of the phoneme.

The second psychological feature of the phoneme is its *function as a distinguisher*. The phoneme is a sound which distinguishes the meanings of words. The psychological feature of distinguishing meanings is clearly revealed in the moment of formation of phonemes. The appearance of the phoneme is connected with the development of an ability to distinguish meanings; the phoneme appears during the process of development of this ability and is a distinctive herald of this phenomenon.

The next psychological feature of the phoneme is its *constancy*. Shcherba first pointed out the constant nature of the phoneme. Thanks to the constancy of the phoneme we perceive *k* in the words *kot* and *kat* as the same *k*.

There is experimental evidence that the appearance of the constancy of the phoneme is connected with the appearance and development of constant meaning of objects. In connection with this originates the necessity for naming objects and this, in turn, leads to the appearance of words. Constant (that is, phonemic) perception of speech sounds is based on this.

Finally, the fourth psychological feature of the phoneme is *voluntariness* or *intentionality*. The phoneme is a sound which is willfully or intentionally pronounced. The voluntary nature of the phoneme clearly manifests itself at the moment when the phoneme appears in development. We see how the child in the prephonemic stage involuntarily pronounces sounds. Indeed, he does not "pronounce"; rather, the sounds "pronounce themselves." They accompany articulation. The nature of phonemic speech sounds is different. From the moment of the appearance of the phoneme the child begins to pronounce speech sounds voluntarily. It turns out that he is not able to pronounce all the sounds that he had involuntarily pronounced in the prephonemic period. The child, mastering the phonetic system of the language, is absorbed (preoccupied) in observing the sounds of his own speech and is very sensitive to the insufficiency of sounds in his speech and that of others. All of this points to the voluntary nature of the phoneme.

Afterward, with the development of automaticity, the phoneme acquires an involuntary characteristic. But this involuntariness differs from the involuntariness of prephonemic speech. This involuntariness is the product of the generalization of the articulation of phonemes, and at any moment—when necessary—the phoneme can again display its voluntary nature.

In the basic part of the research presented below an attempt is made to experimentally determine how the child moves from prosodic, prephonemic speech to phonemic speech and to trace the phonemic development of child speech.

II. INVESTIGATION OF THE PROBLEM

The study of the origin and natural development of phonemic perception of speech was the problem undertaken in this experimental research. It was impossible to limit oneself to the formal registration of facts in the organization of this research. Rather, it was necessary to work out a method which would correspond to the actual course of development of phonemic perception in the child. This problem proved to be quite difficult and required a great deal more time and effort than the actual study of the facts themselves.

1. In Search of a Method

The basic difficulty lay in the fact that it was necessary to work out a method that would reorganize the attitude of a one-year-old child to objects and to words referring to objects. The object and the word should receive a constant meaning in the child's perception. It was necessary to cultivate in the child such an attitude to the designated object that this given object would be seen as a socially established meaning, that is, denotative meaning.

However, for the one-year-old child the objects surrounding him have a very limited meaning defined by immediate physiological needs. Thus, for example, the bottle first of all stands out as an object which "feeds" him with milk. Only in the course of further development, in the second half of the first year, does the child enter into new and more complex relations with the objective reality. He cognizes the diversity of object properties and aspects of objects. The object acquires a constant meaning for the child which does not depend on unstable and dynamic needs.

This makes it possible to give a one-year-old child problems whose solutions demand singling out of differences between objects on the basis of differences in their stable and objective qualities.

In the experiments the child was given the task of *distinguishing* objects. During the process of continuous training he began to acquire the habit of comparing objects. Words were included in the operation of differentiation. Each object received its own name. The child had to learn to relate the given word only to a definite object. Here the child had to overcome the tendency to relate the same name to different objects.

At first the child tended to relate the name not to the object itself but to the actions associated with the given object. The following are two examples.

Lyusya Luk'yanova (a girl aged 0;11,29), who had not yet pronounced a single word, dropped an object which previously in the experiments had been called a *kat* several times. At this moment, for the first time, she pronounced "*kat'*": This was her very first word. To verify this the object was again given to her, but in such way that she again dropped it. When the object fell on the floor, the girl again pronounced "*kat'*" and pointing with her finger, demanded that the object be picked up for her. The experimenter picked up the object and said: "Lyusya, this is *kat, kat.* Say *kat.*" The girl looked at the experimenter, pointed with her finger to the object, but did not utter a sound. But, the object had only to disappear from her field of vision when she began anxiously to look for it and pronounced "*kat', kat'.*" It became evident that she pronounced *kat* only when a need arose to get back the object that had disappeared.

Would she use the same word *kat* to refer to the disappearance of a different object, known to her by a different name?

In order to receive an answer to this question, an object with the name *dok* was chosen. The girl distinguished it from *kat*. The object was presented in the same conditions so that Lyusya could drop it. When the object fell, Lyusya demandingly pronounced "*kat*'." This was repeated in this fashion several times. Thus, it is shown that Lyusya does not relate *kat* to a definite object. *Kat* is rather an expression of her diffuse experience connected with the disappearance of an object.

Another example: Tolya Tret'yakov (a boy aged 1;5) very willingly pronounced after the experimenter the word *bak*. But the experimenter had only to point at an object which Tolya knew to have the same name and ask him: "What is this?" Then Tolya grew silent, poking the object with his finger. When the object disappeared, Tolya, looking for it, pronounced "*ak*." The experimenter asked "Where is *bak*?" [*Gde bak?*] Tolya spread his hands and said in distress, "*baka*." How happily he rushed later to the object, when he saw it! Afterwards an object with the name *kub* was shown to him. Tolya pronounced "*kuba*" several times after the experimenter. But when he was asked: "Tolya, what is this?" he remained silent. When *kub* disappeared, Tolya looked for it in distress muttering "*ak, ak*."

Similar experiences occurred with many children. After continuous efforts I was able to create in the child the need and the interest to distinguish and compare objects and words. Only then did the child begin to understand what was asked of him. He began to relate a word, given as a name for a particular object, only to that object. In connection with this he began to phonemically distinguish between different words as well.

The following is a description of the full series of experiments:

1. The experimenter came to the child with an object. He named the object with a word, such as *bak*, and worked with the child until he was convinced that the child correctly related the given word to the object.

2. On another day the experimenter came to the child with a new object and named it with a different word, for instance, *zub*. Again the experimenter brought the child to the point of correctly relating the given word to the object.

3. After this, both objects were shown to the child. He was faced with the task of correctly relating the acquired word to the object on the basis of distinction between those two objects. Children could usually solve this problem after a certain amount of training.

4. Afterwards, the experimenter showed a third object to the child and named it, for instance, *mak*, in opposition to *bak* The child correctly related the given word to the object.

5. *Zub* was then shown together with *mak*. The child distinguished these words and objects in the same way as *bak* and *zub*.

The critical phase of the experiment came next:

6. Three objects were placed in front of the child: *bak*, *mak*, and *zub*. The problem consisted in making sure that the child distinguished between *bak* and *mak*, that is, could he distinguish these words phonemically.

Further experiments were not carried out with children who handled the problem of phonemic distinction correctly from the very start. For the purpose of research it was necessary to conduct experiments with children who did not yet possess the ability to perceive words phonemically, since it would then be possible to trace the origin and development of phonemic perception during the course of experimentation.

But how can one finally be convinced that a child really can distinguish the objects and the words related to them? The child can sometimes accidentally correctly relate the name to the object. It was necessary to free the experiment from these biases. The following six systematic methods were worked out for that purpose.

1. *Pointing to the object.* The child was asked to point out a definite object from among a number of other objects. The position of the object among others was often changed. If the child *always* correctly pointed at the named object among others whose names differed phonemically from the name of the object sought, then one could attest to the ability to perceive phonemically relevant differences between sounds.

2. *Giving of the object.* The child was asked to give the named object to the experimenter. If the child always correctly chose the named object from a number of objects, whose names differed phonemically from the name of the object, and gave it to the experimenter, then one could attest to the ability to make a phonemic distinction.

3. *Placement of an object.* The child was asked to place different objects, whose names were phonemically different, in certain places of the room. If the child *always* correctly carried out the assignment, one could attest to the presence of a phonemic distinction.

4. *Finding the object.* The child was asked to find one of the objects whose names were phonemically different. If the child *always* carried out the given problem, one could attest to the presence of a phonemic distinction.

5. *Operation of one object in relation to another object.* The child was asked to put one object upon another. Their names were phonemically different from one another. If the child *always* carried out the problem without mistakes, one could attest to the presence of a phonemic distinction.

6. *Substitution of objects.* This method requires detailed description. It was prompted by the children themselves.

There were cases when children gathered together for a collective experiment. Usually the collective experiment was done when the children showed the ability to clearly perceive the phonemically relevant differences in given phonemic contrasts. Once two girls, Lyusya Skachkova (1;8) and Nina Lalyantzeva

(1;8), were called in for the experiment. They were playing with three objects whose names were *mak*, *bak*, and *bok*. Lyusya had a toy named *mak*. Nina had *bak* and *bok*. The experimenter said to Nina: "Put *bak* on the windowsill, Nina." Nina carried out the assignment correctly and returned to the experimenter. At the same time Lyusya, unnoticed, came up to the window and took away the toy called *bak*, which for some reasons she liked, and in its place put the object called *mak* on the windowsill. Then the experimenter turned to Nina and said: "Nina, go and bring me *bak*." Nina quickly ran to the window and, disappointed, returned with the toy *mak*. The toy called *bak* had disappeared. Suddenly, she noticed that toy in Lyusya's hands and ran toward her.

After this, frequent use was made of this complicated method of differentiation. If the child *always* carried out the given task, one could attest to the presence of the phonemic distinction.

For decisive proof of the ability to perceive a phonemic contrast, three or four and sometimes all six methods described above were used on one child. The methods were selected according to the age of the child. The last two methods were successful only with older children.

The research required special attention to the *structure* and *character* of words presented to the child. A word had to differ from other words by only one phoneme. In addition, the word had to be short, in order that a definite sound, differentiating meaning, would be predominant in the child's perception. For that reason only *monosyllabic* words were chosen for the experiments. In this manner it was fairly easy to deal with the problem of word structure.

The determination of the *character* of words was a more complex matter. Since the subjects were Russian children, it seemed desirable to use monosyllabic words in the Russian language. However, the selection of concrete words led to such difficulties that this initial plan had to be abandoned. The experiment at hand required words whose meaning was not only concrete but also material. It turned out that in the Russian language there are very few monosyllabic words with material meaning. This had already been noted by Voyachek. He said, "If one tries to select words from a dictionary that will be suitable for investigation of auditory word perception he will see how difficult it is to find homogeneous monosyllabic words" (1906, p. 44).

Further, the experimental words had to be grouped in definite phonemic series, whose separate units would be phonemically different from each other in specific ways. There are very few words in Russian that satisfy all of these conditions.

Finally, it was necessary to select words and objects which would be equally unfamiliar to the child, otherwise the equivalence aspect of these objects and words would be destroyed.

In order to satisfy the enumerated conditions it was necessary to select "artificial words," that is, words that were specially made up for the experiments. This was possible because in the perception of the preverbal child there is no real psychological difference between words of the native language and artificial words. This was confirmed completely in an experiment comparing Russian and artificial words differing by the same phoneme.

However, in making up *artificial* words it was necessary to overcome new difficulties. The basic requirement of all the artificial words was that the sounds and sound clusters correspond to the phonetic structure of the Russian language; that is, the sounds of these words had to be Russian. For this reason the artificial words made up for this experiment were reviewed by the Russian phonologists Academician L. V. Shcherba and Professor S. I. Bernshteyn.

In addition, it was necessary to specially choose objects that would go with the corresponding artificial words. From a pedagogical point of view it would be silly, for example, to take a small iron which is very familiar to the child and call it *bom*. *Bom* is usually the sound of a bell. This difficulty was resolved in two ways: (1) In some cases the object was changed to correspond to the word. For example, a stone was put inside the little iron to produce a jingling sound; then, the designation of *bom* corresponded in an established way to the object. (2) In the majority of cases solid geometric figures were used: wooden pyramids, cones, and so on. Usually children do not learn the names of these objects until they are much older.

Then it was necessary to solve the problem of *the position in the word of the sound to be changed*. It is evident that this sound must stand out as far as possible in the child's perception of the word. Is the initial or the final sound of a word perceived better?

A control experiment was set up in order to resolve this question. Zina Popova (1;6) could, in the very first trials, easily distinguish not only *b* and *m* but also sonorants in word-initial position. She distinguished between objects carrying the names *lot* and *mot*. However, if the words were pronounced in the reverse order *tol* and *tom*, that is, with the sound contrast at the end of the word, then Zina began to mix up the objects upon simultaneous presentation of them. This was also found with other children when they had begun to phonemically distinguish sounds at the beginning of words. Thus, the pilot study showed that the time of appearance of phonemic distinction of sounds also depends on the place of the sound in the word. Children distinguish the sounds at the beginning of words earlier than at the end of words.

In the course of long preliminary experiments the method was gradually worked out and word lists were compiled. During these experiments it was found that the phonemic distinction of speech sounds does not appear at once. We began to see *a definite sequence in the phonemic development of child speech.*

2. Tracing Phonemic Development

The following phenomenon is frequently observed. A child distinguishes between words with different sound combinations (*b'im* and *dok*), but does not distinguish words where only one phoneme is different (*b'im* and *bom*).

However, this is not caused by deficiency of speech perception or articulation. The cause lies in what it is which determines the very appearance of verbal hearing and voluntary articulation: the child's attitude toward words and the naming of objects. The following is one example.

Tolya Tret'yakov (1;5) and Lyusya Skachkova (1;6) stood out from other children because of their vivacity and talkativeness. During the experiment these children constantly repeated all the words pronounced by the experimenter. They could distinguish between the pronunciation of the following phonemically distinct words: *bak-mak, b'it-m'it, b'ik-m'ik*. On this basis one could draw the hasty conclusion that they do distinguish words on a phonemic basis. However, nothing could be more erroneous than this conclusion. One has to notice under what conditions the children can distinguish the pronunciation of these words. Tolya and Lyusya distinguished words phonemically only when they repeated them after the experimenter. However, one had only to ask them to name the objects to which these phonemically distinct words referred and the children would look in bewilderment either at the objects or at the experimenter, pronouncing some indefinite sound. When they were asked to give these objects, they usually confused them and were displeased when their mistakes were pointed out.

The changes in their relation to objects and words began to appear much later. At first the children rushed joyfully when they saw the toys; they played with them and repeated any word said by the experimenter. Later they began to wait for the experimenter to give names to the toys. If the experimenter for some reason was slow in naming an object, they would demand a name, poking their finger at the object. The name of the object for them became a property of the object. Object naming became a *need* for them.

In the process of the appearance of a need for naming, there also arises a *constant relationship of the word to the object. Word meaning* arises in its elementary form.

All this leads to the appearance of phonemic perception. The child begins to treat the sounds of the pronounced word differently. He begins to understand what the experimenter demands of him. He waits to respond until his own sign of approval which for him becomes the best incentive. The experiment becomes full of intellectual experiences of the child.

Zina Popova, a quiet and alert girl, once, while changing to a more difficult phonemic distinction between sounds, got confused and answered incorrectly. This made her cry. Then the experimenter asked her to distinguish the words and toys she already could discern. She quieted down and felt better.

Another incident happened to Tolya Tret'yakov. He could accurately distinguish the vowel sounds. It was decided to move on and work with him on distinction of presence and absence of consonants. Tolya, who could easily differentiate the vowels, was confused in distinguishing the presence of consonants. He listened very hard to the words pronounced by the experimenter. He seemed to feel the difference but for some reason did not trust himself and suddenly refused to answer. Nothing could make him answer. At the same time he willingly responded to the differentiation of vowels. Only somewhat later was it possible to overcome the negative feelings that had been aroused in him.

Such is the picture of the child's experiences during the appearance of phonemic differentiation between sounds.

Phonemic differentiation does not appear suddenly. Gradually, from one experiment to another, the principle of sequence becomes apparent in the child's mastery of the phonemic relations of the language. Then the thought occurred about the existence of a natural sequence in phoneme formation, and with it the problem of investigation of this sequence.

The aforementioned Zina Popova, who stood out among other children because of her intelligence and attentiveness, had already differentiated the consonants *b* and *m* (*bak* and *mak*) in the first trials. But she could not differentiate *d* and *z* (*dup* and *zup*). In trials for differentiation of vowels Zina accurately differentiated *o* and *u* (*tol* and *tul*), and *u* and *a* (*buk* and *bak*). Another child, Nina Kalyantzeva,[4] differentiated the vowels in exactly the same manner as Zina. The remaining children could not discriminate any speech sounds phonemically. A special series of experiments on discrimination of vowels and consonants was tried with Zina and Nina. Both girls accurately differentiated between the vowels *o* and *i* (*kot* and *kit*) and *u* and *a* (*zuk* and *zak*). A dissimilarity occurred between them in the differentiation of consonants. Zina clearly differentiated *b* and *m* (*bak* and *mak*) while Nina could not differentiate between these consonants. Could Nina discriminate between *b* and *p*? Maybe Nina's perception in this case would be better than that of Zina, who could not differentiate these consonants. The result, however, turned out to be negative. Zina and Nina both confused *bak* and *pak*. Thus, Zina and Nina discriminated the vowels. Zina also discriminated between *b* and *m*. Nina could not yet discriminate any consonants.

The conclusion consists in that *vowels are phonemically discriminated earlier than consonants.* After the discrimination of vowels comes the discrimination of consonants. Which consonants are these?

Zina could not discriminate *d* from *z* or *b* from *p*, but she distinguished *b* from *m* and among the sonorant consonants *lot-mot*, *mak-nak*, and *lak-rak*. Nina could not make these discriminations.

A complex problem occurred in establishing which consonants Nina could discriminate if, in general, she could already discriminate the consonants phonemically. Once the experimenter came up to Nina with the following words: *os*, *mos*, *pos*, *bos*. The tests showed that Nina still could not distinguish *m* from *b* (*mos-bos*), *m* from *p* (*mos-pos*), and *b* from *p*. But she could discriminate *mos-os*, *bos-os*, and *pos-os*. This shows that Nina perceived the presence of a

---

[4] The names and ages of children, along with other information about their development can be found in Appendix B.

consonant—she distinguishes between a phoneme and a "zero phoneme"— but she still cannot distinguish the actual consonants. The proposed conclusion that follows is that *discrimination between the presence and absence of a consonant appears earlier than the differentiation of consonants.*

Is it possible that the differentiation between the presence and absence of a consonant appears before the differentiation of vowels, that is, before the differentiation of phonemes in general? In order to solve this problem an experiment in differentiation of the presence and absence of consonants was carried out with four children who still could not distinguish among vowels. This experiment demonstrated that none of the children could distinguish the presence or absence of the consonants. They got confused in differentiating the presence and absence of consonants in the same way as they got confused in differentiating vowels. What is important is that in the process of these tests the phonemic differentiation began to appear in two of the children. However, perception of the presence of consonants was not registered.

In this manner the experiment established that *the differentiation of vowels appears before discrimination between the presence and absence of a consonant.* Therefore, the first step in the phonemic development of child speech is the differentiation of vowels. The second step in phonemic development is the appearance of the differentiation between the presence and absence of consonants. Afterwards differentiation between consonants begins to appear.

The experiments with Zina Popova demonstrated that the first differentiation of consonants is made on the basis of sonority. From further experiments it became clear that the differentiation between sonorant and obstruent consonants appears before differentiation among the sonorants themselves.

An experiment with Tolya Tret'yakov confirmed this fact. This boy clearly distinguished *m* from *v*, but could not discriminate between *m* and *l*; he distinguished *m* from *g* but did not discriminate between *m* and *z*, and so on.

As to Zina Popova, she already easily discriminated between sonorant consonants. It is striking that she distinguished sonorant consonants from articulated obstruents—although not all of them. She distinguished sonorant and articulated obstruents such as *m-b, m-d, m-g,* but could not discriminate *m-v, m-z,* or *m-ž.* This was somewhat surprising. Evidently, some differentiation exists in discrimination of sonorants and various articulated obstruents. What is the principle of this differentiation?

The conclusion was self-evident: The very first discrimination is between sonorant and stop consonants, and then, after the discrimination between sonorant consonants themselves, there appears the distinction between sonorants and spirants. But soon this hypothesis had to be rejected. Once, during the experiments in discriminating *m* from *z* with Zina and Nina, it was observed that when asked "where is *mak?*" and not clearly pointing to the toy, the children quietly, as if to themselves, pronounced "*mak,*" but when questioned "where is *zak?*" they pronounced "*dak*" (Zina) or "*tak*" (Nina). All attempts to motivate them to pronounce *z* correctly were in vain.

This motivated us to observe the children's articulation. It turned out that they pronounced spirant consonants imperfectly. Thus, imperfection in distinction between sonorants and spirant obstruents perhaps could be explained not by acoustic qualities of spirants but by their articulational features. *Articulation*, and not only hearing, evidently influences the phonemic development of child language; in any case, articulation brings significant amendments in this development.

This conclusion was decisively corroborated when Zina began to pronounce *v*, but at first it was a bilabial *w*. Then she began to clearly distinguish *m* from *v*. At the same time, not having mastered pronunciation of *ž* (she replaced it with *d*), she could not distinguish *m* from *ž*. Tolya Tret'yakov, however, who even prior to starting discrimination between sonorants and obstruents, could say *v*, at the appearance of this discrimination distinguished at the same time between *m* and *b*, and *m* and *v*. But *ž*, which he replaced by the sound *z*, could not be distinguished from *m*.

On the other hand, the same children, who did not yet master the pronunciation of liquid consonants (*r*, *l*), still could clearly distinguish them. This last fact served as a condition against overevaluating the role of articulation in the process of phonemic development. In some cases the child's hearing, regardless of the absence of corresponding articulation, can define the phonemic discrimination. Besides, there is no necessity for complete ability to pronounce the phonemes in order to discriminate them. Sometimes some approximation to the correct pronunciation of the sound is sufficient for eliciting discrimination of the phoneme from others. However, phonemes not clearly pronounced by the child are discriminated significantly later than those phonemes which the child pronounces clearly.

Thus, a definite sequence began to appear in the phonemic perception of consonants: *First comes discrimination between sonorant and articulated obstruents; then discrimination among the sonorants begins, and finally, discrimination between sonorants and nonarticulated obstruents appears.*

Experiments further demonstrated that following the discrimination between sonorants and nonarticulated obstruents, *discrimination between stops and articulated spirants* appears: *b* versus *v*. Nonarticulated spirants began to be discriminated from stop consonants significantly later. Zina Popova succeeded in discriminating *b* from *ž* only with great effort. She began to discriminate them only when, instead of the usual substitution of *d* for *ž*, she began to pronounce *ž* as a sort of sound complex: *d* + *ž*.

Following the advice of Academician Shcherba, we conducted a special investigation of discrimination between hard and soft (palatalized and unpalatalized) consonants, in order to find out what place this discrimination occupies in the general ontogenetic sequence of phonemic development. The elucidation of this question is especially important in the phonemic speech development of the Russian child, since the discrimination between palatalized and unpalatalized consonants is phonemic in Russian.

Zina Popova, who already discriminated stops and spirants, could easily discriminate between palatalized and unpalatalized consonants. Nina Kolyant-zerva and Tolya Tret'yakov, who were at the level of discriminating sonorant consonants, could also discriminate palatalized and unpalatalized consonants. Vova Sukhanov, who could only discriminate between sonorants and articulated obstruents, could not discriminate palatalized and unpalatalized consonants. Parallel experiments were conducted with him in discriminating between sonorant consonants and discriminating between palatalized and unpalatalized consonants. It became evident during these trials that *discrimination of palatalized and unpalatalized consonants appears earlier than discrimination between sonorant consonants.*

Following Shcherba's advice, a special investigation was conducted on discrimination of consonants of different localization. Zina Popova easily discriminated phonemes of different localization. Tolya Tret'yakov and Nina Kalyantzeva, who already discriminated between stops and spirants, could only distinguish labials from nonlabials: *b-d, b-g, v-z, v-ž, v-x.*

They could not discriminate between prelingual and postlingual consonants. Vova Sukhanov, who could discriminate sonorants and nonarticulated obstruents, could not distinguish between labial and lingual consonants. Other children (Lyusya Skachkova and Lyusya Stepanova), after being able to discriminate sonorants and nonarticulated obstruents, began to discriminate between labial and lingual consonants. The discrimination between stops and spirants came afterwards.

These facts demonstrate that discrimination between consonants of different localization comes at different times: labial and lingual consonants begin to be discriminated earlier than stops and spirants; prelingual and postlingual consonants are discriminated later than the discrimination between stops and spirants.

The next fact we established was that discrimination of voiced and voiceless consonants appears very late. This was somewhat surprising. It was natural to assume that an eight-month-old child, who could discriminate between *ba* and *pa*, had a general discrimination between voiced and voiceless consonants. Experiments made it necessary to reject this hypothesis and place discrimination between voiced and voiceless consonants at the end of the development of phonemic speech perception.

How can one explain what is, at first sight, the contradictory phenomenon that the child distinguishes between *b* and *p* in his speech when he is eight months old, but begins to discriminate them phonemically later than other consonants, even later than those consonants which he had not yet mastered in infancy? In reality this contradiction is only illusory. Once again this demonstrates the specificity of phonemic perception of speech, which is connected with the development of the child's activity and consciousness and with restructuring of his needs. A child who discriminates *ba* from *pa* at eight months and earlier is compelled to discriminate them, because this discrimination is connected with his immediate physiological needs. These needs can force a child to distinguish the finest sound nuances and to differentiate the most refined pronunciation of sounds. But when the infant crosses over to a different aspect of speech sound discrimination called forth in a completely different situation and not connected with immediate needs, then the perception of speech sounds reveals different characteristics. The experimental situation was aimed at developing new, object-mediated needs—the need to name an object and the need to discriminate names. In such a situation the child began to perceive and discriminate speech sounds in a different manner: he began to perceive and discriminate *phonemically*.

In this situation it was apparent that *voiced* and *voiceless* consonants begin to be discriminated much later. Only the discriminations between *"hushing" and "hissing" sibilants, and between liquids and y come later.*

This concluded the first exploratory stage of the investigation. The problem, as noted above, was to find a general sequential pattern in the phonemic development of child speech perception. The following sequence was revealed: first to emerge is the discrimination of vowels, then distinguishing the presence of consonants, and finally discrimination between different consonants. The consonants are discriminated in the following sequence:

1. Discrimination between sonorants and articulated obstruents
2. Discrimination between palatalized and nonplatalized consonants
3. Discrimination among sonorants
4. Discrimination between sonorants and nonarticulated obstruents
5. Discrimination between labials and linguals
6. Discrimination between stops and spirants
7. Discrimination between pre- and postlingual consonants
8. Discrimination between voiced and voiceless consonants
9. Discrimination between "hushing" and "hissing" sibilants
10. Discrimination between liquids and *y*.

On the basis of this sequence, it was possible to conduct a systematic investigation, using a sufficiently large number of children, in order to establish *ontogenetic stages in the phonemic development of child speech.*

3. Ontogenetic Stages of Phonemic Development

The experiment revealed a regular sequence in the phonemic development of child speech. With the exception of some individual differences in the development of hearing and voluntary articulation in the second year of life, it is possible to outline schematically the ontogenetic stages of phonemic development.

The First Phonemic Stage (discrimination of vowels). Acoustic and phonemic investigation confirm the fact that *the vowels are perceived better than the consonants.* First, the vowels are more sonorant than the consonants and thus are perceived better. Second, individual vowels are repeated in adult

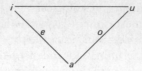

Figure 1a.

speech more often than consonants. Peshkovskiy (1925), in his statistical analysis of several passages of Russian oral speech, established that out of 10,000 sounds there are 5353 consonants and 4647 vowels. If one takes into account that in the Russian language there are five times fewer vowels than consonants in number of types, then one finds a fairly large frequency of occurrence of vowel types in speaking and hearing speech. On the average, vowel tokens are found five times more frequently than consonant tokens. However, not all the vowels are discriminated by the child at once. There are even vowels which, in certain instances, are discriminated later than some consonants.

The experiments on discrimination of vowels were based on the vowel triangle (see Fig. 1a).[5] The experiment showed that, out of all the vowels, *a* is singled out first. By isolating the sound *a* from the general group of vowels, the child seems to be dividing the vowels into two parts: *a* and non-*a*.

One can assume that the initial discrimination of *a* versus non-*a* is determined, in the first place, by the acoustic characteristics of the vowel *a*. The vowels form the following ascending series according to the pitch of the main formant, that is, the characteristic area of auditory frequencies of each vowel, where the partial tones have increasing power of phonation: *u, o, a, e, i.* The vowel *a* occupies a middle place in this series. It is known that auditory sensitivity is greatest precisely in the middle of the pitch range; the sounds in the middle range are the most audible. On this basis, *a* could be defined as "the most audible sound" of all the vowels.

The primordial isolation of the vowel *a* is determined not only by the acoustic features of the sound. In discriminating this sound, children are directed also by visual perception: they attentively follow the movement of the experimenter's mouth.

The vowels in the non-*a* group (*i, e, u, o*) are not immediately discriminated from one another. As the results of the experiment show, first comes the discrimination of *i-u, e-o, i-o, e-u.* Finally, there emerges discrimination of the vowels *i-e, u-o.*

Data on the phylogenesis of speech also indicate later discrimination of the vowels *i-e, u-o.* Usually the vowels *a, i,* and *u* are considered to be the oldest vowels; *e* and *o,* which are located in the vowel triangle between *a* and *i* and between *a* and *u* appear much later. There are languages in which, up to

---

[5] At this stage the child does not discriminate between palatalized and nonpalatalized consonants; therefore it was possible to experiment with the vowel *i.*

this day, only *a*, *i*, and *u* are discriminated phonemically. These languages include: Lake [a Caucasian language], Arabic, modern Persian, and others. In the ancient Semitic language even *i* and *u* are not discriminated phonemically, that is, there is only a phonemic distinction between *a* and non-*a*.

The later differentiation of *i-e* and *u-o* is explained, first of all, by the acoustic proximity of these vowels. Substitution of *o* for *u* and *e* for *i* is encountered frequently. Voyachek observed that "the vowels *o* and *u* have a low bass characteristic and can be discriminated only across a small distance" (1911, p. 1224).

The early discrimination of *i-u* and *e-o* is not only acoustically determined. These vowels are sharply distinguished in their articulation. The vowels *i* and *e* are pronounced without the use of the lips, while *u* and *o* require participation of the lips. This distinction is undoubtedly reflected in the child's visual perception.

The late discrimination of *o-u* and *e-i* is also observed in the speech of the child. Unfortunately, there are no precise observations of this tendency. Sikorskiy observed that *o* and *u* are so little differentiated in common words it is hard to tell which one the child is pronouncing. The same should be said of *e* and *i* (1899, p. 140).

Thus, there are three stages in the phonemic development of vowel perception (see Fig. 1b). First stage: discrimination of *a* and non-*a*; second stage: discrimination of *u-i*, *o-e*, *u-e*, *o-i*; third stage: discrimination of *u-o*, *i-e*.

The Second Phonemic Stage (discrimination of the presence of consonants). First the child *notices the presence or absence of extra sound*. This is very characteristic of child perception. A significant change occurs in his habit of comparison. His hearing is obviously perfecting itself. He gradually begins to notice the presence of an extra sound in comparing such words as *bok* and *ok*, *vek* and *ek*, and others. Thus he first perceives the consonant sound as "something": only afterwards does discrimination between consonants appear. Distinction of the presence of consonant sound is a preparatory stage for discrimination between consonants.

Unfortunately, it was impossible to establish the presence of such a preparatory stage in regard to discrimination of vowels. In a certain sense the initial distinction of *a* and non-*a* is such a step. In the same way the child

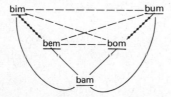

Figure 1b. First stage: ——— discrimination of *a* from other vowels. Second stage: – – – – – discrimination of *i-u*, *e-o*, *i-o*, *e-u*. Third stage: ●—●—●—● discrimination of *i-e*, *u-o*.

separates the vowel *a* from the general group of vowels and notes its presence in distinction from other vowels, in discriminating the presence of a consonant the child separates "the consonant as something" from a general group of consonants and notices its presence.

Experimentation revealed a phonemic sequence, as shown in Figure 2. Except for the voiceless consonant *x*, I made use of voiced consonants, being guided by the fact that voiced consonants are more easily perceived than voiceless. Figure 2, which reflects the actual course of the experiments, shows that the child is always reminded of the previous stage of discrimination, a fact which is necessary to have established, since the child frequently perceived the presence of consonants earlier than he was able to discriminate the vowels *o-u* and *e-i*. Finally, as can be seen in Figure 2, I constantly tried to catch the beginning of the following stage of discrimination in the child.

The Third Phonemic Stage (discrimination of sonorants versus articulated obstruents). A characteristic feature of the child's perception is that he separates sounds of a definite group from the general flow of adult speech and distinguishes this group from the remaining speech sounds. This is vividly manifested in the process of consonant discrimination. *At first the child singles out the sonorant consonants from the general group of consonants.* It seems as if he divides the sound group of consonants into two parts: sonorants and nonsonorants, that is, obstruents.

Data on the phylogenesis of speech likewise indicates such a stage in the phonetic development of language, where only sonorants and obstruents were

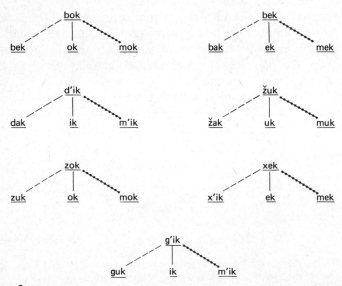

Figure 2.

phonemically discriminated. Differentiation among obstruents comes significantly later. There are languages in which to this day only sonorant and obstruent consonants are discriminated: Tamil, Tasmanian, Australian languages, and others.

The original isolation of sonorant consonants can be explained by the fact that they, of all consonants, are the closest to the vowels.

However, the child does not distinguish all sonorant consonants from obstruents at the same time and to the same extent. As mentioned above, the articulated obstruents are discriminated earlier than the nonarticulated ones. At this stage of phonemic development we encounter for the first time the influence of articulation on the phonemic development of speech. Up to this point, hearing has played the leading role in the establishment of regularities in phonemic development. From this moment articulation starts to contribute its own corrective factors in this development. A child who has mastered certain sounds can discriminate them faster than a child who has not mastered the same sounds. This does not mean that in respect to the ontogenesis of speech one can wholly accept the position of S. I. Bernshteyn, who writes: "One can maintain that it is absolutely true that we hear only those speech sounds which we are able to pronounce" (1937, p. 15). The example introduced by this very author refutes his categorical proposition. A six-year-old girl replaced r with a bilabial consonant w, but could discriminate these sounds when hearing them. One can only say that sounds which are not yet mastered by the child are discriminated later than those sounds which the child pronounces. On the other hand, there are cases in which the child, for example, substitutes t for v and at the beginning of discrimination of t-v begins to pronounce v as a t and then as a bilabial w. The previous identification of t and v has been destroyed.

Therefore, one can say that a child who discriminates a certain phonemic opposition to a certain extent also differentiates pronunciation of the sounds of this opposition. Sometimes this differentiation in pronunciation consists only of some insignificant sound nuance, but the appearance of this sound nuance signals the disintegration of the previous identification, and the discrepancy in the pronunciation of these sounds will gradually increase until the formation of qualitatively different sounds.

The Russian linguist Aleksandrov carefully observed the gradual development of his son's sound articulation. This boy at the end of his first year of life consistently substituted r for f, b for v, and d'/t' for r/z/ž. During the age period of 1;0–1;4 he began to distinguish these sounds, but not at once. Aleksandrov noted the use of bilabial w as a transitional sound from r to f and from b to v; from d'/t' to r/z/ž the transitional sound was y (1883, p 86).

Sikorskiy also noted the phenomenon of gradual development of child articulation in his observations:

The children who replaced the sound k by t in the beginning actually used a more or less specific and clear t in all cases indiscriminately where t or k was encountered, but later, they reserved a much more distinct *t* for cases in which this sound actually should have been used. For words beginning with *k* they placed their tongue not near the edge of the teeth, but significantly further, so that their *t* was not a dental *t* but a palatal *t*. Finally, we could be convinced of the existence of further transitional phases. At a certain point the children began to use three different *t*s: one typical dental *t* in those cases where this sound really applied; and two other *t*s in addition: a palatal *t* and a cacuminal *t*, freely varying in situations calling for *k* (1899, p. 155).

Sikorskiy observed a similar phenomenon in the development of articulation of other sounds.

The facts noted above reveal *an interaction between hearing and articulation* in the process of phonemic development. They point to an intimate connection between the two features. Discussing whether hearing determines the development of articulation or articulation determines the development of hearing, the ontogenetic facts speak for a two-way interaction of hearing and articulation. Their interaction in the phonemic development of the child is revealed by the fact that sonorants and articulated obstruents are discriminated first, and only much later does there appear a distinction between sonorants and the nonarticulated obstruents *z*, *x*, and *ž*.

The third phonemic stage is shown in Figure 3.

The Fourth Phonemic Stage (discrimination of palatalized and nonpalatalized consonants).   After the division of consonants into sonorant and articulated obstruents comes the division of all consonants into palatalized and nonpalatalized. Here again interaction of hearing and articulation manifests itself.

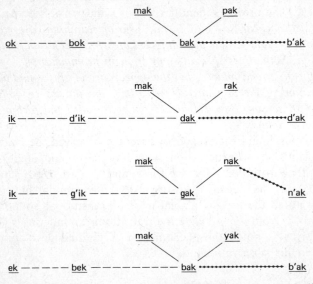

Figure 3. Third stage: ————. Preceding stages. ————. Following stage: ●—●—●—●.

Those consonants, which the child distinguishes later in pronunciation, are also late to be phonemically differentiated on the basis of palatization.

The Russian child discriminates palatalized and nonpalatalized consonants comparatively early; however, this cannot be explained simply in terms of articulation and hearing. Here the linguistic peculiarities of these phonemes in the Russian language manifest themselves. First, in Russian (unlike English, French, and German) this distinction is of semantic significance. Second, the frequency of alternation of palatalized and nonpalatalized consonants plays a role in Russian. Peshkovskiy's data (1925) show that in most cases the child encounters one palatalized consonant for every two nonpalatalized consonants.

The fourth phonemic stage in its relation to the previous and the following ontogenetic stages is shown in Figure 4.

The Fifth Phonemic Stage (discrimination of sonorant consonants). The child, having separated the consonants into sonorant and obstruent, palatalized and nonpalatalized, *passes on to differentiation of sonorant consonants and then obstruent consonants.* He divides the sonorant consonants into two groups: (1) nasals, (2) liquids and *y.* There is reason to assume that in contrasting nasals and liquids the child singles out nasals earlier. They are very easily

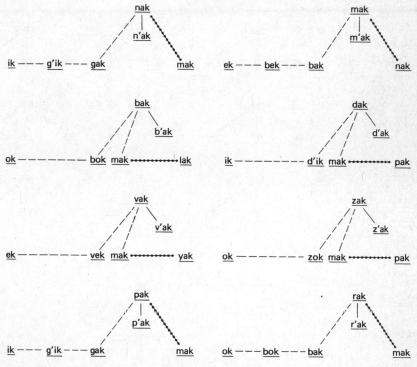

Figure 4. Fourth stage: ————. Preceding stages: – – – – – . Following stage: ●—●—●—●.

articulated sounds. Liquids, as a rule, are not articulated at all in the second year of life. Thus, again the importance of articulation in the phonemic development of speech manifests itself.

Later, the intranasal distinction emerges, and following it, the intraliquid distinction.

The initial intranasal distinction undoubtedly confirms the fact that, in contrasting the nasals and liquids, nasal consonants are singled out first.

It is necessary to stress that a child clearly distinguishes liquid consonants at an age when he, as a rule, still does not use them. It seems that this fact contradicts the previous theory about the interaction of hearing and articulation. But this is, in my onion, but an illusory contradiction. When one speaks about interaction between any two variables, A and B, this does not mean that this interaction is simple. Interaction, on the contrary, assumes the possibility that in one case A acts upon B, while in another case B acts upon A. There are cases in which articulation prevails over hearing. This can be observed when the nasal consonants are singled out instead of the liquids, regardless of the fact that the liquids are more sonorant than the nasals. On the other hand, there are cases in which hearing prevails over articulation. This is the case in the intraliquid distinction. During the process of discriminating consonants,

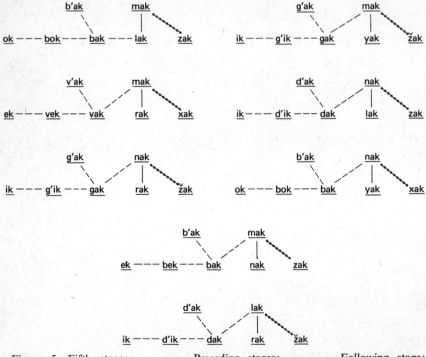

Figure 5. Fifth stage: ————. Preceding stages: – – – – –. Following stage: ●—●—●—●. *Note*: Discrimination between liquids and *y* emerges after stage X.

a child has to have some kind of support in order to isolate a certain group of sounds out of the general stream of adult speech sounds. In some cases, auditory perception of sound serves as that support factor and in some cases it is the articulation of the sound.

The child discriminates liquids and *y* later than other phonemic oppositions precisely because a child of one to two years of age cannot distinguish them from each other either acoustically or by articulation. There is nothing that the child can lean upon.

The intrasonorant distinction is shown in Figure 5.

The Sixth Phonemic Stage (discrimination of sonorants and nonarticulated obstruents).   In the process of transition toward the distinction of obstruents, the child succeeds in decisively differentiating *between sonorants and nonarticulated obstruents.* In this case nonarticulated obstruents are not fully pronounced spirants (*z, ž, x*). The absence of adequate articulation of spirants undoubtedly influences the ability to distinguish them from sonorants. This distinction appears quite late. Figure 6 presents the distinction between sonorants and nonarticulated obstruents.

The Seventh Phonemic Stage (distinction between labial and lingual).   The obstruents are divided first of all on the basis of position. Moreover, the primary differentiation of consonants on the basis of position is quite primitive. *At first the child discriminates only labial and lingual consonants.* The labial-lingual distinction was already noted during the course of intranasal distinction. Now, however, the child has mastered the labial-lingual distinction for all consonants.

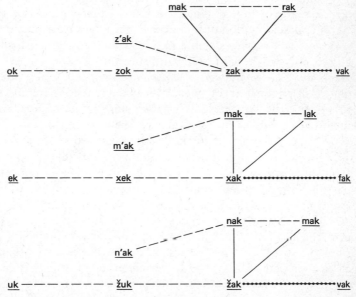

Figure 6. Sixth stage: ─────. Preceding stages: ─ ─ ─ ─. Following stage: ●─●─●─●.

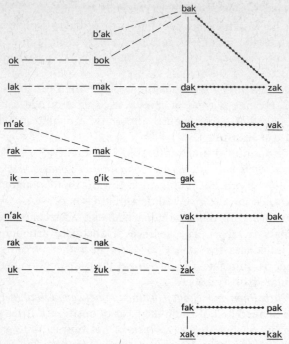

Figure 7. Seventh stage: ————. Preceding stages: – – – – –. Following stage:
●—●—●—●.

First, the labial-lingual distinction is conditioned by articulational features. The imperfect articulation of lingual spirants can be explained by the considerably later differentiation of those consonants. One can assume that besides hearing, vision also plays a definite role in the labial-lingual distinction.

Figure 7 shows the labial-lingual distinction.

The Eighth Phonemic Stage (distinction between stops and spirants). During transition to discrimination of lingual consonants, the differentiation of stops and spirants emerges. A considerably earlier singling out of stops as compared to spirants has already been noted above. The stop consonants are also articulated by the child earlier than the spirants. Consequently this stage allows the child to distinguish stop from nonstop obstruents, that is, spirants.

Data on speech phylogenesis indicate such a stage in phonetic development, in which the obstruent consonants are phonemically separated into two groups only: stops and spirants. The voiced-voiceless distinction comes later. There are languages in which to this day only stops and spirants are distinguished phonemically: Papuan, Tasmanian, some Bantu languages, and others.

Data on speech phylogenesis substantiate the position that there is a psychological process of isolation of a certain group of sounds from the general sound aggregate of language. The phonemic distinction takes place precisely as a result of such isolation. According to the phylogenesis of speech this fact is exceptionally clearly seen at the stage of discrimination of stops and spirants.

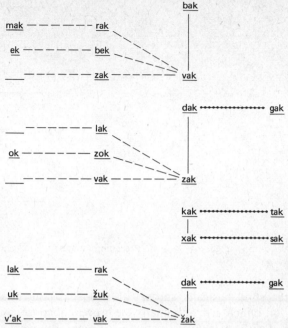

Figure 8. Eighth stage: ———. Preceding stages: – – – – –. Following stage: ●—●—●—●.

In answering the question of the manner in which the distinction of stop and spirant consonants appears, some linguists assert that the spirants emerge on the basis of the stops. They emerge as something different from the earlier isolated stop consonants. We have ascertained this very fact in the child.

Figure 8 shows the differentiation between stops and spirants.

The Ninth Phonemic Stage (distinction between pre- and postlingual consonants).   Discrimination between prelingual and postlingual consonants requires exact articulation of these consonants. Positioning of the tongue comes to the child with difficulty. Many children replace postlingual consonants by prelinguals, and vice versa. Imperfect articulation concomitant with imperfect hearing results in a much later distinction of these consonants.

Figure 9 shows the differentiation between pre- and postlingual consonants.

The Tenth Phonemic Stage (distinction between voiced and voiceless consonants).   The distinction of voiced and voiceless consonants comes comparatively late. This distinction is complicated not only by the fact that there is only a very fine acoustic nuance between these sounds but there is also a close similarity in articulation between voiced and voiceless consonants which confuses the child. He must not be guided by the similarity in articulation but must sharpen his auditory perception in order to discriminate the finest nuances. He must be guided only by his hearing and nothing else.

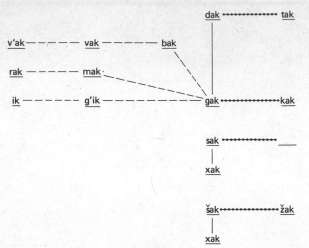

Figure 9. Ninth stage: ————. Preceding stages: – – – – –. Following stage: ●—●—●—●.

Thus, the child basically starts with acoustic differentiation of sounds, then articulation is included, and finally the process of consonant discrimination comes to an end with acoustic distinction once again. But what a great difference there is between the primary and the final acoustic differentiation!

In the case of the initial distinction of sonorants and articulated obstruents there is a comparatively crude and primitive acoustic differentiation of consonants. The child at this stage articulates very few consonants. He is guided mainly by his hearing. In the case of the final distinction of voiced and voiceless consonants the child has already reached greater perfection. In reaching this point the child has traversed a complicated course of development in regard to the interaction of hearing and articulation. He is obliged to master not only the articulation of certain sounds in order to orient himself in distinguishing these sounds, but he must also possess the ability to distinguish sounds acoustically regardless of their articulational similarity.

The data on speech phylogenesis undoubtedly confirm the late phonemic distinction of voiced and voiceless consonants. Some languages, mentioned above, still do not distinguish this opposition phonemically: Tasmanian, Papuan, some Bantu languages, and others.

Figure 10 shows the voiced-voiceless distinction.

The distinctions between "hushing" and ' hissing" sibilants and between liquid consonants and y emerge very late. One of the most difficult linguistic problems is the problem of the appearance of the distinction between "hushing" and "hissing" sibilants. A considerable number of languages do not discriminate these sounds. A very fine differentiation of the movements in the front part of the tongue and a maximal perfection of hearing is necessary to discriminate between "hushing" and "hissing" sibilants. It is even harder to

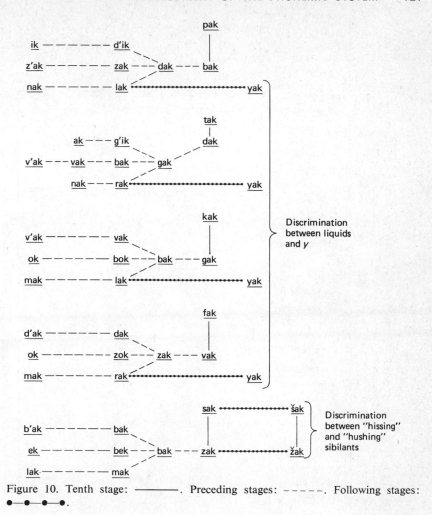

Figure 10. Tenth stage: ————. Preceding stages: — — — —. Following stages: ●–●–●–●.

differentiate liquid consonants from *y*. A child, as we know, does not discriminate them by articulation, and in contrast to the differentiation of voiced and voiceless consonants, he does not discriminate the liquids from *y* by phonation either. Regardless of the greater perfection of children's hearing, at the end of the entire series of experiments they could discriminate these sounds only with great effort.

III. GENERAL CONCLUSION

The experimental evidence has demonstrated certain regularities in development of phonemic speech perception in early childhood. Phonemic perception emerges in connection with the development of semantics in child

TABLE 1 SEQUENCE OF APPEARANCE OF PHONEMIC STAGES IN INDIVIDUAL CHILDREN

Children \ Phonemic Stages	I Distinction of vowels	II Distinction of presence of consonants	III Distinction of sonorants and articulated obstruents	IV Distinction of palatalized and nonpalatalized consonants	V Distinction of sonorants	VI Distinction of sonorants and nonarticulated obstruents	VII Distinction of labials and linguals	VIII Distinction of stops and spirants	IX Distinction of pre- and postlinguals	X Distinction of voiced and voiceless	XI Distinction of "hushing" and "hissing" sibilants	XII Distinction of liquids and y
Rima Barykina	1	2	3	6	4	5	7	—	—	—	—	—
Lida Bakhurina	1	2	3	6	4	5	7	8	9	10	12	11
Shura Budakova	1	2	3	4	5	6	7	—	—	—	—	—
Vitya Fedchin	1	2	3	4	5	6	7	—	—	—	—	—
Vova Grunkov	1	2	3	6	4	5	7	—	—	—	—	12
Nina Kalyantzeva	—	—	3	—	5	6	—	8	9	10	11	12
Nina Karaséva	1	2	3	4	5	6	7	8	9	10	11	12
Pasha Khokhlov	1	2	3	4	5	6	7	—	—	—	—	—
Katya Kotova	1	2	3	4	5	6	7	9	8	11	10	12
Zina Kupavtzeva	1	2	3	6	4	5	7	9	10	8	12	11
Lyusya Kurtakova	1	2	3	6	4	5	7	9	10	8	12	11
Tanya Osokina	1	2	3	4	5	6	7	—	—	—	—	—
Zina Popova	—	—	3	—	—	6	—	8	—	10	11	12
Lyusya Skachkova	1	2	3	4	5	6	7	8	9	10	11	12
Lyusua Stepanova	1	2	3	4	5	6	7	8	9	10	11	12
Yulya Strizhakova	1	2	3	4	5	6	7	8	9	10	11	12
Vova Sukhanov	1	2	3	4	5	6	7	9	8	11	10	12
Tolya Tret'yakov	1	2	3	—	5	6	—	8	9	10	11	12

NOTE: Roman numerals indicate general sequence of stages; Arabic numerals indicate the sequence of development for each individual child.

speech, which reorganizes both the perception of speech sounds and their articulation. The development of hearing and articulation, in turn, influences the order of development of perception of the various phonemes of the language.

As shown in Table 1, the order of appearance of phonemic stages in different children reveals the role of these factors in the phonemic development of child speech. As can be seen in the table, the majority of the children (67 percent) display a uniform sequence in the appearance of phoneme perception. These children are guided by the acoustic and articulational features of the sound system of the language. One third of the children deviated from the general sequence of phonemic development. Some of them (22 percent) acquired the acoustic features much more rapidly; others (11 percent) acquired the articulational features much more rapidly. These deviations, however, are observed only in certain stages of the development of phonemic perception, and therefore do not change the general pattern of phonemic development.

On the whole, the investigation points to two main periods of phonemic development: *the period of vowel discrimination and the period of consonant discrimination.* (See Table 2.) The child divides the whole sound stream of language into two parts, first of all singling out the vowels and discriminating them from the consonants.

Thus, the period of vowel discrimination is the first level in the phonemic speech development of the child and forms *the first phonemic stage* of this development. This first stage is further subdivided into three substages: (1) discrimination of *a* and non-*a*; (2) discrimination of *i-u, e-o*; discrimination of *i-o, e-u*; (3) discrimination of *i-e, u-o*.

The period of consonant discrimination is complex and multilevel. The perception of the presence of consonants serves as a distinctive introduction to this period. It is a sort of preparatory level in the discrimination of consonants. In the general scheme of phonemic development the discrimination of the presence of consonants represents the *second phonemic stage*.

Two other important levels in the discrimination of consonants follow thereafter. At first the consonants are divided into sonorants and obstruents. This is the third phonemic level in child speech development. This level is divided into two stages. One of them is the *third phonemic stage* of child speech development and it consists of the discrimination of sonorants and articulated obstruents. The other consists of the discrimination of sonorant and non-articulated obstruents appearing after other levels of discrimination and constituting the *sixth phonemic stage*. It is conditionally included into the fifth level of phonemic development. Following the separation of consonants into sonorants and obstruents, there comes the distinction between palatalized and nonpalatalized consonants. This is the fourth level of the child's phonemic development and constitutes the *fourth phonemic stage*.

Afterwards comes the discrimination among the sonorant and obstruent consonants themselves. This forms the last two levels of phonemic speech development.

TABLE 2   GENERAL PATTERN OF PHONEMIC DEVELOPMENT.

SEQUENCE OF DEVELOPMENT				
PERIOD	LEVEL	STAGE	SUBSTAGE	PHONEMIC DISTINCTION
First (distinction of vowels)	First (distinction of vowels)	First (distinction of vowels)	First	Distinction of *a* vs. other vowels
			Second	Distinction of *i-u, e-o* *i-o, e-u*
			Third	Distinction of *i-e, u-o*
Second (distinction of consonants)	Second preliminary (distinction of presence of consonants)	Second	—	Distinction of presence of consonants: phoneme = consonant vs. zero phoneme (*bok-ok, vek-ek, d'ik-ik*)
	Third (distinction of sonorants and articulated obstruents)	Third	—	Distinction of sonorants and articulated obstruents: *m-b, r-d, n-g, y-v*
	Fourth (distinction of palatalized and non-palatalized consonants)	Fourth	—	Distinction of palatalized and non-palatalized consonants: *n-n', m-m', b-b', d-d', v-v', z-z', l-l', r-r'*
	Fifth (distinction of sonorants)	Fifth (distinction of sonorants)	First	Distinction between nasals and liquids + *y*: *m-l, m-r, n-l, n-r, n-y, m-y*
			Second	Intranasal distinction: *m-n*
			Third	Intraliquid distinction: *l-r*
		Sixth	—	Distinction of sonorants and non-articulated obstruents: *m-z, l-x, n-ž*
	Sixth (distinction of obstruents)	Seventh	—	Distinction of labials and linguals: *b-d, b-g, v-z, f-x*
		Eighth	—	Distinction of stops and spirants: *b-v, d-ž, k-x, d-ž*
		Ninth	—	Distinction of pre- and postlinguals: *d-g, s-x, š-x*
		Tenth	—	Distinction of voiced and voiceless consonants: *p-b, t-d, k-g, f-v, s-z, š-ž*
		Eleventh	—	Distinction of "hushing" and "hissing" sibilants: *ž-z, š-s*
		Twelfth	—	Distinction of liquids and *y*: *r-y, l-y*

The distinction of sonorants takes place on the fifth level of phonemic development and constitutes the *fifth phonemic stage*. It is subdivided into the following three substages: (1) distinction between nasals and liquids + *y*; (2) intranasal distinction; (3) intraliquid distinction.

The distinction between liquids and *y* appears very late and constitutes the *twelfth phonemic stage*. This stage is conditionally included in the sixth phonemic level of speech development.

The distinction of obstruents occurs at the sixth phonemic level and constitutes the following stages:

Seventh phonemic stage—distinction of labials and linguals
Eighth phonemic stage—distinction of stops and spirants
Ninth phonemic stage—distinction of pre- and postlinguals
Tenth phonemic stage—voiced versus voiceless distinction
Eleventh phonemic stage—distinction of "hushing" and "hissing" sibilants.

Afterwards comes the *twelfth phonemic stage*—the distinction between liquids and *y*.

This sequence of phonemic speech development in early childhood is shown in Table 2.

REFERENCES

Aleksandrov, A., Detskaya rech'. *Russkiy filologicheskiy vestnik*, 1883, **10**, 86–120.
Baudoin de Courtenay, J. A., *Versuch einer Theorie phonetischer Alternation*, 1895.
Bernshteyn, S. I., Stikh i deklamatsiya. In *Russkaya rech'*, 1927.
Bernshteyn, S. I., *Voprosy obucheniya proiznosheniyu*, 1937.
Goyer [Hoyer], A., and G. Goyer. Pervyy period yazykovoy deyatel'nosti rebënka. In N. A. Rybnikov (ed.), *Detskaya rech'*. Moscow, 1927.
Gvozdev, A. N., Usvoyeniye rebënkom rodnogo yazyka. In N. A. Rybnikov (ed.), *Detskaya rech'*. Moscow, 1927.
Kiterman, B., Rebënok i chuvstvo ritma, *Golos i rech'*, 1913, No. 2.
Menchinskaya, N. A., *Dnevnik materi*, Ms. (n.d.).
Peshkovskiy, A. M., Desyat' tysyach zvukov. Sb. statey. 1925.
Rau, N. A. Vospitaniye ritma i slukhovogo vnimaniya u glukhonemykh doshkol'nikov v svyazi s kul'turoy rechi, *Voprosy defektologii*, 1930, No. 5.
Rybnikova-Shilova, V. A., *Moy dnevnik*. Orël, 1923.
Shcherba, L. V., *Russkiye glasnyye v kachestvennom i kolichestvennom otnoshenii*, 1912.
Shmidt, O., *Slovar' Volika*, Ms. (n.d.).
Sikorskiy, I. A., O razvitii rechi u detey, Sb. nauchno-literaturnykh statey, Vol. 2, 1899.

Sokolov, N., *Zhizn' rebënka.* Moscow, 1918.

Teplov, B. M., *Psikhologiya muzykal'nykh sposobnostey.* Moscow, 1947.

Voyachek, V. I., O noveyshikh metodyakh ispytaniya funktsii slukha, *Novoe v meditsine*, 1911, No. 22.

Voyachek, V. I., Sovremennye issledovaniya slukha rech'yu, *Russkiy vrach*, 1906, No. 2.

APPENDIX A: TRANSCRIPTION

[*Editor's note*: The Russian, German, and English words are given by Shvachkin; the transliteration has been provided by the editor. This system of transliteration of Cyrillic applies only to Shvachkin's linguistic examples and artificial words in the text.]

Vowels

а (акр) = a
з (зра) = e
и (ил) = i
о (он) = o
у (ум) = u

Consonants

п (пол) = p б (бак) = b
ф (фут) = f в (вол) = v
т (том) = t д (дол) = d
с (суп) = s з (зуб) = z
ш (щаг) = š ж (жук) = ž
к (кол) = k г (год) = g
м (мак) = m w (walk– = w
н (нуль) = n English
л (лук) = l
р (раб) = r
х (хан) = x [compare German *ch*,
j (jung— = y   as in *Loch*]
German

[Palatalized consonants are followed by an apostrophe, for example, n']

APPENDIX B: LIST OF SUBJECTS

Name	Sex	Age at Beginning of Experiment	Age at End of Experiment	Phonemic stages Investigated
Rima Barykina	F	0;10	1;6	I–VII
Lida Bakhurina	F	1;6	2;0	All
Shura Budakova	F	1;2	1;7	I–VII
Vitya Fedchin	M	1;4	1;8	I–VII
Vova Grunkov	M	1;1	1;6	I–VII
Nina Kalyantzeva	F	1;5	1;11	III, V, VI, VIII–XII
Nina Karasëva	F	1;3	1;9	All
Pasha Khokhlov	M	1;3	1;7	I–VII
Katya Kotova	F	1;5	1;11	All
Zina Kupavtzeva	F	1;4	1;9	I–VII
Lyusya Kurtakova	F	1;3	1;10	All
Lyusya Luk'yanova	F	0;11,22	0;12,23	—
Tanya Osokina	F	1;1	1;9	I–VII
Zina Popova	F	1;6	1;11	VI, VII, X–XII
Lyusya Skachkova	F	1;6	2;0	All
Lyusya Stepanova	F	1;1	1;9	All
Yulya Strizhakova	F	1;2	1;10	All
Vova Sukhanov	M	1;4	1;11	All
Tolya Tret'yakov	M	1;5	1;11	I, III, V, VI, VIII–XII

INTONATION •

Very few systematic investigations have been made of the development of sentence intonation in children. One obstacle to investigation is the lack of widely accepted, comprehensive linguistic analyses of adult intonation. Lieberman's review of the field of intonation (Lieberman, 1967) devotes a whole chapter to child development but offers no generalizations beyond the very first stage, where he hypothesizes that there is an innate physiological basis for the "breath-group" which segments speech into sentences in many languages. He observes also that the intonation of the breath-group takes on a linguistic function before the child has acquired many of the distinctive features of the language around him. The Russian study included here offers better evidence than previously available about the development of intonation, but without making any attempt at linguistic analysis.

Note that some information on intonation appears in several other selections in this volume (Engel, "From sound to phoneme"; Chao) and useful general comments can be found in other works such as Lewis (1951) and Weir (1966). A small study by Evelyn Pike (1949) shows that an infant can be trained to mimic certain intonation contours. An interesting recent study (Kaplan, 1969) demonstrates that eight-month-old children can discriminate regularly between a falling and rising sentence contour spoken with normal stress.

—C.A.F. and D.I.S.

Development of Speech Intonation in Infants during the First Two Years of Life
—— *R. V. Tonkova-Yampol'skaya*

Speech has two basic modes for communicating information—speech sounds and intonation.

The acoustical characteristics of speech are not of direct import for its perception since it is not the physical properties of sounds that are recognized (i.e., frequency of fundamental tone, intensity of vibrations, total resonant

Razvitiye rechevoy intonatsii u detey pervykh dvukh let zhizni. *Voprosy psikhologii*, 1968, **14** (3), 94–101. Translated from Russian by Michael Vale and edited by Dan I. Slobin. Translation reprinted from *Soviet Psychology*, 1969, **7** (3), 48–54, with the permission of International Arts and Sciences Press.

energy), but the timber, loudness, pause patterns, rhythm, and tempo of speech, and its duration and differentiation in time. Thus, speech perception is mediated by the properties of verbal hearing, the system of linguistic meanings, and the semantic content of speech (2). Ideas, feelings, and volitions are the components of semantic content, and are conveyed by various intonations that give speech its communicative finish (1, 7).

Intonation has definite physical characteristics that are interrelated and, in each instance, manifest a unique structure. It is precisely this structure that enables intonation to be perceived directly as a unity with a certain communicative import, e.g., assertion, interrogation, etc. Persons speaking different languages make statements, ask questions, and the like, in similar fashion to the extent that the intonations of statements, questions, imperatives, and exclamations are similar in the different languages, although, of course, if a language is not known, one cannot be cognizant of all the intonational nuances peculiar to it. In other words, the *intoneme* is a functional unit with a typical pattern consisting of various intonational elements (1). If different intonemes prove to have certain invariant features, then the study of the development of intonational structures properly falls within the scope of the general problem of speech development.

In investigating the development of speech intonation in infants up to two years of age, we concentrated on three basic questions:

1. Does the cry of a newborn infant have any intonational structure?
2. What are the intonations in the cooing and babbling of infants during the first year of life? Can they be shown to have a communicative value?
3. What are the characteristics of the intonational repertory of infants during the second year?

We studied the development of intonation in 170 infants, including 30 newborn infants (one to six months old) in the Infant Ward of the Regional Clinical Hospital of the L'vov Maternity and Child Protection Department and 140 children up to two years of age (10 infants for each month of age up to one year, and 20 infants between one and two years old). These children were observed by age group. They were cared for either at home or in the L'vov Municipal Children's Nursery No. 24.

As a method we employed electroacoustical analysis: the vocal responses were recorded on magnetic tape, with a Reporter-III tape recorder having a frequency range of 40–10,000 cycles/sec. The recording was done under suitable acoustical conditions. The sounds were transmitted from the tape to an electrical device (LEFIPR intonograph) that analyzed the basic physical characteristics of the sound. (The LEFIPR intonograph was built in the Laboratory of Experimental Phonetics and Speech Psychology of the Thorez First Moscow State Pedagogical Institute of Foreign Languages, V. A. Artemov, Director.)

The sound intonogram was recorded on motion picture film and

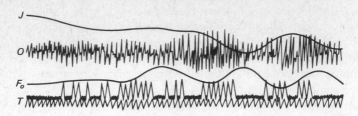

Figure 1. General appearance of intonogram: I—sound intensity; O—sound oscillogram; F_o—fundamental tone frequency; T—time.

contained: (1) a sound oscillogram, 0; (2) fundamental tone frequency, F_o; (3) sound intensity, I; and (4) 1/500-sec. time divisions, T (Fig. 1).

The intonograms (534 in all) were analyzed statistically. Only data with a probability percentage exceeding 95 on the Weber table were used.

In addition to making the tape recordings, we observed the behavior of the children (in particular, their emotional state). The audible intonational nuances of the various sound combinations in the children's speech were noted by parents and nursery attendants.

Even from the mere observation of the children's behavior, it was evident that, throughout the immediate postnatal period and the first month of life, their communicative abilities were limited to information on disagreeable sensations (hunger, wet diapers, pain, etc.), which the infants announced with a cry.

During the second month, the communicative bonds with adults widened, and sounds of discomfort and placid cooing could be distinguished. Sounds of happiness, and then laughter, appeared during the third month. Thereafter, until the sixth month, the semantic content of speech sounds was confined to these four forms: discontent, placid cooing, happiness, and laughter, although the number of speech sounds increased.

The communicative content of these sounds was perceived directly by observers on the basis of intonation, since a sound perceived, for example, as "eu" could be an expression of either happiness or discomfort.

During the second half-year, the intonational capacities were further augmented. It is especially to be noted that new forms of intonational expression appeared at greater intervals from the third month onward. Exclamatory delight and a calmer, satisfied sound were not differentiated in the intonation of happiness until the sixth month. A requesting intonation was discernible from the seventh month; a questioning intonation did not appear until the second year (Fig. 2).

Next, we compared the forms of infant intonation with the intonational structures of adults.

First, we attempted to ascertain whether there were any objective criteria by which the vocal signals of infants could be identified with adult speech.

An analysis of infants' intonograms revealed a gradual approximation of

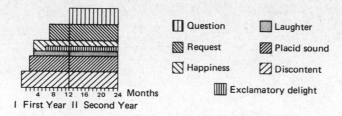

⊞ Question	▦ Laughter
▨ Request	▧ Placid sound
◨ Happiness	▨ Discontent
▥ Exclamatory delight	

4   8   12   16   20   24   Months
I First Year   II Second Year

Figure 2. Development of intonational forms with age.

intonations in infant speech sounds to the intonational structures of adults (1). For this we compared the typical adult intonational forms with the "intonations" of infants.

Thus, in adults, the pitch of the fundamental tone and the intensity of articulation [*intensivnost' proiznosheniya*] vary together and rhythmically in intonations of offense, remonstration, and threat. In intonations of assertion, enumeration, etc., the fundamental tone rises and remains at a certain level, while the intensity of articulation first rises and then falls. In intonations of surprise, consternation, and questioning, the fundamental tone first rises, then falls, and finally rises again, while the intensity varies in reverse order. In command, persuasion, invitation, and request, the intensity of articulation rises slightly, and then falls, while the fundamental tone rises sharply, and then falls abruptly at the end of the sentence (Figs. 3–6).

It is interesting that the intonation of discomfort in adults fully coincides with its counterpart in children from the immediate postnatal period onward. That is, after acquiring the communicative value of an intonation of discomfort during the first month of life, the intonational pattern in the cry of a newborn infant then retains its form and meaning throughout the entire subsequent lifetime (see Fig. 3).

Although it was difficult to discern audibly a difference in the calm intonations of infants during the first month of life, nevertheless a more detailed

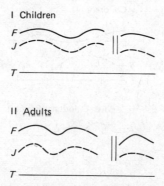

Figure 3. Structural pattern of intonation of discomfort in adults and children.

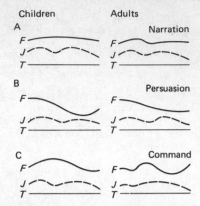

Figure 4. Calm intonations: A—"indifferent" intonation (2–7 months); B—"expressive, calm cooing" (7–10 months); C—"insistent" intonation (10 months to two years).

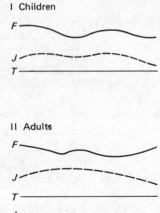

Figure 5. Intonation of happiness.

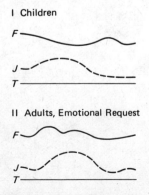

Figure 6. Intonation of request.

acoustical analysis of intonograms revealed definite differences in their structure, so that it was possible to compare a given form of infantile intonation with various logical intonations of adults.

Thus, from the second through the seventh month, an "indifferent intonation" was discerned in children (Fig. 4A) that was structurally comparable to the intonation of assertion, enumeration, and comparison in an adult.

The seventh month marked the appearance of an "expressive calm cooing" (Fig. 4B) that resembled an intonation of affirmation in adults. The number of such intonations rose sharply during the ninth month. An "insistent intonation" appeared in calm sounds in the tenth month (Fig. 4C); this was similar to the intonation of persuasion and insistent command in adults. The frequency of occurrence of this type of intonation also increased markedly with age. Whereas during the tenth month the placid sounds of infants made up 25 % of this type of intonation, their frequency rose to 33.3 % during the second year of life (see Fig. 4).

In acoustical analysis, intonations of happiness give a pattern similar to that of intonations of consternation in adults. This refers to the happiness intonation before the sixth month and the intonation of exclamatory delight during subsequent age periods. Actually, happiness intonations of children are always very emotional. A structural analysis shows a considerable rise in the frequency of the fundamental tone F_o at the end of a "happy" phrase (see Fig. 5).

Adults have two basic, distinguishable request intonemes, viz., an emotional request and a polite request. From the seventh month of life to the end of the second year, children employ intonations that are structurally similar to an emotional request. The dynamics of the envelopes of the fundamental tone frequency and the intensity are almost identical to those exhibited in an adult intonation (Fig. 6).

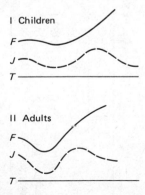

Figure 7. Intonation of question.

TABLE OF FUNDAMENTAL TONE FREQUENCY AND INTENSITY OF ARTICULATION

Forms of Intonation	F_{max}			F_{min}			IV_{Fo}	I_{max}			I_{min}			IV_{I}
	M	m	δ	M	m	δ		M	m	δ	M	m	δ	
Discomfort	539.2	14.2	193.1	339.7	8.5	116.1	37%	9.55	0.5	6.5	1.9	0.18	2.42	80.1%
Placid sounds	423.9	11.6	187.5	280.1	62.6	107.4	33.9%	6.3	0.27	4.2	1.88	0.05	0.7	80.7%
Happiness	627	31.3	248.3	303.1	16.3	130.6	51.6%	7.93	1.07	4.4	2.14	0.13	1.007	73.02%

A questioning intonation does not appear until the second year, but is from the outset similar in structure to an adult questioning intonation (Fig. 7).

The table presents the averaged maxima and minima of the fundamental tone frequency ($F_{o\ max}$ and $F_{o\ min}$), the interval IV_{Fo}, which is the ratio between these values expressed as a percentage, the maxima and the minima of the intensity of articulation (I_{max} and I_{min}), and the interval between them. In addition, the value K is given; it represents the coefficient of the relationship IV_{Fo}/IV_I, from which the homogeneity (or heterogeneity) in the dynamics of the interval increments of F_o and I may be determined.

From the table it is evident that each group of intonations has a specific pattern of basic acoustical characteristics within an envelope of fundamental tone frequency and intensity.

We may summarize the above data as follows:

It is known that speech exhibits an ontogenetic pattern of development. The first cry of a newborn infant is a biologically based phenomenon evoked by stimulation of the subcortical respiratory center. Later the cry acquires communicative characteristics, and for quite a long period remains the sole form of communication between the child and adults. During the first months of life, a child has only his cry as a means of attracting the attention of an adult to his discomfort. At the same time, an analysis of the electroacoustical characteristics of an infant's cry (6) convinced us that, in spite of redundancy, those characteristics are dominant that later appear as the basis of the electroacoustical characteristics of adult speech.

However, even though a child is potentially capable of articulating phonemes, its speech development during the first six months of life is manifested primarily in intonational structure, which continues to predominate in importance until the end of the first year. Actually, the first articulated speech sounds of an infant appear during the second month; but, since these sounds have no linguistic sense, an adult responds not so much to the sound content as to the intonational nuance. An adult responds adequately to intonations in cooing and babbling noises of an infant in the same way as persons speaking different languages understand each other through the basic forms of intonation.

As indicated above, even the cry of a newborn infant has a primary intonational structure that is manifested as a direct proportionality between the envelope curve of the fundamental tone frequency F_o and the envelope curve of the intensity I. This fact testifies to the biological nature of this primary intonational pattern, since an adult speech structure characteristic for a given form of intonation is determined by differentiations of varying degree between the frequency of the fundamental tone F_o and the intensity I. These values convey various information in adult speech; in other words, they are dependent on cortical control.

After an adequate response of an adult to a cry, this primary intonational structure acquires its communicative significance in the form of a so-called intonation of discomfort and remains unchanged throughout the entire subsequent lifetime. An intonation of discomfort or offense in adult speech preserves a form basically identical to the primary intonational pattern of an infant's cry.

Other intonational forms of vocal signals are developed on the basis of this primary intonation. Their development can be observed in two ways: (1) aurally, in the adequacy of perception, and (2) in an analysis of the interrelationships among the acoustical characteristics underlying the audible intonational structures.

Both ways are equally valuable and complement each other in interpreting the results obtained. However, only a structural analysis of physical characteristics can illuminate the process of intonational development (see Figs. 3–6).

To elucidate how other intonational forms develop from the primary intonational pattern, one must refer back to the forms of vocal communication an adult employs in attending to a child during the earliest period of life. In the first place, the mother uses calm and happy intonations, and the evolution of this form of intonation can be observed in children. As has already been stated, calm intonations appear at the age of two months in an infant. This coincides with the fact that the time of active waking increases from the age of two months onward (5). In addition, according to N. I. Kasatkin (3), a stable auditory reflex also appears at the age of two months. From the age of three months, infants are able to aurally differentiate homogeneous sounds, and intonations of happiness and, later, laughter appear in their cooing. This is evidence of the role of an auditory feedback in the development of speech articulation.

During the second six months of an infant's life, adults introduce an intonation of request ("make pattycake," "give me your hand," etc.), and this is gradually reflected in the vocal signals of the child.

The fact that, during the period from three to six months, new forms of intonation do not appear (indeed, from the third month to the end of the first year of life only one intonational signal is added to the child's repertory of expressions, namely, request) can be explained by two considerations. First, during this time the child firmly establishes its ability to modulate various emotions with its voice; and, secondly, the first year of life is a period of accumulation of an increasing number of sound combinations, which during the 10th to 12th month are formed into the first conceptual words (3–10 words by the end of this period). The number of words increases to approximately 200–400 words by the end of the second year; during the first half of the second year, the vocabulary increases slowly, whereas, during the second half, the increase is very rapid (provided vocal contact of the child with adults is sufficient). It is clear that such a quantitative jump requires much nervous energy, which is concentrated primarily on assimilating the verbal content of language.

Consequently, during the second year the intonational repertory of a child's speech acquires only one addition, an interrogative intonation, which is necessary for further development of vocal communication. However, vocal communication is quite impossible without specific intonations since speech acquires communicative specificity, logical structure, and volitional and emotional nuances only through intonation. Hence, intonation is developed and mastered much earlier than conceptual words and individual sounds.

The substance of this report may be summarized in the following points:

1. Speech development in children begins with development of intonations.

2. A definite intonational pattern is observable even in the cry of a newborn infant. In this pattern the intensity of the articulative movements is not differentiated from their vibrational frequency, i.e., F_0 and I are not yet differentiated. Hence, the primary intonation of a newborn infant's cry is initially devoid of linguistic meaning. After acquiring a communicative value, this intonational pattern becomes fixed as an intonation of discomfort in older children and adults.

3. In contact with adults, a child acquires new forms of intonation on the basis of intonations employed by adults. The appearance of the same intonations in the vocal sounds of children as adults use in addressing them indicates the presence of verbal-auditory feedbacks in the "adult-child" system, the adult playing the dominant role.

4. Intonations of placid cooing appear from the second month, and the third month marks the appearance of intonations of happiness. During the sixth month, the happiness intonation is differentiated into happy exclamations and contented noises. From the seventh month an intonation of request appears; at the beginning of the second year the intonation of interrogation is added. The communicative content of these intonations is adequately perceived by adults.

5. The aforementioned forms of intonation of speech sounds are not identical in structure to corresponding intonemes of adults, but are to a considerable extent similar to them. For this reason it is possible to follow the formation of speech intonations in the development of these sounds.

6. In observing the development of intonations, it is also possible to evaluate the participation of cortical activity in speech development on the basis of the law of integrative proportions. First, differentiation between the basic tone frequency F_0 and the intensity of articulation I is an indication of cortical control of speech organs. Secondly, the development of intonation in children on the basis of intonations used by adults is to a certain extent an indication of the establishment of conductive pathways between verbal-auditory and vocal-motor cortical analyzers and speech organs. It is conceivable that the development of intonations, together with the perfection of sound

pronunciation, promotes the evolution of cortical and peripheral analyzers during the first year of life to the level necessary for articulation of phonemes.

REFERENCES

1. Artemov, V. A., K voprosu ob intonatsii russkogo yazyka. In *Eksperimental'naya fonetika i psikhologiya rechi*, Vol. VI. Moscow, 1953.
2. Artemov, V. A., O vzaimootnosheniyakh fizicheskikh svoystv, vosprinimayemykh kachestv, yazykovykh znacheniy, i smyslovogo soderzhaniya rechi, *Vop. Psikhol.*, 1960, **6** (3).
3. Kasatkin, N. I., *Ocherk razvitiya vysshey nervnoy deyatel'nosti u rebenka rannego vozrasta*. Moscow, 1951.
4. Luriya, A. R., Rol'rechi v psikhicheskom razvitii rebenka, *Vop. Psikhol.*, 1958, **4** (5).
5. Maslov, M. S., Detskiy organizm i sreda. In *Mnogotomnoye rukovodstvo po pediatrii*, Vol. I. Moscow, 1960.
6. Tonkova-Yampol'skaya, R. V., K voprosu izucheniya fiziologicheskikh mekhanizmov rechi, *Zh. Vyssh. Nerv. Deyat. Pavlov*, 1962, No. 1.

SEGMENTATION •

One line of psycholinguistic investigation attempts to follow the development of the child's competence in recognizing and producing phonological and grammatical elements such as phonemes and words. A somewhat different line of study could attempt to follow the development of the child's "linguistic consciousness" in this connection, that is, his ability to deal explicitly with these elements. As reading teachers are well aware, a child may understand perfectly the difference between a *bill* and a *pill* and use both words satisfactorily but be unable to localize the difference and give explicit recognition to the initial segments as such. Similarly, word boundaries and other grammatical boundaries may figure in the child's behavior without his being familiar with such concepts as "word." (See Bogoyavlenskiy [this volume] for a study of Russian children's conscious awareness of suffixes; Karpova [1955, 1967] for a study of Russian preschoolers' ability to break sentences into words.)

Studies of linguistic consciousness in little children are rare, but the experiment reported below by the Soviet psychologist Zhurova gives interesting data on children's ability to isolate initial phonemes. The observations recorded in the brief note by the prominent Norwegian linguist Borgström show that his preschool child in some sense "knew" where syllable boundaries and word boundaries fell and that the word boundaries took precedence. (The paper by Brown, Cazden, and Bellugi, reprinted in this volume, presents indirect evidence of children's knowledge of word and phrase boundaries.)

—C.A.F. and D.I.S.

Language Analysis as a Child's Game

—— Carl Hj. Borgström

In August 1953, quite by accident, I was able to note down the limited material of the ten analyzed utterances which are reproduced below.

This was the situation: a seven-and-a-half-year-old boy, who had not yet begun school and who could read and write nothing but his name and individual letters and numbers, was making believe that he was writing. As he put script-like scribblings on a piece of paper, he would loudly and clearly pronounce sentences or words. He made pauses between segments in his speech and spaces between sections of what he wrote. The two types of segments were obviously supposed to correspond to each other. It was then possible to examine where he had segmented the utterances. He thought up by himself what he would write; only numbers 2 and 4 below were suggested by me. These I spoke quickly and without pause.

The utterances are reproduced in a rather crude transcription, very nearly corresponding to the phonemic transcription I have used previously. Since I did not want to hinder his game by asking him to repeat anything, I did not get too many phonetic details. The colon indicates length; in number 5 I have shown half-long by a raised dot. The acute accent indicates stress and tone 1 (single tone), the grave accent indicates stress and tone 2 (double tone). I am uncertain about how much length and stress some of the final syllables, which were pronounced in isolation, really had. A hyphen represents pause between the segments.

1. / i´:-må´r:-re´s:- ri`ŋ:te- mo´:r./
2. /vi´:-ska´l:- çö`:pe- apelsi´:- ne´r- på´:-tå´:ge./
3. /få´:r-jei´- lå´:v-å´:-rö`:-ke (or rö´:-ke´?)./
4. /kre`m:er-hu´:s./
5. /nei`le-la´· k·- ke´n-æ´:r-bo` ṭ:e./
6. /mo´:r-å´:-jei´-ha´:r-få´t:-sti`k:liŋ-er./
7. /i´:-da´:g-ska´l:-jei´-rei`se./
8. /jei´-vi´l:-i`k:e-rei`se./
9. /kni´:ven-li´g:er-ve´:-si`:dnamei´/
10. /jei´-ha´:r-ly´s:t-å´:-bi`n:e-e´:n-e´l:er-to´:-ty`:ver-i´:-e´:n-sno´:r./

These represent:

1. I morges ringte mor. 'Mother phoned ("rang") this morning.'
2. Vi skal kjøpe appelsiner pa toget. 'We will buy oranges on the train.'
3. Får jeg lov å røke? 'Am I allowed to smoke?'

Språkanalyse som barnelek. *Norsk Tidsskrift for Sprogvidenskap*, 1954, **17**, 484–485. Translated from Norwegian by Robert Sayre and edited by Charles A. Ferguson. Reprinted by permission of the author and Universitetsforlaget, Oslo, Norway.

4. Kremmerhus. 'Kremmerhus' (a cone-shaped paper container for candy).
5. Neglelakken er borte. 'The nail polish is gone.'
6. Mor og jeg har fått stiklinger. 'Mother and I got some seedlings.'
7. I dag skal jeg reise. 'Today I'm going on a trip.'
8. Jeg vil ikke reise. 'I won't go on a trip.'
9. Kniven ligger ved siden av meg. 'The knife is beside me.'
10. Jeg har lyst å binde én eller to tyver i en snor. 'I want to tie up one or two thieves in a rope.'

Most of the segments are either *word formatives* (*ordformer*) or *syllables*. Notice the syllable division in /må′r:- re′s:/ and /la′·k·- ke′n/; there was clearly a pause between the syllables, each of which had a clearly pronounced /r/ or /k/, respectively. The word formatives seemed to represent a principle of higher order than the syllables; syllable boundaries are not marked in conflict with word boundaries, for example, /ly′s:t - å′:/, /vi′l: - i`k:e/, /lå′:v - å′:/. On the other hand, syllable boundaries are sometimes marked in conflict with morpheme boundaries within word formatives: /apelsi′: - ne′r/, /rö`: - ke/, /la′·k· - ke′n/. Division of word formatives into morphemes occurs rarely. In /sti`k: liŋ - er/ it is probably really a syllable which was separated out, but he was not able to place /ŋ/ in initial position of an isolated syllable. I do not recall whether the pause was completely clear in this example. Compound sentences are separated into their components (see numbers 4 and 5). Groups of *word formatives* which were taken together without a pause occur at the end when he started to become tired of the game (see number 9).

Small words like /å/ (for "å" and "og") are segmented off along the lines of other *word formatives*, while inflectional morphemes are not separated. For the most part, the analysis corresponds to the general use of spacing and hyphen in writing.

Some additional information on the child is perhaps in order. His first language was Norwegian, but he lived for a while in Sweden and Finland and speaks quite good Swedish and perhaps a few words of Finnish. In general he keeps Norwegian and Swedish apart, except that certain features of Swedish phonetics (intonation and vowel pronunciation) can often be noticed in his Norwegian. He finds it entertaining to translate words and expressions from one language to another. This situation may have sharpened his sense for language analysis. It would be interesting if someone could observe a similar game with other children. The game must, however, come spontaneously, in any event, without a lot of introductory explanations.

The Development of Analysis of Words into Their Sounds by Preschool Children

—— *L. Ye. Zhurova*

Sensation and perception undergo intensive development during the first years of an infant's life. One of the sensory processes that is earliest to take shape is phonemic hearing.

As has been demonstrated by the studies of N. Kh. Shvachkin (1948), an infant is able, as early as seventeen months of age, readily to distinguish words differing by but a single phoneme, and can grasp the fine differences between voiced and voiceless, soft and hard consonants.

In the writings of A. N. Gvozdev (1948) and N. Kh. Shvachkin, a detailed analysis has been presented of the infant's mastery of the phoneme as his oral speech develops. This is a complex process that passes through a number of successive stages. At first the infant masters the over-all rhythm and melody of speech. At this stage it is not the phoneme but the intonation and rhythm that acquire an element of meaning for him. At the next stage in the development of the child's speech, the acoustic picture of a word becomes meaningful, but the general semantic diffusion characteristic of that stage is paralleled by phonetic diffusion. The infant's mastery of words is built entirely upon the establishment of gross acoustic differentiations among words. The infant operates with sounds that, at the beginning, have only a very approximate correspondence with the norm. Gvozdev and Shvachkin explain the progress from prephonemic to phonemic speech in terms of the infant's attempts to make his speech intelligible to those around him; that is, the advance to phonemic perception and reproduction of speech occurs in the infant "under the influence of semantics" (N. Kh. Shvachkin).

The development of the infant's speech occurs along with that of his cognitive activity, and reflects this development. Phonemic hearing, like all sensory processes, constitutes "a subordinate factor in the general course of change in the interrelations between the infant and his environment, and in the general course of development of the child's activity" (Zaporozhetz, 1963). In the first months of the infant's life, rhythm and intonation constitute adequate means for expressing the content that is meaningful to the infant at that age. This is why he reacts only to components of the speech of adults which are significant to him. The further development consists primarily of the addition of grammatical complexities to the child's speech and to the enrichment of his vocabulary. Inasmuch as grammatical and vocabulary differences become fixed in the form of sounds, the infant has to master the acoustic units existing

Razvitiye zvukovogo analiza slov u detey doshkol'nogo vozrasta. *Voprosy psikhologii*, 1963, **9** (3), 20–32. Translated from Russian by William M. Mandel and edited by Dan I. Slobin. Translation reprinted from *Soviet Psychology and Psychiatry*, 1964, **2** (2), 11–17, with the permission of International Arts and Sciences Press.

in the speech of adults. The unit of sound is taken to be that element of sound which, when changed, results in change in meaning. S. K. Shaumyan (1958) observes, in particular, that when the young child masters the phonemic aspect of speech, only those refinements are mastered which are necessary for the differentiation of words in his particular language.

Thus, phonemic hearing is established in the infant by the age of two: the child has good comprehension of adult speech addressed to him, and is himself able to speak.

However, studies of the speech of older preschool children made in conjunction with teaching them to read and write show that even in six- and seven-year-olds, phonemic hearing is often not yet established (Khokhlova, 1950; Ol'shannikova, 1958). This conclusion is made on the basis of the fact that older preschool children are incapable of identifying individual sounds in words.

We thus come up against a paradox: on the one hand, the infant is capable of distinguishing sound complexes by the age of two. On the other hand, children of the middle and older preschool age groups are incapable of distinguishing individual sounds in a word. The questions arise: are these two abilities characteristics of the same process? Is the inability of the child to differentiate a sound in the word something that may be explained by the fact that phonemic hearing has taken shape inadequately in him, and that he *does not hear* that sound? And may one hold that, in the course of the further development of the acoustical and articulatory apparatus of the child, this ability to differentiate a sound in a word gradually takes shape in him?

The recognition and reproduction of speech by a child of early preschool age differs fundamentally from the isolation of individual sounds in a word, which is necessary in teaching older preschool children to read and write. For one thing, the difference lies in the fact that, in the former situation, it is impossible to speak of any conscious analysis whatever of the sounds of a word.

The articulation of a child of early preschool age is characterized by assimilation of the speech of adults as he hears it. The child encounters entire acoustic complexes of varieties of words which he must then discriminate into sound, and pronounce. N. I. Zhinkin emphasizes that phonemes themselves are in general incapable of being pronounced, and "the syllable is that material device which alone makes any pronunciation possible" (1958). Thus, at this stage the child does not as yet deal with isolated sounds as units of speech. The task of identifying an individual sound within a word does not face a young child in his normal life activity, inasmuch as communication with those around one does not make it necessary to be able to single out the individual sounds in a word. Therefore, it is natural that experimental efforts to find, in preschool children, the ability to perform acoustic analysis of a word have been unsuccessful (Detsova, 1950).

The task of acoustic analysis of a word is first posed to a child (and is, specifically, *posed*, and does not arise spontaneously) when the effort to teach him to read and write begins, because except for this, no artificial discrimination of the individual sounds in a word is necessary.

Sound analysis is a particular operation upon the words of a language. In order to understand this activity, one must understand the structure of language. Modern theories of language depict it as a sort of two-dimensional structure in which one plane represents a given objective meaning and the other constitutes a form associated with this objective content. The acoustic and written forms of speech are, in the final analysis, identical in content (when we speak of content here, we have reference to the objective reality reflected therein). The written form of speech depicts the acoustic; that is, the acoustic form is the content of the writing, which expresses the same meaning as does the acoustic form. The task of sound analysis arises specifically at that moment of transition from the oral, acoustic form of speech to the written. The major difficulty encountered in establishing a one-to-one relation between the acoustic and graphic forms of speech is to be found in the following. The acoustic form is a structural formation, inasmuch as the pronunciation of a particular sound is determined by its association with others, while in the graphic form of speech no such structuring exists: a letter has a canonical expression in writing, regardless of which letters are written to right and left.

Acoustic analysis is difficult for a child for the further reason that, in analyzing a word into sounds, depriving it of its usual syllabic pronunciation, and in pronouncing each syllable by its component sounds, we completely distort the word, and its meaning is lost. Naturally, a child of preschool age will refuse to work with such a "broken-down" word.

Consequently, in order to teach a preschool child acoustic analysis of words, it is necessary to find a means of breaking up the structure of the word under which the particular pronunciation of the sound due to its position in the word is retained. Moreover, inasmuch as, in acoustic analysis of a word, the unit which the child is called upon to identify is a sound, the word must be pronounced not by syllabication (as in the usual form of pronunciation) but by sounds. This type of articulation is not natural and must be taught.

In our work we tried to determine whether it is possible to teach preschool children (including those at the younger end of this scale) to perform that formal operation with words of which acoustic analysis consists. We held that the experimental situation in which this instruction would occur must meet two requirements:

1. The task of differentiating a sound in a word must be posed within a situation interesting and comprehensible to a child anywhere in the preschool age group. This is attainable if acoustic analysis is used as a means of solving a basically playful task.

2. The children must be given a comprehensible and clearly defined means of discriminating a sound in a word. This means must correspond to the demands indicated above—that is, children must be taught to pronounce a

word in such fashion that the breakdown of its structure does not change that which is specific to the pronunciation of the individual sound.

The *first series* of experiments posed the goal of teaching children to discriminate the first sound in the word.

The experiments were run in Moscow Kindergarten No. 253 with children in the 3–4, 4–5, and 5–6 age groups (10 per group) and with 25 in the older group (6–7).

Before the game began, the child was shown, with his own name as example, what was meant by the first sound in a word. This was done as follows. The experimenter asked the child his name and then repeated the name, omitting the first sound:

> EXPERIMENTER: What's your name?
> SUBJECT: Sasha.
> EXPERIMENTER: Asha?
> SUBJECT: No, Sasha.

The experiment continued in this manner until the child himself, or with the aid of the experimenter, discriminated the first sound in his name. The child then had a playhouse put in front of him and was instructed as follows: "Animals live in this house—a fox, a mouse, a cat, a dog, a squirrel, a goat, a horse, a sheep, a little pig, and a walrus. A stream runs around the house, but you can get to it over a bridge. But this isn't an ordinary bridge; it's a magic bridge. See, the Wise Crow sits on its railing. He asks whoever comes to the bridge for the first sound in his name. Those who give the right answer may cross, but the bridge falls down under those who give the wrong answer. The animals came to the bridge, but they couldn't cross because they don't know how to speak and don't know the first sounds in their names. Now you help the animals; you get them across the bridge." The child was then given a toy animal which he led across the bridge, answering on the animal's part to the questions put by the experimenter.

Our experiments showed that all the children of preschool age were able to cope with the task of isolating the first sound in a word, but that the process occurred differently at different stages in the child's development.

Children in the three to four age group could not grasp the explanation of what constituted the first sound in a word when their names were utilized as the example. They responded only upon the appearance of the playhouse and the animals, and therefore the instruction had to be repeated. However, during the game itself, instead of pronouncing the first sound alone, they uttered the entire word, but presented the initial sound separately beforehand (we termed this type of utterance "intoning"):

> EXPERIMENTER: Who's coming?
> SUBJECT (Olya A.): Doggie [*sobachka*].

EXPERIMENTER: What's the first sound in your name? [*Kakoy pervyy zvuk v tvoyem imeni?*]
SUBJECT: D-d-doggie [*s-s-sobachka*].

Thus, children of three or four understand very well what they are supposed to do at the request of the experimenter, and isolate excellently the first sound in the ten words offered them, but without separating the first sound from the word. Pronunciation of individual sounds was achieved by pronouncing the desired word, singling out the first sound, and then asking the child to name the first sound alone (we continue below to cite the record of the experiment with Olya A.):

EXPERIMENTER: You're not supposed to say the whole word; say only the first sound: d-d-doggie . . . d-d-d [*Ne nuzhno govorit, vse slovo, skazhi tol'ko pervyy zvuk . . .*].
SUBJECT: d-d-d.
EXPERIMENTER: Who's coming?
SUBJECT: (*leading a bear over the bridge*). A bear, bruin [*medved', mishka*].
EXPERIMENTER: What's the first sound in your name?
SUBJECT: B-b-bear [*m-m-medved'*].
EXPERIMENTER: You're not supposed to say the whole word, only the first sound. Listen: b-b-bear.
SUBJECT: B-b-b.
EXPERIMENTER: That's all! Only the first sound!

Thus, after several repetitions (three to six), it was possible to get three-year-olds to single out the first sound in the word, but it was necessary for the experimenter to pronounce the full word, with intoning. As soon as the experimenter ceased to single out the first sound in the word, the child did likewise, and it was impossible to make him proceed to pronounce the separate sound alone. It must be remarked that children of three to four in this experimental situation were interested in the game as such: they enjoyed taking the animals over the bridge, were interested in how the animals live in the house, and so forth. They regarded the isolation of the sound in the word as an unwelcome addition to the game. There were cases in which three small children flatly refused to continue the game and would not accept the task of separating the sound from the word.

Children of four to five listened attentively to the experimenter's explanation of what constitutes the first sound in a word. But they reacted to erroneous pronunciation of their names not so much in protest as in bewilderment; none of the subjects in this age group were able to say what the experimenter's error was. During the game all the children, when pronouncing the word, had recourse to intoning for isolation of the first sound, and only thereafter could they name it, pronouncing it separately. Two of the ten needed the same kind of help from the experimenter as those in the three to four group (that is, they uttered the sound only after the experimenter isolated it in pronouncing the word). All the other children isolated the first sound very clearly in pronouncing the word, and then named it. In some children, words starting with stop consonants (*belka, koshka*) caused difficulties, and the children began to pronounce these words without singling out the first sound, but by syllabication. The experimenter's help was needed in intoning these words, after which the children themselves began to identify the first sound.

SUBJECT (Valerik Yu.):   Billy-goat [*kozel*].
EXPERIMENTER: What's the first sound in your name?
SUBJECT: Bill-ee-goat [*ko-zel*].
EXPERIMENTER: But what's the first sound?
SUBJECT: me-eh-eh-eh.
EXPERIMENTER: No, now listen: b-b-billy-goat [*k-k-kozel*].
SUBJECT: B-b [*k-k*].

The first sound is isolated in distinctive fashion in the speech of children with speech defects, such as those who cannot pronounce the letter "l."

EXPERIMENTER: Who's coming?
SUBJECT (Vova M.):   *Yoshad'* [*loshad'* 'horse'].
EXPERIMENTER: What's the first sound in your name?
SUBJECT: *Yo.*
EXPERIMENTER: *Yo?*
SUBJECT: No, I can't say it.
EXPERIMENTER: *R-r?*
SUBJECT: No, not like that.
EXPERIMENTER: *L-l?*
SUBJECT: Yes.

We see that the inability to pronounce a sound correctly does not signify the inability to discriminate it in the word and to differentiate it from others. Thus, even in cases in which a child of preschool age is incapable, due to some articulatory inadequacy, of pronouncing a sound correctly (usually, a sonorant or sibilant sound), he hears it clearly, differentiates it accurately from others, and isolates it in the word.

For the first time in the preschool years, independent isolation of the first sound in a word (using the subject's name as the example) appears in children of ages five and six. (Children of three to five learned this from the experimenter in the course of receiving instructions.) All of these children responded to the experimenter's first request to pronounce their own names slowly, doing so very precisely by syllable. But when asked to emphasize and single out the first sound, the intoning phenomenon appeared.

EXPERIMENTER: Tell me, what's your name?
SUBJECT (Igor' O.):   Igor'.
EXPERIMENTER: Your name is Gor'.
SUBJECT (laughs):   No, Igor'.
EXPERIMENTER: So I'm saying it wrong?
SUBJECT: No.

EXPERIMENTER: Then what am I saying wrong?
SUBJECT: (*No response*).
EXPERIMENTER: Tell me your name once again.
SUBJECT: I-gor'.
EXPERIMENTER: Your name is Gor', is that what you're saying?
SUBJECT: No, I'm not saying that; I'm saying: "I-gor'."
EXPERIMENTER: So what am I saying wrong? What am I forgetting to say?
SUBJECT: You're saying "Gor'," and you should say "I-i-gor'."
EXPERIMENTER: When I say "Gor'," what am I forgetting to say?
SUBJECT: I-i-i.

It is interesting that in the process of experiment, when there are difficulties in intoning (when the word begins with a stop consonant), children return to syllabic breakdown of the word.

Fifty percent of the children in this age group were able to isolate the first sounds in their names on their own, while the others readily mastered the explanations of the experimenters.

In the course of the game, half the children did not have recourse to intoning, and at once named the first sound in the word (these were specifically the children who independently intoned their names during the period of instruction), while with the others the experiment proceeded in approximately the same manner as with those in the four to five age group. It is interesting that in the five-year-olds some difficulty was induced by words starting with stop consonants. However, unlike the four-year-olds, they understood clearly what the source of the trouble was.

EXPERIMENTER: Who's coming?
SUBJECT (Sasha I.): *Belka* [squirrel].
EXPERIMENTER: What's the first sound in your name?
SUBJECT: *Bel-ka* . . . No, not like that . . . *Belka* . . . How does it go? . . . I can't do it.
EXPERIMENTER: *B-b-belka.*
SUBJECT: *B-b* . . . right?

When the next word of this type comes up, Sasha I. seems to recognize this and isolates the first sound by intoning (although previously he had not had recourse to intoning) and names it.

Children of five and six differ sharply from the younger preschool children in their behavior during the experiment. They are interested specifically in the play with words, in its formal, and not meaningful aspect. They continue the game with pleasure after the experiment is brought to an end.

The experiments with six- to seven-year-olds were modified somewhat, as it is quite obvious that the task of singling out the first sound in the word is quite simple for children in this age group and does not require incorporation into a game in this manner. First, the six to seven group played the group game, "Who pays attention?" in the course of which it was explained to the children (on the basis of their names) what the first sound in a word is. The experimenter pronounced some particular sound. In response to this, the children whose names began with the given letter had to raise their hands. In cases of error (when, for example, Tanya stood in response to the experimenter's pronunciation of the sound "V"), the experimenter would intone the first sound in the child's name, then pronounce the given sound and compare these sounds along with the children. This comparison had to be made twice, after which these errors ceased. Then all the children in the group (25) participated in a single experiment, in which they were required to pronounce the first sound in the same words as the three- to six-year-olds in their game, but outside the game situation. All the children in the group readily grappled with the task. No single individual had recourse either to intoning or even to mere pronunciation of the word. For example:

EXPERIMENTER: *Medved'*.
SUBJECT: *Me.*
EXPERIMENTER: *Belka.*
SUBJECT: *Be.*

Some children, instead of pronouncing the first sound ("meh," "leh," and so on), uttered the first syllable ("*mi*," "*li*"), but no child in the oldest group singled out the first sound in the manner done by the children in the youngest and middle age groups, whom we either specifically instructed in intoning (the youngest) or elicited intoning (the middle group: "m-m-m," "l-l-l"). Investigation showed that those children who knew their letters pronounced the first letter as it is pronounced in the alphabet. Those children, however, who did not know the alphabet, pronounced syllables. It is interesting that use of intoning by the experimenter immediately changed the child's response. Thus, Sasha B., in answer to the question as to what was the first sound in the word *sobaka*, answered: "*soba*." But then:

EXPERIMENTER: What is the first sound in the word *s-s-sobaka*?
SUBJECT: *S-s-s.*

The first series of experiments demonstrated that when the device of intoning was introduced, all children of preschool age were able to cope with the task of singling out the first sound in the word.

However, the task of singling out the first sound is simpler than that of identifying the middle and final sounds. We decided to determine whether children of preschool age, making use of the method of intoning with which they had been provided, would be able to manage the isolation of the final sound in the word. The difficulties in this task were due primarily to the fact that, in the Russian language, the final sound is almost never pronounced distinctly, but is often "swallowed," as it were.

For the second series of experiments, the same experimental situation was employed as in the first. The subjects were the same, and therefore the mode of intoning and subsequent isolation of the sound did not have to be explained in detail. All that was done was to demonstrate intoning to the child and to isolate the final sound, using his name as example: "*Igor-r'-r*," the final sound "*r*'," and so on.

Children of three to four continued stubbornly to intone the first sound in the word, and only after the experimenter demonstrated the intoning of the final sound in *each word* were they able to carry out this assignment, but without enunciating the sound separately or naming it. We succeeded in this with only two children, but only after the experimenter had demonstrated several (five to seven) times. The remaining children refused to continue the game.

In isolating the final sound in the word, children of four to five proceeded to the type of activity characteristic of three-year-olds in isolating the first sound. Whereas, upon isolation of the first sound in the word, four-year-olds very carefully intone the individual sound and then name it, in the second series of experiments, however, they first listened to the experimenter intone, then imitated him, and it was only after the repeated intoning by the experimenter that they enunciated the sound in isolation.

EXPERIMENTER:	Who's coming?
SUBJECT (Luyba D.):	*Lisa* [fox].
EXPERIMENTER:	What's the last sound in your name?
SUBJECT:	(*No reply*).
EXPERIMENTER:	*Lisa-a-a* . . . What's the last sound?
SUBJECT:	*Lisa-a-a.*
EXPERIMENTER:	You say the word well, correctly . . . *Lisa-a-a* . . . Then what's the last sound?
SUBJECT:	*A-a-a.*

It was found by chance that the names of nine out of ten subjects in this age group terminated with vowels. The very first time that a word was encountered which ended in a vowel, all the children refused to say it. Thus, in the experiment with Andryusha S., the word *morzh* [walrus] was given him after the word *belka* [squirrel].

EXPERIMENTER:	Who's coming?
SUBJECT:	*Morzh.*
EXPERIMENTER:	What's the last sound in your name?
SUBJECT:	I don't know about that.
EXPERIMENTER:	Now listen: *morzh-zh-zh* . . . What's the last sound?
SUBJECT:	I still can't say it.
EXPERIMENTER:	Why can't you? Now listen: *morzh-zh-zh* . . . Say that.
SUBJECT:	(*very uncertainly*). *Morzh-zh-zh.*
EXPERIMENTER:	Very well said. Simply wonderful!
SUBJECT:	*Morzh-zh-zh.*
EXPERIMENTER:	Right. The last sound we hear is *zh-zh-zh*. Right?
SUBJECT:	Right. *Morzh-zh-zh* . . . *zh-zh-zh* . . . Like *zhuk* . . . [beetle].

Thereafter the identification of the final consonant sound followed the pattern already described.

The only subject whose name ends with a consonant, Valerik K., found no difficulty in his first encounter with a word ending in a vowel. (It would seem that a very important fact here is that the experimenter always demonstrated the intoning of the final sound to him.)

In the second series of experiments, too, the children in the five to six group also slipped back one step. It is interesting that this was observed in every child without exception. Children who did not have recourse to intoning in the first series in this case intoned over the course of the entire experiment, while those who had independently intoned all the words in Series I now began to have need of help from the experimenter.

Among the five-year-olds there was a particularly clear-cut manifestation of the importance of the particular word with respect to which instruction was being given: one ending with a vowel or with a consonant. We adduce the records of experiments with two children.

Igor' O. (name ends in consonant, and first word in experiment, *medved'*, caused no difficulty).

EXPERIMENTER: Who's coming?
SUBJECT: *Lisa.*
EXPERIMENTER: What's the last sound in your name?
SUBJECT: *Lis-sa . . . S-s-a.*
EXPERIMENTER: No, you didn't say that word right. You're supposed to say *Lis-a-a-a.*
SUBJECT: *A-a-a.*

There were no further mistakes.

Serezha Ch. (in the first words, *lisa* and *belka*, the last sound was very clearly intoned and named).

EXPERIMENTER: Who's coming?
SUBJECT: *Loshad'.*
EXPERIMENTER: What's the last sound in your name?
SUBJECT: *Loshad' . . .* How do I do it here? *Lo-shad' . . .* I don't know.
EXPERIMENTER: *Loshad'-d'.*
SUBJECT: *D',* is that it?
EXPERIMENTER: Yes, right.

The next word was correctly intoned by the child himself.

But despite the fact that, as we have already observed, five-year-olds switched to the mode of operation characteristic of four-year-olds working on the easier task, they, unlike the four-year-olds, understood, in this series of experiments as well, wherein their difficulties lay. Thus, Sasha I., who easily intoned the words *lisa* and *belka*, had difficulties with the word *loshad'*.

SUBJECT: *Loshad'* is like *belka. (In the first series of tests Sasha had had trouble in intoning* belka.)
EXPERIMENTER: Why?
SUBJECT: Remember, that was hard too. I don't know how to say it.

EXPERIMENTER: *Loshad'-d'.*
SUBJECT: *D'*, then.

Later, when presented with the word *medved'*, Sasha asked the experimenter: "Now you say this one for me too."

Thus, the second series of experiments showed that intoning as a means of activity in singling out a letter in a word is absolutely necessary for preschool children. When the structure of a word is resolved into its components in this manner, no change occurs in the manner in which the individual sound within the word is pronounced. Thanks to this, and by means of intoning, even children of the younger preschool age are able to isolate individual sounds in a word. Moreover, we are now in a position to distinguish several different stages and levels of activity in isolating a sound in a word. These levels are in a definite genetic sequence. The level at which the child functions is determined in each given instance not only by the child's age but also by the nature of the material (the position of the sound singled out and its articulatory characteristics).

As in the first, so in the second series, we organized the activity of the child in isolating the sound in the word in a particular manner. We showed him what the first (or last) sound was, and provided a means for isolating it. In both series, sound analysis served the child as a means of solving the basic play task: that of getting the animal into the house via the bridge. But perhaps if the sound analysis itself were made the object of the activity, that is, if the child were offered a game of speech as such—a procedural game with a word— the task of isolating a sound in a word would prove easier and the sound analysis would be performed by the child independently, without instruction. The third series of experiments was carried out to test this hypothesis.

Five identical dolls, differing only by the colors of their jackets, were offered to the subject. The following instruction was given: "Here are five little boys. They look very much alike; you can't tell them apart at all" (at which point examination of the figures followed). "Then their mother thought up a way to tell them apart. She made different jackets for them and named them as follows:

The boy with the yellow jacket is Yan [*zheltaya—Zhan*]
The boy with the red jacket is Ran [*krasnaya—Kan*]
The boy with the blue jacket is Ban [*sinyaya—San*]
The boy with the white jacket is Whan [*belaya—Ban*]
The boy with the green jacket is Gan [*zelenaya—Zan*].

Do you want to play with them? Then you have to remember their names."

In matching the names of the dolls to the colors of their jackets, the experimenter lightly emphasized the first sound in these words ("y-yellow," "Y-yan"), but did not particularly focus the children's attention on this, nor was it explained to them what the first sound in a word was.

During the game the figures were first arranged in the same sequence in which they had been named in the period of instruction. They were then shuffled and the child was then required to identify them at random, and then to name them.

The experiments were run with children in Moscow Kindergarten No. 1065 (16 aged four to five, 18 aged five to six, and 10 aged six to seven). All the children participating in this series of experiments were classified into two groups: (1) those capable of distinguishing and naming the figures and (2) those incapable of doing so. Inasmuch as children of different ages falling into a single group acted in absolutely identical fashion, we will provide a description and analysis of the materials of this series not by ages but by the mode of operation of the subjects.

In the first group, which proved capable of dealing with the problem readily, we found all the children from six to seven, 7 (of 18) of five to six, and 2 (of 16) from four to five.

The differences between the children were limited simply to the fact that the older children did not make a single mistake in the course of the entire experiment, while among the younger there were, at first, occasional errors not dependent upon the articulatory characteristics of the first sound in the words. There were errors both in the sounds *Zhan*, *Zan*, and *San*, which are easy to pronounce, and in *Kan* and *Ban*, which begin with stop consonants and are therefore hard to intone. No child in this group had recourse to identification by intoning of the first sound in naming the color of the jacket or the figure. However, all the children in the younger age group and some in the six to seven group named the color of the jacket before naming the figure.

EXPERIMENTER:	Who's that?
SUBJECT (Olya Z., five):	Green. Gan.
EXPERIMENTER:	Who's that?
SUBJECT:	Red. Ran.
EXPERIMENTER:	Who's that? (Yan.)
SUBJECT:	Whan . . . Oh, I made a mistake! But he's yellow; that means he's Yan.

After the completion of the experiment, all the subjects, when asked how they knew the names of the little boys, cited the jacket colors. All the children in this group were capable of answering the question as to what the names of boys in pink, violet, and other jackets would be (these were colors not dealt with in the instructions).

The subjects in the second group (11 children of five to six and 14 children of four to five), despite the fact that each figure was presented to them up to 30 times (the maximum number of presentations to the children in the first group was 14) were still unable to distinguish the relationships between the first sound in the color designation and the name of the doll. We cite a typical record (Lyuda S., 5 years, 4 months):

EXPERIMENTER: Who's that?
SUBJECT: Whan.
EXPERIMENTER: What's the color of his jacket?
SUBJECT: Green.
EXPERIMENTER: Then what's his name?
SUBJECT: Then it's Whan.
EXPERIMENTER: No, you said it wrong. Now Listen, he has a g-green jacket . . . What's his name?
SUBJECT: Ran.

Thus, a simple running through of all the names followed.

Sometimes the child accidentally gave a correct answer. But when the researcher asked: "How did you recognize him?" the answer invariably was: "But I know him," or "But I remembered it." Naturally, no child in this group was able to answer a question of the type: "What would the name of a boy in a pink jacket be?"

The results of the third series of experiments proved to be considerably inferior to those in Series I: whereas in the first series all the children in the four to six age group dealt successfully with the task of selecting the first sound in the word, in the third series, only 12 percent of those in the four to five age group carried out the task, and 39 percent of those in the five to six age group.

How is so large a difference to be explained? As we demonstrated in the description of the first series, it was necessary, in order for a sound to be singled out in a word, to carry out the following procedures with all the children of four to five and with 50 percent of those five to six: to pronounce the word, then to hear the intoning by the experimenter, and finally to pronounce the words oneself with an intoned isolation of the first sound. Only thereafter did the children pronounce the sound separately. The younger the children and the more difficult the intoning of the sound (as in the case of stop consonants), the more extended the work in isolating the sound from the word. However, in the third series of experiments, the factor of instruction is eliminated and the experimenter does not show the children how to separate the sound from the word; he does not teach them to intone. The child must, *in some way*, segregate the sound from the word by himself. We emphasize that children who coped with the experiment task in the third series did so in a manner that was unknown to us, performing "in their heads" the entire operation leading to segregation of the sound, and therefore all the stages required to segregate a sound in a word as described by us in presenting the results of the first and second series of experiments had already been eliminated in these children, and what was left was only the simplest of schemes in the older pre-school children: from the word directly to the segregation of the sound.

Thus, our experiments showed that the ability to isolate a particular sound in a word is not, in a child of preschool age, a simple single-stage act manifested spontaneously. In order for the preschool child to learn to resolve a word into its component sounds, he has to be given a mode of operation with this word. He must be taught how to differentiate sounds in a word so that, when this is done, the structure of the word is not violated. The segregation of sounds in a word by means of intoning constitutes such a method. Using this method, children of preschool age are able to deal readily with the task of sound analysis of words.

REFERENCES

Detsova, A. V., Razvitiye osoznaniya zvukovoy storony rechi u detey dosh- kol'nogo vozrasta, unpublished dissertation, Department of Psychology, Moscow State University, 1950.
Gvozdev, A. N., *Usvoyeniya rebenkom zvukovoy storony russkogo yazyka.* Moscow: Akad. Pedag. Nauk RSFSR, 1948.
Khokhlova, N. A., Sravnitel'noye psikhologicheskoye izucheniye zvukovogo analiza slov det'mi-doshkol'nikami, unpublished dissertation, Department of Psychology, Moscow State University, 1950.
Ol'shannikova, A. Ye., Formirovaniye obobshchennogo umstvennogo deystviya zvukorazlicheniya, *Dokl. Akad. Pedag. Nauk RSFSR*, 1958, No. 3.
Shaumyan, S. K., *Istoriya sistemy differentsial'nykh elementov v pol'skom yazyke.* Moscow: Akad. Nauk SSSR, 1958.
Shvachkin, N. Kh., Razvitiye fonematicheskogo vospriyatiya rechi v rannem vozraste, *Izvestiya Akad. Pedag. Nauk RSFSR*, 1948, **13**, 101–132. [Translation in this volume: The development of phonemic speech perception in early childhood.]
Zaporozhetz, A. V., Razvitiye oshchushcheniy i vospriyatiy v rannem i doshkol'nom detstve, *Tezisy doklada na II Vsesoyuznom s"yezde psikhologov,* 1963.
Zhinkin, N. I., *Mekhanizmy rechi.* Moscow: Akad. Pedag. Nauk RSFSR, 1958.

/r/ •

Of the various elements in the sound systems of child language, *r*-like sounds seem to have received the most detailed attention, possibly because they tend to be acquired later and often have well-recognized defective pro- nunciations. The characterization of *r*'s is a serious problem in phonetic analysis, since the range of sound types which are recognized as *r*'s is quite broad, including such different phenomena as tongue-tip flaps and trills, strongly retroflex continuants (for example, in varieties of English), near sibilants (for example, in varieties of Spanish), and postvelar continuants and trills of various kinds (for example, French uvular [R]). There is apparently no clear articulatory or acoustic invariant as a core feature for all these sounds (Tarnóczy, 1948, pp. 71–77; Heffner, 1960, pp. 146–150; Ladefoged, 1964, pp. 29–30; Chomsky and Halle, 1968, pp. 317–318). The phonological functions of *r* are also very varied: in particular languages the /r/ may belong with the semivowels (*w*, *y*, and so on), the apical obstruents (*t*, *s*, and so on), both, or neither, in terms of phonetic patterning and grammatical alternations (Troubetzkoy, 1949, pp. 156–158; Hockett, 1955, pp. 120–122; Chomsky and Halle, *loc. cit.*). Although Troubetzkoy maintains that most languages have two liquids (/l/ and /r/), Jakobson (1968, pp. 57–58) points out that very many languages have only one and adduces this fact in relation to the child's late distinction of two liquids. Also, almost all careful studies of child phonology show some interplay of liquids and semivowels. For example, at one stage a child may combine several adult phonemes into one, with positional variants phonetically similar to the respective adult phonemes; for example, one such possible pattern is adult /w y r l/ → child [y-], [-w]. (See Ferguson, 1968, and references.)

The Rūķe-Draviņa paper, on the basis of a study of four children, offers some details on phonetic varieties of *r*, and the one by Engel, based on her son's speech, describes a late stage in the mastering of *r*. In all five cases the children: (1) first acquired an /l/ corresponding in part to adult /l/ and /r/, then acquired the *l-r* opposition, and finally, if at all, any further sonorants (for example, Czech ř, Latvian *r*); (2) the /r/ first appeared in the cluster /tr/; and (3) postvocalic *r* was at one stage omitted or replaced by length or vocalic glide. Menyuk and Anderson (1969) further document the relation between /r/ and the other liquids and semivowels in English. Similar phenomena have been observed in other languages, including French and Russian, but there are also counterinstances in English and other languages. (See, for example, the Shvachkin and Moskowitz studies reprinted in this volume.) Before further generalization is attempted, other languages must be investigated where the phonetic nature and grammatical functions are different (for example, languages with a large number of laterals, or where /r/ or /n/ interchange grammatically).

—C.A.F.

An Example of Linguistic Consciousness[1] in the Child
—— *Walburga von Raffler Engel*

In observing the development of language in the child, we are faced by the challenging and unresolved question of the relative role of automatic response versus arbitrary choice in language. While it is well known that at an early age the substitution of consonants follows very regular patterns, little or no research has been done on the particular stage of linguistic development

Un esempio di "linguistic consciousness" nel bambino piccolo, *Orientamenti pedagogici*, 1965, **12**, 631–633. Translated from Italian by Yole Correa and edited by Charles A. Ferguson. Reprinted with the permission of the author and the publisher.
[1] Term used by the most prominent living specialist on child language, the German-American linguist Werner F. Leopold, in his *Bibliography of Child Language*, Evanston, Ill., 1952, p. 67.

when the child becomes consciously aware of the automatic nature of the substitutions.[2] This awareness appears to give rise to a reaction which I would call "conscious effort."[3]

At the age of three and a half years my son was capable of pronouncing correctly all the sounds of the Italian language with the exception of *r*. Speech therapists are generally in agreement that the various types of *r* are among the latest sounds to be correctly produced.[4] The point I wish to make, however, is that at this very same period my son was perfectly conscious of the difficulties he was encountering in the pronunciation of the *r*.

He would often pause briefly before a word containing an initial *r* or before this phoneme in word medial position. When he was 3 years and 5 months old I asked him to pronounce better the word "ragazza" ['girl'], which he had rendered as *lagatsa*. In response, first he gave me a challenging look and then with an impish smile he said: *bambina* [another word for 'girl'].

When the child was 3 years and 6½ months old I recorded during two consecutive days all his words containing the phoneme *r*. The list of these utterances appears to confirm—at least for this late period—the Gutzmann variant of the Schultze principle, that is, the principle of least phonetico-muscular effort.[5]

At times the *r* was replaced by the other liquid, and this appears to be the most frequent case:

Roberto (his own name)	*loberto lobeǝto*
	(the form with shwa [ǝ] in place of the
	second *r* occurred later the same day)
ragazza 'girl'	*lagatsa*
rompo 'I'm breaking'	*lompo*
racconta 'story'	*lakkonta*

[2] A good example of the regularity with which such substitution occurs is provided by the late French linguist Marcel Cohen's little son, for whom at 2 years 10 months "the establishment of this word (*poule* 'hen') leads to a transitory phonetic state in which every complex of labial + vowel + labial becomes dental + vowel + labial: *tomber* 'fall': *tôbe* → *tôbe*; *poupée* 'doll': *pupe* → *tupe*. (Marcel Cohen, Cinquante années de recherches linguistiques . . . , Paris, 1955, "Sur les langages successifs de l'enfant," pp. 97–111. The original work was in 1924 and was first published in *Mélanges M. Vendryes*, Paris, 1925, pp. 109–127.

[3] Walburga von Raffler Engel, *Il prelinguaggio infantile*, Brescia, 1964, §10.

[4] Robert West, *The Rehabilitation of Speech*, New York, 1957; ch. XI, "Case Study and Evaluation," § The Chronology of Speech Development, pp. 299–300. In this significant book the phonemes are not classified in absolute order of their first appearance. The author, instead, observed at what age the normal English-speaking child should be capable of producing these sounds correctly in the context of words of the language.

[5] See Clara and William Stern, *Die Kindersprache; eine psychologische und sprachtheoretische Untersuchung*, 3d ed., rev. (The first edition of this key work in research on child language was written by the German psychologists in 1907), Leipzig, 1922; Vol. I, p. 146. See also the American psychologist George K. Zipf, *Human Behavior and the Principle Least Effort*, Cambridge, Mass., 1949.

At times, instead, the *r* was replaced by a central vowel:

Roberto	for the form *lobɘɘto* see above
carne 'meat'	*kaɘne karne* (alternated during the same day)

or by a glottal stop:

carote 'carrot'	*kaʔote*

or by a nasal:

cacciatore 'hunter'	*kačatone*
colore 'color,' 'paint'	*kolone*

or by a geminate of the following consonant:

Borko (nickname of a Yugoslav uncle)	*bokko*

or by the voiced labio-dental spirant:

brutto 'ugly'	*bvutto*
tiro liro là (from a record)	*tivo livo là*

or by the voiced bilabial fricative:

ore 'hours'	*owe*

or by the voiceless velar fricative:

carta 'paper'	*kaxta karta* (the correct form *karta* occurred first on the same day)

or by an abrupt onset:

rosso 'red'	*'osso rosso*
rosa 'rose'	*'oza*

An entire syllable was omitted if *r* occurred as part of an unstressed syllable in final position:

lettere 'letters'	*létte*
Gregorio 'Gregory'	*gregó*

This appeared with consistency as opposed to the occasional omission of a syllable not containing an *r* in similar position.

At times the *r* was replaced by a very slight compensatory pause:

francese 'French'	*f|ancese*

Correct pronunciation always occurred if the *r* was adjacent to a preceding or following voiceless dental consonant:

Roberto	*loberto*
l'altra parte 'the other part'	*laltra parte*
la parte rossa 'the red part'	*la parte rossa*
la lavatrice 'the washing machine'	*la lavatriče*

The perfect production of the word:

aurora 'dawn'	*aurora*

is more difficult to explain because in other intervocalic positions the *r* had been replaced (*ore* becoming "owe"). Perhaps the correct production of the first *r* was caused by the preceding *u*, which is the vowel corresponding to the bilabial consonant which had served him to replace *r* in "owe."

Correct production of *r* had occurred also for *carne*, *carta* as well as in his name, *Roberto*, on the very same day on which the same words had been replaced by other sounds. Likewise, the first *r* in *Gregorio* (*gregó*) was successful.

It seems clear that the instability in articulation was the result of attempts at correct pronunciation which were sometimes crowned with success, sometimes not.

The Process of Acquisition of Apical /r/ and Uvular /R/ in the Speech of Children

——*Velta Rūķe-Draviņa*

1. That the rolled apical /r/ is one of the sounds with which small children have particularly great difficulty, is a fact well known to both experts and people in general.

When in the year 1941 Roman Jakobson formulated one of his theses ("Gegensätze, welche in den Sprachen der Welt verhältnismässig selten vorkommen, gehören zu den *spätesten* lautlichen Erwerbungen des Kindes"),[1] he also included /r/ among the last of the phonemes learnt in the speech of children.

In order to examine the above-mentioned thesis of R. Jakobson I have assembled material dealing with sound-learning in the cases of two Czech children and two Latvian children, one of the latter having had—at a comparatively early stage—contact with Swedish in the form of the southern

From *Linguistics*, 1965, **17**, 58–68. Reprinted by permission of the author and Mouton and Company.
[1] R. Jakobson, *Kindersprache, Aphasie und allgemeine Lautgesetze* (Uppsala, 1941), p. 43 (now also in his *Selected Writings*, I, The Hague, Mouton, 1962). [Translation: *Child language, aphasia and phonological universals*, The Hague: Mouton, 1968.]

Swedish (Skåne) dialect. This material enables us to follow the process of sound-acquisition by children learning a Slavonic, a Baltic, and a Germanic language. An important factor in this connection is that these languages have at their command not only the opposition /l/:/r/, but also /r/:/ř/ (in Czech)[2] or /r/:/ŗ/ (in Latvian),[3] and that the /r/ in the dialect of Skåne is pronounced as a uvular /R/ in contrast to the rolled apical /r/ in Czech and Latvian.

The Czech material has been gathered from the excellent investigations of K. Ohnesorg, *Fonetická studie o dětské řeči* (Prague, 1948) (herein referred to as O I), and *Druhá fonetická studie o dětské řeči* (Brno, 1959) (referred to as O II), which describe the process of learning sounds by a Czech boy (Karel, born 18th October 1942) and a Czech girl (Marie, born 1st March, 1944).

The material in connection with Latvian and southern Swedish is derived from a monograph by the present writer[4] covering the development of speech in the case of a Latvian boy (Dainis, born 10th September 1949), who, during his school-days, gradually became bilingual (Latvian and Swedish), and his sister (Sarma, born 9th February 1956), who became acquainted with Swedish already in the preschool age. When necessary, examples have been supplemented by the author's own observations made in Sweden concerning other Latvian and Swedish children.

2. A comparison of the facts gathered in connection with the Czech and Latvian children shows an almost surprising similarity regarding the acquisition of /r/ and its allophones.

In the speech of the two Czech children and the two Latvian children, /r/ was among the last sounds learned.

In all four cases /r/ first appeared after the /l/ sound had developed. The absolute point of time varies somewhat, but the *relative* sequence remains the same. (In the case of Karel /r/ appeared for the first time 3;2,26 (O I, 39), in

---

[2] /r/ and /ř/ are apico-alveolar trills, and /ř/ is opposed to /r/ by its stridency; cf. H. Kučera, *The Phonology of Czech* ('s-Gravenhage, Mouton, 1961), pp. 30–31. Seen historically, /ř/ < /ŕ/, and "schon bei einer Bildung wie dem russischen ŕ entwickelt sich, bei Verstärkung des Expirationsdrucks, leicht ein spirantisches Nebengeräusch. In der Regel bleibt jedoch das russische palatalisierte r noch völlig sonor . . ." (O. Broch, *Slavische Phonetik*, Heidelberg, 1911, p. 51). Cf. also J. Vachek, "The Place of the Sound /ř/ in the Structures of Slavonic Languages," *Sbornik Praci Filosofické Fakulty Brněnské University*, 1963, A11, p. 81–92.

[3] Even the Latvian /r/ is an apico-alveolar trill, with 2–3 vibrations; /ŗ/ differs from /r/ only that even the middle portion of the tongue is raised somewhat, the tip of the tongue vibrating slightly; cf. A. Laua, *Mūsdienu latviešu literārās valodas fonētikas jautājumi* (Rīgā, 1961), p. 48; J. Endzelīns, *Latviešu valodas gramatika* (Rīgā, 1961), § 86c, pp. 180–181; ZA Valodas un literatūras institūts, *Mūsdienu latviešu literārās valodas gramatika*, I (Rīgā, 1959), § 65 (pp. 32–33), § 112 (pp. 60–61).

[4] The first part (*Zur Sprachentwicklung bei Kleinkindern*, 1: *Syntax*) was published in Lund, 1963; the other parts are being prepared for publication.

all positions first at 3;7–3;8 (O I, 39), in the case of Marie, first at 3;11–4;1 (O II, 40); Dainis learned /r/ 4;7–5;0, Sarma 4;8–4;11).[5]

Last of all the Czech /ř/ was acquired: by Marie slightly later (4;5) than by her elder brother Karel (3;10) (cf. O II, 41), but in both cases it was the last sound of all.

A partial agreement exists also as regards the distribution of the first /r/-sounds in the speech of children:

In the case of the Czech children /r/ appeared first in the sound-group /(-)tr-/ (e.g., /patro/ O I, 39; II, 40), and also in the case of the Latvian boy the real process of acquisition of /r/ began with a peculiar vibrating /l/ (as a substitute for the /r/ of normal speech) in the sound-group /tr/ (cf. /tlīs/—with the vibrant l—(= trīs 'three'), together with some other words with /tr-/ 4;2, while the first real /r/ in a similar position started with 4;7).

In the case of the Latvian girl the process of sound-development was more complicated, but even there /tri-, trī-, trie-/ were found again among the most frequent groups during the period when the /r/ was developed quickly, 4;8,16–4;8,22.

Further points of correspondence are also found regarding the sounds substituted for /r/, as well as concerning the sequence in which these substitutes occurred, before the normal /r/ was learned.

In all cases it was /l/ which appeared as the *last* substituting sound immediately before the acquisition of /r/ (O I, 39; O II, 40). As a direct consequence of this, during a certain period there appeared, immediately after the appearance of /r/, sporadic cases of hypercorrect /r/ instead of /l/ in the case of all the children, who were watched. In the speech of the Latvian girl hypercorrect forms of /r/ for /j/ were also noted, owing to the fact that the last substitutes for /r/ in her speech were /j/, /l/ and (with a short interval following thereafter) /l/.

In the case of the Czech boy, as well as those of the two Latvian children, the uvular /R/ functioned during a certain early period here and there as a substitute for /r/ (heard in the speech of their environment),[6] cf. the chronological sequence of substitutes:

Karel: h — l — ch — /r/ omitted — pause instead of /r/ — R — l — (ł) — r (O I, 39).

---

[5] The point of time thereby corresponds relatively well in the case of both the Latvian children, in spite of the fact that the girl's general speech development during the earliest years of life progressed at a somewhat slower rate than the boy's. According to the observations of the present writer, a number of Latvian children learn to pronounce this sound about a year earlier than the above-mentioned two children. According to I. and M. Bolin, "Psykologiska och språkliga iakttagelser rörande en svensk flicka," *Svenskt arkiv för pedagogik*, 8 (1920), pp. 49–50, the Swedish girl Ann-Mari learnt already at 2;11 to pronounce the /r/ of central and northern Swedish in most Swedish words.

[6] O. Jespersen, *Børnesprog* (København, Kristiania, London, Berlin, 1923), p. 19, also mentions such a uvular /R/ in the speech of children, not appearing in the normal speech in question.

Dainis: /r/ omitted — R — u̯ (v) —j ‖ u̯ (v) — i̇ j l — r.
Sarma: ρ — R — u (v) — d — j — j ‖ i̇ — l — r.

In the Czech girl's speech, on the other hand, no record of /R/ as a substitute for the rolled apical /r/ is found, cf. Marie: /r/ omitted—pause instead of /r/ – j – u̯ – (k) – l – r (O II, 40).

As regards all the three children, who used /R/ now and then during the first two years of their lives, this was nevertheless a question of a sporadic occurrence, which after six months disappeared from their speech and during a relatively long period was replaced by other substituting sounds, first attaining the correct pronunciation /r/ after a number of years, or appearing again—as in the case of the Lettish girl—as the southern Swedish uvular /R/. The chronological sequence of substitute-sounds for the Czech /r/ in the following words may serve as an illustration:

1. *aeroplan/ēroplān, ēro/*:
   ðRo 1;1,6, aʲRo 1;1,28, ð 1;1,29, ēlo 1;9, 9, ē/loplān 2;3,22, ēloplān 2;7,10, ēroplān 3;7,10 (O I, 69);
2. */papír/*:
   papi· 1;10,20, papiR 1;11,7, pa/pilet 1;11,23, papíl 2;0,21, do papíltu 2;5,28, papíl 2;9,2, na papíle 3;1,29, na papiže 3;2,7, papírek 3;6,29, na papíře 3;9,13 (O I, 122).

Quite early in the speech of small children one comes across also the bilabial /ρ/-sound, e.g., interjection /bRR/[7] in the case of Marie 1;7,17 (O II, 83). This sound occurred quite often in the case of both the Latvian children during the babbling stage, and in the case of the one-year-old girl this bilabial /ρ/ had, during a short period, the function of some meaningful words ('car,' somewhat later 'harmonicon,' 'motor,' etc.).

The rolled apical /r/, on the other hand, was never registered during the first two years of life, neither in the case of the Czech children nor in that of the Latvian children, not even during the babbling period, when occasionally even such sounds, missing in the normal language in question, emerge.

As a further observation it may be mentioned that neither the Latvian boy nor girl learned to pronounce the /r/-mouillé of Latvian, although both parents use this sound, and in spite of the fact that the children, as a result of close personal contact with the members of their family circle during the first years of their lives, assimilated all the other elements of their native language. Thus /r/ was the only Latvian sound not acquired by the children from the language of their parents, and the phonological opposition /r/:/r̦/, which characterizes the Latvian of their parents (e.g., /baru/ 'crowd' (acc.) vs. /bar̦u/ 'I scold', /garam/ 'breath, spirit, mind' (dat.) vs. /gar̦am/ 'long' (dat.)) was lacking in their speech. If, during their school-days,· they were especially

[7] Ohnesorg uses the symbol /R/ for the bilabial r; in this paper the Greek rho is used, in accordance with, e.g., R.-M. S. Heffner, *General Phonetics* (Madison, 1960), p. 136.

requested to repeat a Latvian word containing the /r/-mouillé, this sound was most frequently substituted by /R/, i.e., with the uvular sound, which the children at that time knew from their Swedish.

3. As far as I know, up to the present time nothing has appeared in linguistic literature describing the development of sounds in the case of bilingual children who, already in infancy, have learnt to speak two languages, of which one has the rolled, apical /r/ together with the opposite /r/:/ŗ/, and the other has, on the other hand, the uvular /R/.[8] I therefore consider it well justified to subject here the difficulty of the Latvian girl in assimilating these two /r/-sounds to a more detailed analysis. The distribution of /r/ and /R/ during the first stage of development of /r/-sounds deserves special interest, as such a thorough analysis can lead to conclusions having a more universal significance.

At 4;6,25 the Latvian girl was able, for the first time, to pronounce the bilabial /ρ/ in the interjection /ρū!/ which is used as a call to a horse to stop. (This sound which had appeared during an earlier period, had disappeared during 2;0-4;6, so that it had to be learned again.) Both the unvoiced and the voiced variant were repeated with enthusiasm during the following days, and the latter was maintained also in the adjective /brūns/ 'brown' instead of /br-/.

The process of assimilation of the real /r/-sound began first from and with 4;8, first with the uvular /R/ which was spoken in her southern Swedish (Skåne-dialect), but which appeared a little later also in occasional Latvian forms.

At about 4;8,8 more words with /R/ were registered in the girl's Swedish, while the /r/ in her Latvian continued to be substituted by (most frequently) /j/, /d/ or the omission of this consonant. A typical example from this period: (in answer to her mother's question as to the name of her playmate) /zviēdiski tuõ meîtiņu saûc KǎRin, latviski Kãjina/ 'the little girl is called KǎRin in Swedish and Kãjina in Latvian.'

When the girl was directly requested to say the sound /r/, she said /R/; as soon as she read[9] or articulated individual *words*, the /r/ was substituted by /j/ or some other sound, not /R/.

At 4;8,8-4;8,15 several Latvian words with /R/ appeared side by side with Swedish words with this sound. Above all /R/ was registered in such words which, in very much the same form, occur both in Latvian and Swedish,

---

[8] Some interesting observations are to be found in B. Malmberg's "Ett barn byter språk. Drag ur en fyraårig finsk flickas språkliga utveckling," *Nordisk tidskrift*, 21 (1945), pp. 170–181, dealing with the case of a four-and-a-half-year-old Finnish girl, who at that age learned to speak the dialect of Skåne and, doing so, acquired also the burred /R/ of that dialect along with or (later) instead of the apical /r/ of her mother tongue. Unfortunately, this particular question has not been dealt with more thoroughly in Malmberg's analysis.
[9] At this age interest for writing and reading was awakened, and the girl could already write (in print style) easy words and also her own name, Sarma.

e.g., in the names of persons. Some other established utterances, from 4;8,14: /kâ saûc zviẽdiski (= in Standard Latvian zviẽdriski) zeķtu.Ri?/ 'what is "corset" in Swedish?', /kâ tuôReĩz/ 'as on that occasion,' /viênā viêtâ mẽs ʒêRa:m/ 'we drank at a (certain) place.'

At 4;8,16 there emerged for the first time the rolled apical /r/ (= normal Latvian r) in forms where /r/ stands directly before /i/, /ī/, e.g., /turi 'turi Juri!/ 'catch! hold! Juris!' (a humorous play on words), /Pẽterîtis/ 'Peter' (dim.), /Jurîtis/ 'George' (dim.), /Vari, Vari, kuô tu dari?/ 'Varis, Varis (a boy's name), what are you doing?', /darīji/ 'thou didst,' /kuô tu vari, tuo tu dari!/ 'what thou canst (do), that do (thou)' and similar expressions.

On the other hand /R/ was heard in other phonetic positions, e.g., /SaRma/. Three days later the first examples with /tri-/, /kri-/, /gri-/ alongside /-aja/ or /-ala/ as a substitute for /-ara/ — with /r/ between /a/ — were established.

At 4;8,21 the substitution of other sounds for /r/ was still very inconsistent and partly depended upon the phonetic surrounding, cf. /puñči/ (with bilabial /p/ instead of /br-/) 'skirt,' /SaRma/ 'Sarma,' /saûsiņš ar siẽRu/ 'biscuits and cheese,' /griêze griêza juʒîšuos (= rudzîšuos)/ 'the corn-crake called in the rye(field),' /tã i (= ir) vienîgā Griẽtiņas kũzīte (= krūzīte), kas dẽj {(= dẽr)/ 'it is the only cup of Greta's (dim.) which will do,' /ka:dəreĩz nupikt un papasît (= kādreiz nuopirkt un paprasīt)/ 'to buy at some time and to ask,' /riti, riti, rīta jasa (= rasa)/ 'roll, turn over, morning dew' (= the beginning of a Latvian folk-song). The uvular /R/ was also heard in the spelling of isolated words.

At 4;8,22 /l/ emerged more frequently than hitherto as a substitute for /r/: /Pẽtelītis/ 'Peter' (dim.), /kalalis/ (= karalis) 'king,' /kalaliene/ (= karaliene) 'queen,' but—with /r/ omitted—/kũzīte/ (= krūzīte) 'a little cup,' /pasīt/ (= prasīt) 'to ask' and—with /R/—/man, piemẽRam/ 'me, for example,' /šuôReĩz/ 'that time.'

At 4;8,27 the girl succeeded in producing /r/ also in the sound group /ra-/, which nevertheless in the beginning sounded something like /ʰra-/ and which did not appear in all words with /ra-/, cf. two examples established the same day: /rakstīt/ 'to write' but /jaûdât/ (= raudāt) 'to cry.' With a certain amount of effort she was able to pronounce the apical /r/ even in her first name, but with a short vowel element after the /r/: /Sar'ma/ (she usually said /SaRma/).

The vacillation was in other respects quite considerable, cf. /vaĩjâkus papīrus (= vairākus papīrus)/ 'more papers,' /id' (= ir)/ 'is' 4;8,29, /baûcu ‖ braûcu ‖ blaûcu (= braucu)/ 'I drive' 4;9,0, hypercorrect forms /trĩrumā (= tīrumā)/ 'in the field' 4;9,0, /trĩras (= tīras)/ 'clean,' plur., /nᵘo rūras (= nuo jūras)/ 'from the sea' 4;9,1.

At 4;9,2 /r/ appeared instead of the earlier /R/ even when pronouncing disconnected sounds (when writing the letter /r/ and in similar situations) and also in a larger number of words both in the intervocalic position and after a consonant as well as in final position: /pⁱemẽram/ (which replaced the earlier pronunciation /pⁱemẽRam/) 'for example,' /draûsmīgi/ 'terribly,' /viênmẽr/ 'always,' /var ‖ vai̯/ 'can.'

At 4;9,8 the first example was noted with /r/ in the middle of the word after a short or long vowel immediately before the consonant: /cẹtuʳtā/ 'in the fourth,' /Kāʳlis/ 'Karl,' although this /r/ was considerably weaker than in other positions. In many other words the /r/ was still omitted before a consonant, e.g., /tuku pupa/ 'scarlet runner,' /pimdiena (= pirmdiena)/ 'Monday' 4;9,11. At this point there appeared several instances of hypernormalisms or metatheses, as, for example, /rẽriṇi (= jẽriṇi)/ 'little lambs,' /krupes (= kurpes)/ 'shoes,' /stripâk (= stiprāk)/ 'stronger,' /pagruduos (= pagudruos)/ 'shall think about.'

The point 4;10 can be designated as the border for the following period, when most of the words with /r/ in the girl's pronunciation agreed, as a rule, with the Standard Latvian norms, cf. /braûcu/ 'I drive,' /zir̃ks/ 'horse,' accusative /zir̃gu/, /sir̃c/ 'heart,' accusative /sirdu/ (= sirdi), /sprîdi/ 'span' (acc.), /ṇir̃b/ 'it glitters' 4;8,1.

Still after 4;10,15 it was possible now and again to hear isolated forms with /R/ instead of Latvian /r/, only, however, in exceptional cases. The girl's big brother immediately understood such a pronunciation as an impermissible deviation from the Latvian mother tongue, and after his ironic or humorous remarks, the girl understood immediately to correct her pronunciation to the right form with /r/. This rolled apical /r/ is retained even now in her mother tongue, and replaces even there the /r/-mouillé of Latvian (which she hears every day in her parents' Latvian but not that of her big brother).

In her Swedish the Latvian girl pronounced /R/ in complete conformity with the dialect of Skåne spoken in her surroundings, and even according to the opinion of her schoolteacher no sound occurred in her pronunciation (during the second year at school) which showed any difference between her speech and that of her schoolmates in the same class, who spoke in the dialect of Skåne. As an interesting detail it may be added that in the conversation between Sarma and her little Swedish friend, recorded on a tape 4;8,27, a sound was registered alongside /R/ similar to /h/ or /j/ (exclusively in a position before an /i/), e.g., /jiktikt/ (= riktigt) 'right,' i.e., with the same substituting sound which was used at that stage instead of the Latvian /r/.

A comparison of the acquisition of /r/ and /R/ in the speech of the Latvian girl's big brother, who came into nearer contact with the dialect of southern Sweden for the first time in school at the age of seven, can prove to be of methodological importance. The sporadically occurring bilabial /ρ/ 1;0 and 1;5 together with /R/ in disconnected forms 1;5-1;7 (e.g., /uRu 'uRu!/ interj. 1;5, /āaRā! uRu uRu!·'outdoors! urru urru!' 1;5, /muRu muRu/, interj. 1;11, /baRbâ/ (= darbā) 'at work' 1;11) vanished from the boy's speech during the second, third, and fourth years of his age, and /r/ was substituted by /j/—/v/—/l/, until at 4;2 /tlīs/ (with a vibrating /l/) appeared for the first time, and during 4;4-4;6 the rolled apical /r/ with the utmost vigorous vibrations, which with enthusiasm was demonstrated in the word /kur̃pe/ 'shoe,' somewhat later in the intervocalic position, then in /r-/ and gradually in more complicated consonant groups. After the age of five the boy pronounced /r/ in all forms in harmony with the Latvian norms. He never learned /ŗ/ at all, and substituted that sound with the same /r/, e.g., /jũra/ (= jũŗa/ in his parents' pronunciation).

His first school-teacher was from Uppsala, and spoke High Swedish, but most of the pupils in the class were from Skåne. The Latvian boy who, during the first months, could follow the language used in teaching only with great difficulty, learned Swedish during the first year at school, and assimilated even the /R/ as pronounced in Skåne (when eight years old). During a certain period this newly-acquired /R/ also appeared in some words in his Latvian. This period lasted, however, but a short time, and the distribution of /r/ and /R/ remained so, that /r/ was retained for the mother tongue while /R/ was retained for his Swedish. During the following years full use was made of these two "r"s in such a way that one or the other form of pronunciation was applied without the slightest difficulty for other foreign languages with which he came in contact, e.g., /R/ for French, /r/ for Russian, etc.

4. The results of the investigation here presented give an illuminating example of R. Jakobson's thesis that the oppositions which are seldom represented in the languages of the world are learnt last in the speech of children. This is seen most clearly in the acquisition of the Czech /ř/, which is one of the most unusual sounds in the languages of the world, and of the Latvian /ŗ/, which does not include even the whole sphere of the Latvian language (the opposition /r/:/ŗ/ is confined to a little dialect group in Latvia).

Even the assimilation of a single liquid demands a relatively long time and a certain effort on the part of the little child, and the second liquid is first learnt later as one of the last sounds in the child's speech. Still more time is necessary before the third liquid can be acquired. It can happen that children who have already learnt the opposition /l/:/r/ cannot assimilate the opposition /r/:/ŗ/ at all, despite the fact that the language of their surroundings has the latter opposition at its disposal.

The process of acquisition of the oppositions /r/:/ŗ/ and /r/:/ř/ in the speech of little children throws light upon the speech changes in, respectively, the Baltic language and the Slavonic language in question:

The frequency of /ŗ/ is extremely low in Latvian,[10] and the area with the opposition /r/:/ŗ/ diminishes in Latvia nearly each year, and includes today a considerably smaller number of dialects than was the case at the beginning of the century.[11] The new spelling reform of 1946 also bears witness to this general tendency, for this reform abolished the letter /ŗ/ from the Latvian

---

[10] V. Rūķe, "Lauthäufigkeit in der lettischen Schriftsprache," *Årsbok 1948/49* (Slaviska institutet vid Lunds universitet) (Lund, 1951), pp. 161, 162, and 164.

[11] Cf. also J. Endzelins, *Latviešu valodas gramatika* (Rīgā, 1951), § 86, pp. 180–181; V. Rūķe, "Kurzemes un Vidzemes lībiskais apgabals," *Filologu Biedrības Raksti,* 20, pp. 91–93; Valdis, J. Zeps, *Latvian and Finnic Linguistic Convergences* (Bloomington and The Hague, 1962), p. 82.

alphabet and /ŗ/ is regarded no longer as an independent phoneme, but as a facultative or individual allophone of /r/ and is represented by the same symbol /r/.

In the whole of the Balto-Slavonic language group the opposites /r/:/ŗ/ are easily nullified.[12]

Even the Czech /ř/, which is quite the last sound assimilated by Czech children, seems to be quite labile in Czech on the whole: its pronunciation often causes the schoolchildren dyslalia[13] and /ř/ becomes lost at times even in the speech of adults.[14]

The examination shows that of the two variants—the rolled apical /r/ and the uvular /R/—the latter gives cause for the less difficulties and is acquired by the little child earlier than /r/. From this point of view /R/ can be said to be an easier sound and to have a greater power of expansion.

/R/ can appear in the speech of children already at an early stage, even in those cases where this sound is missing in the speech of the environment (cf. /R/ in the cases of the Czech boy and of the two Latvian children). If the child's uvular pronunciation finds support in the speech of the environment the /R/ is acquired by the child quite quickly in all words (cf. the Latvian girl's southern Swedish pronunciation).

If such a support is lacking in the speech of the adults, the /R/ disappears from the child's speech, and the rolled /r/ is substituted again by other sounds (for example, /j/, /d/ or /l/), till the child—not unusually first of all after a long time—acquires the correct apical, vibrating /r/ in accordance with the norms of the mother tongue.

The easier pronunciation of the /R/ and its greater power of expansion explain why Swedish children acquire /R/ if only *one* of the parents has that sound in his or her speech, and why it is more usual for children from central and northern Sweden to begin to speak with a burr in surroundings where the burr is not heard, than on the contrary.[15] Therein also lies, so far as can be judged, the explanation of the rapid advance of the /R/ in Northern Europe at the cost of the rolled apical /r/.[16]

In speech contacts in infancy, where the one language has /R/ at its command and the other /r/, the /R/ has a better chance of intruding and of replacing the /r/ even in the other language. The speech development of the Latvian girl serves as a clear illustration of such a struggle between /R/ in her

---

[12] O. Broch, *Slavische Phonetik* (Heidelberg, 1911), p. 51; see also J. Vachek, "The Place of the Sound /ř/ in the Structures of Slavonic Languages," *Sbornik Prací Filosofické Fakulty Brněnské University*, 1963, A 11, p. 81.

[13] O II, p. 141.

[14] According to statements in R. Jakobson's *Kindersprache, Aphasie und allgemeine Lautgesetze*, p. 44, the Czech colonists in Russia substitute the voiced variant with ȝ and the voiceless variant with ʃ.

[15] See also V. Cederschiöld, *Barnspråk* (Stockholm, 1944), pp. 40–43.

[16] G. Sjöstedt, *Studier över r-ljuden i sydskandinaviska mål* (Lund, 1936), p. 221 ff.

southern Swedish and /r/ in her Latvian mother tongue. It took some time before the /R/ sound, which had extended even to a certain number of Latvian words, disappeared again from the girl's Latvian and was replaced by the normal Latvian rolled, apical /r/.

This analysis of an individual case explains the speech phenomenon occurring and quite widespread in southern Sweden, that children speaking both a Baltic language and southern Swedish easily adopt just this uvular /R/, even in their mother tongue (which has /r/).

Many examples in the above-mentioned analysis show that this sound borrowing begins easiest of all in such words which sound almost the same in both languages in contact, i.e., where the pronunciation of the /r-R/-sound is (practically) the only one which makes a difference in forms with the same meaning in both languages, e.g., Swedish *Karlsson*—Latvian *Karlsons*, Swedish *karta*—Latvian *karte*, Swedish *grupp*—Latvian *grupa*, Swedish *giraff*—Latvian *žirafe*.

It would be worth while to investigate as to whether the *phonetic* borrowing element in the case of bilingual individuals on the whole does not have its beginning in just such words which occur in both languages in approximately the same form. The general observation that it is usual to take over borrowing elements from a structurally similar language easier than from a more remote language also appears to indicate that such can be the case.

Part Two

GRAMMAR

The topic headings in this volume serve organizational rather than theoretical purposes. The clean breaks between "phonology," "syntax," and "semantics" have no correspondingly clear reality in linguistic theory or practice. The reader will find material on grammar in the first section of the book—especially in the papers by Chao and Burling. Matters of phonology reappear in the remainder of the volume. And the line between syntax and semantics can barely be drawn at all. Broadly speaking, the papers in the second part of the book deal with the ways in which the child constructs and combines words to express meaning. There are numerous recent works which the reader can explore in order to acquire a rudimentary feeling for questions of grammar. Among them are: Bolinger (1968), Dinneen (1967), Jacobs and Rosenbaum (1968, 1970), Langacker (1968), and Lyons (1968, 1970). The first part of the paper by Brown, Cazden, and Bellugi, reprinted here, provides a useful orientation to transformational grammar and its application to analysis of child language, and the paper by Antinucci and Parisi provides an introduction to generative semantics.

The first paper in Part II is an attempt by one of the editors (Slobin) to integrate the growing literature on grammatical development into a theoretical framework combining psychology and linguistics. Findings on the acquisition of some 40 different native languages contribute to the formulation of "suggested universals in the ontogenesis of grammar" which the reader can check against the papers in this volume and against future research. Slobin's paper provides a theoretical and bibliographical background to the second part of the anthology. (The references to Slobin's paper are included in the general bibliography at the end of the volume.)

169

The remaining papers in the volume represent a broad range of issues, research methods, and languages, spanning a time range from children born before World War I to children born during the Vietnam War. Several major themes can be traced through these papers. All of the investigators are committed to the position that child speech reflects underlying mental structures of some sort. As Klima and Bellugi put it (p. 341): "It has seemed to us that the language of children has its own systematicity, and that the sentences of children are not just an imperfect copy of those of an adult." The central problems are how to characterize this systematicity and how to account for its development and eventual convergence with the structures of adult language.

If one were to arrange the following papers chronologically by date of writing, one would have a fair summary of the development of linguistics in the twentieth century. There is a curious curvilinearity in this history, as there is in much of the history of social science. The early diarists (Guillaume, Gvozdev, and others not reprinted here) are just as concerned with *what* the child is trying to say as *how* he is saying it.[1] Though unsystematic in their semantics and their psychology, they are concerned with linking linguistic development to mental development in the child. They are also concerned with relating the processes of language development in the child with the historical processes of language change.[2] These questions of semantic intent, cognitive development, and language change are with us again, illuminated by new developments in current psychology and linguistics. Between these two ends of the curve lies the period of emergence and development of the systematic psycholinguistic study of child language in the late fifties and early and mid-sixties—a period in which there was far more attention to the *form* of child speech than to its *content* and *function*.

Around 1960, three similar projects were launched, studying the beginning stages of grammatical development in American children. The investigators were Roger Brown, Colin Fraser, and Ursula Bellugi at Harvard; Susan Ervin (now Ervin-Tripp) and Wick Miller at Berkeley; and Martin Braine at Walter Reed, in Maryland. Key papers from these three projects are included in the section on English syntax. (For the beginning stage of the Harvard project, see Brown and Fraser [1963].) When the first findings were publicized, it became clear that the three projects had independently arrived at very similar descriptions of the structure of two-word utterances. The descriptions, arising from the practices of taxonomic grammar, were based on patterns of word distribution in recorded utterances. Word classes were distinguished and rules of combination proposed. The same sorts of classes and rules emerged in the three studies (compare

[1] Among the diarists, Lewis (1936, 1937) is especially sensitive to questions of semantic development. See Blumenthal (1970) for a valuable historical account of child language study.

[2] This question of ontogenetic-phylogenetic parallelism is also evident in more recent European writing (Rūķe-Draviņa, reprinted below; and Slama-Cazacu, 1962).

Braine's "pivots" and "X-words," Miller and Ervin's "operators" and "non-operators," and Brown and Fraser's "functors" and "contentives"). This was a definite advance from earlier descriptions of child language, in that the classes and rules were based on independent analysis of child speech samples, rather than simply transferred from adult grammar. The "child as linguist" came into his own and has been growing and changing ever since, with the growth and changes in linguistic theory.

A central question—which remains with us—is the question of what is learned by the child. The answers go from (1) Braine's "structural formulae" and Miller and Ervin's "relatively systematic arrangement of classes" through (2) Brown, Cazden, and Bellugi's "system of rules that derives an infinite set of well-formed sentences and assigns them correct structural descriptions" to (3) Bloom's "inherent semantic relations that underlie the juxtaposition of words" and Antinucci and Parisi's "set of well-formed semantic representations and . . . the means for mapping these representations onto surface structures."

Braine (1963a) at first attempted to answer this question of what is learned in terms of psychological learning theory, proposing that the child learns the positions of words in sentence frames. This led to a heated exchange with proponents of transformational grammar (Bever, Fodor, and Weksel, 1965a,b; Braine, 1965)—a controversy which seems to have benignly died away as developmental psycholinguists became more involved with developments in transformational grammar (but see Staats [1971] for a current exposition of an orthodox behaviorist approach to language acquisition). The studies moved from surface structure descriptions and simple phrase structure rules to considerations of transformations—first from the vantage point of Chomsky's *Syntactic structures* (1957) (see the papers in this volume by Klima and Bellugi, Miller, Ervin-Tripp), and then from the vantage point of "*Aspects*" (Chomsky, 1965) (see Brown, Cazden, and Bellugi, below). The concern shifted to the child's knowledge of transformational rules, and it became clear that the course of syntactic development could be explained, in part, in terms of increasing complexity of the rules underlying child speech (Brown, Cazden, and Bellugi; Klima and Bellugi; Miller; Braine ["Three suggestions . . ."]).

As the characterization of what is learned changed, the debate about how it is learned changed as well. Since transformation rules and linguistic deep structures cannot be immediately perceived in the speech the child hears, the problem of accounting for the acquisition of grammar became more complex. A debate on "nativism" versus "empiricism" began in the mid-sixties (see Chomsky, 1965, 1966, 1968; Katz, 1966; papers in Hayes [1970], Slobin [1971], Smith and Miller [1966]) and continues on subtly shifting ground, becoming more and more concerned with acquisition models and processing strategies (see Bever, 1970a,c, 1971; Braine, 1971a; Ervin-Tripp, 1970a; Roeper, below; Slobin, below).

By the end of the decade, however, transformational grammar itself was changing rapidly, as linguists became more and more troubled with the place of semantics in their theories (see the papers in Fillmore and Langendoen, 1971; Jacobs and Rosenbaum, 1970; Lyons, 1970). Developmental psycholinguists began to feel that much had been omitted from their structural descriptions of child speech, and they began once again to pose questions of meaning and semantic intent (see the papers below, under the headings "The Two-Word Stage Reconsidered" and "Semantics"). It is instructive to compare the paper by Miller and Ervin-Tripp, written in 1961, with Bloom's paper, based on her 1968 dissertation. Miller and Ervin note in passing the phenomenon of "structural homonymity"—namely, that the same structure can have more than one meaning in child speech: *Susan sweater on* meant 'Susan has her sweater on,' while *Mommy sweater on* meant 'Mommy, put my sweater on me.' What was an uncomfortable sidelight in distributional analysis becomes a crucial example in semantic analysis. Bloom uses a similar example (*Mommy sock* in either a possessive or subject-object meaning) to show that the child's underlying semantic intentions are richer than the surface form of his utterances and proposes a transformational apparatus to go from semantically interpretable deep structure to phonologically interpretable surface structure in child speech. The new attention to semantic intent, unlike the early diary studies (for example, Guillaume), does not pass over the complexities of grammatical structure. Attention is devoted both to surface structures and to underlying semantic structures.

We are now at a stage of search for adequate and sufficiently rich models of child language. Brown's paper proposes a taxonomy of "structural meanings" (see Blount, 1969; Kernan, 1969; Schlesinger, 1971; Slobin, 1970). McNeill speaks of the central role played by the "basic grammatical relations." The question of the functions of utterances re-emerges (see Gruber's "performative" and "reportative" utterances, Brown's "operations of reference" and "relations," Antinucci and Parisi's "requests" and "descriptions," Braine's "ostensive" and "predicative" sentences). Eve Clark asks about "the pragmatic and semantic reasons for a child's choice of one syntactic form over another in a particular situation" (see also Huttenlocher, Eisenberg, and Straus, 1968; Huttenlocher and Straus, 1968; Slobin, 1966c, 1968b; Turner and Rommetveit, 1967). Most recently, Antinucci and Parisi, working from a generative semantics framework, go below the level of words, seeking underlying "semantic configurations" which can be "lexicalized" in various ways in various languages and contexts. (And, beyond the confines of this book, the old question of child language and language change has re-emerged in a new light—for example, see Kiparsky [1968, 1970], Bever and Langendoen [1972].)

There are a number of structural aspects of child language which are examined repeatedly in the various papers gathered together here, and the interested reader may wish to hunt some of them down in detail with the help of the following brief "index" of central questions. (For authors represented more than once in this anthology, a subscript indicates which paper is referred to.)

Meaning of first words: Antinucci and Parisi; Braine$_2$; Gruber; Guillaume$_2$
Meaningful use of stress and intonation: Braine$_1$; Burling; Chao; Engel$_1$; Miller and Ervin-Tripp; Tonkova-Yampol'skaya
Ability to segment utterances into linguistic units: Bogoyavlenskiy; Borgström; Brown, Cazden, and Bellugi; Burling; Guillaume$_2$
Negation: Bloom; Brown, Cazden, and Bellugi; Klima and Bellugi; McNeill and McNeill;' Miller
Question formation: Brown, Cazden, and Bellugi; Chao; Klima and Bellugi; Miller
Sentence conjunction: Clark; El'konin

A problem of structural analysis which has barely been faced, however, is the feasibility of using linguistic theory as a model for the mental structures underlying child speech (or, for that matter, adult speech). The issue of "psychological reality" of linguistic models is a deep and general problem in psycholinguistics. Watt (1970) has cogently argued that "mental grammar" does not equal "linguistic grammar." But such arguments have yet to be fully elaborated in developmental psycholinguistics.

In addition to concern with *structure*, another major theme runs through the papers below—the theme of *process*. How does the child come to know his language? The processes which have been most commonly cited—imitation and reinforcement—receive ample attention and turn out to be of marginal significance. We have devoted an entire section to papers on imitation, and we point out some of the key issues in the introduction to that section. The roles of parental input and parental feedback are thoroughly explored by Cazden and by Brown, Cazden, and Bellugi, who come to the conclusion that: "It seems, then, to be truth value rather than syntactic well-formedness that chiefly governs explicit verbal reinforcement by parents—which renders mildly paradoxical the fact that the usual product of such a training schedule is an adult whose speech is highly grammatical but not notably truthful" (p. 330).

Along with the development of theoretical questions in developmental psycholinguistics, there has been an impressive development of research methods. The increasing attention to meaning has brought techniques for recording and assessing situational variables and the child's comprehension of speech. Ingenious means have been devised for eliciting speech from children and for determining what aspects of linguistic messages are attended to. In the papers which follow, the reader will find a great array of research techniques for determining what children can say and, to a lesser extent, what they can understand. As yet, however, there have been only beginning attempts to relate all of these tasks and skills to more general issues of cognitive and perceptual development (see Bever, 1970a; McNeill, 1970). The following paper makes a preliminary attempt at bringing these many issues together.   —D.I.S.

Cognitive Prerequisites for the Development of Grammar[1]

—— *Dan I. Slobin*

Every normal human child constructs for himself the grammar of his native language. It is the task of developmental psycholinguistics to describe and attempt to explain the intricate phenomena which lie beneath this simple statement. These underlying phenomena are essentially cognitive. In order for the

Revised version of "Developmental psycholinguistics," in *A survey of linguistic science*, edited and copyright by William Orr Dingwall. College Park: University of Maryland/ Linguistics Program, pp. 298–400. Reprinted by permission of William Orr Dingwall.
[1] The growth of the ideas set forth in this paper has been greatly stimulated by discussion with many students and colleagues. It is a pleasure to acknowledge some of them here: H. David Argoff, Melissa F. Bowerman, Ursula Bellugi, Thomas G. Bever, Roger Brown, L. Dezső, Susan Ervin-Tripp, John Gumperz, Paul Kay, Jonas Langer, David McNeill, Melanie Mikeš, Lubisa Radulović, Grace Wales Shugar, Peyton Todd, Plemenka Vlahović. Part of the work reflected here has been supported by the Language-Behavior Research Laboratory of the University of California at Berkeley, which is supported by PHS Research Grant No. 1 RO1 MH 18188-02 from the National Institute of Mental Health. This support is gratefully acknowledged. This paper was originally presented at the Fifth Meeting of the Southeastern Conference on Linguistics (SECOL V), University of Maryland, May 9, 1971. My thanks to the organizer of that meeting, William Orr Dingwall, for allowing me to reprint this paper here.
    The references to this paper are included in the general bibliography at the end of the volume.

175

child to construct a grammar: (1) he must be able to cognize the physical and social events which are encoded in language, and (2) he must be able to process, organize, and store linguistic information. That is, the cognitive prerequisites for the development of grammar relate to both the *meanings* and the *forms* of utterances. This paper represents a preliminary attempt to explore these cognitive prerequisites in the light of cross-linguistic comparison of the ontogenesis of grammar.[2]

The past decade in developmental psycholinguistics has brought a vast increase in our knowledge of how English-speaking children acquire their native language.[3] The present decade promises to place those findings in broader perspective. Developmental psycholinguists are beginning to reach out to other language communities, in order to study children acquiring other native languages and in order to make contact with the findings of foreign colleagues (see table). At the same time we are beginning to relate our work to the psychology of perceptual and cognitive development (see papers in Hayes, 1970). Developmental psycholinguistics is thus moving from particularism to universalism in two significant ways: from the particularism of English to the acquisition of language in general, and from the particularism of linguistic development to cognitive development in general. We are just beginning to sense the intimate relations between linguistic universals and cognitive universals, and are far from an adequate developmental theory of either.

The psychology of cognitive development promises an eventual universal theory of the growth of the mind (see, for example, papers in Mussen, 1970). The psycholinguistic aspects of this theory will require detailed information on the acquisition of a variety of native languages. The value of cross-linguistic comparison, of course, is to avoid drawing conclusions about child language development which may, in fact, be limited to the acquisition of languages like English. The hope is to find similar developmental processes in different sorts of languages. At present, we have suggestive acquisition data on at least 40 languages from 14 or so major language families (see table). Although the data for most of these languages are still rather scanty, striking developmental uniformities can be discerned (Bowerman, 1970; Braine, 1971b; Slobin, 1970). To the extent that a universal course of linguistic development can be confirmed, a language-free acquisition model is called for (see Bever, 1970a; and papers in Slobin, 1971b). Such a model bases itself on the assumption that the child brings certain operating principles to bear on the task of learning to speak,

---

[2] For background on the methods and results of the Berkeley cross-cultural studies of language development see: Blount, 1969; Ervin-Tripp, 1969, 1971; Kernan, 1969; Slobin, 1967, 1969a, 1970; Stross, 1969, 1970; Talmy, 1970.

[3] The research on English child language development carried out in the sixties is too vast to list in a bibliographical footnote. The interested reader can find broad bibliographical coverage and valuable comment in the following recent and forthcoming publications: Braine, 1971b; Brown, in press; Ervin-Tripp, (forthcoming); Hayes, 1970; McNeill, 1970; Menyuk, 1969; Slobin, 1971b; and, of course, in this volume.

regardless of the peculiarities of the particular language he is exposed to. In this paper I will present some first guesses as to the nature of some of these operating principles.

My major concern here is with the *order* of development of various grammatical devices and with the child's strategies for organizing language. This focus leaves aside the problems of how language *begins* in the child, and why linguistic universals exist. That is, I take for granted the fact that all human children are able to learn language, and ask: Are there common orders of acquisition of different linguistic features across languages?

AVAILABLE MATERIAL ON THE ACQUISITION OF 40 DIFFERENT NATIVE
LANGUAGES*

INDO-EUROPEAN FAMILY
  Romance Branch

Romanian:	Slama-Cazacu (1957, 1960, 1962, 1968)
Italian:	Antinucci and Parisi (1972, in press); Frontali (1943–1944); Parisi (in press); Parisi and Antinucci (1970)
French:	Bloch (1913, 1921, 1924); Cohen (1925, 1933, 1962); de Boysson-Bardies and Mehler (1969); Ferreiro (1971); Ferreiro and Sinclair (1971); Grégoire (1937, 1947); Guillaume (1927a,b); Pichevin (1968); Sinclair-de-Zwart (1967)
Spanish:	Gili y Gaya (1960); Kernan and Blount (1966)

  Germanic Branch

English:	(See footnote 3.)
Dutch:	Kaper (1959)
German:	Ament (1899); Lindner (1882, 1885, 1898, 1906); Grimm (1971); Park (1970); Roeper (1972a,b); Scupin and Scupin (1907); Stern and Stern (1907)
Danish:	Jespersen (1916); Rasmussen (1913, 1923)
Swedish:	Bolin and Bolin (1916, 1920); Söderbergh (1971)
Norwegian:	Borgström (1954); Ravem (1968, 1970)

  Slavic Branch

Russian:	Bogoyavlenskiy (1957); Dingwall and Tuniks (in press); El'konin (1958); Feofanov (1958, 1962); Gvozdev (1948, 1949); Karpova (1955, 1967); Leont'yev (1969); Markova (1969); Menchinskaya (1957); Mukhina (1969); Pavlova (1924); Popova (1958); Rozengart-Pupko (1963); Slobin (1966a,b; 1968c); Sokhin (1959); Ushakova (1970); Zakharova (1958)
Polish:	Kaczmarek (1953); Pfanhauser (1930); Shugar (1971); Skorupka (1949); Smoczyński (1955); Szuman (1968); Wawrowska (1938); Zarębina (1955)

AVAILABLE MATERIAL ON THE ACQUISITION OF 40 DIFFERENT NATIVE
LANGUAGES*—continued

INDO-EUROPEAN FAMILY

	Czech:	Pačesová (1968); Průcha (1971); Sedláčková (1967)
	Slovenian:	Kolarič (1959)
	Serbo-Croatian:	Mikès (1967, 1971); Mikeš and Vlahović (1966); Pavlovitch (1920); Radulović (forthcoming)
	Bulgarian:	Denev (1969); Gheorgov (1905, 1906, 1908); Kospartova (1969); Manova-Tomova (1969)

Baltic Branch

    Latvian: Rūķe-Draviņa (1959, 1963)

Greek Branch

    Greek: Drachman and Malikouti-Drachman (1971)

Armenian Branch

    Armenian: Geodakyan and Kurginyan (1970); Tutundzhyan (1971)

Indo-Iranian Branch

    Hindi: Christian (1971b)

    Gujarati: Christian (1971a)

    Bhojpuri: Christian (1971b)

SEMITIC FAMILY

    Hebrew: Bar-Adon (1971); Grossman and Scholes (1971); Scholes and Grossman (in press)

    Arabic: Omar (1970)

SOUTH CAUCASIAN FAMILY

    Georgian: Imedadze (1960)

URALIC FAMILY

    Hungarian: Balassa (1893); Dezső (1970); Deže and Vlahović (in press); Endrei (1913); Kelemen (1970); Kenyeres (1926, 1927); MacWhinney (forthcoming); Meggyes (1971); Mikès (1967, 1971); Mikeš and Vlahović (1966); Mikes and Matijevics (1971); Simonyi (1906)

    Finnish: Argoff (forthcoming); Bowerman (1970)

    Estonian: Vihman (1971)

TURKIC FAMILY

    Turkish: Slobin (in preparation)

KOREAN FAMILY

    Korean: Park (1969)

JAPANESE-RYUKYUAN FAMILY

    Japanese: Kuniya (1969); McNeill (1966a); McNeill and McNeill (1968); McNeill et al. (1971); Murai (1970); Murato (1968); Nakazima (1969–1970); Ohwaki (1933); Okubo (1967); Sanches (1968, 1970); Takahashi (1967)

HAN CHINESE FAMILY

    Mandarin: Chao (1951)

AVAILABLE MATERIAL ON THE THE ACQUISITION OE 40 DIFFERENT NATIVE
LANGUAGES*—*continued*

BODO-NAGA-KACHIN FAMILY
Garo:	Burling (1959)

AUSTRONESIAN FAMILY
Samoan:	Kernan (1969, 1970); Talmy (1970)
Lun Bawang [Murût]:	Garman, Griffiths and Wales (1970)

EASTERN SUDANIC FAMILY
Luo:	Blount (1969, 1970, 1971)

ATHAPASCAN FAMILY
Navaho:	Spolsky (1970)

MAYAN FAMILY
Tzeltal:	Stross (1969, 1970)

QUECHUMARAN PHYLUM
Quechua:	Solberg (1971)

NATURAL SIGN
American Sign Language:	Bellugi and Klima (in preparation); Schlesinger and Meadow (1971)

---

* This is not a complete list of all available material; for fuller bibliographical information see Slobin (1967, 1972) and Slama-Cazacu (1969). In addition to the languages listed above, I am aware of ongoing research on the following 13 native languages: Slovak, Ukrainian, Albanian, Persian, Kurdish, Tamil, Koya, Thai, Tagalog, Tok Pisin (Neo-Melanesian), Swahili, Zulu, and Yucatec Maya. A listing of ongoing investigations and addresses of researchers can be found in Appendix A of Slobin's bibliography (1972). The language classification (with the exception of American Sign Language) comes from Voegelin and Voegelin (1966).

LANGUAGE-DEFINITIONAL UNIVERSALS

In order to begin at this point, therefore, it is necessary to take as given what may be referred to as "language-definitional" universals. That is to say, children (and adults) everywhere have the same general definition of the form and function of language. Everywhere language consists of utterances performing a universal set of communicative functions (such as asserting, denying, requesting, ordering, and so forth), expressing a universal set of underlying semantic relations, and using a universal set of formal means (such as combinable units of meaning, made up of combinable units of sound, etc.). Furthermore, language —everywhere—is grammatical, in the sense that the meaning of a message is not fully determined by any combination of the meanings of its elements. In all language which I will consider—child and adult—there is a non-direct relation between the surface, acoustic form of messages and their underlying meanings. It is in no way surprising that children should define language in the same way as adults: indeed, they could not learn language if they did not share this definition. In fact, one could argue that human language could not be so defined if it were not so defined by children, because, in a profound sense, language is created anew by children in each generation. Language-definitional universals are what David McNeill calls "strong linguistic universals," and I follow his proposition that such universals reflect "a specific linguistic ability and may not be a reflection of a cognitive ability at all" (1970, p. 74). While much argument has centered on the issue as to whether language-definitional universals are innate, I will avoid this issue here, and merely point to them as basic linguistic capacities which are prerequisites to the questions which I want to consider (cf. Bever's "basic linguistic capacities" [1970a]). We will meet the child at the point when he knows there are meaningful words which can be combined to produce meaningful utterances. And at this point we will pose the queston advanced above: Are there common orders of acquisition of different linguistic features across languages?

CONTENT AND FORM IN CHILD SPEECH

The first and most obvious point that comes to mind is that language is used to express the child's cognitions of his environment—physical and social—and so a child cannot begin to use a given linguistic form meaningfully until he is able to understand what it means. It should be possible, then, to rank linguistic forms in terms of the psychological, or cognitive complexity of the notions they express. For example, no one would expect a child to be able to form conditionals before he could make assertions, to make statements about time before making statements about place, and so on. Is it possible, then, to trace out a universal course of linguistic development on the basis of what we know about the universal course of cognitive development? (Can one take Piaget as a handbook of psycholinguistic development?)

In fact, many such expectations (including those suggested above) are supported by data. The earliest grammatical markers to appear in child speech seem to express the most basic notions available to the child mind. For example, in languages which provide a vocative inflection, this is typically one of the earliest grammatical markers to emerge in child speech (Hungarian, Serbo-Croatian [Mikès, 1967; Mikeš and Vlahović, 1966]; Polish [Shugar, 1971]). One of the earliest semantic relations to be formally marked in child speech is that of verb-object. In order languages, like English, this relation is marked early by consistent word order. In languages which provide an inflection for marking the object of action (accusative), this is typically an extremely early inflection to emerge—often the first (Finnish [Argoff, forthcoming], Latvian [Rūķe-Draviņa, 1959, 1963], Russian [Gvozdev, 1949; Imedadze, 1960]). In Luo the first inflections are subject and object affixes on verbs (Blount, 1969). In every language for which relevant data are available, there is an early form of negation in which a negative particle is affixed to a simple sentence. In languages as diverse as English, Arabic, Czech, Latvian, Japanese, and Samoan, early yes-no questions are formed by rising intonation.

Numerous findings such as these offer support for the notion that the first linguistic forms to appear in child speech will be those which express meanings consistent with the child's level of cognitive development. But striking surprises occur in some languages. For example, yes-no questions in adult Finnish are not formed by rising intonation, but by attachment of a question particle to the word questioned and movement of that word to the front of the sentence. And, strangely enough, Melissa Bowerman, in her recent dissertation on Finnish acquisition (1970), reports that little Finnish children simply do not ask yes-no questions—at least not in any formally marked way. And Margaret Omar, in a recent disseration on the acquisition of Egyptian Arabic (1970), reports that the noun plural "is the most difficult and latest aspect of the language structure to be mastered; older children in this study erred in pluralizing even familiar nouns" (p. 367). And older children, in her study, meant children as old as 15! The reason apparently lies in the extreme complexity of plural marking in Arabic. Briefly: there is a small class of regular plurals, but most nouns fall into a large number of fairly irregular classes in regard to plural formation. There is also a special dual form; a distinction between pluralizing "counted" and "collected" nouns (for example, "trees" as a group, or "trees" as a collection of individual trees); what is more, the numerals 3–10 take the noun in the plural, while numerals above 11 take the singular.

So although one can talk about order of acquisition in terms of semantic or cognitive complexity, there is clearly a point at which formal linguistic complexity also plays a role. I think we can learn a good deal from discovering just what constitutes formal linguistic complexity for the child. If we can order linguistic devices in terms of their acquisition complexity, we can begin to understand the strategies used by the child in arriving at the grammar of his language. To put it the other way, a definition of what is simple for a child to acquire is a definition of the child's first guess as to the nature of language. The child must successively modify such first guesses until he ends up with the conception of language shared by the adults in his community.

Studies of bilingual children yield valuable suggestions as to what sorts of formal devices may be simpler to acquire than others. If a given meaning receives expression at the same time in both languages of a bilingual child, this suggests that the formal devices in the two languages are similar in complexity. For example, Imedadze (1960), studying the linguistic development of her Russian-Georgian bilingual daughter, noted the simultaneous emergence of the genitive and the instrumental in both languages. She concludes that: "The ease of acquisition and the simultaneous appearance of these forms of the genitive and instrumental cases can only be attributed to the fact that these forms express the very same semantic relationships in analogous fashion [in Russian and Georgian]."

If a given semantic domain receives expression earlier in one of the two languages, a difference in formal complexity is suggested. A useful example comes from studies by Melanie Mikeš and Plemenka Vlahović of Serbo-

Croatian—Hungarian bilingual children in Northern Yugoslavia (Mikès, 1967; Mikeš and Vlahović, 1966). Well before they were two years of age, two bilingual girls were productively and appropriately using a variety of Hungarian case endings on nouns indicating such locative relations as illative, elative, sublative, and superessive—that is, in plain English, the children were using inflections to express the directional notions of 'into,' 'out of,' and 'onto,' and the positional notion of "on top of.' At the same time they had barely begun to develop locative expressions in Serbo-Croatian, which requires a locative preposition before the noun along with some case inflection attached to the end of the noun.

Now, the fact that this cross-linguistic discrepancy occurs *within* a single child speaking both languages, rather than between two monolingual children, poses a central question in clear focus: When the child speaks Hungarian, she appropriately uses directional and positional locative inflections, and one is confident to credit her with the semantic intentions to express such notions as 'into,' 'onto,' and so forth. What are we to say of the same child, however, when she fails to grammatically signal such intentions with the corresponding prepositions when speaking Serbo-Croatian? It seems clear to me that if, for example, she puts a doll into a drawer, saying, in Serbo-Croatian, "doll drawer," we must credit her with the same semantic intention as when, describing the same situation in Hungarian, she adds an illative inflection to the word for 'drawer.'

The point I am trying to make, of course, does not depend on the child's bilingualism. The example merely illuminates the general proposition that a child's underlying semantic intentions can contain more information than his surface utterance. The speech of very young children is nearly always interpretable in context, and the very young child is neither able nor feels constrained to express his total intention in a single utterance. Lois Bloom (1970) has made this point abundantly clear in her recent book describing early grammatical development in three American children. For example, a child said "Mommy sock" in two different situations: when mommy was putting a sock on her, and when she picked up mommy's sock. Bloom is confident in labelling the utterance in the first situation as "subject-object," and the second as "genitive," and I think she is right. Previous descriptions of children's grammar were too bound to surface characterizations of word distribution, and failed to differentiate between the several meanings of homonymous utterances, such as "Mommy sock" (e.g., Braine, 1963b; Brown and Fraser, 1963; Miller and Ervin, 1964). More recent approaches to child language (and to linguistic theory) pay increasing attention to the semantic substratum of speech, and to the functions of utterances (e.g., Antinucci and Parisi, this volume; Bloom, 1970; Blount, 1969; Bowerman, 1970; Brown, in press; E. Clark, 1970, 1971, this volume; H. Clark, 1970; Cromer, 1968; Ervin-Tripp, 1970a,b, 1971; Kernan, 1969; Parisi and Antinucci, 1970; Schlesinger, 1971; Slobin, 1970; Talmy, 1970).

To sum up thus far: Cognitive development and linguistic development do

not run off in unison. The child must find linguistic means to express his intentions. The means can be easily accessible (as, for example, the Hungarian
locative), or quite unaccessible (as, for example, the Finnish yes-no question or
the Arabic noun plural). The problem is: What makes a given linguistic means
of expression more or less accessible to the child?

In posing the question in these terms, I am assuming that there is a fairly
autonomous development of intentions to express various semantic notions.
This claim must be defended before answering the questions of relative access-
ibility of formal linguistic devices, for one may be tempted to pose the counter-
argument that grammar plays a leading role in cognitive development.

THE PRIMACY OF COGNITIVE DEVELOPMENT

Let us return to the Hungarian–Serbo-Croatian bilingual example, and
agree that we will assess semantic intention on the basis of the use of utterances
in clear contexts, and not on superficial linguistic marking of such intentions.
We will probably find, on deeper investigation, that the child intends to express
the same locative relations when speaking either language. (The only alternative
to this approach would be to claim that the problem of expressing locatives in
Serbo-Croatian is such a bother to him that he avoids speaking of moving and
placing objects when speaking Serbo-Croatian. I think this alternative can be
safely rejected—though it is, of course, open to investigation.)

Why the precocious marking of locative expressions in Hungarian, then?
One line of argument would be to say that the abundance of clear locative
inflections in Hungarian drew the child's attention to the relevant notions, and
that he learned them earlier than if he had been speaking only Serbo-Croatian.
This is a sort of Whorfian notion of linguistic determinism on the grammatical
level, and I think it will turn out to be false when all the data are in. It seems
unlikely that the structure of a particular language would draw attention more
clearly to the possibilities of putting in, taking out, and so on, than would a
child's everyday experience. It is difficult to imagine children *not* talking about
such things. And, in fact, the cross-linguistic data suggest that children begin to
express basic locative notions by noun-noun and noun-verb combinations at
the two-word stage in all languages. Two-word utterances in Serbo-Croatian,
Bulgarian, Russian, English, Finnish, Hebrew, and Samoan all seem to express
the notions of 'in' and 'into,' 'on' and 'onto,' and 'from'—at first with no
inflections or prepositions. This can be quite reliably assessed from context, as
when a Russian child said the equivalent of "pot stove," pointing to a pot on
the stove; when Roger Brown's famous "Adam" said "put box" when putting
something into a box; and so on. In addition, locative notions are expressed
at early stages by prolocatives and demonstratives, such as the English "there,"
"innere," "on," and the like, and their equivalents in Bulgarian (Gheorgov,
1908), German (Leopold, 1939; Park, 1970), Finnish (Argoff, forthcoming), and
other languages.

Furthermore, the order of acquisition of locatives seems quite certainly to be based on a sequence of cognitive development which goes beyond language. For example, Parisi and Antinucci (1970), following the work of Piaget, suggest an order of acquisition of locatives based on the development of spatial notions from simple topological notions (expressed by terms like "in" and "on"), to locatives involving notions of dimensional or Euclidean space (like "in front of," "below," "beside"), to locatives expressing more complex spatial notions (like "along" and "through"). They present some preliminary evidence from Italian children supporting this order of acquisition, and all of the cross-linguistic work of which I am aware supports a sequence such as this.

If the order of acquisition of locative notions is an aspect of general cognitive development, it does not seem likely to me that the development of these notions is very amenable to linguistic manipulation. Although the general question is not at all closed, a good deal of work emanating from Piaget's research institute in Geneva suggests that the rate of cognitive development cannot be significantly altered by teaching the child the vocabulary needed in order to function at a higher level of cognitive development (Sinclair-de-Zwart, 1967, 1969). On the basis of current findings and theory (Furth, 1969; Piaget, 1967, 1970), it seems to me that the pacesetter in linguistic growth is the child's cognitive growth, as opposed to an autonomous linguistic development which can then reflect back on cognition. As Piaget has put it: ". . . language is not enough to explain thought, because the structures that characterize thought have their roots in action and in sensorimotor mechanisms that are deeper than linguistics" (1967, p. 98).[4]

The argument that language is used to express only what the child already knows can be supported by another line of evidence, coming from an examination of linguistic development from both a *formal* and a *functional* point of view. Studies which have considered the supposed intended meanings of children's utterances support a far-reaching principle which could be phrased as follows: *New forms first express old functions, and new functions are first expressed by old*

---

[4] A related argument for the primacy of cognitive development comes from linguistic analyses of Samoan child speech carried out by Talmy (1970). In one of the first studies to apply a complex modern semantic theory to child language data, Talmy was repeatedly impressed by the children's early command of semantic rules. He notes (pp. 12–13): ". . . it is clear . . . that the children make many grammatical errors—often in omitting functor words and affixes—and make few semantic errors—either in the assignment of correctly delimited ranges and correctly filled-in componentry to lexical items, or in applying these lexical items correctly to realworld events. . . . Apparently the developing child achieves a close approximation of the adult semantic map and its use before he does the same for the adult grammar. One might tentatively conclude that the human language-acquisition mechanism is geared to a primacy and integrity in content-words and a secondariness in grammatical form, is sooner attuned to a control over organically-interrelated implicit components than to the expression of temporally-concatenated overt components, and is organized to manifest the expressively meaningful before the mechanical aspects of communication."

forms. It turns out that this is a familiar principle in the psychology of cognitive development, and it is not surprising to find it in linguistic development as well. For example, Werner and Kaplan state (1963, p. 60):

> wherever functional shifts occur during development, the novel function is first executed through old, available forms; sooner or later, of course, there is a pressure towards the development of new forms which are of a more function-specific character, i.e., that will serve the new function better than the older forms.

Numerous examples could be offered from grammatical development in support of this principle. I will mention only a few.

We already have the locative example. The use of utterances in context indicates that locative relations are intended; when the appropriate new forms enter—be they prepositions, postpositions, inflections, or what have you—they will be new forms expressing old functions.

Roger Brown (in press, Chap. II, pp. 120–121) has performed a detailed analysis of the emergence of inflections in the English of the three children who have been studied in great longitudinal detail at Harvard. He discovered that the first verb inflections to emerge marked just those functions already implicit in verb use at the previous stage, when all verbs were unmarked. At the beginning stage, when verbs occurred simply in their bare, uninflected form, Brown noted that they were used to express four kinds of meanings: (1) "naming an action or state . . . of temporary duration and true at the time of the utterance," or (2) referring to the immediate past, or (3) as a statement of the child's immediate wish or intention, or (4) as an imperative. The first verb markings to emerge were used to express just these functions: (1) the progressive *-ing*, (2) the past tense, and (3) catenative verbs ("gonna," "wanna," and "hafta"). The last function, the imperative, continues, of course, to be expressed by an uninflected verb in English, but Brown notes that "please," as an imperative marker, entered at about the same time as these other verb markings. Brown also found that his three children understood the semantics of possession well before they attained the possessive inflection. In all of these cases, then, the appearance in child speech of a new formal device serves only to code a function which the child has already understood and expressed implicitly.

How does a child go about expressing a new meaning—that is, how does he find the linguistic means for newly-developed cognitive notions? Here we have the other half of the principle proposed above: *New functions are first expressed by old forms.* Richard Cromer (1968) found many examples of this principle in studying the development of temporal expression in English. For example, shortly before emergence of the perfect tense, his subjects attached "now" and "yet" to statements about the past, producing utterances which performed the same function as the perfect tense (for example, "I didn't make the bed yet";

"Now I closed it"). Such forms were soon replaced by the perfect ("I haven't made the bed"; "I've closed it"). Here it is clear that cognitive development has given rise to semantic intentions for which new means of expression must be forged. In fact, children's temporary idiosyncratic linguistic forms often are cues to the fact that the development of a new notion has engendered a search for new means of expression. Miller and Ervin-Tripp (forthcoming) note this explicitly in their longitudinal studies:

> In all cases [of idiosyncratic rules], it appears that the non-standard rules developed because the child's semantic development had outstripped his formal grammatical development.

Acquisition of the complexities of English auxiliaries and negatives provide many familiar examples, as when my three-year-old daughter said such things as "Anything is not to break—just glasses and plates" [= 'Nothing is breakable except glasses and plates'], or, when recovering from an illness, "I must have getting weller and weller."

The picture we have so far, then, is the following: In order to acquire language, the child must attend both to speech and to the contexts in which speech occurs—that is, he must be trying to understand what he hears, and be trying to express the intentions of which he is capable. This means that he must have both cognitive and linguistic discovery procedures available—in order to formulate internal structures which are capable of assimilating and relating both linguistic and non-linguistic data, and which are capable of realizing intentions as utterances. The emergence of new communicative intentions must bring with it the means to decode those intentions in the speech the child hears, and this makes it possible for him to discover new means for expressing those intentions. Cromer summarizes this argument cogently in his thesis (1968, pp. 218–219):

> prior to the development of particular cognitive abilities, the child has been exposed to forms, structures, and words—some of these with a very high frequency—which he fails to acquire. For example, forms of the perfect tense are found in the mothers' utterances from the earliest protocols, and though the child has a span sufficient to produce these and has the elements to do so at his disposal [i.e., auxiliary "have" and past participles], he does not produce the perfect tense until after age 4:6. He has been barraged by a multitude of time words, but he does not use entire classes of these sometimes for years.
>
> On the other hand, once certain cognitive abilities have developed, we begin to find that the child uses forms he had been previously using only in particular limited ways, to refer to and express new ideas. . . . Furthermore, once certain cognitive abilities have developed, we also find an active search for acquisition of new forms. Suddenly forms (and words!) which the child has been exposed to for years become a part of his own speech.

A METHOD FOR REVEALING LANGUAGE ACQUISITION STRATEGIES

Given the primacy of cognitive development in setting the pace for the development of linguistic intentions, it follows that many linguistic forms cannot appear in the child's speech until he is capable of grasping their meaning. If the stages of cognitive development are universal—as I would like to believe—than a very strong developmental psycholinguistic universal can be set forward: *The rate and order of development of the semantic notions expressed by language are fairly constant across languages, regardless of the formal means of expression employed.* (Note that this proposition applies to semantic *intentions*, rather than the formal marking of intentions. Thus, for example, Brown's children would be credited with the four verb meanings, in this sense of intention, at the stage when all of their verbs were in the root, uninflected form.)

If this universal is true, and if communicative intentions can be reliably assessed from a combination of contextual and partial linguistic cues, then we have a powerful research tool for probing the information processing devices used and developed by children to understand speech and to construct grammars. What is needed is a taxonomy and coding scheme for pre-linguistic intentions. We are beginning to develop such a system at Berkeley, in the hope that it will be possible to establish a stable and universal sequence of pre-linguistic communicative intentions.[5] If this is the case, then one can measure the lag between the appearance of a communicative intention and the mastery of the conventional linguistic form which the child's native language offers for the realization of that intention. (See footnote 6 for a criterion of mastery.) The lag between the first attempts to express a meaning and the acquisition of the relevant linguistic forms should vary from language to language, determined by the psycholinguistic complexity of the formal means used by a particular language to express the intention under consideration. With sufficient information on the sorts of formal devices which appear difficult to learn, we will be in a position to make a much clearer formulation of the capacities and strategies involved in language acquisition. It is necessary to compare formal devices used to express the same semantic intentions in order to insure that the children studied are at roughly the same level of cognitive development, and that the devices are used for similar purposes.

A TEST CASE: DEVELOPMENT OF LOCATIVE EXPRESSIONS

In effect, this research tactic attempts to separate the bilingual child into two monolingual children who are following the same sequence of communicative intentions. A useful test case of the proposed method, therefore, begins with

[5] The current version of our analysis is based on an enrichment of Fillmore's "case grammar" (1968). A similar approach is currently being followed by Martin Braine at Santa Barbara (personal communication). Francesco Antinucci and Dominico Parisi, at the Istituto di Psicologia in Rome, are developing what promises to be an extremely valuable model on the basis of generative semantics (see the paper by Antinucci and Parisi reprinted below).

a re-examination of locative development in the Hungarian–Serbo-Croatian bilingual girls mentioned above. Our procedure will be to compare development of the formal means of locative expression in several languages; to propose a developmental universal based on inductive generalization of these findings; and to propose a psycholinguistic operating principle which may be a partial determinant of the general finding. The locative example will clarify the procedure.

You will recall that the development of Hungarian locative inflections was in advance of Serbo-Croatian locative prepositions. Why should the Hungarian locative expressions be easier for the child to acquire? In order to attempt an answer, it will be necessary to look briefly at the grammatical devices for locative expression in the two languages. Hungarian has an abundance of nominal inflections which express combinations of position and direction. For example, with the word *hajó* 'boat,' there are forms such as *hajóban* 'located in the boat,' *hajóból* 'moving out from inside of the boat,' *hajótól* 'moving away from next to the boat,' and so on. The inflections are all monosyllables, and systematically encode position, motion toward a position, and motion away from a position. They apply to all nouns (there is no grammatical gender in Hungarian). Serbo-Croatian, like English, has a number of prepositions which encode locations: the equivalents of "in," "on," "from," and so on. And, like English, some of these prepositions encode direction (as English "to" and "from"), while some do not distinguish between direction and position (compare: "Put it *in* the box" and "It is *in* the box"). In addition, unlike English, Serbo-Croatian encodes the distinction between position and direction by means of noun inflections. The accusative is used when an ambiguous preposition like *u* 'in' is used directionally, and the locative case is used when such a preposition is used positionally (e.g., *kuća* 'house,' *u kuću* 'into the house,' *u kući* 'located in the house'). The situation is even more complex in Serbo-Croatian, because of a variety of semi-arbitrary pairings of preposition with case. For example, *blizu* 'near,' *do* 'as far as,' and *iz* 'from/from out of' must take genitive nouns; *k* 'towards' takes the dative; *pri* 'at/near' takes the locative; etc. In both Serbo-Croatian and English, position vs. direction is sometimes uniquely signalled by one preposition or compound preposition (such as "towards," "out of," and so on), and sometimes one preposition fails to distinguish between the two senses (as "in" and "on"). Serbo-Croatian is more complex, however, in that every preposition governs a noun inflection. Sometimes this inflection is meaningful, distinguishing position from direction, and sometimes it is redundant. Furthermore, the particular phonological realization of a given inflection is determined by the gender and by the final sound of each particular noun.

Why, then, is the Hungarian locative acquired before the Serbo-Croatian locative in bilingual children? In the most general terms, it seems obvious that the Hungarian means of locative expression is simpler: the locative marker is always at the end of the noun only, always unambiguously and consistently indicates both position and direction to or from. The example demonstrates—at the very least—that a system which can be described by a small set of consistent and regular rules is easier to learn than one less consistent and regular—even by children under the age of two. But we can go beyond impressionistic statements such as these. The value of such cross-linguistic examples—I have proposed—is to teach us something about the ways in which children process speech.

The Hungarian locative is expressed by noun *suffixes*. This fact may facilitate acquisition, in that the end of a word seems to be perceptually salient. Little children will often imitate only the last part of a word, saying, for example, *raff* for *giraffe* in English, *sáyim* for *mixnasáyim* in Hebrew (Bar-Adon, 1971), *ḥibb* for *ᶜam-yḥibb* in Arabic (Omar, 1970), etc. Unstressed initial syllables, prefixes, and prepositions are very frequently omitted in child speech, as virtually all observers have noted. Furthermore, evidence from Czech, where all words receive initial stress, suggests that the ends of words are perceptually salient even if unstressed. Pačesová (1968), reporting on a detailed longitudinal study of a Czech boy, presents numerous examples of omission of initial stressed syllables in Czech child speech. She notes that if "stress were to be the relevant factor in the abbreviating operation, the syllabic prepositions, being stressed in Czech, should have been early in appearance and, as for shortening, they should have been preserved, which is certainly not the case" (p. 205).

Another argument for perceptual salience of word endings comes from studies in acoustic phonetics. A paper by Kim Oller (1971) has brought to my attention the fact that phoneticians have noted the existence of final-syllable lengthening in many languages (e.g., Russian [Zlatoustova, 1954]; Swedish [Lindblom, 1968]; English, Spanish, German, French [Delattre, 1966]). Oller (p. 13) entertains a suggestion of Ernest Haden (1962) "that final-syllable lengthening cues listeners to the fact that a linguistic unit has terminated." Thus there is additional support for the argument that word endings attract the child's attention.

In regard to our bilingual example, this suggestion of differential perceptual salience could be checked carefully by having children imitate Hungarian and Serbo-Croatian sentences and note what is omitted. This check remains to be carried out, but other evidence supports the suggestion that part of the difference in ease of acquisition has to do with the pre- or post-nominal location of locative markers in the two languages. The prepositions are missing from the earliest stages of Serbo-Croatian monolingual child speech, and inflections begin to emerge before prepositions (Mikès, 1967; Mikeš and Vlahović, 1966; Pavlovitch, 1920). Inflections are word-final, and would be more perceptually salient on the above interpretation. The best support for this suggestion is the finding that Serbo-Croatian children begin to express the difference between position and direction by adding noun inflections rather than prepositions.

Additional evidence comes from cross-linguistic comparison. Russian, which is extremely similar to Serbo-Croatian, demonstrates the same pattern of prepositional and inflectional acquisition described above (Gvozdev, 1949). The first locatives are noun-noun combinations, as in the example given earlier of "pot stove." At the next level, the first inflections emerge, and the child distinguishes between position and direction by contrasting the locative case with the dative and accusative cases. At this stage the child is expressing the locative notions 'in' and 'into,' 'on' and 'onto,' and 'towards,' using inflections and no prepositions. Later, when prepositions emerge, it is first just *these* prepositions which are used—performing the same functions as the earlier prepositionless utterances. Several months later a flood of prepositions comes—the equivalents of "under," "behind," "through," "along," and so on.

Rūķe-Draviņa (1959, 1963) presents the same picture in Latvian, with early inflectional marking of 'in,' 'on,' and 'from,' and later emergence of prepositions. She notes that: "Endings, as case markers, generally occur earlier than the corresponding prepositions" (1963, p. 141); and that prepositions are learned gradually, with difficulty, and are often omitted even after they emerge in Latvian child speech.

In English, too, prepositions tend to be omitted in early child speech, but the English-speaking child has no inflections available to use in the place of prepositions. When prepositions do emerge in English, the first ones are "on" and "in" (Brown, in press, chap. II), followed almost immediately by a large number of other prepositions (Brown, unpublished data). It is as if the child had to develop to the point where he could attend to prepositions; he then uses them first for well-practiced locative notions, and quickly develops the means for expressing a wide range of such notions.

The suggestion of perceptual salience can be approached obliquely in English. Well before the acquisition of prepositions, English-speaking children are using locative verb particles like "on," "off," "down," and so on. These tend to occur towards the ends of utterances in adult speech addressed to the child: "Put the shirt on," "Take your shoes off," and so on. Some of these particles are frequently present as one-word utterances (Braine, 1963b; Leopold, 1939; Miller and Ervin, 1964). The same is true of analogous German verbal particles, such as *ab, an, auf, mit,* and so on (Leopold, 1939; Park, 1970). By contrast, Slavic verbal particles of this sort are prefixed to the verb (the equivalents of "down-fall," "off-take," etc.). Grace Shugar (1971), in longitudinal studies of Polish child speech, reports that locative verbal prefixes of this sort emerge at the same time as prepositions in Polish—that is, relatively later then they do in English. For example, *od* 'off of/away from' emerges simultaneously as a verb prefix (e.g., *odjechał* 'rode away,' *odpadł* 'fell down') and as a preposition (e.g., *od mamy* 'away from mama'). Since the Polish locative particles are placed before the verb, they are probably at the same level of perceptual saliency as prepositions.

Thus the argument is that if a language expresses locative notions by means of inflections and post-verbal particles (and, by extension, postpositions), acquisition of the verbal expression of locative notions will be facilitated. This can now be checked by comparison with other languages of this sort. Preliminary data on the acquisition of Turkish (my data), Finnish (Argoff, forthcoming), and Korean (Park, 1969)—all similar to Hungarian in this respect—suggest that this is the case. The argument can now be re-phrased, by inductive generalization, as a suggested universal of grammatical development:

> *Universal: Post-verbal and post-nominal locative markers are acquired earlier than pre-verbal and pre-nominal locative markers.*[6]

This developmental universal is undoubtedly not limited to the expression of locatives. In fact, it seems to reflect a general early tendency on the part of the child to attend to the ends of words when scanning linguistic input in a search for cues to meaning. This is a sort of general heuristic or *operating principle* which the child brings to bear on the task of organizing and storing language. Phrased roughly, one can say that the following is one of the basic "self-instructions" for language acquisition:

OPERATING PRINCIPLE A: Pay attention to the ends of words.

We have seen this operating principle reflected in data on word imitation and in the acquisition of locative expressions. It is also evident in the acquisition of other inflectional systems. For example, accusative and dative inflections are very early acquisitions in inflected languages like Russian, Polish, Serbo-Croatian, Latvian, Finnish, Hungarian, and Turkish—where they are realized as noun suffixes. But these inflections are relatively late in the acquisition of German (Stern and Stern, 1907), where they are realized as forms of pre-nominal articles. English articles are also lacking at early stages of development. It is not the semantic nature of articles which accounts for the omissions in German and English, because the Bulgarian article, which is a noun suffix, appears early in child speech (Gheorgov, 1908). Apparently Operating Principle

---

[6] The notion of "earlier" is crucial to the understanding of such proposed developmental universals. There are two operational criteria of "earlier": (1) If both means of expression are available in a given language, one will appear in development at a younger age than the other. This can be ascertained in either longitudinal or cross-sectional studies. If A and B are linguistic devices taken to be ordered in psycholinguistic complexity, one would expect to find a given child using either A or both A and B, but not B alone. (2) If only one means of expression is available in a given language, the relevant variable is the time from first reliable *unmarked* intention to express the notion encoded by the linguistic form and the first reliable and appropriate use of that form. Only longitudinal study is applicable in this case. Brown (in press) has proposed a useful criterion of reliable and appropriate mastery of a linguistic form. He suggests that one examine the contexts in a corpus of child speech in which a given grammatical form is obligatory, and set an acquisition criterion in terms of "output-where-required." He has found it useful to define mastery of grammatical morphemes as appropriate production in 90% of obligatory contexts. For purposes of cross-linguistic test of a universal, one would measure the lag between the intention to express the content encoded by A and B and the mastery of A or B in terms of Brown's 90% criterion. The lag between emergence of communicative intent and the acquisition of A should be shorter than the lag between the emergence of intent and the acquisition of B.

A is at work here as well, making it relatively difficult for the child to detect German inflections. The principle also accounts for the finding (Grégoire, 1937) that the first negative element in early French speech is *pas*—the final member of the separated pair *ne . . . pas*.

All of these findings taken together suggest a general developmental universal, based on the supposition that Operating Principle A is one of the first operating principles employed in the ontogenesis of grammar:

> *Universal A1: For any given semantic notion, grammatical realizations in the form of suffixes or postpositions will be acquired earlier than realizations in the form of prefixes or prepositions.*[7]

In order for this universal to be manifested, a number of language-definitional universals must be taken for granted (e.g. that there are words, that the meaningful unit is smaller than the word, that sounds can express grammatical relations as well as make reference, and so on). In addition, the emergence of inflections requires at least one other basic operating principle:

OPERATING PRINCIPLE B: The phonological forms of words can be systematically modified.

Numerous observers have reported a period of playful modification of words which precedes the emergence of inflections. Werner and Kaplan, reviewing the European diary literature, note (1963, p. 155):

> there are some indications reported in the literature which suggest that long before the child grasps the role of form-changes as grammatical devices, he grasps the fact that forms of vocables may be modified to express some qualification of, or affective reaction to an event.

They cite many examples of playful reduplication, suffixing, and so forth. In languages which provide inflectional diminutive or affectionate forms, such inflections are among the first to emerge. Shugar (1971), for example, cites early Polish diminutives for names (e.g., *tatunia* [= *tata* 'father'] and *mamunia*

---

[7] Greenberg (1957) presents a closely related argument in terms of the psycholinguistic bases of linguistic change. He explores Sapir's observation, corroborated by his own experience, "that prefixing is far less frequent than suffixing in the languages of the world" (p. 89). Greenberg adduces a number of possible psychological causes for a regular historical development away from prefixes to suffixes and finally to isolating linguistic systems. Greenberg examines this phenomenon as an example of the role of psychological factors in language change. The suggestions made here about attention to suffixes in child language development provide an important link to his chain of reasoning. (Of course, additional sorts of psycholinguistic factors will have to be introduced to account for development of an isolating language into either a prefixing or a suffixing one. In consonance with the present argument, however, Greenberg notes that the latter course of historical development is more frequent [p. 93].)

[= *mama*]) and for other words (e.g., *śliweczka* [= *śliwka* 'plum'] and *jabłuszka* [= *jabłko* 'apple']). Pačesová (1968, p. 216) gives remarkable examples from the early speech of a Czech boy who inserted extra syllables into adjectives in order to intensify their meanings. For example, the child had the following series for the adjective *veliký* 'big': [velikej]—[velika:nskej]—[velikana:nskej]—[velikan-ana:nskej]; and *malý* 'little' was changed to: [mali:]—[maliŋki:]—[malineŋki:]—[malilineŋki:]—[malulilineŋki:].

Children frequently experiment with the forms of words before they discover the meanings of particular formal changes. For example, Rūķe-Draviņa (1959) gives numerous examples of the early noncomprehending use of linguistic forms in Latvian:

> The inflections -*a*/-*e* (nominative) and -*u*/-*i* (accusative) are used in free variation as alternative pronunciations of nouns at age 1;6, not being differentiated for the two case meanings until 1;8.

> The plural ending is occasionally attached to nouns referring to singular objects before the acquisition of the pluralization rule.

> Masculine and feminine adjectives are first used indiscriminately, ignoring the gender of the associated noun.

In all of these Latvian examples the form in adult speech is salient (according to Operating Principle A) and is fairly regular. A similar example is the English plural, which sometimes appears in early child speech as an alternative pro-nunciation of nouns.[8]

Operating Principles A and B present part of an explanation for the

---

[8] It should be noted that there are considerable individual differences between children in their propensity to play with form when not expressing meaning. For example, of the two girls studied by Roger Brown, Eve had a period of free variation of singular and plural forms, whereas Sarah did not use the plural inflection until she could use it correctly. The problem of individual differences between children in their approaches to language acquisition has not been addressed frequently in developmental psycho-linguistics, but is obviously of great importance—especially in light of the typically small samples required by longitudinal research methods. Wick Miller (1964a) has made a valuable observation in this regard:

> There are individual differences in grammatical development . . . some children are more prone to invent their own grammatical patterns, patterns that have no relationship to adult patterns. The early grammatical rules for some are limited and quite regular, and for other children they are more variable and more difficult to define. Some children are quite willing to speak at almost any time, whether or not they have the appropriate grammatical structures at hand to express their thoughts, whereas others are more reserved in this regard, and will avoid talking at all, or will use a clumsy circumlocution. . . . I am inclined to think that the variations that are closely tied to formal features of language reflect innate individual differences.

relative ease of acquisition of Hungarian locative inflections: the inflections are presumably perceptually salient, and the child is presumably prepared to manipulate the forms of word endings in his production. These principles both relate to ongoing speech processing—the deployment of attention in speech perception and the production of grammatical markers in speaking, although they also have implications for the kinds of linguistic rules which will be formed. Another set of determinants of ease of acquisition has to do more directly with rule organization factors—both simplicity and consistency of rules from a formal point of view, and semantic consistency. In the Hungarian system the locative marker is directly bound to the noun, while in the Serbo-Croatian system it is divided between a pre-nominal preposition and an inflection. In addition, the choice of formal markers for locative expression is semantically consistent and non-arbitrary in Hungarian, but is much less principled and orderly in Serbo-Croatian. A full answer to the question posed in our test case, therefore, will require operating principles for rule formation as well as for language processing. Principles of this sort will be advanced later in the paper, in connection with broader ranges of data. (See Operating Principles D and G, below.) The test case has played its role in demonstrating the types of cognitive prerequisites to grammatical development which can be revealed by the method outlined above.

Broadly speaking, there are three classes of such prerequisites: (1) those related to the underlying semantics of utterances, (2) those related to the perception and production of speech under short-term constraints, and (3) those related to the organization and storage of linguistic rules.[9] The first class of prerequisites falls within the domain of the general psychology of cognitive development; the remaining prerequisites must be elaborated by developmental psycholinguistics. These are essentially *language processing variables* which can be conceptualized in terms of *operating principles* such as those proposed above. A number of such operating principles, and the predicted developmental universals which flow from them, will be proposed in the last section of this paper. Such operating principles guide the child in developing strategies for the production and interpretation of speech and for the construction of linguistic rule systems. The operating principles function within a framework of constraints on linguistic performance. These constraints must be considered before enumerating specific operating principles in more detail.

---

[9] Cf. the distinction made by Braine (1971a) in his recently-proposed "discovery-procedures" model of language acquisition between (1) concept learning, (2) the scanner, and (3) the memory component. The operating principles proposed here are aimed at specifying some of the properties to which the scanner is sensitive and some of the organizational features of the memory. In addition, Braine's model posits a preferential order or hierarchy among the properties noticed by the scanner. The property hierarchy (cf. Chomsky's "simplicity metric") for a given language would result from the application of the operating principles (e.g., the suggested preference for word-final markers), as well as a possible preferential order of application of some operating principles.

CONSTRAINTS ON LINGUISTIC PERFORMANCE

By and large, the language processing variables to be discussed below are determined by the fact that human language is produced and received in rapid temporal sequence. That is to say, because we communicate through the rapidly-fading, temporally-ordered auditory modality, we must have strategies for quickly programming and deciphering messages. The sorts of processing variables considered here are therefore closely linked to general perceptual and performance-programming principles. Some of them may well be special biological adaptations for language processing, or may have evolved in connection with language—but the issue of evolutionary origin need not be decided here.[10]

The constraints on linguistic performance are both short-term and long-term. The short-term have to do with the ongoing use of speech, and the long-term with the storage and organization of the linguistic system. Child and adult alike must operate under pressures of fading signal and fading auditory image; child and adult alike must have ready access to stored linguistic rules in programming and interpreting utterances. Although short-term sentence processing span increases with age, similar performance constraints are present in childhood and adulthood. Bever (1970a,c) has proposed that certain linguistic structures are not found in human language because they cannot be processed perceptually; it is likewise true that certain linguistic structures are not found in child language because they exceed the child's processing span. Because this span increases with age, it is evident that many universals of linguistic development are based on increasing temporal scope of processing operations. This is, of course, true of speech production as well as speech perception.

Processing span at first is quite literally limited to the number of terms which can occur in an utterance. Almost all investigators report a two-word (or two-morpheme) stage of development. During this period the child can typically express such relations as agent-verb, verb-object, and agent-object, but cannot unite all three terms into a single utterance. The advance from two-word to three-word utterances involves filling in a three-term sequence with fragments which earlier occurred as two-word utterances (cf. Brown, in press, Chap. I; Bowerman, 1970). That is, with maturation, the child reaches the point at which all of the sub-parts of an agent-verb-object sentence can be spoken in a single utterance. Adjective-noun combinations, which also occur earlier as two-word utterances, can be combined into three-word sentences as well, but this requires deletion of one of the other terms—generally the subject—producing verb-object strings with a nounphrase in object position. Thus the child can say, for example,

---

[10] It may well be that human skills associated with auditory pattern perception, production and perception of rapid temporally-ordered auditory sequences, and so forth, originally evolved to subserve the function of linguistic communication. Once evolved, however, such skills can be applied to a broader range of functions. For example, music may owe its existence to skills originally evolved for linguistic purposes.

"Mama drink coffee" and "Drink hot coffee," but not "Mama drink hot coffee."

At this early stage, then, output length limitations are quite severe—literally limited to words rather than to structures or to linguistic operations. Such limitations do not occur in adult speech, and this aspect of development seems purely to be based on maturation of a very simple sort of short-term processing capacity. At somewhat later stages, however, one finds the same sorts of processing limitations as in adult linguistic performance—but down to child scale. For example, both adults and children have difficulty dealing with material interposed between related parts of a sentence (cf. Operating Principle D, below). The only important age difference is in terms of how much material can be interposed without losing track of one's place in a sentence. For example, children may have difficulty in dealing with a doubly modified object noun between verb and particle—as in "He called the little old lady up"—whereas adults may tolerate a longer intervening string. But for both children and adults short-term limitations constrain the amount of material which can be interpolated before production or interpretation of utterances breaks down. In similar fashion, children are limited in the number of grammatical operations which can be performed in an utterance (Bellugi, 1968), but this limitation does not differ in kind from limitations on adult linguistic performance.

I am proposing, therefore, that the short-term limitations under which children operate—beyond the very early limitations on absolute sentence length—are universal human limitations on sentences processing, and that they are based on general perceptual and information-processing principles. The nature of their development can be revealed by the general psychology of perceptual development.

Constraints on production and comprehension are intimately related—especially in child speech, where the forms the child uses in his own speech must be those he has been able to perceive in the speech of others. Thus the operating principles proposed below relate closely both to comprehension strategies (cf. Bever's "perceptual mapping rules") and to the sorts of linguistic rules originally preferred by the child. To a great extent, the form of linguistic rules is determined by the short-term processing limitations, because the rules refer to a system which is represented in the auditory-acoustic modality, and because they must be called into play during rapid speech processing. In fact, at the beginning levels, it could be that there is little difference between short-term processing strategies and linguistic rules. That is to say, the child's knowledge of language—beyond the definitional knowledge proposed at the outset—is represented chiefly by the techniques he uses to interpret and produce sentences.[11]

[11] Beyond these language-specific constraints, however, many linguistic universals are undoubtedly shaped by general constraints on the kinds of rules which the human mind can function with. I suspect that if other complex domains were formally described to the extent that language has been so described we would find similar constraints on the abstract structure of rules.

SUGGESTED UNIVERSALS IN THE ONTOGENESIS OF GRAMMAR

In the remainder of the paper I propose some very specific language processing strategies. The approach is to define a set of presumably universal operating principles which every child brings to bear on the problem of language acquisition. From these operating principles, a number of more specific strategies can be derived, finally resulting in language-specific strategies for the acquisition of aspects of a given native language. Although the operating principles and universals have been arrived at through the same procedures spelled out in the locative test case reviewed above, the format in the following section is more terse, working down from broad operating principles to suggested developmental universals, summarizing data which support those universals (marked by § in the text below). The universals are hopefully phrased in such a way that they can be supported, modified, or abandoned in the light of future research.

Word Order

One of the earliest and most pervasive operating principles has to do with attention to order of elements in an utterance. It seems that a basic expectation which the child brings to the task of grammatical development is that the order of elements in an utterance can be related to underlying semantic relations.

OPERATING PRINCIPLE C: Pay attention to the order of words and morphemes.

Universal C1: The standard order of functor morphemes in the input language is preserved in child speech.

§ No observers report deviant orders of bound morphemes. Burling (1959) found that post-verbal and post-nominal morpheme order was always correct in Garo, where long strings of ordered affixes occur. The same is true of Turkish, Finnish, and Hungarian child speech. The elements of the English auxiliary phrase always occur in their proper order (e.g., "has not been reading," "will not be able to come," etc.).

Universal C2: Word order in child speech reflects word order in the input language.

The phrasing of this universal is purposely vague, because the data are, as yet, imprecise. Earlier, limited data had suggested that children would adhere to fixed word order regardless of the degree of freedom of word order in the input language (Slobin, 1968c). More recent data (Bowerman, 1970) indicate considerable individual differences between children in this regard.

§ Word order in child speech is typically reported as more consistent in languages with fixed word order (e.g., English, Samoan) as opposed to languages with relatively more freedom in this regard (e.g., German, Slavic languages, Finnish, Turkish). (But see Burling [1959] and Braine [1971] for examples of deviant word order in English child speech.)

§ American children tend to retain word order in sentence imitation (Brown and Fraser, 1963; Fraser, Brown, and Bellugi, 1963), whereas Polish children (Shugar, 1971) and Russian children (Dingwall and Tuniks, in press) frequently change word order in imitating sentences.

§ A Finnish child studied by Bowerman (1970) seemed to have acquired the dominant word orders of adult Finnish by the time his mean utterances length was 1.42 morphemes. Bowerman presents the following figures on the frequency of occurrence of various orders of subject, verb, and object in the speech of the child and his mother (figures represent numbers of utterances in recorded natural conversation):

	CHILD	MOTHER
SV	44	47
VS	4	5
VO	4	16
OV	1	3
SVO	7	32
OSV	1	0
OVS	0	1
VSO	0	1
SOV	1	1

Universal C3: Sentences deviating from standard word order will be interpreted at early stages of development as if they were examples of standard word order.

§ Fraser, Bellugi, and Brown (1963) found that English-speaking pre-schoolers would interpret passive sentences as if the order of elements were subject-verb-object. For example, "The girl is pushed by the boy" is matched with a picture of a girl pushing a boy. In other words, children's interpretations conform to the order principle, but reverse meaning. Bever (1970a, p. 298) has proposed as a general strategy of English sentence interpretation: "Any *Noun-Verb-Noun* (NVN) sequence within a potential internal unit in the surface structure corresponds to *actor-action-object*." He presents extensive data in support of this strategy. McNeill (1970, p. 124) proposes a similar strategy.

§ Conjoined sentences referring to two temporally ordered events are first given the interpretation that order of mention matches order of occurrence, even if the conjunction indicates otherwise (E. V. Clark, 1971; Cromer, 1968; Hatch, 1969). (E.g., it is relatively more difficult for children to understand sentences of the form "Event 2 *after* Event 1" and "*Before* Event 2, Event 1" than sentences of the form "Event 1 *before* Event 2" and "*After* Event 1, Event 2.")

§ Universal C3 is apparently applicable even in inflected languages, which allow more flexibility of word order than English. Roeper (this volume) investigated German children's attention to word order and inflection. The standard word order for German imperatives is verb-indirect object-direct object (V-IO-DO), with inflected articles indicating the roles of IO and DO. The inflections make it possible for adults to vary the order of the two nouns without losing sense or grammaticality. When offered V-DO-IO sentences for imitation, some children tended to switch articles, placing the dative article on the first noun and the accusative on the second. That is, children showed their command of the inflections *and* their reliance on word order: they interpreted the first noun after the verb as the indirect object, and inflected the article preceding that noun accordingly. Similarly, in a comprehension task, Roeper found that V-DO-IO sentences were frequently comprehended as if they were V-IO-DO. Thus in both imitation and comprehension many children tended to rely on word order over inflections as a guide to grammatical relations.[12]

§ C. Chomsky (1968) and Cromer (1970) have demonstrated that children have difficulty in correctly interpreting sentences of the type "John is easy to see," where the surface subject corresponds to the. object in deep structure. Children as old as six interpret the first noun in such sentences as subject.

Surface Preservation of Underlying Structure

Psycholinguistic research suggests another sort of operating principle which is tied to the fact that speech is produced and processed sequentially in a rapidly fading modality. In its most general form, this principle states that interruption or rearrangement of linguistic units places a strain on sentence processing—both in production and reception. In other words, there is a pressure to preserve the internal or underlying structure of linguistic units in their surface manifestations. A number of strategies can be related to this principle—both strategies for speech perception and strategies for the formation and use of rules of production.

OPERATING PRINCIPLE D: Avoid interruption or rearrangement of linguistic units.

Universal D1: Structures requiring permutation of elements will first appear in non-permuted form.

§ English yes-no questions first appear in non-inverted form (e.g., "I can go?"); inversion of subject and auxiliary is also absent in the first forms of wh-questions (e.g., "Where I can go?") (Brown, Cazden, and Bellugi, 1969; Klima and Bellugi, 1966).

[12] The operation of language processing variables can also be discerned in the process of language change (cf. Bever and Langendoen, 1971). For example, inflections are replaced by word order in the development of pidgin forms of a language, thus suggesting that order is a more basic device than inflections. It is also probably the case that all languages make use of word order as a basic linguistic means of signalling underlying relations, while the use of inflections is not universal.

§ The first relative clauses in English appear in sentence-final position without inversion (e.g., "I know what is that") (Menyuk, 1969).

Universal D2: Whenever possible, discontinuous morphemes will be reduced to, or replaced by continuous morphemes.

§ Slavic case inflections are first used to express the contrast between position and direction, in the absence of prepositions—i.e., the locative notion is, at first, not marked on both sides of the noun (as discussed above).

§ The first form of the English progressive is the verbal inflection *-ing* with no pre-verbal auxiliary (Brown, in press, Chap. II; and many others).

§ The first form of French negation is *pas*, the final part of the discontinuous morpheme, *ne . . pas* (Grégoire, 1937).

§ The discontinuous Arabic negative /*ma-. . .-š*/ is acquired later than the prefixed negative /*miš*/ by Egyptian children, although both are equally frequent. Children under 3;6 have a general negation rule of /*miš*/ + S, even when incorrect by adult standards (e.g., /*huwa miš rāḥ*/ instead of /*huwa ma-rāḥ-š*/ 'he not went'). Above 3;6, the discontinuous /*ma-. . .-š*/ is never substituted for /*miš*/, but the opposite substitution does occur (Omar, 1970).

Universal D3: There is a tendency to preserve the structure of the sentence as a closed entity, reflected in a development from sentence-external placement of various linguistic forms to their movement within the sentence.

§ Early negative forms in English are attached to primitive sentences ("No do this"), later moving within the sentence ("I no do this" and, with auxiliary modal development, "I can't do this") (Bellugi, 1967; Klima and Bellugi, 1966; Menyuk, 1969; Snyder, 1914).[13]

§ Finnish yes-no questions require attachment of a question particle to the word questioned, and movement of that word to the front of the sentence. Acquisition of this form of question is exceptionally late in Finnish children (Argoff, forthcoming; Bowerman, 1970). An earlier form of yes-no question in Finnish child speech consists of a sentence-final interrogative particle (S + *vai* or S + *yoko*) (Argoff, forthcoming).

§ Sentence-final relative clauses ("I met a man who was sick") are earlier to develop than embedded relative clauses ("The man who was sick went home") (Brogan, 1968; Menyuk, 1969; Slobin and Welsh, this volume).

[13] But Shugar (1971) reports early sentence-internal placement of a negative particle in Polish, and proposes: "It would seem that relative freedom of word position in sentences as well as experience with diminutive infixes might facilitate such re-arrangements within linguistic units like sentences in the Polish language."

Universal D4: The greater the separation between related parts of a sentence, the greater the tendency that the sentence will not be adequately processed (in imitation, comprehension, or production).[14]

§ Brogan (1968), in analyzing unpublished imitation data gathered by Carolyn Wardrip, found that sentences (1) and (2) were easy for preschoolers to imitate, while (3) posed considerable difficulty:

(1) He knows how to read because he goes to school.
(2) I saw the man who fell down.
(3) The man that fell down ran away.

Note that sentence length and number of embedded sentences do not account for these findings. What is difficult is not embedding, but *self*-embedding, as exemplified in (3). Similar findings are reported by Menyuk (1969); Slobin and Welsh (this volume), and Smith (1970).

Clear Marking of Underlying Relations

Children scan adult sentences for cues to meaning, and are aided by overt morphological markers which are regular and perceptually salient. Such markers probably play a similar role in production, helping the child keep track of where he is in the transition from thought to utterance. With maturation and psycholinguistic development, the child develops an increasing ability to derive deep structure from minimal cues. Bever (1970a, p. 350) has set forth "a view of sentence complexity according to which the more internal structure material that is implicit in the external structure, the harder the sentence, since the child must contribute more information to the sentence himself."

Children apparently prefer that grammatical functors be not only present wherever possible, but also that they be clearly marked acoustically. In fact, functors may be more clearly marked acoustically in child speech than in adult speech. Levina has noted that for Russian children

> clarity and accuracy of pronunciation appear first of all in the inflections. At the same time the word stem continues to sound inarticulate. . . . The work carried out by the child in connection with rudimentary distinctions of grammatical meanings . . . facilitates more articulate perception of the acoustic composition of words at this stage (quoted by Leont'yev, 1965, p. 101).

Rūķe-Draviņa (1963) notes that in Latvian child speech newly acquired conjunctions and other connecting words are stressed, even if unstressed in adult speech.

---

[14] This is, in fact, not a developmental universal, but a statement of a general psycholinguistic performance constraint. As pointed out above, the only age difference is in severity of the constraint. Watt has phrased this universal in terms of a "theory of cumulative assignments" (1970, p. 151): ". . . psycholinguistic parsing complexity increases with the amount of deep structure whose correct assignment is postponed; with the length of sentence over which the postponement must be carried; and with the complexity of misassignments whose rescission returns the processor to an earlier point in the sentence."

OPERATING PRINCIPLE E: Underlying semantic relations should be marked overtly and clearly.

Universal E1: A child will begin to mark a semantic notion earlier if its morphological realization is more salient perceptually (ceteris paribus).

§ The notions of "more salient perceptually" and "*ceteris paribus*," of course, are in need of more precise definition. Operating Principle A and the discussion of locative expressions offer some support for Universal E1. (Cf. early acquisition of the Hungarian locative inflections, the Bulgarian suffixed article -*at*/-*ta*/-*to*, etc.)

§ The Hungarian–Serbo-Croatian bilingual children acquired the Serbo-Croatian accusative inflection -*u* earlier than the corresponding Hungarian inflection -*t*, using it on words of both languages.

§ The development of the passive is late in Indo-European languages, where it typically requires several morphological changes, as well as a change in word order in many languages. By contrast, the Arabic passive is learned early by Egyptian children (Omar, 1970), where it is formed by a prefixed /it-/ on the past tense of the verb, with obligatory agent deletion and preposing of under- lying patient. Although several factors are at play in this comparison, the marking of the passive by a single clear prefix is probably one of the reasons for its early acquisition in Arabic.

§ The following finding, reported by Shugar (1971) for Polish child language development, suggests a role for perceptual salience in inflectional development: "The following oppositions emerged: singular vs. plural in nouns, verbs, and pronouns; first vs. second person singular in verb endings; nominative vs. accusative case for feminine nouns; masculine vs. feminine gender both in pronouns and verb-endings. Most of the above differentiations seem to rest upon a new phonological acquisition: an acoustically clear differentiation of /a/ and /e/."

Universal E2: There is a preference not to mark a semantic category by ∅ ("zero morpheme"). If a category is sometimes marked by ∅ and sometimes by some overt phonological form, the latter will, at some stage, also replace the ∅.[15]

§ The Russian noun singular accusative is marked by ∅ for masculine non-human and neuter nouns. Such nouns are first marked with the acoustically salient feminine accusative -*u* by Russian children (Gvozdev, 1949; Pavlova,

---

[15] It may be necessary to draw a distinction here between marked and unmarked categories (Greenberg, 1966). Children do not insist on an inflectional marker for the nominative case in the Slavic languages, although such overgeneralization is technically possible. Little English-speaking children are content to leave the third person verb singular uninflected (a category which is generally unmarked in the world's languages), while they overgeneralize the plural (e.g., "sheeps") and the past tense (e.g., "cutted") to all possible cases.

1924; Slobin, 1966a, 1968c; Zakharova, 1958). The very same is true of Serbo-Croatian language development (Mikeš and Vlahović, 1966; Pavlovitch, 1920).

§ Gvozdev's (1949) Russian child used the masculine and feminine *-ov* for all plural genitive nouns, replacing the feminine plural genitive Ø.

§ Arabic nouns are given in the singular (Ø) with numerals over 10; but Egyptian children tend to use plural noun forms with all numerals (Omar, 1970).

Universal E3: If there are homonymous forms in an inflectional system, those forms will tend not to be the earliest inflections acquired by the child; i.e. the child tends to select phonologically unique forms, when available, as the first realization of inflections.

§ The first noun instrumental inflection used by Russian children is the masculine and neuter *-om*, rather than the more frequent feminine *-oy* (Gvozdev, 1949; Pavlova, 1924; Slobin, 1966a; 1968c; Zakharova, 1958). The suffix *-om* has only one homonym (masculine and neuter locative adjective inflection), while *-oy* represents five homonymous inflections (singular adjective inflections for masculine nominative and feminine genitive, dative, instrumental, and prepositional cases).

Universal E4: When a child first controls a full form of a linguistic entity which can undergo contraction or deletion, contractions or deletions of such entities tend to be absent.

§ Bellugi (1967) has noted the clear enunciation of "I will"—even in imitations of sentences containing "I'll"—at a developmental stage at which special attention is paid to the auxiliary system.

§ Slobin and Welsh (this volume), in a longitudinal study of elicited imitation, found numerous examples in which their subject supplied elements in her imitation which had been optionally deleted in the model sentence (e.g., Model: "I see the man the boy hit." Child: "I see a man who a boy hit.")

Universal E5: It is easier to understand a complex sentence in which optionally deletable material appears in its full form.

§ This statement is a version of Bever's suggestion that "the child ... has some difficulty with constructions that depend on active reconstruction of deleted internal structure" (1970a, p. 351). Psycholinguistic research on adults, such as that carried out by Fodor, Garrett, and Bever (1968), has shown that multiply self-embedded clauses are very difficult for adults to understand (e.g., "The pen the author the editor liked used was new"). There are, presumably, too many interruptions to keep track of. Such sentences can be made significantly easier for adults to understand if each embedded clause is marked by a relative pronoun (e.g., "The pen which the author whom the editor liked used was new") (Fodor and Garrett, 1967; Hakes and Cairns, 1970). The notion here is that one scans a sentence perceptually, searching for cues to underlying meaning, and that the relative pronoun facilitates a particular strategy for interpreting multiply embedded sentences—namely, that in a sequence of *noun-relative pronoun-noun-transitive verb*, the first noun is object and the second subject of the following verb.

Children, of course, cannot understand multiply self-embedded sentences, but they can begin to understand sentences with one embedded clause. For example, Charles Welsh and I found that a two-year-old girl could imitate many sentences with embedded clauses marked by relative pronouns, and that her imitations showed that she understood the appropriate underlying relations (e.g., Model: "The man who I saw yesterday got wet." Child: "I saw the man and he got wet."). Note that her imitation has preserved meaning, showing that she was able to decode the structure, but that she has avoided interruptions in her version. She gives back the full forms of the two underlying sentences, supplying the deleted repetition of the subject: "I saw the man" and "He got wet."[16] (This is further evidence for Operating Principle D.) At this stage of development, the child is unable to interpret sentences from which the relative pronoun has been deleted (e.g. Model: "The boy the book hit was crying." Child: "boy the book was crying"). These structures were clearly beyond her competence at this level, and were treated as word lists. (Cf. the example given above under Universal E4, drawn from a later stage in the development of the same child. In that example the deleted relative pronoun is supplied by the child in her imitation, indicating her ability to interpret the deletion, along with the need to mark the relative clause overtly with the pronoun in her own production.) (Slobin and Welsh, this volume).

§ Olds (1968) found that boys aged seven, nine, and eleven responded more quickly to instructions in which a relative pronoun was present (e.g. "The piece that your opponent moved may be moved two spaces") than to the corresponding shorter sentences from which the pronoun had been deleted (e.g. "The piece your opponent moved may be moved two spaces").

§ C. Chomsky (1969) and Olds (1968) found that children were less likely to misinterpret the verbs "ask" and "tell" when a pronoun indicated the underlying subject of an embedded sentence. For example, (1) and (2) were more difficult to interpret than (3) and (4):
(1) Ask Laura what to feed the doll.
(2) Tell Laura what to feed the doll.
(3) Ask Laura what you should feed the doll.
(4) Tell Laura what she should feed the doll.

Overregularization

Perhaps the most widely-noted aspect of child speech has been children's tendency to overregularize or overgeneralize. Virtually every observer has noted some examples of analogical formations, over-extension of regular principles,

---

[16] Note that this example also shows that the perception rules are not identical to the production rules. That is, the child can retrieve meaning from structures which she cannot yet produce.

etc., and a comprehensive list of examples cannot be attempted here. Rules applicable to larger classes are developed before rules relating to their subdivisions. There is a tendency to apply a linguistic rule to all relevant cases. In short:

OPERATING PRINCIPLE F: Avoid exceptions.

Universal F1: The following stages of linguistic marking of a semantic notion are typically observed: (1) no marking, (2) appropriate marking in limited cases, (3) overgeneralization of marking (often accompanied by redundant marking), (4) full adult system.

§ A classic example is the development of the English past tense, as represented by the following schematic sequence of stages of strong and weak forms in past tense contexts: (1) break, drop; (2) broke, drop; (3) breaked, dropped; (4) breakted, dropted; (5) broke, dropped (Slobin, 1971a).

§ Stage (3) can consist of substages of successive overgeneralizations, in which one form drives out another (cf. the discussion of "inflectional imperialism" in Slobin, 1968c). For example, Russian children first use the masculine and neuter *-om* inflection for all singular noun instrumentals; then replace this with the feminine *-oy*; and only later sort out the two inflections (Zakharova, 1958). Similarly, Russian children first use the feminine past tense for all verbs, regardless of the gender of subject noun; then use only the masculine for all verbs; followed by a period of mixed usage and eventual separate marking of verb past tense to agree with gender of subject noun (Popova, 1958).

§ The Arabic plural has a number of irregularities and inconsistencies, as described earlier in this paper (a large number of irregular forms; a separate dual; singular nouns with numerals over 10; separate forms for "counted" vs. "collected" senses of given nouns). The regular feminine plural suffix is widely overgeneralized, and "was strongly preferred for pluralizing nonsense nouns by children of all ages" (Omar, 1970, p. 375).

Universal F2: Rules applicable to larger classes are developed before rules relating to their subdivisions, and general rules are learned before rules for special cases.

§ Gvozdev's (1949) Russian child did not distinguish between mass and count nouns, requiring that every noun have a singular and a plural form. Thus he pluralized mass nouns (*bumagi* 'papers'), counted mass nouns (*odna sakhara* 'one sugar'), and invented singulars for plural nouns which have no singular forms in Russian (e.g. **lyut* as the singular for the collective noun *lyudi* 'people'). Similar phenomena have been frequently reported for English-speaking children.

§ Masculine animate nouns take a special accusative inflection in Russian. Subdivision of the noun class into the categories of animate and inanimate masculine for purposes of accusative inflection is typically late in Russian children, who prefer to use a single accusative form for all nouns (Gvozdev, 1949; Solov'yeva, 1960).

§ C. Chomsky (1969) found late acquisition of the special rules involved in the use of the verbs "promise" and "ask" in English. "Promise" is a special case in that it violates the "Minimal Distance Principle" (Rosenbaum, 1967) generally used to decide on the subject of an infinitival complement verb; e.g., in (1) the subject of the complement verb is "Bill," but in (2), where "promise" appears, the subject is "John."

(1) John wanted Bill to leave.
(2) John promised Bill to leave.

"Promise" *consistently* violates the Minimal Distance Principle, while "ask" is *inconsistent*—cf. (3), where "Bill" is the subject of the verb in the complement, and (4), where "John" is the subject:

(3) John asked Bill to leave.
(4) John asked Bill what to do.

While "promise" is consistently exceptional, "ask" is inconsistent. Chomsky found that full comprehension of "promise" came at an earlier age than full comprehension of "ask," suggesting that it is easier to learn a consistent exception than an inconsistent exception.

Semantic Motivation for Grammar

The overgeneralizations engendered by Operating Principle F are always constrained within semantic limits. The child applies an appropriate inflection or function word within a grammatical class, failing to observe a detailed subdivision of that class, but errors in choice of functor are always within the given functor class. There are numerous examples in the cross-linguistic data of the principle that rules relating to semantically defined classes take precedence over rules relating to formally defined classes, and that purely arbitrary rules are exceptionally difficult to master (see footnote 4). Simply stated:

OPERATING PRINCIPLE G: The use of grammatical markers should make semantic sense.

Universal G1: When selection of an appropriate inflection among a group of inflections performing the same semantic function is determined by arbitrary formal criteria (e.g. phonological shape of stem, number of syllables in stem, arbitrary gender of stem), the child initially tends to use a single form in all environments, ignoring formal selection restrictions.

§ The examples cited under Universals E2 and F1 also support Universal G1. For example, a common error in both Russian and Serbo-Croatian child speech is to use the frequent and perceptually salient feminine accusative -*u* on masculine and neuter nouns as well as feminine nouns. But, when it is used, the -*u* inflection is added only to nouns, and not to other parts of speech, and only to indicate the direct object of action or the goal of directed movement. Thus the proper inflection is picked to express semantic intention (accusative inflection), though the child does not yet follow the subselections within that class on the basis of gender and phonology. For each particular grammatical case category, the Slavic child apparently selects one salient case ending to express the semantic of that case in connection with all nouns. The underlying grammatical rule, therefore, is semantically appropriate, but only formally deficient.

§ In languages requiring agreement between adjective and noun, case and number agreement is acquired before gender agreement. In Russian, for example, the child uses a single adjective inflection for each case and number combination, but does not make gender distinctions (e.g., one singular nominative for all genders, one plural nominative, etc.) (Gvozdev, 1949).

§ Mikeš and Vlahović (1966) report for Serbo-Croatian that case distinctions and the singular-plural contrast are acquired before gender distinctions (both selection of gender-conditioned noun inflection and agreement between noun and modifier in gender). They note that children stop themselves before expressing proper gender much more frequently than for other grammatical decisions.

Universal G2: Errors in choice of functor are always within the given functor class and subcategory.

§ Gvozdev (1949) points out that although there are many confusions as to the proper suffix to employ within a given Russian case category, the child never uses one case instead of another. For example, although the Russian child uses an instrumental noun inflection which fails to agree with the noun in gender, he does not express the notion of the instrumental case by means of a dative inflection, a verb tense inflection, etc.

§ English-speaking children at first fail to appropriately subdivide prepositions according to their detailed semantic functions, but do not confuse prepositions with conjunctions or other parts of speech, and so forth. Miller and Ervin note, in summarizing their longitudinal study: "The children seldom used a suffix or function word with the wrong lexical class" (1964, p. 26).

Universal G3: Semantically consistent grammatical rules are acquired early and without significant error.

§ A Samoan child studied by Kernan (1969) had learned to appropriately use the articles *le* + common noun and *'o* + proper noun/pronoun at the two-word stage. Thus a choice of articles based on a clear semantic feature —[⊥ human]— was acquired at a very early stage of development.

§ Roger Brown (in press, Chap. II) has found that the English progressive is the only inflection which never overgeneralizes in American child speech. That is, children never add the progressive to "state" verbs, saying things like "wanting," "liking," "needing," "knowing," "seeing," or "hearing"; but they freely use the progressive with a large number of "process" verbs. Brown argues that there is a clear semantic distinction between verbs which take the progressive inflection and those which do not. Those not allowing the progressive all indicate involuntary *states*, while those allowing the progressive indicate *processes* which can be voluntary when predicated of people. This is the only subclassification of English words, for inflectional purposes, which is semantically principled. There is no principled basis for remembering, for example, that some verbs form irregular past tenses, or that some nouns have irregular plurals. These lists must be learned by rote, and the result is that such forms are overregularized in child speech. It is easier to apply a rule uniformly than to block it for unprincipled reasons, and so, long after they show their knowledge that one cannot say "I am knowing," children persist in saying things like "I knowed" and "two sheeps."

CONCLUSION

What has been sketched out on the preceding pages is only an outline of what some day may evolve into a model of the order of acquisition of linguistic structures. It has several major components, all of which must be elaborated. The first component, I have argued, is the development of semantic intentions, stemming from general cognitive development. The child, equipped with an inherent definition of the general structure and function of language, goes about finding means for the expression of those intentions by actively attempting to understand speech. That is to say, he must have preliminary internal structures for the assimilation of both linguistic and non-linguistic input. He scans linguistic input to discover meaning, guided by certain ideas about language, by general cognitive-perceptual strategies, and by processing limitations imposed by the constraints of operative memory. As in all of cognitive development, this acquisition process involves the assimilation of information to existing structures, and the accomodation of those structures to new input. The speech perception strategies engender the formation of rules for speech production. Inner linguistic structures change with age as computation and storage space increase, as increasing understanding of linguistic intentions leads the child into realms of new formal complexity, and as internal structures are interrelated and re-organized in accordance with general principles of cognitive organization. All of these factors are cognitive prerequisites for the development of grammar. While we can disagree about the extent to which this process of developing grammars requires a richly detailed innate language faculty, there can be no doubt that the process requires a richly structured and active child mind.

REFERENCES

The references to this paper are included in the bibliography at the end of the volume.

INFLECTIONS

All languages show fundamental similarities in grammatical structure, but there is enormous variation in detail. Languages differ greatly, for example, in the variety, scope, and regularity of their inflectional devices. Some languages signal grammatico-semantic relations between words chiefly by features of order, intonations, and function words (like English prepositions), while other languages make extensive use of inflectional affixes, accent shifts, and the like, yielding paradigmatic sets such as case systems (Latin *mensa* 'table [subject]': *mensae* 'of table': *mensam* 'table [direct object],' and so on). The categories identified by inflectional systems are not only relational; they may be inherent, as marking genders, inflectional classes, and the like (for example, *mensae* 'of table': *libri* 'of book': *maris* 'of sea,' and so on, same case but different genders and declensions). Thus in acquiring full adult competence in his native language the child must master all the particular formal, phonological means used in the language for the expression of such underlying grammatical categories as case, number, gender, person, tense, aspect, and the like.

The development of inflectional systems in language is just a special instance of grammatical development, but since inflectional systems are so limited and readily describable as compared to whole grammars, the study of them has already yielded valuable insights and promises to contribute further to our understanding of the processes of child language development. The chief sources of knowledge about the development of inflectional systems have been two: the careful diarylike studies of individual children carried out by such linguists as Gvozdev and Rūķe-Draviņa and the kind of experimentation typified by the Anisfeld and Tucker and Bogoyavlenskiy studies.

All the papers reprinted here point to the fact that the child acquires the basic *functions* of an inflectional system before mastering particular details of *form* of inflections. For example, Russian children use the various noun cases in semantically appropriate fashion at an early age, although they fail to select the appropriate suffix within a given case (for example, the instrumental) on the basis of gender and phonological chracteristics of the given noun. Thus they may use a single instrumental suffix (for example, the masculine and neuter -*om*) for masculine, neuter, and feminine nouns of various types. In similar fashion, English-speaking children show mastery of the past tense inflection when they say such things as *comed*, though they have not yet mastered the past tense form of that particular verb. Such phenomena of overregularization or overgeneralization are demonstrated repeatedly in both the observational and experimental studies reported in this section and are discussed theoretically in the preceding paper by Slobin. The selection of temporary dominant forms is determined by a complex of factors, such as frequency, perceptual salience, number of semantic functions performed by a given suffix in the language, and so forth. The data presented in this section will allow the reader to formulate his own hypotheses about the determinants of the child's selection and use of particular inflectional forms to express various semantic and grammatical categories. (The development of inflections is also examined in the following papers, found elsewhere in this volume: Burling; Brown, Cazden, and Bellugi; El'konin; Ervin-Tripp; Fraser, Bellugi, and Brown; Miller and Ervin-Tripp; Roeper.)   —C.A.F. and D.I.S.

ENGLISH •

The papers in this section represent the best of the two major approaches to child language study: experimentation and naturalistic observation. Anisfeld and Tucker have refined and extended the classic study carried out by Jean Berko (now Jean Berko Gleason) in Roger Brown's laboratory in 1957–1958 (Berko, 1958). Berko's great methodological contribution was to elicit children's productive control of various inflections by presenting nonsense syllables in contexts requiring inflections. (Brown [1957] had developed a similar method to test children's *comprehension* of inflections and function words). For example, if a child encounters a *bik* and asserts that two of them should be called *biks*, one can credit him with control of this particular plural inflection. This technique, also independently devised in the Soviet Union by Bogoyavlenskiy (this volume), has served as a valuable and popular tool in developmental psycholinguistics.[1] Anisfeld and Tucker explore the technique in great depth, using both production and recognition tasks. In a series of continuing studies (Anisfeld, Barlow, and Frail, 1968; Anisfeld and Gordon, 1968; Bryant and Anisfeld, 1969) Anisfeld and his co-workers have shown that children's sense of inflectional rules is more general and more subtle than revealed by Berko's technique alone. In an ingenious and careful series of experiments, they have offered children pairs of nonsense syllables systematically contrasting the distinctive features of final consonants. For example, the child is asked if he prefers *nark* or *narf* as the plural of *nar*. The results show that children define the plural inflection in terms of distinctive features, preferring the nonsense inflections /f, v, š, č, j/, which share the features of stridency and continuance with the regular plural inflections /s, z/. In a similar vein, Slobin (1971a) has found evidence that children have a general rule of final dental consonant for the past tense inflection in English.

While the Anisfeld and Tucker paper exemplifies the rise of experimental method in child language study begun by Berko and Brown, Courtney Cazden's paper shows how much can be learned from careful longitudinal study of natural conversation. (The papers by Wick Miller and Susan Ervin-Tripp, reprinted in

---

[1] Miller and Ervin-Tripp (this volume) have found, in their longitudinal study, that ability to apply an inflection to a nonsense word typically emerges about a month after application of the inflection to real words in spontaneous speech.

the next major section of this volume, represent a fruitful combination of the experimental and longitudinal methods.) Cazden's analysis of Brown's longitudinal data casts additional light on the problem of morphological development.[2] The longitudinal, naturalistic data give clear evidence of the order of emergence of various inflections, showing both individual differences and striking parallels in the development of the three children studied. (For fuller detail, see Brown, in press). Such data also allow for the inference of children's sentence processing strategies. For example, Cazden finds that "the three children supplied the plural correctly when the requirement was within the noun phrase before they did so when the requirement extended across the noun phrase boundary. These data suggest that one aspect of language development is the extension of linguistic dependency relations across larger units" (see Slobin, this volume). The data also allow for analysis of parental speech. Cazden found that parental training, in the form of expansions of child speech, played no discernible role in the acquisition of inflections (see the general conclusion of Brown, Cazden, and Bellugi [this volume] on the ineffectual role of reinforcement in grammatical development.) In a similar vein, both Cazden and Guillaume point out that frequency of occurrence in adult speech of a given linguistic form is not a reliable predictor of its use by the child. Numerous studies have demonstrated that children are more sensitive to regularity than frequency in making use of adult speech as a data base for rule induction.   —D.I.S.

English Pluralization Rules of Six-Year-Old Children[1]

—— Moshe Anisfeld and G. Richard Tucker

A detailed investigation of the nature of the pluralization rules of 6-year-old children is reported in this paper. This research tries to determine the extent of the child's acquisition of the standard rules of adult speakers of English and to

[2] In addition to the papers by Brown; Brown, Cazden, and Bellugi; and Klima and Bellugi in this volume, the following studies have been carried out on data from the longitudinal study of the children whom Roger Brown has named "Adam," "Eve," and "Sarah"; Bellugi, 1967, 1968; Brown, 1965, 1968, in press; Brown and Bellugi, 1964; Brown and Hanlon, 1970; Cromer, 1968; McNeill, 1966b; Slobin, 1968a, 1971a.

From *Child Development*, 1968, **38**, 1201–1217. Reprinted by permission of the authors and the Society for Research in Child Development, Inc.

[1] The authors wish to thank the Protestant School Board of Greater Montreal as well as the University Settlement of Montreal for their interest and cooperation. The third experiment of Study 2 was conducted in Halifax, Nova Scotia, by Joan C. Christie and Sharon J. Morehouse under the direction of M. Anisfeld. This research was conducted while G. R. Tucker was a Woodrow Wilson Fellow. The research reproduced herein was performed pursuant to a contract with the U.S. Department of Health, Education and Welfare, Office of Education. Additional support was received from the Defence Research Board of Canada, grant 272-83, through the courtesy of W. E. Lambert.

uncover any peculiarities in children's representation of the singular-plural relation.

The correct choice of plural allomorph for regular English nouns is determined by the final phoneme of the singular form of the noun. Three alternatives are available. The plural allomorph /iz/ is used after the sibilants /s, z, š, ž/ and the affricates /č, ǰ/ as in the words *glasses*, *noses*, *rashes*, *garages*, *watches*, and *packages*. The allomorph /s/ is required after all voiceless consonants /p, t, k, f, θ/ as in the nouns *maps* and *paths*, and /z/ appears after all other phonemes as in the words *dogs* and *beds*. A more complete description of these rules is given by Francis (1958).

How are such rules acquired? Presumably, the child discerns patterns of regularities in the adult speech to which he is exposed and induces rules to account for these regularities (see, e.g., Brown and Fraser, 1963; Chomsky, 1965, pp. 47–59). From the words, phrases, and sentences that he hears, he abstracts certain rules which he uses until additional information causes him to revise them. This additional information may take the form of exposure to new vocabulary, experience with irregular sequences, or corrections by parents. He will modify his rules repeatedly to incorporate these new data, although a lag may exist between exposure to relevant data and active use of new rules based on those data (Ervin, 1964, p. 174; Menyuk, 1964, p. 545).

Because the child may not yet have been exposed to all pertinent linguistic information, his rules may be different from those of the adult community. Chomsky (1964a, p. 7), for instance, noted: "It is by no means obvious that a child of six has mastered this phonological system in full—he may not yet have been presented with all of the evidence that determines the general structure of the English sound pattern." With regard to plurality, some investigators (Ervin and Miller, 1963, pp. 123–124; Weir, 1962, p. 70) have suggested that a numeral preceding a noun may be construed by the young child as a sufficient marker of plurality, resulting in such constructions as "two book" and "one-two shoe." Such observations suggest that any attempt to study the nature of the child's pluralization rules must focus not only on his knowledge of "adult" rules but also on any other rules which he may adopt temporarily.

In studying the child's methods of pluralization, one cannot infer that the child lacks knowledge of certain rules if he does not apply them in particular situations. It is necessary to determine "the kinds of structures the person has succeeded in mastering and internalizing, whether or not he utilizes them, in practice" (Chomsky, 1964c, p. 36). In order to minimize situational effects in studying the child's competence, it is important to test him with both "productive" and "receptive" kinds of tasks (Brown and Berko, 1960). The child reveals one aspect of his competence when he produces utterances on demand, in accordance with linguistic rules, and another when he recognizes instances of correct usage of these rules.

A technique for inferring receptive control of grammatical rules from a picture identification task has been described by Fraser, Bellugi, and Brown (1963). In a typical example, the child is shown a picture of one sheep jumping and another of two jumping. Then *E* says: "The sheep is jumping," and the child must point to the correct picture. Various grammatical contrasts can be tested by this procedure.

A similar technique has been developed by Berko (1958) for the study of productive control of morphological rules. Among other things, she investigated the child's ability to produce the plural form of nonsense syllable names. Berko showed the child a picture of a cartoon animal which she assigned a nonsense name: "This is a *wug*." She told the child that another animal had come along: Now "there are two of them." She showed him a picture of the two animals and said: "There are two——," expecting the child to supply the plural form *wugs*. She was interested in the child's ability to produce the three regular plural allomorphs.

Berko gave her figures new names so that if the child answered correctly she could infer that he had used a rule and that he had not merely relied on his memory for a particular plural name previously heard. She selected a number of nonsense words whose plurals were formed with the allomorphs /z/ and /iz/ as well as one (*heaf*) for which adults allowed either /s/ (*heafs*) or /z/ (*heaves*).

The results showed that children in the age range of 4–7 years made approximately 67 per cent errors with the names requiring /iz/ but only 25 per cent errors with names requiring /z/. Berko also found that most children had an appropriate model in their lexicon for the /iz/ form, since 91 per cent of them could correctly form the plural of the word *glass*. Because of their limited experience with /iz/, however, young children may not have yet induced the relevant rule and, therefore, are unable to extend this form to new situations. Errors typically took the form of no response or repetition of the singular form.

Although this was a carefully conduced study, several limitations restrict the inferences which may be drawn from it. First, Berko tested only productive control of pluralization rules and did not attempt to study receptive control. Further, the children were required, at all times, to produce a plural form, having been given the singular form. A broader understanding of the child's concept of singularity-plurality may be gained from an analysis of his ability to produce the singular form when he has been given the plural form. Since, in the plural-singular sequence, the child has only to drop the plural marker, one might expect him to make fewer errors in this sequence than in the singular-plural sequence. Even this task, however, may cause the child considerable difficulty. On the phrase level, Huttenlocher (1964) reported that "preschool children have difficulty in dividing common word sequences" (p. 264). On the word level, Bruce (1964) found that children of the mental ages of 5 and 6 were unable to analyze words into their sound constituents. They could not report what was left of a word after the elision of one of its phonemes. Bruce suggested that this inability to fractionate is due to the cohesiveness of word sound patterns in the child's experience. It is thus possible that children may have difficulty in extracting the singular root from a plural form.

Berko's study was also limited by her use of an unequal distribution of the three allomorphs. This precludes making all possible error comparisons. Finally, she always structured the task in the same way: "There are two——." Her phrasing provided the child with both morphological and syntactic constraints which determined the response more fully than if she had said: "Now tell me what you see in the picture."

In general, however, Berko's approach seems to be useful for the exploration of the child's morphological rules, and we decided to extend her methods in studying what kind of rules the child has abstracted from the information available to him in the English language.

PILOT STUDY

In an exploratory study, two methods were used to investigate the child's linguistic concept of singularity-plurality: a Production task similar to Berko's in which the child was also asked to produce a singular name having been given the correct plural name, and a Recognition task in which the child had to choose the best name for a picture.

The Ss were 18 kindergarten pupils with a mean age of 5 years, 6 months. The parents of the Ss in this study and in the other studies to be reported were skilled laborers, businessmen, or professionals. The Ss in all studies were native speakers of English.

Brightly colored pictures of cartoon animals which had been given nonsense names were used. Thirty-six names were used in the Production task, and six in the Recognition task. The names were always chosen so that /s/, /z/, and /iz/ appeared equally often as the plural suffix. Berko's method of presentation, modified to take account of the considerations mentioned, was used for the Production task.

In the Recognition task, E showed S either a singular or plural picture and said both the singular and plural forms of a nonsense name. He asked S to choose the word which sounded "best" to him as a name for the picture. "Would you call this picture [either singular or plural] *wib* or *wibs*?"

After S had replied, E reinforced a correct answer by saying "good" or said "no" to a wrong answer. If S answered incorrectly, an error was recorded, but S was asked to try again. Finally, E supplied the correct answer.

In the Production task, the children made many errors with /iz/ names (41 per cent) but successively fewer with /s/ names (32 per cent) and with /z/ names (28 per cent). Statistical analysis (significance of difference between proportions; Ferguson, 1959) revealed that only the difference between errors with /z/ and with /iz/ was significant ($z = 2.86, p < .02$). Berko had also found more errors with /iz/ than with /z/. In the Recognition task, however, the error pattern was distinctly different from that of our Production task and from that of Berko's. The children made few errors with the /iz/ names (19 per cent) but considerably more with both the /s/ names (36 per cent) and with the /z/ names (28 per cent). These differences among allomorphs in the Recognition task were not significant, possibly because of the small number of items used.

In many instances, the errors in the Production task took the form of no response or repetition of the given name unchanged. More frequently, however, *S* would repeat the name as given and add, appropriately, a singular or a plural numeral to it. He would, for example, produce such responses as *five hesh* and *one zams*. This suggested that the child might be using numerals as alternative markers to distinguish singular from plural nouns.

Two main findings thus appear in the pilot experiment: the apparent use of numerals by some children to mark singularity and plurality, and the distinctly different pattern of errors in the Production and Recognition tasks. To explore these findings further, two series of experiments were conducted. In the first (Studies 1 and 2 below), we tried to examine special rules which the child might use; and in the second (Study 3), we studied his performance on a variety of Production and Recognition tasks to explore the nature of the child's pluralization rules in relation to the standard rules of adult English speakers.

STUDY 1: THE ROLE OF NUMBERS IN PLURALIZATION

A Production task was administered to 14 kindergarten pupils with a mean age of 6 years, 1 month to examine the hypothesis that the young child uses numerals to mark plurality. Six grade 5 students were given the same task as the younger *S*s to ascertain whether the rules studied indeed governed the responses of more mature speakers. The fifth graders performed without error.

The procedure was that of Berko's original task in which a plural response was always required. Twelve pairs of pictures were used. Each pair consisted of a singular picture assigned a name by *E*, and a plural picture used to elicit *S*'s response. When the plural picture was shown to *S*, he was asked to say what he saw in the picture. The plural picture contained two, three, or many (12–15) similar figures. Names were assigned according to the following procedure. Two lists of 12 names were constructed and alternated among *S*s. Names of the two lists formed corresponding minimal pairs. For example, *tek* appeared on the first list; therefore, *teg* appeared on the second. The names were constructed from words which contained the final phonemes /b, d, g, p, t, k, č, ǰ, š, ž/. Each of these ten phonemes was represented once in the list except for /č/ and š/, which appeared twice. Thus, six names required /iz/ for pluralization, three required /s/, and three required /z/. More names pluralized by the addition of /iz/ were used because the Pilot Study had shown that it was more difficult for *S*s to produce plural names with this marker than with /s/ or with /z/. If number is an alternate marker of purality, *S*s should readily use numbers with names whose standard plural forms they cannot produce. In other words, there should be a greater proportion of number responses in cases where the standard marker is omitted (incorrect responses from an adult point of view) than in cases where the standard marker is used (correct responses from an adult point of view).

Analysis revealed no significant difference in number of errors with the two lists ($t = .19$) so the data were pooled for further analysis. Table 1 shows the

TABLE 1   DISTRIBUTION OF RESPONSES IN STUDY 1

| | CORRECT RESPONSES | | INCORRECT RESPONSES | |
	WITH NUMBERS	WITHOUT NUMBERS	WITH NUMBERS	WITHOUT NUMBERS
/s/	17/42 = .40	11/42 = .26	10/42 = .24	4/42 = .10
/z/	22/42 = .52	13/42 = .31	5/42 = .12	2/42 = .05
/ɨz/	14/84 = .17	22/84 = .26	38/84 = .45	10/84 = .12
Total	53/168 = .32	46/168 = .27	53/168 = .32	16/168 = .09

distribution of number responses. These are expressed as ratios because of the unequal distribution of allomorphs. The proportion of errors with numbers (.32) was greater than that (.09) without numbers ($t = 4.86, p < .01$). But there was no corresponding difference in the Correct Response category. When numbers were used, significantly more errors and significantly fewer correct responses occurred with /ɨz/ than with either /s/ or with /z/ ($t > 2.69, p < .02$). But there were no differences among allomorphs in either the Correct or the Incorrect category when numbers were not used. These findings indicate that when Ss encountered a difficult item (usually one involving an /ɨz/) for which they could not produce the correct adult plural form, they at least appended a number to the singular form. Numberless incorrect responses were very infrequent (.09). But when the standard adult form was known to the children they were not so careful to avoid numberless responses (.27). It thus seems that 6-year old children do not consider numbers equal in status to the standard markers but, rather, as substitutes to fall back on when the proper marker is not known.

STUDY 2: A "PLURALIZATION BY ADDITION" RULE

In the recognition task of the Pilot Study, the children performed better in choices between singular and plural forms involving the /ɨz/ allomorph than in choices involving the other two allomorphs. Since the singular and plural forms of /ɨz/ words differ by two phonemes while forms of /s/ and /z/ words differ in only one, these results suggested that the child possessed a rule which could be called "pluralization by addition." Quite simply, this rule states that the plural form of a name is the singular form with something appended to it.

Three experiments were designed to investigate the "pluralization by addition" rule. The Ss in each of the first two experiments were six kindergarten pupils with a mean age of 5 years, 11 months. These Ss later participated in Study 3. In one experiment, S was shown a singular picture, while E said: "This is called *waf*." The E then showed S a plural picture and asked him to choose the better of two names for the second picture. The choice was always between the original singular name and a longer name formed from the original root word. In one-half (six) of the cases, a -k was added to the singular, for example, *wafk*;

and in the other half (six) -*kren* was added, for example, *wafkren*. The results clearly indicate a strong preference for the longer forms as plurals. In only two of the 72 trials did *S*s choose the original singular form to serve also as the plural form. The nearly unanimous choice (97 per cent) of the longer forms over the nonchanged forms precluded a comparison between the terms ending in -*k* and those ending in -*kren*. It was thus impossible to evaluate the original hypothesis which gave rise to this experiment.

A second experiment indicated that the general rule was one of addition, rather than a rule to choose a different word for plurality. In this study, words such as *wafk* were presented as the singular form, and *S*'s choice for plurality involved either a form in which the final -*k* was dropped (*waf*) or a longer word with -*kren* added (*wafkren*). Again, the results were nearly unanimous. The longer form was chosen as the plural on 70 out of 72 occasions (97 per cent), which implies a rule of "pluralization by addition."

One further experiment indicated that the general rule was one of addition, rather than a rule to choose a word different in sound. In this experiment, ten CVC syllables (e.g., *bip*) were presented as the singular form, and *S*s' choice for plurality involved either a form in which a vowel change had occurred (e.g., *bop*) or a singular syllable with a suffix added (e.g., *bipum*). Ten different suffixes were used. There were twenty *S*s in this study, ranging in age from 4 years, 6 months to 7 years, 2 months, with a mean age of 5 years, 11 months. They were tested in their homes during the summer. Results again support the notion of an addition rule. The number of *S*s who chose each of the ten suffixes is as follows: -*en* (15), -*it* (13), -*ik* (15), -*in* (15), -*of* (13), -*or* (11), -*up* (14), -*lin* (19), -*um* (13), and -*sit* (17). For the ten suffixes combined, the longer forms were preferred over those with vowel change in 72 per cent of the trials ($t = 4.97$, $p < .001$). The lower level of preference (72 per cent vs. 97 per cent) for the longer form in this task as compared to the earlier two tasks could reflect the greater likelihood of a vowel change serving as a plural marker in English than no change or shortening performing this function. However, it could also be due to differences in *S*s and experimental setting.

It thus appears that, even before the child has fully mastered the specific plural suffixes of English, he possesses a general rule to mark the plural by adding onto the singular code. Cross-cultural comparisons are needed to determine whether this addition rule is due to the influence of English or reflects a tendency for isomorphic coding, that is, to increase the linguistic code when the referent is increased.

STUDY 3: THE CHILD'S MASTERY OF THE STANDARD ENGLISH PLURALIZATION RULES

In the Pilot Study, different error patterns were found on the Production and the Recognition tasks. In the Production task, more errors occurred with /iz/ than with either /s/ or with /z/; whereas, in the Recognition task, fewer errors occurred with /iz/ than with either of the other two. These results, suggesting that the two tasks involved different processes, seemed to warrant further investigation.

METHOD

Subjects

The Ss were 36 kindergarten pupils with a mean age of 5 years, 11 months.

Materials and Procedure

Brightly colored pictures of cartoon animals were drawn on $8\frac{1}{2}$ × 11-inch yellow paper. These cartoon animals were given nonsense names. Figure 1 shows several sample pictures. Nonsense names for each task were selected from a list of 36 words and were systematically rotated among tasks. The names were constructed from words which contained the final phonemes /f, k, p, t, b, d, g, m, t, v, s, z, ǰ, ž, č, š/. Names were distributed so that /s/, /z/, and /iz/ appeared equally often as the plural suffix.

There were three Production and three Recognition tasks. Each S performed either the three Production or the three Recognition tasks. The order of task presentation was balanced among Ss. The Ss were tested alphabetically.

The E gave directions to S using a sample series of five or six pictures of real objects. The examples required both singular and plural responses. No S began any phase of the testing until he responded correctly to the sample pictures.

In all tasks, E said "good" when S replied correctly and "no" when he was wrong. In the latter case E, recorded an error but encouraged S to try again. The E finally provided S with the correct answer.

Six varieties of errors were possible. Within each task, S's errors were tallied separately for the items which required a plural response (Plural errors), and for the items which required a singular response (Singular errors). Within each of these two categories, S could commit an error by failing to supply or to delete one of the three allomorphs /s/, /z/, or /iz/. Twelve responses were elicited on each task.

Production Task 1: Words with Pictures. Task 1 was similar to the Production task of the Pilot Study. Twelve pairs of pictures were used: six singular stimulus-plural response pairs and six plural stimulus-singular response pairs. In the singular stimulus case, E showed S a single figure and named it. Then S was

Figure 1. Sample of pictures used in Study 3.

shown another picture with several of the same figures, and *E* attempted to elicit a plural response from him. For example, in the singular stimulus-plural response conditions, *E* showed *S* a picture and said: "This is a *pash*. [*S* repeated *pash*.] Several others (or, another) have (has) come along to join him. [The picture with several figures was shown to *S*]. Now tell me what you see in the picture." This item requires a plural response with the allomorph /iz/—*pashes*.

In the plural stimulus-singular response case, *S* was provided with the name for a plural picture and requested to produce the name for a singular picture. For example, *E* showed *S* a picture and said: "These animals are called *pashes*. [*S* repeated *pashes*.] Some (or, one) of them have (has) gone away. [The picture with a single figure was shown to *S*.] Now tell me what you see in the picture." This item requires a singular response with the allomorph /iz/ deleted— *pash*.

Production Task 2: Words Alone. Task 2 was similar to Task 1 except that no pictures were used. There were 12 items in this task: six requiring singular responses and six, plural. The *S* was told to "pretend that one *wib* was here. [*S* repeated *wib*.] Now pretend some others (or, another one) come(s) along. What would there be now?" This item requires a plural response with the allomorph /z/—*wibs*. In every task, instructions were appropriately modified when a singular response was required.

Production Task 3: Tell a Story. Task 3 required *S* to "Tell a Story" about a cartoon animal(s). Twelve pairs of pictures were used as in Task 1. In Task 3, however, the animal(s) in the second picture of each pair was always drawn performing some action. The *S*'s job was to describe the picture. The *E* showed *S* a picture and said: "This is a *gop*. [*S* repeated *gop*.] Some others (or, another) have (has) come along to join him. [*S* was shown a picture of *gops* jumping rope.] Can you describe what you see in the picture?" This item required a plural response with the allomorph /s/: "I see the *gops* jumping rope." The answer was scored correct if the appropriate form of the name was mentioned in the description disregarding the description itself.

Recognition Task 4: (1P, 2N). In Task 4, *S* was shown one picture (1P) while *E* said a pair of nonsense names (2N). For example, *E* showed *S* a single figure and said a pair of nonsense words (*maj-majes*). The *S* was instructed to choose the "best" name for the picture. In this example, a singular response, *maj*, would have been correct. Six singular and six plural pictures were used.

Recognition Task 5: (2P, 1N). In Task 5, two pictures (one singular and one plural, but each of different animals) were shown to *S*, while *E* said one name. The *S* had to point to the picture named by *E*. If *E* said *him*, *S* had to point to the singular picture. If he failed to do this, a "Singular error" was recorded. Twelve pairs of singular and plural pictures were used.

Recognition Task 6: (2P, 2N). In this task, a pair of pictures was shown to *S* while *E* said a pair of names (*zop-zops*). The *S* had to point first to one picture as *E* again said the name, and then to the other named picture. Six pairs of singular and plural pictures were used.

RESULTS

Analysis of variance (repeated measures design; Winer, 1962) for the three Production tasks revealed a significant difference among allomorphs ($F = 9.23$, $p < .01$) and among tasks ($F = 3.28$, $p < .05$). The interaction was not significant ($F = 1.33$). Table 2 shows the mean number of errors by allomorph for each of the tasks. Comparisons among allomorphs within each task were evaluated using t test for correlated data. Significant comparisons are indicated. In all other comparisons, $t < .88$. In each task, significantly more errors occurred with /iz/ than with either of the other two allomorphs. There were no significant differences between words with /s/ and with /z/ in any of the three Production tasks. These results replicated the findings of the Pilot Study and Study 1 concerning the distribution of errors with the three allomorphs in a Production task.

Table 2 shows the distribution of errors in the Production tasks for the six items requiring a plural response versus the six items requiring a singular response. For each task, comparisons were made between total Singular errors and total Plural errors. Although more Plural errors occurred in every task, the difference was significant ($t = 2.94$, $p < .01$) only for Task 1 (Words with Pictures). The total number of Plural errors for all three tasks combined was also significantly larger than that of Singular errors ($t = 2.50$, $p < .05$).

TABLE 2   DISTRIBUTION OF SINGULAR AND PLURAL MEAN ERRORS ON PRODUCTION TASKS

Task	Singular	Plural	Total	Significant t Values
1. (Words with Pictures):				
/s/	0.17	0.44	0.61	2.90
/z/	0.11	0.33	0.44	3.52
/iz/	0.45	1.06	1.51	
Total	0.73	1.83	2.56	—
2. (Words Alone):				
/s/	0.28	0.28	0.56	6.32
/z/	0.39	0.33	0.72	7.14
/iz/	0.88	1.28	2.16	
Total	1.55	1.89	3.44	—
3. (Tell a Story):				
/s/	0.22	0.17	0.39	3.79
/z/	0.22	0.34	0.56	2.91
/iz/	0.50	0.94	1.44	
Total	0.94	1.45	2.39	—
Total	3.22	5.17	—	—

Note.—In each task, the first t value is for the /s/ vs. /iz/ comparison and the second for the /z/ vs. /iz/ comparison. All t's are significant at the .01 level, two-tailed tests.

Analysis of variance for the three Recognition tasks revealed a significant difference among tasks ($F = 26.24$, $p < .001$) as well as significant interaction ($F = 3.80$, $p. < .05$), but the difference among allomorphs was not significant ($F = 1.83$). This was likely due to the virtual absence of errors on Task 6 (2P, 2N). Table 3 shows the mean number of errors by allomorph for each of the three Recognition tasks. No comparisons were possible within Task 6 because of the virtual absence of errors. In the other two Recognition tasks, significantly fewer errors occurred with /z/ than with either /s/ or with /ɨz/. There were no differences ($t < .88$) between errors with /s/ and with /ɨz/. This pattern of errors for the three allomorphs was also obtained in an exploratory study using only three Recognition tasks. This distribution of errors by allomorph is distinctly different from that of the Production tasks.

No significant differences were found between number of Singular and Plural errors for either the Individual tasks or the combined totals. Table 3 also shows this distribution.

Comparisons among all six Production and Recognition tasks show that Task 6 is significantly easier than any of the other five tasks ($t > 2.90$, $p < .01$) and that Task 2 (Words Alone) is significantly harder than Task 3 (Tell a Story; $t = 2.12$, $p < .05$) and Task 4 (IP, 2N; $t = 2.30$, $p < .05$). All other comparisons yielded t values below 1.56.

TABLE 3   DISTRIBUTION OF SINGULAR AND PLURAL MEAN ERRORS ON RECOGNITION TASKS

TASK	SINGULAR	PLURAL	TOTAL	SIGNIFICANT t VALUES
4. (IP, 2N):				
/s/	0.28	0.50	0.78	
/z/	0.17	0.17	0.34	3.49
/ɨz/	0.33	0.33	0.66	2.91
Total	0.78	1.00	1.78	—
5. (2P, 1N):				
/s/	0.78	0.44	1.22	
/z/	0.33	0.17	0.50	3.74
/ɨz/	0.56	0.50	1.06	2.65
Total	1.67	1.11	2.78	—
6. (2P, 2N):				
/s/	0.06	0.06	0.12	—
/z/	—	—	—	—
/ɨz/	—	0.06	0.06	—
Total	0.06	0.12	0.18	—
Total	2.51	2.23	—	—

Note.—In each task, the first t value is for the /s/ vs. /z/ comparison and the second for the /z/ vs. /ɨz/ comparison. The first three t's are significant at the .01 level and the last one at the .05 level, two-tailed tests.

DISCUSSION

Consider first the child's *productive* control of pluralization rules. Table 2 indicates that the same pattern of errors by allomorph occurred for all three Production tasks. There were significantly more errors with /iz/ than with either /s/ or /z/, and there was no difference between the number of errors with /s/ and with /z/. The greater difficulty of /iz/ is probably due to the child's limited experience with nouns taking this allomorph.

The finding that the children performed better when they were given the plural and required to produce the singular than when the task was reversed indicates that they can, to some extent, analyze a plural word into a stem and a plural marker.

In spite of the similar distribution of errors by allomorph in the three Production tasks, differences did occur among the tasks in total number of errors. Words Alone (Task 2) was the most difficult task, probably because requirements of this task were not constantly emphasized through pictures. Fewer errors were made in the better-structured Words with Pictures task (No. 1) where the pictures helped define the task requirements for the Ss. The easiest Production task, Tell a Story (No. 3), also well defined by pictures, captured the interest and enthusiasm of the children.

Despite the differences in level of difficulty, the Production tasks exhibit a characteristic pattern of errors distinguishing them from the Recognition tasks to which we now turn. Although the Recognition tasks also share a common pattern of errors by allomorph, they differ more among themselves than the Production tasks. We will, therefore, discuss separately each Recognition task.

Task 6 (2P, 2N) was the easiest of all six tasks with only three errors in 216 trials. In this task, S was shown both the singular and plural pictures of an animal while E said both the singular and plural forms of a name. The S was required simply to match the names with the pictures. The child can perform accurately on this task if he matches isomorphically the longer code with the larger number of objects and the shorter code with the single object. Perfect performance on Task 6 does not require any other knowledge.

Such one-to-one matching is not possible in Task 4 (1P, 2N) where S is given only one picture and asked to choose the better of two names for it. This task is, nevertheless, fairly easy because S can draw on the simple generalization from English singular-plural relations that plural nouns are longer than singular nouns. This information is sufficient for deciding which of the two names is plural and which is singular. Study 2 has demonstrated that 6-year-old children are able to apply this generalization when asked to choose between a longer and a shorter name for a plural referent. However, the occurrence of differences among allomorphs indicates that Ss did not exclusively depend on this generalization.

Task 5 (2P, 1N), in which a single name was offered to the child and he was required to select the picture (out of two) that best suited the name, was more difficult than the other Recognition tasks partly because the two pictures within each pair differed not only with respect to number of animals but also with respect to kind of animals. This may have rendered Task 5 less well defined than the other Recognition tasks.

The different levels of difficulty of the various tasks reveal some aspects of the mental operations underlying performance on these tasks; some other aspects are reflected in the distribution of errors. The pattern of errors in the Recognition tasks is distinctly different from that in the Production tasks. In the Production tasks, /s/ and /z/ were of equal difficulty, and /iz/ was significantly harder than each of them; whereas in the Recognition tasks, more errors occurred with /s/ and with /iz/ than with /z/.

In Task 4, this distribution of errors can be explained by reference to the fact that in English only a few singulars end in a /consonant + z/cluster—*lens* and *adze* are the only cases that come to mind. Consequently, when the child is given a choice between a CVC name and a CVC + /z/ name, he can draw on this information and readily decide that the CVC + /z/ is the plural. In the case of /s/, the decision is not so easy, as many common singular nouns have a /consonant + s/ in final position (e.g., *tax*, *wax*, *fence*, *horse*). This accounts for the greater error score for /s/ than for /z/ in Task 4. In the case of /iz/, the difficulty may be due to the availability of singular nouns ending in /vowel + z/ (e.g., *maze*, *breeze*) and to the presence of /s/ and /z/, and sounds similar to these plural markers in the final positions of the singular alternatives (e.g., *tass* vs. *tasses*, *bez* vs. *bezes*, *kush* vs. *kushes*). Thus in choices involving /iz/, the child could mistakenly consider either both names as singulars or both as plurals. These considerations would explain why fewer errors were obtained in Task 4 with /z/ than with either /s/ or with /iz/.

There was no difference between the number of Singular and Plural errors on Task 4. This can be explained by reference to the fact that both in the case when the picture depicted a single animal (an occasion for the occurrence of Singular errors) and in the case when it depicted several animals (an occasion for the occurrence of Plural errors), the singular *and* the plural forms were given to the S who was required to choose the appropriate one of the two. In *both* the singular case and the plural case, Ss could respond correctly by identifying either the singular form or the plural one, and, by a process of elimination, arrive at the complementary form. Since recognition of either the singular or the plural form could contribute to a Correct response, no difference between the number of Singular and Plural errors would be expected.

Task 5 (2P, 1N) was the most difficult Recognition task. It was, in fact, more difficult than two Production tasks (Words with Pictures and Tell a Story). Nevertheless, the error pattern by allomorph in Task 5 is quite different from that of the Production tasks and exactly like that of Recognition Task 4. In Task 5, as in Task 4, significantly fewer errors occurred with /z/ than with either /s/ or with /iz/, and there was no significant difference between errors with /s/

and with /ɨz/. In the cases where the name offered was a plural one, the explanation proposed for the distribution of errors in Task 4 obviously applies here too. Names ending in /consonant + s/ and in /vowel + z/ are not as reliably plurals as are names ending in /consonant + z/. When the name is in singular form, the plural-sounding endings of the nouns taking /ɨz/ in the plural (e.g., *ress, niz, pash*) could lead the child to regard the singulars as plurals. If this suggestion is accepted, it would account for the greater number of errors made with /ɨz/ than with /z/. But why were there more errors with unvoiced singulars (those taking /s/ for pluralization) than with voiced singulars (taking /z/)? Perhaps in deciding whether a particular name is singular or plural, *S* tried, covertly, to generate the complementary form; and since the complementary form of unvoiced singulars (ending in /consonant + s/) is not as obviously plural as that of voiced ones (ending in /consonant + z/), *S* had greater difficulty in identifying the unvoiced CVC names as singular than the voiced CVC names.

The finding that there were fewer Plural than Singular errors in Task 5, although not significantly so, deserves comment because it goes contrary to the trend in all other tasks. This difference may mean that the presence of a plural allomorph is more suggestive of plurality than its absence is of singularity, possibly because irregular plurals have a singular shape.

CONCLUSIONS

Two general conclusions are suggested by the results of the above experiments.

a) In studies of retention, recognition memory is commonly distinguished by its sensitivity to memory traces too faint to be picked up by recall techniques. But both methods are viewed as assessing the same underlying process; recognition is considered merely a finer measure of the same thing measured crudely by recall. Similarly, in language studies, recognition and production methods are usually distinguished in terms of degree of difficulty. The present findings challenge the general validity of characterizing the difference between recognition and production procedures solely in quantitative terms. In the experiments described in this paper, level of difficulty did not differentiate Recognition tasks from Production tasks, only the pattern of errors did. The two procedures were seen to have tapped different aspects of the *S*s' linguistic knowledge. While in production tasks, *S*s had to depend mainly on the information contained in the rules governing English pluralization, in the recognition tasks, they could have drawn, and in many cases did draw, on the generalization that, in English, plurals are longer than singulars and that few singulars end in /consonant + z/ clusters.

b) The second lesson we have learned from the described experiments is that in studying particular linguistic rules one should not ignore other linguistic information available to the *S*s. Although English pluralization rules do not prohibit the formation of singular nouns ending in /consonant + z/, nevertheless the rare occurrence of such nouns had an effect on *S*s' responses in our experiments. It should always be kept in mind that when a *S* participates in an experiment designed to investigate a particular segment of linguistic rules, his responses need not be guided solely, or even mainly, by these rules. The *S* has access to a larger store of knowledge—including grammatical rules, language habits, statistical facts—than the *E* is investigating and is able to bring this knowledge to bear on the problem at hand. More generally, one can say with Humboldt and Chomsky, and against Wittgenstein, that the whole totality of language is "present to the mind as a permanent background for each act of language use" (Chomsky, 1964b, p. 24).

REFERENCES

Berko, Jean, The child's learning of English morphology, *Word*, 1958, **14**, 150–177.
Brown, R. W., and Jean Berko, Psycholinguistic research methods. In P. H. Mussen (ed.), *Handbook of Research Methods in Child Development*. New York: Wiley, 1960. Pp. 517–557.
Brown, R. W., and C. Fraser, The acquisition of syntax. In C. N. Cofer and Barbara Musgrave (eds.), *Verbal Behavior and Learning: Problems and Processes*. New York: McGraw-Hill, 1963. Pp. 158–197.
Bruce, D. J., An analysis of word sounds by young children, *British Journal of Educational Psychology*, 1964, **34**, 158–170.
Chomsky, N., Comments for Project Literacy meeting, *Project Literacy Reports,* September 1964, No. 2, 1–8. (a)
Chomsky, N., *Current Issues in Linguistic Theory*. The Hague: Mouton, 1964. (b)
Chomsky, N., Formal discussion. In Ursula Bellugi and R. W. Brown (eds.), The acquisition of language, *Monographs of the Society for Research in Child Development*, 1964, **29**, No. 1 (Serial No. 92), 35–42. (c)
Chomsky, N., *Aspects of the Theory of Syntax*. Cambridge, Mass.: M.I.T. Press, 1965.
Ervin, Susan M., Imitation and structural change in children's language. In E. H. Lenneberg (ed.), *New Directions in the Study of Language*. Cambridge, Mass.: M.I.T. Press, 1964. Pp. 163–189. [Reprinted in this volume.]
Ervin, Susan M., and W. Miller, Language development. In H. W. Stevenson (ed.), *Yearbook of the National Society for the Study of Education*, 62, Part I. Chicago: Chicago University Press, 1963. Pp. 108–143.
Ferguson, G. A., *Statistical Analysis in Psychology and Education*. New York: McGraw Hill, 1959.
Francis, W. N., *The Structure of American English*. New York: Ronald Press, 1958.
Fraser, C., Ursula Bellugi, and R. W. Brown, Control of grammar in imitation, comprehension, and production, *Journal of Verbal Learning and Verbal Behavior*, 1963, **2**, 121–135. [Reprinted in this volume.]

Huttenlocher, Janellen, Children's language: word-phrase relationship, *Science*, January 17, 1964, **143**, (3603), 264–265.

Menyuk, Paula, Syntactic rules used by children from preschool through first grade, *Child Development*, 1964, **35**, 533–546.

Weir, Ruth W., *Language in the Crib*. The Hague: Mouton, 1962.

Winer, B. J., *Statistical Principles in Experimental Design*. New York: McGraw-Hill, 1962.

The Acquisition of Noun and Verb Inflections[1, 2]

—— *Courtney B. Cazden*

When analyses of language development are based on a corpus of spontaneous speech, the researcher must question the representativeness of his corpus. If a particular construction does not appear in a certain transcription of the child's speech, is it missing from the child's linguistic competence or only from this sample of his performance?

One way to separate the absence of a construction in the child's competence from the rarity of that construction in his performance is to look for the frequency of forms in contexts which make them obligatory. Each of these contexts in the child's speech can be considered a learning trial, and the proportion of times in which the child performs appropriately can be charted as that proportion changes over time. For such analyses one needs features for which clearly defined contexts exist even in the telegraphic speech of young children. Noun and verb inflections fit this criterion well.

The present paper will report on the acquisition of five noun and verb inflections by Adam, Eve, and Sarah, three subjects of a 5-year study of language acquisition (Brown and Bellugi, 1964; Bellugi, 1967; Brown, Cazden and Bellugi, 1968). When the study was begun, Adam's and Eve's fathers were Harvard graduate students, while Sarah's father was a clerk in a local supermarket. Neither of her parents had gone beyond high school. All analyses are based on tape recordings of spontaneous parent-child conversation made weekly or biweekly in each child's home.

Figure 1 on page 296 gives a small-scale view of the language development

From *Child Development*, 1968, **39**, 433–438. Reprinted by permission of the author and the Society for Research in Child Development, Inc.

[1] This research was supported by Public Health Service grant MH-7088 from the National Institute of Mental Health to Roger Brown. Previous versions of this paper were presented at a colloquium, Eliot Pearson Department of Child Study, Tufts University, March 1967; at the biennial meeting of the Society for Research in Child Development, New York City, March 1967; and at the annual convention of the Speech and Hearing Society of the Province of Quebec, Montreal, May 1967.

[2] [For additional comments on Roger Brown's research project, from which this work stems, see editorial introduction to the paper by Brown, Cazden, and Bellugi, below. —Ed.]

of the three children for the period discussed here. The horizontal axis is age. The vertical axis is mean length of utterance (MLU)—a useful summary of the result of the development process even though it tells nothing about that process itself. Roman numerals I–V indicate five points in the developmental continuum at which the children can be compared with MLU held constant.

First, acquisition of the five inflections is charted: plural and possessive inflections on nouns and present progressive, regular past- and present-indicative inflections on verbs. Second, the role of parent speech is examined. Finally, systematic errors of commission are categorized.

THE ACQUISITION OF INFLECTIONS

Criteria were established for asserting that an inflection was required in a particular utterance. Following are some of the criteria for plurals with examples of omitted inflections from the children's speech:

Number.—Required after all numbers except 1: "Two minute."

Linguistic.—Required on count nouns after such modifiers as "more" or "some": "More page."

Interaction.—Required for discourse agreement: "Shoe" in response to parent's question, "What are those?"

Normally plural.—"Stair" ("upstairs").

Routines.—Either public, like nursery rhymes and the names of cartoon characters—"Mr. Ear" ("Mr. Ears")—or private, like Eve's telegraphic version of her mother's oft repeated explanation of father's work—"Make penny Ema' Hall" ("He's making pennies in Emerson Hall").

Any one criterion was sufficient, but multiple coding was frequently necessary.

The entire set of transcriptions from I and V was used. On the above criteria, inflections were coded as supplied correcty when required (S_c), supplied in inappropriate contexts (S_x), or required but omitted (O). Overgeneralizations in form (OG)—"Somes" or "I seed it"—were also coded.

In some analyses the relations between S_c, S_x, and O were charted as they changed over time. In other analyses a point was established at which a certain inflection can be said to have been acquired. Those points were then compared within each child's language system and across the set of three subjects. Point of acquisition is defined as the first speech sample of three such that in all three the inflection is supplied in at least 90 per cent of the contexts in which it is clearly required.

Noun Inflections

Of the two noun inflections, plurals reached the point of acquisition before possessives in Adam's and Sarah's speech. In Eve's speech, they reached criterion at the same time, suggesting that a phonological constraint may have been operating on both.

TABLE 1   PERIODS IN THE DEVELOPMENT OF THE PLURAL INFLECTION

PERIOD	AGE IN MONTHS	POINT(S) IN FIG. 1	$S_c/(S_c + O)$	$S_x(S_x + S_c)$	$OG/(S_x + S_c)$
			EVE		
A	18–19	I	.00	.00	.00
B	20–22	II	.15 (14/(14 + 78))	.00	.00
C	23–24	III	.86 (136/(136 + 22))	.07 (10/10 + 136))	.05 (8/146)
D	25–27	IV–V	.98 (217/(217 + 4))	.005 (1/ (1 + 217))	.03 (7/218)
			ADAM		
A	—	—	—	—	—
B	27–29	I–II	.36 (32/(32 + 57))	.00	.00
C	30–32	—	.68 (142/(142 + 67))	.15 (25/25 + 142))	.01 (2/167)
D	33–42	III–V	.94 (927/(927 + 58))	.06 (54/(54 + 927)).	04 (40/981)
			SARAH		
A	—	—	—	—	—
B	27–30	I	.13 (11/(11 + 74))	.00	.00
C	31–33	—	.86 (124/(124 + 21))	.03 (4/(4 + 124))	.00
D	34–49	II–V	.98 (722/(722 + 12))	.04 (28/(28 + 722))	.03 (23/750)

Table 1 summarizes data on the acquisition of plurals by the three children. The first column gives the ratio of S_c to the total required; the second and third columns give the ratio of S_x and OG to the total supplied. The first two rows for Eve thus read as follows: at 18–19 months, which include I on the graph, Eve used no plurals. At 20–22 months, which include II, she used them 15 per cent of the time they were required, with no errors and no overgeneralizations.

In Table 1 the developmental continuum for each child has been broken at three places to yield four periods. Period A is defined by the absence of the inflection. Adam and Sarah had gone beyond this point when our transcriptions began. Period B is defined by occasional production with no errors or over-generalizations. This period is present in all three children's development. In period C production increases markedly, and errors and overgeneralizations appear. Finally, in period D, the inflection attains the arbitrary criterion of 90 per cent correct use.

These three divisions do not have the same status. The break between C and D is clearly an arbitrary imposition. The meaning of the break between A and B, signaling the onset of the inflection, is unclear. But the break between B and C represents a significant developmental phenomenon, because systematic errors and overgeneralizations provide convincing evidence that the child has a productive rule. Werner (1957) differentiated between quantitative change (no matter how abrupt) in the frequency of some behavior and qualitative change. Later he described the "de-differentiation (dissolution) of existing, schematized or automatized behavior patterns" (1957, p. 139) as one of the processes by which simple behavior is reconstructed into more complex behavior. Such a dissolution of existing behavior patterns seems to be taking place in the qualitative break between periods B and C.

The pattern of no use, followed by infrequent but invariably correct use, followed only later by evidence of productivity, characterizes the development of many features of the children's speech. A hypothesis suggested by these data is that the child begins to operate with stored fragments of speech he has heard (not just an immediately preceding utterance), which are somehow tagged liberally for semantic information on the verbal and nonverbal context and only later are gradually subjected to analysis for the acquisition of productive rules. This hypothesis is consistent with Ervin's (1964) finding that imitations per se are not progressive and with McNeill's suggestion that "a child's additions to competence are made through his comprehension" (1966, p. 81).

Tables 2 and 3 give finer details of two developmental patterns and, correspondingly, more striking examples of regularities across the three children. Table 2 shows an enlarged close-up of one subset of plurals, those required on linguistic criteria. The linguistic criteria can be divided into requirements that are contained within the noun phrase and requirements that extend across the noun-phrase boundary. For example, in the noun phrase "some crayons," "crayons" must be pluralized because it is a count noun following "some." That is a requirement within the noun phrase. In "Those my crayons," however, "crayons" must be pluralized because it is a predicate nominative which must agree with the subject "those." Here the requirement extends across the noun-phrase boundary. With striking consistency, the three children supplied the

TABLE 2 PROVISION OF PLURAL INFLECTION IN TWO LINGUISTIC CONTEXTS

	AGE IN MONTHS	WITHIN NOUN PHRASE	ACROSS NOUN-PHRASE BOUNDARY
Eve	18–27	.89 (48/54)	.30 (3/10)
Adam	27–42	.77 (124/162)	.43 (26/61)
Sarah	27–49	.83 (67/81)	.54 (12/22)

TABLE 3 PROVISION OF POSSESSIVE INFLECTION IN TWO LINGUISTIC CONTENTS

	AGE IN MONTHS	WITH NOUN	ELLIPTIC	OG
Eve	18–24	.07 (9/138)	.69 (11/16)	5
Adam	27–33	.16 (21/130)	.86 (37/43)	36
Sarah	27–39	.06 (2/33)	1.00 (8/8)	2

plural correctly when the requirement was within the noun phrase before they did so when the requirement extended across the noun-phrase boundary. These data suggest that one aspect of language development is the extension of linguistic dependency relations across larger units.

A related but simpler hypothesis was not confirmed. Because a child's programing span is limited, it seemed possible that during the learning period the utterances which included plurals would be on the average shorter (not counting the plural morpheme itself) than their counterparts with plurals omitted. Supporting examples were found of isolated noun phrases which included plurals and noun phrases in longer utterances which did not. But computation of mean length showed no clear pattern across the three children. The hypothesis suggested by Table 2 still assumes a limit on programing span, but it does not assume that the limit is on the accretion of morphemes of equal unit, like beads on a string. Rather, it assumes that morphemes have differential cognitive weight depending on structural complexity.

In Table 3, the evidence shifts from plurals to possessives. Here we find another regularity in the contexts in which an inflection first appears. The normal form for expressing possession is noun plus possessive inflection plus noun— "That's Daddy's hat." In the alternative elliptic form, the final noun is deleted —"That's Daddy's." Table 3 shows that for the period up to the criterion of 90 per cent accuracy, all three children were more apt to supply the possessive inflection in the elliptic context.

The data are particularly clear on this point for Sarah because of a conversational routine which served to test Sarah's use of the possessive inflection at intervals. Sarah's mother frequently asked, "Whose girl are you?" to which Sarah was supposed to reply, "Mommy's girl." The first time she answered correctly was at 38 months. Before that we find: only one instance of possessive inflection plus noun (at 28 months) and that an imitation of her mother's preceding utterance; 10 instances of the routine answered "Mommy girl"; 21 other instances of omitted inflections, all with final noun; 8 instances of inflection supplied, all elliptic; 2 (the only two) instances of overgeneralizations—"Where mines?" and "I drink hims."

This finding is particularly interesting because the three mothers used the normal form 7–20 times as often as the elliptic form. The proportion of elliptic to all possessives in a sample of 2,800 utterances from each mother was: Eve's mother, 3 out of 62; Adam's mother, 3 out of 37; Sarah's mother, 7 out of 50. Two possible reasons for this discrepancy between what the children heard and what they produced are confounded. First, even though the children heard the elliptic form much less frequently, the inflection may be more noticeable in that context. Second, the elliptic form is less redundant and more critical to meaning. The relative importance for unambiguous communication was shown by a remark of Sarah's after a trip to get an ice-cream cone. She told her mother, "I shared Daddy's." Only the inflection signified that it was the ice-cream cone and not Daddy that was divided up.

Verb Inflections

In the analysis of verb inflections, the present progressive *ing* form was counted only when it was attached to the main verb. "Got" was excluded from all counts because its past status is uncertain and its colloquial uses have peculiar aspects which make interpretation difficult. Often the children used unmarked verbs where some inflection was clearly required. But unless there was a clear indication of which inflection should have been supplied, these cases were excluded from analysis.

Despite these simplifications, the findings on verb inflections are fragmentary, probably because the verb system is one of the most complicated parts of English grammar. Because there is no one-to-one relation between linguistic forms and temporal reference, application of requirement criteria probably produces more wrong interpretations with verb inflections than with nouns. Furthermore, verb inflections cannot be easily separated from the complex system of English auxiliaries. For example, the past- and present-indicative inflections appear only in declarative sentences. In both questions and negatives, the markers for tense and person shift to the dummy auxiliary "do":

He walked. Did he walk? He didn't walk.
He walks. Does he walk? He doesn't walk.

The relation of verb inflections to the auxiliary system complicates the child's learning as well as the researcher's analysis. Sometimes an adult model is not helpful:

MOTHER: Did you write it already?
CHILD: Write already.

Sometimes an expansion even leads to regression:

CHILD: Because I caught . . .
MOTHER: What did you catch?
CHILD: I catch my bicycle.

To the extent that the child's learning is helped by adult speech which precedes as a model or follows as an expansion, the past- and present-indicative inflections pose special problems. Parent speech uttered with identical intent cannot provide the same assistance as it may for other constructions.

Of the three verb inflections, the present progressive appeared first in all three children, reaching criterion between II and III. The sequence of acquisition for regular past and present indicative was less consistent. By V, Sarah had attained our criterion of 90 per cent accuracy on both, Eve had attained only the past, and Adam only the present indicative.

The appearance of "be" auxiliary forms with the present progressive— "I'm going" or "We're playing"—was added to the analysis because the required contexts are clear and errors of interpretation therefore unlikely. None of the children reached criterion on the auxiliary by V. The percentages of auxiliaries supplied in the final three transcriptions range from 18 for Eve to 79 for Sarah. Eve supplied auxiliaries in questions first, but this seems to be an idiosyncratic phenomenon. Adam was more apt to include them in declaratives, while Sarah showed no bias either way.

Adam and Sarah both occasionally used a form of "be" without *ing*, while Eve did not. These utterances seemed to have different derivations in the two children's language. In Sarah's speech there were nine instances, all of them "I'm" plus verb, such as, "I'm play with it" and "I'm twist his head.' These constructions are probably reduced catenatives conveying intention rather than referring to ongoing action. In Adam's speech, only one utterance was counted as Auxiliary without *ing*—"Dey are stand up." But there were many instances of "its" plus verb, such as, "Its go up" and "Its went away." Elsewhere (Brown et al., 1969), Adam's use of "its" has been analyzed as a temporary segmentation error which led him to consider "its" as a variant of "it" in subject position, perhaps because in his mother's speech "it" was followed much more often by "is" than by a main verb.

Differences in Rate of Acquisition

Any comparison of developmental phenomena across children requires a metric for that comparison. The conventional metric is chronological age. Because Adam, Eve, and Sarah have been equated at five points on MLU, comparison on this basis is also possible. The three children's acquisition of inflections has been analyzed on both cases of comparison. Chronological age and mean length of utterance in this research are comparable to chronological age and mental age in studies of intellectual development. Like mental age, MLU is a single global measure. Equating children on such a measure may yield additional information on the relative development of more specific abilities.

When we compare the children in relation to age, the order of development is clear: Eve way out in front, Adam second, and Sarah third. This is what one would expect from Figure 1. Eve at V was 27 months old, the age of Adam and Sarah at I. But if age is ignored, the order changes as shown in Table 4. By II, when all three children had a MLU of 2.25, only Sarah had achieved criterion in one of the inflections, plurality; by IV, when all three children had a MLU of 3.50, she had five inflections, Eve had four, and Adam only two. Where criterion was not reached by V, the percentage of supplied to total required is given in the last column. Note the much higher percentage of Sarah's auxiliaries with the present progressive.

Cazden (1968) reported that Sarah acquired plurals before Eve and Adam in terms of MLU and suggested a relation to the higher density of plurals in Sarah's mother's speech. With more evidence, this suggestion must be amended. The relative advancement of Sarah at particular MLU values is not restricted to plurality.

TABLE 4   COMPARISON OF ACQUISITION OF INFLECTIONS ON BASIS
OF MLU

	I	II	III	IV	V
Eve	—	—	*ing*	Plural Poss. Past	.77 pres. indic. .18 aux.
Adam	—	—	Plural *ing*	—	Poss. Pres. indic. .91 past .23 aux.
Sarah	—	Plural	*ing*	Poss. Past Pres. indic.	.79 aux.

Several additional pieces of evidence are now available on the relative grammatical competence of the three children when mean length of utterance is held constant. First, Bellugi (1967, p. 209a) found that the auxiliary-verb system developed earlier in Sarah (before IV) than in Eve and Adam (at IV). She also found that of the three children, only Sarah used tag questions ("Now you can see, can't you?") by V. "Tag questions are of particular interest in the language acquisition process, since they involve knowledge of a good deal of [grammatical] apparatus . . . and very little meaning" (Bellugi, 1967, p. 149). Finally, Brown tabulated the presence and absence of all required functors at II and V. Functors include inflections and also articles, prepositions, etc.— everything except the content words: nouns, verbs, adjectives, and adverbs. At both points, Sarah supplied required functors a higher proportion of the time than Adam and Eve did. At V, the percentage of functors still missing was: Eve, 43; Adam, 20; and Sarah, 15 (Brown, unpublished memorandum, 1966).

In interpreting this evidence, consider only the two extremes—Eve and Sarah. If, at a particular MLU value, Sarah supplied more required functors, then Eve's speech contained proportionately more content words. An abnormal proportion of content words to functors characterizes what we call telegraphic language (Brown & Bellugi, 1964)—the language of telegrams ("Arrive Saturday" instead of "I will arrive on Saturday") the language of note-taking, and the language of young children. It is a highly informative language, since functors can be guessed from context, whereas content words cannot. So we can say that Eve conveyed more information for the same overall mean length than Sarah did. Eve's utterances were a more telegraphic version of a more informative and less predictable utterance, while Sarah's utterances were a less telegraphic version of a less informative and more predictable utterance.

These two patterns can be labeled macrodevelopment and microdevelopment, respectively. Macrodevelopment refers to the elaborateness of the semantic or plan for speaking, while microdevelopment refers to the successful execution of whatever plan has been formulated. They represent relative advance in more cognitive or more strictly grammatical aspects of the total language-acquisition process. Evidently, synchronization of the two aspects can vary in ways which are masked by the global measure of mean length of utterance. An increase in mean length is just a quantitative accretion, while an essential characteristic of development is "movement over time toward complexity of organization" (Harris, 1957, p. 3). Complexity and length do increase together at these early ages, but the complexity summarized by a certain mean length is not the same in all details for all children.

Eve had undoubtedly caught up in the provision of functors by the time she reached Sarah's age, probably long before. But Sarah was less behind in her provision of functors than in what she was trying to say. Alternatively, and perhaps more simply, prediction of level of language development on the basis of MLU, a measure of performance, underestimated Sarah's linguistic competence. Perhaps differences in intelligence between the two children (about which we have no information) affected language performance more than competence. Perhaps communication patterns in the home provided different degrees of stimulation for the child to use whatever competence had been attained.

THE ROLE OF PARENT SPEECH

Brown and Bellugi (1964) hypothesized that a form of parental response termed "expansions" might provide especially useful information for the acquisition of grammar. Cazden (1965) was unable to confirm that hypothesis in a manipulative experiment and found instead that the provision of well-formed but non-contingent models was more helpful to the grammatical development of 12 lower-class Negro children. Because we considered this small experiment inconclusive, we have probed further into the effects of expansions and models on the growth of specific aspects of grammatical development such as inflections.

Each child utterance identified as S_c, S_x or O was coded for the adult utterance which immediately followed. If a child's utterance which contained an omitted or inappropriate inflection was followed by an adult utterance which contained the appropriate inflection, it was coded E for expansion whether or not the entire utterance was an expansion of the child's utterance. Note that for the particular purpose of this analysis expansions are defined less restrictively than usual (cf. Brown and Bellugi, 1964). Note also that an expansion of an inflection supplied but inappropriate can be termed a "correction," as when the child says "foots" and the mother immediately says "feet." If the child's utterance was followed by an adult utterance which contained the noun or verb in the same form as the child's utterance, it was coded M for imitation. Finally, if the child's utterance was followed by an adult utterance which did not contain the relevant noun or verb at all, it was marked N. From these analyses we can determine the percentage and absolute frequency of parental expansions.

TABLE 5   ACQUISITION OF INFLECTION AND TWO FEATURES OF
PARENT SPEECH

	Summed Ranks of Order of Emergence on Basis of Age	Summed Ranks of Order of Emergence on Basis of MLU	Proportion of Parent Expansions I–V	Frequency of Parent Models in 2,800 Utterances
Eve	5.0	11	0.45 (191/427)	499
Adam	12.5	12	0.51 (348/679)	576
Sarah	12.5	7	0.29 (86/294)	471

Because of their greater density, noncontingent models of the five inflections were counted in only a sample of parent speech. This sample consists of
the four sets of 700 parent utterances which immediately precede II, III, IV,
and V in the children's speech. It is the sample used in the comparison of normal
and elliptic possessives in parent speech.

Table 5 shows the relation between order of emergence of the five inflections on two bases of comparison—age and MLU—and the provision of parental
expansions and models. Order of emergence is given in summed ranks which
range from 5 to 15—first to last of the three children on the five inflections.

The difference in modeling frequency among the parents is small. This
finding was anticipated because of prior evidence of a common pattern of
mother-child conversation in the three homes. But the difference in proportion
and frequency of expansions is considerable. Sarah's telegraphic utterances
which omit inflections were followed much less frequently by a parent utterance
which included the appropriate inflections than was the case for Adam and Eve.
We knew that Sarah's mother provided the lowest density of expansions. In
fact, discovery of the relation between rate of parental expansions and rate of
child language development in terms of chronological age was one basis for the
hypothesis that expansions aid the acquisition of grammar (Brown and Bellugi,
1964). Table 5 shows that Sarah received fewer expansions in absolute frequency
as well, even though the period of time covered was 23 months for Sarah and
only 9 months for Eve.

The negative relation between expansion rate and order of emergence in
terms of MLU is surprising. Sarah received the fewest expansions, yet her
language system was relatively the most advanced in the provision of inflections.
It is hard to reconcile this finding with the hypothesis that expansions should
provide the most usable information for the acquisition of all types of functors.
Comparison of Eve's and Sarah's development suggests that particular forms
of parent interaction have less effect on more strictly grammatical aspects. Basic
grammatical structures seem to be learned despite differences in the child's
linguistic environment, while how children use language to express ideas may
be more vulnerable to environmental variation.

INFLECTIONAL ERRORS

The foregoing analyses have been based on errors of omission. But the systematic or analogical errors of commission which children make are even better guides to their linguistic knowledge. One way to categorize errors is to start with the levels of Chomsky's (1965) generative grammar and fit the rules which the children violate to them. The levels constitute parts of the adult speaker's knowledge of his language. The syntactic component of generative grammar has four levels: phrase-structure rules, lexical-subcategorization rules, transformational rules, and morphophonemic rules. Inappropriate inflections fall into the last three, which will be discussed in turn. Table 6 gives frequencies by level, and examples, of all types of errors involving the use of inflections except number agreement.

TABLE 6   INFLECTIONAL ERRORS

TYPE OF VIOLATION	NO. OF CHILDREN	NO. OF TOKENS	EXAMPLES
	SUBCATEGORIZATION RULES		
Parts of speech			
Adjectives	2	3	"Dat greens."
Adverbs	1	1	"Look how she stand ups."
Noun and verb subcategories			
Noun: mass-count	2	11	"Going put some sugars."
Noun: pronoun	3	10	"Let me have somes."
Verb: process-status	2	5	"I seeing Fraser."
Verb: transitive-intransitive	1	1	"I falled that down."
	TRANSFORMATIONAL RULES		
Wh question	3	5	"It doing dancing."
No. and tense markers			"Does it works?"
in question and negation	3	15	"I didn't spilled it."
Compound nouns	1	3	"Streets lights."
	MORPHOPHONEMIC RULES		
Wrong allomorph	2[a]	5[a]	"You pull my pantses down."
Regular-irregular:			
Plural	3	32	"Two mans."
Possessive	3	43	"Where mines?
Present indicative	1	4	"The milkman doos."
Past	3	50	"Why Paul waked up?"

[a] Only inappropriate provision of /əz/ allomorphs included.

Subcategorization Rules

According to Chomsky (1965), each word in a person's lexicon has a set of tags or syntactic features which govern the slots in which that word can be placed (strict subcategorization rules) and the words in other slots with which it can co-occur (selectional rules). For example, the noun "boy" is a count noun (and so can be pluralized), a common noun (and so can be preceded by an article), and a human noun (and so can be the object of a verb like "frighten"). When a word enters a child's lexicon, it does not enter with the full set of syntactic features correctly attached. Vocabulary development in children involves both acquisition of new words and addition of new features, with their restrictive implications, to words already learned. Morphological overgeneralizations, or more accurately underdifferentiations, can serve as tracers to linguistic categories which are still immaturely formed.

The first major division among words in a child's lexicon is the division into parts of speech—noun, verb, etc. Children so rarely overgeneralize these boundaries that we may fail to notice how easy this learning seems to be despite ever present opportunity for error. While noun and verb inflections are being learned, one might expect children to add them to words that are not nouns or verbs. Instances of such errors are very rare—three tokens of plural inflections added to adjectives and only one token of a misplaced verb inflection ("stand ups"). Because violations of part-of-speech boundaries are just as rare in Miller and Ervin's (1964) records, it is all the more curious that one of their subjects, Susan, added a past to the same particle—"stand up-ed." A segmentation error may make "stand up" a single unit to the child, or the adverbs of separable verbs may tend to take on a verbal force.

Below the level of parts of speech, four kinds of violations of lexical-subcategorization rules occurred. Plurals were extended to pronouns (a subdivision of nouns, complementing common nouns, and proper nouns) like "somes" and to mass nouns like "sugars." There were five instances of a possible violation of the process-status distinction among verbs, all with "seeing" or "having," as in "I seeing Fraser." These are verbs to which *ing* can be added with some meanings but not others: "I'm having lunch." but not "I'm having a dress on." There were no overgeneralizations to status verbs that can never take *ing*, not even to verbs of high frequency in the children's speech like "want" or "know.' (In British English the rules are different; in England and Scotland one frequently hears "wanting" and "needing.") Finally, there was one instance of an intransitive verb used transitively—"I falled that down." In this case, the inflectional error itself belongs in the morphophonemic category below, but the presence of the inflection confirms the structural analysis of the utterance. Of these four kinds of subcategorization errors, violation of the mass-count subcategorization of nouns is the most common. Why it should be more difficult for children than the process-status division among verbs is unclear.

Transformational Rules

Inappropriate inflections can result from missing or inadequate transformational rules which govern the permutation and deletion of linguistic units. First, the rules for answering *Wh* questions are overgeneralized to one kind of question where the rules do not work. While a complete answer to "What is he eating?" is "He is eating candy," the answer to "What is it doing?" is not "It doing dancing." But that is the kind of answer given for a brief period by all three children. Second, failure to shift inflections for number (in the present indicative) or tense (in the past) to the auxiliary verbs in questions and negatives produces utterances like, "Does it works?" and "I didn't spilled it." Third, Adam's utterance "Streets lights," may represent violation of the rules for forming compound nouns.

Morphophonemic Rules

Morphophonemic rules govern pronunciation and relate the syntactic and phonological parts of the grammar. Two kinds of violations occur: first, provision of the wrong allomorph (*knife-es* or *pantses*) and, second, failure to observe the division between regular and irregular forms of the plural (*mans*), possessive (*mines*), present indicative (*doos*), and past (*maked*).

It it easy to understand why children make so many errors with these irregular forms. Because the division between regular and irregular is an arbitrary one, rote learning is required in each case. They are particularly interesting because the irregular forms are often used correctly by the child before he starts to overgeneralize. Of the overgeneralized past forms, 11 of the 32 types used by Adam, Eve, and Sarah had appeared earlier in our records with the correct irregular form. For example, Eve said "comed" three times between 25 and 27 months after she had previously used "came" correctly 11 times between 20 and 22 months. McNeill (1966) argued from similar data that children are more creatures of rules than creatures of habit. Temporary coexistence of the correct irregular form and the overgeneralization is common in our records. Following are months in which Sarah used "went" and "goed":

Went:	27	32 ...	47	48	49	50
Goed:			47		49	

The irregular forms may start out as separate lexical items with no past meaning for the child. If so, it is surprising that only 5 tokens out of 50 are formed with these irregular forms as the stem, as in "tored." With plurals a higher proportion of the overgeneralizations, 11 out of 32, are added to the irregular stem, as in "feets." Note that *ing* is never added to the wrong stem; words like "tooking" never occur despite the high frequency of the irregular verbs.

While this way of looking at children's errors seems potentially productive,

the particular analysis suggested here should be considered only a first approximation. Generative grammar is itself undergoing continuous development, and
even if it were stabilized, alternative explanations of child speech would remain.
    One important question is the psychological status of the construct "levels
of the grammar." Consider again the set of lexical-subcategorization rules.
Chomsky suggested that "degree of deviance" can be scaled from most deviant
to least: violation of a lexical category ("Sincerity may virtue the boy"), conflict
with a strict subcategorization feature ("Sincerity may elapse the boy"), and
conflict with a selectional feature ("Sincerity may admire the boy") (Chomsky,
1965, pp. 152–153). The last type produces anomalous sentences which have not
been discussed here. Such a scale corresponds roughly to the frequency of errors
in children's speech, and one wonders if it also corresponds to the sequence
of acquisition. This cannot be true in any simple sense. Transformational rules
start to develop before categorization rules are completely acquired, and some
morphophonemic rules have to be acquired before any speech can be produced.
But in relative degree of differentiation and completeness, there may be an interesting correspondence.
    Another question arises from individual differences in error rate. Adam
was more prone to overgeneralizations than Eve and Sarah. See, for example,
the relative frequency of overgeneralized possessive in Table 3, Adam also
produced more anomalous sentences. For instance, he said, "Dey talking,"
about two irons that face each other on the ironing board. This may indicate
late learning of the restrictions on subjects with which "talking" can co-occur,
or it may be a deliberate metaphorical extension. Generalizations before and
after differentiation are different phenomena, but one wonders if the roots of
childish error and mature creativity are in this case somehow related.

REFERENCES

Bellugi, U. H., The acquisition of the system of negation in children's speech.
    Unpublished doctoral dissertation, Harvard University, Cambridge, Mass.,
    1967. [To be published by M.I.T. Press.]
Brown, R., and U. Bellugi, Three processes in the child's acquisition of syntax,
    Harvard Educational Review, 1964, **34**, 133–151.
Brown, R., Cazden, C. B. and U. Bellugi, The child's grammar from I to III. In
    J. P. Hill (ed.), *Minnesota Symposium on Child Development*. Vol. 2. Minne-
    apolis: University of Minnesota Press, 1968. Pp. 28–73. [Reprinted in this
    volume.]
Cazden, C. B., Environmental assistance to the child's acquisition of grammar.
    Unpublished doctoral dissertation, Harvard University, Cambridge, Mass.,
    1965.
Cazden, C. B., Some implications of research on language development for pre-
    school education. In R. D. Hess and R. M. Bear (eds.), *Early Education:
    Current Theory, Research and Practice*. Chicago: Aldine, 1968. Pp. 131–142.

Chomsky, N., *Aspects of the Theory of syntax*. Cambridge, Mass: M.I.T. Press, 1965.

Ervin, S. M., Imitation and structural change in children's language. In E. Lenneberg (ed.), *New directions in the study of language*. Cambridge, Mass.: M.I.T. Press, 1964. Pp. 163–189. [Reprinted in this volume.]

Harris, D. B., Problems in formulating a scientific concept of development. In D. B. Harris (ed.), *The concept of development*. Minneapolis: University of Minnesota Press, 1957. Pp. 3–14.

McNeill, D., Developmental psycholinguistics. In F. Smith and G. A. Miller (eds.), *The Genesis of Language: a Psycholinguistic Approach*. Cambridge, Mass.: M.I.T. Press, 1966. Pp. 15–84.

Miller, W., and S. Ervin, The development of grammar in child language. In U. Bellugi and R. Brown (eds.), The acquisition of language, *Monographs of the Society for Research in Child Development*, 1964, **29**, 9–34. [Reprinted in this volume.]

Werner, H., The concept of development from a comparative and organismic point of view. In D. B. Harris (ed.), *The Concept of Development*. Minneapolis: University of Minnesota Press, 1957. Pp. 125–148.

FRENCH •

The Development of Formal Elements in the Child's Speech

——*Paul Guillaume*

MORPHEMES

The formal elements are generally noticed rather late. They are slow to appear in the child's speech. The almost universal rule for these expressions is that they remain *latent* in the forms of the sentences clearly imitated from utterances in which these morphemes play a discernible part. The formal theme appears in the shape of the sentences, the intonation, the accent, sometimes even in certain inflections; but the morpheme—above all, the unstressed one—remains absent. Let us verify this by looking at a variety of grammatical devices.

Spatial relations are very early understood by the child, but the prepositions expressing them long remain latent in the child's speech. He simply juxtaposes meaningful words; these words, besides, refer to a situation in which it is clear how people, parts of the body, objects, and so on, are related in space. Examples: *Bobo tête* (=hurt head, that is, j'ai mal *à* la tête = my head is sore[1])

Pages 216–229 from "Le développement des éléments formels dans le langage de l'enfant," *Journal de Psychologie*, 1927, **24**, 203–229. Translated from French by Eve V. Clark and reprinted by permission of Presses Universitaires de France.

[1] [Translator's note: There is no preposition in the corresponding English sentence.]

(16;26).[2] *Coca sière* (gateau épicière = cake grocer, that is, je vais acheter un gateau *chez* l'épicière = I'm going to buy a cake *at* the grocer's). *La chaise assis-là* (= the chair sit there, that is, je veux m'asseoir *sur* la chaise = I want to sit *on* the chair). *Pas le feu, pas du feu* (= not fire, that is, pas *près* du feu = not *near* the fire) (23;17). *Mis sa poche* (= put his pocket, that is, mis *dans* sa poche = put in his pocket) (22;7). *La cheminée* (= mantelpiece, that is, *sur* la cheminée = *on* the mantelpiece). In reality, at least in the last examples, one sees a model close to the actual expression that has been formed, although the preposition is still perceived in a confused way. In the same way, the child at first imitates the spatial question without using *où* (= where); there is no possible doubt about the meaning of the question: [Où] *il est?* (= [where] he is?) (22;7), [Où] *il est l'autre de maman?* (= [where] it is, mama's other one?); [Où] *il est maman chérie?* (= [where] it is, dear mama?).

Attribution and the possession of an object are also relations that are accessible to the child. The child's own name and, from sixteen months on, the pronoun *moi* (= me; disjunctive or emphatic form) nearly always have this meaning (*à moi* = to me, mine; *pour moi* = for me). Later on, the object is named, but it is simply juxtaposed to the name of the possessor: *Taté papa* (le café de papa = dada's coffee). Notice that at this stage, the child clearly understands the questions "A qui?" (= whose [is it]?), "Pour qui?" (= who [is it] for?) and replies to them by giving someone's name (*moi* = me; *Ahmed* = Ahmed) (16;26).

When two clauses are linked, the conjunction is at first latent: *Donne le couteau* [pour] *couper la belle dame* (= give the knife [to] cut the pretty lady) (P., 22;7). *Tu vas voir* [comme je] *fais la musique* (= you are going to see [how I] play music); *Elle veut pas* [que] *je le fais* (= she doesn't want me [to] do it). All these facts are too well known for us to have to emphasize them here. Likewise the omission of the article, pronoun, and auxiliary verb are frequently characteristic of the child's utterances.

As the influence of the imitated sentence model increases, the morphemes begin to appear in the child's speech. Different stages could probably be distinquished, just as in sentence construction, until mastery of the process has been completed. Thus, under the influence of still ill-defined models, the child will hesitate between several symbols or mistakenly use one for another. L. (25;17) says: *Gentil auprès de moi . . . gentil à moi* (= nice *near* me . . . nice *towards* me, that is, gentil *pour* moi = nice *to* me). P. (20;11) says: *Monter à papa* (= climb *to* papa, that is, monter *sur* papa = climb *on* papa) and *A pon à feu* (la soupe est à feu = the soup is *at* stove, that is, la soupe est *sur* le feu = the soup is *on* the stove). He also says *sous* (= under) when he means *sur la table* (= on the table). *A* (= on, to, at) has a very general meaning for some time and is placed wherever there should be a preposition; then it gradually relinquishes some of its uses (notably as an indication of possession) to *de* (= of, from) as the rules of the

----

[2] The first figure indicates the months, the second the days, of the child's age.

language are assimilated more correctly. Stern gives a curious example of excessive generalization of *von* (= of, from) which became a "universal" preposition in the speech of one of his children.

Let us go one step further. The meaning of the morpheme comes from its primitive indefiniteness which gives way to specificity as a result of numerous models upon which new usages are more closely built. But—and this is a vital indication for us of the child's personal creative activity—certain peculiarities of form are still not clear when the general rule of usage has already been made explicit. Thus we find more or less awkward regularizations which indicate a somewhat gross mastery of the processes. Thus *ton* (= your, masculine singular) and *mon* (= my, masculine singular) are often replaced by *de toi* (= of you) and *de moi* (= of me): *la cuiller de papa et celle de moi* (= spoon of papa and spoon of me) (23;10). *Du, au, des* (= of, partitive of the; = to the/at the; = of, plural partitive/of the, plural) are still a source of difficulty: *A bras* (au bras = in/on [the] arm) (P., 20;11). *Celui de le monsieur* (= that of the man; *de le* is obligatorily contracted to *du* in French) (23;10). In the speech of some other three-year-olds, we still find: *à les chemises* (= on/to the shirts; obligatory contraction of *à les* to *aux*), *près de les soldats* (= close to the soldiers; obligatory contraction of *de les* to *des*), and so on. A more curious effect of the awareness of the necessary existence of the morpheme is that the child, in many utterances where its existence is not obvious, because it has been absorbed into a neighboring word of which it is part, reduplicates it in some way. One child of three years says: *Tu la l'ôtes.* [Ne] *la l'ôte pas* (= you take-it it off. Don't take-it it off; *la* is redundant beside *l'* in *l'ôte*[*s*]). Another child says: *Moi la l'ai vue* (= me, [I] saw-it it; *la* is redundant), *Il la l'ouvre* (= he opens-it it). The elided pronoun (*l'*) not being very salient, the child is adding the nonelided form also. For analogous reasons, he says: *à chez le marchand* (= at at-the shopkeeper's; *à* = at is redundant in combination with *chez* = at the house of) and (L., 21;22): *Donne-moi des sous pour à Jeanne* (= give me some pennies for-to Jeanne; *pour* = for is redundant in combination with *à* = to). In these examples, the formal theme is applied to a material theme for which a special formal model is suitable. The child is as yet unfamiliar with this model, but he at least shows that he is in possession of the necessary rules by his not recognizing the exceptions.

INFLECTIONS

Let us analyze what goes on in the schoolboy's mind when he constructs a form in some language learned by studying didactic works and not by everyday usage. For example, he wishes to translate "il commande" (≐ he commands) into Latin. He forms the infinitive "command*er*" (= to command) and finds *imperare* in his Latin dictionary. He then separates this word into a stem *imper-* and an ending. Returning to his grammar, he sees from the model conjugation of the verb *amare* (= to love) set out in terms of the stem plus its endings that the form *-at* is characteristic of the person, tense, and mood that he ought to use.

He therefore arrives at the form *imperat*. The material theme here is "the verb *imperare*," which leads to the stem *imper-*; the formal theme is present in his mind in some form like "third person singular, present tense, indicative mood," which results in the ending *-at*. But what "shape" do the material and formal themes take in the child who is learning his mother tongue through usage?

It seems that the material theme can be only the primitive drive for verbal expression which would be suggested by the situation because of previous habits; for example, the word sentence or the simple sentence which was used at a more primitive stage of language acquisition.

The aspect of the situation which predominates in the mind, the orientation of interest, the words that the child has just said or heard, and so on, cause variations in the verbal suggestions. We will show with examples the variability of the basis of the future inflection. In a form like: *elle va buver* (= she is going to drink; infinitive form *buver* instead of adult *boire*), we must not only consider the ending in *-er* but also the stem *buv-* which is also found in the form *buvu* of the past participle. We find that the idea expressed by "the verb *boire*" tends to be presented here in the form *buvons* (first person plural, present tense), *buvez* (second person plural, present), *buvais* (first person singular, imperfect) . . . , and not in the forms like *bois* (first person singular, present), *boirai* (first person singular, future), and so on. The action of the former forms must be very pervasive, since although the form *bu-* seems to be the source of the *u* in *buvu*, it has not done away with the influence of the stem *buv-*. In fact, when this child later says: *elle boivait* (third person, feminine singular, imperfect), she has built on forms like *boit* (third person singular, present), *boivent* (third person plural, present). The same child says: *Vous avez fini de me batter* (= you have finished smacking me; *batter* used for *battre*) probably under the influence of *Vous me battez* (second person plural, present) rather than under that of *bat* (third person singular, present), *battu* (past participle). She says: *Elle veut éteigner* (= she wants to put the lights out; with *éteigner* replacing *éteindre*) because the idea expressed by "the verb *éteindre*" has been accidentally perceived in the forms *éteignez* (second person plural, present), *éteignais* (first person singular, imperfect) and not in the forms *éteindre* (infinitive) or *éteinte* (past participle, feminine). (It is possible that the child habitually addressed as *vous*—the formal form of "you"—will be extremely familiar with the forms *buvez, battez, éteignez*.) But, in the same child's speech six weeks later, I heard *éteindé* and *éteindu* (both for the past participle *éteinte*) which are clearly derived from *éteindre*. If she says *Il a couré* (= he has run) (and not *couri* or *couru*) it is probably because she feels the influence of *il court* (= he runs), in which the final consonant cannot be distinguished from that of first conjugation verbs, and not of *il veut courir* (= he wants to run) for example. *On s'en allera, on s'en allerait* are based on the infinitive *s'en aller* (= to go away) and not on the very familiar *on s'en va* (impersonal third singular, present = "we're going"). If we find the extraordinary form *prendu* occurring beside *pris* (= taken, past participle) which is both familiar and frequent in the speech of the children we observed, it is because at that point, *prendre* (= to take, infinitive) is active. *On ouvrera* (for third person singular, future) comes from *on ouvre* (third person singular, present); *ouvri* (for the past participle) comes from *ouvrir* (= to open, infinitive). Although G. has just said: *Je ne veux pas sortir* (= I don't want to go out), he must also be under the influence of *sors* or *sort* (first and third person singular, present) when he forms the future tense: *sorrai* immediately afterwards. *J'en voulerais* (for first person singular, conditional) has a "conditional" form but also a material theme: *je voulais* (first person singular, imperfect) and not *je veux* (first person singular, present). It is *mordre* (= to bite, infinitive) or *ils mordent* (third person plural, present) which leads to the *d* in *il m'a mordé* (= he bit me) and not the form *mord* (third person singular, present) in which the *d* is silent. When M.C. says *Elle morde* (= she bites), the same material theme is the source, but when Rob says *Il va la mor* (= he is going to bite her), it is the form *mord* which is active. The infinitive *assir* comes from *assis* (= seated, past participle) and not from *asseoir* (= to sit, infinitive) which is just as familiar to the child.

Thus the material theme appears under various guises in different circumstances, with their determinism being generally very clear. But how is the formal theme, in its turn, presented? Its reality consists of the structure of the sentence to which it is related. We have seen above that the structure of a sentence can acquire a relative independence with respect to *certain* of its terms. The sentence may be begun without *every* element having already been chosen. The child may begin a sentence and leave it in mid-air, groping for a word that he may not find and for which he will give a more or less suitable equivalent. Certain aspects common to a whole series of situations rely on a sentence "framework" which has still to be separated into its individual parts.

It seems as if there are instances in which the material theme is simply inserted into the empty place awaiting it in the sentence mold without, however, adapting itself in any way by modifying its primitive form. It behaves like an invariable word. There is certainly an analogical creation in the construction of the sentence, but not in the inflection of the word. The formal motif lacks precision; it outlines the textures of the phrase better than the particular forms of the words. We can interpret some of the preceding examples in this light. Here are some more: *Moi il m'assis* (= he sits me down): transference pure and simple of the familiar participial form (*assis*) to a personal mode. *J'ai peur que ça fait* (for *se fasse*, subjunctive; = I'm afraid that'll happen); *pour qu'on la met* (for *mette*, subjective; = so as to put it on). The numerous examples of *tient* (third person singular, present) used as the infinitive or participle are of this order: *Je fais les faire tient* (for *tenir*, infinitive; = I make them stick on), *il a tient* (for *tenu*, past participle; = he/it held). Similarly, *Pour qu'il se salit pas* (for *ne se salisse*, subjunctive; = so that he doesn't get himself dirty) ... *Les trois qui dort* (for *dorment*, third person plural, present; = the three who are sleeping) ... *Il va la mor* (for *mordre*, infinitive; = he's going to bite her). *Des madames elle est assis* (for *elles sont assises*, with plural feminine agreement; = the ladies are sitting down)

(23 months). *Je vas te tue* (for *tuer*, infinitive; = I'm going to kill you) (23;5). *Tu t'en ailles?* (for *vas*, present indicative; = you're going away?); *elle ne peut pas tourne* (for *tourner*, infinitive; = she can't turn round), and so on.

However, there are only fugitive traces of this period visible. The adaptation of the word to the structure begins very early on: it is then that we find wrong inflections, abnormal regularizations. It is remarkable that the child has been using numerous verb forms for a long time before he makes a single mistake. These forms, though, were correct only because they were simply reproductions. The mistakes are an indication that the child has begun to form his own constructions. It is only then that, from the psychological point of view, true conjugation begins. I heard the first wrong inflection in my son's speech when he was two years old: *Tu servis maman?* (for *tu sers*, second person singular present; = you are helping mama [to food]?), and in my daughter's speech (23;7): *Vous avez fini de me batter?* (for *battre*, infinitive; = you have finished smacking me?) . . . *Il a couré* (for *couru*) (23;11); *elle m'a fait rier* (for *rire*, infinitive; = she made me laugh).

There are two cases possible here:

1. The function of the word, that is, the structure of the sentence it belongs to, completely determines its form, its inflection. Thus, in French, the future, conditional, and imperfect tenses have characteristic endings.

The function does not completely determine the form. There are several declensions and conjugations. A form is not entirely determined when one knows that it is a dative or a participle. The participle in French, for example, may end in *é*, *i*, or *u*. It is clear that, at this level, the mold or schema of the sentence is not enough to produce the inflection. A second model must come into play to achieve this precision. Besides the model of the sentence, there is the formal theme which provides a special model of inflection.

The second case is the most general one in the problems of inflection. There is rarely a simple or unique correspondence between grammatical function and form. The endings can vary with no change of function, and, inversely, one ending may represent several different functions.

Where the function unequivocally determines the form, we might say that, without the intervention of a particular "example," the general "rule" operates directly. For example, depending on whether the child expresses his intentions or tells of an accomplished fact, he will mentally begin a different type of utterance: *Je vais* . . . (= I am going to . . .) followed by an infinitive, or *J'ai* . . . (= I have) followed by a participle. In German, the first type tends to determine in advance that the verb must be in the infinitive, although this is not yet determined materially, ending in *-en*. The second case calls for an initial syllable *ge-* on the participle. Formal elements of the word may appear before the word itself or else emerge at the same time. But in French, under the same conditions, neither the infinitive nor the participle have a specific, unique form. The former may end in

-er, -ir, -oir, -re (for the child, at least three of these conjugations are active). The latter may end in -é, -i, -u (all three forms are active). There is no partial anticipation of the form of the word which might support an "awareness of rules." A linguist would doubtless be able to state the rules in a fairly complicated way. The forms of some verbs are attached to one among them, for example, to the infinitive which becomes the center of the system somehow, and the expression *par excellence* of the idea contained in the verb. But it is not enough to establish a relationship between the endings; one must know how to articulate them in conjunction with the rest of the word. This seems to require a distinction between the fixed stem and the system of movable endings. In what mysterious "implicit" form could we visualize this complex rule operating in the mind of the two-year-old child who is beginning to conjugate verbs? How often has man learned his language through practice, without knowing its grammar, when he painfully searches to "abstract out" from everyday usage the rule that he does not know, and formulates it inaccurately, either too broadly or too narrowly, in unsuitable terms.

Before the difficulties of interpretation which are raised by the hypothesis about the action of a general rule, we might think about what is involved in particular models. If we assume, for the reasons given above, that a participial form like *buvé* derives from a material theme such as *buvez*, for example, we should also add the influence of pairs like *lavez-lavé, donnez-donné*, so that the form is completely determined. The form is built up on a proportional basis and may involve whole sentences rather than isolated verb forms. In other words, it is a question of analogical constructions based on examples rather than on a rule. Actions of this sort do not have the same rigor as the application of a rule: they leave room for the complex influence of the ending of the material theme, of its stem and of its meaning in the choice of the formal model. Resemblances may interact without having been analyzed or precisely defined, and, depending on the influence of the moment, the formal theme itself may vary.

It is this variability which actually appears in some of our examples. We have explained certain cases of it by allowing for the primitive material theme's variability: this, for example, would sometimes give the forms *buv-*, sometimes the forms *boiv-*, to the verb *boire* (= to drink). Elsewhere, we have pointed out that this theme could be inserted anyhow into the sentence (infinitive: *tient*) or could be inflected. In the latter case, we have to distinguish the correct and incorrect inflections (*tenir* versus *tiendre*). These facts alone would point to the instability of all the influences in play here. P. (24;2) uses *mouri,* although he knows the form *mort* (= died, past participle). One child (36;3) says within the space of a few minutes: [Je] *vas le faire tient* (for *tenir; =* I'm going to make it hold) and [Je] *vas le faire tiendre* (*ibid.*). There are examples of such alternations in the speech of several subjects. Another child (36;9) says: *Il va tiendre . . . tu vas tenir*, and so on. The same child tries to open a door: *Peux pas l'ouvrir* (= can't open it); I help him and says: "*Regarde elle est . . .*" (= look, it is) and he correctly finishes: *Ouverte* (= open). A moment later he tries by himself, succeeds, and says: *Ça y est: elle est ouvrie* (= there you are: it's open). R. (24;10) says successively: *m'a pris mon lit* (= took my bed away) and (incorrect) *me l'a prendu* (= took it way from me). Let us leave aside all the correct forms for which it is difficult to judge whether they are personal constructions or simply remembered forms. What is most remarkable is the case where the two forms are both constructed from the same material theme but with different endings: for example, *buvé* and *buvu*, *éteindé* and *éteindu*. We have to suppose that this is the action of different formal models, one for the first conjugation and another for the fourth conjugation. It would be interesting to collect more examples like these: ours are too few for us to draw any firm conclusions about these points.

It is possible that conjugation has become completely independent of individual models in the adult who is in full possession of his grammatical habits; this seems to be true even for those rare instances where the adult has to actually create a form. He knows a large number of verbs: their influence could become anonymous. We cannot, however, always draw conclusions from adult to child: in particular where the child knows only a small number of verbs. Forms like *viendre* and *tiendre* (the latter is very frequent among the children I have been able to observe) are substituted for words as familiar as *venir* (= to come) and *tenir* (= to hold). The verbs that may have served as models that children of that age would know are few in number (*éteindre* = to turn off [lights]; *prendre* = to take; *rendre* = to give [back]; *descendre* = to go down; *entendre* = to hear; *vendre* = to sell; *défendre* = to defend, forbid). The gap between the hypothesis about a general rule and the hypothesis about individual models has become very small. It is not impossible to suppose that, initially, there is specific imitation of some words. Similarly, in looking at the history of a whole category of words, one often discovers some strange fact or an historical accident. Sometimes one is aware of being inspired by a famous phrase, by a classical allusion, by a word said by someone specific under particular circumstances. The law of imitation, in speech as in action, involves gradual emancipation from the primitive model, insofar as the model is determined individually. The speaker ends up by depending only on the characteristics common to this model and to any others.

We ought to be able to specify these models. Since it is clearly impossible to reconstitute the unstable determinism of such analogical creations, we shall restrict ourselves to a few conjectures.

We are tempted to attribute a decisive role to the most frequent forms, to those the child knows best and which he uses most often. We shall start with data from observations of such familiar forms. We have records, collected previously, of the conversations of nursery school children: as the children, left free to talk and play, ended up by taking no notice of the observer, their dialogue is a sample of their natural, habitual speech. Here are the results of some statistical investigations of the verb, based on the infinitive forms of the four conjugations in French.

NUMBER OF USES

First conjugation	1,060	36.2%
Second ,,	173	6.0
Third ,,	670	22.8
Fourth ,,	1,036	35.0
Totals	2,939	100

Notice the number of verbs from which these forms derive when each verb is counted only once however many times it is used, and whatever forms it occurs in (these children were aged between two and four years):

NUMBER OF VERBS

First conjugation	124	76.0%
Second ,,	10	6.1
Third ,,	8	4.9
Fourth ,,	21	13.0
Totals	163	100

One fact is obvious from these raw statistics, and it is the only thing we can learn from them. First conjugation verbs are far more frequent (they represent three quarters of the total number of verbs), but the number of uses is far from being proportional to the number of verbs. In fact, the third and fourth conjugations contain very few verbs, but these are by far the most frequently used.

Let us examine this in more detail. The most frequently used verbs in the latter conjugations are *être* = be (491), *avoir* = have (320), *faire* = make, do (185), *vouloir* = want (129), *mettre* = put (102), *prendre* = take (93), *voir* = see (78), *tenir* = hold (75), *pouvoir* = be able (55). In the first conjugation, besides the irregular verb *aller* = go (177), which only nominally belongs here, the only verbs used more than fifty times are *donner* = give (85), *tomber* = fall (78), and *casser* = break (54). If frequency is the only thing to be taken into account, the child must be faced with a series of fairly different models, mostly irregular ones, either because they take their forms from different stems or because they have different and sometimes mixed conjugations.

What is there for the child besides conjugation? Clearly we must avoid the fallacious picture of the rich selection of symmetrical forms presented in our grammars. Certain forms are extremely rare or else late to appear. Here are a few more statistics. Consider the (regular) verbs of the first conjugation. The plural of the personal mode is practically nonexistent: I have not a single example in my notes (except for some imperatives).

I find 280 examples of the first three persons of the present indicative or imperative (for example, *donne* = give!) ending in -*e* mute. The participle (for example, *donné* = given) occurs 240 times, and the infinitive (for example, *donner* = to give) 213 times. These are three essential forms, the others are rare (eight occurrences of the imperfect, 23 of the future, 11 of plural imperative, and that is all). The frequency of the participle may be explained by its use as an adjective or by its combination with the auxiliaries in the passive and in the compound tenses of the active voice. The frequency of the infinitive comes from the construction introduced by *pouvoir* (= to be able), *vouloir* (= to want, wish), *aller* (= to go), or by *pour* (= in order to). If we note that certain forms are acoustically identical (the infinitive and the participle in the first conjugation, the present indicative and the participle in the second conjugation and, so on), the number of types of inflection is decreased still further.

These facts indicate that in addition to frequency, which undoubtedly plays a part, other causes are present in analogical creation, and that the more regular verbs, independently of their frequency, have particular influence. It is remarkable sometimes to see the more usual forms regularized by others which are less so. *Prendre* and *tenir* are, as we have seen, among the most frequently used verbs: all their forms are known and are used correctly most of the time. However, this does not prevent regularizations like *prendu, prendait,* or *tiendre, tiendait.* The forms *pris, tenir,* in view of their frequency, present considerable resistance to these constructions, yet cannot always prevent them: the models having such strong influence can only be verbs like *entendre, descendre,* and so on, which are less frequent than those they "rule," but they are most regular. We do *not* see the inverse process where a verb as common as *prendre* gives rise to forms analogous to *je prenais, j'ai pris,* and so on, in verbs like *descendre.*

How should we interpret the influence of such regularity? For a verb to become a model, it is probably necessary for its different forms to acquire a psychological unity, become a natural "whole." If we go back to the schema for a proportional model, the two terms in relation must be a couple such that the body of the word offers a characteristic and recognizable structure in its transformations which thus appear as variations on the same theme and not on independent themes. It is not a question here of the dissociation which grammatical analysis operates between the stem and the ending: the phenomenon is on another level psychologically. It has to be compared to the effects produced by an analogy of rhythm and design in two members of a musical phrase. Doubtlessly, the first models are nonconstructed forms, learned haphazardly through usage; brought together in sentences, they may act upon each other, becoming organized simultaneously by meaning and musical form. When the child repeats: *Donne-moi* (= give me) . . . *il m'a donné* (= he gave me) . . . *il me donnera* (= he'll give me) . . . *il va me donner* (= he's going to give me), and so on, the simple proximity of these sentences already makes for the fact that these forms are no longer strangers to one another. They are linked by assonance. There is all the more reason to argue in the same fashion for the forms which have been actively constructed upon one model: they are the most active models for new constructions, a regularized and, above all, regularizing form.

However, many of the forms that we have ranged among the most frequent are unfit to produce this type of effect. They are borrowed from several different stems (*je vais, aller* = I go, to go) or have several alternations in the stem (*je veux, je voulais* = I want, I wanted; *prendre, pris* = to take, took/taken). They are often monosyllables in which the stem is confounded with the ending. These words are scarcely separable from the expression as a whole in which they occur. Lastly, frequency itself ends up by masking analogies. The form never has to be constructed because it is too familiar in each of its uses. *Avoir, être, faire* (= to have, to be, to do/make), and so on, are hardly ever regularized, save in a few rare forms (*vous faisez* for *vous faites* = you plural do/make).

There are grounds for comparing inflection and derivation. The child, working from certain familiar words, forms others from them by adding the endings of nouns, adjectives, or verbs according to particular models. We have gathered few examples of this compared to the large numbers cited by Stern in the speech of German children. This is probably because derivation is a more active and a freer process there than in our language (this is still more true when it comes to creating new words through compounding). In some cases—and, it seems, in the speech of the youngest children—nouns are formed from verbs by simple insertion of a usual form of the verb (the material theme) into the noun slot of a certain type of sentence (the formal theme). L. (22;27) says, in talking about a billiard ball: *C'est une* ROULE (= it's a "roll"). Another child of 26 months also calls a billiard ball *a rouroule* (= a roll-roll). Another child (35 months) calls a pipe *une* FUME (= a "smoke"). There is no adaptation of the form of the word in these instances to its new function (as in the case of the child saying: *il va tient* for *il va tenir*). In contrast, an older child calls a billiard ball *un rouleau* (with a noun ending added to the verb, *-eau*). He has just mentioned *un grosier* (for *groseille* = berry) and qualifies it with *petoyer* (from *petot*, a popular name for "gooseberry"). In the latter instances, there is a noun ending attached to the word, probably under the influence of a determinable model. Naturally, it would be exceptional to be able to trace the actual origin of the process.

We have seen the main parts of the sentence built up, from the state of grammatical nondifferentiation in the first stages up to the moment at which the child knows how to manipulate the different parts according to the rules of language. Can we draw any conclusions from this study about the much-debated question of the relation between the development of language in the child and the historical development of languages in general?

A certain parallelism between ontogeny and phylogeny seems as plausible in this domain as elsewhere. The assimilation of a language involves to some degree its reconstruction and its recreation. From early on, we have seen that the child's language ceases to be a mosaic of ready-made expressions applicable to each situation. It is certainly difficult to know in each particular case whether the child repeats or reconstructs, whether he copies or imitates freely.

However, independently of the conjectures arising from continuous observations, the regularization of irregular forms is a sure index of imitation in the speaker. This is a paradoxical fact, as it is the mistakes made which confirm the (incomplete) knowledge of the rules of the language. Whether it is a question of a semantic or a grammatical rule, it is not transmitted by the language itself. A word is always used in a sentence, and the sentence is used in particular concrete circumstances. Efforts are needed to dissociate the meaning of each word, and additionally to estimate from a number of different uses the exact limits of the general meaning, the rule for all the possible uses. Still more efforts are needed to separate out the value of the morphemes or inflections from the whole structures in which they appear initially as ornaments devoid of meaning. The child has to be capable of making these efforts, and the ideas underlying them must be accessible to him. There are certain easy routes for access to these ideas: they are frequently the same ones that languages have followed in the course of their evolution and that the child, in turn, takes up in learning his language. The assimilation of a complex and learned language first of all requires that it be simplified and impoverished in its vocabulary, grammar, and syntax. Therefore, as we have seen, the child's first grammatical categories will be neither nouns nor verbs, but the names of people and the names of things initially associated with an undifferentiated expression.[3] The latter, through a new process of dissociation, will gradually evolve into designations of acts or attitudes of the speaker towards his experience. But what does the child do during this progress? He is still imitating because *certain* of our substantives are really the names of people, of things, *certain* of our verbs designate real actions, and so on. He has only to chose what he needs from what we offer him. The habits formed in this way will act as guides in understanding other uses, in gradually enlarging the grammatical categories without breaking the primitive mold of the sentence. If the child first assimilates the spatial function or the possessive function of prepositions, he finds these uses (as well as others) in the language he is imitating; it is always a question of a simple choice. On the other hand, he finds no trace of the historical origin of these morphemes as concrete, autonomous words. Thus his assimilation will not reproduce that stage and his expression will be analytic from the very first. To sum up, it is not necessary to believe in some mysterious internal necessity which causes the individual learning language to go *via* the tortuous routes of history. The only similarity lies in the degree to which the route is constrained by certain logical and psychological necessities for assimilation in a complex organism. The ontogenetic "repetition" is not history: repetition is rather a selection of models offered by the language in its actual state, which includes still-living witnesses of a primitive age as well as acquisitions due to superior forms of culture.

[3] [Translator's note: See "The first stages of sentence formation in children's speech," Guillaume, 1927, this volume.]

LATVIAN •

On the Emergence of Inflection in Child Language: A Contribution Based on Latvian Speech Data

—— *Velta Rūķe-Draviņa*

(1) Previous investigations of child language, as far as these have been carried out by linguists, have dealt only to a limited extent with morphology, so that the remark made by Karl Bühler in 1922 about the development of inflectional syntax is still pertinent today: "We have hardly taken the first step in this marvelous area of investigation. . . ."[1]

This is due above all to the fact that the analysis of morphological phenomena in child language is a more difficult and complicated task than, for instance, the establishment of the inventory of sounds or of the vocabulary. The description of the morphological and syntactic characteristics of the speech of a small child is only possible if one has already acquired a good view of the phonetic situation of his language.

The majority of previously published linguistic studies of child language have furthermore been limited to the first two years of the child's life.[2] However, since the appearance of inflection usually begins around the end of the second year, the development of declensional and conjugational systems falls outside the scope of such investigations.

In addition, most of the studies have been carried out within the confines of the Germanic languages, which are not rich in inflections and which therefore do not offer much data for morphological development. In most Slavic and also Baltic languages, however, inflection plays a very important role. For this reason, one would hope that rules of general validity for the appearance of declensions and conjugations could be drawn from studies of the speech of Baltic and Slavic children. It is conceivable and, based on the present investigation, even demonstrable that some general morphological rules concerning the development of inflection in child language can be established. These rules may also be valid for all inflectional world languages, in much the same way as Roman Jakobson[3] hypothesized with respect to sound development.

In the evaluation of speech data from small children, attention may be

---

Zur Entstehung der Flexion in der Kindersprache: Ein Beitrag auf der Grundlage des lettischen Sprachmaterials, *International Journal of Slavic Linguistics and Poetics*, 1959, 1/2, 201–222. Translated by Robert Sayre and edited by Charles A. Ferguson and Dan I. Slobin. Reprinted with the permission of the author and Mouton and Company.
[1] K. Bühler, "Vom Wesen der Syntax," *Festschrift Karl Vossler* (1922), p. 83.
[2] See references (to 1946) in Werner F. Leopold, *Bibliography of Child Language.* Evanston, 1952.
[3] R. Jakobson, *Kindersprache, Aphasie und allgemeine Lautgesetze.* Uppsala, 1941 [English translation: Mouton, 1968.]

directed to several other important factors. Thus one should not leave out of consideration the fact that the study of child language is simultaneously the study of living colloquial speech. The speech of adults is mirrored in the child, of course, but to a certain extent the environment also adapts itself to the child.

Of special importance is the fact that many linguistic processes are easier to observe in the language of small children than in the language of adults because they can be followed over a shorter amount of time. The forms emerge and are changed, so to speak, right before our eyes (ears), while similar changes in language history take decades or even centuries. In this respect, observations made in the area of child language can sometimes throw light on the development of forms within the history of the respective standard language.

(2)   Unfortunately there are but few thorough investigations into the morphological problems of child language in the inflectionally rich Slavic languages. The most important are found in Polish, primarily in the works of L. Kaczmarek,[4] P. Smoczyński,[5] and S. B. Pfanhauser.[6] For Bulgarian, I. A. Gheorgov's article of 1908 can be mentioned.[7] The observations made on the language of several Russian children at the end of the last century are unimportant.[8] Scientific interest in these problems has just recently been renewed, above all in the work of A. Gvozdev[9] and K. Chukovskiy.[10]

My work, as far as I know, is the first and so far the only work done on the Baltic languages. The data and the conclusions presented in this paper are actually taken from a monograph (at present in manuscript) on the language development of a Latvian boy in Sweden. The notes were recorded daily during the period from 0;6 to 3;1 and—with less precise regularity, but nonetheless at least once a week—continuing until the end of the fourth year (1950–1953). It may be added that during the observation period contact with Swedish or any language other than Latvian was so insignificant as to be totally discounted. Only material which was considered pertinent for this paper was selected from the comprehensive corpus.

(3)   A few introductory remarks may first be appropriate. What does the appearance of inflection in the speech of children really mean? In contrast to the manner in which the young child imitates sounds or words, simple imitation is

[4] L. Kaczmarek, *Kształtowanie się mowy dziecka*. Posen, 1953.
[5] P. Smoczyński, *Przyswajanie przez dziecko podstaw systemu językowego*. Lodz, 1955.
[6] S. Brenstiern Pfanhauser, "Rozwój mowy dziecka," *Prace Filologiczne*, 15, Warsaw, 1930, pp. 273–356.
[7] I. A. Gheorgov, *Ein Beitrag zur grammatischen Entwicklung der Kindersprache*. Leipzig, 1908.
[8] A. Aleksandrov, "Detskaya rech'," *Russkiy filologicheskiy vestnik*," 10, Warsaw, 1883, pp. 86–120; B. Blagoveshchenskiy, "Detskaya rech'," *Russkiy filologicheskiy vestnik*," 16, Warsaw, 1886, pp. 71–101.
[9] A. N. Gvozdev, *Formirovaniye u rebenka grammaticheskogo stroya russkogo yazyka*. Moscow, 1949.
[10] K. Chukovskiy, *Ot dvukh do pyati*. Moscow, 1955. [English Translation: University of California Press, 1963.]

not sufficient in the acquisition of morphological and syntactic characteristics. Here it is a matter of acquiring certain linguistic features which can then be extended analogically to a whole series of similar phenomena.

The emergence of morphological markers is probably closely connected with the child's general level of phonetic development. It is, of course, well known from historical linguistics that extensive phonetic changes result in the restructuring of the whole inflectional system.

It is not enough for the young child to have reached a specific level of phonetic competance to ensure the proper use of an ending. For instance, it is not sufficient to be able to pronounce final -s in accordance with the rules of the corresponding standard language. Only when this -s is acquired as the mark of a certain case category and transferred analogically to other words can one speak of the acquisition of -s as a case ending. Only in this way can we understand why a certain sound will sometimes be used in a particular word by the child while the same sound is absent in another word, even though the phonetic conditions in both forms are the same. The explanation is actually that the morphological function of this sound is not the same in both cases and that the child has not progressed far enough in his language development to discover all these functions.

Let us illustrate this with an example from the speech of the Latvian boy we have observed. At 1;11 the child had already acquired the case ending -s for the genitive singular, but not yet for the nominative plural. Thus a sentence noted on 8/18/51 contains the genitive form *with* -s, while the immediately following plural form lacks it: *tu iśa tẹts mañta* (= *tur iekšā tētes mañtas*)[11] "there inside /are/ Papa's things." In the standard language both cases in both words end in -s: genitive singular *tētes* (from *tēte*) and nominative plural *mañtas* (from *mañta*). Only a few weeks later, when -s had clearly become the mark for the plural category for the child, did this ending appear in the nominative plural.

It must be further stressed that in the preceding investigation it is not a question of the passive comprehension of the content of various inflectional forms, but rather a question of the acquisition of *formal* linguistic means which serve to express the content. The child actually understands the meaning of the various case or verbal forms long before he is able to use the particular endings actively in his own speech—in the same way that the small child can perceive the various sounds of his environment well, even when he himself is not capable of imitating these sounds. As early as 1;6, for instance, the meaning of the interrogative pronoun *kas?* "who?, what?" and the accusative *kuo?*

---

[11] In parentheses are repeated the corresponding forms as they would have appeared in the language of the environment. In rendering the child's speech, I have used the transcription customary for Latvian dialect texts; since the official Latvian orthography is based largely on phonetic principles, it is fairly easy to detect how much the forms pronounced by the child deviated from their models. Also, several individual formations were in use in the family which do not completely agree with the norms of the written language, for example, *mẹm̃mẹ* or *mẹm̃me* "Mama."

"whom?, what?" was quite clear. A dialogue between the mother and the child noted at 1;7 indicates that even the dative *kam* "to whom?" was correctly understood:

MOTHER: *kam tad Daȋnis duôs ʒeȓt ka·kao?* "to whom will Dainis [you] give cocoa to drink?"

CHILD: *aćiś!* (= lācis) "the bear" [nominative]

The child had thus correctly understood the content of the question with the dative *kam?* But since the inflection of his language was not complete at this time, he responded with the formally nominative case (*lācis* instead of *lācim*).

It should be further emphasized that it is not a matter of *direct* repetition of the inflectional form, which the child had just heard from the speech of the adult, but rather of the independent active use of such forms. (In immediate imitation the word always appears in a phonetically more correct form!)

(4)   In the following I will give a general sketch of the process of inflectional development in the Latvian child I observed. First a few words about the structure of the DECLENSIONAL SYSTEM.

The first beginnings of different case endings were noted at 1;7: individual cases like accusative *ka-ku* (= *katlu*) "the kettle" in contrast to nominative *ka-ka* (= *katls*) "the kettle." But a rapid process of development in the inflections first occurred in the last month of the second year (1;11). At this time, that is, at the end of the second year, general language development was already quite advanced. The child possessed a fairly rich vocabulary, even if in somewhat phonetically imperfect form—the total sum of actively used, recorded words had already risen to something over 600. With respect to the composition of the vocabulary by word classes, he had mastered, in addition to substantives, quite a few verbs, a large number of adjectives and adverbs, interjections and onomatopoetic words, the numerals 1–3, and also certain pronouns. Conjunctions and prepositions were, however, still completely missing (the only exception was *bez* "without," which appeared sporadically). The child's language was also quite well developed syntactically, so that six-term sentences appeared frequently. Two sentences will serve as an illustration of the general level of language development. Both occurred in the last months of the second year. The first example (1;10): *Daȋ opã gūzu nęs* (= *Daȋnis opã! gruozu nęs*) "Dainis hop!, the basket carries," that is, "I pick up the basket [and] carry." The interjection (*opã*) has taken up the function of a verb here with perhaps the meaning "lift up"; the conjunction *un* "and" is not yet in the language of the child. Instead of a construction with the personal pronoun "I" and the corresponding verb form (*es paceļu* "I lift up") we find here a means of expression which is characteristic of both adult baby talk and child language, namely, the child speaks of himself in the third person. The object *gūzu* already demonstrates the accusative ending *-u* even though phonetically this form deviates quite strongly from the model in adult speech—*r* is lacking, the rising-prolonged intonation used by the child does not correspond to the falling or broken tone with which this word is pronounced in standard Latvian.

A second example from 1;11: *tu nãk at'õ tũ ćèju* (= *tur nãk aũto* [*pa*] *tuo ceļu*) "there comes an auto that way." Here, too, the deviation from the standard language is greatest with respect to phonetic shape. The instrumental form with the proper ending is already present, but the appropriate preposition *pa* is missing.

At this stage of general language development, then, inflections began to emerge. In the formation of the declensional systems, the individual cases developed in the *singular* somewhat earlier than in the plural. The first formal difference developed in the nominative and accusative singular (-*a*, -*e* contrasting with the accusative -*u*, -*i*) during the period 1;7–1;9. The first nominative and accusative endings had actually appeared one month earlier (1;6) but were, however, used interchangeably, that is, accusative form with nominative meaning and vice versa, for example, nominative and accusative *bumba*//*bumbu* (= nominative *bum̃ba*, accusative *bum̃bu*) "ball" or nominative and accusative *mẽm̃me*// *mẽm̃mi* (= nominative *mẽmme*, accusative *mẽm̃mi*)[12] "Mama." The case form was thus already present, but the real sense of the form was not. Only after a few months did the case form acquire the proper content.

The locative singular appeared as the third inflection one month after the separation of nominative and accusative, and with the appropriate ending (1;8–1;10). (In Latvian the locative is formed without a preposition!) One month later (1;11) the genitive singular was added and, at the beginning of the third year, the dative singular. At this point, around the end of the second year, all of the singular case endings of Latvian had emerged in the child's language except for the vocative and instrumental singular.[13] The vocative, however, does not always have an ending that is distinct from the nominative even in the standard language and there are certain constructions in Latvian in which the instrumental is identical to the accusative, that is, when used without a preposition.

The formal separation of *number* developed somewhat later than the separation of case. Only at the end of 1;11, when the nominative and accusative case endings had already emerged, did -*i* (in *o*- and *iío*- stems) appear as the first mark of the nominative plural.

Although occasional forms with the plural ending -*i* appeared around 1;8, they were still used with singular meaning, for example, *ú:ta źi-ģi* (= *uõtrs*

---

[12] *Mẽmme, mẽm̃me,* or *mẽm̃m* was, at this time, an idiosyncratic formation of the family language which had partially arisen as an adaptation to the child's pronunciation. In the literary language *ē*- stems end in -*e*.

[13] This by no means indicates that the concept of possession was foreign to the child up to this time. The meaning of possession or belonging can be expressed by uninflected juxtaposition, for example, *Daĩ da* (=*Daĩņa dãrziņš*) "Dainis'(s) stroller," that is, "my stroller" (at the age of 1;5), or at 1;6 the cry of protest *Daĩ!* (=*Daĩņa!*) "[they are] Dainis's!" that is, "they are mine!" when someone took the child's things from him.

ziřgs) "the other horse." The plural form was therefore already present phonetically but the concept of plural *ending* was still lacking. On the other hand the child also said *d'ivi kupe* (= *divas kuřpes*) "two shoes" during this time, where the formally singular ending had the content of a plural or dual. The concept of plurality was already there, although without the formal marking of the plural form. At 2;0 both -*as*/-*es* and -*a*/-*e* forms were still used for nominative plurals with *ā*- and *e*- stems.

The assertion by Clara and Wilhelm Stern that the separation of number in child language occurs significantly earlier than case separation[14] is thus not supported by the conclusions drawn above from Latvian speech data. Even psychologically, the priority of *formally* marked plural forms does not seem to me to be urgently needed, for the concept of plurality can easily be expressed by the formally singular form with the addition of a number, "many," or "several," in much the same way as it can be treated, for example, in the Germanic "standard" languages, (German *zwei Pfund*, Swedish *tre glas*, and so on). Comparable examples from the Latvian child's speech are: *d'iv aṁpa* (= *divas laṁpas*) "two lamps" (1;7) or *d'iv ķeṁpe* (= *divas ķeṁmes*) "two combs" (1;7), where the number "two" is followed by a formal singular.

The Latvian child's development with respect to the acquisition of the plural sign corresponds remarkably to the observation which Leopold made with his English-German speaking children;[15] the -*s* was acquired as genitive singular case ending one month earlier than as nominative plural ending (for Leopold the respective dates were 1;10 and 1;11, in my case, 1;11 and 2;0).

At the end of the second year and in the first month of the third year, the accusative, dative, locative, and finally the genitive plural were also added. The instrumental forms in both numbers were still missing insofar as they appear in Latvian with the preposition.

As already mentioned, the formal separation between nominative and accusative singular was the very first. Last of all, in contrast, were those case forms which are formed in Latvian with the aid of prepositions, that is, the instrumental forms. This probably based on the fact that the prepositions belong to those word classes which the child acquires very late. Only at the age of 2;4 did the child begin to use the first prepositions, more frequently (*bez* "without" and *pēc* "after"), but some prepositions (for example, *uz* "on") appeared as late as during the first half of the fourth year.

The complete paradigm at the beginning of the third year appeared as follows:

[14] Clara and Wilhelm Stern, *Die Kindersprache* (Leipzig, 1907), p. 221.
[15] "When we compare the chronology of the plural ending and of the possessive ending, which are phonetically closely parallel, we find that the possessive was introduced one month earlier (1;10) than the plural (1;11). Neither was well established by the end of the year." Werner F. Leopold, *Speech Development of a Bilingual Child*, Vol. 3 (1949), p. 84.

ā- STEMS

Nominative Singular	*mãja* (= *mãja*) "the house"[16]
Genitive Singular	*mă:js* (= *mãjas*: with the meaning of "from the house")
Dative Singular	? (Only once was an unusual form with dative meaning recorded: *faŭt'am* // *faŭt'ajam* [= *spaĺvai*] "to the feather")
Accusative Singular	*bum̃bu* (= *bum̃bu*) "the ball"
Instrumental Singular	*mãju* (= *uz mãju*) "toward home"
Locative Singular	*mãjā* (= *mãjā*) "at home"
Nominative Plural	*apᵃs* (= *lapas*) "the leaves"
Genitive Plural	*mañt* (= *mañtu*) "of the things"
Dative Plural	*cũka:m* (= *cũkãm*) "to the pigs"
Accusative Plural	*apᵃs* (= *lapas*) "the leaves"
Instrumental Plural	*kãjãm* (= *kãjãm*) "on foot"
Locative Plural	*ŭkâs* (= *ruokâs*) "in the hands"

ē- STEMS

Nominative Singular	*męm̃mę* (= *męm̃mę*) "mama"
Genitive Singular	*męm̃m-s* (= *męm̃mes*) most often noted with the meaning *pie męm̃mes* "to mama"
Dative Singular	*męm̃męi* // *męm̃mę* (= *męm̃mei*) "to mama"
Accusative Singular	*męm̃mi* (= *męm̃mi*) "mama"
Instrumental Singular	*męm̃mi* (= *ar męm̃mi*) "with mama"
Locative Singular	*mẽjê* (= *mēlē*) "in the tongue"
Nominative Plural	*kupe* // (a few weeks later) *kuřpes* (= *kuřpes*) "shoes"
Genitive Plural	?
Dative Plural	?
Accusative Plural	*bĭ:ds* (= *biĺdes*) "the pictures"
Instrumental Plural	*kupę̃m* (= *uz kuřpēm*) "on the shoes"
Locative Plural	?

o- STEMS

Nominative Singular	*dâ͞s* (= *dārzs*) "the garden"
Genitive Singular	*fàka* (= *uz vāka*) "on the lid (of a kettle)"
Dative Singular	?
Accusative Singular	*fàku* (= *vāku*) "the lid"
Instrumental Singular	*dâzu* (= *uz dārzu*) "toward the garden"
Locative Singular	*dâzā* (= *dārzā*) "in the garden"

---

[16] Only those case forms actually heard are indicated. Since the same word was usually not recorded in all cases, I have sometimes cited as examples several nouns belonging to the same stem class.

o- STEMS—*continued*

Nominative Plural	*mati* (= *mati*) "the hairs [hair]"
Genitive Plural	*ęzęju* (= *ęzęru*) "of the seas, lakes"
Dative Plural	?
Accusative Plural	*mat-s* (= *matus*) "the hairs [hair]"
Instrumental Plural	*dīǵim* (= *pie diegiem*) "with (other) yarns"
Locative Plural	*matũs* (= *matuôs*) "in the hair"

i̯o- STEMS

Nominative Singular	*âc′ⁱs* (= *lâcis*) "the bear"; *śùn* (= *suns*) "the dog"
Genitive Singular	*śùṇ* (= *suṇa*) "of the dog"
Dative Singular	*âćim* (= *lâcim*) "to the bear"
Accusative Singular	*âci* (= *lâci*) "the bear"
Instrumental Singular	*naźi* (= *ar nazi*) "with the knife"
Locative Singular	*sapī* (= *skapī*) "in the closet"

Nominative Plural	*kàśîśi* (= *kāsīši*) "the little hooks"

No other words of the *i̯o* stems were recorded in the plural at this time.

u- STEMS

Nominative Singular	*męds* // *mêds* (= *mędus*) "honey"
Genitive Singular	?
Dative Singular	?
Accusative Singular	*mę:du* (= *mędu*) "honey"
Instrumental Singular	*t′ĭ:gu* (= *uz tirgu*) "to the market"
Locative Singular	*vidu:* (= *vidŭ*) "in the middle"

i- STEMS

Nominative Singular	*aē* (= *acs:* in the child's environment usually pronounced *aē*)
Genitive Singular	*nać kęk* (*naktskrękls*) "of the nightshirt"
Dative Singular	?
Accusative Singular	*isapt'i* (= *izkapti*) "the scythe"
Instrumental Singular	*isapt'i* (= *ar izkapti*) "with the scythe"
Locative Singular	*a:ũsi* (= *ausi*) "in the ear"

Nominative Plural	*aćiś* (= *acis*) "the eyes"
Genitive Plural	?
Dative Plural	?
Accusative Plural	*àusi* (= *ausis*) "the ears"
Instrumental Plural	*kùtim* (= *ap krūtim*) "around the chest"
Locative Plural	*aći* (= *acīs*) "in the eyes"

I wish to emphasize in general that the acquisition of the various morphological markers took place gradually and that the dates given above for the appearance of the various case endings are only approximate. It was nearly always the case that sporadic beginnings of a new formal case difference emerged several months earlier. This is probably simply an indication that the process of development of a new inflectional category had already begun. Only after a shorter or longer time did this ending become regular in the child's speech. There were also cases, however, in which these first starts completely disappeared in the following months, only to reappear later. (The same is, of course, true for the acquisition of verb inflections.)

The acquisition of the various case endings in the plural proceeded at a quicker rate than in the singular, probably because the content of the corresponding case in the singular had already become clear to the child.

Also, the case endings did not appear completely simultaneously in all the stem classes.

The starting point for the acquisition of a specific ending lay primarily in those sentences which were repeated often in the speech of the parents, so that the child imitated first the entire phrase, together with the corresponding case form, and then transferred the abstracted case marker to other similar words. Especially interesting, in my opinion, is the observation that the child affixes such abstracted case endings to those forms which, according to their phonetic shape in the child's language, belong to stem classes differing from the model in the language of the environment. Compare, for example, (1;10) accusative singular *baʒi* (= *baznīcu*) "the church" to nominative singular *baʒe* (= *baznīca*) or accusative singular *aĩvi* (= *laĩvu*) to nominative singular *aĩve* (= *laĩva*). Since the forms *baʒe* "the church" and *aĩve* "the boat" end in -*e* in the child's language, they are both treated as *ē*- stems, taking the accusative singular ending -*i*, in complete agreement with the general rules of declension in Latvian. Such cases clearly indicate that the child already correctly understands the alternating relationship between the nominative and accusative endings and that he is able to apply the case markings even when there is no direct model in the language of his environment.

A further oddity which one could observe in the construction of the declensional system was that some case forms appeared only rarely in the child's speech, in contrast to other frequently used cases, such as the nominative and accusative.

The dative forms of the singular appear especially rarely. In the beginning of the third year, when declension was generally well developed, only a few words were recorded in the dative form, and even these occurred with an ending that was incorrectly transferred from another stem class. At 1;11 to 2;0, to be exact, the dative singular ending -*am* was recorded for several feminine *ā*- stems instead of the expected -*ai*, for example, *aũkam* (= *aũklai*) 2;0 "to the string," *Guñtam* (= *Guntrai*) 2;0 "to[a girl named]Guntra," *faũťam*, (= *spalvai*) 2;0 "to the feather." Apparently the ending of the *o*- stems or masculine *ā*- stems was incorrectly extended to the feminine *ā*- stems. The masculine *ā*- stem *puĩka* "boy," which in the nominative singular likewise ends in -*a*, and which has the dative form *puīkam*, could well have served as the model, especially because this word was frequent in the speech of the adults. In the following years, as late as the eighth year, the reverse was observed in the inflection of this word in the child's speech: the masculine *ā*- stem *puika* "boy" was considered as feminine *ā*-stem because of its ending -*a* and was declined accordingly, even with respect to gender, for example, dative singular *puīkai* (= *puikam*) "to the boy," nominative plural *tās nejaukās puīkas* (= *tie nejaukie puikas*) "these impudent boys."

The tendency was therefore clear—the child attempted in one way or another to create an "order" in the declension of words ending in -*a* and to bring them all into agreement.

Remarkable in this regard is the fact that it was primarily the dative forms which varied so greatly in the child's speech. Even in the Latvian vernacular, in the various dialects, the dative endings demonstrate an especially great instability and numerous variations, which have often arisen as analogical extensions. In this respect the child's speech offered a good parallel to similar phenomena in the standard language.

(5) The inflection of the ADJECTIVE proceeded, for the most part, parallel to the noun inflection. Formal distinction in gender developed somewhat earlier than distinctions in case endings. At 1;10 the masculine and feminine of the nominative singular were already formally differentiated; for example, masculine *aps* (= *labs*) "good," feminine *aba* (= *laba*); masculine *śaps* (= *slapjš*) "wet," feminine *śapa* (= *slapja*); masculine *męĩjs* (= *męĺns*) "dirty," feminine/ *męĩj* (= *męĺna*).

In the preceding months such feminine adjective forms had also been used with masculine nouns, and vice versa, for example, 1;6 *ada a-śa* (= *adata asa*) "the needle[is]sharp," but also *aʒi aśa* (= *nazis ass*) "the knife[is]sharp." In other words, again the *form* was first imitated and then later the child began to differentiate these masculine and feminine forms correctly *by content*.

At the age of 2;4, when the nominal inflection was generally already completed, the definite forms of the adjective came into use, for example, *pęĩēkās kups* (= *pęĩēkās kurpes*) "the grey shoes," *sakanᵘôs tâp-s* (= *saȓkanuôs tārpus*) "the red worms" (accusative plural). Occasional definite adjective forms were recorded for the first time around 1;10 (accusative singular *mazo: śuku* (= *mazuo suku*) "the small brush" accusative singular *gajô bići* (= *gaȓuo biksi*) "the long pants," but it was quite a long time before such early starts became regular forms in the child's language.

The earliest and most firmly developed was the inflection of the demonstrative pronoun *tas* "this," feminine *tā* "this," even somewhat earlier than the declension of the nouns. An expression noted from 1;10 may serve as an instructive example for the priority of the pronominal endings: *tā kupe* (= *tā kuȓpe*) "this shoe" next to *tās kupe* (= *tās kuȓpes*) "these shoes," where the characteristic plural ending -*s* was already present in the demonstrative pronoun but not in the noun form.

I also noticed several hypercorrections where the pronominal ending of the definite adjective was transferred to the corresponding case of the noun. That was the case, for example, in the dative (instrumental) plural; compare the fluctuation between *ŭgajãm* and *ŭgãm* (= *uôgãm*) "(with the berries" (1;11–2;0) or a sentence recorded about the same time: *Daĩ ŭtà pŭgajam* (= *Daĩnis ruõtaļãjas* [*ar*] *puõgãm*) "Dainis plays with the buttons," where the boy himself immediately corrected the form *pŭgajam* to *pŭga:m*.

It was thus possible to follow in the child's language the same process which at one time in the history of the Latvian language had caused the nouns to lose their nominal endings and to be declined exactly like the (indefinite) adjectives.

(6)   We can now turn to CONJUGATION. The verbal system developed later than the declensions. The formal differentiation of the tenses emerged earlier than the personal endings. The first tense forms to be formally distinguished were the present and future (mostly concerning immediately impending events, sometimes also with imperative meaning). At 1;10 future forms of other verbs were added to the forms already present (namely *i* (= *ir*) "is," *bi* (= *bij*) "was" and *bus* (= *bûs*) "will be"): for example, future *duś* (= *duôs*) "will give," along with present *dũd* (= *duôd*) "gives"; future *ĩs* (= *iẽs*) "will go," along with present *ĩt* (= *iẽt*) "goes"; future *ʒẹš̄* (= *dzeȓs*) "will drink," along with present *neʒẹj* (= *nedzer*) "does not drink"; future *ņèms* "will take," along with present *ņèm* (= *ņem*) "takes."

The present forms served to express the past at this time (1;10), for example: *daḱi ņem* (= *dakšiņu ņēma*) "[Dainis] took the fork [in his hand]."

The first past tense forms to be different from the present and future appeared at 1;11, for example, *śãve-ja* (= *stãvẽja*) "stood," along with *śã͏ų* (= *stãv*) "stands"; *kit* (= *krita*) "fell" as opposed to *kìt* (= *krìt*) "falls"; *dabu-ja* (= *dabũja*) "got, received" as opposed to *dabu* (= *dabũ*) "gets"; *vaĩʒe* (= *vajadzẽja*) "one needed" as opposed to *vaĩga* (= *vajag*) "one needs." The past tense forms at the end of the second year were still quite rare compared with the high frequency of the present and future forms.

Compound tense forms (*ir redzẽjis* "has seen," and so on) were recorded only much later. These begin around 2;1 (for example, *tũ Daĩ'nàu ẹʒẹ́jś* (= *tuõ Daĩnis nav redzẽjis*) "Dainis didn't see that," that is, I didn't see that) and become somewhat more frequent at 2;4.

It is noteworthy that the various tense forms were first constructed with the auxiliary verb *bũt* "to be, to have." Compare, for example, at 1;6 *bu* (= *bûs*) "will be" (future), *nàu* (= *nav*) "there is not" (present), from 1;7 on *i//iį* (= *ir*) "is," from 1;9 on also *bi* (= *bij; bija*) "was "(past).

The PERSONAL ENDINGS developed significantly later than the separation of tenses. The first verb forms in which one could detect an ending with certainty were the forms of the third person. Since Latvian has only one ending in the third person of both numbers, it is impossible to tell whether this form was singular or plural. The appearance of the verbs in exactly the form of the third person is quite understandable when one considers that the frequency of third person verb forms is very high in speech. Furthermore, adults most often speak in the third person, both about themselves and about the child, when in conversation with young children, and avoid the personal pronouns "I" and "you" so that the frequency of the third person verb forms becomes still greater.

As in the Latvian "Tamian" dialect, this unitary third person ending also served for the first and second persons.

After the period of this unitary verb form the first opposition to appear was the first person singular, and at about the same time (1;11), also the first person plural. The third person form continued to be used for the second person, as well. At 2;1 the child had the appropriate ending for the second person singular of the indicative (occasional imperative forms were used much earlier). The second personal plural ending was acquired last—at 2;7, along with the corresponding personal pronoun *jūs* "you (plural)." The ending appeared nearly simultaneously in the indicative and imperative, for example, *tâ jūs vajat eʒɛ̂t, kuô?* (= /vai/ *tâ jūs varat redzêt? kuó?*) "Can you see that? Hm?" (2;7) and *nãciet!* (= *nãciet!*) "come! (plural)."

It was also observed that the development of the personal endings stood in close temporal relation to the acquisition of the corresponding personal pronoun. Even the verb forms of the second person singular indicative appeared simultaneously with the pronoun *tu* "you (singular)": (2;1) *tu vãji putu!* (= *tu vãri putru*) "you're cooking mush." (The imperative forms of the second person were present earlier since the pronoun is not necessary here.)

In the child's language the formal opposition between personal endings developed earliest in the future tense and then in the present and past, for example, 1;11 *ɛ́ś te śɛ̂dɛ̂śu* (= *es te sêdêšu*) "I will sit here" and *âb divi śɛ̂dɛ̂sim* (= *abi divi sēdēsim*) " [we] both will sit"; while the first person plural is first noted in the present at 2;0: *mɛ̃s ɛ̂dàm* (= *mẽs ɛ̂dam*) "we're eating," and occurs a month later (2;1) in the past: *mɛ̃s bãzãm iśa tãdu* (= *mẽs bâzãm iekšã tâdu*) "we stuffed one-of-those in."

Just as in the development of tense forms, it was noted in the development of personal endings that the forms of the auxiliary *būt* preceded the other verbs. So, for example, the form for the first person plural *bija:m//bijâm* (= *bijām*) "we were" was already present at 1;11.

Around the end of the third year the endings for all three persons were present, even though occasional verb forms did deviate significantly from the norms of standard Latvian. For example, numerous analogical formations for the past tense appeared. The third person form *i* (= *ir*) "is" was long used for all persons; at 2;4 the boy attempted to replace this form in the first person with the analogical construction *i ju* (= *iru*) "[I] am." Only at the beginning of the fourth year did the standard form *ɛsmu* "I am" appear in the proper form, as did the first person plural *ɛsam* "we are."

As far as MOOD is concerned, the indicative and imperative emerged nearly simultaneously: the first records begin at 1;9. The imperative was long confined to the second person singular; only from 2;7 on were forms with the second person plural noted. The third person command came sporadically for the first time at 2;1 (*i' sāu!* = *lai stāv!*) "let him stand!" and became frequent only later on.

At the age of 1;11 the formal contrast between imperative and indicative was already developed in at least some verbs, for example, *nãc śupu!* (= *nãc šuřpu!*) "come here! (singular)" contrasted with *nãk* (= *nãk*) "come"; *nȩ̂-ȩj!* (= *neej!*) "don't go! (singular)" contrasted with *ĩt* (= *iȇt*) "go(es)"; *nûtaĩsⁱ!* (= *uztaisi!*) "make! (singular)" contrasted with *tâisa* (= *taĩsa*) "make(s)"; *śat'ī!* (= *skatiȇs!*) "look (singular)" contrasted with *śatâ* (= *skatâs*) "look(s)."

The original imperative form was often used incorrectly with an indicative meaning, for example, *mȩm̃mȩ âudi* (= *mȩm̃mȩ, raudâs*) "Mamma will cry" (actually "Mamma, cry!") or *maĩśi* (= *maĩsa*) "stirs" (actually "stir! [singular]").

Thus we find in child language a phenomenon corresponding to one found elsewhere in the Baltic-speaking area, namely, the interaction between imperative and indicative forms.

The debitive emerged a few months later. The first example was recorded at 2;0: *Daĩnim jà-ĩt gūtã* (= *Daĩnim jā-iȇt gul̃tā*) "Dainis must go to bed," that is, "I must go to bed."

Optative forms as well as the relative mode, in contrast, were not used by the child during the period of observation, that is, up to the fifth year.

Occasional *reflexive* forms were already present at 1;10 (in the third person), although the active form could be used just as well at this time to express reflexive meaning. Some examples are: *nùʒȩjⁿôs* (= *nuodzȇruôs*) "I drank," *nùkàtⁿôs* (= *nuokārtuosies*) "will be settled" (2;1).

The *passive* construction was hardly observed at all during the first four years, only in occasional expressions such as "made," "ended." Even in colloquial Latvian of adults, however, passive constructions with the auxiliary verb *tikt* or *tapt* are not numerous.

Nonfinite verb forms were acquired noticeably later than finite forms. Only at the end of the second year and beginning of the third year did the child acquire the *infinitives* with all four characteristic endings: for example, *śaĩgât* (= *staigât*) "go, walk," *guvȩ̂t* (= *gulȩ̂t*) "sleep," *dañcũt* (= *dañcuôt*) "dance," *aśi:t* (= *rakstît*) "write."

Last of all to emerge were the PARTICIPLES, in a specific order. The first to appear were the perfect passive participles (1;11): *miźûc* (= *mizuôts*) "peeled," plural *miźûti* (= *mizuôti*). These forms first became frequent around 2;1 when the passive tenses formed with these participles became more frequent: *i:mȩtâti zȇm viśⁱ kućĩśi* (= *izmȩtāti pa zemi visi klucĩši*) "all the blocks are scattered on the floor."

After 2;0 the present participles in *-ams* emerged and at 2;2 the first instance of the gerund in *-uot* appeared: *ȩ́ś pa-iku śȇźuot* (= *es paliku sȇžuot*) "I kept sitting." The gerund became somewhat more frequent at 2;4.

Finally, the child began to use the past active participle also. At 1;11 such forms of the auxiliary verb *būt* "to be" were already present: *biis//bīs* "been," *nebiis* "not been." These forms of other verbs became frequent after 2;4; simultaneously with these participles also came the compound tenses which use them (perfect): *tie i apẹduśi viš^as kūk^as* (= *tie ir apẹduši visas kūkas*) "they have eaten up all the cakes," *es nav dāzis* (= *es neẹsmu drāzis*) "I have not cut."

On the basis of the foregoing Latvian data one can, with due caution and reservations, draw some conclusions, provided that one supplements the data with observations on the language development of a number of other Latvian children and adduces investigations of other languages. The following may be of general validity with respect to the development of inflection in child language:

1. Syntactic development in child language seems in general to begin earlier than the development of the morphological markers used to express these syntactic relationships.
2. In general, the end of the second year and the first half of the third year seem to be the most usual periods in which the declensional systems are developed in child language.[17]
3. Conjugation develops, as a rule, somewhat later than declension, so that even at the end of the fourth year the finer features of the verbal system are often not yet present in the correct form.

The reason for the late emergence of verb inflection should be sought in the general structure of the child's psyche and therefore also in child *language*. Verbs, as word categories, also appear later than nouns in child language. Second, verbal inflection is closely bound to the emergence of personal pronouns, but these are acquired by the child fairly late since they require a greater ability for abstraction and relativity. The verb system, moreover, at least in Baltic languages, is characterized by greater variety and abundance of forms, which greatly hinders the acquisition of these various linguistic elements during the first two or three years.
4. The sequence of acquisition of inflections depends to a certain extent on the general structure of the corresponding language, for example, on the relative frequency of certain case forms in the colloquial or family speech. Those languages whose systems are more similar will correspond to each other also in the processes of development in child language. In my opinion, it is no accident that the sequence of the inflections recorded for the Latvian boy corresponded on the whole to the formation of declension and conjugation in Polish children, in any case, at least better than, for example, corresponding to the language development of Bulgarian children. (There is unfortunately no comparable material for the closely related Lithuanian language.) The child has, of course,

---

[17] The language development of the Latvian child observed for this study was, at least in morphological, lexical, and syntactic respects, earlier and more rapid than the average.

the model of the normal language of his environment—even if he selects only certain linguistic elements and continually reshapes and combines them.

In my opinion, much of the lack of overlap in language development of children of different nationalities can be explained by the diversity in the character of the respective languages. Let us take an example.

On the basis of observations on his own children and similar observations of several other Western investigators, W. Leopold believes that the forms of the verb "to be" emerge very late in the language of the child and that they perhaps belong to those words which the child acquires last of all.[18] Although Latvian belongs to those languages in which the subject and predicate can be joined without "is" (for example, *māte laba* "mother [is] good"), forms like "is," "will be," "was" appeared very early in the Latvian child's language. In fact, the child used the tense forms of this verb earlier than those of other verbs.

In reviewing the total recorded data, it seems that the explanation of this difference between the language development in English–German-speaking children on the one hand, and the Latvian child on the other, lies in the difference in the usage of these verb forms in the respective languages. In Latvian one often uses the forms *ir* "is," *nav* "is not," *būs* "will be," *bija* "was" in instances where one would answer with *ja* or *nein* in German, *yes* or *no* in English, *ja, jo,* or *nej* in Swedish. Even the first sentences which contained *nàu* (= *nav*) and *i* (= *ir*) were used in situations when a strong affirmative or negative was intended; at 1;6 (for the first time) *nàu!* "there is none," 1;7, *śau-ía i!* (= *slaũḳi ir!*) "there *are* hand towels!" (in response to a skeptical statement by the mother that there were perhaps no towels), or at 1;9 *mẽm̃m 'i mãja*) (= *mẽm̃me' ir mãjā*) "Mother *is* certainly at home."

Something similar is important with respect to the individual case categories. In languages which, for example, make frequent use of the genitive, in places where other languages would use the accusative or dative, one can expect the probability to be greater that the child will acquire the genitive ending earlier.

Therefore it does not seem to me to be possible to postulate an exact sequence among case endings that would have any general validity, and in this respect I agree with the Sterns. Surely much depends on the character of the individual language in question. It appears, however, that the formal contrast between nominative and accusative (or that case which has the function of direct object) will be created early and that those cases which are expressed by prepositions will be formed later because the child acquires prepositions as a word class quite late.

The present and future verb forms should be expected first even though much depends on the characteristics of the verbal system of the respective

---

[18] "The verb 'to be,' as a full verb meaning 'exist,' 'be located' and as a copula linking a subject, implied or expressed, with the real predication, was always omitted. The copula is phonetically unemphatic and semantically not essential. Many standard languages can do without it, . . ." Werner F. Leopold, *Speech Development of a Bilingual Child*, Vol. 3 (1949), p. 93.

languages. In German, where the present tense can also express the future, there is, so to speak, no pressing need for a formally distinct future tense form, so that the Sterns were able to observe the emergence of a formal preterite earlier than the future in their children.

So far as mood is concerned, the imperative and indicative appear to develop earliest.

(5) Further generalizations should probably not be made, at least at the present time. First, a larger number of monographs on language development, especially on inflectional systems are needed from the languages of children of diverse nationalities.[19] Individual studies of this type are indispensable in order to be able to differentiate among idiosyncrasies of the specific child, characteristics of the whole language or language family, and, finally, putative general developmental rules of most, if not all, of the inflectional languages of the world.

RUSSIAN •

Russian and English have been the two most widely investigated languages in ontogenetic perspective. Beginning in the late nineteenth century (Aleksandrov, 1883; Blagoveshchenskiy, 1886) and culminating in the monumental work of A. N. Gvozdev (1948, 1949), Russians contributed significantly to the literature of child language diaries popular before the rise of systematic psycholinguistics. And Soviet pedagogical psychologists and psycholinguists have carried out scores of scientific investigations of language development in the last twenty years (partly abstracted by Slobin [1966a] and reviewed in Ervin-Tripp and Slobin [1966] and Slobin [1966b, 1966d]; a recent guide to Soviet psycholinguistics can be found in Slobin [1969b]).

An important impetus to Soviet interest in language development has been the practical task of raising infants and very young children in public nurseries—both day nurseries and boarding institutions. Influenced by pedagogical demands, much work on child language takes the form of training experiments. This orientation goes back to the thirties and Vygotsky's wise suggestion that intelligence tests should measure not the child's performance at a single point in time but rather his ability to improve this performance with instruction or aid: "The discrepancy between a child's actual mental age and the level he reaches in solving problems with assistance indicates the zone of his proximal development. . . . With assistance, every child can do more than he can by himself—though only within the limits set by the stage of his development"

---

[19] Mildred C. Templin also mentions the pressing importance of monographs depicting language development in children: "In order to learn more about the actual development and interrelationships of language skills, longitudinal studies must be done. It is through these that the interrelations of language as it is developed will be better understood." *Certain Language Skills in Children* (Minneapolis, 1957), p. 152.

(Vygotsky, 1962, p. 103). Accordingly, a frequently used technique, exemplified by the Popova study which follows, is to take a group of children in a given age range and require them all to perform a certain linguistic task. The performance of each child is then qualitatively analyzed, and a classification of performances is set up. The average age of children falling into each performance category is calculated and an attempt is made to establish an ontogenetic sequence of performance types on the basis of such cross-sectional data. Various training procedures are then instituted, and it is generally found that certain training procedures are most effective with children at given stages, that rapid advance is more possible in some stages than in others, and so forth. An outstanding feature of this research is the use of long-term training experiments, stretching over weeks or months of a young child's life (see Shvachkin, this volume). Children as young as nine months have served as subjects in such studies (Mallitzkaya, 1960).

The three studies reprinted here, along with the Shvachkin and Zhurova studies reprinted in Part I, are classic examples of Soviet research in developmental psycholinguistics. Popova studied gender agreement; Zakharova studied case inflections; and Bogoyavlenskiy, like Jean Berko in the United States. (1958), studied children's ability to attach suffixes to unfamiliar words (diminutive, augmentative, and agentive endings).

A few words about Russian grammar will orient the reader to the three papers and to El'konin's summary of Gvozdev's diary, which appears in the following section of this volume. There are three genders, almost always unequivocally marked by the noun ending in the nominative case. Generally, nouns ending in consonants are masculine; feminine nouns end in -a; neuter nouns in -o (which, when unstressed, is indistinguishable from the feminine). Nouns ending in palatalized consonants, however, may be either masculine or feminine. There are six grammatical cases (nominative, genitive, dative, accusative, instrumental, prepositional), and case inflections vary with gender (for example, *karandash* 'pencil': *karandashom* 'by means of a pencil'; *avtoruchka* 'fountain pen': *avtoruchkoy* 'by means of a fountain pen'). Adjectives are also inflected for case and gender, agreeing with the head noun. However, the phonological form of the adjective inflection rarely coincides with that of the noun inflection (for example, *bol'shoy karandash* 'big pencil' : *bol'shim karandashom* 'by means of the big pencil').

Use of grammatical case is determined by semantic criteria (for example, dative of indirect object) and by a variety of arbitrary and semiarbitrary criteria, such as the case requirements of particular verbs, prepositions, or sentence forms. For example, one *learns* something (*uchit'sya*) in the dative, but *masters* something in either the instrumental (*ovladevat'*) or the accusative (*usvaivat'*), depending on the verb. One walks *up to* (*k*) a friend in the dative, does something *with* (*s*) him in the instrumental, brings something *for* (*dlya*) him in the genitive, talks *about* (*o*) him in the prepositional, and so on.

Some of these inflections are examined in the Zakharova study. Popova explores another corner of the system, namely the use of gender suffixes on past tense verbs (which must match the gender of the subject noun). Bogoyavlenskiy deals with noninflectional noun suffixes, exploring children's grasp of agentive suffixes and of the rich affective tools of the Russian language in the realm of diminutive and augmentative suffixes. El'konin's summary of Gvozdev's diary (next section) echoes many of the experimental findings presented in the following three papers.   —D.I.S.

Grammatical Elements of Language in the Speech of Pre-Preschool Children

——M. I. Popova

In investigations devoted to the study of the child's acquisition of the grammatical structure of language, attention has usually been centered on characteristics of the child's formation of grammatical generalizations on the basis of generalizations of concrete object relations reflected in the grammar (Serebrennikova, 1953; Sokhin, 1955; Zakharova, 1955). The facts of child speech development, however, show that children master some language forms long before understanding the corresponding object relationships. For example, the correlative forms of present and past tense of the verb appear in child speech toward the end of the second year of life (Gvozdev, 1949), that is, before his acquisition of temporal relationships. This is even more obvious in the acquisition of the category of noun gender, which reflects actual sex distinctions in animate nouns only, while remaining purely formal in inanimate nouns. Therefore, the question of the acquisition of formal grammatical elements has remained unanswered. This raised the necessity for study of the child's acquisition of those grammatical forms which either do not carry any object relationships or in which these relationships are too difficult for a child of pre-preschool age to grasp. It became necessary, therefore, to discover the conditions which promote the acquisition of morphology and to study the nature of the verbal activity of the child when linguistic material itself is a manifestation of objective reality.

The grammatical category of gender was investigated as the most characteristic morphological feature of nouns. This category is devoid of lexical significance, preserving it only to some degree in male and female names of persons and animals. We studied acquisition of the purely morphological significance of gender—that is, strictly obligatory agreement.

The research therefore centered on the study of the acquisition of agreement by pre-preschool children, on their orientation in creating interdependent word combinations, and on the conditions which facilitate the process.

Grammatichiskiye elementy yazyka v rechi detey preddoshkol'nogo vozrasta. *Voprosy psikhologii*, 1958, **4** (3), 106–117. Translated from Russian by Greta Slobin and edited by Dan I. Slobin.

Complexity of the problem resulted in the division of the experiment into three stages, each devoted to a solution of a single problem. The first stage was used to determine the presence of particular features in the agreement of nouns and verbs in the past tense.[1]

For this task we chose various verbs: *prishel(a)* [came], *ubezhal(a)* [ran away], *pel(a)* [sang], *upal(a)* [fell], *yel(a)* [ate], *pil(a)* [drank], as well as four series of animate and inanimate nouns representing the basic variety of masculine and feminine forms. The first series consisted of animate nouns in which the gender differences were expressed either semantically (*mal'chik, devochka* [boy, girl]) or morphologically by ending and by declension type (animal names: *verblyud* [camel], *volk* [wolf], *sobaka* [dog], *lisa* [fox]). The second series consisted of animate nouns representing the category of gender most clearly, in that gender is also expressed by the grammatical juxtaposition of the names of male and female animals. These nouns form semantically related pairs in which feminine gender is marked either by ending only or by suffix and ending (*yëzh—yezhikha* [he- and she-porcupine]). The third series consisted of nouns which the child hears and pronounces at an early age (*papa, mama, dyadya* [uncle], *tëtya* [aunt]). These words are peculiar in that they form pairs with identical number of syllables and with a uniform ending (*a* or *ya*), while belonging to different genders (*papa-mama*). In masculine nouns the morphological feature (ending) does not correspond to the sex of the object [but the verb past tense is masculine —Ed.]. The fourth series consisted of inanimate nouns in which the ending determines the gender (*kubik* [block], *kukla* [doll]).

In order to familiarize the children with all the words, we conducted games with words of the first and third series, and a number of pictures were drawn for the words of the second and fourth series. During each of these series and games, the experimenter would first ask a question with a verb in the past tense plural [same for all genders—Ed.]: *"Kakiye zveri ubezhali v les?"* [Which animals ran away to the forest?] *"Kakiye igrushki upali na pol?"* [Which toys fell on the floor?] Then the experimenter would proceed with the story, answering the questions with subject-predicate sentences (*zayats ubezhal* [the rabbit ran away], *lisa ubezhala* [the fox ran away]; *myach upal* [the ball fell], *kukla upala* [the doll fell]). Whenever possible, the experimenter would demonstrate the actions of the people and animals. Stories were repeated two or three times to each group and the children's ability to answer questions was fully checked. Some children had to be taught individually. In the days that followed,

---

[1] [Editor's note: Russian has three genders—feminine, masculine, and neuter. Commonly, feminine nouns end in *-a*, masculine in consonants (zero), and neuter in *-o*; however, a number of masculine animate nouns end in *-a*. (There is also a variety of less common endings, each of them unique to a given gender except for certain palatalized consonants, which may be masculine or feminine.) The past tense of the verb carries a gender suffix—zero for masculine, *-a* for feminine, and *-o* for neuter (reduced, when unstressed, to be indistinguishable from the feminine). There is also adjective-noun agreement in gender.]

individual discussions were conducted with the purpose of checking the degree of the child's acquisition of correct agreement and of the level of acquisition of agreement of gender of nouns and of past tense verbs. During the discussion the child was asked: *"Rasskazhi, Slava, kakiye zveri peli na yëlke?"* [Tell me, Slava, which animals were singing in the fir tree?] Full sentence answers were demanded: *"Slon pel. Tigritsa pela."* [The elephant was singing, The tigress was singing.] The two-part structure of this sentence is very elementary but is, at the same time, a complete syntactic unit.

Observations of 55 children, between the ages of 1;10 (1 year 10 months) and 3;6 (3 years 6 months), were conducted in two Moscow nurseries. Altogether approximately 9,000 answers were analyzed (8,914).

Children tested on the agreement of nouns with past tense verbs produced both correct and incorrect answers which showed, in the analyses, that gender agreement was established in only 13 children (24%; age 2;3–3;6; 8 boys, 5 girls), and that the remaining 42 children (70%; age 1;10–3;5; 15 boys, 27 girls) did not yet form the correct agreements. Depending on the features of the agreement, the children were divided into four groups which represent different stages of acquisition of agreement in the following discussion.

Children of the first group (22 subjects; age 1;10–3;2; 7 boys, 15 girls) most often used feminine gender in agreement (percentage of correct answers with masculine words: 0–34; with feminine words: 70–100).

Children of the second group (9 subjects; age 2;6–3;3; 4 boys, 5 girls) most often used masculine gender in agreement (percentage of correct answers with masculine words: 75–100; with feminine words: 0–40).

Children of the third group (11 subjects, age 2;2–3;5; 4 boys, 7 girls) confused both genders in approximately similar ratio (percentage of correct answers with masculine words: 45–82; with feminine words: 40–90).

The fourth group included the children who formed predominantly correct agreements (percentage of correct answers in both genders: 75–100).

The data presented in Table 1 show that predominance of agreement with feminine gender declines with age; predominance of agreement with masculine gender increases, and correct agreement remains on approximately the same level.

Analysis of response shows that in all four groups the character of the

TABLE 1   DISTRIBUTION OF SUBJECTS INTO GENDER-AGREEMENT GROUPS ON THE BASIS OF AGE

| | | PERCENTAGE OF SUBJECTS IN EACH GENDER-AGREEMENT GROUP | | | |
| | | 1 | 2 | 3 | 4 |
AGE	N	FEMININE	MASCULINE	MIXED	CORRECT
1;10–2;6	25	52	8	16	24
2;7–3;0	18	39	17	22	22
3;1–3;6	12	17	33	25	25

agreement is identical for each group, but with a different degree of prevalence of a gender, depending on the words in the series. Thus, there is not much difference of agreement of the two genders in the first and fourth series of words: first group of masculine words: 11 percent correct answers in the first series and 10 percent in the fourth; for feminine words: 94 and 95 percent in the second group: 95 and 87 percent, and 16 and 19 percent; in the third: 67 and 70 percent, 70 and 62 percent in the fourth: 90 and 91 percent and 91 and 95 percent. Among the two series, agreement in the second and third series is distinctly different. Words of the second and third series promote a change in the agreement by the majority of children in each group (90–95 percent).

In the Russian language there is a contradiction in the nouns themselves in their determination of the gender of the past tense verb in the agreement. Usually, words different in structure are also different in gender (*myach-mashina* [ball-car]; *mal'chik-devochka* [boy-girl]), but there are words similar in structure and endings, but also different in gender (*papa-mama*); there are words with identical root but with different suffixes and endings, differing in gender (*kozël-koza* [he– she-goat]); finally, there are words with identical stems and different endings, but of the same gender (*zayats-zayka*) [hare-little hare]. Such distinctions between nouns make acquisition of agreement more difficult because there is no single basis for working out generalizations. Nevertheless, the experiment showed that change in the character of agreement is directly dependent on the noun structure.

Feminine words of the second series (*tigritsa* [tigress], *slonikha*, [she-elephant], *yezhikha* [she-porcupine]) were acquired as varieties of masculine words by all the children with predominantly correct agreements. Children expressed this during the experiment:

> Vova V. (3;0) *"Slonikha poyekhal na yëlku. On poyekhal na yëlku v zoopark."* [Elephant (fem.) went (masc.) to the fir tree. He went to the fir tree in the zoo.]

> Nadya K. (3;5) *"Slonikha pel na yelke. Tetya, pokazhi, kak on pel?"* (asking the experimenter). [Elephant (fem.) sang (masc.) on the fir tree. Auntie, show how he sang.]

> Some subjects made the following comments: *"Slon, yëzh—eto on; slonikha, yezhikha, tozhe on, tol'ko bol'shoy."* [Elephant (masc.) and porcupine (masc.) are he; elephant (fem.) and porcupine (fem.) are also he, but big.]

As a result, in almost all groups of children, in the agreement of words of the second series, there is an increase in correct answers for masculine words (by 7–19 percent), while quite a high percentage remained in the feminine words (31–82 percent). In the agreement of words of the third series, the results are the opposite: the percentage of correct answers in masculine words decreases (by as much as 35 percent) and increases in feminine words (by about 15 percent).

The result of the experiment showed that change in the nature of agreement is directly related to the morphological features of words, namely, to noun endings. This leads to the conclusion that concrete-material content connected with designation of sex is only a partial basis for generalization in the agreements with verbs but does not serve in most cases. The basis of the formation of agreement lies in the child's orientation to the formal feature of the noun.

Following are examples of orientation to the noun form in the fourth group among children who have acquired correct noun agreements:

1. For the word *loshad'* [horse], only 28 percent of the answers were correct. This shows that the [palatalized] ending of this word orients the child to the masculine form of the past tense verb. Especially significant is the fact that the majority of the children, after pronouncing the word with the masculine verb form: *Loshad' poyekhal, loshad' ubezhal* [horse (fem.) went (masc.), horse (fem.) ran away (masc.)], immediately contrast it with: *A loshadka poyekhala, loshadka ubezhala* [little horse (fem. dim.) went (fem.), little horse (fem. dim.) ran away (fem.)].[2]

2. Children who have basically mastered correct agreement make errors with words such as *papa, dyadya, dedushka* [father, uncle, grandfather], often using the feminine form of the past tense verb: *"Dyadya sidela na loshadke"*; *"Moy papa zabolela"*; and so on [Uncle was sitting (fem.) on the little horse; My father got sick (fem.)].

3. In all the cases in which children pronounce nouns incorrectly (*slona* instead of *slon, tigra* instead of *tigr*) the verb form always corresponded to the noun form ending.

In Pavlov's theory of conditioned connections we find the statement that the same association takes place between two neighboring words as between a light and a sound, without the special reinforcement of unconditional stimuli. "Temporary nervous connection is the most universal physiological phenomenon in the animal world and in the human world. It is also psychological in nature— what the psychologists call "association," whether it is the creation of connections of various actions, impressions, or of letters, words, and thoughts" (Pavlov, 1949, p. 56). This association of two neighboring words is the basis of the acquisition of correct agreement.

It can be assumed that from the moment the past tense verb appears in child speech a strong union is formed between the verb and the noun, and that the verb is pronounced in the feminine regardless of the gender of the noun. This type of connection may be termed as belonging to the first type. Generalization

---

[2] [Editor's note: The fact that *loshad'*, ending in a palatalized consonant, is feminine must be rote-learned, as nouns ending in palatalized consonants are either feminine or masculine. *Loshad'* is thus not morphologically marked for gender, while the corresponding diminutive form, *loshadka*, bears the characteristic feminine ending. The children apparently treat *loshad'-loshadka* as a male-female pair for 'horse.']

of the first type accounts for the long predominance of feminine forms in agreement between nouns and past tense verbs.

The following hypothesis can be established in connection with the problem of the stage of predominantly feminine forms in agreement:

1. The feminine gender is the most strongly and clearly marked of the genders. It has one type of ending in the nominative (*-a* or *-ya*) while the masculine gender has various endings (*-b*, *-v*, *-g*, *-d*, *-zh*, and so on).

2. In child speech there is a common tendency, stretching over a long period, to pronounce open syllables. Instead of the whole word, children pronounce only one syllable at an early age; and later, words of the type *mal'chik*, *myach*, *tigr*, *slon* are pronounced as *mal'chka*, *myachka*, *tigra*, *slëna*.

3. An analysis of children's vocabulary (taken from diary materials) showed that about 70 percent of the words end in *-a*.

Accumulation in the vocabulary of masculine forms of past tense verbs creates conditions for formation of the second type of connection with masculine gender predominant in the agreement. The displacement and complete replacement of the first type by the second is based on generalization of the new connections of the second type.

Generalization of connections of the first and second types creates obstacles in orienting to the form of the word. Only in the stage of confusion do favorable conditions for orientation arise. Generalization becomes replaced by differentiation of both types of connections in accordance with gender differences of nouns.

The result of the experiment led to a further question: what conditions favor orientation to the form of words in the process of acquisition of correct agreement from among the variety of forms encountered by the child in the process of verbal communication? The second stage of the investigation was devoted to the solution of this question.

The second stage consisted of a teaching experiment for the purpose of ascertaining the conditions which promote orientation of pre-preschool children to a purely linguistic phenomenon (word ending). The goal was to single out the endings and generalize them in the agreement of nouns and past tense verbs.

Teaching was conducted four times a week over the course of two months, using a certain group of nouns and verbs. Stories were made up with nouns like *ptichka*, *yëzhik*, *belka*, *krokodil*, *stol*, *truba*, and so on [little bird, porcupine, squirrel, crocodile, table, pipe]; and with verbs in the past tense: *begal(a)*, *sel(a)*, *lezhal(a)*, *prishel(a)*, and so on [ran, sat, lay, came]. All objects, animals, and their actions were presented in drawings. The subject was allowed three days in which to become familiarized with the teaching process, so as to be able to answer questions easily. In most cases children memorized short stories easily and were able to tell them with pictures. The experimenter would first demonstrate the correct pronunciation of verbs and nouns, marking the endings with a louder voice. Then the question was posed:

EXPERIMENTER: *"Rasskazhi, Sasha, kakiye igrushki lezhali u Mishki na stole?"*
[Tell me, Sasha, what toys lay on Misha's table?]
SASHA (2;5):   *"Truba lezhala, stul lezhal . . ."* etc. [pipe, (fem.) lay (fem.), chair (masc.) lay (masc.)].
EXPERIMENTER: *"Chto delali yёzhik i ptichka v komnate u okhotnika?"* [What were the bird and the porcupine doing in the hunter's room?]
SASHA: *"Ptichka letala, yёzhik begal; ptichka zasnula na stole, yezhik zasnul v shlyape."* [the bird was flying, the porcupine was running; the bird fell asleep on the table, the porcupine fell asleep in the hat].

The experimenter always corrected wrong answers: *"yёzhik zasnula* [porcupine (masc.) fell asleep (fem.)]. No, that's wrong, you should say *yёzhik zasnul."* Correct answers were verbally reinforced: "That was right; correct." Teaching continued until correct agreements were formed with all the given words. After this children were given other words to work with.

This method was applied to 12 children, aged 2;6–3;4, after they had been observed during different stages of the acquisition of agreement (Table 2).

Teaching showed the following: not all children were able to form correct agreements despite numerous repetitions by the experimenter of some words and their equal repetition by the children. From the five in whose agreements feminine forms were predominant, one child was able to form correct agreement after 180 repetitions; the other four children after 312–534 repetitions were still unable to do so. Of the seven children in whose agreements either the masculine form was predominant or there was a confusion of genders, three children needed 216, 258, and 438 repetitions, respectively. Only four children needed a

TABLE 2   RESULTS OF THE FIRST TEACHING METHOD

	SUBJECT	AGE AT THE END OF TEACHING	STAGE OF GENDER AGREEMENT AT THE BEGINNING OF TEACHING	NUMBER OF REPETITIONS OF AGREEMENT BY THE CHILD	STAGE OF GENDER AGREEMENT AT THE END OF TEACHING
1.	Natasha M.	2;8	I	534	III
2.	Sasha B.	3;2	I	528	II
3.	Ira Kh.	2;11	I	312	II
4.	Nadya M.	3;5	I	204	III
5.	Olya I.	2;9	I	180	IV
6.	Toma O.	3;4	II	438	IV
7.	Yura G.	3;6	II	84	IV
8.	Tanya F.	3;0	II	216	IV
9.	Tanya L.	3;1	III	218	IV
10.	Galya R.	3;0	III	84	IV
11.	Voba S.	3;0	III	60	IV
12.	Yulya K.	2;10	III	12	IV

relatively small number of repetitions (84, 60, 12); three of these children were at the highest stage (III) at the beginning, and the other was at II.

Thus, correct agreements were formed by the children who were in the third stage (gender confusion) before the experiment. Correct agreements were more difficult to form for the children who used mostly masculine forms before the experiment (Stage II) and for those who used mostly feminine (Stage I).

Having followed the process of the acquisition of agreement, we concluded that in some children irregularities in the acquisition of agreement (for example, time needed for a stage, different degree of predominance of different genders at different stages) do not, on the whole, disturb the process of acquisition, which is more or less uniform for everyone. Succession of stages takes place in a definite order: I: predominance of feminine; II: predominance of masculine; III: confusion of both genders; IV: correct agreement. There were only a few cases of deviations, for example, Stage I returns after Stage II, but is soon replaced by III.

The duration of predominance of masculine or feminine gender is caused by generalization of the agreement connections which become fixed in the child's speech. These connections are, actually, constantly reinforced because they are correct in some cases. Words which correspond in fact to a certain type of connection (feminine type 1, masculine type 2) inhibit extinction of connections which do not correspond to grammatical norms.

During observation of the acquisition of gender agreement, it was noted that only in Stage III was a child able to correct his mistakes (this was not observed in either I or II). Correction of errors gives the opportunity to pronounce the verb in both masculine and feminine forms.

It is popular in pedagogical practice to believe that exercise or frequent repetition of a given form is a determining condition for the acquisition of grammar. The results of our teaching experiment showed that although repetition has a role in the process of acquisition, it is not the only basic and important condition.

Correcting mistakes in a child's pronunciation is not the same as correcting expressions which do not correspond to reality (the child says that he put the bear *na yashchik* [on the drawer], when he should say *v yashchik* [into the drawer]). And it is something quite different again to correct a child's expressions when they are pronounced correctly but express the action without the correct grammatical agreement (*volk prishla v teremok* [the wolf (masc.) came (fem.) to the tower], or *lisa prishel v teremok* [the fox (fem.) came (masc.) to the tower]). In this case, a simple exercise of repetition by both the experimenter and the subject of the correct gender agreement either does not lead to formation of a correct agreement through orientation to the form of the word, or it will lead to it only with great difficulty.

Thus it was found that mere accumulation of verbal experience in nursery conditions, without a special organization of the linguistic material which would facilitate orientation to the phonetic aspects of words, does not accelerate the acquisition of gender agreement. This made it necessary to organize instruction so as to orient the child to formal features of words—to the gender endings of nouns.

For this purpose, a third stage of the experiment was designed to include child speech in practical activities, making linguistic forms the object of activity. It was necessary to establish correct agreement not only in those children who confused genders or used predominantly masculine forms before the beginning of instruction, but also among the children who used mostly feminine forms. The essence of the teaching technique was the following. When agreement was correct, the experimenter would reinforce it verbally and would allow the child to carry out a desired act. If the agreement was incorrect, the subject was shown his mistake verbally and not allowed to complete the action.

Teaching was conducted with the game *Teremok* [tower]. Children were asked to lead animal figures into a tower (lion, elephant, tiger, squirrel, goat, fish). If the experimenter's question, *"Kto poshli v teremok?"* and *"Kto prishli v teremok?"* [Who went (plural) into the tower? Who came (plural) to the tower?], was answered with a correct agreement, the tower doors would open and the animal could enter. If the answer was incorrect, the doors would not open and the mistake was pointed out by the experimenter. If the child corrected his mistake without the experimenter's assistance, the doors would open; if he did not, the experimenter would not open the door, he would point to the mistake again by pronouncing the correct agreement, and the game would continue with different animals.

Teaching was conducted among 20 children, aged 1;11–3;4. In this group, 13 children used mainly feminine gender, three used masculine, and four had a more or less equal confusion of the two genders. The results are presented in Table 3.

This second teaching method proved to be quite effective. All children were able to form correct agreements; the number of repetitions needed for the acquisition was reduced; and 25 percent of the children achieved correct agreement in a very short time (during the first three days in which repetitions and corrections were no longer counted).

Under these conditions, the acquisition of agreement has certain characteristic aspects. Shortening of Stages I, II, and III preceding correct agreement was observed. In some children Stages II and III were insignificant: Stage II was by-passed when children jumped to Stage III from I and went on to IV, or went from II directly to IV. Also, a sort of curtailment of the process was observed when some children formed correct agreements without going through the stages.

Most children learned to correct their mistakes almost from the first day of learning, and some children did not make any mistakes during the whole learning period. When taught according to the first method, children acquired such skills only at Stage III, and when taught by the second method, at Stages I or II. The teaching experiment showed that the necessity of a fast transition

TABLE 3   GENDER AGREEMENT BEFORE AND AFTER TEACHING

Name	Age at the End of Teaching	Stages of Gender Agreement at the Beginning of Teaching	Number of Repetitions of Agreement by the Child	Stage of Gender Agreement at the End of Teaching
1. Lena Z.	1;11	I	0	IV
2. Inna B.	2;3	I	0	IV
3. Ira F.	3;3	I	0	IV
4. Alexandr D.	2;1	I	12	IV
5. Masha P.	2;3	I	24	IV
6. Andrey E.	2;9	I	36	IV
7. Yura Zh.	3	I	36	IV
8. Nadya K.	2;7	I	48	IV
9. Tanya K.	3;1	I	60	IV
10. Yevgeniy S.	2;3	I	84	IV
11. Lyuda M.	2;1	I	132	IV
12. Valya D.	2;2	I	156	IV
13. Lyusya P.	2;6	I	192	IV
14. Slava G.	3;4	II	24	IV
15. Nina P.	2;8	II	156	IV
16. Lyusya Sh.	3;1	II	156	IV
17. Voya M.	2;3	III	0	IV
18. Galya Yev.	2;6	III	0	IV
19. Natasha M.	3;2	III	36	IV
20. Valerik S.	2;4	III	84	IV

to the correction of mistakes makes the children pronounce not one but two verb forms, masculine and feminine, which speeds up the acquisition.

It had become clear during the experiment that the already formed agreements (with predominance of either gender) become obstacles not only in orientation to the form of the word but in simple repetition of the correct form after the experimenter. For a long time, some children (Nadya K., Zhenya S., Slava G., Lyuda M., Nina P., Valya D., Lyusya P.) were unable to pronounce the verb form after the experimenter and instead kept repeating the form they had fixated. It was as if these children did not "hear" what the experimenter was saying, as if they had become "deaf" for a while.[3]

In order to switch the children from pronouncing one form to the other it was decided to conduct teaching on the basis of those nouns which require the past tense of a verb contrary to the one predominant in the child's agreement system at the moment. For example, if feminine was strongly predominant in the agreement, then feminine words would be excluded from teaching and only

[3] In both the first and second teaching methods the number of repetitions pronounced by the experimenter was equal to that of the child.

masculine words were left. This method was used in order to limit the spread of generalization of agreement by excluding those words which promote its appearance and fixation. As soon as we switched to learning words of different genders, the old connection gradually disappeared and a new one appeared. After some time, the words excluded earlier would be reintroduced. The new connection became predominant but was soon followed by the stage of gender confusion.

As soon as the child would start using the past tense verb in both forms, it became possible to teach nouns of different genders given in the contrasts; this was, finally, followed by the acquisition of correct agreement.

In order to check how firmly correct agreement had been learned in such a short time, additional observations were conducted two weeks after the completion of the second method of teaching. For this purpose, animate and inanimate nouns unfamiliar to the children were used. Among these words there were nouns in which the morphological ending does not correspond to the actual gender of the referent. This was done in order to determine whether children direct themselves toward the gender of the ending of the word.

Results showed that of the 16 children observed, 15 formed mostly correct agreements (more than 90 percent correct answers); thus the speed of the acquisition did not influence its stability. Almost all children preserved the capacity for correcting their mistakes which had been acquired in the learning process.

In forming agreements between verbs and nouns in which the ending does not correspond to the gender of the referent (*mishka* [bear], *zayka* [little hare]), many incorrect answers were received (44–88 percent) and, as a rule, mistakes were not corrected. This shows that orientation to the form of the word appears even when the gender of the verb is determined not by the form, but by the gender of the noun.[4]

Thus, special organization of the child's linguistic activity promotes rapid formation of generalized orientation towards the phonetic features of words.

When the experimenter gives the child a ready-made correct agreement to repeat (first method), the child is not faced with the necessity of manipulating linguistic material; what takes place is a simple juxtaposition of phrases. The forms of either nouns or verbs are not in themselves significant elements. This is not the case in the second teaching method, where in order to find correct endings the child must actively approach the word structure. As a result of his practical activity with the sounds of words, the child is faced with a choice of two different forms of the past tense verb. In the experiment, the child's success depended on the correct choice of the verb form. This speeded his skill in correcting mistakes. As a result, correct agreement between noun and the past tense

---

[4] [Editor's note: These nouns are semantically masculine, although the -*ka* (diminutive) ending is morphologically feminine, and require the masculine form of the verb. The subjects, however, tended to give the feminine past tense, demonstrating orientation to formal, rather than semantic, features of the nouns.]

verb was achieved on the basis of the child's orientation to formal features of nouns.

The investigation allows us to draw the following main conclusions:

1. Acquisition of gender agreement is a process consisting of several stages which follow each other in a given sequence when special teaching is absent: I—predominance of feminine gender in agreement; II—predominance of masculine gender; III—confusion of both genders; IV—correct agreement.

2. The child's orientation to the form of nouns is the basis for correct acquisition of agreement.

3. Two types of connections are established in child speech in the course of communication: (1) noun and feminine verb form, (2) noun and masculine verb form.

4. Predominance of either masculine or feminine gender in the agreement is caused by generalization of these types of connections. Generalized connections become fixed for a long time because they happen to be correct for some nouns and are reinforced by reality, and are thus justified.

5. In our first experimental condition, in which the subject heard and repeated only correct agreements and was systematically corrected for errors, the process of acquisition of correct agreement went through all the stages. Under these conditions the child did not work actively with phonetics, and as a result orientation to the formal features of nouns was inhibited. The most important condition for orientation to the phonetic form of words is an organization of the child's activity with words in which orientation to sound is a crucial aspect of the success of the entire activity (second teaching method). Such conditions facilitate acceleration of movement through all of the intermediate stages of agreement, or even by-passing of the intermediate stages.

6. Analysis of our data demonstrates that orientation to formal features of words appears very early in children—even before mastery of word meanings —and that, under appropriate conditions, even children of pre-preschool age are capable of full orientation to formal features of words.

REFERENCES

Gvozdev, A. N., *Formirovaniye u rebenka grammaticheskogo stroya russkogo yazyka*. Parts I and II. Moscow: Akad. Pedag. Nauk RSFSR, 1949.

Pavlov, I. P., *Polnoye sobraniye trudov*, Vol. 3, 1949.

Serebrennikova, N. P., K voprosu ob ovladenii det'mi-preddoshkol'nikami elementami grammaticheskogo stroya yazyka. Cand. dissert., Leningrad, 1953.

Sokhin, F. A., Nachal'nyye etapy ovlandeniya rebenkom grammaticheskim stroyem yazyka. Cand. dissert., Moscow, 1955.

Zakharova, A. V., K voprosu o razvitii grammaticheskogo stroya rechi u detey doshkol'nogo vozrasta. Cand. dissert., Moscow, 1955.

Acquisition of Forms of Grammatical Case by Preschool Children

—— *A. V. Zakharova*

Psychologists and educators investigating the process of speech development in children have long explained the practical mastering of language norms on the basis of the child's so-called "language feeling," or "verbal instinct" (Ushinskiy, 1945), which they designated as "the unconscious generalization" of language material (Bozhovich, 1946).

The task of our investigation was to ascertain the system of connections underlying the acquisition of a given grammatical category, from the point of view of the fullness, correspondence to grammar, and degree of generalization of such connections. The material under study consisted of the acquisition of the case forms of nouns by preschool children. The investigation was also concerned with the process of the child's acquisition of case forms: (1) the basis used by the child for the construction of such forms and (2) determination of the conditions and factors which aid the more successful accomplishment of this process.

To clarify these questions, observations of children's speech were conducted during collective and individual conversations with them and during storytelling with pictures using certain nouns in different cases. In addition, a series of experiments with the following methodology was conducted. Children were presented with certain concrete materials requiring the use of different cases of words belonging to different genders and types of declensions. In order to determine the degree of generalization of systems of connections underlying the acquisition of case forms, the children were asked to decline familiar and nonfamiliar words, which were given in the nominative form by the experimenter. At the same time, the child's ability to bring adjectives into agreement with given nouns was checked in order to determine whether the child correlated the syntactic definition of the noun gender with its practical reference to some type of declension. To this end, the method of determination of the size and color of play objects was used.

Two hundred children, age three to seven, were included in this experiment.

Analyses of the data obtained enabled us to reach the following conclusions.

1. Initially, a child acquires case endings without orienting himself to the endings of words in the nominative (that is, not orienting himself to the gender of the nouns). First of all, he organizes systems of connections which secure the semantically correct usage of grammatical forms (case inflections), corresponding to the circle of meanings of each grammatical case, that is, first of all the child constructs intercase stereotypes for the use of endings.

Usvoyeniye doshkol'nikami padezhnykh form. *Dokl. Akad. Pedag. Nauk RSFSR*, 1958, **2** (3), 81–84. Translated from Russian by Greta Slobin and edited by Dan I. Slobin.

2. However, this initial stage of the child's analytic-synthetic activity is accompanied by a wide generalization: within individual cases "dominant" endings appear, which are used for making forms from nouns of all declension types (for example, in the instrumental case, the ending -*om* becomes widely used, in the accusative, the ending -*u*, and so on). Overgeneralization of certain endings is conditioned by their wide usage in the language and by their more marked phonetic shape, thanks to which they are the strongest of all morphemes expressing the meaning of a given case.

3. Along with this initial differentiation of case forms on the basis of their meaning, the child proceeds with a more delicate analysis: he begins to differentiate the use of certain inflections within every case, relating them to certain types of words; that is, he is working out intracase stereotypes. This process is tied to the acquisition of noun gender by the child and is based on his orientation toward the form of the word (its ending) in the nominative. The formation of these systems of connections takes place in a definite sequence and embraces the whole preschool period.

The earliest forms that preschool children differentiate into separate systems are inflections of feminine nouns ending in -*a* (first declension) and inflections of masculine nouns with hard endings (second declension). What contributes to a quick establishment of this system of connections is the fact that in the Russian language the -*a* declension (mostly feminine) and the declension with a zero ending (mostly masculine), are, indeed, the strongest and the most influential, because of their outstandingly clear grammatical shape.

Declensions of feminine and masculine nouns ending with a soft (palatalized) consonant are acquired by the children only toward the end of preschool age. When declining these nouns, the younger preschool children still do not always use gender for the basis, and consequently, within each case they often use those endings which have been more firmly acquired as the clearer endings of the case (for example, in the genitive they say *net tsirkuli* instead of *tsirkulya* [there's no compass], in the instrumental, *lovim setem* instead of *setyu* [catching with a net], and so on). Older children, when declining these nouns, orient themselves mostly toward their gender; however, some of them attribute feminine nouns to masculine gender and thus give them second declension endings (for example, in the genitive, *net trostya* instead of *trosti* [there's no stick], in the dative, *k trostyu* instead of *k trosti* [to the stick], in the instrumental, *trostem* instead of *trostyu*).

In little preschool children the neuter nouns are sharply broken into two declension types: the correct use of paradigmatic cases of nouns with stressed endings is quite quickly established, while more time is needed to acquire the principles of forming oblique cases for nouns with unstressed endings.

When changing nouns with a stressed -*o* ending (of the type *okno, zerno* [window, seed]), children often pronounce a form of the nominative case instead of that of one of the oblique cases. Otherwise, children construct forms of these cases correctly.

When declining neuter nouns with unstressed ending (of the type *shilo, lukoshko* [awl, little basket]), the little preschool children confuse, in many forms, the endings of the first and second declensions; the older preschool children, when declining words of this type, orient themselves, in most cases, toward their endings in the nominative: pronouncing them like nouns with an *-a* ending, they use endings of the first declension type in all cases, but when taking the ending for a reduced *-o* they use endings of the second declension in all the cases.

4. The syntactic definition of noun genders by children (on the basis of agreement with adjectives or replacement by pronouns) confirms the conclusion that the little preschool children, when constructing case forms do not always orient themselves toward the gender of the noun, or its ending in the nominative. Despite a correct syntactic definition of the gender of the nouns, children of this age often construct case forms incorrectly. Among the older preschool children, the syntactic definition of gender in most cases coincides with the choice of the system of paradigms. Only in exceptional cases, in neuter words with unstressed endings, can one notice the use of second declension endings by attributing the word to feminine gender.

5. Comparison of noun declensions of familiar and unfamiliar words leads to the conclusion that where a system of declensions is acquired by the child— that is, where corresponding systems of generalized connections have been formed—there he can create all forms easily, including declensions of words heard for the first time; where a corresponding system has not been formed, the child makes identical mistakes in familiar words as in those whose initial form (that is, the nominative) was supplied by the experimenter.

Experiments show that in order to produce forms correctly, it is very important for a child to assimilate the structure of the word in the nominative. Little children have difficulties assimilating words which are phonologically more or less complicated. When repeating such words after the experimenter, they shorten their structure and give them other endings (mostly, strong endings of the first declension). In these cases when, at the beginning of the experiment, the child pronounces two forms—with correct and with altered endings—he also often confuses the endings of different types of declensions when declining the word, despite prior numerous repetitions of the correct initial form of the word. This can possibly be explained by the fact that the child becomes somewhat disoriented as far as the gender of the noun is concerned, so that the strongest ending within each case appears, since, when difficulties arise, the revival of the earlier created forms and of the stronger connections takes place much faster. This also explains the fact that some children, when in doubt in changing a word, use the more firmly acquired nominative case instead of the forms of the oblique cases.

6. In the process of constructing case forms of unfamiliar words, children often pronounce them aloud with different endings, as if deciding in this manner which form would be the correct one in the given case, correcting themselves and deciding on the ending only after that. The choice of the correct endings through oral repetition of some of them can probably be explained by the fact that the additional sound and kinesthetic signals from the speech organs, entering

the cerebral cortex during the process of repetition, facilitate control over the speech activity of the child and in cases of difficulties assist in the correct choice of a grammatical form.

Observations of children's speech show that one may encounter, in the younger preschool children, independent corrections of grammatical forms constructed from the familiar words as well. This is evidence that the systems of connections developed in the cortex of the child's brain during the process of speech acquisition have not yet become completely automatic. A child works out the necessary speed of verbal reaction only in the process of speech practice which becomes more developed and more complicated under the demands of verbal communication and of the growing complexity of sentence structure.

Mastery of the grammatical system and of the wide variety of grammatical tools of language facilitates the child's deeper comprehension of surrounding reality and is a necessary condition for the development of his thinking.

A child masters the grammatical system of language in the practice of verbal communication with those around him, directly copying their speech. Thus, correct and well-defined speech of the educator and his demands on the child's speech are very important for successful development of this process.

During the child's development, the process of mastering the grammatical system of the language takes on a more conscious and goal-oriented character. Therefore, it is necessary to constantly direct the child's attention to his speech, to correct all the wrong forms he uses and make him repeat them correctly several times; that is, it is necessary to assist in an active acquisition of these forms. Along with this, at later preschool ages one can conduct special games and tasks directed toward practical mastery of the grammatical structure of the language.

REFERENCES

Bozhovich, L. I., Znacheniye yazykovykh obobshcheniy. *Izvestiya Akad. Pedag. Nauk RSFSR*, 1946, No. 3.

Ushinskiy, K. D., *Izbrannyye pedagogicheskiye sochineniya.* Uchpedgiz, 1945.

The Acquisition of Russian Inflections

—— *D. N. Bogoyavlenskiy*

Children's word creation indicates that when mastering speech, a child enriches his vocabulary not only by learning "whole words," but also by making use of the morphological elements of language. In order to check such a fact, we conducted a small research project with the goal of ascertaining the degree

Excerpted from D. N. Bogoyavlenskiy, *Psikhologiya usvoyeniya orfografii* [*The psychology of acquisition of orthography*]. Moscow: Akademiya Pedagogicheskikh Nauk RSFSR, 1957, pp. 261–271. Translated from Russian by Greta Slobin and edited by Dan I. Slobin.

to which a child understands and uses certain suffixes in word creation. The first series of experiments was devoted to checking the understanding of the suffixes -ënok- [diminutive],[1] -ishche- [augmentative], -nits- [agentive], and -shchik- [agentive].

In order to find out whether the child understood the meaning of these suffixes, we attached suffixes to words formed from stems unfamiliar to the child: lar, explained to the child as an animal; lafit, a sweet kvass drink, and kashemir, a beautiful fabric. The experiments were conducted individually with children aged five to six. We explained the meaning of the experimental word, describing various concrete attributes of the "animal," of the "kvass," and of the fabric. Then the child was asked: "Who do you think is larënok, larishche, lafitnitsa, kashemirshchik?" If a child had difficulties with the answer, leading questions were asked: "What is the difference between lar, larënok, larishche? What is the difference between kashemir and kashemirshchik?" and so on.[2]

In cases where the task was not understood by the child, we would introduce these words into a "fairy tale" which we would tell him. Here is an example of one of them:

"Once upon a time there was a lar in the woods. (Do you know who a lar is? It's an animal with thick fur, with sharp teeth, and a very short tail). He would go walking alone in the woods and he felt very lonely. One day a larënok came up to him. They began to play together and the lar cheered up. They built a little house and begin to live in it. Once, while they were sleeping, they were awakened: someone was breaking down their door. Larënok looked out of the window and saw a strange larishche."

Further on, the story tells of how the lar and the larënok fooled the larishche and saved themselves. In the construction of this "fairy tale" we omitted all indication of the height and the size of the lars.

Eight children, aged five to six, took part in the experiment with the word lar. All of them answered the control questions correctly. Some of them did so right away, some after hearing the story. Here are examples of their answers:

Nadya M.

EXPERIMENTER: Who is a lar?
NADYA: An animal.
EXPERIMENTER: And who is larishche?
NADYA: Also an animal
EXPERIMENTER: What is the difference between them?
NADYA: Lar is big.
EXPERIMENTER: And larënok?
NADYA: He is little.

[1] [Editor's note: roughly pronounced -yónək.]
[2] [Editor's note: The form of the Russian questions is: A kak ty dumayesh', kto takoy larënok? Kakaya raznitsa mezhdu larom, larënkom i larishchem?]

Yulya D.

EXPERIMENTER: Who is a *lar*?
YULYA: A little baby.
EXPERIMENTER: And a *larishche*?
YULYA: That's mother, she was breaking the door in order to eat them and satisfy her hunger.
EXPERIMENTER: Well, but who is bigger: the *lar* or the *larishche*?
YULYA: The *larishche*.

Nina M. (without the fairy tale)

EXPERIMENTER: Who is a *larënok*?
NINA: That's a kind of a rabbit.
EXPERIMENTER: And who is a *larishche*?
NINA: I don't know. (After the fairy tale, though, she correctly points out the difference in the size of the animals.)

The experiment demonstrated that although children had to deal with unfamiliar words, they had good comprehension of the suffixes *-ënok-* and *-ishche-*.

The suffixes *-shchik-* and *-nits-*, however, turned out not to be as familiar. After the fairy tale in which we explained *kashemir* and told how it was made from thin little threads, without mentioning the word *kashemirshchik*, only two out of five children defined the word *kashemirshchik* correctly on the basis of its suffix.

EXPERIMENTER: Who is *kashemirshchik*?
NINA: It's a man.
EXPERIMENTER: What does he do?
NINA: He turns a handle and gets *kashemir*.

In other cases, children answered that a *kashemirshchik* is a kind of a machine, or simply refused to answer, saying that they had "forgotten." The suffix *-nits-* turned out to be easier for the children, but it was also more difficult to manage than suffixes *-ënok-* and *-ishche-*.

The results of these experiments confirm the data from previous observations and show that the understanding of certain morphological elements of speech opens the meaning of new and unfamiliar words to the child.

Unfamiliar words created with the help of familiar suffixes are easily differentiated by the children according to the indications of meaning carried by the suffixes.

But the question arises of the role played here by the outer form of the words which are being changed. This question has a special theoretical significance in differentiating practical verbal knowledge from grammatical knowledge. A school child, who has learned the morphological structure of words, can not only see the semantic differences between words with different suffixes but can effortlessly distinguish the suffix from the word stem, because the meaning of the suffix is firmly associated with the concrete form of its expression.

To what degree do preschoolers associate the differentiation of the semantic words carried by the suffixes with differentiation of those material elements of words which serve as carriers of these differences? This question is connected, then, with the problem of abstraction in speech acquisition. Without touching upon the essence of this problem, we wanted to answer these questions in relation to a given concrete case. With this goal in mind, we worked with the children who had correctly differentiated the semantic nuances between words with diminutive and augmentative suffixes, trying to turn their attention to the formal difference between the words *lar, larënok,* and *larishche.* At this point we explained the problem to the children in more or less this way: "You were right in saying how the animals differ from each other; one is small, one is big; and now turn your attention to the words I am saying: *lar - larënok*; what is the difference between them?"

Despite repeated verbal presentation of these words, not one of the children who had easily managed the semantic differentiation of these words could give an answer in this case. The children either smiled shyly or simply remained silent without an attempt to analyze the sounds of the words.

The first experiment was followed by another with the same children. The second experiment differed from the first in that it dealt with the active word creation of the child. In this series we gave the child an unproductive word and asked him to make it into a word with a given semantic nuance. In order to make the child's word creation independent, we presented words for which the diminutive form was either rarely used or was unusual in children's speech.

Thus, in contrast to the preceding experiment, here the meaning of the suffix was given, while its linguistic form was unknown. We familiarized the child with the root word, asked him its meaning and whether he had ever seen such an object, told him more about it, showed him pictures, and so on, and then asked the following questions: "Tell me, what would you call a baby ostrich, giraffe?" and so on.[3] The results are shown in the table.

As can be seen in the table below, there is a total of 57 responses received from the children. Only one of these answers (*zhuravel'* [crane]) does not correspond to the semantic task of giving a diminutive form. In one case we encountered a refusal of word creation. In all the other answers the semantic task was carried out and the children did not use any but diminutive suffixes in word creation. Here are the suffixes: *-ënok-, -ik-, -chik-, -k-, -echek-, -ochk-, -ichek-, -ichk-.*

It is evident that the children's choice, from among the wealth of suffixes in the Russian language, of just those suffixes which carry the meaning of the diminutive is not accidental. To the contrary, such a choice shows that children have completely mastered the generalized meanings of the given suffixes.

The fact that children's word creations did not always correspond to the

---

[3] [Editor's note: The form of the Russian question is: *Skazhi, kak budet' nazyvat'sya detenysh strausa?*]

Root Word	Number of Children	Children's Derivations[a]
zhiraf [giraffe]	9	zhiravënok, zhilënok, zhiravki (plural), zhuravchiki, zhurafki, zhiraflenok (2), zhuravel' [crane], zhirafchik
ovës [oats]	5	ovsënok (2), oveslënok, oveshchik, and one refusal to form a derivation
zhelud' [acorn]	5	zhulënok, zheludënok (2), zheludchik (2)
dub [oak]	5	dubënok (3), dubik, dubchik
lev [lion]	7	l'vënok (2), levënok, levchonki (plural), rebënok [child], lefënok, levchik
straus [ostrich]	5	strauski (2), stravinki (plural), strausënok (2)
puzyrëk [vial]	9	puzyrënok (3), malen'kiy [little] puzyrëk (2), butylochka [little bottle] (2), puzyrëchek
nos [nose]	5	nosënok (2), nos, nosik (2)
volk [wolf]	4	volchatki (plural) (2), volchonki (plural) (2)
gvozd' [nail]	3	gvozdichek, gvozdënok, gvozdichki

[a] The numbers in parentheses show the number of children who gave identical answers.

literary norms of language does not contradict this basic fact. The "free" use of suffixes only shows that children do not yet differentiate some of the additional conditions for the use of diminutive suffixes. So, for example, children use the suffix -ënok- for both animate and inanimate objects (zhiravlënok [giraffe], levënok [lion], and puzyrënok [vial], dubënok [oak], and so on), when, according to grammatical rules, the suffix -ënok- is used only with words designating animate objects, and so on.

This also applies to many other cases of the use of suffixes which show that in the given case children had violated some norm of the language. However, one should note that limitation in the use of some suffixes is conditioned or caused by purely phonetic reasons. So, for example, from words with stems ending in g, k, kh, only the forms with suffixes -ok- are created (krug - kruzhok [circle - little circle], bok - bochok [side - small side]); with sibilant stems, only the suffix -ik- is used, for example, klyuchik, dozhdik [little key, little rain], and so on. Both of these suffixes are possible for forming the diminutive from other stems (dub-dubok-dubik).

In any case, by the time he is seven, a child has mastered a great variety of suffixes of the Russian language. A. N. Gvozdev (1928), observing the development of this aspect of his son's speech, enumerated more than 60 different suffixes of nouns alone, as used in the child's neologisms. Among these suffixes one finds various categories of meanings: diminutive and endearing suffixes, suffixes marking the young of animals, augmentative suffixes, suffixes of feminine person, of objects, of state and action, and some others. Yet, despite their variety, what is remarkable is the absence of suffixes used for forming abstract nouns of the type -ost'-, -est'- (smelost', svezhest' [courage, freshness]); -ota-, -eta- (dobrota, nishcheta [kindness, poverty]); -izna- (belizna [whiteness]). This latter condition supports our data on the suffixes -nits- and -shchik-.

Apparently, the sequence of acquisition of Russian suffixes depends, to a great degree, on their meaning. Acquisition of abstract noun suffixes requires a certain level of intellectual development in the child. Only under these conditions can words with such suffixes enter the child's speech experience and, later, become abstracted as meaningful elements of language.

All of these facts dealing with the process of word creation show that, when mastering vocabulary, a child depends not only on the assimilation of whole words taken from adult speech but that he also uses the meanings of separate grammatical elements of the word. This makes it possible for him to understand words and to create them himself, from familiar roots, prefixes, and suffixes. Therefore, the notion of the enrichment of the child's vocabulary through memorization of whole words should be considered inadequate. Our data allow us to understand this process as a creative one, directed toward mastering the word-building elements of language and toward the construction of speech.

However, in order to understand the process of speech development correctly it is important to study not only the products of this development but also to conduct analyses of this process aimed at answering not only the question of *what* the child acquired but also the question of *how* he did it. This point has remained inadequately treated in our presentation thus far because it requires longitudinal methods of investigation. Such material is found in the work of A. N. Gvozdev (1949). The importance of this investigation for speech psychology lies, first of all, in its method. This is a longitudinal investigation in which the author-linguist systematically presents all the language forms which emerge consecutively in child speech and in which he observes further changes as they take place.

Gvozdev's data show that the process of distinguishing the morphological elements of language from whole words begins at the age of one year and ten months. The "mistakes" in child speech, which are like those found in neologisms, give evidence of their independent use. When "making mistakes" the child uses forms which he could not have heard from adults. When, for example, he says *ishchit'* instead of *iskat'* [to look for something], he constructs a verb form using separate morphemes: the present tense stem -ishch- and the suffixes -i- and

-t'-, which he has singled out from other words. Gvozdev notes that morphological elements begin to be distinguished simultaneously in a series of grammatical categories (verbs, nouns, and so on). He gives further evidence that as early as about the age of three a child uses all the basic inventory of prefixes, suffixes, and inflections of Russian in his speech. But mastering declension and conjugation as definite systems of endings continues up to the age of seven (and even later in detail).

This kind of study of the consecutive appearance of certain morphemes in child speech completely confirms the suppositions which he expressed when discussing the experiments with suffixes. Gvozdev also comes to the conclusion that the sequence in which the mastering of certain morphemes takes place depends on the nature of their meanings. Thus, for example, the meanings easiest for a child are the plural of nouns, diminutive and nondiminutive nouns, the imperative mood, and the past tense of the verb. These and some other meanings are acquired by the child even before he is two. They are distinguished by their especially concrete and graphic meanings, or by the especially important role which they play in the child's communication with others (for example, the imperative, which expresses different desires).

The more difficult abstract ideas are acquired last by the child. For example, such a seemingly simple grammatical category, from the formal point of view, as the conditional aspect (attachment of the particle *by* to a form of the past tense) begins to appear in child speech only at about the age of three, although the form of the past tense has already figured in his speech for a long time. Here the author notes that the obstacle in the use of the conditional is probably the fact that it expresses a supposition and not something that exists in reality.

The acquisition of the category of gender also appears to be extremely complex due to its lack of a definite meaning, despite the fact that gender is encountered by the child at every step. These examples show that learning of grammatical categories is influenced by the character of their meanings (abstractness) and by their practical role in the life of the child.

Difficulty of acquisition is also influenced by the variegated expression of the same case among nouns of different types. Thus, among all the forms of the accusative the one acquired first is the accusative with the ending *-u* (*sestru* [sister]), because this ending has one meaning and because it is not duplicated in other cases. For a while this ending becomes the child's universal means for expressing the meaning of the accusative of every word (*day listochku* [give me a leaf], *goni barashku* [chase the sheep], *rubit' polenu* [to chop wood]).

At the same time, the single meaning of the instrumental, though expressed by different endings (*-oy* and *-om*), is not easily acquired. The meanings of some suffixes are hard to differentiate and are constantly confused with one another. A child says *mamochkom* instead of *mamochkoy* [by mama], *lozhkom* instead of *lozhkoy* [with the spoon], *za supoy* instead of *za supom* [for the soup], *pod* *komodoy* instead of *pod komodom* [under the chest], or *nozhnik* and *nozhinshchik*, *vrunevka* and *vrunikha*, and so on.[4]

These data show that the most important factor in the acquisition of morphemes is their regularity. Stern (1915, p. 95) already mentioned the significance of this regularity, and later Guillaume (1927), but they could not explain adequately either these or other analogous factors which showed that frequency of repetition of some morpheme in a language is not sufficient guarantee of its acquisition. However, the role of regularity becomes obvious if one realizes that it merely signifies a more regularly expressed connection between a definite meaning and certain form. Thanks to this, the generalization of the meaning of this form and its comprehension take place under especially favorable circumstances.

In the analyses of the experiments with suffixes we have already noted that children, while correctly understanding the diminutive function of the suffixes, still use their various forms with a certain degree of freedom. Gvozdev also notes a similar situation. In child speech a period can be observed during which morphological elements, different in form but with the same meanings, are used in each others' places. Thus, for example, the differentiation in meaning of the singular and plural takes place very early (1 year, 11 months), but the differentiation of case endings within the same case takes place between the ages of five and seven. Therefore, in child speech there is often a situation when some category of language is used correctly according to its meaning, but is used chaotically as far as its form is concerned.

On the basis of this finding, Gvozdev concludes that "acquisition of a given grammatical meaning precedes acquisition of its external expression" and that "semantics is the primordial nucleus which further directs the acquisition of all grammatical means of expression of individual categories."

Thus, investigation of speech on the ontogenetic level shows that semantics is the main motive force of speech development, and the process itself takes the form of continuous active "search" by the child for linguistic tools for the expression of meanings, while gradually approaching the system of grammatical forms which is characteristic of the given language.

It is, therefore, possible to maintain that all the major events which unfold in the process of speech development are connected with the child's acquisition of grammatical elements of language. Therefore, any study of the vocabulary and

---

[4] [Translator's note: *Nozhnik* is probably the child's diminutive of *nozh* 'knife,' where the correct diminutive would be *nozhik*. This may be the child's creation of a singular form from *nozhnitsy* 'scissors,' which is a diminutive plural. *Nozhinshchik* is probably an attempt to form an agent from *nozh*, although such a form does not exist in adult Russian. *Vrunovka* is a feminine noun derived by the child from the masculine *vrun* 'liar,' where the correct feminine form is *vrun'ya*. The child's insertion of *-ov-* is probably based on analogy to such masculine-feminine pairs as *vor-vorovka* 'thief,' *Vrunikha* is another plausible substitute for *vrun'ya*, analogous to such masculine-feminine pairs as *tkach-tkachikha* 'weaver.']

syntax of child speech which does not take this fundamental fact into consideration cannot give a full picture of the psychology of speech acquisition.

It should be noted that it is only in the initial stage of speech development that memorization of ready-made verbal clichés exhausts the contents of this process. As soon as the child acquires a certain supply of whole words or combinations of words, the grammatical elements of language singled out by the child begin to play a primary role. They are acquired gradually and separate forms are not memorized mechanically, but in connection with their verbal function and with their meaning. . . .

REFERENCES

Guillaume, P., Le développement des éléments formels dans le langage de l'enfant. *J. Psychol. norm pathol.*, 1927, **24**, 203–229. [Reprinted in this volume.]

Gvozdev, A. N. Znacheniye izucheniya detskogo yazyka dlya yazykovedeniya. *Rodnoy yazyk i literatura v trudovoy shkole*, 1928, No. 3. [Also in A. N. Gvozdev, *Voprosy izucheniya detskoy rechi*. Moscow: Akad. Pedag. Nauk RSFSR, 1961, pp. 9–30.]

Gvozdev, A. N., *Formirovaniye u rebenka grammaticheskogo stroya russkogo yazyka*. Moscow: Akad. Pedag. Nauk RSFSR, 1949. [Also in A. N. Gvozdev, *Voprosy izucheniya detskoy rechi*. Moscow: Akad. Pedag. Nauk RSFSR, 1961, pp. 149–467.]

Shtern, V. [Stern, W.], *Psikhologiya rannego detstva*. St Petersburg, 1915. [Transl. of *Psychologie der frühen Kindheit*. Leipzig, 1914.]

SYNTAX

In this section we bring together studies in which primary attention is paid to the sentence and its constituents. The developmental span covered goes from the very beginnings of syntax with simple two-word combinations to the complex embeddings and relative clauses of the late preschool period. The basic outlines of the syntactic system are universally acquired by four or five, and most investigations have stopped at this age. Recently, however, psycholinguists have become interested in syntactic development after five, and several studies have begun to probe the mastery of complex details and special cases which continues through the school years (C. Chomsky, 1968; Cromer, 1970; Kessel, 1970; Olds, 1968). (Other psychological traditions have long been interested in later stages of language development: there are numerous pedagogically oriented studies, especially German and Russian [for example, Huth, 1919; Nazarov, 1964]; valuable experimental studies come from Heinz Werner's school of developmental psychology [Asch and Nerlove, 1960; Werner and Kaplan, 1952].)
—D.I.S.

ENGLISH •

The Harvard Children

The following two papers, along with the papers by Brown and by Cazden reprinted elsewhere in this volume, stem from a landmark project begun by Roger Brown at Harvard's Center for Cognitive Studies in 1962. The grammatical development of the three children called "Adam," "Eve," and "Sarah" has been studied more intensively than that of any other children to date. The project has included Samuel Anderson, Ursula Bellugi, Melissa F. Bowerman, Courtney B. Cazden, Gloria Cooper, Richard F. Cromer, Colin Fraser, Jean Berko Gleason, Camille Hanlon, Edward S. Klima, David McNeill, Dan I. Slobin, and others. The work is being summed up masterfully by Roger Brown in monographs to be published by Harvard University Press (Brown, in press). (For additional reports on aspects of this project and its findings, see Bellugi, 1967, 1968; Bowerman, 1970; Brown, 1965, 1968, in press; Brown and Bellugi, 1964; Brown and Hanlon, 1970; Cromer, 1968; McNeill, 1966a, 1970; Slobin, 1968a, 1971a.)

The paper by Brown, Cazden, and Bellugi, written in 1967, applies the then-current version of transformational grammar (Chomsky, 1965) to a description of the first three phases of child language studied by Brown *et al.* The strategy followed was to write a transformational grammar of the speech of each child at each phase (ultimately, five phases were considered) and compare the course of development of the three children. Striking parallels were found in these three pictures of independent development.

Brown, Cazden, and Bellugi devote a good deal of attention to parental speech—both as input and response to the child—and find no strong evidence for parental training as a determining factor in grammatical development. One variable they consider in detail is frequency of occurrence of grammatical forms in parental speech (see also Cazden, this volume; Bowerman, 1970; Brown and Hanlon, 1970). They find great similarity between the mothers of the three children in relative frequency of use of a number of forms, and they do find that children seem to be sensitive to this variable: "The important general fact is that there seems to be something like a standard frequency profile for mother-to-child English, a profile that children match within their competence at any given time, and in this profile great inequalities exist even among very simple and familiar constructions" (p. 325). The more frequent forms also tend to be less complex in formal linguistic terms, so that the interrelated variables of frequency and complexity cannot be easily sorted out (see Brown and Hanlon, 1970). It is clear, however, that the frequency profiles of mother-to-child speech are quite different from those of adult-to-adult speech (see Drach *et al.*, 1969; Ervin-Tripp, 1971). The speech directed at children is thus a special style, characterized by brief, grammatical sentences of a limited range of structures.

In a very large number of speech communities around the world children receive primary speech input from other children rather than mothers. Yet the course and rate of language development seem to be quite similar in all cultures studied to date (Slobin, 1970). Slobin (1969a) examined this problem in one case which allowed for direct comparison between mother-to-child and child-to-child speech. Claudia Mitchell Kernan, in studying language development in the black ghetto of Oakland, California, noted that two- and three-year-olds spend a good deal of their time interacting with older children rather than with mothers. Slobin compared the frequency profiles given by Brown, Cazden, and Bellugi for mothers with relative frequencies of the very same grammatical forms in the speech of two black girls of four-and-a-half and five. The profiles are almost identical, suggesting that mother-to-child English may not be strikingly different in grammatical form from child-to-child English. If this suggestion finds further support, it may well be that children, universally, are exposed to a special simplified version of the language of their community. The simplification may come about either because the speech input comes from immature speakers or because adults make a special selection of grammatical forms when speaking to children.   —D.I.S.

The Child's Grammar from I to III[1]
—— *Roger Brown, Courtney Cazden, and Ursula Bellugi*

A group of us at Harvard are engaged in a longitudinal study of the development of grammar in three preschool children. One of the children, Eve, is the daughter of a graduate student, Adam is the son of a minister who lives in Boston, and Sarah is the daughter of a man who works as a clerk in Somerville. Eve's and Adam's parents have college educations; Sarah's parents have high school degrees. The principal data of the study are transcriptions of the spontaneous speech of the child and his mother (occasionally also the father) in conversation at home. For each child we have at least two hours of speech for every month that he has been studied; sometimes as much as six hours. Sarah's records are entirely transcribed in a phonetic notation that includes stress and intonation. The other children's records are not in phonetic notation except at a few points where some particular hypothesis made the notation necessary.

Figure 1 identifies an initial developmental period which has been the focus of our analyses thus far. The initial period has been defined in terms of the means and ranges of utterance length, terms external to the grammar. The period begins, for all three children, when the mean was 1.75 morphemes and ends when the mean was 4.0 morphemes. The longest utterance at the lower bound of the interval was 4 morphemes; at the upper bound, 13. Mean length of utterance is useful as a rough term of reference for developmental level in this early period but it grows more variable and less useful with age.

As can be seen from the figure, the children were not of the same chronological age when the study began: Eve was eighteen months; Adam and Sarah were twenty-seven months. We selected these three children from some thirty considered on the basis of matched initial performance rather than age. At the end of the period for analysis, Eve was twenty-six months, Adam forty-two months, and Sarah forty-eight months. In terms of the utterance length the rates of development of the three children may be ordered: Eve, Adam, Sarah.

The research is directed at two general questions. What does the child know of the structure of English at successive points in his development? By what processes does he acquire his knowledge? The most explicit, comprehensive, and systematic form in which adult knowledge of grammar has been represented is the generative transformational grammar (Chomsky, 1957; 1965). A generative

From *Minnesota Symposia on Child Psychology*, Vol. 2, John P. Hill, ed., University of Minnesota Press. Minneapolis, © 1968, University of Minnesota. Reprinted by permission of the authors and the publisher. (Originally published under the names of Roger Brown, Courtney Cazden, and Ursula Bellugi-Klima.)
[1] This research was supported by Public Health Service Research Grant MH-7088 from the National Institute of Mental Health.

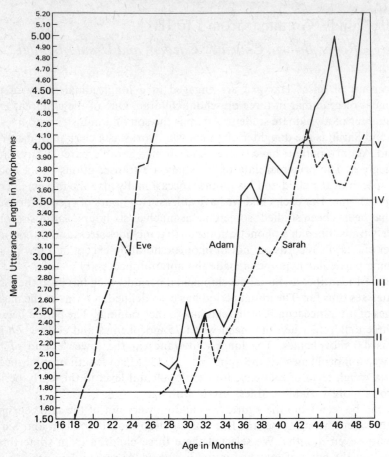

Figure 1. Mean utterance length and age in three children. The horizontal lines I-V represent five points for which generative grammars are being written.

grammar is a system of rules that derives an infinite set of well-formed sentences and assigns them correct structural descriptions. The most demanding form in which to pose the question of the child's knowledge of structure at any time is to ask for a generative grammar that represents his knowledge. We are attempting to write such grammars for the three children at each of five points in the initial developmental period. These points are marked with lines and Roman numerals in Figure 1; they fall at nearly equal intervals across the period. For the grammars we make detailed distributional analyses of seven hundred utterances from each child.

A complete annotated grammar is between fifty and a hundred pages long, and so none is presented here. We do, however, present portions of a single grammar, the one written for Adam at III, to illustrate the kinds of knowledge such a grammar is designed to represent. Then, using Adam III as a kind of temporary terminus, we provide a descriptive overview of developments in the first period. Following this we offer more detailed discussions of two specific developments: segmentation into morphemes and the construction of wh questions. Finally we review what we have learned about the role of "training variables" in grammar acquisition.

A PORTION OF ADAM III

The sentence *Where those dogs goed?* was not actually created by Adam in III; it is a composite that illustrates more of the interesting features of his grammar than does any single sentence he actually formed. Let us follow the derivation of this composite sentence using the grammar constructed for Adam at III.

The grammar is a set of mechanical procedures or algorithms for generating sentences and assigning structural descriptions to them. The generation in question is "logical" rather than "psychological," in the sense that the grammar does not constitute a model of practical processes by which sentences might actually be produced or understood. The grammar is psychological in that it is supposed to *represent* Adam's knowledge about the organization of sentences, and it is presumed that this knowledge somehow enters into actual production and comprehension.

The structure of grammatical knowledge is not given in any direct and simple way in spontaneous speech. It is worked out from spontaneous speech by a process of inference that is far from being either mechanical or certainly correct. The process is something like trying to fit together the pieces of an immense jigsaw puzzle and something like the process of trying to decipher an unknown Minoan script but not at all like the process of doing experiments in a psychological laboratory. We operate on the general assumption that the child's terminal state of knowledge is of the kind represented by current transformational grammars (e.g., Chomsky, 1965; Katz and Postal, 1964; Klima, 1964). However, we do not simply attribute to each sentence that the child produces the analysis that would be appropriate to that sentence if it were produced by an adult; if we were to do that, the inquiry would be largely vacuous. Insofar as the child's particular sentence—and all related sentences—depart from adult forms the grammar is tailored to the departures. The most informative departures are analogical errors of commission, such as *goed* in the sample sentence. Harder to interpret, but still important, are errors of omission, such as the absence of the auxiliary *did* from the sample sentence. Omissions in a sentence are at least easy to detect, but omissions in the distributional range of a form are harder to detect and harder to interpret since it is necessary to weight the probability that an omission is simply a consequence of the size of the sample that has been taken. Finally, all the errors that occur must be considered in comparison with conceivable errors that do not occur. Even this full procedure will not render the construction completely determinate in all respects. The indeterminacies are tentatively resolved by assigning the usual adult representation insofar as that representation does not depend on forms that have never appeared in the child's speech. We shall be able to illustrate most aspects of this process in what follows.

The Phrase Structure Level

A phrase structure rule in adult grammar rewrites a single symbol into symbol(s) distinct from the one rewritten. Roughly speaking, the phrase structure represents the adult's sense of hierarchical grouping in a sentence—the feeling that a sentence cracks or breaks up into natural major constitutents which in turn break up into natural smaller constituents. It also represents such basic sentence relations as are called in traditional grammar subject of a sentence, predicate of a sentence, object of a verb, and so forth. The phrase structure includes everything essential for a complete semantic interpretation, but it does not necessarily order elements as they are ordered in the ultimate surface structure.

In the list of phrase structure rules and derivation below each derivation begins with the symbol S for *sentence*, not because Adam is supposed to have a generic intention to compose a sentence which precedes the composition of any particular sentence, but because the grammar is a kind of extended definition of the meaning of *sentence*. The first rule of the phrase structure rewrites S into Nominal and Predicate and a set of abstract morphemes symbolized as imp, wh,

LIST OF PHRASE STRUCTURE RULES AND DERIVATION

RULES OF PHRASE STRUCTURE	DERIVATION OF "WHERE THOSE DOGS GOED?"
1. S → ([imp/wh]) (neg) Nominal-Predicate	wh-Nominal-Predicate
2. Predicate → [MV/Cop]	wh-Nominal-MV
3. MV → Vb (Comp)	wh-Nominal-Vb-Comp
4. Vb → (Aux) V (Prt)	wh-Nominal-Aux-V-Comp
5. Aux → [V^c/B+ing/Past]	wh-Nominal-Past-V-Comp
6. Comp → [Adverb/Nominal (Adverb)]	wh-Nominal-Past-V-Adverb
7. Cop → B-Pred	
8. B → [be/β]	
9. Pred → [Det/Nominal/Adverb]	
10. Adverb → [Loc/Adv/Prep Phr]	wh-Nominal-Past-V-Loc
11. Loc → [somewhere/Adv/Prep Phr]	wh-Nominal-Past-V-somewhere
12. Prep Phr → Prp[Nominal/Adv]	
13. Nominal → [something/NP]	wh-NP-Past-V-somewhere
14. NP → (Det) N	wh-Det-N-Past-V-somewhere

Symbols do not all have exact equivalents in the terminology of traditional grammar so translations are only suggestive. The exact sense of each symbol is given by the grammar itself.

( ): optionality

[x/y]: mutual exclusivity of
x and y

Adv: adverb

Adverb: adverbial

Aux: auxiliary

B: *be* or β

B+ing: progressive aspect

β: should contain *be* form but
does not

Comp: complement

Cop: copula

Det: determiner or descriptive
adjective

imp: imperative

Loc: locative adverbial

MV: main verb

N: noun

neg: negative

NP: noun phrase

Past: past tense

Pred: predicate adjectival,
nominal, or adverbial

Prp: preposition

Prep Phr: prepositional
phrase

Prt: particle

S: sentence

V^c: catenative verb

V: verb

Vb: verbal

wh: interrogative

and neg. These last three represent the germs from which, respectively, imperatives, interrogatives, and negatives can be developed. The abstract morphemes do not stand for any particular words but provide the occasion in adult grammar for transformations that result in a great variety of imperative, interrogative, and negative expressions. The abstract morphemes are in parentheses; sentences need not be either imperative, interrogative, or negative. In the derivation of a declarative affirmative sentence none of the abstract morphemes is selected. The imp and wh symbols are in brackets to indicate that the symbols are mutually exclusive; a sentence is not simultaneously imperative and interrogative.

The second rule of the phrase structure makes a fundamental division among predicates. The symbol Cop (for *copula*) expands either as a form of *be* or as β, which ultimately has no phonological representation (Adam produces sentences such as *That my book* which should contain a *be* form but do not). Sentences with Cop are sometimes called equational sentences. The verb (or its absence) is followed in such sentences by a noun phrase (NP) functioning as predicate nominative or an adverbial (Adverb) or a descriptive adjective (included in Det which means *determiner*). Sample sentences are *That's a clock*, *Doggie is here, Doggie big*. The main verb (MV) form of the predicate may, if the verb is transitive, be followed by a NP functioning as direct object which may in turn be followed by some sort of adverbial (Adverb). Intransitive verbs take adverbials but not direct objects.

In Rule 4 the auxiliary (Aux) is introduced and in Rule 5 it is rewritten. These rules are somewhat different from the rules that represent adult use of the adult auxiliary. What kinds of distributional facts about Adam's speech suggest the rules we have written? Adam's Aux is introduced into MV but not Cop; the adult auxiliary would be introduced into both. The adult rule represents the fact that adults combine *be* forms with Past (e.g., *was*) and with auxiliary verbs (e.g., *I want to be*) and with progressive (B + ing) aspect (e.g., *He is being good*) as well as combining main verbs with these operations. Adam, on the other hand, never combined *be* with auxiliary operations. The division between equational and main verb sentences lies deep in Adam's grammar precisely because he includes Aux in the one and not the other.

In Rule 5 Aux is rewritten as three constituents: catenative verbs (V^c) such as *wanna, gonna,* and *hafta*; the progressive aspect (B + ing) which produces such forms as *walking* and *eating*; the Past morpheme which produces such forms as *walked* and also *feeled*. Why are the three constituents collected together and placed before the V? The description is not in accord with the surface characteristics of Adam's relevant sentences, for, although the catenatives do precede verbs on the surface, the progressive and past inflections are affixed to the ends of verbs. At a later point in the grammar, in the transformational component, there has to be a rule that transposes stems and affixes so as to produce the correct surface order. In that case why set them wrong in the first place? For several reasons. In the first place, as a means of representing the relation of mutual exclusion which obtains among the three auxiliary elements in Adam's speech. He never combines two or more auxiliaries to say such things as *I was eating* or *I wanted to eat*, though adults of course do. Deeper motivation for the Aux constituent derives from the requirements of the transformational component. In the construction of imperatives, for example, Adam never uses an auxiliary. He says *Please read* but not *Please reading* or *Please wanna read* or *Please readed*. It is convenient to be able to exclude all of the possibilities at once by forbidding the use of all auxiliaries in imperatives and for that you need an Aux constituent. Behind the convenience, of course, is the fact that catenative verbs, progressives, and pasts are distributed in sentences as if they were, on some level, one thing.

These are some of the considerations that shape the first five rules. How does one use the rules to construct a derivation? The derivation of a sentence is, essentially, the pathway through the rules that will yield the sentence. There must be such a pathway for every sentence and none for non-sentences. One constructs a derivation by applying the rules to successive strings, making those (permitted) choices which will in the end produce the intended sentence. The first step of the derivation in the list on page 298 might be read, "the symbol S is rewritten, by Rule 1, as 'wh-Nominal-Predicate.' " Since the intended sentence is to be an interrogative, wh is chosen from among the optional abstract morphemes. The intended sentence is to contain a main verb (*go*) and so MV is selected by Rule 2. The sentence will also contain a locative, and since these develop out of the complement (Comp), that constituent must be added by Rule 3. There is to be a Past auxiliary, and Rules 4 and 5 accomplish its selection.

And so the derivation proceeds. The last line, sometimes called the "preterminal" string, still does not look much like the sentence *Where those dogs goed?*

Instead of the interrogative word *where*, we have the abstract interrogative morpheme wh and the locative "somewhere." This last is not the word *somewhere* but rather is a dummy element standing for an unknown, or unspecified, locative. The *where* interrogative will be derived by transformation from the wh element and the dummy locative. The preterminal string contains, in place of the lexical items *those*, *dog*, and *go*, symbols for the categories (or parts of speech) to which these items respectively belong: Det, N, and V. In the next level of the grammar the category symbols will be replaced by appropriate lexical items, and the result will be a terminal string: "wh-those-dog-Past-go-somewhere."

The Subcategorization Level

If determiners, nouns, and verbs from the lexicon were allowed freely to replace the category symbols Det, N, and V in the preterminal string underlying the sample sentence, the results would often be ungrammatical. In addition to *those dogs go*, we might have *a dogs go*, *those Adam go*, *the stone knows*, and what not. There are, in English, restrictions on the co-occurrence of lexical items forbidding many of the combinations that the phrase structure rules alone permit. These restrictions have traditionally been formulated in terms of lexical subcategories. For example, among nouns, those that may take determiners are said to belong to the subcategory of common noun, such as *dog*. Nouns that may not take determiners are proper nouns, such as *Adam*. Nouns are also subcategorized on other principles; count nouns (including *dog*) may be pluralized, whereas mass nouns (e.g., *air*) may not. How is subcategorization to be represented in the present grammar? We shall illustrate the general character of the rules with reference to one constituent of the sample sentence, the subject Nominal, which is represented in the preterminal string as Det-N and in the surface sentence as *those dogs*.

Each entry in the lexicon of the language is going to be assigned certain syntactic features (such as $+$ct for count nouns) that represent certain distributional potentialities of the lexical items. In addition, the lexical category symbols in the last line of the phrase structure derivation—such as Det, N, and V—are going to expand into complex symbols that also contain syntactic features. The complete symbol will be a kind of grappling hook with a set of syntactic features constituting a denticulate surface shaped to retrieve only the right kind of item from the lexicon.

The complex symbol is, first of all, marked with the name of the major category (e.g., $+$N). In the lexicon all nouns (e.g., *dog* in the subcategorization rules and derivation, below) are assumed to be similarly marked. Now we have the first level of subcategorization, sometimes called strict subcategorization. This involves the assignment to each complex symbol of syntactic features which are simply its frames or contexts stated in category symbols. It is as if one were to scan the preterminal string, to take note of the fact that each category occurs in the context of certain other categories, and then to enter those category contexts which restrict the selection of lexical items. In our own example the symbol N

LIST OF SUBCATEGORIZATION RULES AND DERIVATION

	SUBCATEGORIZATION RULES	
LEXICAL CATEGORY	CATEGORICAL CONTEXTS	OTHER SYNTACTIC FEATURES
N → [+N][a]	N → [+Det__]; [−Det__]	N → [+ct]; [−ct]
		N → [+no]; [−no]
Det → [+Det][b]		Det → [__[+ct]N]; [__[−ct]N]
		Det → [__[+no]N]; [__[−no]N]

DERIVATION

Preterminal string	wh-Det-N-Past-V-somewhere
Complex symbol expansion	N → [+N, +Det__, +ct, +no]
	Det → [+Det, __[+ct]N, __[+no]N]
Replacement by lexical items	*dog*, [+N, +Det__, +ct, +no]
	those, [+Det, __[+ct]N, __[+no]N]

[a] Lexical entry: *dog*, [+N, +Det__, +ct, ±no]
[b] Lexical entry: *those*, [+Det, __[+ct]N, __[+no]N]

occurs in the context Det__. When, therefore, N is replaced by a particular noun from the lexicon, that noun must be of the kind that may be preceded by a determiner—in fact, by a common and not by a proper noun. The facts can be expressed by assigning the complex for N the contextual feature [+Det__], by assigning all common nouns in the lexicon (including *dog*) this same feature, and by adopting a replacement rule which allows the complex symbol for N to be replaced by only those lexical items with matching syntactic features.

From Rule 14 of the phrase structure we know that *in general*, which means across all sentences, determiners are optional before nouns. In the particular sentence under derivation, however, there is to be a determiner before the noun and the fact must enter into the derivation. The need for specification of a contextual feature arises only, but always, where there is in the phrase structure an optional environment for a lexical category. Contextual features are needed at several points in Adam's grammar. By assigning verbs the contextual features +__NP and −__NP, for instance, it is possible to retrieve transitive verbs when they are required and intransitives when they are required.

At the next level in the expansion of the complex symbol, syntactic features are added which are not defined in terms of the categories of the preterminal string. In the case of the nouns in a sentence the syntactic features are context-free—that is, they are selected without reference to other complex symbols in the sentence. The syntactic features added to the symbols for determiners and verbs are context-sentitive—they are selected with reference to markers already added to nouns. Such rules are sometimes called selection rules. By this arrangement other words are made to agree with nouns rather than nouns with them. For English, in general, and also for Adam III, the selectional dominance of the noun is not just a convention, but it is rather a representation of certain facts about sentences.

The symbol N in our present derivation acquires the marker +ct rather than −ct and the marker +no rather than −no. It is then equipped to retrieve a count noun from the lexicon, a noun marked $+$ct as *dog* is on page 36. Lexical entries for nouns will not be marked $+$no but rather $\pm$no, to indicate that they may be pluralizied, or else $-$no, to indicate that, like *air*, they may not be pluralized. These markers, and in addition a marker that indicates whether a noun is human ($+$hum) or not, are needed for nouns in Adam III.

The symbol Det acquires syntactic features in a context-sensitive manner, taking its lead, as it were, from the head word in the noun phrase. Since that head word, the N, has the features $+$ct and $+$no, the determiner to accompany it must have features which comprise a matrix to the noun's patrix. Det requires the features [__[$+$ct]N] and [__[$+$no]N]; the features require that the determiner drawn from the lexicon be one able to modify count nouns in the plural.

The fully expanded complex symbols for our sentence (there would be one for V as well as N and Det) serve to select lexical entries. The general lexical rule (which need not be stated in the formal grammar, since it constitutes part of the definition of derivation) is, Where a complex symbol is not distinct from a lexical entry the latter can replace the former. The lexical entry for *dog* is one of those common count nouns that can replace the symbol for N in the present derivation, and *those* is among the entries that can replace the symbol for Det. These processes are illustrated in the rules and derivation on page 36.

The Transformational Level

The phrase structure and subcategorization levels together comprise what has been called the base structure of a grammar. In a derivation the base structure yields a structural string of morphemes such as wh–[those dog]$_{Nominal}$ [Past–go]$_{Vb}$–somewhere; this string contains only some of its labeled bracketings. Tranformational rules map such underlying strings into new structured strings that are closer to actual sentences. Transformations delete, substitute, and permute elements—as phrase structure rules cannot. Roughly speaking, transformations represent the feeling native speakers have that the members of a certain set of sentences are related to their counterparts in another set by a single function.

LIST OF TRANSFORMATION RULES AND DERIVATION

TRANSFORMATION RULES[a]

XIV. Wh incorporation for MV sentences:
  wh–Nominal–Vb(Nominal)–somewhere *implies* wh$+$somewhere–Nominal–Vb (Nominal)
XIX. Affixation of Past[b]:
  χ^1–[Past]$_{Aux}$–V–χ^2 *implies* χ^1–V$+$Past χ^2

DERIVATION

Base: wh–[those dog]$_{Nominal}$[Past–go]$_{Vb}$–somewhere
XIV: wh$+$somewhere–those–dog–Past–go
XIX: wh$+$somewhere–those–dog–go$+$Past

---

[a] The numbers assigned the rules are those they carry in the full grammar.
[b] χ^1 and χ^2 simply stand for any other sentence constituents.

Adam III includes twenty-four transformational rules. Some of the grammatical functions they perform are: agreement in person and number for subject and verb; agreement in number for subject and predicate nominative; creation of such elliptical possessives as *yours* and *mines*; and deletion of subject *you* from imperatives. In the derivation of our sample sentence, transformations are needed to transpose an affix and stem and to incorporate *somewhere* into wh. The rules and the steps in the derivation appear in the list above. A transformational rule describes the structure of the kind of string to which it is applicable; there will generally be an indefinite number of strings that satisfy that structural description. In an actual derivation it is a particular string that is transformed.

The Morphophonemic Level

Rules on this level really belong to the phonological component, but to bring the derivation of our composite sentence to a recognizable form we need to use two of them. They are: xv, wh + somewhere→*where*, and xxiv, $[\chi]_v$ + Past→χ + $-ed$. Rule xxiv results in the erroneous form *goed*. The occurrence of this error marks the absence from Adam III of the adult morphophonemic rule, $[go]_v$ + Past→*went*. In terms of the conventions with which we are working, then, the error in question is a superficial one. It can be corrected by adding a single rule which does not disturb the remainder of the grammar in any way.

Now that we have a general picture of the children's competence at III, let us characterize in a general way developments between I and III.

OVERVIEW OF DEVELOPMENTS BETWEEN I AND III

Figure 1 indicates that there are large differences in rate of linguistic development among Adam, Eve, and Sarah but the order of events is, for these three unacquainted children, strikingly uniform. So much so that it is possible to describe developments between I and III in a way that is true of all. This is not to say that there are no differences among the children. One that is especially consistent and interesting concerns the rate of production of ungrammatical and anomalous forms. Adam produced these at about four times the rate of either girl—he spoke of "talking crackers," said his nose could "see," addressed the microphone as if it were a person, and said, "It's went," "Why I can't do that," and "That a my book." The girls were more literal and, except for telegraphic omissions, more often grammatical. From other data we have seen and from what parents tell us, there is evidently great individual variation among children on this dimension; probably it explains the very different notions of language development that particular psychologists derive from their own children. When the girls made errors, they were the same kinds of errors that Adam made. For that reason we have assumed that the induction and hypothesis-testing involved is common to the three and simply more copiously externalized by Adam. He gives us a richer print-out, and so we more often cite evidence from his records than the girls'.

Types of Sentences

From I to III the children seem to be working chiefly on simple sentences. This is not to say that all or even most of the children's *utterances* were complete simple sentences. It is rather to say that the most complex constructions they produced were simple sentences, that they never (or almost never) conjoined or embedded simple sentences. We do not find such sentences as *John and Mary laughed*, *The man you saw is here*, or *I want you to eat*.

In saying that the children from I to III seemed to be working on the structure of simple sentences it is necessary to make explicit the fact that we do not intend to make two related but stronger claims: We do not claim that in I and III the children learned nothing about conjoining and embedding; it is possible after all, that some restriction on performance prevented them from revealing in spontaneous speech all that they had learned. Nor do we say that the children's knowledge of the simple sentence was complete before they started to embed and conjoin; that is clearly untrue. In III there were a few instances of embedding and at that point all three children still had a great deal to learn about simple sentences. Auxiliary elements were only occurring singly; there were no combinations. There were no passives and only the simplest reflexes of negativity. There were no tag questions, and indeed, well-formed yes-no questions of all kinds were missing. Clearly, embedding and conjoining do not wait upon the development of complete knowledge of simple sentences.

What sorts of simple sentences were the children working on from I to III? Declarative-affirmative sentences, of course, but we shall leave till last the description of these, since most of the knowledge involved is not specific to them but is common to all sentences. In addition to declarative-affirmative sentences, the children were working on negatives, imperatives, and interrogatives. We saw in Adam III that these are developed, in transformational grammar, from the abstract morphemes neg, imp, and wh. From the beginning of our records, that is, from I, the children gave evidence of understanding the meaning of these morphemes. What they lacked was the transformational rules which develop surface structures expressing these morphemes. These rules were missing entirely in I. In III there were eight to twelve transformational rules serving this purpose, only a fraction of the adult rules, and some of them were not proper adult rules at all.

René Spitz (1957) says the the child begins at about fifteen months to shake his head as an intentional negative signal, usually having the sense of resistance to some attempt to influence him. In I, we find this signal and also the word *no* used to resist imperatives and to answer yes-no questions. We also find *no* added initially to several kinds of utterance: *No fall, No put, No picture in there*, and so forth; this seems to be the child's own invention. In II and III the *no* forms were supplemented by *can't*, *won't*, and *don't*. It seems unlikely to us that these were related transformationally, as they are in the adult language, to *can*, *will*, and *do*—unlikely because the affirmative modal auxiliaries had not appeared at this time. The forms seemed simply to be a set of preverbal forms introduced by obligatory transformation when the neg morpheme was in the base structure of a sentence with a main verb.

Imperative sentences in adult grammar are derived by transformation out of underlying strings containing the morpheme imp and having *you* as subject and *will* as auxiliary. This analysis is motivated by such adult sentences as, *Go chase yourself* and *Come here, will you?* Neither reflexives (*yourself*) nor tags (*will you*) occurred in early child speech, and so the facts justifying the adult analysis were lacking. In the recording sessions at home one could often be quite sure that a child's sentence had an imperative meaning, but there was nothing in the surface form of his imperative sentences that could serve as a reliable sign of this meaning. To be sure, such sentences were often produced without explicit subject, as are adult imperatives, but the children also very often omitted the subjects of sentences clearly intended to be declaratives. What happened between I and III was that the subjectless sentences came to be ever more nearly restricted to the imperative, but it was not exclusively imperative even in III. In addition, there were a few words the child learned to use after I (especially *please* and *gimme*) which may be confidently interpreted as imperative markers.

Very few of the linguistic reflexes of imperativity developed, then, in this first period, but from the start in I there were indications that the child understood the imperative meaning. This evidence on the responsive side lay in the child's compliance with or (at least as often) resistance to the force of a parental imperative. On the performance side the evidence lay in the child's occasional persistence in using certain constructions again and again to accomplish some effect in a resistant adult.

Interrogatives are of two basic types: yes-no questions and wh questions. We shall leave for a later section the description of wh questions. From I to III the child's yes-no questions were identifiable by rising intonation but not, consistently, by any other feature. It was as if he asked, "Yes or no?" by speaking any sentence or sentence fragment with questioning intonation. Well-formed yes-no questions, with the subject and the first member of the auxiliary transposed, appeared later than III.

The grammatical structure of declarative affirmative simple sentences is represented almost entirely by the base component of a grammar, the phrase structure and subcategorization rules. All of this structure is relevant also to negatives, imperatives, and interrogatives, but these three kinds of sentence include something more—rules in the transformational component. There are several kinds of knowledge represented by the base component: relations within a sentence, hierarchy of constituents, and subcategorization or co-occurrence restrictions. We shall say something about each of them.

Basic Sentence Relations

The basic relations are those called subject of the sentence, predicate of the sentence, and object of the verb. So far as our materials permit us to judge, the child's knowledge of these relations (which, in English, are chiefly expressed by order) undergoes no development. He seems to express the relations he means to express from the very start. At any rate, there are few detectable errors in all the records. In most utterances it is clear that the intended subject and object are the constituents found in subject and object position—for instance, *I dump trash out, I making coffee, You need some paper*. It is unlikely that the child intended to convey the reversed relations, *Trash dump me out, Coffee making me, Some paper need you*. There are in the records a handful of exceptions in which the intended object seems to be in subject position—*Paper find, Daddy suitcase to get it, Paper write*—but these are the only exceptions in thousands of well-ordered sentences.

The precision with which the child expresses basic sentence relations is important, since these relations are probably linguistic universals and so may themselves be organizations preformed in the human brain. Perhaps subject and object relations are to the child what nut-burying is to the squirrel, an innate pattern requiring only a releaser to set it in operation. Perhaps, but we shall not want to draw that conclusion until we have more data. The children we have studied scrupulously preserve sentence word order not only with respect to basic relations but also with respect to the order of articles, adjectives, auxiliary verbs, adverbs, and all other words. In imitation tasks they omit words but seldom confuse order. This may be a general feature of imitation in children or perhaps only a feature of the imitation of speech. The accurate expression of sentence relations by children learning English may, therefore, be a kind of incidental consequence of the fact that English expresses these relations by word order. We should like to know how well the relations are expressed by children learning a language that expresses subject and object relations by case endings (see Slobin, 1966, for some evidence concerning Russian).

Constituents

The Aux is a constituent that developed in the period I–III. In I, all main verbs occurred in unmarked generic form. In II and III, the same set of operations on the verb developed in all three children, the progressive, the past, and a set of semi-auxiliary verbs we called catenatives. Most prominent among the catenatives are *gonna, wanna,* and *hafta*. The three operations on the verb are represented as a constituent Aux for reasons already described.

The constituent NP was present even in I but underwent consolidation and elaboration between I and III. The constituent status of the NP even in I is attested to by the fact that the children quite consistently responded to questions in *Who* or *What* with some sort of NP. This equivalence in the exchanges of discourse is evidence that the many particular NP's were organized together. In adult speech, the NP has four principal functions in simple sentences: in equational sentences it serves as subject and as predicate nominative, and in main verb sentences as subject and direct object. For the children, the NP had these four functions from the start. At any rate some sort of NP served each function, but, whereas an adult will use every sort of NP in all positions, in the children's speech at I, each position seemed to require a somewhat different formula for the

NP. Subjects of equational sentences were often impersonal pronouns (especially *that* and *it*), but predicate nominatives never were. Subjects of main verbs were almost always names of persons or animals, whereas direct objects were almost always names of inanimate things. Subject NP's in both kinds of sentence, at I, never consisted of more than one morpheme—a simple pronoun or noun. Object and predicate nominative NP's at I were, on the other hand, somewhat more complex; they might consist of two nouns (e.g., *Adam book*) or a determiner and noun (e.g., *my book*). If we write a grammar that stays close to the sentences actually obtained at I, we must include four distinct versions of NP, which makes a fragmentary grammar strangely unlike the adult form. One of the things that happened between I and III was that the four NP's came to resemble one another closely enough so that a single NP symbol, one rewritten by a single set of rules, could be entered in all four positions. In addition, the NP grew in complexity in all positions.

There are, finally, constituents that had still not developed by III. These include the adverbials Time and Manner. There were occasional time and manner expressions in the children's speech by III, but they were few. Most importantly, the children at III were not giving grammatically appropriate answers to time (*When*) and manner (*How*) questions. Of the adverbials, the locative is by far the first to develop. It is clearly present even in I.

Strict Subcategorization

The progressive inflection (*-ing*) emerged for all three children between I and III. In adult English, this inflection is not used with all verbs. So-called "process" verbs (*sing*, *walk*, *eat*, and so forth) freely take the progressive, whereas "state" verbs (*need*, *equal*, *know*, and *like*) do not. To say *I am singing the song* is quite correct, but *I am knowing the song* is strange. The process-state subcategorization of verbs can be represented, in an English grammar, in the expansion of the complex symbol for V. A choice is made between two features which represent contexts at the level of the phrase structure, the features $[+ [be + ing]\_\_]$; $[- [be + ing]\_\_]$.[2] These features are entered also in relevant verbs in the lexicon. The interesting fact is that these rules were already needed for the children's grammar at III because the children observed the subcategories and made no mistakes of the type *I liking candy* or *I wanting a book*. Such mistakes were not absent simply from the samples used for the grammars; they were absent from all data over the full range I–V.

David McNeill (1966) has argued that children must have innate knowledge of a hierarchy of subcategories corresponding to whatever hierarchy may prove to be a linguistic universal. The complete absence of subcategorization errors in connection with the progressive inflection seems to support McNeill's position—or, at any rate, does so if the following interpretation of his position is acceptable.

---

[2] The form be+ing refers to English grammar, whereas the form used earlier, B+ing, refers specifically to the grammar of the children in this study.

If we ask what could possibly be universal and therefore innate about the process-state distinction, the answer must surely be the underlying semantic principle. The distributional facts, such as the rule for *-ing*, are known to be specific to particular languages. How could an innate process-state distinction forestall inflectional errors? Something like this would have to be true: As the meaning was learned of each new verb like *walk*, *eat*, *need*, and *like*, the semantic entry would have to include all innate subcategorization features as well as individual elements of meaning. In short, *walk* would from the first be tagged as a "process" and *need* as a "state."

When at a later time the child attended to distributional facts peculiar to English, such as the fact that some verbs are inflected with *-ing* and some not, he would have a set of ready hypotheses to explain the cleavage. He would test to see whether it was governed by one or another of the preestablished, universal subcategorizations. And of course the process-state subcategorization defines the proper dotted line for *-ing*. It is somewhat as if a child learning to recognize coins kept track of all the attributes that are ever significant in a coinage system —color, weight, size, design, texture, and so forth. Then when he first encountered the distributional facts of monetary exchange, such as the fact that two coins of one kind equal one of another, he would quickly see which of the perceptual attributes he had been keeping track of were useful.

The absence or error in connection with a semantically principled subcategorization is one prediction of the "innateness" hypothesis, and this prediction is confirmed in the case of the progressive. However, one easily thinks of other predictions that are not confirmed. The division of nouns into mass and count subcategories is semantically based and as likely to be universal as the process-state division, but the children were, at V, still making some errors in their use of the noun subcategories. Some subcategorizations in English are unprincipled (i.e., they have no semantic base)—for example, the verb subcategories that take regular and irregular inflections for Past. Not surprisingly, children make many mistakes in cases like these, where rote learning of the subcategory membership of each verb is really the only possibility. In fact, errors in this connection are often heard in the elementary school years; they are to be expected. But if the children have innate subcategories, should they not, on first encountering unprincipled cleavages, act as if they expected one or another of the innate principles to govern the cleavage? On first encountering the fact that some verbs take *-ed* and some do not, a child ought to test the hypothesis that all of the former verbs might be processes and the latter states, the hypothesis that the former might be transitives and the latter intransitives, and so forth. There is no trace of anything of the kind in our data.

The full story is too long to tell, but our present best guess is that the absence of error with *-ing* is not to be attributed to innate subcategorization. And, in general, we have not found any reason to believe that subcategories are innate other than the usual reason—it is exceedingly difficult to determine how they are learned.

Noncategorical Syntactic Features

Plural number in English is marked by inflection of the noun; this inflection, like the progressive, was entirely absent in I and often present by III. The expression of number in English is vastly more complicated than the expression of something like progressive aspect. For example, there must be agreement in number between a head noun and its determiners, between a subject noun and a predicate nominal, and between a pronoun and its antecedent noun. Number and person together, as features of a subject noun, determine the form of the verb: *walks* or *walk*, *is* or *are*. In Adam III, number is introduced in the base structure in the form of two context-free syntactic markers in the complex symbol for the noun: [+no] and [−no]. There are related markers for the complex symbol of Det and for many lexical items. There are three transformations and several morphophonemic rules.

The development of number in the three children illustrates nicely the difference between deep and superficial acquisition of a grammatical feature. In terms of chronological age, Eve began to inflect nouns some fourteen months earlier than did Sarah. However, when Eve first used plurals she made many mistakes in all aspects of number agreement, whereas Sarah, from the start, made almost no mistakes. What this means is that in Eve's grammar, number first appears as a low-level morphophonemic rule which, in effect, says that nouns have an optional pronunciation with a terminal sibilant. The introduction of this rule leaves the rest of Eve's grammar undisturbed. For Sarah, number enters in the base structure and effects complex changes in the total grammar. So we see that Eve was not always so far in advance of Sarah as the simple mean length of utterance index alone would indicate. And we see that acquisitions that may look alike if only certain words or endings are examined may look very unlike when the total distributional pattern is examined.

In summary of this overview, it is correct to say that the child's early grammar comprises a base structure not very different from that of the adult grammar and a syntactic transformational component that is rudimentary in III and almost totally absent in I. This is not the same as saying that children directly speak base-structure sentences. It is not clear what that statement could mean since morphophonemic and phonetic rules are required to make sentences of the underlying strings. But the underlying strings themselves seem to be chiefly those that can be generated by the base.

SEGMENTATION INTO MORPHEMES

In order to learn grammar, a child must segment the speech he hears into morphemes because morphemes are the ultimate units of grammatical rules. There are short-run regularities that can be formulated in smaller units, the segmental phonemes, but the long-run regularities that render an infinite number of meanings constructable and interpretable cannot be formulated in terms of phonemes.

It may be useful to imagine an erroneous segmentation into morphemes and what its consequences would be. Consider the following set of utterances that a child might easily hear: *My book, Your book*; *My bike, Your bike*; *My birthday, Your birthday*. If we let a slash mark represent a morpheme cut, then this segmentation is erroneous; *Myb/ook, Yourb/ook*; *Myb/ike, Yourb/ike*; *Myb/irthday, Yourb/irthday*. These morphemes look odd in print, but they represent sound combinations that are, in English phonology, easily pronounceable— think of *scribe* and *orb*, *Ike* and *oops*.

Suppose the child who has segmented in the above fashion goes on to store the contexts of each morpheme to the (unintentional and unconscious) end of discovering general and meaningful construction rules. The result may be represented in part as:

> *myb*, [__*ook*, __*ike*, __*irthday*]
> *yourb*, [__*ook*, __*ike*, __*irthday*]
> *ook*, [*myb* __, *yourb* __]
> *ike*, [*myb* __, *yourb* __]

Myb and *yourb* have identical context entries distinct from the entries for *ook* and *ike*, the latter two being themselves identical. In these circumstances it would be reasonable to infer the existence of two morpheme classes ($C_1 \rightarrow myb$, *yourb*; $C_2 \rightarrow ook$, *ike*, *irthday*) and of a construction signifying possession which is created by selecting class members in proper sequence ($C_1 - C_2$). These inferences founded on a mistaken segmentation do not lead anywhere. For the small set of utterances that preserve the artificial co-occurrence of certain morphemes and a subsequent /b/ phoneme, the segmentation would appear to work. Given *my b/rake* and *my b/and*, the child could construct *your b/rake* and *your b/and* with approximately correct meaning. However, outside this artificial range his false morphemes would not work. He would not hear *the ook, the ike, the irthday* or *myb pencil, myb doggie, yourb Mommy*. And he would find unanalyzable such new possessives as *my pencil, my doggie, my Mommy, your pencil*, and *your doggie*.

Compare the results of a correct segmentation. The context entries would look like this:

> *my*, [__ *book*, __ *bike*, __ *birthday*]
> *your*, [__ *book*, __ *bike*, __ *birthday*]
> *book*, [*my* __, *your* __]
> *bike*, [*my* __, *your* __]

One morpheme class would represent a start on possessive pronouns, and the other a start on count nouns. A construction rule written in terms of these classes correctly anticipates *your brake* from the occurrence of *my brake*, *my band* from *your band*, and so on in an indefinite number of cases. Furthermore, the tentative morphemes *book, bike, birthday, my*, and *your* will recur with approximately the same meaning in such new constructions as *the book, my old hat*, and *your good friend.* A correct segmentation is repeatedly confirmed by its continuing ability to unlock regularities and structural meanings. An erroneous segmentation is a false trail winding off into the desert.

Judging from our materials, and from what we know of the materials of others, morpheme segmentation errors such as *myb pencil* or *the ook* are uncommon. It is easy to overlook the segmentation problem in child speech because there is so little evidence that it exists. The evidence we found in the fine structure of our data suggests that segmentation is a real problem in the sense that it is something a child learns but that it is also a problem for which he has highly effective solution procedures.

For example, Adam produced in an early record the sentence *It's big.* What was the status in Adam's grammar of the form *'s* (or *is*)? In adult grammar, *is* is a morpheme distinct from such other morphemes as *it* and *big* and organized closely with *am* and *are* as forms (allomorphs) of the verb *be.* We find in Adam's records certain errors of commission suggesting that *is* was differently organized for him. He produced hundreds of well-formed equational sentences with *it* as subject, but he also produced a large number of odd ones. The following are representative: *It's fell* (Sample 14), *It's has wheels* (Sample 21), *It's hurts* (Sample 17), and *It's went on the top* (Sample 22). The form *is* has no place in these sentences and seems to have been imported into them as an onhanger of *it.* Perhaps, then, the adult polymorphic form *its* was a single unanalyzed morpheme for Adam. How does this hypothesis fare when tested against all the relevant evidence?

Suppose the hypothesis were wrong, and Adam was, in fact, learning to organize *is* in the correct, adult way. What errors ought he then to have made? Since *is*, as a form of *be*, is closely related to *am* and *are*, we should expect the several forms to have occasionally displaced one another in Adam's sentences through disregard of the features of the subject noun phrase that are supposed to select them. There ought to have been such errors as *I is, we is, I are*, and *he am.* There were no such errors in Adam's early records, and that fact supports the conclusion that *is* was not at first organized as a form of *be.*

In certain contexts *is* is obligatory: in such reduced equational sentences as *it big*, and in sentences with a verb inflected for progressive aspect, such as *it going.* When Adam began sometimes to produce an audible *is* in such contexts, he did not, for many months, always do so. On the same page of a protocol, it is quite usual to find otherwise identical sentences with and without *is.* Of course, adults too do not always sound all their segmental phonemes, but this particular reduction, from *it's* to *it*, is not one that adults make. Its occurrence in Adam suggests that for him *it's* and *it* were just varying pronounciations of one morpheme.

The range of *is* in Adam's early records were restricted in an important way. The word *it* is an impersonal pronoun and substitutes for impersonal noun phrases. When such noun phrases themselves occur as subjects of equational sentences and with verbs inflected for progressive aspect, an adult uses *is*—for example, *The top is big*; *The top is spinning*. In such cases, during the many months when we believe *it-s* was organized as a single morpheme, Adam always failed to produce *is*—that is what should happen if our hypothesis is correct. If, on the contrary, *is* were a separate morpheme, the difference between its invariable absence with noun phrase subjects and its only occasional absence with *it* as subject would be unaccountable.

There is another revealing restriction of range. If *it's* were simply a variant of *it*, then it ought to have occurred sometimes in all the sentence positions that *it* ever fills. As the third column of Table 1 shows, *it* was an object of a verb more often than it was a subject. An adult would never use *it's* as a pronoun object, but our hypothesis about *it's* predicts such errors for Adam. If *it's* were a simple variant of *it*, he ought to have formed such sentences as *get it's* and *put it's there*. As the third column of Table 1 shows, he never made such errors.

The forms *it* and *it's* were in perfect complementary distribution. This is not a phonologically conditional complementary distribution of the kind that obtains for the several forms of the regular plural inflection in English. In the phonologically conditioned case the several forms are perfectly predictable, so the variation among them is always redundant, and the descriptive linguist (e.g., Gleason, 1961; Harris, 1942; Hockett, 1947; Nida, 1948) considers the forms to be allomorphs of one morpheme. The complementary distribution that obtains for *it* and *it's* seems to be conditioned by grammatical role (sentence subject versus verb object), and in such cases the linguist does not necessarily conclude that the forms are allomophs or variant forms.

Many languages use inflectional forms to signal the role of a word in a larger construction. When nouns are involved (the most familiar instance), we speak of cases. Subject and object case (or nominative and accusative) are marked in Sanskrit, Latin, Greek, Finnish, and many other languages (Gleason,

TABLE 1   THE FORMS *IT* AND *IT'S* IN EARLY ADAM SAMPLES

Samples	*It* as Subject, *Is* Required as Verb[a]		*It* as Subject, *Is* Forbidden as Verb[b]		*It* as Object, *Is* Forbidden to Occur[cd]
	Is Absent	*Is* Present	*Is* Absent	*Is* Present	*Is* Absent
5–7		1			73
8–10		2	1		106
11–13		4	2		89
14–16	4	6	8	2	94
17–19	3	33	2	10	132
20–22	3	54		18	112

[a] For example, *It's big*; *It's going*.
[b] For example, *It hurts*; *It went*.
[c] For example, *Get it*; *Put it there*.
[d] No sentences with *is* present appeared in the sample.

1961). In English, nouns are not inflected for case; nominative and accusative forms are distinguished by word order (e.g., *John saw Mary* versus *Mary saw John*). However, Adam used *it* and *it's* as if *'s* or *is* were a nominative case ending. If *it* and *it's* were organized in this way, then *is* was a separate morpheme, and we are incorrect in suggesting that *it's* was a single form, a variant of *it*. The possibility is an interesting one. Since case is a common syntactic device in the languages of the world, it is reasonable to suppose that case should be among the hypotheses about linguistic structure that the human mind would be disposed to entertain and test (Chomsky, 1965; Foder, 1966). Much of the distributional data available to Adam would seem to have confirmed this hypothesis, and he might reasonably have organized the facts about *it* and *it's* in this way until more data motivated reorganization. However, for various reasons that cannot be detailed here, it is quite clear that Adam's *is* was not functioning as a case ending. The conclusion that best fits all the evidence is that *it* and *it's* were allomorphs of a single morpheme, their occurrence conditioned by grammatical role.

Errors of segmentation were rare in Adam, Eve, and Sarah, but *it's* was not the only case. The clearer instances[3] include: *I'm, that-a, drop-it, get-it, put-it, want-to, have-to, going-to, another-one, what-that*, and *let-me*. These pairs have two characteristics which, taken together, distinguish them from pairs that were correctly analyzed. The first characteristic is a phonetic one. *It's, wanna, lemme, put-it*, and indeed, all pairs in the set are regularly run together by adults as if they were in fact single words (Heffner, 1949). This is to say that the morpheme boundary is not in these pairs marked in any way whatever—the pairs all lack the open juncture phoneme ($/+/$) which marks the majority of morpheme boundaries in English. Perhaps, then, children are usually able to avoid segmentation errors because they regularly cut the stream of speech at just those points where $/+/$ occurs. This, however, is not a simple claim.

How are children able to recognize $/+/$? It is not a phonetically simple feature. To be sure, when detectable pauses occur in a sentence, it is usually at morpheme boundaries; pause is thus considered one of the phonetic manifestations of $/+/$. The difficulty is that pause is only an intermittent feature. How is $/+/$ identified more generally?

Consider the pairs *nitrate* and *night-rate, slyness* and *minus, mark it* and *market*. There need be no actual pause in either member of a pair, but still there is an audible difference in the amount of aspiration on the $/t/$, in the duration of the vowel $/ay/$, and in the release of $/k/$. For each pair there is a phoneme that takes two somewhat different forms. In order to be able to classify the related but

---

[3] Brown and Bellugi (1964) previously interpreted some portions of the relevant evidence in other ways. For instance, errors like *That a my boot* and *That a your car* were thought to indicate that Adam had adopted a mistaken rule permitting articles to precede every sort of nominal other than pronouns. Such errors as *drop it book* and *get it pencil* suggested that Adam, in learning to substitute pronouns for noun phrases, was making both explicit. In certain points of detail, previously overlooked, the view here that *that-a, drop-it*, and *get-it* were all unanalyzed single morphemes provides a closer fit to the data than do the previous interpretations.

different sounds as single phonemes and so to simplify description, the linguist creates the junctural phoneme $/+/$ and assigns to it the phonetic features distinguishing a pair (Harris, 1951). The phonemic transcriptions will then look like this: /nayt+reyt/, /slay+nɨs/, /mark+ət/, /naytreyt/, /maynis/, /markət/. It follows that the phonetic values of $/+/$ are a disjunctive set and elaborately so. It follows also that $/+/$ is not itself a segment at all, since aspiration, duration, and the like have no existence apart from particular vowels and consonants. The open juncture, in short, is an invention of linguistic science designed to simplify language description. How could a child possibly learn to recognize $/+/$ and use it to segment the speech he hears?

The /t/ one hears in *night rate* occurs also at the ends of words (e.g., *night* or *right*) and so can occur terminally in complete utterances, whereas the /t/ of *nitrate* is never terminal. Similary, the /ay/ of *slyness* can be terminal (as in *sly* or *die*), but the /ay/ of *minus* cannot. And, in general, that form of a phoneme which is found within utterances at morpheme boundaries is found also in final position in total utterances, but the form found within utterances internal to a morpheme is never final in a total utterance. A child might learn that. He might learn also to give special status to utterance-internal consonants or vowels that assumed the forms they ordinarily assumed in utterance-final position. In fact, he might learn to make morpheme cuts at just these points and to make contextural entries in terms of the resultant units.

When a child first begins to produce polymorphemic utterances, he has for some time been producing single-morpheme utterances. Suppose that he has made independent entries for all of these—both the one-morpheme utterance like *dog* and the polymorphemic utterances like *my dog*; at this point, the polymorphemic utterances might simply have the status for him of longer words. Suppose now that an internal analysis routine is activated which involves retrieving two entries at a time and comparing them, phonemically, from left to right. Suppose, further, that he returns to storage pairs with unlike first phonemes but retains for further analysis pairs that start out identically. Let him then make a tentative morphemic cut at the first point of phonemic divergence in the pair. Let him finally look up the resulting segments to see if there are already independent entries for them—as there usually would be if they were morphemes— and mark as morphemes just those segments having prior entries. If he picked a pair like *br/eak* and *br/ing*, he would cut them as indicated, would find no prior entries for any of the segments, and would not mark them as morphemes. However, a pair like *my/dog* and *my/cat* would yield segments with prior entries, and a child who started with this pair might soon discover that cuts yielding morphemes by his original criteria regularly coincided with terminal vowels and consonants (or, one might say, with $/+/$). Thereafter he could make segmentation cuts wherever terminal phonemes occurred without regard to either identical sequences or prior entries. By this account, the value of $/+/$ is discovered from its correlation with more primitive criteria. It is possible, however, that the terminal vowels and consonants are themselves the most primitive criterion of morpheme segmentation.

Although errors of segmentation seem only to occur across boundaries unmarked by open juncture in adult speech, it is far from the case that every such unmarked boundary will give rise to an error of segmentation. Adults will run together *Pop's here* as well as *It's here*. But Adam organized *is* as a feature in the pronunciation not of any noun but only of the pronoun *it*. Probably the important factor here is the second characteristic, which helps to define the pairs erroneously organized as single morphemes. Each such pair was characterized by a high transition probability in the speech mothers addressed to their children. After the first member, the second was more frequent by far than any other morpheme. Nouns like *Pop* or *Adam* sometimes appeared as subjects of equational sentences, but they also often appeared as subjects of main verbs—too often, apparently, for Adam to make the mistake of thinking *is* belonged to the nouns. *It*, on the other hand, appeared hundreds of times a day as the subject of equational sentences but seldom, surprisingly seldom, as the subject of any other verb. The high transitions in these pairs have nothing to do with grammar, of course, but are simply accidental statistical features of mother-child interaction. They demonstrate that bias in the language sample to which a child is exposed can, in an extreme case, result in a partly erroneous formulation of the underlying grammar.

It is important to make it perfectly clear that the evidence for segmentation errors is not simply, or even primarily phonetic. We are not relying on the fact that Adam's version of *it's* often sounded like *iss* or that his rendering of *want to* sounded like *wanna*. The important evidence is distributional: the fact that Adam said *It's hurts*, for instance, and that he said *I want to play* but never *I want you to play*. When, at length, the children corrected their few segmentation errors and reconstrued the forms of *be* and articles, the evidence was again distributional and in some cases dramatically clear. In the case of Adam's *a*, for example, the form appeared for nineteen samples in only a restricted portion of its proper range—chiefly with *that* as pronoun subject.[4] Then, in Samples 20 and 21, the full range quite suddenly filled out, and *a* appeared with noun phrases in isolation, noun phrases functioning as subjects of sentences, noun phrases in locative questions, and so forth. We do not yet know what causes reconstruction of forms at one time rather than another.

TRANSFORMATIONS IN Wh QUESTIONS

Wh questions are those using an interrogative word from the set *who, whom, what, where, when, why,* and *how*. Contemporary generative grammars of English (e.g., Katz and Postal, 1964; Klima, 1964) do not all derive wh questions in just the same way, but they all do use transformational rules to represent the

---

[4] The form appeared also with a few strictly transitive verbs where, as with *that*, it seems to have been a feature of pronunciation. Representative errors are: *have a two minute, get a one.*

TABLE 2   SYSTEMATIC RELATIONS AMONG QUESTIONS AND ANSWERS

CONSTITUENTS TO BE SPECIFIED	NORMAL QUESTIONS[a,b]	OCCASIONAL QUESTIONS[a,c]	POSSIBLE ANSWERS[a]
Subject nominal	*Who* will read the book?	*WHO* will read the book?	*John* will read the book.
Object nominal	*What* will John read?	John will read *WHAT*?	John will read *the book*.
Predicate nominal	*What* is that?	That is *WHAT*?	That is *a book*.
Predicate	*What* will John do?	John will *do WHAT*?	John will *read the book*.
Locative adverbial	*Where* will John read?	John will read *WHERE*?	John will read *in the library*.
Time adverbial	*When* will John read?	John will read *WHEN*?	John will read *this evening*.
Manner adverbial	*How* will John read?	John will read *HOW*?	John will read *slowly*.

[a] Wh words and the substitutes for them are italicized.
[b] The derivation of normal questions follows: Base: Wh–John–will–read–something; Preposing and Wh incorporation: Wh + something–John–will–read; Transposition: Wh + something–will–John–read; Morphophonemic: What–will–John–read.
[c] Words with all letters capitalized receive heavy stress and rising intonation.

systematic relations between these questions and the declaratives that answer them. Wh questions begin to appear in good quantity and variety at Level III; indeed, the composite sentence derived with rules from Adam III was such a question. The question here is whether there is, in the form of these questions, evidence directly supporting the notion that the child acquires implicit knowledge of the kind represented by the transformational rules of the adult grammar. The brief discussion here is drawn from a full research report (Brown, 1968) which presents the evidence for all wh questions in all the protocols from I through V.

Table 2 sets out some adult questions and answers so as to expose the systematic relations among them. Consider first the two middle columns. Each question in "normal" form stands alongside a semantically equivalent, but less frequent "occasional" form, in which the wh word is in final position and is to be spoken with heavy stress and rising intonation. If someone said, "John will read the telephone book," one might respond, "John will read *what?*"—this response is an occasional form. The occasional form for the subject nominal— the first entry—is unlike the others in the column in that the wh word appears initially, its normal position.

The occasional forms (except the subject nominal) are all related to their normal counterparts by the same function. In describing the function let us take the occasional form as the base or starting point. The normal form can be created from the occasional in two steps: The first would move the wh word from final position to initial position; we call this preposing. The second would interchange the subject of the sentence and the auxiliary; we call this transposing. The same two steps will generate all the questions of the second column from their re- spective counterparts in the first column. Essentially, these two steps are the transformational rules used in adult grammar to derive wh questions. The main difference is that normal questions are not derived from actual occasional questions but from underlying strings that are similar to the occasionals.

Consider now the sentences of the last column, which are examples of well-formed answers to the questions standing opposite them. Question and answer differ in the words that are italicized in each case and only in these words. The italicized words in the answers may be said to stand in place of the italicized wh words—in the *exact* place, the very sentence locus of the wh word, for the occasional questions. The normal questions, we know, shift the place of the wh word. The material italicized in the answer is the material most directly responsive to the question. Indeed it is the only essential part of the answer. "What will John read?" "*The book.*" "When will John read?" "*This evening.*" In fact, each interrogative word is a kind of algebraic x standing in the place of a particular constituent of the sentence, the constituent identified in the left column of Table 2. The wh word asks for specification of that constituent. It marks the spot where information is to be poured into the sentence, and the form of the wh word—whether *who*, *what*, *where*, or *when*—indicates the kind of infor- mation required.

A transformational grammar of adult English can represent the systematic relations of Table 2 in the following way. Associated with each of the sentence constituents there is a stand-in element symbolized as "someone," "something," "somewhere," "sometime," and "somehow." The derivation of a wh question begins in the phrase structure with the selection of the interrogative morpheme wh. Then, from the constituent which is to be specified in a well-formed answer, the stand-in element is selected, rather than some particular NP, Loc, or whatever. The phrase structure derivation terminates in an underlying string which is just like the string for the occasional question except that the stand-in element stands where the interrogative words stand in the occasional questions of Table 2. In the derivation of normal questions, a first transformation preposes the stand-in element and incorporates it into wh, and a second transformation transposes the order of the subject NP and the first member of the auxiliary. A morphophonemic rule rewrites the wh + stand-in component as the appropriate interrogative word: wh + something as *what*: wh + someone as *who*; wh + somewhere as *where*, and so forth. The derivation rules and sample strings are represented in the note to Table 2.

Production of a Hypothetical Intermediate

The composite sentence derived by Adam III was *Where those dogs goed?* and not *Where did those dogs go?* How is Adam's form related to the derivation of the normal adult form? It is a sentence that would be produced by the rules in the note to Table 2 if the second transformation, the one that transposes subject and auxiliary, were simply omitted, and if the morphophonemic rules followed upon the preposing transformation alone. In short, Adam seems to have given phonetic form to a structure that is generated by the adult grammar as a hypothetical intermediate, a structure not actualized as a question by adults. The composite form is, in this respect, representative of all Adam's wh questions in III and for many months after III. Eve and Sarah both also constructed these preposed wh questions, though not in such quantity as did Adam. Table 3 represents the relation between the children's version of various wh questions and the two varieties of well-formed adult questions.

A Transformation in Discourse

The derivation rules loosely described in the note to Table 2 and presented in explicit form in Adam III presuppose the establishment of such major sentence constituents as NP and Loc, since the stand-in elements are associated with these constituents. As seen in the Overview of Developments between I and III (pp. 304–310), there was good evidence of the existence of these constituents from early in the records. The most persuasive evidence was the children's ability to answer *who* and *what* questions with noun phrases and *where* questions with locatives. We also reported in the Overview that adverbials of time and manner did not seem to be organized as constituents in I to III, since the children did not make grammatically appropriate answers to *when* and *how* questions. If the responsive constituents were not organized as such, then *when* and *how* questions

TABLE 3   THE CHILD'S Wh QUESTION AS A HYPOTHETICAL
INTERMEDIATE IN ADULT GRAMMAR

Occasional Questions[a]	Child's Questions[b]	Normal Questions[c]
Who will read the book?	Who will read the book?	Who will read the book?
John will read *what*?	What John will read?	What will John read?
That is *what*?	What that is?	What is that?
John will do *what*?	What John will do?	What will John do?
John will read *where*?	Where John will read?	Where will John read?

[a] Words in italics receive heavy stress and rising intonation.
[b] Derivable from occasional questions by preposing.
[c] Derivable from occasional questions by preposing and transposing.

could not be derived in the children's grammar by the kinds of rules we have proposed. It is consistent, therefore, to find that Adam in III was still not making *when* and *how* questions.

In another respect, Adam's performance in III seems not to have been consistent with the rules. He produced a large number of *why* and *why not* questions. But in all of the prior sixteen samples he had only once answered a *why* question in a way that could possibly be considered appropriate. In this case, then, we seem to have the construction of the question occurring before there is any evidence on the responsive side that the relevant grammatical organization exists.[5] We have also, incidentally, a demonstration that, in language development, comprehension need not always precede production.

When we look at Adam's *why* and *why not* questions in their actual discourse setting, we find something unexpected and interesting: they were often closely related to an immediately antecedent declarative from his mother. Table 4 contains a set of mother's declaratives and Adam's *why* responses. Some of the differences between members of these pairs are not peculiar to *why* questions. For instance, the telegraphic reduction process that eliminates *was*, *-ing*, and *a* from the adult sentence is quite general in child speech. Setting aside such nonspecific differences, Adam's questions are a simple function of his mother's antecedent declaratives: the word *why* is placed in front of the declarative. Table 4 also has a set of questions in *why not*, and these, too, have apparent bases in the mother's speech. Setting aside a few details, what happens is that the words *why not* are added in front of the mother's negative declaratives. In creating these questions, Adam seems to have been operating with a rule very like the preposing transformation.

Where did Adam's *why* and *why not* transformations come from? Once in a

---

[5] Adult *why* questions cannot be derived in a way directly parallel to other wh questions. We have not gone into the details because they do not alter the fact that Adam produced such questions when his responses gave no evidence that he could analyze them correctly with respect to either grammar or semantics.

TABLE 4   *WHY* AND *WHY NOT* QUESTIONS FROM ADAM 17–19 WITH APPARENT BASES

MOTHER'S DECLARATIVES	ADAM'S QUESTIONS
Why	
He was playing a little tune	Why he play little tune?
see a seal	Why you see seal?
You bent that game	Why me bent that game?
Well, because she wanted to	Why she want to?
I think it's resting now	Why it's resting now?
Why Not	
I guess I'm not looking in the right place	Why not you looking right place?
Because you weren't careful	Why not me careful?
I don't see any	Why not you see any?
You can't dance	Why not me can't dance?
You're going to have to buy another one and give it to Ursula because you're breaking that one	Why not me break that one?

long while, his mother produced a *why* question as a direct follow-up of a declarative and repeated in her *why* question the proposition expressed in the declarative. Probably Adam was attempting to imitate this performance, but his imitation did not come out right. Suppose the antecedent declarative were "He can't dance." Mother would follow this with "Why can't he dance?" Adam's version, on the other hand, would be "Why he can't dance?" Mother not only preposed *why*, she also transposed the subject and auxiliary in the manner of the adult grammar. Adam only preposed. Probably he copied according to his present understanding—as children also do when they pretend to drive a car or read a newspaper. Perhaps his imitation took the form it did because that form was close to the general operation that Adam was using with his other wh questions.

So we do have some evidence that the knowledge represented by transformation rules in the derivation of wh questions was learned by the children. They did not simply start to produce well-formed questions at a given point in time. All three children first produced a simpler form that would result from the application of just one of the two transformations required. And Adam—always the one to make interesting errors—also created *why* questions in circumstances that suggest the application of the same single transformation to declarative bases supplied by his mother.

THE ROLE OF TRAINING VARIABLES

Whatever the processes by which children acquire grammar, their primary data come from the speech they hear. Part of our work has consisted of attempts to isolate antecedents in the child's linguistic environment which may affect the rate or quality of the child's development. By antecedents we do not mean global variables like social class, but specific features of parental speech and parent-child interaction.

We have learned something about the effects of two aspects of variation in the speech to which a child is exposed: variation in the frequency with which particular constructions are produced or "modeled," and variation in the frequency with which particular reactions are made to a child's utterances. The reactions we have studied are expansions, occasional forms of wh questions, and expressions of approval and disapproval.

The work has progressed through three phases: first, discovery of relations between parental speech and rate of language development in our three subjects; second, a manipulative experiment with different subjects to test a hypothesis derived from those observations; and third, more detailed analyses of relations within our longitudinal data.

Preliminary Observation and an Experiment

When we began work several years ago, one of the first things we noticed was the frequency with which parents responded to the young child's telegraphic utterance[6] by echoing what the child said and filling in the missing functors. If the child said *Eve lunch* or *Throw Daddy*, the parent often responded with the nearest complete sentence appropriate in the particular situation—*Eve is having lunch* or *Throw it to Daddy*. Brown and Bellugi (1964) called such responses expansions, and suggested that they might provide optimal data for the acquisition of grammar. It was not their intention to suggest that the child learned grammar by storing the expanded versions of his telegraphic utterances, since he could not in this way learn more than the finite set of sentences he had at some time attempted to produce. Brown and Bellugi recognized that expansions were only data, and that grammatical knowledge was a system of general rules somehow derived from data. They argued, however, that the data provided by expansions were maximally relevant and seemed to be delivered with ideal timing.

At the same time, we have always realized that the relevance and timing of particular forms of interaction may have no importance for the acquisition of grammar. It is quite possible that the adult need do nothing but "model" the language—that is, provide samples of well-formed speech. When evidence is limited to natural observations, it is not possible to separate the effect of expansions from the effect of the amount of well-formed speech that the child hears. The mothers of Adam and Eve responded to the speech of their children with expansions about 30 per cent of the time. Sarah's overall language development was slower, and her mother expanded fewer of Sarah's utterances. But Sarah's

---

[6] We have not in this paper discussed the telegraphic aspect of the child's early sentences, since that was a major topic of such earlier papers as Brown and Fraser (1963) and Brown and Bellugi (1964). In I, II, and III, however, the speech of the three children was extremely telegraphic, as the data on page 296 indicate.

mother also talked less to her child in general. In our samples of three parents, expansion rate and general volubility varied together, and their effects on language acquisition could not be teased apart.

A manipulative experiment was designed to separate these two aspects of the child's language environment and to compare their effects (Cazden, 1965). The subjects were twelve Negro children, aged twenty-eight to thirty-eight months. They were all attending a private day-care center in Boston, where thirty children under three and a half years were cared for by one adult. Four matched trios were formed on the basis of the child's chronological age, talkativeness, and initial level of language development as judged by his mean length of utterance during an orientation period. Within each trio the children were randomly assigned to one of three treatment groups: expansion, modeling, or control.

The expansion group received forty minutes per day of intensive and deliberate expansions. The modeling group received exposure to an equal number of well-formed sentences that were not expansions. One of two tutors trained for this research talked with each child in these two groups in an individual play session every school day for three months. The sessions were held in two small rooms normally used only for naps; both were equipped with toys and books selected to stimulate conversation. The play sessions were monitored at regular intervals during the three-month period to ensure the separation of the critical interaction variables. Children in the control group received no treatment, but they were brought into the treatment rooms every few days so that they stayed familiar with the materials and the tutors.

Tape recordings were made of each child's speech at the beginning, middle, and end of the three-month period. The tapes were transcribed by a secretary who was trained by a linguist on our staff and who was ignorant of the treatment assignment of the children. The transcriptions were then coded according to strict rules. The dependent variables were six measures of language development: one was a test of the child's ability to repeat sentences, and five measured aspects of the child's spontaneous speech—mean length of utterance in morphemes, noun phrase index, verb complexity, copula index, and type-of-sentence index (the last four indexes were devised for this research).

Two statistical analyses were used to test the hypothesis that expansions would be the most effective treatment. First, the six dependent variables were considered separately. A two-way analysis of variance (treatment x tutor) was computed for the post-test scores on each measure separately, with the pretest scores on that same measure as a covariance control. Then, in order to compare the children on their overall growth on the six measures considered together, growth was operationally defined as the sum of the child's six gain score ranks, and Friedman's nonparametric two-way analysis of variance was used to test the significance of group differences. In neither analysis was there any evidence that expansions aid the acquisition of grammar. Contrary to our hypothesis, modeling was the most effective treatment.

Before speculating on possible explanations for these results, we need to examine what happens when forms of interaction which naturally co-occur are experimentally separated. Originally, we assumed that modeling without expansion had no positive features of its own, but this turns out not to be the case. If a child says *Dog bark* when a dog is indeed barking, the expanding adult says *Yes, the dog is barking*. The non-expanding adult who desires to maintain a reasonable discourse sequence—as our tutors did—has to contribute a related idea, such as, *Yes, he's mad at the kitty* or *Yes, but he won't bite*. Thus, a treatment which focuses on grammatical structures confines the adult to expanded echoes of the child and limits the ideas to the child's presumed meaning, whereas a treatment that focuses on the idea extends that idea beyond the presumed meaning of the child and introduces more varied words and grammatical elements to express those related ideas. In natural conversation, parents often provide both grammatical expansions and semantic extensions. Our tutors were asked not to do this, in order to keep the distinctions between the experimental treatments as sharp as possible.

Three reasons can be suggested for the results. Cazden originally proposed that richness of verbal stimulation might be more important than the grammatical contingency of the adult response. If we consider the learning of syntactic rules to be akin to concept formation, then learning may be aided by variation in non-criterial attributes—for instance, the particular noun stem in the case of inflection for plurality. If the process of first language learning is akin to construction of scientific theory, in which hypotheses are tested against available data, then a meager set of data may be disadvantageous. We have seen that bias in the mother-to-child sampling of the possibilities of English grammar caused Adam to make the segmentation error revealed in such a sentence as *It's fell*.

Miller and McNeill (1969) suggest an alternative explanation. When an adult attempts to expand a child's telegraphic utterances far more often than parents spontaneously do, some of the expansions probably misinterpret the child's intended meaning. Instead of facilitating the acquisition of grammar, such erroneous expansions may mislead the child and interfere with his learning.

Still a third explanation is possible, separately or in conjunction with either of the previous two. Artificial elevation of the expansion rate may depress attentional processes in the child. We know from many current studies of child development that stimuli of a certain degree of novelty—not too familiar and not too strange—command the greatest attention. The acquisition of language should be facilitated by those environmental events that enhance the child's attention to the adult's utterance and to relevant features of the verbal and non-verbal context in which it is spoken. In these particular experimental treatments, a greater degree of novelty may have been attained in the modeling treatments. We do not consider this experiment conclusive; all we can say is that the benefits of expansions remain unproved.

Training Variables in the Longitudinal Data

In the last two years we have gone back to the longitudinal data on Adam, Eve, and Sarah to look more carefully for evidence of the effects of parental speech. In selecting dependent variables, we have learned to reject measures of the child's performance in favor of better indicators of the child's grammatical knowledge. We have substantive findings on the independent variables of expansions and modeling, occasional questions, and expressions of approval and disapproval.

Grammatical Knowledge versus Performance. In certain facts about construction frequency there lies a major trap for the student of child speech who is interested in the development of knowledge of grammar: the first fact is that in mother-to-child speech the various constructions that English grammar permits are of grossly unequal frequency; the second is that the frequencies are astonishingly stable across the three mothers in our study; and the third is that frequencies in child speech, within the limits of the child's competence, tend to match adult frequencies. We have examined frequencies on many levels, from major types of sentence all the way down to the several allomorphs of *be*, and the story is always the same: rank order correlations among the mothers and between each mother and her child ranging from .65 to .90.

Some of the stable inequalities one might have guessed: active affirmative, declarative sentences are much more common than negatives, yes-no interrogatives, or wh interrogatives, and well-formed passives are almost nonexistent. Others are easy to understand but are not likely to have occurred to anyone who has not counted: the impersonal pronouns *it*, *this*, and *that* as sentence subjects almost always have their allomorph of *be* (*is*) as verb, whereas the personal pronouns *I*, *you*, *he*, and so forth as subjects have a main verb much more often than an allomorph of *be*; *where* questions are very much more frequent than *when* or *how* or *why* questions; catenative semi-auxiliaries like *wanna* and *gonna* are much more frequent than the modal auxiliaries *will* or *can*, and *may* and *must* are seldom heard; the progressive inflection -*ing* is much more frequent than the regular past -*ed*, and irregular pasts (e.g., *ran*, *saw*, *did*) are more frequent than regular pasts; and so on. The important general fact is that there seems to be something like a standard frequency profile for mother-to-child English, a profile that children match within their competence at any given time, and in this profile great inequalities exist even among very simple and familiar constructions.

Consider two examples in detail: major sentence types and expressions of possession. If we set an arbitrary frequency in child speech as a criterion of emergence—for example, the occurrence of three instances of a given type of sentence in each of three consecutive samples of seven hundred utterances—we find a high rank order correlation between parental frequencies and order of emergence in the child for twenty-four types of sentence—affirmative, declaratives, negatives, yes-no interrogatives, and wh interrogatives using, respectively, lexical verbs or *have* or *be* or *will* or *can* or *may*. Lexical and *be*-verbs in declarative sentences are the most common in all three mothers and appear first in the speech of all three children. But suppose we entertain the extreme hypothesis that all twenty-four verbs enter the child's competence simultaneously. Because the probability that a given construction will attain an arbitrary criterion varies with its standard frequency in mother-to-child English, and because these frequencies are grossly unequal, lexical and *be*-verbs would appear first on a strict basis. The student of child speech might then conclude that the hypothesis of simultaneous development was false when it could indeed still be true. Highly stable orders of construction emergence, in terms of an arbitrary frequency criterion, are not inconsistent with the possibility that the children in question know how to form all the constructions from the start but produce them with unequal frequency.

The same misleading performance match appears when we relate individual differences in construction frequencies among the children to differences in their mother's speech. For instance, one of the first individual differences we noted was Eve's tendency to use N + N constructions far more often than Adam or Sarah did. At I, the frequencies of N + N in 700 utterances were: Eve, 66; Adam, 40; Sarah, 10, of which 8 were imitations. In looking for an explanation, we thought it possible that the speech of the three mothers might differ in the frequency with which sentences were spoken from which N + N constructions might be telegraphically derived. The best match to the rank order of the children was the particular subset of parental N + N constructions that express possession, such as *Daddy's chair*. In the first 1,253 utterances of each mother, these frequencies were: Eve's mother, 31; Adam's mother, 24; Sarah's mother, only 6. This is an extremely interesting relation. One can hypothesize that territoriality and property rights are more important in homes where father is a graduate student, and that this is related to the child's tendency to use the N + N construction. But it is not sufficient evidence that greater frequency in parent speech produces earlier learning in the child. It is the antecedents of grammatical *knowledge* we are seeking, not influences on performance.

There are various ways out of the trap, all involving data that are better indexes of knowledge or competence than is an arbitary frequency of production. One can consider child frequencies against a background of known stable adult frequencies and so set frequency criteria that are not entirely arbitrary; one can consider frequencies of forms in contexts that make them obligatory; one can consider the pattern of omissions in the total distributional range of a form; one can consider the adequacy of the child's responses to adult questions and assertions; and above all, one can use the child's analogical errors of commission. In analyses of the relation of child speech to parental speech, the frequency of forms in contexts that make them obligatory has proved an especially useful measure. Each of these contexts in the child's speech can be considered a learning trial, and we can compute the proportion of times in which the child performs appropriately as that proportion changes over time.

**TABLE 5   EVE'S PERFORMANCE IN SUPPLYING VARIOUS PREPOSITIONS
IN SAMPLES 7–12 COMPARED WITH EVE'S MOTHER'S MODELING
FREQUENCIES AND EXPANSIONS IN SAMPLES 1–6**

Preposition	Mother's Modeling Frequencies 1–6	Mother's Proportion of Expansions 1–6	Proportion Correct in Eve 7–12
On	157	.57 (25/44)	.90 (82/92)
In	142	.61 (20/33)	.92 (147/159)
With	54	.64 (7/11)	.67 (29/43)
Of	33	.50 (1/2)	.70 (14/20)
For	32	.40 (2/5)	.69 (11/16)
To	31	.00 (0/3)	.78 (7/9)

Further Evidence on Expansions and Modeling.   Because we considered the manipulative experiment inconclusive, we have probed further into the effect of expansions and modeling on the growth of specific aspects of grammatical knowledge in our three subjects. We have charted the emergence of prepositions in Eve's speech and of appropriate answers to four kinds of wh questions and five noun and verb inflections in all three children.

Table 5 presents the data for the emergence of Eve's prepositions. Two findings are of interest: First, for any given preposition, both the frequency with which it is modeled and the frequency (but not proportion) of expansions are strongly related to the point at which that preposition is regularly supplied by the child in all the phrases requiring it. In Samples 1–6, Eve's mother uses *in* and *on* approximately three times as often as she uses *with*, *of*, *for*, or *to*. In Samples 7–12, Eve supplies *in* and *on* correctly at least 90 per cent of the time, and the proportion correct for each of the other four prepositions is between .67 and .77.

Second, there is no relation at all between modeling frequency of particular phrases—*in there* versus *in the wastebasket*—and the point at which the child produces that phrase with the preposition in place. A given preposition appears in all the phrases requiring it at about the same time, and it does not matter whether the particular phrase has been often modeled by the mother or not. This is a good example of how parental speech aids the induction of general rules but does not provide models for imitation as such.

With wh questions, we can determine what proportion of a given type elicits semantically and grammatically appropriate answers from the child. Four wh-adverbial questions are rather well matched in grammatical (though probably not in semantic) complexity, but they differ greatly in parental frequency. For all three mothers at II, the order of frequency is locatives first (about three fourths of the total), then causal, manner, and time—in other words, *where*, *why*, *how*, and *when*. This rank order matches the rank order of proportion of appropriate responses from the children at V except for questions about time, for which the data are too few to be reliable. Pooled data for the three mothers and children are presented in the accompanying tabulation.

	Frequency of Mother's Questions	Proportion of Children's Appropriate Responses
Locative	228	.64 (29/45)
Causal	29	.40 (14/35)
Manner	18	.11 (1/9)
Time	7	.50 (1/2)

Before turning to the emergence of inflections, another comment on method is in order. For relating child behavior to parental behavior in a sample of more than one child, two approaches are possible. The child's language can be related to antecedents in his parent's speech, and this relation then compared across the dyads; no direct comparison of the children is made. The preceding analyses of twenty-four verb forms, prepositions, and answers to wh questions were of this type. Alternatively, differences in the language of the children can be related to differences in the language of their parents. The preceding analysis of N + N constructions was of this type. Here, direct comparison of the children is required, and the experimenter faces the question of a metric for that comparison. We have analyzed the emergence of inflections in both ways.

The five regular inflections which emerge betweeen I and V are the plural and possessive inflections on the noun and the present progressive, regular past, and present indicative inflections on the verb. For this analysis we used as a criterion of emergence the first sample of three, such that, in all three, the child supplies the inflection in at least 90 per cent of the contexts in which they are clearly required. The charting of this aspect of development is a long story in itself and will be reported in detail elsewhere. We shall describe here only the data for the correlations between the sequence of emergence and three features of the child's linguistic environment: the proportion of times in which his omitted inflections are expanded by the parent during the entire period I–V, the absolute frequency of those expansions, and the frequency with which the inflections are modeled in four examples of seven hundred parental utterances which immediately precede Levels II, III, IV, and V of the children's speech.

First, we computed rank-order correlations for each child separately. For all three children, order of emergence within the child's language system is more strongly related to the frequency with which the inflection is modeled by the parent than it is to the proportion or frequency of expansions. The only statistically significant positive correlation is with frequency of modeling for Sarah, $\rho = .90$ ($p < .05$).

We have also looked for relations between differences among the children and differences among their parents. It is here that a metric for comparing the children is required. In the above analysis of N + N constructions, the three children were compared at II; the metric, therefore, was mean length of utterance. A more conventional metric is age. We have analyzed individual differences in the order of emergence of inflections on both bases of comparison—the contrast in outcomes is itself informative.

When we compare the children on the basis of age, the order of development is what one would expect from the figure on page 296: Eve way out in front, Adam second, and Sarah third. But when we ignore age and compare the children on the basis of mean length, the rank order of the children changes sharply. At II, when all three children have a mean length of 2.25 morphemes, only Sarah has reached the 90 per cent criterion on any inflection (plurality). By IV, when mean length has increased to 3.50 morphemes, she has reached criterion on five inflections, Eve has on four, and Adam on two. Data tabulated independently for the percentage of missing functors (everything except nouns, verbs, adjectives, and adverbs) at II and V yield the same relation: for Eve, 81 per cent of the functors were missing at II and 43 per cent at V; for Adam, 83 per cent at II, 20 per cent at V; and for Sarah, 74 per cent at II, 15 per cent at V.

Looked at in this way, the relative position of Eve and Sarah is reversed. At any given mean length value for utterances, Sarah is handling inflections and functors in general more successfully than Eve. Conversely, since Eve's speech contains proportionately more content words than Sarah's, her utterances are more informative. Eve has undoubtedly caught up in the provision of functors by the time she reached Sarah's age, probably well before. The point is that Sarah is less behind in the provision of obligatory functors than in what she is trying to say.

Table 6 shows the relation between order of emergence of the five inflections on these two bases of comparison (age and mean length) and proportion and frequency of expansions and frequency of modeling in parent speech.

As one would expect from the previous discussion of mother-child communication patterns, the difference in modeling frequency among the parents is small. But the difference in proportion and frequency of expansions is considerable: Sarah's telegraphic utterances omitting inflections are followed much less frequently by a parent utterance including the appropriate inflection than are Adam's and Eve's. This we expected from our observation of differential expansion rates at the beginning of our work. What is surprising is the negative relation between expansion rate and order of emergence in terms of mean length

TABLE 6   EMERGENCE OF INFLECTIONS AND TWO FEATURES OF PARENTAL SPEECH

CHILD'S SPEECH	EVE	ADAM	SARAH
Inflections			
Order of emergence,[a] by age	5	12.5	12.5
Order of emergence,[a] by mean length	11	12	7
Proportion of parental expansions	.45	.51	.29
	(191/427)	(348/679)	(86/294)
Frequency of parental models	499	576	471

[a] Order of emergence is given in summed ranks which range from 5 to 15—first to last of the three children on the five inflections combined.

of utterance. Sarah receives the lowest density of expansions, yet her language system is relatively the most advanced in the provision of inflections. It is hard to reconcile this finding with our original hypothesis that expansions should provide the most usable information for the acquisition of all types of functors.

Expressions of Approval and Disapproval. It might be supposed that syntactically correct utterances come to prevail over those that are incorrect through the operation of positive reinforcement and punishment on the part of adults. Because events subsequent to a child's speech are infinitely various, one can never be sure that there is no event which functions as a reinforcer or punishment. In practice, however, we know that certain events such as signs of approval or disapproval are likely to function in this way. The proposition "Syntactically correct utterances come to prevail over syntactically incorrect utterances through the selective administration of signs of approval and disapproval" is a testable one.

The proposition cannot be true for the natural case of parents and children at home unless parental approval and disapproval are in fact appropriately contingent on syntactical correctness. If the reactions *are* appropriately contingent, then they may or may not have the effects proposed. For this analysis, we worked with samples II and V. The general plan was to contrast the syntactic correctness of the population of utterances followed by a sign of approval— *that's right, very good*, or just *yes*—with the population of utterances followed by a sign of disapproval—*that's wrong* or *no*. The results are simply stated: there is not a shred of evidence that approval and disapproval are contingent on syntactic correctness.

What circumstances did govern approval and disapproval directed at child utterances by parents? Gross errors of word choice were sometimes corrected, as when Eve said *What the guy idea*. Once in a while an error of pronunciation was noticed and corrected. Most commonly, however, the grounds on which an utterance was approved or disapproved in Levels I–V were not strictly linguistic at all. When Eve expressed the opinion that her mother was a girl by saying *He a girl*, her mother answered *That's right*. The child's utterance was ungrammatical, but her mother did not respond to that fact; instead, she responded to the truth of the proposition the child intended to express. In general, the parents fitted propositions to the child's utterances, however incomplete or distorted the utterances, and then approved or not according to the correspondence between proposition and reality. Thus, *Her curl my hair* was approved because the mother was, in fact, curling Eve's hair. However, Sarah's grammatically impeccable *There's the animal farmhouse* was disapproved because the building was a lighthouse, and Adam's *Walt Disney comes on on Tuesday* was disapproved because Walt Disney came on on some other day. It seems, then, to be truth value rather than syntactic well-formedness that chiefly governs explicit verbal reinforcement by parents—which renders mildly paradoxical the fact that the usual product of such a training schedule is an adult whose speech is highly grammatical but not notably truthful.

Interaction Routines with Occasional Questions. In describing the systematic relations that underlie the grammar of wh questions, we introduced in

Table 2 the forms called occasional questions because we believe they are a great help in making those relations clear in explicit form to adults. We naturally wonder, therefore, whether the occasional questions also help make the relations clear in implicit form to children. The mothers of Adam, Eve, and Sarah produced such questions in two circumstances, which may be represented as follows: First, *say constituent again*—(a) Child, "I want milk," Mother, "You want what?" Child, "Milk." or (b) Child, "Put milk in glass." Mother, "Put milk where?" Child, "In glass." Second, *constituent prompt*—(a) Mother, "What do you want?" Child, no answer. Mother, "You want what?" or (b) Mother, "Where will I put it?" Child, no answer. Mother, "I will put it where?"

The say-constituent-again interaction occurred when mother found a part of a child's utterance unintelligible. She then repeated what she had understood and replaced the constituent which was the locus of unintelligibility with the right kind of wh word. Since the wh word appeared in the sentence position of a constituent, the result was an occasional question. The occasion was unintelligibility in a constituent, and the child's response was repetition of the constituent displaced. The mother's question is essentially a request to say the constituent again and that is the name we have given to this kind of interaction. What should such exchanges be able to teach the child? Perhaps, the membership of each type of sentence constituent—members of NP, for example, are just those terms, of whatever complexity, that can be replaced by *what*.

The constituent-prompt interaction was initiated by the mother. She asked a question in the normal form—"What do you want?"—and received no answer. She then reformulated the question as "You want what?" which is, incidentally, an occasional question. She was, in effect, turning the question into a sentence completion item, and since the mothers usually resorted to this prompting form when the normal form had failed, they must have felt that it was easier to process. In our materials, the occasional form was, in fact, more likely to elicit an appropriate answer than was the normal form. What should exchanges of this type be able to teach the child? Fundamentally, the equivalence of particular normal and occasional questions—equivalents are questions that replace one another when no answer is forthcoming.

A large amount of structural information is revealed in these two interactions with unusual clarity because of the use of the occasional question. It must be possible to discover the systematic relations that underlie the grammar of wh questions without the benefit of the occasional question, since many children who learn English do not have attentive mothers around to echo and prompt them. However, it may be easier to discover the relations if the middle term is often heard. It may be accidental, but in our records, the occasional form was used much more frequently by the mothers of the two children whose grammatical understanding developed more rapidly, Adam and Eve: in samples of seven thousand parental utterances, Adam's mother produced occasional questions at the rate of 1 in 57 utterances; Eve's mother at the rate of 1 in 80; Sarah's mother at the rate of only 1 in 146.

Whether or not the occasional questions prove to be helpful for the discovery of wh grammar, it seems likely that the many kinds of grammatical exchange in discourse will prove to be the richest data available to the child in his search for a grammar. It may be as difficult to derive a grammar from hearing unconnected static sentences as it would be to derive the invariance of quantity and number from simply looking at liquids in containers and objects in space. The changes produced by pouring back and forth and by gathering together and spreading apart are the data that most strongly suggest the conservation of quantity and number. We suspect that the changes sentences undergo as they shuttle between persons in conversation are, similarly, the data that most clearly expose the underlying structure of language.

We have examined the effect on the child's development of grammatical knowledge of two aspects of the speech he hears: variation in the frequency with which particular constructions are modeled and variation in the frequency of particular parental responses—expansions, expressions of approval and disapproval, and occasional questions. There is a small amount of evidence that modeling frequency does affect the acquisition of knowledge. With regard to the parental responses of expansion and approval-disapproval, the present evidence is that neither has any effect on the development of grammatical knowledge. The role of occasional questions is still unknown. Our own interest in isolated training variables is giving way to an interest in the structural information latent in various forms of linguistic interaction. Perhaps we shall someday find that linguistic environments at home do vary significantly in structural richness but that any single form of response is an unreliable index of this variation, even as age of weaning has proved an unreliable index of something more important—general child-rearing attitudes.

REFERENCES

Brown, R., The development of wh questions in child speech, *Journal of Verbal Learning and Verbal Behavior*, 1968, **7**, 279–290.
———, and Ursula Bellugi, Three processes in the child's acquisition of syntax, *Harvard Educational Review*, 1964, **34**, 133–151.
Brown, R., and C. Fraser, The acquisition of syntax. In C. N. Cofer and Barbara S. Musgrave, eds. *Verbal Behavior and Learning*. New York: McGraw-Hill, 1963, pp. 158–197.
Cazden, Courtney B., Environmental assistance to the child's acquisition of grammar. Ph.D. thesis, Harvard Univer., 1965.
Chomsky, N., *Syntactic Structures*. The Hague: Mouton, 1957.
Chomsky, N., *Aspects of the Theory of Syntax*. Cambridge, Mass.: M.I.T. Press, 1965.
Fodor, J. A., How to learn to talk: Some simple ways. In F. Smith and G. A. Miller, eds., *The Genesis of Language*, pp. 105–122. Cambridge, Mass.: M.I.T. Press, 1966.

Gleason, H. A., *An Introduction to Descriptive Linguistics*, rev. ed. New York: Holt, 1961.

Harris, Z. S., Morpheme alternates in linguistic analysis, *Language*, 1942, **18**, 169–180.

Harris, Z. S., *Methods in Structural Linguistics*. Chicago: University of Chicago Press, 1951.

Heffner, R. M. S., *General Phonetics*. Madison: University of Wisconsin Press, 1949.

Hockett, C. F., Problems of morphemic analysis, *Language*, 1947, **23**, 321–43.

Katz, J. J., and P. M. Postal, *An Integrated Theory of Linguistic Descriptions*. Cambridge, Mass.: M.I.T. Press, 1964.

Klima, E. S., Negation in English. In J. A. Fodor and J. J. Katz, eds., *The Structure of Language: Readings in the Philosophy of Language*, pp. 246–323. Englewood Cliffs, N.J.: Prentice-Hall, 1964.

McNeill, D., Developmental psycholinguistics. In F. Smith and G. A. Miller, eds., *The Genesis of Language*, pp. 15–84. Cambridge, Mass.: M.I.T. Press, 1966.

Miller, G. A., and D. McNeill. Psycholinguistics. In G. Lindzey and E. Arsonson, eds. *Handbook of Social Psychology*. Reading, Mass.: Addison-Wesley, 1969.

Nida, E. S., The identification of morphemes, *Language*, 1948, **24**, 414–441.

Slobin, D. I., The acquisition of Russian as a native language, in F. Smith and G. A. Miller, eds., *The Genesis of Language*, pp. 129–148. Cambridge, Mass.: M.I.T. Press, 1966.

Spitz, R. A., *No and Yes: On the Genesis of Human Communication*. New York: International Universities Press, 1957.

Syntactic Regularities in the Speech of Children[1]
—— Edward S. Klima and Ursula Bellugi

Klima and Bellugi begin with adult transformational rules (Klima, 1964), defining the end point toward which child grammar will develop. This paper, based in large part on Bellugi's dissertation (1967), explores the development of negatives and questions in depth. Wick Miller (below) reports similar findings from the Berkeley study. These studies describe the surface forms

Reprinted from J. Lyons and R. J. Wales, ed., *Psycholinguistics papers* (Edinburgh: Edinburgh University Press, 1966); copyright © 1966 by Edinburgh University Press. Reprinted with revision by permission of the authors and Aldine-Atherton, Inc.

[1] This work was supported in part by the Joint Services Electronics Project under contract BA 36-039-AMC-03200 (E), in part by the National Science Foundation Grant GP-2495, the National Institute of Health Grant MH 0473-05, the National Aeronautics and Space Administration Grant NSO-496, the U.S. Air Force ESD contract AF 19(628-2487), and Public Health Service Research Grant MH7088-04 from the National Institute of Health.

of negative and interrogative utterances and the syntactic transformations underlying those forms. More recently, Lois Bloom (below, and 1970) has raised the issue of the various meanings of negation in English child speech, and David and Nobuko McNeill (below) have done the same for Japanese, arriving at similar descriptions of the semantic development of negation in the two languages.

Klima and Bellugi devote attention to comprehension as well as production, making use of children's response to adult questions. This technique has been developed in detail by Susan Ervin-Tripp (1970a), yielding valuable insights into the strategies used by children in formulating answers to questions.

The following study, like that of Miller, reveals the development of general linguistic operations applicable across a great variety of sentence types (for example, auxiliary attachment, preposing, transposing). In another study, Bellugi (1968) has suggested that there are mechanical limits ("sentence programming span") to the number of such operations which a child can perform on a single sentence at given stages of development. For example, at the stage in which Adam could *transpose* subject and auxiliary for yes-no questions and *prepose* wh-question words, he could not perform both operations on one sentence *(Can he ride in a truck?* but *What he can ride in?)* At a later stage, with an increase in sentence programming span, Adam was able to perform both operations on a single sentence, but failed to transpose when a third operation—negation—was involved *(Why can he go out?* but *Why he can't go out?)*. Bellugi demonstrated this phenomenon clearly in a sentence elicitation game she played with Adam, who was to ask questions of a puppet shaped like an old lady:

BELLUGI :   Adam, ask the Old Lady where she can find some toys.
ADAM   :   Old Lady, where can you find some toys?
BELLUGI :   Adam, ask the Old Lady why she can't run.
ADAM   :   Old Lady, why you can't run?

Bellugi concludes: "In his responses, all affirmatives were inverted, all negatives were not. The interpretation . . . fits with the notion of a limit on the permitted complexity at one stage" (1968, p. 40).

Roeper (below) raises similar questions in his studies of German acqusition. He finds that German children have much less difficulty with inversion than do English-speaking children, and proposes that a given rule may be mastered earlier if it occurs in a wide range of different grammatical contexts. Whereas English inverts subject and auxiliary only for questions, German uses subject-verb permutation in a number of different sentence types.
—D.I.S.

What we have set as our goal is the grammatical capacity of children—a part of their general linguistic competence. The question, of course, is how to arrive at this competence. The utterances produced—which might seem to be a direct access to competence—cannot give the total answer. There is really no way to determine which of the child's utterances are grammatically non-deviant in terms of his own grammar. And even if the grammatically nondeviant utterances could be reliably determined, they could only give hints as to the total grammatical capacity of the child, which includes not only what has been produced (or understood) but also what could be produced (or understood). The situation is the same as that involved in describing our own adult grammar if we limited ourselves to what had been uttered over some short period of time and faithfully gave equal weight to everything uttered, no matter how it actually came out. What is actually done, in analyzing the adult language, is to select. Sentences are selected which are felt intuitively to be most free of deviances, and then one goes beyond the mere corpus to develop a more structured theory that excludes sentences which are wrong grammatically (i.e., which present clear deviances) and that explains the status of the other cases. The range of difficulties that face the analyst in describing the language of children on the basis of their utterances should be illuminated by examining a sketch of grammatical structure in adult English.

Approaching the grammar of child language from the other direction answers certain of the problems—that is, from the point of view of the child's ability to understand sentences. Sentences the child understands describe the scope of his grammar more accurately than those he produces, just as with the adult. But if the child's "understanding" of adult sentences is examined, there is some evidence to suggest that the child comprehends sentences according to his existing grammar. Where comprehension involves syntactic characteristics not present in the child's utterances it seems that this does not represent a relatively rich grammar coupled with a much poorer production device, but rather a limited grammar coupled with a liberal perceptual device that sifts out or bypasses unfamiliar material. As an example, with children whose speech did not contain passives, we tested comprehension of the passive construction, using pairs of pictures. One picture showed a cat being chased by a dog, and another a dog being chased by a cat. When the children were asked to show *The cat is being chased by the dog*, a number of them pointed to the picture of the cat chasing the dog.[2] This suggests that these children may have been processing the passive sentences as if they were active sentences, i.e., in terms of usual *Subject-Verb-Object* relations, sifting out the unknown material, specifically the passive auxiliary and the agentive preposition. We plan to use as much information on comprehension of syntax as possible in investigating the grammar of children.

A striking characteristic of the language acquisition situation is the fact that the particular linguistic ability that develops in the individual child as he gradually masters his native language is grossly underdetermined by the utterances

---

[2] Colin Fraser, Ursula Bellugi, and Roger Brown, " Control of Grammar in Imitation, Comprehension, and Production," *Journal of Verbal Learning and Verbal Behavior*, **22** (1963). [Reprinted in this volume.]

he hears. Not only does he understand, produce, and recognize as perfectly normal countless sentences he has never heard, but he will recognize as deviant in some way or other countless utterances that he has heard produced during his linguistically formative years. The child will recognize as deviant all the various slips of the tongue, false starts, interrupted completions, and noises that are present in our everyday utterances. Given the external characteristics of language acquisition, the psycholinguist asks: How do any two children—to say nothing of those of a whole speech community—arrive at anywhere near the same language? How does a particular language—each time it is acquired by a child—keep from changing radically? Since language does not change radically in this situation, there must surely be some general principles at work, and it is the principles underlying language acquisition which we want eventually to illuminate.

But first, prior questions must be investigated. If one looks closely at the development of speech in children who have heard totally independent language environments during the early period of language acquisition, it may well be that each will follow an independent path in his grammatical growth and syntactic patterns. And if the limitations on what the child produces have little relationship to his grammatical capacity, one would not expect that a study of children's speech would reveal regularities in the order of appearance of structures across children. We propose to investigate the development of negative and interrogative structures in the speech of three children in order to examine some of these aspects of language development.

THE LANGUAGE ACQUISITION PROJECT

We have as data for this research a developmental study of three children whom we have called Adam, Eve, and Sarah in previous reports with Roger Brown and his associates. Tape recordings of mother-child interchanges were made regularly in the children's homes. Each child was followed by a different investigator. The families were totally unacquainted and independent of one another, and each child heard a different set of sentences as "input." The children were beginning to string words together in structured utterances when we began the study. One child was 18 months old, another 26 months, and the third was 27 months old; however, all three were at approximately the same stage of language development.

For each child, then, there are two to four sessions of the speech of the mother and child per month as data. These sessions were tape recorded and later transcribed together with a written record made at the time of the recording which includes some aspects of the situation which relate to the meaning of the interchange. In order to describe stages in development we picked two end points in terms of mean utterance length. The first period is from the first month of study for each child—i.e., the mean utterance length is about 1.75 morphemes; the last is from the month in which the mean utterance lengths approach 3.5

morphemes for each of the three children; and the second period is between the two (see Figure 1, p. 296).

Each period represents several thousand child utterances. From the total speech we isolated the negative statements and the questions for analysis, and have suggested outlines for a study of the development of these systems in the children's speech. We have used the children's utterances and evidence about the children's understanding of these constructions in the language of others, in attempting to consider the children's developing grammatical capacities.

I. NEGATION IN ENGLISH

To begin, let us touch on some of the linguistic facts about the terminal state toward which the children are progressing, that is, the syntax of English negatives and interrogatives. We shall consider *Neg* as a formant which combines with parts of the sentence to constitute negation in the sentence. Among the realizations of *Neg* are the negative particle *not* and its contracted form *n't* (e.g., *It isn't true*), and a small set of negative words including the negative pronouns *nobody* and *nothing* (*Nobody came*), the negative determiner *no* (e.g., *No students passed*), the negative adverbs *never* and *nowhere*. Although there are many complexities in the total picture of negation in adult English that do not occur at all in the early periods, the basic facts about negation in simple sentences are all relevant—in particular the form and position of the negative formant.

Negation and Auxiliary verbs. The negative particle *not* appears most simply in conjunction with the auxiliary verbs (*Aux*) in English and is generally contracted with them in speech. Consider first the modal auxiliaries (*M*) (*will, can, may, must, could, would, shall, should*, etc.) and notice that the negative particle is located after the first auxiliary verb of the sentence if there is one. Compare these sets of affirmative and negative sentences:

The man will finish today.	*The man won't finish today.*
The baby can sit up.	*The baby can't sit up.*
He will have been doing it.	*He won't have been doing it.*

In sentences in which *be* comes first in the verb phrase (whether as progressive (*be–PrP*) or passive (*be–PP*) auxiliary) or as main verb, the negative particle follows *be*, as it does *have* when the latter is auxiliary for the perfect (*have–PP*) and occurs first in the verb phrase and also, restrictedly, when *have* is the main verb:

They are coming here.	*They aren't coming here.*
Her face is red.	*Her face isn't red.*
I have done it.	*I haven't done it.*
I have time for that.	*I haven't any time for that.*

In each case, the contraction of the negative element with the auxiliary is optional. One can say either *They cannot go* or *They can't go*, although the latter seems more frequent in informal speech.

The negative element is not attached to other main verbs, nor does it stand in place of an auxiliary; thus we do not say *I wantn't it or *I not want it, but rather I don't want it.[3] The auxiliary verb do occurs in negative sentences with the particle not where the affirmative version of a sentence does not have an auxiliary verb, and not only carries the negative particle but also the tense marker (T). He made it is the affirmative sentence corresponding to He didn't make it. Thus auxiliary do is left unspoken in affirmative declaratives and imperatives—except under special conditions as in Do be quiet and He did so leave.

Negative imperative.   We analyze negative imperatives as having auxiliary do followed by the negative formant, then optionally you (or an indefinite anybody), then the imperative modal auxiliary (Imp) (which in certain circumstances is realized as will or can), and finally the main verb:

> Don't be late, will you!
> Don't you do that again.
> Don't anybody move.

Negation and Indefiniteness.   Special cases aside, sentences of standard English permit only one negative formant per main verb. The presence of such a negative formant provides an appropriate condition for the occurrence of one or more indefinites (Indef) (any, anybody, anything, anywhere, ever) as subject, objects, or other complement to the main verb in the same environments in which indeterminates (Indet) (some, somebody, something, somewhere, once) occur in the corresponding affirmative declaratives and imperatives. Compare the following sets:

You have some milk.	You haven't any milk.
Give me some more.	Don't give my any more.
I want something.	I don't want anything.
Somebody left something.	Nobody left anything.

We shall describe this negative coloring as the conversion of indeterminates into indefinites in the context of a negative formant. However, no indefinites may precede the form representing the final realization of the negative formant, whether this form is the negative particle not/n't or a negative word (e.g., nobody). Thus Nobody left anything is grammatical but not *Anybody left nothing. Note particularly in this respect the special form of active-passive pairs.

> Nobody saw anything new.
> Nothing new was seen by anybody.

and not *Anything new was seen by nobody which would be predicted by the identity, otherwise holding, between object of the active and subject of the passive, on the one hand, and subject of the active and agent of the passive, on the other. We capture this fact by assuming that the negative formant

---

[3] An asterisk preceding an utterance means that this is not a grammatical sentence of English.

combines with an indefinite (or the first of several indefinites) which is then realized as a negative word (*any* as *no*, *anybody* as *nobody*, etc.), obligatorily if the indefinite precedes the main verb and all its auxiliaries; otherwise, optionally. Compare the single possibility *Nobody saw him* with the alternates of its corresponding passive *He wasn't seen by anyone* and *He was seen by nobody*.

Negation not included in this study.   The sections described above cover the problems which arise in relation to negatives in the children's speech as far as we have considered it in this study. Symptomatic of sentence negation in adult English is the possible occurrence of an *either*-clause (*I didn't like it and he didn't either*); the negative appositive tag (*I don't like dogs, not even little ones*); and the question tag without *not* (*He's not going is he?*). None of these occur in the children's speech in these early stages. Affixal negation does not occur either (*unfortunately, impossible, unmade*), nor do inherently negative words like *doubt, reluctant*.

This discussion comprises part of what we mean by the negative system and the auxiliary system in adult English; that is, the occurrences and non-occurrences involving those parts of the grammar. We will try to capture the nature of these systems by a set of rules something like those on the following pages, although undoubtedly as more is learned about grammatical systems in general and about English in particular, the form of these rules will be different. We feel that in their present state they do at least capture the spirit of this part of the grammar in a way that is compatible with other aspects of the grammar of English. One can think of the rules as giving some verifiable substance to our claim that these occurrences and nonoccurrences fit together in some systematic way.

RULES FOR NEGATION IN ADULT ENGLISH

The verb phrase with its auxiliaries has at one level in its derivation the following possible forms:

$$[T - do]_{Aux_1} (Neg) \left[\begin{Bmatrix} Imp \\ M \end{Bmatrix} (have - PP)(be - PrP)(be - PP) \right]_{Aux_2}$$

$$\left[\begin{Bmatrix} V \\ be \\ have \end{Bmatrix} (NP) \cdots \right]_{VP}$$

or after contraction of *not* to *n't*:

$$[T - do\,'(Neg)]_{Aux_1}$$
etc.

This represents the underlying structure after certain transformations (the details of which are not important in this study) have already operated; for example, the positioning of the negative formant, the occurrence of the passive auxiliary.

Transformations:

I. Replacement of *do*:

$$T - do - (Neg) - \begin{Bmatrix} M \\ have \\ be \end{Bmatrix} \Rightarrow T - \begin{Bmatrix} M \\ have \\ be \end{Bmatrix} - (Neg) - \phi$$

II. Negative Coloring:

1. $X^1 - Indet - X^2 - Neg - X^3 \Rightarrow X^1 - Indef - X^2 - Neg - X^3$

2. $X^1 - Neg - X^2 - Indet - X^3 \Rightarrow X^1 - Neg - X^2 - Indef - X^3$

(if *Neg* is treated as occurring initially in the underlying string, then a simpler formulation is possible.)

III. Formation of Negative Words
   1. Obligatory

$$X^1 - Indef - X^2 - Neg - X^3 \Rightarrow X^1 - Neg + Indef - X^2 - \phi - X^3$$

   2. Optional

$$X^1 - Neg - X^2 - Indef - X^3 \Rightarrow X^1 - \phi - X^2 - Neg + Indef - X^3$$

IV. *Do* Deletion:

$$T - do - V \Rightarrow T - \phi - V$$

or, expanded to include imperatives as approximately:

$$T - do - (Imp) \begin{Bmatrix} V \\ be \\ have \end{Bmatrix} \Rightarrow T - \phi - (Imp) \begin{Bmatrix} V \\ be \\ have \end{Bmatrix}$$

NEGATION IN CHILDREN'S SPEECH

What it is that the child learns in becoming a mature speaker of the language is, of course, the whole system which we have tried to capture by the rules above, and certainly not those particular tentative rules. It should be understood that when we write rules for the child grammar it is just a rough attempt to give substance to our feeling about, and general observations demonstrating, the regularity in the syntax of children's speech.

We have intentionally allowed ourselves much freedom in the formulation of these rules. Even within this freedom we feel that at the very earliest stages perhaps we fitted the language unjustifiably to what we assume to be the underlying structure of adult language. These rules reflect but certainly do not describe completely the utterances produced by the child. Whenever possible we took into consideration comprehension of utterances; but comprehension, like speech, only reflects grammatical capacity. Our aim in both cases is to find basic regularities.

One of the ultimate objectives in describing such regularities is to discover—given the child's own linguistic abilities as they have developed at some particular stage and given the utterances that he hears—what system or possible systems the child will ascribe to the language. We are interested in the basis for particular constructions; notably those that characterize the language of all three children.

Not very much is known about how people understand a particular sentence or what goes into producing one; but something is known about the systematicity of adult language. It has seemed to us that the language of children has its own systematicity, and that the sentences of children are not just an imperfect copy of those of an adult.

Are there hazards in considering the grammar of a child's language from the point of view of his speech? Of course there are many. One possibility is that the limitations on what is produced have nothing at all to do with the grammar but have to do with factors of memory, immediate requirements of explicitness, and the like. However, if this were the case, one would not expect the order of appearance of certain structures, and in particular certain systematic "mistakes," to be regular across children. We want to emphasize here that we are not dealing with the expression of semantic concepts on the part of the child, or of basic grammatical notions like subject function and transitivity; rather we are concerned with the way he handles lower-level syntactic phenomena like position, permutability, and the like.

Period 1. The sentences we want to describe from Period 1 are taken from the protocols of all three children:

More . . . no.
No singing song.
No the sun shining.
No money.
No sit there.
No play that.
No fall!
No heavy.
No want stand head.
No Mom sharpen it.
No Fraser drink all tea.

Unless otherwise noted, the sentences included in this study represent large numbers of like utterances in the children's speech, and are not to be considered isolated examples but rather reflections of recurrent structures occurring in the children's spontaneous speech. Notice that there are no negatives within the utterances, nor are there auxiliary verbs. The element which signals negation is *no* or *not*, and this element either precedes or follows the rest of the utterance.

Let us refer to the elements *Mom sharpen it, more, the sun shining,* in the above sentences as the *Nucleus*. Notice incidentally that there seems to be limited structure to the nucleus. The sentences consist largely of nouns and verbs without indication of tense or number. Inflections, prepositions, articles, adjectives, adverbs, and auxiliary verbs rarely occur.

The negation system at Period 1 can be considered as follows:

$$\left[\begin{Bmatrix} no \\ not \end{Bmatrix} - Nucleus \right] \quad \text{or} \quad [Nucleus - no] \tag{1}$$

At this stage, there is no clear evidence that the child even understands the negative embedded in the auxiliary of adult speech, without at least some reinforcement. During this early period, the mothers often reinforce their negative statements as in *No, you can't have that,* to insure the children's comprehension of the negative impact of the sentence. What is interesting in the speech of the child at this stage is that he employs extremely limited means for negative sentences in his own speech, and the same system is repeated in all three subjects. In subsequent periods there may indeed be an initial sentence adverb *no*, but this initial element is not a sufficient or even necessary part of sentence negation.

The rule for negation that we have given serves many negative functions in the child's speech at Period 1.

> ADULT: Get in your high chair with your bib, and I'll give you your cheese.
> CHILD: No bibby.
> ADULT: Oh, you don't want your bibby?
>
> ADULT: Well, is the sun shining?
> CHILD: No the sun shining.
> ADULT: Oh, the sun's not shining?
>
> (An adult leans over to talk to the child. Child looks up and puts up a hand in warning.)
> CHILD: No fall!

Period 2.   Some of the sentences we want to describe, again from all three children, are as follows:

> *I can't catch you.*
> *I can't see you.*
> *We can't talk.*
> *You can't dance.*
> *I don't sit on Cromer coffee.*
> *I don't want it.*
> *I don't like him.*
> *I don't know his name.*
> *No . . . Rusty hat.*
> *Book say no.*
> *Touch the snow no.*
>
> *Don't leave me.*
> *Don't wait for me . . . come in.*
> *Don't wake me up . . . again.*

That not "O," that blue.
That no fish school.
That no Mommy.
There no squirrels.

He no bite you.
I no want envelope.
I no taste them.

A characteristic of child language is the residue of elements of previous systems, and the sentences produced might well be described as a coexistence of the rules at Period 1, and a new system. Let us begin with a basic structure something like

$$S \to NP - (Neg) - VP \tag{2}$$

where the formant *Neg* has as possible lexical representatives *can't, don't, not,* and occasionally *no.* The auxiliary verbs can be thought of as occurring in the speech of the children only when accompanied by a *Neg*, since it is a fact that the auxiliary verbs do not occur in questions or declarative utterances at this stage. They occur only in negative sentences, and in these limited forms. This first rule can be related to the shape of sentences by the following rules:

$$Neg \to \begin{Bmatrix} no \\ not \\ V^{neg} \end{Bmatrix} \tag{3}$$

$$V^{neg} \to \begin{Bmatrix} can't \\ don't \end{Bmatrix} \tag{4}$$

where the particular selection of the negative is determined by the Main Verb with *don't* and *can't* restricted to occurrence before instances of nonprogressive main verbs.

Two auxiliary verbs appear in the negative form, *don't* and *can't*. These are considered as lexical representations of V^{neg} since there are no occurrences of *I can do it, Can I have it?, He shouldn't have it, They aren't going,* etc., but only instances of the sort described above. The negative element is also found within the sentence, but not connected to an auxiliary verb, as in *He no bite you.*

There are a number of sentences with *no* or *not* followed by a predicate. There is a limited class of subjects in this set. The negative imperative has appeared in the speech of all three children, in the form *Don't leave me.* In the previous period the imperative form was presumably *No fall.* There is at this period an affirmative imperative as well, as in *Come here* and *Do It.* There are hardly any sentences with indefinite determiners or pronouns, but there are by now personal and impersonal pronouns, possessive pronouns, articles, and adjectives.

It is clear that the child understands the negative embedded in the auxiliary of the sentence by this period. For example:

MOTHER: Oh, we don't have any bread.
CHILD: We have buy some.

MOTHER: He doesn't have a ball,
CHILD: Why not he have ball?

There is also evidence that the child uses negatives to contradict a previous proposition either expressed or implied, as in

MOTHER: Did you play in the snow?
CHILD: No, play sunshine.

MOTHER: You told me to sit on it.
CHILD: No, you sit there.

Period 3.   A sample of the sentences to be described, again from all three children:

Paul can't have one.
I can't see it.
This can't stick.
We can't make another broom.

I didn't did it.
Because I don't want somebody to wake me up.

I don't want cover on it.
I don't . . . have some . . . too much.
You don't want some supper.
You didn't caught me.
You didn't eat supper with us.
I didn't see something.
Paul didn't laugh.
I didn't caught it.

I gave him some so he won't cry.
'Cause he won't talk.
Donna won't let go.

No, I don't have a book.
No, it isn't.
That was not me.
I am not a doctor.

This not ice cream.
This no good.
They not hot.
Paul not tired.
It's not cold.

I not crying.
That not turning.
He not taking the walls down.

Don't put the two wings on.
Don't kick my box.
Don't touch the fish.

I not hurt him.
I not see you anymore.
Ask me if I not made mistake.

In the speech of the children, the modal auxiliaries *do* and *be* now appear in declarative sentences and questions, as well as in negative sentences; so we can now begin with a basic structure like

$$S \rightarrow NP - Aux - VP \tag{5}$$

and suggest some such rules as follow:

$$Aux \rightarrow T - V^{aux} - (Neg) \tag{6}$$

$$V^{aux} \rightarrow \begin{Bmatrix} do \\ can \\ be \\ will \end{Bmatrix} \tag{7}$$

where *be* is restricted to predicate and progressive and is optional, *can* and *do* are restricted to nonprogressive main verbs.

Transformations:
 I. Optional *be* Deletion:

$$NP - be \rightarrow NP - \emptyset$$

II. *Do* Deletion:

$$do - V \rightarrow V$$

In the speech of the children at this period the negative auxiliary verbs are now no longer limited to *don't* and *can't*, and the auxiliary verbs now appear in declarative sentences and questions, so that the auxiliary verbs can be considered as separate from the negative element of the sentence.

Indeterminates now start appearing in the children's speech, in affirmative utterances as *I want some supper* or *I see something*. The children's negative sentences have the form *I don't want some supper* and *I didn't see something*. The negative versions are clearly not imitations of adult sentences, and indicate that the complex relationship of negative and indefinite has not yet been established. Examples of indefinite coloring are rare, and do not appear with any regularity until subsequent stages.

RULES FOR NEGATION IN CHILDREN'S SPEECH

Period 1

$$\left[\begin{Bmatrix} no \\ not \end{Bmatrix} - Nucleus \right]_S \quad \text{or} \quad [Nucleus - no]_S \tag{1}$$

Period 2

$$S \rightarrow NP - (Neg) - VP \tag{2}$$

$$Neg \rightarrow \begin{Bmatrix} no \\ not \\ V^{neg} \end{Bmatrix} \tag{3}$$

$$V^{neg} \rightarrow \begin{Bmatrix} can't \\ don't \end{Bmatrix} \tag{4}$$

where the particular selection of the negative is determined by the main verb with *don't* and *can't* restricted to occurrence before instances of nonprogressive main verbs.

Period 3

$$S \rightarrow NP - Aux - VP \tag{5}$$

$$Aux \rightarrow T - V^{aux} - (Neg) \tag{6}$$

$$V^{aux} \rightarrow \begin{Bmatrix} do \\ can \\ be \\ will \end{Bmatrix} \tag{7}$$

where *be* is restricted to predicate and progressive, *can* and *do* to nonprogressive main verbs.

Transformations:
 I. Optional *be* Deletion

$$NP - be \Rightarrow NP - \emptyset$$

 II. *Do* Deletion

$$do - V \Rightarrow V$$

II. INTERROGATIVES IN ENGLISH

For questions in adult English, we represent the interrogative nature of the sentence by the formant Q, with which may be associated (*a*) interrogative words (represented here by *Wh* + *Indet* in various functions, ultimately realized as *what, who, which, where, how, why*); or (*b*) the sentence as whole in the form of a *yes/no* question represented here by *Wh* preceding the major parts of the sentence, i.e., *Q-Wh-NP-Aux-VP*. In direct *yes/no* questions, *Wh* has no lexical realization, whereas in the corresponding indirect questions it is realized as *whether*. Compare *Will John leave?* with *They wonder whether John will leave*. In adult English, either the whole sentence may be questioned (a *yes/no* question) or one or more parts may be questioned (an interrogative word question).

If Q and either an interrogative word ($Wh + Indet$) or the Wh of yes/no questions precede the *entire* subject noun phrase of the sentence, then that noun phrase and the first auxiliary verb are inverted. If the interrogative word is part of the subject, then there is no inversion. Thus *What will that person make?* and *Will that person make something?* but no inversion in *Which person will make something?* Auxiliary *do* is unspoken, unless some element (e.g., the subject because of inversion) intervenes between *do* and the main verb. (Recall that in negation, the negative particle also had the effect of preserving the otherwise unspoken auxiliary *do*.)

RULES FOR QUESTIONS IN ADULT ENGLISH

$$S \rightarrow Q - Wh - NP - Aux - VP$$
$$VP \rightarrow (\text{as on bottom p. 339]})$$

$$NP \rightarrow \begin{cases} \ldots \\ Wh + Indet \text{ (provided that } Q, \text{ but not } Q - Wh, \text{ introduces } S) \end{cases}$$

Transformations:

I. Replacement of *do*:

$$T - do - (Neg) \begin{Bmatrix} M \\ have \\ be \end{Bmatrix} \Rightarrow T \begin{Bmatrix} M \\ have \\ be \end{Bmatrix} (Neg) \, \emptyset$$

II. Interrogative Preposing (optional):

$$Q - X^1 - Wh + Indet - X^2 \Rightarrow Q - Wh + Indet - X^1 - X^2$$

III. Interrogative Inversion:

$$Q - Wh \, (+ Indet) - NP - Aux_1 - X \Rightarrow Q - Wh \, (+ Indet) - Aux_1 - NP - X$$

IV. *Do* Deletion:

$$T - do - V \Rightarrow T - \phi - V$$

QUESTIONS IN CHILDREN'S SPEECH

Period 1. The questions to consider, from all three children, are

Fraser water?
Mommy eggnog?
See hole?
I ride train?
Have some?
Sit chair?
No ear?
Ball go?

Who that?
Why?
What(s) that?
What doing?
What cowboy doing?

Where Ann pencil?
Where Momma boot?
Where kitty?
Where milk go?
Where horse go?

Again, one can consider the elements *Fraser water, Mommy eggnog, Ann pencil, milk go*, in the above questions as the nucleus. As with the negative, in Period 1 there is very limited structure to the nucleus, which consists primarily of nouns and verbs without indication of tense and number.

The questions without an interrogative word can be thought of as $Q^{yes/no}$ – *nucleus*, where the *yes/no* marker is expressed as rising intonation. There are no other identifying characteristics of *yes/no* questions in adult English, since there are no auxiliaries, and there is no form of subject-verb inversion. From the contexts of mother-child interchange, it seems that these rising intonation sentences are frequently responded to by the adult as if they were *yes/no* questions. The formulation suggested is

$$S \rightarrow Q^{yes/no} - Nucleus \qquad (8)$$

The *Wh*-questions can be described as a list which includes only a few routines that vary little across the three children. The most common questions are some version of *What's that?* and *Where NP (go)?* and *What NP doing?* It is not at all clear that the *What* in *What cowboy doing?* has any relationship to a grammatical object of the verb *do* (that is, that it is a special case of *Q*-nucleus where the particular interrogative occurs as the object of *do*). What might be said, with reservation, is that, indeed, there is a relationship in the child's speech between sentences like *go NP* and *where NP go* but that the special interrogative form is bound to the particular word *go* and does not at all have the generality of the adult structure. Paraphrases of the above questions for the child might be *I want to know the name of that thing; I want to know what you call that action;* and *I want to know the location of that (previously present) object.* One might tentatively suggest a formulation as follows:

$$S \rightarrow Q^{what} - NP - (doing) \qquad (9)$$
$$S \rightarrow Q^{where} - NP - (go) \qquad (10)$$

Let us take as an example the interrogative word questions in which the object of a verb is the missing constituent and has been replaced by a preposed *what*. If one looks at the set of these questions, which the mother asks the child in the course of the samples of speech, one finds that at Period 1 the child generally does not respond or responds inappropriately, as in

MOTHER: What, did you hit?
CHILD: Hit.

MOTHER: What did you do?
CHILD: Head.

At this period, then, the children are producing questions that only superficially resemble those questions in which the object of a verb has been questioned and preposed, and they do not understand this construction when they hear it.

Period 2.   Some of the questions to consider are

See my doggie?
That black too?
Mom pinch finger?
You want eat?
I have it?

Where my mitten?
Where baby Sarah rattle?
Where me sleep?

What book name?
What me think?
What the dollie have?
What soldier marching?

Why you smiling?
Why you waking me up?

Why not he eat?
Why not me sleeping?
Why not . . . me can't dance?
Why not me drink it?
You can't fix it?
This can't write a flower?

There is some development in the superficial structure of the sentences since Period 1. Notably, pronouns have developed, articles and modifiers are more often present, some inflections (present progressive and plurals) occur, and the verb phrase may include a prepositional phrase or preverb. There are no modal auxiliaries in affirmative sentences, and only two negative modal forms (*don't* and *can't*). There are few indeterminates or indefinites.

There seems to be a gradual development of rules and not necessarily the wholesale replacement of one total system by another. Constituent questioning is developing. Although the interrogative word *what* appears in sentences which have a missing object, there are nonetheless occurrences of that interrogative without those conditions. It is perhaps premature to associate this word in each case with a specific deleted constituent of the sentence. But certainly there is already some association of what will be referred to as zero interrogative constituent and the interrogative introducers *what*, *where*, and *why*. That is, in

Period 2 Q^{what} (perhaps also Q^{where}) has begun in its function of requesting the information that would be supplied by a specific syntactic constituent of the sentence (the object of a verb) and the questioned constituent is left blank. We suggest that the child's question *What the dollie have?* may well have some such structure as

$$Q^{what} - [the\ dollie]_{NP}\ [[have]_V\ [\phi]_{NP}]_{VP}.$$

and that already there is a general relationship between introductory *what* and the occurrence, without an expressed object noun phrase, of any verb like *have*. In Period 2, there is still no inversion of subject and verb in *yes/no* questions.

By this period there are appropriate answers to most questions. The responses reflect that the child understands that the object of a verb or preposition is being questioned:

MOTHER: What d'you need?
CHILD: Need some chocolate.

MOTHER: Who are you peeking at?
CHILD: Peeking at Ursula.

MOTHER: What d'you hear?
CHILD: Hear a duck.

We suggest for Period 2:

$$S \rightarrow \begin{Bmatrix} Q^{yes/no} \\ Q^{what} \\ Q^{where} \\ Q^{why} \end{Bmatrix} Nucleus \qquad (11)$$

$$Nucleus \rightarrow NP - V - (NP) \qquad (12)$$

$$NP \rightarrow \begin{Bmatrix} \cdots \\ \phi \text{ if the sentence is introduced by } Q^{what} \end{Bmatrix} \qquad (13)$$

Period 3.   The questions to consider are

Does the kitty stand up?
Does lions walk?
Is Mommy talking to Robin's grandmother?
Did I see that in my book?
Oh, did I caught it?
Are you going to make it with me?
Will you help me?
Can I have a piece of paper?
Where small trailer he should pull?
Where the other Joe will drive?
Where I should put it when I make it up?

Where's his other eye?
Where my spòon goed?
What I did yesterday?
What he can ride in?
What you had?
What did you doed?
Sue, what you have in you mouth?
Why the Christmas tree going?
Why he don't know how to pretend?
Why kitty can't stand up?
Why Paul caught it?
Which way they should go?
How he can be a doctor?
How they can't talk?
How that opened?
Can't it be a bigger truck?
Can't you work this thing?

Between the previous period and this one many parts of the children's grammar have undergone developments. There is now a class of verbal forms that inverts with the subject in certain interrogatives (*yes/no* questions) and may take the negative particle with it. One particular verb, *do*, occurs only in its function as a helping-verb in inverted questions and negatives, seldom in interrogative word questions. At this point, the system that has been developed bears striking similarities to the adult pattern. Notice, however, that the auxiliary verbs are not inverted with the subject noun phrase in interrogative word questions. There are other aspects that set the child's system apart from the adult language; namely, the child does not produce the full set of sequences of the adult auxiliary system. In the adult system, the possible sequences are (M) $(have-PP)(be-PrP)$; that is, any combination of these, but always in that order, where tense appears always on the first, or if none of these are present, then with the main verb. The children, at this stage, do not produce any combinations of auxiliaries.

Considerable development is found in the children's grammar by this period. In addition to the noun and verb inflections appearing in the previous period, one finds possessive markers, third person singular present indicative, and the regular past indicator. The sentences are no longer limited to simple English sentences. There is considerable development in complexity, and we find relative clauses and other clauses for the first time: *You have two things that turn around; I told you I know how to put the train together; I gon' get my chopper for chopping down cows and trees; Let's go upstairs and take it from him because it's mine.*

Let us begin with the same basic structure as for negatives at Period 3:

$$S \rightarrow (Q \ (Wh)) - NP - Aux - VP \tag{14}$$

$$Aux \rightarrow T - V^{aux} - (Neg) \tag{15}$$

$$V^{aux} \rightarrow \begin{Bmatrix} can \\ do \\ will \\ be \end{Bmatrix} \qquad (16)$$

$$NP \rightarrow \begin{Bmatrix} Wh + Indet \\ \ldots \end{Bmatrix} \qquad (17)$$

Transformations:

I. Interrogative Word Preposing:

$$Q - X^1 - Wh + Indet - X^2 \Rightarrow Q - Wh + Indet - X^1 - X^2$$

II. Interrogative Inversion (characterizing only *yes/no* questions):

$$Q - Wh - NP - Aux - X \Rightarrow Q - Wh - Aux - NP - X$$

III. *Do* Deletion:

$$do - V \Rightarrow V$$

In *yes/no* questions, we have noted that the children invert the auxiliary component with the subject noun phrase appropriately. Affirmative sentences generally have an auxiliary. In interrogative word questions, however, the auxiliary is generally not inverted. The auxiliary form of *be* is optional at this stage, and the auxiliary *do* is not present in the final shape of most of the interrogative word questions.

RULES FOR QUESTIONS IN CHILDREN'S SPEECH

Period 1

$$S \rightarrow Q^{yes/no} - Nucleus \qquad (8)$$
$$S \rightarrow Q^{what} - NP - (doing) \qquad (9)$$
$$S \rightarrow Q^{where} - NP - (go) \qquad (10)$$

Period 2

$$S \rightarrow \begin{Bmatrix} Q^{yes/no} \\ Q^{what} \\ Q^{where} \\ Q^{why} \end{Bmatrix} Nucleus \qquad (11)$$

$$Nucleus \rightarrow NP - V - (NP) \qquad (12)$$

$$NP \rightarrow \begin{Bmatrix} \ldots \\ \emptyset \text{ if the sentence is introduced by } Q^{what} \end{Bmatrix} \qquad (13)$$

Period 3

$$S \rightarrow (Q \ (Wh)) - NP - Aux - VP \qquad (14)$$

For further details see the description of *Period 3* (pp. 350–351).
Transformations (as on p. 352).
  I.   Interrogative Word Preposing
  II. Interrogative Inversion (characterizing only *yes/no* questions)
  III. *Do* Deletion

SUMMARY

The speech of the three children consists primarily of a small set of words strung together at the earliest period we have investigated in two and three word sentences. Among the early systematic aspects of child speech in its step-by-step approximation to the adult system are the following: in the early period the negatives and an ever-growing class of interrogative introducers occur first in the sentence, as sentence modifiers in the basic framework. The association of the interrogative word with other constituents of the sentence is very limited at first, restricted at the beginning to a complement of one or two particular verbs (e.g., *go* in *where NP go*). Only later does the association apply to whole categories, such that the preposing of *Wh* + prefixed elements can be spoken of with any generality. The auxiliary verb emerges first (anticipated perhaps by the optional occurrence of the copula *be*) always associated with negatives (as *can't, don't*). Not until afterwards do the modal auxiliary verbs and *do* appear inverted with the subject, and then only in the *yes/no* questions (i.e. the question not introduced by an interrogative word). At the same time, the modal auxiliary verbs, but not *do*, finally emerge independent of interrogatives and negatives. Not until the next period does the inversion of auxiliary verbs extend to questions introduced by an interrogative word. Negation is embedded in the auxiliary verbs by this third period, but the complex relation of negative and indefinite is not established yet. We have attempted to capture the regularities which we found in the speech of the three children in the rules which we have suggested for negatives and interrogatives.

SYMBOLS

S	Sentence	*T*	Tense marker
Neg	Negative formant	*Wh*	Interrogative word
Q	Interrogative formant	*have – PP*	Perfect
X	Variable	*be – PrP*	Progressive
Det	Determiner	*be – PP*	Passive
Aux	Auxiliary verb	*M*	Modal auxiliary verbs
Imp	Imperative modal auxiliary	+	Incorporated with
		( )	Symbol enclosed is optional
MV	Main verb	[ ] subscript	Node dominating enclosed constituent
NP	Noun phrase		
VP	Verb phrase	{ }	Choose one of list
Indet	Indeterminate	∅	Null
Indef	Indefinite	•	

The Berkeley Children

The study reported in the following three papers was begun at Berkeley in 1960 by Susan Ervin-Tripp (then Susan Ervin) and Wick Miller. It was longitudinal in plan, like the Harvard study, but the interaction recorded was between experimenter and child, rather than mother and child. Five children were followed intensively, and an additional 20 were tested periodically. A number of standardized elicitation measures were applied repeatedly. Also like the Harvard study, it is clear that such projects yield data which take many years to examine. Miller and Ervin-Tripp are working on a summary volume (forthcoming). Aspects of the study are also discussed by Miller (1963, 1964b), Ervin-Tripp (1970a, 1971), and Slobin (1971a).

The first paper, written in 1961, looks for patterns of word distribution in early speech. There is also some attention to functional categories (reference, direction, responsive discourse) and to stress and intonation (rare in most studies of child speech). This paper, along with a report of the beginning phases of Roger Brown's work (Brown and Fraser, 1963), was part of an important S.S.R.C. conference on language acquisition held at M.I.T. and summarized in a volume edited by Bellugi and Brown (1964). That volume contains valuable discussions of child language research by the linguists Chomsky, Halle, and Lees, and by a number of psychologists and anthropologists.

Miller's paper, originally presented at the December 1964 meeting of the Linguistic Society of America, deals with the development of transformations. He found a typical pattern in the five children: slow acquisition of some initial transformations, followed by rapid acquisition of related transformations, demonstrating that: "The children had learned a set of rules that could be applied widely."

The third paper, by Ervin-Tripp, combines papers she delivered in 1963 at the International Congress of Psychologists in Washington and the American Psychological Association convention in Philadelphia. The paper ties in closely with the preceding section of papers on inflections and the following section of papers on imitation. After careful consideration of her data and reasoned argument, Ervin-Tripp is led to the strong conclusion that "there is not a shred of evidence supporting the view that progress toward adult norms of grammar arises merely from practice in overt imitation of adult sentences." (See the comments preceding the section of papers on imitation for further discussion of this problem.)

In a recent paper, Ervin-Tripp (1971) re-examines some of the premises underlying the child language grammars she proposed in 1963. She notes that frequently "grammatical class defined by distribution resulted in constructions which were so semantically diverse as to seem absurd" (p. 207) and discusses an ongoing reanalysis of the data which pays much greater attention to semantic features: "By accepting semantic features as part of the necessary analysis, one finds that such structurally homonymous sequences as noun-noun sentences can be semantically subdivided" (p. 207) (see Bloom, below). She also favors the use of smaller time periods to be covered by a single grammatical analysis, thus rendering the corpus more homogeneous. And she notes: "That analysis is heavily informed, on the basis of a suggestion of Braine [this volume], by groupings of replacement sequences which appear to be alternative formulations of the same semantic substance, sequential in production" (p. 207).

Another important contribution of this third paper is evidence that children begin to overregularize inflections on the basis of very limited contact with regular forms, and that successive sweeps of overregularization patterns reveal the active role of the child's rule inductive capacties.   —D.I.S.

The Development of Grammar in Child Language[1]
——Wick R. Miller and Susan M. Ervin-Tripp

Before describing the development of children's grammar, it is necessary to specify some of the properties of natural languages as used by adults. This is the model presented to the child and the eventual outcome of his development.

It is possible to analyze in all languages two types of constructs (or linguistic units): phonemes and morphemes. There are at least two corresponding systems which can be called the phonological and grammatical levels.[2] While this paper is concerned only with the grammatical level, certain properties of the phonological level will be briefly considered by way of contrast.

The phonetic substance, the raw material of language, can be analyzed into a finite set of mutually exclusive classes. The distinctive features by which the classes are contrasted are few in number. Each phonological system may be described in terms of different privileges of occurrence of the features or the sets of features called phonemes. Phonemes are grouped together into larger units in limited arrangements, and the groupings can be completely described by distributional statements. Thus it is possible to predict *all* possible phonemic shapes.[3] From the standpoint of the learner, the phonemic rules are given. Even

From U. Bellugi and R. Brown (eds.), The acquisition of language, *Monograph of the Society for Research in Child Development*, 1964, **29** (1), 9–35. Reprinted by permission of the authors and the Society for Research in Child Development. (Originally published under the names of Wick R. Miller and Susan M. Ervin.)

[1] The project described in this paper is supported by a grant from the Department of Health, Education and Welfare (M-3813) to the Institute of Human Development, University of California, Berkeley. Facilities have also been provided by the Center for Human Learning under support of the National Science Foundation.
[2] The term "level" has been used in a variety of ways in the linguistic literature. Our use of the term does not apply to the so-called levels within the syntactic system, or the distinction between morphology and syntax. As we use the term, the two levels correspond to what communication theorists call the channel and the message.
[3] Whorf (1940) has given a succinct statement for phonemic sequences in English monosyllables.

nonsense words or coinages normally follow these rules. Imitation of sequences already heard is the normal mode of acquisition and use, and continues with the expansion of vocabulary.

If we turn to the grammatical level, we see many differences. Morphemes, like phonemes, can be grouped into a number of classes, but the nature of the classes is different. The classes can be divided into two groups, which following Fries (1952) we can call lexical and function classes. Lexical classes are large and open and the number of classes is small. English lexical classes include nouns, verbs, and adjectives. A lexical class can normally be divided into subclasses, e.g., English mass nouns, count nouns, proper nouns. In contrast, function classes are small and closed and the number of classes is larger. English function classes include prepositions, conjunctions, interrogatives, noun determiners, and auxiliaries. It is more often possible to point to a simple referent for members of lexical classes than for members of function classes. The contrast between lexical and function classes is often only a relative one, which may mean that it is not always a useful distinction to make in organizing a grammar.

The grammatical productivity of a language is infinite. A speaker can produce utterances which he has never heard before. Unless the words are nonsense or the sentence semantically aberrant, such utterances will be understood by the hearer. This property of grammars is in contrast to the phonological system. Any novel recombination of phonemes, while it may follow phonological distribution rules, is nonsense until or unless conventional meaning is assigned.

Every language has a major predication type formed by placing together two constructions. The predication is *exocentric*—that is, the resulting construction does not belong to the same class as either of the two constituent constructions. In most languages at least one of the constituents of the predication is a member of a lexical class or an expansion of a lexical class, e.g., the English subject is composed of a noun or noun phrase. Most nonpredication constructions are *endocentric*, or expansions in which the head of the construction belongs to the same class as the resulting construction. An example is the noun phrase, *the three boys*, which is an expansion of the noun phrase, *three boys*.

The term *discourse agreement* is used to indicate formal relationships that cross sentence boundaries. They are of two kinds: (a) *class restrictions*, and (b) *verb restrictions*. The first occur in answers to questions. A question has a formal structure, which normally restricts the formal structure possible in the response, and also a semantic content or a request for information. The comparison of two questions illustrates this point; on formal grounds we would expect the following answers:

A: *Where is Main Street?   I don't know.*   or   *Straight ahead.*
B: *Can you tell me where Main Street is?   No.*   or   *Yes.*

Obviously the responses to question B fail to meet the semantic requirements posed by the question. The two questions differ formally but are semantically equivalent.

In addition to "yes-no" questions, there are "or" questions and interrogative word questions. "Or" questions require a choice of an alternative if there is a falling intonation. The short response to interrogative word questions must be a word or phrase belonging to the same class as the interrogative word or words.

Verb restrictions involve the maintenance of tense or auxiliary features across sentence boundaries, and can be characterized as long components of a grammatical category. Compare the following set of sentences:

A: *This ice cream is good.*   *Yes, it is.*
B: *This ice cream tastes good.*   *Yes, it does.*

The initial sentences of A and B are semantically equivalent, but differ formally and require different responses. Verb restrictions can apply to successive utterances of the same or different speakers, but our attention will be focused on situations in which different speakers are involved, in particular when the second speaker is required to answer a "what—do" question.

In this paper we will distinguish three functional categories in the child's utterances. The first may be called *reference* (Skinner's *tacts*). It involves naming or describing and may be accompanied by pointing. Such behavior is initiated by the child and does not necessarily demand a response from another person. The second may be called *direction* (Skinner's *mands*) and demands verbal or active response from the hearer. Such utterances include commands and questions. It is often impossible to discriminate questions from reference utterances of the child. A third category may be called *responsive discourse* and includes informational responses. This category can be initiated by the interlocutor or the child, but we are primarily concerned with this category when initiated by the interlocutor.[4]

A person has two grammatical systems, one for encoding and another for decoding, or an active and passive grammatical system. For the adult, a single grammar can normally account for almost all of both systems. Quite clearly this is not the case with the child. We assume that a child must understand a grammatical pattern before he can produce it. Presumably the decoding and encoding systems at any point in time are not independent. It seems likely that rules could be found for the derivation of one from the other. Such a procedure might be a fruitful way to approach grammatical development. We have little evidence concerning the decoding system at this time.

THE RESEARCH PROJECT

The data mentioned in this paper were obtained in a project consisting of longitudinal testing of 25 children and more intensive text collection from a subgroup of five. Texts for four of the children were collected beginning when the children were about 2. The fifth child, Susan, was added when she was 1.9. Text

---

[4] Linguists frequently distinguish three functions: referential, directive, and expressive; for a recent account see Hymes (1961), and Jakobson (1960).

collection was scheduled to continue for two years. The standardized tests collected from the larger group consisted of three tests: a plural test, a pronoun test, and two forms of a discourse agreement test. The children in the smaller sample were older than the other children in the group.

The texts were at first collected weekly, in sessions of 45 minutes, because of rapid change. As the rate of change decreased and the fluency of the children increased, the frequency of text collection was gradually reduced, until texts were collected at two-month intervals, in two or three sets of closely spaced interviews totaling four or five hours.

The texts were all tape recorded. The transcription was at first phonetic, but later it was made in the normal orthography marked for stress and intonation, with a phonetic transcription only for ambiguous material. The texts also included utterances of the investigator and pertinent contextual information.

The earliest texts were collected in unstructured interviews. As techniques which elicited certain types of utterances were noted, the investigator increasingly structured the interviews. For example, attempts to elicit negatives were made by putting clothes on the wrong doll or puzzle pieces in the wrong place. Doll clothing was used for eliciting possessives. To elicit an interrogative sentence, two dolls were "fed," and the child was told to "ask Joe what he wants to eat." Plurals were produced for nonsense objects made of play-doh. If one of the dolls was left behind, "because he is sick," the child was asked to talk on the toy telephone to find out how "Joe" was, another device for eliciting questions. Telephone conversations with the child tested his reliance on verbal rather than general cues. Techniques that were discovered in this way were incorporated where appropriate into tests for the larger group.

The plural test consisted of 17 items. In each case a toy object or picture was shown, its name elicited, and then two were shown. "Here are two what?" Thus the test did not give the children the option of using a syntactical plural signal rather than a morphological one. The items included certain pairs in which nonsense items (wooden constructions) were given names which had the same final consonant as a familiar word (*boy-kigh*, *block-bik*, *bed-pud*, *horse-tass*, *orange-bunge*). Irregulars were *foot*, *man*, and *house*. The singular of the regular and nonsense words was offered by the investigator if it was not offered by the child. In the case of *foot* and *man*, however, the singular was not offered by the investigator. This procedure was followed in order to determine which form, e.g., *foot* or *feet*, was used by the child as the singular. Testing was stopped on items after they had been contrasted for several months.

On the pronoun test, the child was questioned about pictures, the questions being designed to elicit sentences containing possessives and nominative pronouns varying in number and gender. In the test of discourse agreement, questions tested the class of responses, verb restrictions, comprehension of subject-object distinctions ("Who is he feeding?" vs. "Who is feeding him?") and "why" questions. There were two matched forms alternated each month, using the same pictures.

THE FIRST GRAMMATICAL SYSTEM

The children in our project began forming primitive sentences of two or more words before their second birthday.[5] It is clear that the grammar of these sentences is not identical with the adult model. It is often striking that one can provide a translation of children's utterances into adult utterances by the addition of function words and inflectional affixes. It appears that the children select the stressed utterance segments, which usually carry the most information. Brown and Fraser have called this a "telegraphic" version of English.

Since children's language undergoes a constant process of change through imitation of adult models, it makes sense that it should be describable in terms of its relation to the adult model. There are, however, some utterances which cannot be described as telegraphic speech:

At 2.3 Christy and her baby sister each had a balloon. The baby bit her balloon and broke it. Christy first said *Baby bite balloon*, then pointed to the unbroken balloon and said, *Baby other bite balloon no.*

Between 2.1 and 2.4 Lisa had a particular kind of construction which often generated sentences that had no adult analogue, e.g., *all-gone puzzle.*

A conversation between the investigator and Susan at 1.10:
SUSAN: *Book read. Book read. Book read.*
INV: *You want me to read book? OK.*
SUSAN: *Read book.*

The last example shows a correction by imitation in the direction of telegraphic speech. However, the child's original utterance either was an unpatterned error or represented a productive pattern that deviated from the model.

Is there any kind of system or pattern to the child's first sentences? In attempting to answer this question we will examine some of the text material of Susan (1.9 to 2.0) and Christy (2.0 to 2.3).

Susan

Susan, according to her parents, started putting words together at 1.8 to form multiword sentences. One-word sentences, however, predominated until $1.9\frac{1}{2}$. Thus, the system to be described represents the very beginning of the development of the grammatical level.

---

[5] We will use the term "word" rather than "morpheme" except when the distinction is necessary. A word class of the model language, as opposed to a word class of the child's language, is indicated by an abbreviation and a superscript "m," e.g., N^m and Adj^m indicate model language noun and adjective. Age is indicated by year and month, e.g., 2.4 indicates 2 years and 4 months old.

During this period the most common words in Susan's vocabulary were *off* and *on*. A consistent pattern emerges when the preceding words, classified as to part of speech in the model language, are charted, as in Table 1.

TABLE 1   ANTECEDENTS OF *OFF* AND *ON* (SUSAN 1.9–2.0)

	NOUN	VERB	OTHER	INITIAL	TOTAL
off	28	8	4	1	41
on	29	7	11	3	50

The figures in the chart represent text occurrences, excluding obvious imitations and chain repetitions.

The words that preceded *off* and *on* showed a large amount of overlap, and can be combined into one list, in Table 2. Words marked with an asterisk were

TABLE 2   ANTECEDENT TYPES FOR *OFF* AND *ON* (SUSAN 1.9–2.0)

back	dress	Liz	shoe	that
bandage	dusting	one*	sit*	them*
blanket	fall	pants	snap*	this*
button	fix	paper	sock	this-one
came	flower	piece*	sweater	(neck) tie
chair	hair	salt	take*	
coat*	hat	scarf	(scotch) tape	
diaper	hold*	shirt	tear	

* These words were found only in sentences of more than two words.

found only in sentences of more than two words. Other words have been found in two-word sentences. *This-one* is assumed to have been a unit in Susan's speech.

Most of Susan's sentences with *on* and *off* reflected model sentences with two-word verbs, but a few reflected the prepositional use. Susan used *off* and *on* in a construction which had the shape W + I; W stands for any word(s) and I stands for *off* or *on*. We can call this the particle construction. The W will be defined as the complement, the I as the particle. Most of the characteristics of the particle construction are illustrated in the following example taken from a text at 1.10:

> SUSAN: Hat off, hat off.
> INV: That's more than the hat off. The whole Santa's head [*of a toy Santa Claus*] came off.
> SUSAN: Santa head off. (*Pause.*) Head on. Fix on, fix on.

Class I words had a verbal force. Most of the examples of imitations were imitations of two-word verbs. She was able to construct sentences of this pattern that had no direct adult analogue, e.g., *fix on*; the adult would normally say something like *fix it* or *put it on*. This example also shows that *off* and *on* were opposites for Susan; this may help explain why these two particles were used so much more than other particles.

The particle complement was usually a N^m or noun phrase of the model language, but V^m was not uncommon: *White sweater off*, said while taking her sweater off; *white sweater on*, a request directed to her mother to put her white sweater on her; *salt on*, pretending to salt food; *scarf off*, said while taking her scarf off. The model language provides analogues in which the noun is the object: *I took my sweater off; put my white sweater on! I put the salt on; I took my scarf off.* There are also analogues in which the noun is the subject, but these seem less likely to have been the model for the child: *my sweater is off; my white sweater should be on; the salt is on; my scarf is off.* The fact that there were no sentences like *Susan off* or *Mommy on*, that is, transitive two-word verb sentences of the model analogue with the verb and object deleted strengthens the view that the N^m usually represents the object of action. There were exceptions to this pattern, such as *chair off*, said while taking a teddy bear off a chair.

There were 12 sentences in which the complement was a two-word phrase:

White sweater on.
Blue sweater on.
Mommy sweater on.
Susan sweater on.
Susan coat on.
Bonnie coat on.
This dress off.
Put that on.
That came off.
Miller take off shoe sock.
Shouldn't take off shoe sock.
Let's take off shoe sock.

It will be seen that there was evidence for distinguishing two-word classes that reflected N^m and V^m. It was not clear if Adj^m should be grouped with N^m or kept distinct. Therefore the formulas $N^m + N^m$, $N^m + V^m$, or $V^m + N^m$, and perhaps also $Adj^m + N^m$ can be used to form expansions of the particle complement. The phrases that reflected auxiliary + verb, however, cannot be accounted for in this fashion. *Susan sweater on* and *Mommy sweater on* were ambiguous. In the first sentence a possessive relation was intended and a model analogue would be *Susan's sweater is on* or *Susan has her sweater on*. The second sentence was a request directed to her mother and a model analogue would be *Mommy, put my sweater on me*.

A rather neat pattern was found for the core of Susan's particle construction. There were, however, loose ends. In some sentences the particle was medial, and in a few it was initial:

> *Take off me* (requesting help in taking her scarf off).
> *Sock off Liz* (in imitation of *Let's take the shoes and socks off of Liz*).
> *Snap on off* (said while playing with the snap of a doll's dress).
> *Want to hold on Liz.*
> *Liz her hat back on* (indicating she wanted to put Liz's hat on after it fell off).
> *This one blue one on.*
> *Susan blue one sweater on* (this and preceding sentence were used to indicate she wanted to wear her blue sweater).
> *On tight* (putting her doll more securely on her Kiddy Kar so it would not fall off again).
> *Off of me* (requesting help in taking her scarf off).

No recurrent pattern can be found for these sentences.

Other particles of the model language were common, but none were as common as *off* and *on*. *Up* occurred 15 times: three times after N^m, nine times after V^m, two times after other words, and once in initial position. There are a few examples that fit the pattern described for the particle construction: *sleeves up*, requesting the investigator to roll up her sleeves; *red shoe up*, leaning her shoes against the door sill, pointed up. *Up bed*, indicating she wanted the side of the crib raised, would be **bed up* if it followed the pattern of *off* and *on*. Several sentences were probably learned units, thus accounting for the larger number of V^m than N^m before the particle: *tear up; come up; Susan get up*.

The remaining model language particles were common as a whole, but no single particle was very frequent. A large number of the sentences followed the pattern of the particle construction, but there were a larger proportion of exceptions to the general pattern than were found with *off* and *on*. A good many exceptions seemed to reflect the prepositional uses of the words in the model language.

When Susan's linguistic system became more mature and more closely approximated the model, transitive sentences with two-word verbs were common. The elements that developed into the object and particle were represented at this stage. The verbs less frequently, and the subjects almost never were represented.

The words *this*, *this-one*, and *that* showed certain consistent features. We can designate these three words class II. In initial position they formed the demonstrative construction. *This-one* had the phonological shape /disn/ or /disən/, and appeared to be a unit for Susan. The sequence /-n/ or /-ən/ was distinct from the vocabulary item /wən/ *one*. The demonstrative construction had less semantic consistency than the particle construction. It was usually used to identify an item: *this-one yellow, this book, this-one Joe, that bead*. But it could also be used to indicate location and action or quality (the last two are difficult to separate in Susan's speech): *this on top; this-one on; this-one tear*. The word classes of the model language that followed an initial class II word were also more variable, as shown in Table 3.

TABLE 3   SUSAN'S DEMONSTRATIVE CONSTRUCTIONS (SUSAN 1.9–2.0)

FIRST WORD	SECOND WORD				
	N^m	V^m	ADJ^m	CLASS I	OTHER
this	9	1	1	3	2
this-one	3	3	2	3	4
that	9	1	1	6	6

Class II words were usually in initial position; class I words were usually in medial or final position. However the positional preference is more consistent for class I than for class II.

A third class, labeled class III, may be recognized, consisting of *a* (19 occurrences), *the* (nine occurrences), and *(an)other* (11 occurrences). Excluding some examples of *a* (discussed below), class III preceded a N^m or a noun phrase of the model language, except in: *a red* (in answer to *What kind of an apple is that?*); *is that the blue mine?; have another blue.* In addition *a* was found in a few sentences in medial position before words where *a* was inappropriate: *up bed, (side?) a bed*, requesting that the investigator raise the side of her crib; *this a Bonnie pants; have a pants; this-one a Joe?; I know a that; these a Liz pants; this a back on; this a Joe?; mine, all a mine.* Shortly before Susan said *have a pants*, she had said *here a lemon* in imitation of her mother's sentence *here's a lemon.* Sentences like *here's a lemon* and probably also phrases like *all of* (/ə/) *mine, piece of* (/ə/) *toast* provided the model for Susan's pattern. The *a* seemed to have

TABLE 4   CLASS CONTINGENCIES IN SUSAN'S TWO-WORD SENTENCES (1.9–2.0)

SECOND WORD	FIRST WORD										
	I	II	III	A	B	C	D	E	*It*	*More*	TOTAL
I	—	10	—	6	45	—	—	1	—	—	62
II	—	—	—	6	1	—	1	—	—	1	9
III	—	—	—	—	—	—	—	—	—	—	—
A	—	3	—	1	26	—	1	—	—	—	31
B	—	10	8	18	26	4	6	1	—	3	76
C	—	3	1	—	4	—	—	2	—	—	10
D	—	1	—	4	5	1	—	7	—	—	18
E	—	4	—	12	10	1	—	—	—	1	28
it	—	—	—	6	—	—	—	—	—	—	6
more	—	—	—	—	—	—	—	—	—	—	—
Total	—	31	9	53	117	6	8	11	—	5	240

NOTE.—Thirty-seven sentences that include the following words have been excluded: *night-night, I, me, my, mine, he, you, her, them, one, two, no, what, now, too, please, bye, like*, and *right* (in *right here*).

the function of dividing the sentence into two parts. This function was restricted to a two-month period from 1.9½ to 1.11½.

Eight words have been assigned to three classes. The remaining words in Susan's vocabulary were either less frequent or less consistent and cannot realistically be assigned to classes by the methods used for setting up classes I, II, and III. Are we justified in lumping the remaining vocabulary items into one large undifferentiated class? If we group the remaining words into the word classes of the model language and examine only two-word sentences, we find a certain pattern emerges. The results are given in Table 4. Sentences that included

TABLE 5　DEMONSTRATIVE SENTENCES FOR CHRISTY (2.0–2.3)

That	That's	This	Thatsa	This a	Thata	'sa
blue					blue	
broken			broken			
chicken	chicken					
dolly	dolly					
eye	eye					
elephant			elephant			
go		go				
hat	hat					
Joe	Joe					
pants	pants					
pretty			pretty			
truck	truck		truck	truck		truck
yellow	yellow					
			cup		cup	
airplane	bus	one	car	A	doggy	arm
blocks	milk		coffee		horse	baby
bowl	quack-quack		girl			block
cat			owl			boy
Christy's			pig			ear
Daddy's			plane			lion
dolly's						rabbit
fish						Wick
horsie						
huke*						
kitty						
neck						
pin						
pink						
po*						
Sarah						
turn						
yellow						

* *Po* and *huke* were the names of two nonsense shapes of play-doh.

I, me, my, mine were excluded because these words came in late in the period and were replacing *Susan. What* is also excluded because it represented a late development. A number of other words were excluded either because they were rare and their class membership was difficult to assign, or because they appeared to belong to learned formulas. Prepositions and particles have been lumped into one class.

Class A reflected V^m. There was only one example of A + A (*want talk*). The most common patterns were A + B and B + A. There were only six examples of A + *it*, but these comprise all the examples of *it. It* seemed to function as a suffix for class A words, and perhaps marked a subclass of A, words that reflected transitive verbs in the model. Class B reflected N^m and was common before classes A, B, and I, and after class A. Class C, which reflected Adj^m, was not common. The words reflected a variety of subclasses in the model language. Classes B and C show similar patterns and we cannot be sure they represent two classes in Susan's speech. If N^m and Adj^m words belong to one class in Susan's linguistic system, we would expect to find examples of Adj^m + I, because the pattern N^m + I was so common. Class D represents locative adverbs, and class E prepositions and particles of the model. These two classes cannot be sustained by the evidence presented in the table. The words represented in D and E might be aligned in a different fashion but the evidence is too meager to group these words with confidence. There were not many examples of *more*, but the evidence seems to indicate that the word belongs to class III.

Christy

A somewhat different pattern is found in Christy's grammatical development. The following paragraphs are based primarily on two-word sentences collected during 12 hours of recorded texts. The most common type of sentence began with *that*. The various initial elements of these sentences along with the following words are listed in Table 5. The lists may be pooled into one in view of the similarity of the lists and gradation of phonetic shapes represented by each category: /dæ, dæ?, dæt, dæ, da, dat, dɔ, as, dæs, dædæ, dæda, dæa, æta, dætsa, dœsa dæza, zæza, æza, sa, dæsa, za, sæ, tsa/.

This and *this a* (found before *a, go, one,* and *truck*) and the variants of *that* may be pooled as class I. The items in Table 5 and the items found after *this* (*a*) may be called class A. As a result of this classification, a construction can be identified which we may call the demonstrative construction: I + A↓/↑ (the arrows indicate falling and rising intonation). There were 74 examples of such utterances.

Nineteen sentences began with *the* or *a*. The words which followed were *other*, or class A words. *The* and *a* never terminated a two-word sentence. These words have been designated class II.

The words *in, on, out, away, over,* and *under* appeared in 16 sentences. They both preceded and followed class A and preceded class I. There was one set which followed, but never preceded class A: *away, out*; others which preceded but never followed: *over, under*; and others of dual membership: *in, on*. The

TABLE 6 CLASS CONTINGENCIES IN CHRISTY'S TWO-WORD SENTENCES (2.0–2.3)

SECOND WORD	I	II	III	A	B	C	D	where	what	(an)other	it	TOTAL
I	—	—	—	—	2	—	1	—	1	1	—	5
II	—	—	—	3	5	—	5	—	—	—	—	13
III	74	18	9	41	5	—	3	10	—	8	—	168
A	2	—	—	10	2	—	—	1	—	—	—	15
B	—	—	—	4	2	—	—	—	—	—	—	6
C	—	—	—	—	—	—	—	—	—	—	—	—
D	—	—	—	—	—	—	—	—	—	—	—	—
where	—	—	—	—	—	—	—	—	—	—	—	—
what	—	—	—	—	—	—	—	—	—	—	—	—
(an)other	—	1	—	—	—	—	—	—	—	—	—	1
it	—	—	—	—	2	—	—	—	—	—	—	2
Total	76	19	9	58	18	—	9	11	1	9	—	210

Above the column headers: FIRST WORD

NOTE.—Nineteen sentences were omitted because they contained words of ambiguous class membership from the standpoint of the two-word sentence corpus: *his, walk, oh, no, else, my, right (right here), more, don't, two, both.*

TABLE 7   CLASSES IN CHRISTY'S TWO-WORD SENTENCES (2.0–2.3)

I	this, thisa, that, that's, that'sa, 'sa, thata
II	a, the
III	here, there
A	arm, baby, bus, cat, Christy's, dolly, dolly's, fish, horsie, truck, pretty, yellow, etc.
B	come, doed, flying, go, goes, got, hold, see, sit, sleep, sleeping, turn, want, walking
C	away, in, on, out, way
D	in, on, over, under

words which occurred in first position have been designated class D, and those in second position as class C. The decision to split these words into two classes, in spite of the overlap in membership, is based on the presumed later evolution into prepositions and adverbs or two-word particles. The accent pattern for sentences containing these items was relatively consistent.[6] In 13 out of the 14 cases where the stress was recorded, it occurred on the second word, e.g., *on cóuch, clothes ón*.

In addition to preceding class I and class A, words in class C preceded *there* and *here*, e.g., *in thére* ↑. *There* and *here* may be designated as class III. The words *where* and *what* occurred only in initial position. *Where* only occurred in sentences with falling pitch.

Class A was by far the largest class both in terms of frequency and variety. Included are items which are N^m, V^m, and Adj^m. We may subdivide this category on certain distributional grounds. The sentences *see this*, *hóld it*, *doed it*, and *óther this* were not paralleled by any instances in which N^m or Adj^m occurred in first position in the same frame, in spite of the fact that N^m was far more frequent than V^m. V^m never followed class II, III, or D. The pattern $I + V^m$ was relatively infrequent compared to $A + V^m$. V^m is designated class B, and the occurrences are shown in Table 6. If only two-word sentences are considered, the separation of class A and B is based on weaker evidence than the other class criteria, but it is quite likely that the analysis of longer sentences would confirm this division. On Table 5 the overlap was greatest between *that* and *that's*. If the words ending in *a* are viewed as in fact two words (*this a*, *that's a*), so that the sequences form three-word sentences, it may be seen that there are no cases of V^m in the last four columns, though three appear with *this* and *that*. Such sentences as *you hold this*, *make apple there*, and *take it off* suggest that the analysis of long sequences will require a separate class of verbs. In all cases except *apple eat* the semantic object followed the verb. The semantic actor normally preceded, except in *I carry Christy* which had two objects and *where go eye* and *where go toast, huh* which had an inversion regularly following *where*. There was insufficient evidence for further subdivision of class A.

---

[6] An accented word, defined for Christy's speech in the section on Prosody, is indicated by a primary stress mark.

Christy's grammar included an accentual system. The locative construction consisted of A + Á or A + ÍĬI. Sentences based on the possessive or adjectival analogue of the model consisted of Á + A: *baby róom* (in answer to *Where's the baby?*); *báby book* (in answer to *Is that the baby's book?*); *bíg choochoo*. In a few cases, however, the second item was accented in sentences that had a possessive and adjectival analogue: *baby báll* (in answer to *Is that the baby's ball?*); *baby cár* (in answer to *Whose car is this?*); *a big wádi* (wadi = dog). The first example might reveal imitation of the investigator's stress. The accent pattern was not consistent in the possessive or adjectival construction, in contrast to the locative construction.

Discussion

The partial descriptions for Susan and Christy show that the two language systems were quite different in their details. Some of the differences could be ascribed to the age difference, but others were due to a difference in their language style. There were, however, certain characteristics that applied to the speech of all the children in the project except Harlan, who was beyond this phase of development from the beginning.

A few high frequency words tended to be restricted to a given position in the sentence and tended to define the meaning of the sentence as a whole. The use of these words marked the first step in developing the grammatical system of the model language. These words may be called operators. The classes of operators for Susan and Christy have been labeled with Roman numerals. The difference between operator classes and nonoperator classes is relative rather than absolute. The nonoperator words tend to be grouped into large classes, but the division between the classes is sometimes difficult to make. Part of this difficulty is probably the nature of the data. If a low frequency word does not occur in enough different contexts, class assignments are difficult to make. But part of the difficulty may be the nature of the linguistic system of the child. The instability of class assignment is especially probable in a system based on order and not on additional markers. If a child has only heard a word from adults a few times, his sense of the meaning and the appropriate verbal contexts for that word may be easily changed by new experience. Thus, even though some regularity in order for two classes may exist, vacillation with regard to certain specific items may obscure that regularity. The method of classifying the child's words in part by pure distribution and in part by the word classes of the model language will not adequately account for all of the child's vocabulary, or vacillation of specific items. But the regularity displayed in the tables shows that this method yields information about structure.[7]

---

[7] A grammar cannot be derived from the tables. The tables only show that the elements in the child's sentences are systematized. The best explanation for the systematization is that the child has word classes that have at least some properties of word classes in adult speech. The tables do not tell what the classes are, but they do provide clues.

Operators are defined as those words having high frequency and few members in a class. These properties are found, in adult speech, in function words. The children's operators tended to be derived from adult function words and to be precursors of the function words which characterized a later phase of their own development. The nonoperators were precursors of lexical words. There was some tendency for the most frequent models of operators to be words which could serve as substitutes for lexical classes and carry stress, i.e., pronouns (demonstratives) rather than pure noun determiners, particles of two-word verbs rather than pure prepositions.

If the child used the operators in constructions that had analogues in adult speech, adults reinforced the child's pattern and enabled him to approximate adult patterns more closely. If the operators or constructions did not reflect patterns in the model language, they dropped out. There was one clear example. From 2.1 to 2.4, Lisa used *byebye, no, all-gone, another*, and *please* as operators. These words were used in a construction which consisted of an accented operator plus N^m: *nó toy*, indicating she did not want a particular toy any longer (contrast *no tóy?*, asking if there were any more toys). Many of the sentences can be related to the model only by reversing the order. Thus *all-gone puzzle* (the puzzles had just been put away) would normally be said by the adult as *The puzzle is all gone*, or some such sentence in which the word order is the reverse of Lisa's. It is always possible to find analogues that preserve the child's order, e.g., *It's all gone, the puzzle is* or *That which is all gone is the puzzle*. These are sentences the child is not likely to hear. This construction became less frequent and eventually disappeared.

Most of our analysis has been limited to two-word sentences, and the distinction between endocentric and exocentric constructions cannot apply. It seems clear, however, that this distinction will be needed to account for longer sentences. Most of the child's early constructions have exocentric models, and are probably to be considered exocentric in the child's system also. In addition, many phrases in longer sentences can probably be treated as expansions of single word classes. A characteristic feature of the children's speech was to take a construction that could be a complete predication for them and treat it as an expansion of one part of another construction. Thus the possessive construction in Christy's speech, $Á + A$, can be used as the demonstrative complement: *that Christy rabbit*. This kind of expansion seems to be typical in the early phases, and endocentric features of the model language were weakly represented in the children's language. There are certain problems to this kind of an analysis, however. In Christy's sentence *that one Joe*, *that one* can probably be treated as an expansion of the demonstrative, but in *-'s a one two* Christy was counting and *one two* appears to be an expansion of the development. In *that this shoe*, *that* may be treated as the demonstrative, *this shoe* as the complement, and the complement also as a demonstrative construction. It is not certain, however, that such analysis can be formally sustained.

It seems surprising that the children's relatively systematic arrangement of classes could be sustained with so few overt markers. One explanation may be the relative semantic consistency of English lexical classes for the words in young children's vocabulary, a fact pointed out by Brown (1958b, p. 247). He found experimentally that lexical items with class markers were systematically identified with certain types of referents (*ibid*, p. 251). Thus it may be that regularities of order are aided by the additional cue that is provided by semantic similarities between items in a class. We have very weak evidence on this point, from Harlan. The word *have* in English serves as a verb, but it does not have a meaning of action. Harlan had considerable difficulty in giving *have* the verb markers he used with other verbs. It might be objected that the difficulty stems from its use as an auxiliary, but this is a specialized use that had not yet (at 3.1) appeared in Harlan's speech. Further, *do*, which was used by Harlan both as an auxiliary and main verb, was marked appropriately when *have* was not. Thus we have examples of past tense markers for many verbs, including *do*, at least six months before the past tense was marked for *have*, although contexts in which the past tense would have been appropriate for this verb did occur before that time. At 2.7, after the regular testing of discourse agreement was begun, it was found that Harlan could answer a question about what someone was doing with an appropriate response. Notice that he did not say *having* in response to this question:

> INV: What do you think Paul was doing with the hoe?
> HARLAN: Have.
> INV: Hm?
> HARLAN: Have it.

This is not altogether a clear case, since the semantic peculiarity of *have* is reflected in its lower probability in the -*ing* form in adult usage.

The casual observer is often struck by what appears to be a complete lack of any system in the young child's first speech efforts. The composition of words into sentences appears to be random; any words can be juxtaposed. Our evidence shows this not to be the case. There was a complex system even at the earliest stages, even though it was a much simpler system than the extremely complex adult model. Are we justified in calling the kind of system that a young child has a formal grammar? This depends to a large extent on what a formal grammar is conceived to be.

From the standpoint of a linguist, a grammar can be conceived as a set of rules that will account for the sentences produced by the speaker and will not predict impossible sentences. Vocabulary items have to be assignable to word classes so that new sentences can be generated by operating with the grammar. Normally in natural languages many constructions have stateable and consistent semantic correlates, but it might be debated whether this is a necessary property.

It is obvious from the description of Susan's and Christy's speech that for most generalizations there were exceptions. Some sentences seemed to fall outside the system. Other sentences reversed the patterns that held in all other cases.

It is sentences like *off of me; clean in, in clean* (in Susan's speech); and *I carry Christy; that one Joe; that one two* (counting); *where rattle Christy; big shoe red, red shoe big; apple more; more apple* (in Christy's speech) that cause problems. Almost any rule that allows these sequences allows others that seem impossible.

How shall we know what is impossible with a child? With adult informants one can test a grammatical solution by eliciting paradigmatic material or by asking *Can you say . . .?* This implies that a speaker can distinguish the grammatically impossible from the improbable; Maclay and Sleator (1960) have presented evidence that college rhetoric students could not make the distinction. Yet we do know that adults can correct their own grammatical mistakes. Harlan corrected grammatical errors in his speech. Was this simply recognition that the utterances were improbable?

There seem to be a number of views which could be defended as to whether a formal system existed for Susan and Christy. There were a few generalizations which could be made without exceptions, but these were weak in that they also predicted many sentences that did not appear and were improbable. It might be said they were formal systems, but that they were undergoing change.

Alternatively, it could be said that the statistical tendencies and preferences were precursors of more stable and clearly defined classes. It might be argued that grammatical systems arise first in the child's exposure to differing probabilities in adult substitutions and sequences, which are reflected in a system of regularities which cannot be expressed by exceptionless rules.

THE GRAMMATICAL SYSTEM WITH WORD CLASS MARKERS

Eventually lexical classes could be identified by markers and order, not simply order as in the earlier stage. Nouns were marked by the plural suffix and noun determiners, verbs by verbal suffixes and auxiliaries. At this time it is convenient to describe the child's grammatical system as a simplified grammar of the model, along with added grammatical rules to account for constructions that have no counterpart in the model language.

Most of the mistakes or deviations from the model can be classified as omissions (*I'll turn water off* for *I'll turn the water off*), overgeneralization of morphophonemic combinations (*foots* for *feet; a owl* for *an owl; breaked* for *broke*), the incorrect use of a function word with a subclass of a lexical class (using *a* with mass nouns and proper nouns), or doubly marked forms (adding the possessive suffix to a possessive pronoun, *mine's*). Except for the first kind, these mistakes point to the fact that classes were marked. The children seldom used a suffix or function word with the wrong lexical class, either at this stage or at the earlier stage when markers were not well developed; the only examples of this kind of mistake were provided by Susan: *I by-ed that* where the adult would say *I went by that*, and *stand up-ed* where the adult would say *stood up*. In the second example it could be argued that the *-ed* was not added to the wrong word class, but rather was added to the verb phrase instead of the verb.

Most of our discussion of this stage of development will be centered on the linguistic system of Harlan, who was at this stage of development at 2.2 when we started working with him (the remaining children in the project entered this stage at 2.6 or shortly thereafter).

At 2.2, verbs in Harlan's system could be marked by the past tense suffix -ed, the progressive suffix -ing, the positive auxiliaries can, will, want, going, and the negative auxiliaries can't, won't, don't. The sentence: I pushed it, I can push it was typical. The markers were not always used, however:

INV: It popped.
HARLAN: (To his mother) My balloon pop.
MOTHER: You popped it?
HARLAN: I pop it.

Harlan's parents reported that he had the past tense suffix a few weeks before we began working with him. At 2.2 a few strong verbs were correctly used with the past tense: My Daddy-O went to work; I made a somersault. These forms varied with the base form:

HARLAN: I go boom boom (past tense context).
INV: What'd you do?
HARLAN: I went boom.

Normally strong verbs were unmarked. The -ed form of the past tense was not added to such verbs until 2.5: I breaked that.

At 2.2 the progressive was simply the suffix -ing with no form of the verb to be: Man talking on the telephone. Thus the suffix had the same, or a very similar distribution as the -ed suffix. At 2.3, forms with to be were used sporadically: Man's taking out the baloney. To be was not consistently used until 2.8.

Harlan grouped his auxiliaries into two sets, positive and negative. This resulted from his lack of negative transformations. In addition, he had two auxiliaries that are not in the model language, want and going. These words are analyzed as auxiliaries because they came directly before the verb without the infinitive marker to: I want make two bowls; I going make a pig.

At 2.2 the most common noun markers were the, a, and the plural suffix -s. The markers were sometimes omitted in contexts where they should have been used: I want the duck, I want the duck, I want duck. Other words marked nouns, e.g., some, possessive pronouns, numerals, but they were less frequent.

At 2.2 Harlan indicated the negative with a negative auxiliary, not or isn't: I can't see the pig; That not go right; Isn't a boy. Isn't was used primarily in one-word negations. It was not treated as a negative transformation of is as can be seen in: That piece (puzzle piece) go right over there. (Harlan tried the puzzle piece over there, and found it did not fit.) Isn't. Unfortunately our material does not allow us to say when the negative was first treated as a transformation, but the transformation pattern was present by at least 2.8.

At 2.2 yes-no questions were marked by the rising intonation. The following example at 2.3 indicates that Harlan understood that some sort of inversion should take place:

HARLAN: Want d'you policeman?   /wan juw pliysmæn↑/
INV: Hm?
HARLAN: Want . . . want d'you policeman?   /want | want juw pliysmæn↑/

We have noted that *want* was interpreted by Harlan as an auxiliary, and this may have had some influence on the inversion. But it is clear that Harlan did not understand the function of *do*. The interrogative inversion was used sporadically after this time, and became a productive pattern at 2.8:

INV: You ask Liz what she wants, OK?
HARLAN: D'you want honey, you do? OK.

The elliptical transformation appeared quite suddenly at 2.7, and was common and productive at that time:

INV: Where's the deer going?
HARLAN: Because he is.

INV: How old are you?
HARLAN: Because I am.

INV: Why can't you do it with me?
HARLAN: Because I can't.

INV: When do you eat breakfast?
HARLAN: Because I do.

INV: How did the bird get there?
HARLAN: Because he did.

INV: You've seen this book before, Harlan.
HARLAN: I have?

Emphatic transformations occurred sporadically: *I did turn it off* (2.3); *I did wake up* (2.7).

The above paragraphs show that the verbal transformations involving *do* and other auxiliaries started to come in about 2.3, and became an established feature in Harlan's grammar by 2.8. (Transformations with interrogative words, not treated here, came in a little later; the sentences with interrogative words showed more complicated patterns of development.) The verb restrictions in discourse agreement patterns were fairly well controlled by 2.8.

There seemed to be a correlation between Harlan's grammatical development and the funtional categories described in the introduction. After the development of the verbal transformations and the verb restrictions in discourse agreement, the functional category of responsive discourse was utilized. Since functional categories are more difficult to recognize than formal categories, and since most attention has been focused on the formal categories, this correlation may not be correct. It seems likely that language functions are correlated with grammatical development, whether or not the suggested correlation is correct.

The linguistic system of the child is very unstable. After the word classes are overtly marked, the instability is very noticeable, as the above sketch of Harlan's grammatical system shows. The formal patterns are not set, and the child frequently lapses back into older patterns. It takes a long time for the learned patterns to become automatic.

When the child is able to correct his mistakes, it indicates that he considers certain sentences to be ungrammatical. This is excellent proof that the child has a formal grammatical system. Harlan, the only child to exhibit this ability early, started correcting himself at 2.9, soon after the appearance of verbal transformations and the development of verb restriction in discourse agreement.

PROSODIC FEATURES

Children are good mimics of prosodic features, particularly pitch, and they can give the impression of having the pitch-stress system under control. This may be true from a phonetic, perhaps even phonemic standpoint, but does not necessarily entail the use of the prosodic features in the grammatical system. The rising and falling intonations used to distinguish questions and statements were the only prosodic features consistently found in the linguistic system before the use of class markers. Even this contrast may be later than is generally recognized. The earliest and best record of this contrast is for Susan. In the early records for her at 1.9, many sentences that ended in a level or rising pitch were interpreted as questions. The lack of a falling pitch was often the only indication that the sentence might be a question, and sometimes the context suggested that it was a statement. The adult (parent or investigator) always interpreted the sentence as a question and gave Susan an answer. Susan was over 2 years old before the rising intonation consistently indicated a question. It may be that she learned the intonation by noting which sentences drew a response from the adult.

Prosodic features that had no analogue in the model language were sometimes used in the early period. Christy and Lisa had an accentual system based on pitch and stress. Each sentence had one accented word. The accented word received the last high pitch and/or strong stress. The pitch and stress of the preceding words were variable. Each construction in both children's linguistic system had a particular accent pattern, but the accent pattern was not always adhered to.

All of the children had primary and secondary stress, and a two-level pitch system at the time they developed a linguistic system with marked word classes. The two-level pitch system persisted well beyond this period, probably because two levels are sufficient to indicate most of the grammatical contrasts signaled by the English prosodic system.

INDIVIDUAL DIFFERENCES

We have noted that there were certain features common to the early development of the grammatical level for all the children. Each child had a set of operators, usually derived from function words of the model language, that served as a means of breaking into the model language system. The children did not have the same operators, however. These differences between the children in preferences were clear from the beginning and have persisted in differences in foci of development. It is possible that certain types of patterns or constructions are more compatible than others. Greenberg (1961) has pointed to correlated structures in languages and we might find some patterns in the individual differences between the children at various stages, but our evidence is scant at present.

Lisa had a particularly primitive phonological system. As a result, it was often difficult or impossible to understand her. In addition, final sibilants were absent for a considerable period and she was not able to mark the plural with the suffix -*s*. Instead she used a syntactic device: *one two shoe* meant *more than one shoe*. She later gave this up in favor of other number combinations. According to her mother, she would pick two numbers to indicate the plural, e.g., *eight four shoe*, and then after a few days she would pick up another combination, e.g., *three five shoe*. She finally developed a final /θ/ and was able to say *shoeth*. There may be a relationship between Lisa's syntactic marking of the plural and her earlier use of an operator class which had no adult analogue. In addition, at a later stage of development Lisa seemed to develop some grammatical rules of her own, rules which had no counterpart in the model language.

There are some suggestions in our data that linguistic patterns correlate with some nonlinguistic behavior. Susan's favorite operators were *off* and *on*. Susan was a busy little girl who always taking things off and putting them back on. Christy's favorite operator was *that*, and was used in the demonstrative construction to identify things. When the investigator arrived at Christy's house, she would run into the living room, sit down, and wait to be entertained—wait for the investigator to take toys out of his bag. Most of the children had a favorite toy and a favorite activity. Harlan had no favorite toy, but he had a favorite activity: talking. We found that if we could keep a conversation going he was less apt to throw things. Harlan had the most developed linguistic system of any of the children. He talked early and often. He also made more expressive use of language than the other children: the diminutive baby talk suffix -*y* was productive by 2.5; the expressive pitch pattern /312↑/ was in common use by 2.2.

In the preceding sections we have described a technique in which the child develops the grammatical level by composing, by placing words together to form sentences. A less common technique consists of treating a polymorphemic sequence of the model language as a monomorphemic unit, and then at a later stage of development segmenting the sequence into its proper parts. It is our impression from parental reports that this is more common with second children than with the first born. but still never an important pattern; all of the children in the small group are first born. A third, closely allied technique is the learning, or imitating, of a sentence, understanding the meaning of most of the words and the meaning of the sentence as a whole, but not understanding the grammatical function of the elements. If a number of sentences of a similar pattern are learned, it might be possible for the child to come to recognize the grammatical function of the elements. This technique is rare, or perhaps nonexistent, because the child would probably have to learn by heart a large number of sentences before he happened to learn two that contrasted in the proper fashion. Christy had a number of sentences which appeared to have been memorized, e.g., *where are the shoe?* (2.3). At this time neither *are* nor *is* were productive elements in Christy's speech, and there is no evidence that this or similar sentences were instrumental in her learning the copulative pattern.

DEVELOPMENTAL SEQUENCES

One of the purposes of this study is to describe developmental sequences of linguistic features. While the features studied are those of English, it would be valuable to be able to consider features inherent in any linguistic system. This is difficult to do until more is known about language universals and the prerequisites of language.

The relation between the time of mastery of skills may consist of co-occurrence or of necessary sequence. Sequential orders may arise either because one skill is dependent on the prior acquisition of another, because one is less often practiced, or because they differ in difficulty though are practiced equally. Many of the sequential findings of a normative sort have the third property. They occur because, on the average, it takes a different amount of practice to accomplish one task than another. We would like to separate the logically sequential features. These could be found best in an experimental transfer design, but, whenever in our data there are individual differences in acquisition patterns, some information about sequential dependence can be obtained from studying changes in individual systems rather than group averages.

Viewing the acquisition of phonological contrasts in terms of learning to distinguish features or properties rather than classes, Jakobson (1941) has proposed a developmental order for the phonological system of children. He has suggested that the child successively elaborates a phonological system approaching the adult's by binary division. If he begins with one feature or bundle of features for contrast, he can only have two classes; with two sets of independent features he may have four classes. Within each class he may have sounds which are in many respects phonetically different from the adult model.

Does anything of this sort happen in grammar? We have indicated that grammatical classes and grammatical markers do not have the structural properties of a matrix of features which phonemes have. The classes that are identified in grammatical analysis are not usually marked by features that can then be recombined to define another class. However, at various points in the grammatical-system there are differing degrees of generalization possible. Proper, mass, and count nouns are contrasted by their occurrence with noun determiners, a function class that is unique to this system of classes. The learning of the morphophonemic series in the contrast plural/singular has greater generality. It can also serve in marking possessive nouns, and in marking third person singular verbs. An analogous series marks the regular past tense. At the level of grammatical transformations, a very broad transfer of skills is possible. We may seek for correlations between these related series. For example, though the contrasts plural/singular and possessive/nonpossessive may be acquired at different times for reasons which are semantic or based on frequency, if the contrasts of one are mastered, the other should be too. We have so far only one instance—Harlan—of mastery of both by a child in our study. He gave us productive forms *po-poez* for singular/plural at 2.3 and *Joe-Joez* for possession at 2.4½. At the latter date we find *nizz-nizzez* for singular/plural. But we do not find the possessive *Liz-Lizez* until 2.7. *Joe* and *Liz* were the names of dolls which were used to elicit possession for body parts and clothing, so the opportunity for these contrasts was frequent. This slight evidence does not support the expectation that the morphophonemic contrasts would generalize.

If we turn back to the learning of division into word classes when it first appears, we are limited by the fact that we have only two types of information on which to base our judgment as to the productive operation of classes. One is rules of order with different words. The other is semantic consistency of constructions using these words. At the point at which we first analyzed the children's speech, there were already many classes discernible. Thus we cannot say that at the initial stage before word classes were defined by markers that there was evidence of a first division into two primordial classes which then were subdivided.

If the division into lexical classes is marked by affixes and function words later, then we may expect to find some of the divisions appearing only at the later stage. The division into mass, proper, and count nouns is possible at this point.

In addition to sequences that depend on the availability of markers, some depend on the availability of vocabulary. Thus the rules of order that apply to subclasses of adverbs only could appear after these words enter the vocabulary of children and co-occur in the same sentences.

The earliest forms of markers which we found were inconsistently used. They were the possessive suffix, the plural suffix, *the, and* and *-ing* which were used sporadically. If they were consistent as to class, though, even sporadic use could help identify a class. Thus the first use for these markers may be to identify lexical classes, rather than to distinguish subclasses within lexical classes or to identify constructions. *Want* and *going*, which were used by most of the children of the project as auxiliaries, marked verbs. On the whole, where suffixed and nonsuffixed forms existed, the children preferred the nonsuffixed forms rather than free variants. This was probably in part a phonological problem, since the children had less control of the final consonants than of the other parts of the phonological system.

At the point where subclasses begin to be distinguished so that markers are used as a consistent signal, it is possible to make some simple predictions. For cases with a semantic correlate, a child will first begin imitating forms correctly, and after using a certain number of contrasts correctly will generalize the contrast to new forms. Until enough instances are learned, there will presumably be a delay between these two points. Generalization to irregular cases should occur also; the preferred form for the singular of irregular nouns probably depends on the relative frequency of the singular and plural and relative ease of pronunciation of the two. We already know from Berko's work (1958) that the plural of nouns with final fricatives, sibilants, and affricates tends to be late.

We have tested 25 children with systematic tests of familiar words, irregulars, and nonsense words with a technique similar to Berko's. Nearly always the contrast with familiar forms preceded the contrast with nonsense forms. Naturally, the familiar forms chosen give a rough estimate only. We do not know whether it is the variety of types or the frequency of tokens showing contrasts which is crucial in determining the length of time before generalization occurs.

The average gap for *boy* vs. *kigh* was 2.4 months; for *ball* vs. *kigh* was the same; for *block* vs. *bik* the gap was 1.1 months; for *cup* vs. *bik* 1.5 months. The cases were too few to estimate the gaps for the other contrasts. Thus the child who calls one cup by a different term than two cups might do the same with the nonsense toy *bik* in a month and a half. This analysis was not specific as to the phonological nature of the contrast.

Does the "concept" of plurality generalize; i.e., when one contrast occurs do the others occur soon after? There are artifacts in the restriction on age range provided by the time at which we stopped testing for this paper. For all items except those with fricative, affricate, or sibilant finals, the range between the first contrast to appear and the last was quite short—averaging $2\frac{1}{2}$ months including the nonsense items.

Two irregulars were used as tests for overextension: *foot* and *man*. Of the 15 children who produced a contrast, three said *feet-feets* and 11 said *foot-foots* about the same age as other stop plurals were produced. One child had *foot-footis* first. For 18 children, a contrast between *man* and a plural was offered. For all, the plural was at first *mans*. Two children showed irregular development that can be shown as follows:

SARAH

2.4	bik-biks	tass-tassez	bunge-bunge	man-manz	foot-foots	box-box
2.5	bik-biks	tass-tassez	bunge-bungez	man-manz	foot-footez	box-boxez
2.6	—	tass-tassez	bunge-bungez	man-manz	foot-foots	box-boxez
2.7	bik-biks	tass-tassez	bunge-bungez	man-man	foot-foots	box-bockez
2.9	bik-biks	tass-tass	bunge-bunge	man-man	feet-feets	box-box
2.10	bik-biks	tass-tass	bunge-bunge	man-man	foot-foots	box-box

HARLAN

2.8	bik-biks	tass-tassez	bunge-bungez	man-manz	foot-footez	box-box
2.9	bik-biksez	tass-tassez	bunge-bungez	man-manzez	foot-footsez	box-boxez
2.10	bik-biks	tass-tassez	bunge-bungez	man-manz	foot-footsez	box-boxez
2.11	—	tath-tassez	bunge-bungez	man-men	foot-feet	box-boxez
3.1	bik-biks	tass-tassez	bunge-bungez	man-manz	foot-feet	box-boxez

The vacillation in these series illustrates instability, regression, boredom, or, clearly with Harlan at 2.9, playfulness. Harlan frequently invented games with language.

In sum, the acquisition of the plural contrast followed a simple pattern in most children from noncontrast to acquisition of particular instances of contrast, generalization several months after acquisition of particular instances, and finally, differentiation of irregular forms.

In addition to inflectional suffixes, certain derivational suffixes are used to mark classes. For example, the diminutive or baby talk -*y* was used widely by the children in naming animals—*doggy, horsey*—even when we tried to get them to use the nonsuffixed form for the purpose of testing plurality. However, the suffix was used productively by only one child, Harlan, who produced the following in an argument about a name at 2.5½:

> INV: Really. His name is Cootes. Bill Cootes.
> HARLAN: Billzy the Coooootsy. (*singing*)

Transformations were not found in the earliest linguistic systems. The first to appear were simple (nongeneralized) transformations, such as the progressive (*be* . . . -*ing*), inversion of word order for questions, and the use of auxiliaries with *not*. There were some early interrogative inversions by Christy:

> 2.0 *Where's the arm?*
> 2.1 *Where go toast, huh?*
> 2.4 *Where belong shoe?*
> 2.5 *Where go button, Chrity, huh?*

Soon afterwards the coordinate transformation with *and* appeared. The two-part coordinative transformations (e.g., *both . . . and . . .*) and subordinative transformations have not appeared in our data yet.

Preliminary evidence suggests that discourse agreement features are sequentially ordered. We would expect discourse agreement features involving class restrictions to parallel the sequential development of the classes themselves. Appropriate answers to simple "who/what" questions and "what . . . do" questions came early. Preliminary evidence indicates that the child's adverbs are learned in the order locative, temporal, manner; if true, it might be expected that discourse agreement would proceed in the order where, when, how. In a similar fashion the development of verb restrictions in discourse agreement should follow the development of verb structure.

REFERENCES

Berko, J., The child's learning of English morphology, *Word*, 1958, **14**, 150–177.

Fries, C. C., *The Structure of English*. Harcourt, Brace, 1952.

Greenberg, J., Some universals of grammar with particular reference to the order of meaningful elements. Paper for SSRC Conference on Language Universals, 1961. [Published in J. H. Greenberg (ed.), *Universals of language*. M.I.T. Press, 1962, pp. 58–90.]

Hymes, D. H., Functions of speech: an evolutionary approach. In F. C. Gruber (ed.), *Anthropology and education*. University of Pennsylvania Press, 1961, pp. 55–83.

Jakobson, R., *Kindersprache, Aphasie, und allgemeine Lautgesetze*. Uppsala: Almqvist & Wiksell, 1941. [English trans. by A. Keiler, *Child language, aphasia, and general sound laws*. The Hague,: Mouton, 1968.]

Jakobson, R., Linguistics and poetics. In T. A. Sebeok (ed.), *Style in language*. Technology Press & Wiley, 1960, pp. 350–377.

Maclay, H., and M. Sleator, Responses to language: judgments of grammaticalness, *Int. J. Amer. Ling.*, 1960, **26**, 275–282.

Whorf, B. L. Linguistics as an exact science. Reprinted in J. B. Carroll (ed.), *Language, thought and reality*. Technology Press & Wiley, 1956, pp. 220–232.

The Acquisition of Grammatical Rules by Children

——*Wick R. Miller*

Linguists and parents alike have always found children's speech interesting. In earlier years the interest, in some cases, seemed to be motivated by curiosity. The study of children's speech was not always taken seriously; it was quaint and fascinating, but somehow not really important to an understanding of language. Recent developments of linguistic theory have placed heavy emphasis on the linguistic competence of the native speaker, not just his production, and as a result the acquisition of this competence has placed the study of child language in a more central position in the study of general linguistics.

The data for this paper is a rather large corpus collected over an almost two-year period from a group of five children. It represents a portion of the material collected by Susan Ervin and me as part of a three-year study on the

This paper was presented at the annual meeting of the Linguistic Society of America, New York, December 30, 1964, and is printed here with the permission of the author.

development of grammar in child language. There are certain difficulties in using the materials that represent linguistic production in investigating linguistic competence. The same difficulties are encountered in using a corpus to analyze adult grammar, but they are magnified in the study of children's grammar. More will be said about this later. For the present, I will only point out that the interpretation of the data is not unambiguous, and that in some cases decisions about grammatical productivity are based primarily upon my opinion.

Recent research, our own as well as the research of others, clearly shows that the first multiword sentences of the child are patterned. Whether such patterns can be considered evidence of grammatical structure is debatable, but I would be inclined to think not. At any rate, the patterns grow into a grammar which seems to consist primarily or entirely of phrase-structure rules. Because of the lack of many function words and the resulting abbreviated sentences, Roger Brown and Colin Fraser have aptly characterized the language of the one-and-a-half and two-year-old child as "telegraphic speech." The early grammars are hard to specify because they are highly idiosyncratic in nature. For the most part, the rules seem to reflect reworkings of the adult rules, but sometimes they are made up out of whole cloth and appear to reflect nothing of the model grammar. Children start off on different paths, and it is only when there is a certain amount of convergence that it is profitable to compare the development of the child's grammar with the adult model. This point is reached when the child is about two or two and a half years of age, an age at which many of the phrase-structure rules of adult grammar have been established. This paper will consider the grammatical development from this age to about three and a half. Because of time considerations, I will limit my discussion to a few of the grammatical patterns that must be described in adult grammar by transformational rules.

(When it is stated that a child learns a certain transformational rule, it is to be understood that he has learned a certain grammatical relationship which can be described by the transformational rule. This does not necessarily mean that the child's rule is identical to one found in a transformational grammar, but the two must in some way be isomorphic. The grammatical relations could, of course, be translated into any other adequate linguistic model besides the transformational model.)

Three of the transformations—inversion for yes-no questions, the negative and verb ellipsis—require of the child the same structural analysis and, in certain contexts, the insertion of the auxiliary "do." The occurrences of these transformations are listed in Tables 1–4 for one of the children, Susan; Table 5 lists the estimated age at which each of the transformations became productive for each of the children. The estimates are based not so much on tables, such as those given for Susan, but rather on my judgment as to the quality of the sentences in which they were found. The figures quite probably underestimate the actual age at which the transformations were learned because I did not judge them to be productive until the evidence was conclusive. But I do believe that Table 5

TABLE 1   SUSAN, YES-NO INVERSIONS

AGE	2.2	2.3	2.5	2.7	2.9	3.1	3.6
Do	1	2	11	13	4	25	40
Modals	30	21	37	39	31	72	45
Be	3	3	18	12	6	11	17
	34	26	66	64	41	108	102
do	1	2	8	8	2	15	20
does	0	0	2	3	0	0	6
did	0	0	1	2	2	10	14
	1	2	11	13	4	25	40
will	1	0	1	17	2	2	0
can	5	5	11	13	4	16	3
could	24	13	19	1	14	50	25
Others	0	3	6	8	11	4	17
	30	21	37	39	31	72	45
are	1	3	7	10	1	1	9
is	2	0	11	2	5	10	8
	3	3	18	12	6	11	17

TABLE 2   SUSAN, NONINVERTED MODALS

will	0	2	18	17	9	19	25
can	2	8	25	48	12	32	19
could	0	1	6	4	8	1	12

reflects the true pattern and sequence of development for each of the five children.

The first of these three transformations to be used by Susan was the yes-no inversion, which occurred first at 2.2. At this time almost all of the questions contained the modals "could," "will," and "can." The modal "could," which was by far the most common, was never found in noninverted position, and the other modals, "will" and "can," were seldom found in noninverted position. Thus Susan had not learned to invert the subject and modal, but rather had learned to place the modal at the beginning of the sentence, before the subject. The resulting sentences can be described by a phrase-structure rule with no need to invoke a transformation rule. These sentences were, semantically, not questions but polite requests. Susan said "Could I have the dish" or "Could you make this one" where other children would have said "I want a dish" or "Make

TABLE 3 SUSAN, NEGATIVE

Age	2.0	2.2	2.3	2.5	2.7	2.9	3.1	3.6
Do	0	11	3	8	34	47	50	67
Modals	1	1	4	19	32	14	18	10
Be	0	0	0	6	14	19	9	43
	1	12	7	33	80	80	77	120
do	0	10	3	7	27	33	44	55
does	0	0	0	0	4	3	4	10
did	0	1	0	1	3	11	2	2
		11	3	8	34	47	50	67
am	0	0	0	1	4	4	2	11
are	0	0	0	0	6	6	2	8
is	0	0	0	5	4	8	5	24
were	0	0	0	0	0	1	0	0
				6	14	19	9	43

TABLE 4 SUSAN, VERB ELLIPSIS

Age	2.5	2.7	2.9	3.1	3.6	Age	2.5	2.7	2.9	3.1	3.6
Do	3	15	15	9	19	do	0	6	8	4	10
Modals	4	10	6	6	5	does	2	2	2	2	4
Be	5	10	9	10	24	did	1	7	5	3	5
	12	35	30	25	48		3	15	15	9	19
						am	0	4	3	1	1
will	0	2	1	5	2	are	0	5	3	3	6
can	4	6	3	1	0	is	5	0	3	6	15
Others	0	2	2	0	3	was	0	1	0	0	2
	4	10	6	6	5		5	10	9	10	24

this one." The sentences usually had an intonation pattern 2-3-1 with a falling contour.

During the next period of text collection at 2.3, Susan used "can" a number of times in both inverted and noninverted position. Susan may have learned the inversion rule by this time, but it was not until the next period, at 2.5, that the evidence was unambiguous. At 2.5 there were several noninverted sentences with "could," though the modal was employed more commonly in

TABLE 5   AGE AT WHICH THREE VERBAL TRANSFORMATIONS BECOME PRODUCTIVE FOR FIVE CHILDREN

	SUSAN	CHRISTY	CARL	LISA	HARLAN
Q, Do	2.5	3.0	3.4	3.1	2.10
Q, Modals	2.5	3.1	3.4	3.3	2.10
Q, Be	2.5	3.1	*	3.1	2.10
Neg, Do	2.7	2.10	2.9	2.11	2.3
Neg, Be	2.7	3.1	2.9	3.1	2.4
Elp, Do	2.7	3.0	3.4	3.3	2.5
Elp, Modal	2.7	3.1	*	3.1	2.5
Elp, Be	2.7	3.1	*	3.1	2.5
Cp. appearance of "not" in sentence fragments	2.7	2.8	2.6	2.10	2.4
Cp. when inversion outnumbered simple rising intonation	2.3	3.0	3.4	3.3	2.10

* Had not appeared when last text was collected at 3.4.

inverted order to form polite requests—a common technique that Susan employed throughout the period of the study. At 2.5, Susan applied the inversion rule not only to modals but also to forms of "be" and to the three forms of the inserted "do." Exchanges of the following type were common:

> INV: Ask Liz if she drinks coffee.
> SUSAN: Do you drink coffee?

Before the interrogative inversion is learned, children are able to ask questions by simply using a rising intonation. All five of the children in our sample utilized this technique quite early. Once the inversion was learned, it did not replace all of the questions marked only by intonation since this technique is also available to adults. But it did appear that once the inversion was learned questions of this type outnumbered those marked only by the rising intonation, and that the ratio between the two could be used as a rough index for the time of learning this transformation (Table 6). In most cases, the inverted questions predominated when the transformation was judged to have been learned.

After Susan had learned to properly analyze her sentences for the yes-no inversion, she was in a position to extend the analysis for the negative and verb ellipsis transformation. These two transformations were learned rather rapidly, and Susan clearly controlled them by 2.7. In general, Susan's pattern of

TABLE 6   QUESTIONS MARKED ONLY BY RISING INTONATION VERSUS INVERSIONS FOR FIVE CHILDREN

	2.0	2.1	2.2	2.3	2.4	2.5	2.6	2.7	2.8	2.9	2.10	2.11	3.0	3.1	3.3	3.4	3.5	3.6	3.8
SUSAN																			
Intonation	6	6	37	7		21		4	2		22		10	11				22	
Inversion	0	0	34	26		66		2	0		2		14	16				75	
CHRISTY																			
Intonation			20	49	68	14	3												
Inversion			2	3	1	0	1												
CARL																			
Intonation						23	7		2	29				16		13			
Inversion						5	1		1	5				4		109			
LISA																			
Intonation						12	12	2	2	3	12	22		22	35				6
Inversion						0	2	0	0	0	3	0		13	57				30
HARLAN																			
Intonation				3	9	16	23		13	8	4	33		20	8		18		
Inversion				0	5	0	1		1	8	46	61		60	87		38		

development was typical in that the first transformation was learned rather slowly, but the remaining two transformations were learned more quickly since the structural analysis for the first could be extended to the second and third. But Susan's particular pattern was unique among the five children, in that she learned the yes-no inversion first, whereas the other children learned the negative transformation first.

Christy's development illustrates the more typical pattern. At 2.7 and 2.8 she placed "don't" before the verb to form negative sentences, yielding such sentences as "Doggy don't say byebye" as well as "I don't want it." Since the form "don't" was invariable, the grammatical pattern could be described by a phrase-structure rule. By 2.10 she was able to correctly use "doesn't" and by 3.0 "didn't," indicating that she had now learned the transformational pattern. Sentences of the type "He don't want to" were still found occasionally at 2.10, but these could be considered ungrammatical slips, reversions to the earlier pattern.

Sentence fragments with "not" appeared at about the same time that the negative transformation was learned. Some examples from Susan at 2.7:

> INV: Does she walk yet?
> SUSAN: No, not yet.
>
> SUSAN: She's not through eating. Not through.

Such sentence fragments are quite different from the abbreviated sentences or telegraphic speech of the two-year-old. Susan's response "not yet" indicated the presence of a sophisticated grammatical pattern which allowed her to derive the sentence fragment from "She doesn't walk yet" by the use of a deletion rule.

The elliptical transformation was usually learned last, although one child, Harlan, learned it long before the interrogative inversion. As with the sentence fragments containing "not," verb ellipsis shows a high level of grammatical sophistication, because the child must be able to correctly analyze the sentence and delete the appropriate elements. We have an unusually good check for this transformation because the source sentence was usually present. Some typical exchanges with Christy at 2.10, before she had learned the elliptical transformation:

> INV: Are you gonna make coffee for Liz?
> CHRISTY: Yeah I do.
>
> INV: I'm Joe.
> CHRISTY: No you don't. You're a Wick.

By 3.1 there were a number of exchanges of the following type:

> INV: It's not blue.
> CHRISTY: Yes it is.

These three transformations—yes-no inversion, the negative, and verb ellipsis—appeared to develop as a group, and a general pattern can be observed. The child first learned a formula, or better, a phrase-structure rule, that enabled him to produce sentences which were transformations in adult grammar. Susan started with the inversion of modals in yes-no questions, the remaining children with the negative, usually formed by placing "don't" before the verb. The pattern spread slowly at first so that other kinds of sentences could be included. Once the pattern changed so that the grammatical relations could only be described by transformation rules, the other transformations were learned rather rapidly. The children had learned a set of related rules that could be applied widely.

Questions with interrogative words present the child with a different kind of learning problem. To be able to produce these questions, by adult rules at least, it is necessary to first apply the yes-no question transformation. Yet all of the children in our sample used two interrogatives, "what" and "where," long before they had mastered the yes-no inversion. To produce these sentences, the children had to have rules that would not match adult rules. We have found that it is very difficult to construct grammatical rules that are at variance with adult rules. I have, nevertheless, attempted to write rules that account for Susan's "what" questions at 2.2 (Table 7). I cannot claim that the rule is accurate in the

TABLE 7   RULES FOR FORMING " WHAT " QUESTIONS, SUSAN 2.2

$$\text{(1)} \quad \text{what-sentence} > \text{what} + (-\text{'s}) + \text{NP} + (\text{VP})$$

$$\text{(2)} \quad \text{VP} > \text{verb} + (\text{-ing}) + \left(\left\{ \begin{matrix} \text{NP} \\ \text{prep} + \text{NP} \end{matrix} \right\} \right)$$

The rules correctly predict 23 out of 35 "what" questions.

sense that Susan had exactly this rule, but I do feel confident that she had a rule something like this. All of the children had rules more or less of this sort for both "what" and "where" questions, although it is clear that each child had his own slightly varying rule. All of the children made use of the contracted "-s," which reflected both "does" and "is" in the adult language. The children did not distinguish the different sources of this contraction, as can be seen in the sentence from Lisa at 2.10 "Where is this belong?". Some of the children occasionally added tense to the verb, as in the sentence from Christy at 3.1 "Where it goes?". It can be seen from these examples that the rules produced sentences that, from the adult point of view, were sometimes grammatical and sometimes not; but it may be significant that the ungrammatical sentences were fewer than could be expected by chance.

It is difficult to say when the children developed the adult rules for interrogative questions because they seemed to grow into them rather than learn them. Two factors were probably involved. First, the children probably lapsed back into the earlier rules from time to time before the newer rules were well established. Second, there were probably some ungrammatical slips of the tongue; such slips occur in adult speech, too, but they are more frequent in children's speech, and, in this case, extremely difficult to identify. But it does appear likely that the adult rules were well established within two or three months after the mastery of the yes-no inversion.

Relative clauses are introduced by words that largely overlap the interrogative words. It is not surprising, then, to find that relative clauses appear at about the same time that the child learns to handle interrogative word questions appropriately. Four of the relatives, "what, where, when," and "that," account for most of the examples. The corresponding interrogative word was, for the most part, used more frequently, though not necessarily earlier, than the relative. The major exception was "when," which was used more frequently, as well as earlier, in relative clauses than in questions by all five of the children. It might be expected that the child would apply the question inversion to the relative clause, since the interrogative function was more common. But, in fact, there were no examples of this.

TABLE 8 SUSAN, RELATIVE CLAUSES

Age	2.2	2.3	2.5	2.7	2.9	3.1	3.6
what	4	4	1	1	4	7	14
who	0	0	0	0	0	1	3
that	0	1	0	1	2	2	16
which	0	0	0	1	0	0	0
where	0	0	2	2	0	3	7
when	0	0	2	6	15	7	22
how	0	0	0	1	0	6	12
why	0	0	0	0	0	3	1
	4	5	5	12	21	29	75

The passive can be discussed quickly, because it was not present in the grammars of any of the children by the time the last texts had been collected. In almost every text there were a few sentences that reflected adult passive sentences. For example Susan at 2.7: "He said it was locked." "This is torn;" or Christy at 2.10 "That is broken." The word "broken," in particular, was used very early by most of the children in sentences that reflected adult passives. But the agent, introduced by the preposition "by," was never present, indicating that the child was not using the adult rule. A sentence by Christy at 3.0 was the closest that any of the children ever came to a true passive: "So we won't hurt a car," where she meant "So we won't get hurt by a car"; the order of goal and agent was that of the passive, but the form of the verb and the expression of the agent did

TABLE 9   SUSAN, OCCURRENCES OF "AND" USED TO LINK PARTS OF SENTENCES

AGE	2.2	2.3	2.5	2.7	2.9	3.1	3.6
Nouns	0	0	4	6	12	1	18
Verbs	0	0	4	7	5	10	13
Adjectives	0	0	1	0	0	0	5
Other classes	1	0	0	3	2	0	7
	1	0	9	16	19	11	43
Other uses	3	0	13	39	31	14	100

not follow the adult rule. It seems very probable, however, that this sentence was influenced by adult passive sentences.

The conjunction "and" presents still another kind of grammatical problem for the child. It is used to connect words and phrases that belong to the same class, so that its use presupposes the development of classes. There is good evidence that classes start to develop in the very earliest stages, long before the first appearance of "and" is found. The typical chronological order of class linkage was first nouns and noun phrases, verbs, adjectives, and lastly other things such as prepositional phrases and adverbs. Susan's use of "and" is given in Table 9 and you will note that she varied somewhat from this pattern. The last line of the table, labeled "other uses," is a tabulation of all occurrences that cannot, for one reason or another, be taken as firm evidence for its use in connecting parts of sentences. For the most part, these include the connecting of whole sentences, or the use of "and" at the beginning of a sentence or sentence fragment. When the conjunction occurrred at the beginning of a sentence, its use sometimes seemed inappropriate, and in other cases it was impossible to tell what the child was linking the sentence to. But it was clear in some cases, particularly in the later texts, that the sentences or sentence fragments were additions to the previous sentence, which was spoken either by the child himself or by

TABLE 10   THE USE OF "AND" IN (1) LINKING PARTS OF SENTENCES, AND (2) OTHER USES FOR THREE CHILDREN

CHRISTY	2.4	2.5	2.6	2.7	2.8	2.10	3.0	3.1	3.6
Linking	2	1	0	3	0	3	2	6	16
Other	8	1	0	9	2	12	13	24	31
CARL	2.5	2.6	2.8	2.9	3.1	3.4			
Linking	4	0	5	4	11	23	(4 of the 5 at		
Other	1	2	4	5	17	77	2.8 = imitations)		
LISA	2.7	2.8	2.9	2.10	2.11	3.1	3.3	3.8	
Linking	3	2	5	9	13	23	17	37	
Other	0	4	26	32	11	46	134	67	

some other person. As with the elliptical sentences, the child had become more sensitive to the linguistic environment outside the single sentence, and this accounted for the very large increase of sentences classified as "other uses" around three or three and a half years of age. The appearance of the conjunction in linking parts of sentences coincided with what I have labeled "other uses," indicating that simply the occurrence of "and," regardless of the particular function, was diagnostic of the child's ability to use it as a conjunction. This is the same pattern that was found for "not," which appeared in negative transformations at the same time as sentence fragments.

CLOSING REMARKS

It should be clear that I am *not* trying to write grammars for the language of these five children. It is, of course, very difficult or impossible to derive a grammar from text material alone. In working with adult informants, texts are useful for making preliminary grammatical notes to be later checked by other means. Texts gathered from children can be used in the same fashion. But different techniques must be used for checking since you cannot question a child the way you would an adult informant. Roger Brown and his colleagues have developed some testing techniques for grammatical patterns that allow a choice between two alternatives. Thus to test for the active and passive, the child can be asked to select the pictures in which the truck hit the train, or in which the truck was hit by the train. This technique or variations of it can be used to study a number of grammatical features such as the noun plural suffix, the verb past tense suffix, compounding vs. modification by prepositional phrases, and so on. A number of grammatical patterns that do not lend themselves to formal test situations can be tested informally while collecting text material, and we did this in our study. To test for yes-no inversion, the child would be instructed to "ask the doll if he wants some food"; or for the morphophonemic patterns of irregular verbs we would say, "Ask the doll what he saw yesterday," and the child's response would be either "What did you saw yesterday?" or, "What did you see yesterday?". Having the child imitate sentences or phrases provides another check, since it has been found that children seldom imitate grammatical patterns that are not a part of their own language system. Still another technique is to present the child with a choice such as: "Is it a new red dress, or a red new dress?" The child almost always picks the last of two alternatives if he lacks the appropriate grammatical rules.

There are still many kinds of grammatical patterns, however, for which there are as yet no techniques available for checking, and all our information must come from the study of text materials. In addition there are some grammatical patterns that can probably best be studied from text material, such as the development of deletion rules and of sentence fragments. These are particularly important in the development of grammar since their proper use depends upon responding to the linguistic environment outside of the single sentence, a larger environment which may be provided by the child himself or some other person.

REFERENCES

Braine, Martin D. S., The ontogeny of English phrase structures: The first phase, *Language*, 1963, **39**. 1–13. [Reprinted in this volume.]

Berko, Jean, The child's learning of English morphology, *Word*, **14**, 1958, 150–177.

Brown, Roger, and Ursula Bellugi, Three processes in the child's acquisition of syntax, *Harvard Educational Review*, 1964, **34**, 133–151.

Brown, Roger, and Colin Fraser, The acquisition of syntax, *Child Development Monographs*, 1964, **29**, 43–79.

Brown, Roger, Colin Fraser, and Ursula Bellugi, Explorations in grammar evaluation, *Child Development Monographs*, 1964, **29**, 79–92.

Ervin, Susan M., Structure in children's language. Paper read at the International Congress of Psychology, Washington, D.C., 1963.*

Ervin, Susan H., Imitations in the speech of two-year-olds. Paper read at the American Psychological Association, Philadelphia, 1963.*

Fraser, Colin, Ursula Bellugi, and Roger Brown, Control of grammar in imitation, comprehension, and production, *Journal of Verbal Learning and Verbal Behavior*, 1963, **2**, 121–135. [Reprinted in this volume.]

Menyuk, Paula, Syntactic rules used by children from preschool through first grade, *Child Development*, 1964, **35**, 533–546.

Miller, Wick R., Patterns of grammatical development in child language, *Proceedings of the Ninth International Congress of Linguists, Cambridge, Mass.*, 1962, pp. 511–517. Mouton and Company, 1964.

Miller, Wick, and Susan Ervin, The development of grammar in child language, *Child Development Monographs*, 1964, **29**, 9–34. [Reprinted in this volume.]

* [Editors' note: These two papers, combined, are reprinted in this volume as "Imitation and structural change in children's language," by Susan M. Ervin-Tripp.]

Imitation and Structural Change in Children's Language

——Susan M. Ervin-Tripp

We all know that children's grammar converges on the norm for the community in which they live. How does this happen? One source might be through adult correction of errors and through operant conditioning reinforced by the responses of others. This is probably a relatively weak source of change in

From E. H. Lenneberg (ed.), *New directions in the study of language*. Cambridge, Mass.: M.I.T. Press, 1964, pp. 163–189. Reprinted by permission of the author and the publisher. (Originally published under the name Susan M. Ervin.)

first language learning. We know, for instance, that children learn certain grammatical structures which nobody taught them explicitly, and we also know that often teachers try hard to eradicate some of them. All over the world children learn grammatical patterns whether or not anyone corrects their speech, and there have been cases in which children who were believed for years to be mute have been found employing relatively mature grammatical patterns. A second source of change is maturation. Young children cannot learn grammatical and semantic concepts of a certain degree of complexity, and they produce sentences limited in length. Gvozdev (1961), in a book on child language development in Russian, has presented evidence that, when grammatical complexity is held constant, semantic difficulty is related to the age of acquisition of certain grammatical patterns. For instance, the conditional is learned late. Recent work by Roger W. Brown and his group supports this view. But maturation cannot account for the content of language nor for the particular structures acquired. A third factor affecting language development might be comprehension. We know that, typically, recognition precedes production. We know that people can understand many more words than they ever use. The number of cues for recognition is less than the information needed for accurate production, and in recognition we can often profit from redundancy.

Fraser, Bellugi, and Brown (1963) have recently found that children's imitation of grammatical contrasts regularly surpassed their comprehension, which in turn was superior to their freely generated speech. For instance, they would choose the right picture, or repeat "The sheep are jumping," or "The sheep is jumping," more often than they could speak the right name when a picture was pointed out.

The children in this study were asked to imitate. The real test as to whether imitation is significant as a source of progress in grammar should be based on spontaneous imitations, for children may imitate selectively.

The material to be reported here is merely suggestive. It consists of a study of only five children.[1] It is unique in that I have the advantage of working from careful descriptive grammars for each of the children about whom I shall report. The crucial test is this: Are imitated utterances grammatically different from free utterances? If they are different, are they more advanced grammatically?

Ideally, one would write independent grammars for the imitated sentences and for the freely generated sentences and compare the grammatical rules. Since the number of imitations was far too small, grammatical rules were written only for the free sentences, and then the imitations were tested for their consistency

[1] Conducted with the support of a grant from the National Institute of Mental Health and the facilities of the Institute for Human Development and the Institute for Human Learning at the University of California, Berkeley. The work was done in collaboration with Wick Miller, now Assistant Professor of Anthropology at the University of Utah.

with these rules. This method loads the dice against the similarity of the imitations to the free sentences.

First I shall describe what I mean by a grammar, then define what I mean by imitation, and finally test the hypothesis of similarity.

We collected 250 sentences of two words or more from Donnie (Table 1).

TABLE 1   SENTENCE-GENERATING RULE FOR DONNIE, AGED 2:2

	OPTIONAL CLASSES[a]						REQUIRED CLASS
1	2	3	4	5	6		7
goodness					bead		bead(s)
oh	here(s)				blanket		blanket
oh oh	there(s)	go[b]			bow-wow		bow-wow
oh dear	where(s)		a		car		car(s)
				big	choochoo		choochoo
see			the		Daddy		Daddy
whee	this				kiddy-car		kiddy-car
	that(s)				ring		ring
					truck		truck(s)
					water		water
					etc.		etc.

[a] Classes 1 to 6, selected in that order, may precede 7.
[b] "This" and "that(s)" never precede "go."

At this time, when he was 2 years and 2 months old, his mother reported that he had just begun to put words together. The rule described here accounts for 198 of Donnie's sentences.

Another 16 sentences followed another rule, producing "what's that" and "what's this." There were 35 sentences which could be described by neither rule.

You will see that the following sentences were grammatically consistent:

Blanket water.	Oh, there's a bed.
Bow-wow dog.	Oh, car.
Here big truck.	Oh, dear, the truck.
Where go the car?	Where's a big choochoo car?

We could not account for 7 per cent of Donnie's sentences by any simple rules. These included the following:

Where the more bead?	Go bye-bye Daddy.

Naughty Donnie.	Here's it go.
Go get the truck.	Here's it goes.

What the choochoo car?

Three months later, Donnie's grammar had changed (Table 2). Some of the sentences that we could not account for at the earlier stage have now become more frequent and stable. We now find it necessary to set up a phrase rule for a nominal phrase, which you see in Table 2. Although all the regular sentences at the younger age contained at least one nominal, there are now more frequent

TABLE 2   NOMINAL PHRASE-GENERATING RULE FOR DONNIE, AGE 2:5

	Optional Classes[a]			Required Class
	1	2	3	4
NOMINAL	a	red	all-gone	all-gone
	the	big	ball	ball
		more	bead	bead(s)
			broken	broken
			bye-bye	bye-bye
			choochoo	choochoo
			green	green
			monkey	monkey
			truck	truck
			yellow	yellow
			etc.	etc.

[a] Classes 1 to 3, in that order, may precede 4.

sentences without a nominal phrase (Table 3). We can conveniently divide Donnie's sentences into four types at this age. The largest number, 173, were declarative sentences like "there's a bus," "there's a green," "here's a broken," and "there's all-gone." Ninety-six were nominal sentences like "big yellow," "oh, broken," "yellow broken," or "monkey broken." Another 76 contained "go" or "goes" as in "car go broken," "goes the bubbles," and "there's it go." There were 20 sentences with "have-it," meaning "I want it." For example, "there beads, have-it" and "where the choo-choo, have-it."

These are inductive or descriptive rules or grammars. Alternative descriptions might do as well: our criteria were brevity and completeness. We can test a grammar of an adult language by asking speakers if test sentences are acceptable; with so-called dead, literary languages we can cross-check different sources. With children, our descriptions must be more tentative. For these two-year-olds

TABLE 3   SENTENCE-GENERATING RULE FOR DONNIE, AGE 2:5

1	2	3[a]	4	5	6
oh boy	there(s)	it			
hi	where(s)	all	go	NOMINAL	have-it[c]
no	here(s)		goes		
don't	that(s)[b]				
etc.	this is[b]	NOMINAL			

[a] Multiword sentences contain at least one item from columns 3 to 6, with order as in the sequence of columns.

[b] That(s) and this (is) never precede columns 4 to 6.

[c] Columns 4 and 6 are mutually exclusive.

we found that between 77 and 80 per cent of the sentences could be described by our grammars.

Now we turn to the central issue. Are the spontaneous imitations of these children governed by the same rules as their freely generated sentences? To illustrate, here are some examples of Donnie's imitations at 2.5. You will find the first three are consistent, the last two are not.

"This is a round ring."   "This ring."
"Where does it go?"   "Where's it go?"
"Is Donnie all-gone?"   "Donnie all-gone."
"Is it a bus?"   "It a bus."
"Is it broken?"   "Is broken."

We have confined this study only to overt, immediate repetitions. We have excluded imitations in which there were changes, as in "Liz is naughty," "He's naughty." We found that adult conversations are heavily threaded with such partial imitations and also that they are hard to separate from answers to questions. Judges might easily disagree in judging which were imitations. We kept the clear-cut cases, including exact repetitions, which were few, echoes of the final few words in sentences, and repetitions with words omitted. There were few cases of repetitions with changes in word order. Omissions bulked large in our cases of imitation. These tended to be concentrated on the unstressed segments of sentences, on articles, prepositions, auxiliaries, pronouns, and suffixes. For instance: "I'll make a cup for her to drink" produced "cup drink"; "Mr. Miller will try," "Miller try"; "Put the strap under her chin," "Strap chin." Thus the imitations had three characteristics: they selected the most recent and most emphasized words, and they preserved the word order.

When the imitations have been isolated, the next step is to identify the grammatically consistent sentences. These were of two types. Some used vocabulary that we had included in describing the grammars. As I have said, our rules included lists of words according to classes, or by positions they could occupy.

Some of the imitated sentences included new words that were not on these lists. Any speech sample is selective in vocabulary, and since we were interested in structure and not vocabulary, we arbitrarily included as grammatical any sentences containing a single new word by treating these words as "deuces wild." That is to say, any new word could be assigned to a class so as to make a grammatical sentence. The same rule was used on the residual sentences which were freely generated. Some of these sentences were called ungrammatical simply because they included grammatically ambiguous words.

We used exactly the same rule of procedure for the imitated sentences and for the free sentences in deciding whether the sentence fit the structural rules or not. We made liberal, but equally liberal, provision for accepting new vocabulary in both samples. Thus we can see whether the rules of word arrangement were the same in the two samples (Table 4).

TABLE 4   GRAMMATICAL NOVELTY OF IMITATIONS

	PERCENTAGE IMITATED	PERCENTAGE GRAMMATICALLY CONSISTENT	
		Freely Generated	Imitated
Susan (1.10)	7	88	79
Christy (2.0)	5	91	92
Donnie (2.2)	6	93	100
Lisa (2.3)	15	83	65
Holly (2.4)	20	88	68[a]
Donnie (2.5)	8	91	94
Donnie (2.10)	7	92	91

[a] $X^2 = 9.4$

For all the children except one, Holly, the sentences in both samples were equally predictable from both rules. Donnie was studied at three ages, and there was no change with age in the consistency of his imitated sentences.

But what about Holly? We must move to our second question with her: Were the imitated sentences grammatically more advanced than the free ones, or simply more inconsistent? We shall use three criteria in judging the grammatical maturity of these sentences. These criteria are based on the changes that characterized the children's speech in the months following those we are considering. First, sentence length increased with age. Donnie's sentences at the three ages considered had an average length of 2.2, 2.4, and 2.7 words. Secondly, there is an increase in certain grammatical markers with age, including an increase in the use of articles and pronouns. Finally, there is an increase in adult-like sentence constructions consisting of imperative-plus-object, or subject-verb-object, or subject-verb-adjective, or subject-verb-particle. Examples are "hold it," "he took it," "that's hot," and "they came over."

Using these three criteria, we examined all of Holly's residual sentences, both imitated and free, that did *not* fit the rules of arrangement we had called her grammar. The average length of the free sentences was three words, of the imitated sentences, two words. There were grammatical markers such as articles and pronouns in 62 per cent of the free sentences, and in 28 per cent of the imitated sentences. Half of the free sentences and a third of the imitated sentences were structurally complete, from an adult standpoint. There were no subject-verb-object imitated sentences, but there were six subject-verb-object free sentences, such as "I want play game" and "I don't see Heather car," Heather being Holly's sister.

We are left with a question about why Holly was so different from the other children. It was something of a *tour de force* to write a grammar for Holly. One class, identified as a class by the fact that its members occupied initial position in sentences, included "this-one," "see," "want," and "there." Another heterogeneous class, identified only by the fact that it followed the words just described, include "around," "pull," "raining," "book," and "two." No other child had such a bizarre system, if system it was. Probably Holly's imitations did not fit this system because these were not in fact rules governing her speech. Donnie's rules were far more simple, consistent, and pervasive. It is possible that the high percentage of imitations produced by Holly is related to the fluidity of her grammar. But if it is so, then her imitations were a disturbing rather than a productive factor in her grammatical development.

If we can rely at all on this sample of five children, there is an inescapable conclusion. Imitations under the optimal conditions, those of immediate recall, are not grammatically progressive. We cannot look to overt imitation as a source for the rapid progress children make in grammatical skill in these early years.

A word of caution. I have *not* said that imitation is never important in language learning. In comprehension covert imitation may be important. Possibly imitation aids in the acquisition of vocabulary or of phonetic mastery. Perhaps overt imitation is indispensable in the special conditions of classroom language learning. All I have said is that there is not a shred of evidence supporting a view that progress toward adult norms of grammar arises merely from practice in overt imitation of adult sentences.

FITTING THEORIES TO FACTS

One may take several different approaches in accounting for child language development. We have already touched on one: the imitative view. According to this conceptualization the child makes errors and introduces abbreviations in his effort to approximate sentences he hears. Development is thought to consist of gradual elimination of such random errors.

This point of view is implied in the studies of grammatical development which have counted grammatical errors, omissions, and sentence length as criteria for developmental level. A second view assumes that children have sets of rules like those of adults, since they can understand adults, but that in speaking they have a combination of editing rules and random production errors. Development consists in eliminating the omissions and redundancies arising from these editing rules. A third view would assume that development can be described as the evolution of a series of linguistic systems increasing in complexity, with changes in behavior reflecting changes in the child's syntactical rules.

The data reported below have been collected in a collaborative study with Wick Miller, in which frequent texts were collected from seven monolingual oldest children, and monthly systematic tests were conducted on 24 children, during a period approximately from age 2 to 4.

In English plural inflection, the contrast *dogs* vs. *dog* might be learned as if the two words were unrelated, separate items of vocabulary. Each would be learned by imitation and by association with the appropriate semantic discrimination. Yet imitation will not account for the behavior of adults speaking English. If an adult hears a new word, say, the name of a new tool, such as a *mindon*, he will surely call two of them *mindons*, a word he has never heard. We might say that he has formed a new word by analogy. Such analogic extensions are not explainable as simple generalization, because they occur when both the referent and the word itself are new and clearly distinguishable from previously known words. We found that children formed new plurals in this way when they were between 2 and 3 years old.

We tested children systematically by showing them objects, first singly and then in pairs, and asking for a description. These tests were conducted at monthly intervals. Some of the things we asked about were familiar, such as "boys" and "oranges." Others were new objects, called such things as a *bik*, *pud*, or *bunge*.

If the child learns the plural first in terms of separate items of vocabulary, we would expect him to employ the plural suffix with some consistency with familiar words before he generalized to new words. In fact, this is just what happened. For nearly all the children, there was a time gap between the time when a familiar plural was used and the time when an analogous new word was given a plural. Thus, between the time when the child contrasted *block* and *blocks* and the time when he said that two things called *bik* were *biks*, there was a small but reliable gap of about two weeks. For *car* and *boy* and the analogous *kie*, the gap was about six weeks. For other words the gap was greater. In all cases—*pud*, *bik*, *kie*, *tass*, and *bunge*—the new contrast appeared later than the contrasts the children had heard.

We would expect that this extension to new forms also would occur for the irregular plurals. All of the children, over the period we studied them, regularized the plural for *foot* and *man*. They said *man-mans*, and *foot-foots* or *feet-feets*. Most preferred *foot-foots*. Very few of the children fluctuated between *foot* and *feet*, so although the word *feet* must have been heard by the children, we can clearly see a regularizing influence. If imitation alone were at work, we would have expected fluctuation between *foot* and *feet*.

There was a difference in the time of acquisition depending on form. The English plural form is quite regular and has few exceptions. Its form is governed by certain sound rules. Thus we have *mat* and *mats*, but *match* and *matches*. We can describe this difference by saying that words ending in sibilants, such as *horse*, *buzz*, *match*, *judge*, *marsh*, or *rouge*, add a vowel plus *s*. Children at this age frequently do not distinguish these sounds phonetically—orange may be pronounced unpredictably as *orinch, orinz, orints, orins, orinsh* by the same child. The children all shared the problem of adding *s* to words ending in sibilant sounds. What they did was omit a plural contrast for these words. The usual pattern in the earlier grammars was distinction of singular and plural except for words ending in sibilants, which had the same forms for singular and plural. Occasionally we would have analogies which removed the sibilant, as in singular *bun* plural *buns* for *bunges*, and singular *bok* plural *boks* for *boxes*.

At some point each child produced the regular plural for one of these sibilant words. Quite often, when this happened, the plural for other earlier forms changed. Thus when *box-boxes* first was given, we found such forms as *foot-footses*, or *hand-handses*. Another pattern sometimes appeared. When *tass-tasses* came in, we found *foot-footiz* or *bik-bikiz*.

These changes occurred with children who had previously used the *-s* plural regularly, for *foot*, *bik*, and *hand*. Why did these words change? If we examine the whole range of plurals employed at one of these points in time, we might describe the system as involving two plural forms vacillating unpredictably from *-s* to *-iz*. Alternatively, *-s* or *-siz* were both in unpredictable variation. Surely, at this point, it is clear that the child is employing some common response, whatever you may call it, in using all of these plural forms. A linguist would say the child had a plural morpheme with two allomorphs in free variation. How can a psychologist translate this behavior into terms familiar to him? This is most certainly not behavior learned by accumulated imitation. It is transitory, lasting at most two months, and then is resolved into a system of conditional variation like that of adults.

There are two pieces of evidence here which will not fit a theory that inflection develops through imitation of familiar forms and extension by generalization to new items. One is the fact that *foot* and *feet* do not fluctuate as much as imitation of adults would lead us to expect. The other is that even highly practiced, familiar plurals may be temporarily changed in form by overgeneralization of new patterns. Both these data suggest that analogy in the production of sentences is a very important process and may outweigh the imitation of familiar forms.

Analogy is a familiar process to linguists. Formal similarity is the basis for the construct they call a morpheme. Yet overlaid on the child's systematic analogic forms, or morphemic patterns, we have a gradual accumulation of successful imitations which do not fit the stabilized pattern of the child, in such instances as *oranges* and *boxes*. Eventually these result in a change in the system, which becomes evident in the errors, from the adult standpoint, and in the analogic extensions to nonsense words. The conditioned allomorphs in the adult system—the different plurals in *mats* and *matches*—were imitated one by one at first. Then they produced random fluctuation between the two forms, and later stable responses conditioned by the same features in the phonetic environment as the adult plurals.

Now let us turn to past tense inflection. Our best data are from the group of seven children from whom we collected extensive texts in interviews over a period of time. It is, of course, much harder to elicit a contrast in tense than one in plurality. The semantic cues are less controllable. For this reason we relied on less systematic methods of testing. Now it happens that the English tense system has analogies to the system of plurals. Like the plurals, it has both a regular pattern and irregular forms. There is *walk-walked*, and there is *go-went*. As with the plurals, the specific phonemic pattern depends on the particular final phoneme of the simple verb—we have *pack-packed* and *pat-patted*, when a vowel is added in the suffix. As with plurals, the children used forms that indicated the difficulty of the pattern of adding a vowel—forms such as *toasteded*.

The major formal difference in English between plural inflection of nouns and tense inflection of verbs is the great frequency of irregular (or strong) verbs, whereas irregular nouns are relatively few. It was a surprise to me, in examining verb frequency tables for the children we studied, to find that verbs with regular inflection were few and infrequent in our earliest texts. Therefore, tense inflection begins with the *irregular* forms.

I looked for the first case of extension of the regular past tense suffix which could not have been imitated—for instance *buyed, comed, doed*. The odd, and to me astonishing, thing is that these extensions occurred in some cases before the child had produced *any* other regular past tense forms according to our sample. In some cases the other past tense forms consisted of only one or two words of dubious significance as past tense signals.

Relatively rare was the extension of irregular patterns—though we did find *tooken*. With plurals we had found that extension to new instances followed considerable practice with the regular pattern. Of course, our texts must underestimate the frequency of regular verbs, since they are small samples, but the regularity with which we found such extensions occurring quite early suggests that it takes relatively few instances and little practice to produce analogic extension. Another interpretation is that such extensions can occur with little or no actual contrasts in the child's speech; he may base them on the variety of types employing the regular contrast in the language of the adult. That is, if he can comprehend the contrast in the adult language he may on that basis be led to produce analogous forms.

With plurals, the regular patterns were learned and extended first; children did not waver between *foot-feet* and *foot-foots* but employed *foot-foots* normally. With the irregular past tense forms, the children learned the unique, irregular contrasts as separate items of vocabulary first. Sometimes they were separate even contextually, as in the child who said *it came off* and *it came unfastened*, but *come over here* and *come right back*. Next the children produced analogic past tense forms for these highly frequent words. At the same period in which a child said *did*, he might say *doed*; at the same age at which he said *broke*, he might say *breaked*, and so on. We do not know if there were correlated linguistic or semantic differences between these two versions of the past tense forms. At any event, these productive analogies occurred before we had evidence of practice on the familiar forms from which the analogies presumably stemmed. Whatever its basis in practice, it seems clear that the regularizing or analogizing tendency is very strong.

The learning of syntax is even more difficult to explain. Let us go back before the age of two. In the earliest examples we have obtained, we find that there are consistencies of order between words. A very simple system might be one that produces sentences like *all-gone candy, candy up-there, all-gone book, read book,* and *book read*. Another said *snap on, snap off, fix on*. Notice that these sentences could not all be produced by simple abbreviation of adult sentences. Many of the children's sentences are such imitations, but some have a word order that cannot be explained by simple imitation. Children talk a great deal and they hear a great deal. It is improbable that they could produce the great variety of sentences they do produce from memorized strings of words.

When we introduced words to a child in controlled sentences, he put them into new and appropriate sentences. When told of a nonsense object *that's a po*, or *this is a po*, the child said *here's a po, where's a po, there's a po, the po go up there*, and *poz go up there*. When told *I'm gonna sib the toy*, he later said *I sib 'em*, indicating the appropriate gesture. Yet the form *wem*, in *this is a wem bead*, was not extended. Thus a noun form was productively ultilized in many new contexts, a verb form in one, and an adjective form in none. However slight, at least here is an indication of an analogic extension at the syntactic level.

One explanation which has been offered by several different observers of young children, for instance, Braine (1963), Brown and Fraser (1963), and Miller and Ervin (1964), is that these early systems indicate the beginnings of syntactic classes.

How do such classes develop? Two features of classes have been noted to account for the development of regularities. In children's language, there is greater semantic consistency than in adult language. Brown (1957) has shown that by nursery school age children identify verbs with action, nouns with things. Perhaps groupings into classes of words that can occur in the same place in sentences rest at least partly on semantic similarities. Another feature is that in all these grammars there are some positions where only a few words can occur, but that these words are very frequent. Thus one child started many of her sentences with *thats*. Another ended many of her sentences with *on* or *off*. The words that can occur following *thats* constitute a class, in the same sense that nouns are identified as following *the* for adults. This is not the only way we recognize nouns, but it is almost as useful as a suffix in marking the class. How do we know that these words "go together" in a class for the child? We find that the recorded bed-time monologues of a child described by Weir (1962) were filled with instances of words substituting for each other: *what color blanket, what color mop, what color glass; there is the light; here is the light; where is the light.* Such practice, like the second-language drill in the classroom, could make some words equivalent counters in the game of rearrangement we call language. Thus, both meaning and high frequency of certain linguistic environments seem important in the evolution of syntactic classes.

Clearly, we have evidence that children are creative at the very beginnings of sentence formation. They imitate a great deal, but they also produce sentences which have both regularity and systematic difference from adult patterns. At the same time, within these classes there are always statistical tendencies toward finer differentiations.

As my last example, I will take the grammatical features called transformations by Chomsky (1957). A good instance is the rule for the purely syntactical use of *do* in English. This word appears in a variety of sentence types: in elliptical forms, such as *yes, they do*, in emphatic forms such as *they do like it*, in questions such as *do they like it?* and in negatives as in *they don't like it*. According to Chomsky's analysis, these uses of *do* are analogous and can be described by a single set of related rules in the grammar of adult English.

Let us see how children employ *do*. In the negative, a simple rule for the contrast of affirmative and negative would be simply to add *no* or *not* in a specified place. *He's going* vs. *he's not going; he has shoes* vs. *he has no shoes*. Another procedure would be to contrast *is* with *isn't*, *can* with *can't*, and so on. In both cases, the contrast of affirmative and negative rests on a simple addition or change, analogous to the morphological change for tense or for the plural. Neither rule presents new problems.

Some children had several co-existing negative signals. During the time period, one child had the following: (1) *any* in possession sentences, such as *Joe has any sock* and *all the children has any shirt on*; (2) *not* in descriptions and declaratives, such as *Not Polly*; (3) *don't* in most verb sentences, such as *Don't eat that*, and *I don't like that*. Note that all these utterances can be described in very simple terms without the use of more complex constructs than those needed to account for inflection, or simple syntactic classes.

But as the child acquires verb inflection, more complex rules develop. We say *he goes*, but we do not usually say *he goes not*. Simple addition of *not* is inadequate. We say *he doesn't go*. In the contrast *he can go* vs. *he can't go* there is only one difference. In the contrast *he goes* vs. *he doesn't go* there are two: the addition of the word *don't* in appropriate number and tense, and the difference between *go* and *goes*.

Usually children use *don't* quite early as a negative signal, but as inflections began we found sentences like *Joe doesen't likes it* and *it doesn't fits in here*. In these sentences inflections appeared, but in two places. In an analogous development, *do* appeared early in elliptical sentences as a verb substitute. Thus we find, in response to the remark *there aren't any blocks in this book*, the reply *there do*, and when Wick Miller said *I'm Joe*, the child said *no you don't, you're Wick*. Thus the child had not differentiated subclasses of words used in elliptical constructions, just as the subclasses of inflections of *do* with different number and tense did not appear until later. By age three, this child said *it goes right here, doesn't it?* and *you're named "she," aren't you?*, employing complex constructions which cannot be explained in terms of the simple semantic signals we found in *Joe has any sock*.

Chomsky has described the various uses of *do* in adult English economically as based on the same rule. Does the use of *do* appear concurrently in negatives, interrogatives, ellipsis, and emphasis? Quite clearly this is not the case. As we have seen, *don't* appears early in negatives. It is often the only negative signal. In interrogatives, the question is signaled by question words or by a rising pitch, and *do* is typically not present until months after it appears in negatives or in ellipsis. Thus we cannot infer the process of acquisition from an analysis of the structure of the adult language. Sentences that are described as generated through transformation rules in the adult grammar may be based on different, and simpler, rules in the early stages of the child's grammar. And a rule that may apply to a variety of types of sentences in the adult grammar may develop through quite separate and independent rules in the early stages of the children's grammars.

I have mentioned the development of tense and number inflection, simple syntax, and more complex syntactical processes called transformations. These have all raised certain similar problems of explanation.

In adult language, it has been found necessary to postulate such constructs as morpheme classes, syntactic classes, and grammatical rules. It is not inevitable that similar constructs need be employed in accounting for the earliest stages of language acquisition.

Three different theories of child language development were described earlier. The imitation view assumed that the child imitates adult sentences and gradually eliminates abbreviations and errors as he grows older. A second view assumed that children comprehend adult rules but make random errors in speaking. A third view sees language in children as involving successive systems, with increasing complexity.

In their simplest forms all these positions seem wrong. Let us review the evidence. We found that spontaneous imitations were syntactically similar to or simpler than nonimitations. In examining plural inflection, we saw that indiscriminate imitation would lead us to predict free variation of *foot* and *feet*, but, in fact, one form was usually preferred, and the plural contrast was based on analogic extension. We found it necessary to postulate a plural morpheme to account for the sudden and transitory appearance of forms like *bockis* and *feetsiz*. With verbs, mere frequency of use of a contrast was less important than the variety of types employing it, suggesting again the need for conditions giving rise to a past-tense morpheme, with varied environments for a particular form, before analogic extension can occur.

In children's early syntax, the data are still ambiguous, for it is hard to elicit and identify extensions to new cases. On the one hand, sentences like *fix on, allgone puzzle, I not got red hair*, and *once I made a nothing pie* clearly involve processes of analogic extension. Here we see at least rudimentary classes. On the other hand, in any system we devised, there were indications of incipient subdivision, of statistical irregularities in the direction of the adult model, prior to shifts in the system.

In the use of *do* we found that the adult rule applies equally to the negative, interrogative, elliptical, and emphatic sentence. But among children *do* did not appear at the same time in these types of sentences. The pattern of development, and the rules that might describe usage at a particular point in time, differed for these different sentence types and differed for different children. Yet there were rules; errors were not random.

In all these cases, we find that children seem to be disposed to create linguistic systems. We have not examined the speech of twins, but it seems likely that we would find there a rich source of systematic creation of constructions. It is hard to conceive that children could, by the age of four, produce the extraordinarily complex and original sentences we hear from them if they were not actively, by analogic extensions, forming classes and rules.

At the same time we cannot wholly accept the third position presented— that of idiosyncratic systems. In every instance of systematic change I have examined, there has been some evidence of fluctuation, some evidence of greater similarity to adult speech than one would expect on the basis of the system alone. In addition, in the early stages of some complex rules—such as the use of *do*— we found that there were phases that seemed to rest on rudimentary acquisition of vocabulary. The use of *don't* as an undifferentiated negative signal could be so described.

The shift from one system to another may be initiated from several sources. One is the comprehension of adult speech, another is imitation. The relation of imitation to comprehension has barely been faced in discussions of child language, yet these two must account for the accretion of instances which eventuate in systematic changes.

In language, unlike other intellectual processes, the child can monitor his output through the same channel by which he receives the speech of others. If he knows how—if he can make discriminations and remember models—he can compare his own speech to that of others. Thus, language development involves at least three processes.

It is obvious that there is continual expansion in the comprehension of adult speech. Perhaps comprehension requires some ability to anticipate and hence, at a covert level, involves some of the same behavior that occurs in speech production. But this practice in comprehension alone is not sufficient to bring overt speech into conformity with understood speech. Consider again the phenomenon of so-called twin languages, for instance, or the language skills of second-generation immigrants who have never spoken the parents' first language but understand it, or of second-language learners who persistently make certain errors of syntax after years of second-language dominance, or of some children of immigrants who understand their age peers but speak the English of their parents. More than comprehension is involved.

Another process is the imitation of particular instances by children. What is entailed in hearing and imitation we do not know at this point. The fact that phrases may be uttered long after they are heard, without overt practice, suggests that our study of immediate, spontaneous imitation concerns only a fraction of actual imitation-derived utterances. Yet unless these utterances constitute a systematically simpler sample of all imitated utterances, it is obvious from our analysis of them that syntactical development at least cannot rest on imitation.

The third process is the building by analogy of classes and rules, a process which we infer from the child's consistent production of sentences he could not have heard. Of the three approaches which I offered earlier, I would suggest that the third is closest to the truth but that the accrual of gradual changes under the influence of listening to adults lies at the base of the generalizations and analogies formed by the child. Any system of analysis which omits either the idiosyncratically structured and rule-governed features of children's language or the gradual changes within these rules is contradicted by evidence from all levels of the linguistic behavior of children.

REFERENCES

Braine, Martin D. S., The ontogeny of English phrase structure: The first phase, *Language*, 1963, **39**, 1–13. [Reprinted in this volume.]
Brown, R., Linguistic determination and the part of speech, *J. abnorm. soc. Psychol.*, 1957, **55**, 1–5.
Brown, R., and C. Fraser, The acquisition of syntax. In C. N. Cofer and Barbara Musgrave (ed.), *Verbal behavior and learning*. New York: McGraw-Hill, 1963.
Chomsky, N., *Syntactic structures*. The Hague: Mouton, 1957.
Fraser, C., U. Bellugi, and R. Brown, Control of grammar in imitation, comprehension, and production, *J. verb. Learn. verb. Behav.*, 1963, **2**, 121–135. [Reprinted in this volume.]

Gvozdev, A. N., *Voprosy izucheniia detskoi rechi* (Problems in the language development of the child). Moscow: Academy of Pedagogical Science, 1961.

Miller, W., and S. Ervin, The development of grammar in child language. In U. Bellugi and R. Brown (eds.), The acquisition of language, *Child Developm. Monogr.*, 1964, **29**, 9–34. [Reprinted in this volume.]

Weir, R. H., *Language in the crib*. The Hague: Mouton, 1962.

The Maryland Children

Braine's first paper concerns itself with the structure of the very first two-word combinations to emerge in the speech of three children. It thus deals with an earlier phase than Brown's I and is comparable to the early levels described by Miller and Ervin-Tripp (above) and by Bloom (below). Braine's formulation of "pivotal constructions" has found widespread currency in the developmental psycholinguistic literature (see McNeill, 1966a,b, 1970; and papers in Slobin, 1971b). It has also been in for its share of criticism for lack of attention to semantic features (see the discussion on pp. 171–172.)

Braine discusses more advanced linguistic developments in his second paper: structural homonymity, sentence meanings (predication and ostension), successive mastery of linguistic distinctions. He notes the important phenomenon of "replacement sequences" (see Weir's "build-ups" [1962]) as an indication of constructions and transformations which are in the process of growth in child speech at a given point in development. These issues are explored at length by Braine in a thorough and searching review paper (1971b).

In a number of studies, Braine has explored the learning of miniature language systems as a means of learning about child language acquisition (Braine, 1971a; Smith and Braine, in press). Recently (1971a) he has proposed what he calls a "discovery-procedures" acquisition model—a valuable format for an acquisition model—which raises many important questions for developmental psycholinguistic theory and research.

Because Braine's work began at Walter Reed, we have dubbed his project "The Maryland Children." Since then, however, he has moved to the University of California at Santa Barbara and, most recently, to New York University.

—D.I.S.

The Ontogeny of English Phrase Structure: The First Phase

——*Martin D. S. Braine*

1.1 Students of infants and of language have long wondered over the fact that a structure of such enormous formal complexity as language is so readily learned by organisms whose available intellectual resources appear in other respects quite limited.[1] While a certain amount of work has been done on phonological development, and there has been much speculation about the acquisition of "meanings," development at the morphological and syntactic levels has been relatively little studied.[2] Yet it is perhaps the development at these levels that is the most striking and puzzling.

Before the question *how* the child learns can be broached, the question *what* the child learns has to be answered. The question "What is learned?" can be answered at two levels. The first answer has to be a description of the structure of the language at successive stages of development, and the task is purely one for structural linguistics. At a more interpretative level, the question "What is learned?" is answered by a statement of the nature of the stimulus attributes and relationships which the child learns to distinguish; at this level the task is as much psychological as linguistic, and the answer should in some sense "explain" why the grammar at a particular stage has the structure that it has.

The present paper reports and attempts to interpret the structural characteristics of the first word combinations uttered by three children followed by the writer from about 18 months of age. In the analysis of the data, the

From *Language*, 1963, **39**, 1–13. Reprinted by permission of the author and the Linguistic Society of America.

[1] I am deeply indebted to Dr. and Mrs. Chaim Shatan, Dr. Dorothy Kipnis, and Mrs. Harold L. Williams, parents of the children, for their careful record keeping and continuous cooperation over a long period. The investigation was supported in part by USPHS small research grant M-5116(A) from the National Institute of Mental Health, Public Health Service.

[2] D. McCarthy, "Language development in children," in *Manual of child psychology* (ed. L. Carmichael; New York, 1954), reviews a number of studies which employ traditional grammatical categories instead of treating the child's speech as sui generis. Of greater interest are a number of studies of children's knowledge of English inflexional rules, reviewed by J. Berko and R. W. Brown, "Psycholinguistic research methods," in *Handbook of research methods in child development* (ed. P. H. Mussen; New York, 1960); but these studies use subjects at least three or four years old, who have already mastered much of English phrase structure. Some corpora of utterances by children who seem somewhat more advanced than those reported here have been recently discussed by R. W. Brown and C. Fraser, "The acquisition of syntax," in *Verbal learning and verbal behavior* (ed. C. N. Cofer; New York, 1963), and also by W. Miller and S. Ervin, "The development of grammar in child language," in *The acquisition of language, Child development monographs* (ed. U. Bellugi and R. W. Brown; 1964). Miller and Ervin's paper came to my attention after this article was written; they note some of the same phenomena discussed here. Their term "operator" appears to correspond to my term "pivot."

structural features of the corpora will first be described, then the sequence of development, and finally, from the description of structure an attempt will be made to infer what was learned.

1.2.   To provide a common time scale for each child the month in which the first word combination (i.e., utterance containing two or more words) was uttered will be called the "first month"; this month will be taken as the starting point in all references to the time of an event, e.g., "first four months." The "first phase" in these children refers to the first four or five months on this time scale, and is defined statistically by a low rate of increase in the number of word combinations. In each child the number of different word combinations at first increased slowly and then showed a sudden upsurge around the fifth or sixth month. For example, the cumulative number of Gregory's recorded different word combinations in successive months was 14, 24, 54, 89, 350, 1400, 2500+, . . ., and undoubtedly the sampling was more complete in the earlier than the later months. In each child the upsurge in the number of different word combinations in the fifth and sixth months was accompanied by a marked increase in the structural complexity of utterances. The first phase appears to be fairly well delineated, being characterized not only by a particular temporal span and slow increase in the number of word combinations, but also by a typical and simple structural property which it is the purpose of this paper to describe.

2. PROCEDURE

2.1. Gathering of the corpora. In the case of two children, Gregory and Andrew, the mother or both parents maintained a seriatim written record of their child's spontaneous comprehensible utterances. A "spontaneous" utterance was defined as any utterance which was not a direct imitation or repetition of something said by another person in the previous few seconds. A "comprehensible" utterance was defined as any utterance which the parent could identify with considerable confidence as an attempt to say an English word or morpheme, or a string of English words or morphemes. The parents were instructed not to attempt to represent pronunciation, but merely to record in conventional spelling the word or sequence of words they heard the child say. In the case of word combinations the parents also recorded a paraphrase into ordinary English indicating what they understood by the child's utterance. The written record of utterances was started when the child had an estimated vocabulary of 10–20 single-word utterances (i.e., before the first word combination appeared).[3]

[3] No tape recordings were made of Gregory and Andrew in the early months because of the uneconomically large number of hours spent in recording and listening that would have been required to obtain the small number of word combinations at the child's command. A few tape recordings were made in the fifth month, and after the sixth month a high proportion of each corpus was tape-recorded, the written record being eventually abandoned as no longer practicable. This later material is not discussed here. Comparison of the written record with tape recordings made at the same age revealed that constructions present in the one were always present in the other, and with about equal frequency, a fact which is evidence of the reliability of the written records.

In addition to listing the utterances, the parents also recorded how often each utterance occurred (up to five times). The measure of frequency was included to provide an internal check on the accuracy of the record; it was assumed that utterances heard several times would be less likely to be erroneously recorded than those heard only once. Since the few word combinations that occurred only once did not differ from the others in any discernible way, no distinction will be made when discussing the corpora between utterances occurring once and those occurring many times.

In the case of the third child, Steven, a similar written record was soon abandoned, primarily because serious question arose whether certain sounds were properly identifiable as words. To resolve this question required investigation of phonetic regularities in Steven's speech. The entire corpus was therefore tape-recorded. The material discussed here was obtained in twelve play sessions of about four hours total duration, spaced over a four-week period during the fourth and fifth months. During the play sessions Steven's mother kept a running record of what she understood Steven to say; morpheme identifications were based on a comparison of her written record with the sounds on the tape, made in the light of what had been learned about the phonetic characteristics of Steven's speech.

The fact that the data on Steven were tape-recorded should not mislead the reader into thinking that the morpheme identifications are necessarily more reliable in his case. The major factor affecting the certainty with which a child's words can be identified is the clarity with which he speaks, and Gregory and Andrew spoke more clearly than Steven.

At the time of their first word combination two of the children were 19 months old and the third 20 months.[4]

2.2. "Word" and "word combination." On the assumption that the morphological units of the child's speech might be longer, but would probably not be shorter than the morphemes of adult English, the following somewhat crude distributional criterion was adopted for a "word" (or "morpheme"—no distinction between "word" and "morpheme" will be made for the child's language). Those segments are considered "words" which are the longest segments that cannot be divided into two or more parts of which both are English morphemes that occur in the corpus independently of the others. Thus *ice cream* and *all gone* are each classified as one word in Gregory's speech, since neither *ice* nor *cream*, nor *all* nor *gone*, occur in other contexts or alone.

---

[4] The procedure described leads to a lexical and not a phonemic representation of morphemes. With very young children there are reasons for not making a phonemic analysis preparatory to an investigation at the morphological and syntactic levels. For example, it is not easy to use the 21-month-old as an informant who gives same-different judgments to questions. Moreover, the contrasts that exist are not constant over time. The strong likelihood that a child may hear contrasts which he cannot produce not only means that partially separate analyses of receptive and productive functions would be necessary, but may also lead to a special situation in which phonemic strings would frequently have to be inferred from lexical ones.

However, for Andrew *all gone* is classified as a combination of two words, since *gone* occurs by itself, and *all* occurs independently in *all wet, all dressed*, etc. In line with the criterion, the few expressions in which only one part occurs elsewhere (like English *cranberry*) are treated as single units.

In writing the children's utterances, the morphemic status will be indicated by spacing: where English words are run together (e.g., *howareyou*), they are not separate units by the above criterion.

3. GRAMMATICAL STRUCTURE

3.1.   Gregory. Table 1 summarizes the 89 word combinations uttered by Gregory during the first four months. Over two-thirds contain one or another of a small group of words in first position. Thus, *byebye* occurs in 31 combinations, always in first position; *see* occurs in 15 combinations, always (except for the exclamatory *ohmy see*) in first position; similarly *allgone, big, my, pretty, more, hi*, and *nightnight* recur in first position in two or more combinations. These words will be called "pivot" words, since the bulk of the word combinations appear to be formed by using them as pivots to which other words are attached as required. There is some communality among the words that follow the pivots: six of the words that follow *see* also occur after *byebye*; most or all of the words that follow *hi, my, big, pretty* are also to be found after *byebye*, and some after other pivot words. Although none of the five words that follow *allgone* occur after other pivots, this is probably accidental (cf. *allgone shoe* and *see sock, allgone lettuce* and *byebye celery, more melon, my milk*). The evidence suggests that the pivot words occupying utterance-initial position have essentially similar privileges of occurrence. Accordingly, there is a basis for defining two primitive word classes: a class of pivots (P) to which a few frequently occurring words belong, and a complementary class which has many members, few of which recur in more than one or two different combinations (49 different words follow pivots, 34 of which occur in only one combination). The latter class will be called the X-class.

All words which occur in the frame P(—) also occur as single-word utterances, whereas some of the pivots do not occur alone. There is, therefore, a basis for identifying the X-class with the class of single-word utterances.

Of the 89 word combinations, 64 are PX sequences. Five of the remaining combinations have a recurring element in utterance-final position: *do it, push it, close it*, etc. These appear to exemplify the same kind of pivotal construction as the previous combinations discussed, except that now the pivot is in the final position. *Do, push, close*, etc., all occur as single-word utterances; *it* does not occur by itself. These five combinations may therefore be classified as XP sequences. The remaining 20 combinations appear to have no determinable structure. Some of them are greetings or exclamations (e.g., *hi howareyou*), some are English compound words (e.g., *mail man*), others may well be early cases of later developing forms.

There is no overlap between the 49 words occurring in the frame P(—)

TABLE 1 GREGORY'S WORD COMBINATIONS, FIRST FOUR MONTHS

14 combinations with see (—), e.g.	my mommy	nightnight office	hi plane	allgone shoe
see boy	my daddy	nightnight boat	hi mommy	allgone vitamins
see sock	my milk			allgone egg
see hot		31 combinations	big boss	allgone lettuce
	do it	with byebye (—),	big boat	allgone watch
	push it	e.g.	big bus	
pretty boat	close it	byebye plane		20 unclassified, e.g.
pretty fan	buzz it	byebye man	more taxi	mommy sleep
	move it	byebye hot	more melon	milk cup, ohmy see

and the five words occurring in (—)P. This lack of overlap may be accidental (the fact that the five words which follow *allgone* fail to occur following other first-position pivots has already been assumed to be accidental). However, it is primarily English nouns and adjectives that occur in the context P(—), whereas the words occurring in (—)P are all English verbs; Gregory may be adumbrating a substantive-verb distinction within the X-class. Using subscripts to denote subclasses, the structures employed by Gregory may be summarized as P_1X,

TABLE 2   ANDREW'S WORD COMBINATIONS, FIRST FIVE MONTHS

PIVOTAL CONSTRUCTIONS

all broke	no bed	more car[d]	other bib	airplane by[f]
all buttoned	no down[a]	more cereal	other bread	siren by
all clean	no fix	more cookie	other milk	
all done	no home	more fish	other pants	mail come
all dressed	no mama[b]	more high[e]	other part	mama come
all dry	no more	more hot	other piece	
all fix	no pee	more juice	other pocket	clock on there
all gone	no plug	more read	other shirt	up on there
all messy	no water	more sing	other shoe	hot in there
all shut	no wet[c]	more toast	other side	milk in there
all through		more walk		light up there
all wet			boot off	fall down there
	see baby		light off	kitty down there
	see pretty	hi Calico	pants off	more down there
I see	see train	hi mama	shirt off	sit down there
I shut		hi papa	shoe off	cover down there
I sit			water off	other cover down there

OTHER UTTERANCES

airplane all gone	byebye back	what's that	look at this
Calico all gone	byebye Calico	what's this	outside more
Calico all done[g]	byebye car	mail man	pants change
salt all shut	byebye papa	mail car	dry pants
all done milk	Calico byebye	our car	off bib
all done now	papa byebye	our door	down there
all gone juice		papa away	up on there some more
all gone outside[h]			
all gone pacifier			

---

[a] "Don't put me down."	[f] "A plane is flying past."
[b] "I don't want to go to mama."	[g] Said after the death of Calico the
[c] "I'm not wet."	cat.
[d] "Drive around some more."	[h] Said when the door is shut: "The
[e] "There's more up there."	outside is all gone."

XP_2, or, if one chooses to credit him with the substantive-verb distinction, P_1X_1, X_2P_2.

3.2. Andrew. Andrew's word combinations during the first five months are listed in Table 2. About half the combinations contain *all, I, see, other, no,* or *more* in utterance-initial position; the pivotal mode of construction seems quite comparable to Gregory's, although the individual words are not the same. However, while there was only one second-position pivot in Gregory's corpus, Andrew seems to have several, one of which is a phrase which itself has internal positional structure (*there*, preceded by *down, in, on,* or *up*).

There is some overlap between the sets of words that follow the various first-position pivots, e.g., *all fix* and *no fix, all wet* and *no wet, all shut* and *I shut, hi mama* and *no mama*; but these are the only examples (cf. *other bread* and *more toast*; *other milk, more juice, no water*). There is one case of overlap between the words preceding the second-position pivots: *light off* and *light up there*. More substantial overlap is present between the sets of words preceding second-position pivots and following first-position pivots: 9 of the 19 words that occur in the context (—)P also occur in the context P(—), e.g., *pants off* and *other pants, water off* and *no water, hot in there* and *more hot, sit down there* and *I sit*. Andrew's pivotal constructions may therefore be summarized by the formulae P_1X and XP_2. All words occurring in either P_1(—) or (—)P_2 also occur as single-word utterances; as with Gregory, the X-class may be identified with the class of single-word utterances.[5] But unlike Gregory, there is nothing to indicate that Andrew is as yet developing anything like a substantive-verb contrast.

Of the 102 combinations, 73 are pivotal constructions. In a further 9 combinations a pivotal construction (*all* X) occurs as an immediate constituent of a longer utterance; these (and also *other cover down there*, listed among the pivotal constructions) seem to be early examples of more complex forms belonging to the next phase of development. The remaining 20 combinations have not been classified. Some of them may contain pivot words (e.g., *our car, our door*).[6]

3.3. Steven. Table 3 lists Steven's identifiable word combinations, recorded in twelve play sessions during the fourth and fifth months. The corpus was tape-recorded because the phonetic characteristics of Steven's speech made the

---

[5] Some of the pivots (e.g., *more*) occur as single-word utterances, others (e.g., *all*) do not. Those that occur alone seem also to occur as X-words in word combinations (e.g., *no more, more down there*); they can therefore properly be regarded as belonging to both classes.

[6] In deciding whether utterances containing infrequently occurring words were pivotal constructions, the writer was sometimes guided by the child's subsequent development. For example, although *mail* occurs three times in first position (*mail man, mail car, mail come*), it is not classified as a pivot because there are no further cases of *mail* in first position in subsequent weeks; on the other hand, although *come* only recurs twice in final position, the subsequent uses of it in final position suggest that it is a pivot. Similarly, in Gregory's corpus (Table 1), although *more* and *pretty* only occur twice, they are regarded as pivots because they recur frequently in initial position before X-words in the next month of Gregory's development.

TABLE 3 STEVEN'S WORD COMBINATIONS, TAPE-RECORDED SAMPLE AT END OF FOURTH MONTH

PIVOTAL CONSTRUCTIONS

want baby	it ball	get ball	there ball	that box
want car	it bang	get Betty	there book	that Dennis
want do	it checker	get doll	there doggie	that doll
want get	it daddy		there doll	that Tommy
want glasses	it Dennis	see ball	there high[d]	that truck
want head	it doggie	see doll	there momma	
want high[a]	it doll	see record	there record	here bed
want horsie	it fall	see Stevie	there trunk	here checker
want jeep	it horsie		there byebye car	here doll
want more	it Kathy	whoa cards[c]	there daddy truck	here truck
want page	it Lucy	whoa jeep	there momma truck	
want pon[b]	it record			bunny do
want purse	it shock	more ball	beeppeep bang[e]	daddy do
want ride	it truck	more book	beeppeep car	momma do
want up				(want do)
want byebye car				

OTHER UTTERANCES

bunny do sleep	baby doll	find bear	eat breakfast
Lucy do fun	Betty pon	pon baby	two checker
want do pon[f]	byebye car	pon Betty	Betty byebye car
want drive car	Candy say	sleepy bed	Lucy shutup Lucy shutup Lucy

[a] "Put it up there."
[b] 'Put on' or 'up on' or both.
[c] "The cards are falling."
[d] "It's up there."
[e] "The car that goes 'beeppeep' is falling."
[f] "I want (you) to put (the jeep) on top."

morphemic status of parts of his utterances uncertain. In discussing these characteristics, phonetic symbols will be used. Since no phonemic analysis was made to determine what contrasts he controlled, these symbols are to be understood as identifications by English-speaking listeners; they provide only an approximate indication of the sounds. The lack of a phonemic analysis also makes it impossible to distinguish clearly between allophonic and allomorphic variation.

Steven's pronunciation is extremely variable—much more so than either Gregory's or Andrew's. In particular the last consonant of *that* and *it* takes a variety of forms: [t, d, h, ʔ, ð, tš, ts, z, tz]. Much of this variation is probably allophonic, but a terminal sibilant also appears occasionally after *here* and *there*. Separate morphemic status is not assigned to the terminal sibilant, because forms with and without the sibilant are in free variation, and also because the terminal sibilant, present in the third and fourth months, disappears completely in the fifth and sixth months and reappears only when *is* occurs in other contexts in his speech. In addition to the allomorphs *it* ~ *its*, *here* ~ *heres*, etc., it is possible that *it* and *that* may not be independent morphemes, since there appear to be occasional intermediate forms, e.g. [het, ditz]. (In the latter case, Steven may be trying to say *this*.) The general character of the combinations listed in Table 3 would not be altered by treating *it* and *that* as allomorphs.

From a grammatical point of view the most interesting phonological feature of Steven's speech is the periodic occurrence, at the beginning or in the middle of utterances, of either a front-central vowel, or, somewhat less often, of [d] or [t] followed by a front or central vowel. Steven's family usually identified these as English words—as *a* or *the* before nouns, as *I* before *want*, *see*, *get*, as *to* in such contexts as *want* (—) *do*, as *it* in context *want* (—) *high* or *want* (—) *up*, and as *is* or *of* in appropriate other contexts. Before *that, there, Lucy*, etc., these phonetic entities could not be interpreted. One or another of these elements is present in over 40% of Steven's utterances. The tape-recordings indicate that these elements occur before any word, that their phonetic shape is not affected by the class of the following morpheme and that utterances with and without them are in free variation. While it is quite likely that these elements are an interesting distillate of the unstressed and phonetically often obscure English articles, prepositions, and auxiliary verbs, there is no basis for giving them morphemic status at this stage of Steven's development (although it may be desirable at some later stage). The alternative course will be taken of regarding them as a periodic feature of the intonation pattern. Consistent with this decision is the fact that when these elements occur in utterances of three words or longer, they appear to separate immediate constituents; clearly defined junctures often appear at the same points. Thus, a vowel sometimes occurs at the marked point in *want* (—) *do* and *want* (—) *ride*, but in *want do pon* and *want drive car*, the vowel seems to shift forward: *want do* (—) *pon*, *want drive* (—) *car*. Similarly there is a vowel at the marked point in *there* (—) *byebye car*, but never between *byebye* and *car*. Such marking of immediate constituents, however, has little relevance to the initial phase of development. Neither Gregory's speech nor Andrew's ever shows anything analogous to these elements.

Another feature of Steven's speech which is not present in either Gregory's or Andrew's at this stage is a generalized terminal vocative. No one listening to the play sessions has the least difficulty in distinguishing vocatives from other occurrences of proper names. Whether the intonational cues in Steven's speech alone would suffice to identify vocatives is not clear, since so many other cues are invariably present that it is difficult to find appropriate contrasts in the tape recordings. These terminal vocatives are omitted in Table 3. If one wishes to include them in Steven's grammar, one need only add a rule that, if "S" is an utterance, then "S, (proper name)" is also an utterance.

Table 3 indicates that Steven's word combinations have much the same structural features already described for Gregory and Andrew. Three-quarters of the combinations contain one or another of a small group of words (*want, get, it, there,* etc.) in utterance-initial position. Four combinations contain *do* in final position. In a further four combinations a pivotal construction is an immediate constituent of a longer utterance (*bunny do sleep,* etc). The remaining combinations are not classified.

There is substantial overlap between the sets of words that follow the various first-position pivots. Five of the words that follow *want,* eight that follow *it,* three that follow *see,* and eight that follow *there* occur after more than one pivot: essentially similar privileges of occurrence are therefore indicated for the first-position pivots. Two of the words that precede *do* also occur after first-position pivots. The formulae P_1X and XP_2 again summarize the pivotal constructions. Words occurring in the contexts $P_1(—)$ and $(—)do$ also occur as single-word utterances; there is again ground for identifying the X-class with the single-word utterances.

In Steven's corpus there is much more overlap among the sets of X-words that are found with each pivot than in Gregory's and Andrew's. No doubt this is because all Steven's utterances were recorded in special play sessions, so that there was greater constancy in the environmental stimuli eliciting Steven's utterances.

3.4. The common structure of the three corpora. The following structural properties appear to define the initial phase of development in these children.

(a) There are two word-classes: pivots and X-words. The pivots are few in number; they tend to occur in several word combinations; and each is associated with a particular utterance position. Thus two subclasses are definable, P_1 associated with initial position, and P_2 with final position. The X-class is a large open class containing the child's entire vocabulary except for some of the pivots. X-words tend to recur in relatively few word combinations and do not appear to be tied to a particular utterance position; they occur alone or in the position complementary to that of the pivot word. One but only one of the children (Gregory) gives some evidence for a subdivision of the X-class.

(b) Single-word utterances are X. Multiword utterances are either P_1X or XP_2, the former being much more frequent (for Gregory the formulae may be P_1X_1, X_2P_2).

The occasional utterances in the corpora that are more complex than the above (where a pivotal construction is an immediate constituent of a longer utterance) are taken to be early examples of constructions belonging to the next phase of development.

Structural formulae in linguistics can be construed in a weak or a strong sense. So far it has been asserted only that the sequences P_1X and XP_2 occur and are characteristic. Students of generative grammar, however, give a stronger interpretation to such formulae: the formula PX asserts that any P "can" occur with any X. To construct and test a generative grammar it is necessary to have information not only about grammatical utterances, but also about ungrammatical ones. Information of the latter sort is difficult enough to obtain with adult informants,[7] and seems clearly out of the question with children as young as these. Nevertheless, although it cannot be proved, it seems quite likely that the formulae P_1X and XP_2 are generative. The only alternative hypothesis is that, in the class of all grammatical sentences, some or all of the pivot words have unique sets of cooccurrents, By the fourth month both Gregory and Andrew had a recorded vocabulary of about 250 words, and internal evidence suggests that the true size may have been two or three times as large.[8] If each set of X-words that occur with a given pivot is a random sample from this class (as the generative interpretation of the formulae implies), very little overlap between any pair of such sets would be expected; even taking into account the fact that some X-words occur much more frequently than others and would, therefore, be more likely to appear in any set taken at random, the amount of overlap to be expected is limited, and, though difficult to estimate, seems unlikely to be greater than that actually found in the corpora. There is, therefore, no reason to think that any of the pivot words have cooccurrents which are unique in any special way (with the possible exception of *it* in Gregory's speech).

An objection which has been raised against the assumption that any pivot can occur with any X-word is that it puts into the children's mouths some implausible expressions which seem highly foreign to English. For example, the formulae would allow Gregory to generate *more hot, big dirty, allgone hot*; Andrew to say *see read, other fix, I shirt*; and Steven to say *that do, there up, high do*. This objection is sometimes based on the idea that the children's utterances are a recall, or delayed imitation, of things they have heard adults say. As against this, there are a number of expressions in the corpora which are sufficiently strange to render it most unlikely that the children had heard them, e.g., *see cold, byebye dirty, allgone lettuce, no down, more high, want do pon, there high*. In one child, not reported here, *the* was an early pivot word, yielding such utterances as *the byebye, the up*. Moreover, several "strange" combinations, similar or identical to utterances generated by the formulae, appear in the fifth and sixth months; examples are *more wet, allgone sticky* (Gregory, after washing his hands), *other fix* (= "fix the other one"), *more page* (= "don't stop reading"), *see stand up* (= "look at me standing up"), *this do* (= "do this"). Manifestly, the strangeness of an utterance is no criterion of its grammaticality at this age.

[7] A. A. Hill, "Grammaticality," *Word*, **17**, 1–10 (1961); H. Maclay and M. Sleator, "Responses to language: Judgments of grammaticalness," *IJAL*, **26**, 275–282 (1960).

[8] By the end of the second month the recorded vocabulary was sufficiently large that the parents had difficulty in distinguishing which single-word utterances were new, and they recorded many fewer single word utterances in the third and fourth months than in the second. However, during the first four months 150–200 words were recorded as having been uttered five times or more. There were probably many more less frequently occurring words which were not recorded. Even if the usual rank-frequency relation (Zipf's law, $rf = K$, in which the constant K approximates the total vocabulary, since it is the rank of the least frequently occurring word) fits the single-word utterances poorly, the total vocabulary must be very substantially greater than that recorded.

3.5. Continuity with later development. What is here called the first phase of development has been defined by a certain time period (the first four or five months), a low rate of increase in the number of word combinations, and the presence of a characteristic structural feature (the pivotal construction). In order to justify treating a continuous development as composed of phases described separately, it seems appropriate to add some general remarks about the nature of the next phase.[9]

No claim is made that any discontinuity exists between phases. The pivotal type of construction continues long after the first five months, and new pivot words develop. However, several developments seem to occur more or less together around the fifth and sixth months. Forms in which pivotal constructions enter as immediate constituents have already been mentioned. The development that has most impressed the writer is the appearance of an increasing number of utterances in which an X-word (e.g., an English noun) occupies both utterance positions. Examples are *man car* ("a man is in the car"), *car bridge* ("the car is under the bridge"), *coffee daddy* ("coffee for daddy"). These are not pivotal constructions,[10] but seem rather to exemplify a primitive sentence form, in which both components can be expanded by a PX = X substitution rule, e.g., *man car* expanded to *other man#car*, *man#other car*. The large number of two-word utterances of this general type that appear around the sixth month give a random appearance to many word combinations in that phase of development. It may be this sentence form which has misled some observers into suggesting that children's first word combinations are for the most part mere juxtapositions of words without syntactic constraints.

The development of this sentence form may explain the very sharp increase around the fifth or sixth month in the number of different word combinations uttered. Since the X-class is very large, the addition of an XX construction (or of any construction admitting a large open class in both positions) to the existing PX and XP constructions would at once greatly increase the number of word combinations that the grammar is capable of generating. The statistical change is, therefore, explicable as a consequence of structural change.

4. SEQUENCE OF DEVELOPMENT

The order of appearance of the various word combinations shows a definite pattern. Gregory's third word combination was *see hat*; the next three were *see sock*, *see horsie*, and *see boy*; ten of his first 13 combinations contain *see* in

---

[9] The next phase of development in these children will be fully discussed in a subsequent article. See also the longer discussions of children they have followed by Brown and Fraser, *op. cit.*, and Miller and Ervin, *op. cit.*

[10] They may form constructional homonyms with pivotal constructions, e.g., *bàby cháir* ("little chair": pivotal construction), usually without an intonation break, and *báby # cháir* ("the baby is in the chair"). The two constructions, however, certainly cannot always be distinguished from their intonation alone (# is used here and in the text as a general juncture symbol).

first position. *Byebye plane*, the first word combination containing *byebye*, appeared in the third month; during the remainder of the month nine other combinations occurred containing *byebye* in first position. *Do it*, *push it*, and *close it* were all uttered at about the same time.

In the development of Gregory's language, it appears that from time to time a particular word is singled out, placed in a certain position, and combined with a number of other words in turn, often in quick succession. The words that are singled out in this way are of course the pivots. This sequence of development appears to be quite general. The majority of Steven's first word combinations contain *want* in first position. The same sequence occurs in Andrew's speech: *all* appeared in the first month, *other* did not appear until the third month and occurred in that month in five contexts; *no* and *there* appeared for the first time in the fourth month, both being quickly used in a number of different combinations. Less systematic observations on a number of other children suggest that this kind of development is quite typical of the initial stages of first-language learning (at least for the English language).

Throughout the first few months there is a large expansion of vocabulary. It seems clear that in this period the language expands rapidly in vocabulary by adding new members to the X-class, and that it develops structurally by singling out at intervals new pivot words.

Both functionally and developmentally, the distinction between open and closed word classes in the adult language (nouns, verbs, and adjectives vs. pronouns, prepositions, auxiliary verbs, etc.) seems quite parallel to that between X-words and pivots. The closed classes have relatively few members, and tend to serve in sentences as frames for the open-class words; historically their membership changes slowly. The pivots seem to play a similar role in utterances, also have few members, and add to their membership slowly.

5. WHAT IS LEARNED

It is suggested that a sufficient explanation of the structural features of the first phase is provided by the single assumption that the children have learned the positions of the pivot words, i.e., have learned that each of a small number of words "belongs" or "is right" in a particular one of two sentence positions.[11] While the evidence provided by the corpora might suffice without argument, it seems nevertheless desirable to make explicit the line of reasoning that leads to this inference.

[11] Actually there are two parts to this assertion: (a) that the children learn the positions of certain words, and (b) that a sentence typically has just two positions—first and last. But (b) needs no discussion when utterances are just two words long. In experiments in children's learning of simple artificial languages, reported elsewhere (Braine, "On learning the grammatical order of words," *Psychological review*, 1963) learning positions is explored when "position" in a sentence is defined by successive fractionations, i.e., when a sentence has just two positions, each of which may be occupied by a word or a phrase, and when each constituent phrase in turn may be divided into two positions.

In general, what a subject has learned is diagnosed from the generalizations that he makes. Thus, a naive rat, trained to jump for food towards an upright triangle in preference to a circle, will, when later confronted with a square and a circle, jump towards the square; but when the choices are an inverted triangle and a circle his jumps are randomly directed. The rat's generalizations provide information about what he must have learned in the original training: to jump towards something that an upright triangle shares with a square and does not share with an inverted triangle. Similarly, a child who has learned to indicate the past only by appending /id/, /d/, or /t/ to verbs would be expected to construct by generalization 'incorrect' forms like *singed* and *breaked,* and to inflect nonsense words used as verbs in response to questions in appropriately designed experiments, e.g., *This man is ricking. He did the same thing yesterday. Yesterday he* (—).[12]

What generalization phenomena would be expected to follow from the learning merely of the position of a word? The principal expectation is that the word would be used freely in the position involved, i.e., there should be no restriction on the words appearing in the complementary position. Thus, if *a* is a word whose position (first position, say) has been learned, then the frame a (—) should admit any word in the vocabulary. If this condition does not hold, i.e., if there is some set of words k_1, k_2, k_3, etc., which occur in the frame a(—) and another set l_1, l_2, l_3, etc., which cannot occur in this frame, then either the position of *a* has not been learned (in which case there is some other explanation for the occurrence of ak_1, ak_2, etc.),[13] or something more has been learned over and above the learning of the position of *a* (which accounts for the exclusion of al_1, al_2, etc.).[14]

While a word whose position is learned would be expected to occur in that position with some regularity, the consistency with which a word occurs in a position is not by itself a useful criterion of whether its position has been learned. A word may occur consistently in a specific position without its position necessarily having been learned (e.g., *boat* in Gregory's corpus). Conversely, the fact that a word occurs in both positions is not necessarily a bar to the assumption that the child has learned that it is "right" in one of these positions, since a word may generalize freely in one position and occur only in specific contexts in the other position (e.g., *more* in Andrew's corpus seems to occur freely when in first

---

[12] J. Berko, "The child's learning of English morphology," *Word*, **14**, 150–77 (1958).

[13] For example, in the context (—) *boat*, Gregory places *byebye, pretty, nightnight,* and *big.* These are all pivots. Since the evidence indicates that not any word can precede *boat,* but only a small set, there is no basis for assuming that the position of *boat* has been learned. The occurrence of the specific utterances *byebye boat, pretty boat,* etc., can better be explained by assuming that the positions of *byebye, pretty,* etc. have been learned.

[14] For example, in the context (—) *it*, Gregory places *do, push, close, buzz, move,* and in the context P_1(—) he places such words as *boy, dirty, plane, hurt, mommy,* etc. If the occurrence of only verbs before *it* is not accidental, Gregory has not learned merely the position of *it,* but something more which limits its environment to English verbs.

position, but in second position occurs only in *no more*, i.e., following a pivot). The inference that the position of a word has been learned must be based primarily on the degree to which the word is free from limitation to specific contexts when it appears in a particular position.

It is clear from the earlier discussion of the grammatical structure that the pivots and only these tend to recur in particular positions without limitations on their context. Frames $P_1(—)$ and $(—)P_2$, which freely accept words in the vocabulary, are precisely the forms which would be expected if the children had learned the positions of a few words, and learned nothing else which would limit the occupancy of the complementary position.

6. CONCLUSION

The simplest account of the phenomena of the first phase of development seems to be as follows: out of the moderately large vocabulary at his disposal, the child learns, one at a time, that each of a small number of words belongs in a particular position in an utterance. He therefore places them there, and, since he has not learned anything else about what goes where in an utterance, the complementary position is taken by any single-word utterance in his vocabulary, the choice determined only by the physical and social stimuli that elicit the utterance. As a consequence of this learning, the word combinations that are uttered have a characteristic structure containing two parts of speech. One part of speech, here called pivot, comprises the small number of words whose position has been learned. The other, here called the X-class, is a part of speech mainly in a residual sense, and consists of the entire vocabulary, except for some of the pivots. During this first phase the language grows structurally by the formation of new pivot words, i.e., by the child's learning the position of new words. The language grows in vocabulary by adding to the X-class.

Three Suggestions Regarding Grammatical Analyses of Children's Language

——— *Martin D. S. Braine*

The first suggestion is a methodological one. A fundamental problem in the grammatical analysis of text material from very young children is that there are necessarily many possible grammars which will generate the text utterances. It seems quite possible that grammars could be constructed to account for the same text material which are rather radically different from each other—perhaps different to the degree that one is a finite state grammar and the other is not, or that one finds a subject-predicate distinction where the other does not. A possible

This paper was presented at the Tenth Annual Conference on Linguistics of the Linguistic Circle of New York, March 1965, and is printed here with the permission of the author.

source of this difficulty is that children's texts have been treated as if they were primarily an unordered list of utterances.

To solve this problem it seems necessary to require that a grammar do more than merely describe or generate a list of utterances. That is, children's grammars should be provided with conditions to satisfy additional to the generation of the text utterances. It seems highly desirable that these conditions should be intrinsic to the text material, rather than extrinsic conditions arising from simplicity criteria or coefficients of goodness of fit. To discover appropriate conditions for a grammar to satisfy, we need to investigate texts to inventory what possibly relevant linguistic data they contain. Texts appear to contain much usable information about structure which would not be contained in an unordered list of utterances.

One such kind of linguistic data is provided by "replacement phenomena." In tape recordings one often finds sets of utterances which are obviously structurally related to each other, and which occur within a few seconds of each other on the tapes without change in the environmental stimuli eliciting speech. Examples are *man/car#man/in car#man/in the car*, or *Marty come#see Marty come*, or *Stevie gun#Tommy/Stevie gun#Tommy give gun#Gun#Tommy/gun #Tommy/give Stevie gun#*(Stevie is trying to report that his brother Tommy gave him a gun). Such sets of utterances will be called "replacement sequences."[1] Apart from proximity in time, the utterances of a replacement sequence seem to have the following properties: (a) there is no detectable change in the eliciting situation during the sequence, i.e., nothing happens in the environment to indicate that the utterances are not equivalent in meaning; (b) the longer utterances contain the lexical morphemes of the shorter utterances; (c) the longer utterances are a more recent acquisition than the shorter ones, i.e., the shorter utterances—or utterances structurally like them—are found in texts before the longer forms have developed. In these replacement sequences it seems clear that the child is "building up" the more complex form slowly. It seems reasonable to demand that a child grammar should not only reconstruct the utterances of a corpus but also reconstruct them in such a way as to make sense of the replacement patterns. My suggestion is that a child grammar should generate utterances so that replacing constructions come out as expansions, or transformations, of the utterances replaced.

Replacement sequences provide at least two kinds of linguistic information. First, they indicate the extent and kind of grammatical free variation, and thus provide information analogous to that provided by same-different judgments on utterances (e.g., if we find that on some occasions *man car* is replaced by *man in car*, and on other occasions by *man's car*, we have distributional evidence for a constructional homonym, and, therefore, evidence that the grammar should provide at least two different structural descriptions for some noun + noun

---

[1] Replacement sequences are similar to the stretches of speech that Weir (1962) has called "sequences." However, the present definition is narrower than Weir's.

combinations). Second, replacement sequences provide some information about subordination relations. There appears to be sufficient consistency in what is present and absent that it may be possible to distinguish components present in the shortest utterances (the "head" or "center," perhaps) from the components added in the longer utterances.

About 30–40 percent of the utterances in tape-recorded sessions seem to be part of a replacement sequence. Bringing these sequences into a distributional analysis may place sufficient restrictions on the analysis that at least the main features of structure can be justified. The level of detail at which the grammar becomes indeterminate might then become a function of the amount of material available for analysis. This seems as much as one should ask; all grammars based on text material must become vague at some level of detail.

My next suggestion is empirical rather than methodological. It refers to the age period 24–28 months approximately.[2] The data consist of extensive text material on 4 children, plus some more recent material on my son. Most of the text material consists of tape recordings averaging about one hour a week between 24 and 30 months of age. (However, much of the later material has not yet been analyzed.) In addition, for two of the children during the period 24–26 months the tape recordings are supplemented by some lists of utterances written in conventional spelling by the parents. About half the tape recordings were made in play sessions at which the child, myself, and the mother were present; the other half were made by the parents and sampled language occasioned by a wide range of domestic interactions: mealtimes, having a bath, etc. Most of the material illustrated in the figures comes from one child, Andrew. The text material on Andrew is the most completely analyzed, partly because it is the least voluminous, about 800 different multiword utterances.

The suggestion is that the first English "sentence" consists of a predicate-phrase head, with an optional subject. As evidence, first, the texts contain many replacement sequences in which utterances without subjects are followed by the same utterance incorporating an initial noun phrase. Tables 1 and 2 present examples. Table 1 shows pairs of Andrew's utterances which illustrate that a predicate phrase alone is in free variation with the same predicate phrase preceded by a subject noun phrase. It may be observed that the substitution of subject and predicate for predicate phrase alone occurs regardless of whether the predicate is a noun, verb, or adjectival or prepositional phrase in adult English. Andrew appears to have one simple included-sentence construction, consisting of *see* + sentence, and the table illustrates that in the included sentence in this construction the subject may be present (*see car come*) or absent (*see bang jam*). Table 2 shows similar replacement sequences from two other children.

[2] Data on an earlier period were presented in a previous paper (Braine, 1963). The gathering of the text material was supported in part by USPHS small research grant M-5116 (A) from the National Institute of Mental Health, Public Health Service.

TABLE 1   ANDREW (24–27 MONTHS): PAIRS OF UTTERANCES SHOWING PREDICATE PHRASES WITH AND WITHOUT PRECEDING SUBJECTS

All messy[1]	Change pants	Take a nap
Coffee pot all messy[1]	Papa change pants	Mama take a nap
Put that on	All wet	All gone
Andrew put that on	This shoe all wet	Meat all gone
All done milk[2]	All dressed	No touch
Mama all done toast[3]	Mama all dressed	This no touch

Tape recorded:

More outside[4]	Chair[5]	Plug in
Andrew more outside[4]	Pussy cat chair[5]	Andrew plug in
Want that	More that	Off
Andrew want that	Papa more that	Radio off
That off[6]		
Andrew that off[6]		

In included sentence:

See car come	See blankets all dry
See bang jam[7]	See all broke[8]

[1] "The coffee pot is all messy"
[2] "I finished my milk"
[3] "Mama finished her toast"
[4] "I want to go outside again"
[5] "The cat is on the chair"
[6] "I want to turn that off"
[7] "Look at me banging the jam jar"
[8] "Look at it all broken"

TABLE 2   SEQUENCES IN WHICH A PREDICATE PHRASE IS IMMEDIATELY REPLACED BY SUBJECT + PREDICATE

Stevie (25–26 months):
Cinna toast . . . Betty cinna toast ("Betty is to have some cinnamon toast")
Man . . . Stevie man ("Stevie has a picture of a man on his pants")
Fall . . . Stick fall ("The stick fell")
Go nursery . . . Lucy go nursery ("Lucy went to the nursery")
Push Stevie . . . Betty push Stevie ("Betty pushed Stevie")
Get . . . Lucy get
Crawl downstairs . . . Tommy crawl downstairs
Build house . . . Cathy build house

Jonathan (26–27 months):
Other coffee . . . Daddy other coffee ("Daddy had the other coffee")
Close radio . . . Mommy close radio ("Mommy should close the radio")
Take off . . . Daddy take off . . . Mommy take off ("Somebody take it off!")
Stand up . . . Cat stand up
Hot . . . Meat hot
Back there . . . Wheel back there
On table . . . Wine on table
Up sky . . . Jona up sky ("Jonathan is looking up in the sky")

The second line of evidence for this sentence structure is that there exists a technique which will usually elicit a missing subject. I tumbled on the technique only fairly recently in listening to my son, so I have not been able to check it with the other children. The trick is simply to pretend to misunderstand. For example, my son says *in kitchen*, and it is clear from the context that he intends to convey that his mother is in the kitchen. Deliberately misunderstanding, I say "Your car's in the kitchen? No, the car's over there, see." He corrects me: *mommy in kitchen*. Or again, his ball has rolled under the sofa, and he says, simply, *sofa*. I make a game of getting down on my hands and knees, and look under the sofa and announce "mommy is not under the sofa; mommy's upstairs!" Looking somewhat nonplussed, he hesitates, and then supplies the missing subject: *ball sofa*.

Given this definition of the early sentence form, the majority of utterances are classifiable as "sentences." In particular, most of the large apparently heterogeneous collection of one-word utterances, containing an English adjective, adverb, verb, or noun, come out as sentences consisting of a predicate phrase occurring alone. However, there is one important exception to this generalization: noun phrases occurring in isolation which are used to identify or name objects, pictures, etc., appear to belong to a somewhat different construction. When these are replaced, as they are eventually, by utterances which have something like a sentence form, they are preceded by an introducer, usually *it*, *that*, *here*, or *there*. Let us call these "ostensive" sentences, whether or not the introducer is expressed. It is my impression that, once the simple sentence form has developed, *all* nontrivial utterances can be classified as being either ordinary or ostensive sentences.

My third point has to do with the so-called "telegraphic" character of children's speech, which has been extensively discussed by Roger Brown and his co-workers. My suggestion is that the omissions of elements present in adult speech are due to the child's learning the most fundamental syntactic distinctions (e.g., between subject and predicate, between primary and adjunct predicate positions, between transitive and intransitive predicators) before he has learned some of the more detailed rules for expanding the components of the major syntactic positions. As it were, the higher nodes of the constituent structure are acquired before the intermediate and some of the lower nodes. Tables 3–7 show the main features of Andrew's predicate-phrase structure around 26–27 months of age.

Table 3 illustrates predicate phrase types. The one-term intransitives consist either of a class of intransitive general predicators (G_{intr}, which includes English intransitive verbs, adjectives, and *all*-phrases), or of nominal phrases or of English adverbial phrases (D). In the two-term intransitives G_{intr} always precedes D. Table 4 summarizes the different classes of phrase and indicates that there is a well-defined transitive-intransitive distinction (G_{intr} vs. G_{trans}), although there is no marked verb class. Table 5 shows that G precedes D and that when both occur D_{loc} (locative D) precedes D_t (*now*, *too*). Table 6 sketches what

TABLE 3   PREDICATE PHRASE TYPES (ANDREW)

One-term Intransitives:

(Coffee pot) all messy	(Andrew) sit	(Meat) hot[1]
put away	(Car) come	(Andrew) go
(Meat) all gone	(Shoes) all wet	(Mama) sing
(Pussy cat) chair	(Andrew) time nap[2]	
(Coffee pot) on stove	(Boots) down there	(Milk) in there
(Apple juice) there	(Mama) upstairs	in car
(Kitty cat) outside	(Lunch) now	under chair

Two-term Intransitives:

all messy on stove	sit down there	hot in there
put away there	come downstairs	go in car
all gone outside	all wet now	sing too

Transitives:

(Mama) take a nap	see train	(Mama) fix egg
(Papa) shut the door	(Mama) do dishes	read book
(Mama) all done toast	(Papa) wash face	make toast
(Andrew) take a nap on couch		eat egg too
take a nap too		

[1] "The meat is hot"
[2] "It's time for me to have a nap"

TABLE 4   PHRASE CLASSES (ANDREW)

NP: car, light, coffee, pants, etc.; vacuum cleaner, new shoes, next page, etc.; piece of bread, time bed, etc.; the $+N$, other $+ N$, etc.; this, Mama, Papa, Andrew, etc.; Andrew toast, Papa's tie, Mama chair, etc.

G_{intr}:   hot, bad, busy, etc.; come, go, sit, wash, etc.; no touch, all done, all wet, all dark, etc.

G_{trans}:   fix, do, get, take, wash, make, etc.; all done, all broke, all gone.

D: D_{loc}: there, in there, down there, etc.; up, down, upstairs, outside, etc.; on lap, in car, on the shelf, etc.; down on floor, up in the sky, etc.
D_t: now, too.

appears to be the structure of Andrew's well-developed adverbial phrases, and Table 7 represents the probable structure of his nonostensive sentences. (He has a small number of more complex sentences, e.g., *make coffee hot*, which are presumably early object-complement constructions. These are omitted in Table 7 because they are too few to support analysis.)

Table 8 presents a tentative theory of Andrew's early predicate structure development. It posits a transitory early period in which the only differentiation is into predicates with and without nominal heads. Andrew's idiolect as described (middle quadrangle) develops out of this as two contrasts merge: transitive versus intransitive, and a position contrast. The previous nominal heads

TABLE 5   POSITIONS OF PREDICATE HEADS AND ADJUNCTS (ANDREW)

PREDICATOR + D_{loc}	PREDICATOR + D_t	D_{loc} + D_t
(all) dark outside	all done now	up there now
all broke there	all wet now	up on bed too
all messy on stove	off now	down in cellar too
all done on stove	on too	
fall down there	sing too	PREDICATOR + D_{loc} + D_t
sit down there	vacuum clean too	
off (down) there	away too	all done there now
on there		on there now
hot in there	take a nap too	push there now
	eat egg too	
play outside		
come downstairs		
go in car		
put away there		
(Andrew) some jam there[1]		
make coffee hot on the stove		
take a nap on couch		

[1] "Andrew has (or wants) some jam there"

TABLE 6   STRUCTURE OF LOCATIVE PHRASES (ANDREW)

$$D_{loc} \rightarrow \left\{ \begin{array}{l} \left\{ \begin{array}{l} up \\ down \end{array} \right\} + \begin{array}{c} there \\ \text{-stairs} \end{array} \\ \left(\left\{ \begin{array}{l} up \\ down \end{array} \right\} \right) + \left\{ \left(\left\{ \begin{array}{l} in \\ out \end{array} \right\} + \text{-side} \right) \left(\left\{ \begin{array}{l} in \\ out \\ on \\ under \end{array} \right\} \right) + \left\{ \begin{array}{l} NF \\ there \end{array} \right\} \right\} \end{array} \right\}$$

Examples:

up there	up in the sky	under chair
up on there	down there	on the stove
up on bed	down on floor	out there
up on shelf	down in cellar	in mama room

NOTE: Braces enclose alternative forms. Parentheses around forms indicate that they are optional.

TABLE 7   STRUCTURE OF PREDICATIVE SENTENCES (ANDREW)

$$S_{Pred} \rightarrow (NP) + Pred.\ Phrase + (D_t)$$
$$Pred.\ Phrase \rightarrow Pred + (D_{loc})$$
$$Pred \rightarrow \begin{Bmatrix} G_{intr} \\ (G_{trans}) + NP \\ NP \\ D_{loc} \end{Bmatrix}$$

TABLE 8   TEMPORAL COURSE OF DEVELOPMENT OF MAJOR STRUCTURAL DISTINCTIONS IN ANDREW'S PREDICATE PHRASES

←Period I		Period II: 25–27 mo.		Period III
		INTRANSITIVE PHRASE	TRANSITIVE PHRASE	
Nominal Phrase	1st TERM ONLY	come, sing hot, ready . . . . Equational Nominals	wash face eat cookie read book make toast	Predicate system with three distinctions
versus				1. tr./intr.
Nonnominal Phrase	1st or 2d	inside there	in house on table	2. 1st/2nd 3. V/non-V (nonorthogonal)

distribute themselves into equational nominals, objects of transitive verbs (*Daddy book* > *Daddy read book*), and objects of prepositions (*Pussycat chair* > *Pussycat on chair*). The nonnominal heads similarly distribute themselves among the cells. Later, the verb becomes a marked class via the appearance of the *-ing* ending.

I would like to suggest that the data presented lead to a psychologically simple and very natural conception of the development—namely, that the development consists in the successive mastery of linguistic distinctions, and that the character of the texts comes from the order in which the distinctions are learned and the degree of command over them. Thus, sentences like *Pussycat chair* ("The cat is on the chair"), *Momma more toast* ("Momma wants some more toast"), *Momma away* ("Momma is putting the dishes away") reflect a command of the subject-predicate composition of sentences, but not of the internal structure of predicate phrases; sentences like *pussycat on chair, momma fix egg* ("Momma is fixing an egg") reflect more command over the internal structure of the predicate phrase, but a lack of the phrase structure nodes controlling auxiliary verbs and articles. One would anticipate that differences between children, the extent of which remains to be determined, probably reflect differences in the order of acquisition of features of English structure.

The only other hypothesis I know of which claims to account for the telegraphic character of children's speech is the notion that omissions are due to an "erase" rule which eliminates unstressed syllables during "print out" (i.e., utterances are apparently supposed to be generated pretty much as an adult generates them, but certain components are eliminated at or prior to the arrival of the nerve impulses at the speech organs). I should say that I have never actually seen this suggestion developed in print.[3] There are several difficulties with it. First, it is factually false that only unstressed elements are omitted (e.g., many of the sentences cited in this paper). A second objection is that the earlier stages of development are treated as actually more complex than the later stages—a very unnatural idea—more complex because the young child is assumed to command not only much of English structure, but, in addition, a set of "erase" rules.

It seems to me that the alternative I have suggested provides an explanation of the telegraphic character of children's speech which is both simpler and more natural than the "erase" rule hypothesis.

REFERENCES

Bellugi, U., and R. W. Brown, (eds.), *The acquisition of language, Monogr. Soc. Res. Child Develpm.*, 1964, **29**, No. 1.
Braine, M. D. S., The ontogeny of English phrase structure: The first phase, *Language*, 1963, **39**, 1–13. [Reprinted in this volume.]
Weir, R. H., *Language in the crib.* The Hague: Mouton, 1962.

The Two-Word Stage Reconsidered

As mentioned in the introduction to the grammar section, above, the late sixties saw a move toward deeper semantic analysis of child language: Gruber (1967) reanalyzed pivot constructions in terms of topicalization; Schlesinger (1971) presented a scheme of intentions and semantic relations; Fillmore's (1968) "deep case" grammar attracted a number of investigators (Blount, 1969; Kernan 1969; Slobin, 1970; and others). The following three papers are important contributions to this ongoing reanalysis. Lois Bloom's 1968 dissertation (1970) was the first large-scale attempt to describe early grammatical development in terms of underlying semantics, based on thorough recording of both speech and its situational context. She summarizes her position in the following paper. Gruber, in 1967, also worked from rich contextual data (on film), presenting an analysis of two-word utterances in terms of Austin's "speech acts" (1962) and Ross's (1970) use of these notions in linguistics. And Brown offers a valuable review of available data on early sentences in terms of underlying meanings ("operations of reference" and "relations"). (A much more thorough analysis can be found in Brown [in press].) The current use of videotape in child language studies promises to enrich studies of this sort.

[3] However, there are some suggestions along these lines in Bellugi and Brown (1964, 39–40).

All of the papers show that "pivot structures" can be analyzed in a number of more meaningful ways if attention is paid to context and to the child's inferred semantic intent.

—D.I.S.

Why Not Pivot Grammar?[1]

——*Lois Bloom*

Recent studies of language development have focused attention on the early stages of emerging syntax—the use of two-word and three-word sentences sometime during the second half of the second year of life. A number of investigators have reported similar distributional phenomena in samples of early child speech. When children begin to use two words in juxtaposition there are often a small number of words that occur frequently, in relatively fixed position, in combination with a large number of other words, each of which occurs less frequently. Braine (1963) named this first group of words "pivots"; children's speech has since been described in the literature as "pivotal," and an account of the systematic productivity of early utterances is often referred to in terms of "pivot grammar." The apparent convergence on this point in the literature (in particular, Bellugi and Brown, 1964; McNeill, 1966a) has led to its application to programs for language disorders (see, for example, McNeill, 1966b). However, more recent research (Bloom, 1970) and a careful examination of earlier studies, such as the classic diary study of Leopold (1949), indicate that the time is at hand for a reevaluation of the phenomenon. How real is pivot grammar?

This paper will begin with a review of the original evidence. Subsequently, several important questions will be raised concerning the adequacy of the notion of pivot grammar as an account of what children know about grammar as they begin to use syntax in their speech. Recent evidence of the underlying conceptual relations in children's early speech will be reported, and, finally, this information will be discussed as it relates to possible approaches to language disorders in children.

THE ORIGINAL EVIDENCE

The studies of Braine (1963), Miller and Ervin (1964), and Brown and Fraser (1963) were essentially distributional studies. They viewed children's speech as evidence, potentially, of a distinctive language, and for this reason they were admirably motivated to avoid the classes and categories of adult

From *Journal of Speech and Hearing Disorders*, February 1970. Reprinted with the permission of the author and the American Speech and Hearing Association.
[1] The research described in this paper was supported by PHS grant 5-F1-MH-30,001,03 from the National Institute of Mental Health.

speech in their accounts. As a linguist would approach an exotic language in order to describe its grammar, these investigators looked at large numbers of children's utterances, and described what they saw in terms of classes of words based on their privileges of occurrence. What they found was essentially an orderly arrangement of at least two, possibly three, classes of words. Certain words such as "no," "no more," "all gone," "more," "this," "that," "here," "there," "off," "on," occurred frequently, in fixed position as either the first or second constituent in a two-word utterance, and shared contexts with a larger number of words that occurred relatively less frequently. Braine (1963) referred to the classes as "pivots" and "x-words," Brown and Fraser (1963) referred to "functors" and "contentives," and Miller and Ervin (1964) referred to "operators" and "non-operators."

Only Braine (1963) was discussing a relatively complete corpus. His data consisted of (1) the records kept by the mothers of two boys of all of their first two-word utterances over a period of several months, and (2) tape-recorded samples of a third boy's speech during play sessions. Brown and Bellugi (1964) described only the constituents of noun phrases and the developmental differentiation of the initial position modifier class. Brown and Fraser (1963) and Miller and Ervin (1964) presented for discussion lists of two-word and three-word utterances that demonstrated the distributional phenomenon—for example, utterances with "this" and "that" or "Mum" and "Dad."

McNeill (1966a), using some of Brown's data, presented an extended account of the "pivotal" nature of children's speech. He viewed the original classes of pivots and x-words, or, as he named them, "open" words (because of the apparent tendency of the class to admit new members freely), as the original generic classes from which all the category classes of the adult model ultimately develop, through some sort of differentiation. McNeill (1970) has since refined his distinction between pivot forms and other forms further, in terms of their syntactic features with respect to cooccurrence with noun forms. Essentially, his account specifies all noun forms as an unmarked class in the child's lexicon—the class of "open" words. All other words are marked forms—marked, in the sense that they are identified as occurring only with nouns—the verbs, modifiers, and determiners which constitute the originally undifferentiated "pivot" class.

At least two critical questions can be raised about the adequacy of the pivot grammar notion as an account of children's early speech. First, how does pivot grammar relate to the grammar of the adult, model language? Large enough samples of adult speech would undoubtedly reveal similar kinds of distributional evidence on relative frequency of occurrence (see Zipf, 1965). Certain words such as determiners, pronouns, and other function words or syntactic markers occur more frequently and in more varied linguistic environments in adult speech than do verbs, adjectives, and nouns. However, such rules of grammar as "pivot + open," "open + pivot," or "open + open" have no real analog among the syntactic structures of the adult model. How does the child progress from using pivotal utterances to using utterances that reflect the complex interrelation of rules that is the essence of adult phrase structure? McNeill, in both of the foregoing accounts, attempted to deal with this question. However, his conclusions are based upon certain assumptions—for example, that pivot forms do not occur in isolation, and that two nouns cannot occur together—that simply are not supported in the data.

The second question concerns the adequacy of the pivot grammar account for describing and explaining children's early speech. What does the notion of pivot grammar tell us about what children know about grammar when they begin to use syntax in their speech?

THE ADEQUACY OF A PIVOT GRAMMAR ACCOUNT

The studies just discussed focused attention on the formal syntax of children's speech—on the arrangements of words in utterances. However, such descriptions of the form of speech provide minimal information about the child's intuitive knowledge of a linguistic code. Linguistic expression is intimately connected with cognitive-perceptual development and the child's interaction in a world of objects, events, and relations. The goal of the research discussed here (and reported at length in Bloom, 1970) was to investigate the development of linguistic behavior in relation to aspects of experience related to the speech children use.

The subjects of the study—Kathryn, Eric, and Gia—were the first-born children of white, college-educated, American English-speaking parents. They were each visited in their homes for approximately eight hours over a period of several days. Each sample of spoken language (at six-week intervals) was obtained during the child's (1) play with a selected group of toys, (2) eating, dressing, and toileting, and (3) play with a peer. The syntactic components of generative grammars were proposed for the earliest texts with mean length of utterance less than 1.5 morphemes. The syntactic and semantic development of negation was described until mean length of utterance was approximately 3.0 morphemes (in Bloom, 1970). Kathryn was 21 months old when the study began; Eric and Gia were each 19 months, one week old.

Judgments were made of the semantic intent of utterances, based upon clues from the context and behavior in the speech events in which utterances occurred. Using this kind of information, an attempt was made to propose rules of grammar to account for the inherent semantic relations that underlie the juxtaposition of words in early sentences. The notion of sentence structure implies a pattern of organization—an arrangement of otherwise independent parts that is based on the relationship of the parts to each other—which is something more than simply a sequence of words. The semantic relations that were coded in the children's speech were essentially of two kinds: functional relations with invariable grammatical meaning, and grammatical relations with variable grammatical meaning between constituents in subject-predicate relationship.

Functional Relations: Semantics of Certain Pivot Forms

To begin with, the data from Kathryn, Eric, and Gia contained utterances that were similar to those reported in the earlier studies and described as pivotal: Kathryn's utterances with "no," "this," "that," "more," and "hi"; Gia's utterances with "more" and "hi"; and Eric's utterances with "no," "another," "there," and "it." The children's use of these forms, in terms of semantic intention, could be described with some confidence. "No" most often signaled the nonexistence of the referent named by the second constituent (as in "no pocket"), where there was some expectation of its existence in the context of the speech event. "More" or "another" was used to comment on or to request the recurrence or another instance of an object or event (as in "more raisin" and "more read"). "This" and "that," and "there" were not contrastive in proximal-distal reference, and were used to point out an object or event in the environment (as in "this book," or "this cleaning"). "Hi," which occurred less frequently, was used in a nonsalutatory way as the child took notice of an object, person, or picture (as in "Hi shadow," "Hi spoon," "Hi Jocelyn"). The forms occurred frequently, in fixed syntactic position, with a number of different words, and they shared contexts. All occurred as single-word utterances as well. However, they occurred with specific intent, either in relation to the words with which they were juxtaposed or with inherent relation to something not specified, in the case of single-word utterances. Their use was motivated by their semantic function; they occurred in speech events that shared features of context and behavior. This last point is of considerable importance; certain words occur often in children's speech apparently because of the nature of their referential function. Description of such utterances as pivotal is only a superficial description of relative frequency of occurrence and syntactic position.

Moreover, it turned out that the utterances described as pivotal, in the limited sense just indicated, proved to be a small percentage of the total number of utterances that were obtained from Gia and Kathryn. Only Eric's speech—during the period of time under discussion, when mean length of utterance was less than 1.5 morphemes contained a preponderance of utterances such as have been so far described. The majority of the utterances of Kathryn and Gia presented certain critical problems for a pivot grammar account.

There were certain words in the children's speech that met all the distributional criteria for specification as pivots. The most frequent of these was either "Mommy" or reference to self—either by first name or, in Kathryn's case, "Baby" as well. However, not only did syntactic utterances with "Mommy" occur frequently, but it was also the case that "Mommy" occurred in relatively fixed position. For example, in 32 sentences with "Mommy" in the first speech sample from Kathryn (when mean length of utterance was 1.32), "Mommy" occurred in sentence-initial position 29 times. Moreover, "Mommy" also shared contexts with other forms, for example "Mommy sock" and "no sock," "Mommy haircurl" and "more haircurl."

One immediate objection to "Mommy" as pivot is that "Mommy" is a form having lexical status as a substantive or content word rather than a function word or syntactic marker. There is something intuitively wrong about classing "Mommy" as a function word, and, indeed, there has been a general inclination to avoid such characterization in the literature (see, for example, the discussion in Smith and Miller, 1966).

However, more important reasons for arguing against the distributional evidence that would class "Mommy" as a pivot or function form had to do with the fact that different utterances with "Mommy" meant different things. For example, in the first sample from Kathryn, the utterance "Mommy sock" occurred twice in two separate contexts:

(1)   Kathryn picking up her mother's sock
(2)   Mommy putting Kathryn's sock on Kathryn

It apeared that the difference in semantic interpretation between the two utterances (1 and 2) corresponded to a structural difference in grammatical relationship between the constituents "Mommy" and "sock." In one instance the structure was a genitive relation and in the other the relation between subject and object.

Grammatical Relations

Constructions with two substantive forms (the 32 utterances with "Mommy" and 24 utterances with "Baby" or "Kathryn," for example) were described by Braine (1963) and McNeill (1966a) as the juxtaposition of two x-words or open class words, respectively. But whether such utterances are classed together as "pivot + open" or "open + open," the two instances of "Mommy sock" would have the same structural description in either case, because the surface form of each is the same. Rules that account for utterances in terms of the juxtaposition of pivots and open words cannot account for differences in semantic interpretation. And yet there was strong evidence in the data for ascribing different structural descriptions to utterances with similar surface form but different underlying relationship between constituents. The full argument regarding the correct structural representation of such utterances has already been presented (Bloom, 1970). For the purpose of this paper, it will be pointed out that interpretation of the semantic intent of utterances with two substantive forms provided evidence that the children knew more about grammar at this early stage than merely rules for permitted juxtaposition of two different kinds of words.

There were a number of potential interpretations of the utterances that occurred with "Mommy" in constructions with nouns. The first possibility was that the child had simply named two aspects of a referent, or two referents, within the bounds of a single utterance—a conjunction (for example, "Mommy" and "sock"). If one interpreted children's use of single-word utterances (before and during the emergence of syntax) as labeling or naming behavior, then this would be an intuitively appealing interpretation of the juxtaposition of two noun forms within an utterance. If such were the case, and the two noun forms were simply conjoined without connection or with any possible connection between them, one could reasonably expect the constituents to be named in variable order. If the child had simply named two referents, or two aspects of a referent, there would be no motivation for naming them in a particular order. But the occurrence of "Mommy" in sentence-initial position 29 times in the 32 utterances that included "Mommy" was impressive evidence that the motivation for the order of the constituents was strong.

In addition to the utterances with "Mommy," there were 37 other noun + noun constructions in the first sample of Kathryn's speech and 66 utterances that juxtaposed two nouns in the second sample of Gia's speech (when mean length of utterance was less than 1.5 for each). Clearly, this utterance type was one of the most productive constructions in the speech of both children. Of the total of 135 noun + noun utterances, there were only seven that occurred with no other interpretable relationship between the forms than simple conjunction, for example, "umbrella boot" from Kathryn as her mother walked into the room carrying her umbrella and boots, and "Mommy Gia" from Gia as she looked at a photograph of Mommy and Gia. All of the remaining utterances appeared to present constituents with an inherent relationship between them, although in some instances the relationship was equivocal.

The utterances with two noun forms specified the following grammatical relations (given here in order of frequency): subject-object ("Mommy pigtail"), the genitive relation ("Kathryn sock"), the attributive relation ("bread book"), subject-locative ("sweater chair"), and, marginally, conjunction ("umbrella boot"). However, it was not the case that any two words could occur with any possible relation between them. There were no instances of such other possible relations that could hold between two noun forms as identity ("Mommy lady"), disjunction (either-or relation), or direct-indirect object. If it could be assumed that the unobtained relations existed in the child's experience, for example, giving something to someone (direct-indirect object), then the children's utterances were not merely reflections of nonlinguistic states of affairs. Such selectivity in expression and the impressive consistency of word order provided evidence for assuming that the children's utterances were motivated by an underlying cognitive-linguistic rule system.

The most frequently expressed relationship between two nouns was subject-object. All three children produced verb forms in predicate relation to noun forms in subject-verb and verb-object strings in the early two-word utterances, when subject-verb-object strings occurred only rarely. Utterances that have been described in the literature as simply the cooccurrence of two substantive words (x-word + x-word by Braine [1963], or two open class words by McNeill, [1966a]) could thus be explained in terms of the inherent semantic relationship between the constituents. It was apparent that the children in the study were talking about the relations between actors or agents, actions, or states, and objects or goals, and that the order of constituents reflected the underlying order of basic sentence relations with remarkable consistency—subjects and verbs preceded objects or goals.

The possible grammatical relations were not equally represented in the data. Not only were certain relations more productive than others—that is, they occurred more often in different situations with different words—but the children differed in their use of each. For example, Eric used the verb-object relations first, and utterances expressing this relation were dominant in his speech before he began to use subject nouns in relation to verb forms. The most productive early relationship for Gia and Kathryn was subject-object; Eric never produced such utterances. I. M. Schlesinger (1971) reported the productivity of this structural relationship between two nouns in the early speech of two Hebrew-speaking Israeli children, and Leopold (1949) described its frequent occurrence in the speech of his daughter Hildegard. In the speech of Kathryn, Eric, and Gia, verb-object strings appeared earlier and were more productive than subject-verb strings.

SUMMARY

The children's earliest sentences could thus be seen as expressing two kinds of conceptual relations. In grammatical relations, substantive words such as "Mommy" and "sock" enter into variable grammatical relationship with other words in sentences. Such words are not in themselves relational terms in the sense that they have independent lexical meaning. The children's earliest sentences also expressed functional relations, where inherently relational words such as "more" and "no" operate in linear structure with other (substantive) words to specify a particular relational aspect of such words (or their referents). Spoken alone as single-word utterances, such words manifestly imply such a semantic relationship to some unspecified aspect of experience.

It is not the case that the words the children used—for example, "no" and "more"—have only one meaning. All of the children used "no" subsequently to signal rejection, as in "no dirty soap" (I don't want to use the dirty soap) and, still later, denial, as in "no truck" (that's not a truck, it's a car). In the adult model, "more" is used to express the partitive notion (here is sand—and here is an addition to the quantity of sand, or "more sand"), and the comparative notion as well. The partitive may be a derivative of recurrence, but it is clear that the notion of comparative "more" is a relatively late development. Similarly, substantive forms with essentially constant semantic meaning vary in grammatical meaning in relation to other words in sentences, for example, "*Mommy* push," "push *Mommy*," "*Mommy's* shoe," and "my *Mommy*." The function or use of certain forms is not implicit for the child in the word itself.

Given that children comment on the notions of existence, nonexistence, and recurrence of objects and events, one might well wonder why they should talk about anything else—in the light of what we know to be the achievements of sensory-motor intelligence. Piaget (1960) has described a major achievement in the child's development of thought with the realization of the endurance of objects when removed in space and time. The child learns that objects and events exist, cease to exist, and recur, and so he talks about it. The important conclusion about the development of grammar appears to be that children do not simply use a relatively uncomplex syntactic frame (such as pivot + open); they talk about something, and syntax is learned by the child in his efforts to code certain conceptual relations.

There is a necessary distinction between a speaker-hearer's knowledge of grammar and the notion of grammar as a linguistic account of that knowledge. The nature of the underlying rules that the child uses to speak and understand utterances cannot be described directly. A generative grammar represents a formal linguistic account of how such rules specify the inherent relations in sentences. Such an account specifies the syntax of utterances (the arrangements of forms) that accounts for the semantic relations among the forms, and in this sense there is a crucial relationship between linguistic structure and underlying cognitive function. Indeed, it is difficult to distinguish between cognitive and linguistic categories when accounting for the expressed relations between actors or agents, actions or states, and objects or goals.

It appears that the notion of pivot grammar describes children's early speech in only the most superficial way. Although the notion of pivot speech describes certain distributional phenomena in early utterances, it is clear that children know more about grammar, that is, more about the inherent relationships between words in syntactic structure, than could possibly be accounted for in terms of pivot and open class analysis. If treatment for language disorders in children is ultimately to be derived from a model of normal language development, there is evidence to indicate that a pivot grammar is not the model of child speech to use.

TREATMENT OF LANGUAGE DISORDERS

Several conclusions from this discussion may be applicable to planning treatment of language disorders in children. There are necessary limitations in the extent to which the conclusions of this study pertain to all children learning language, and it would follow that similar limitations apply as well to using these results in evaluating and treating language pathology. Whether or not, and how, the normative data on language development in the literature can or should be directly applied to treating children with delayed language development are important questions (see Bloom, 1967). However, certain observations can be made at this time that should provide hypotheses for research directed toward evaluating procedures for treating language disorders.

First, the results of this study confirmed a conclusion that has been reached in every study of language development of children in the earliest stages of acquiring grammar. Children learn the syntax of language—the arrangements of words in sentences—before they learn inflections of noun, verb, and adjective forms. Although there may be alternation of certain forms from the beginning—"block," "blocks," and "sit," "sits"—the different forms of a word do not occur in contrast. For example, in the early samples, "-s" did not signal a meaningful difference, such as marking reference to more than one block as opposed to reference to only one block without expression of "-s." Thus, children learn word sequences (for example, "throw block") before morphological contrasts (as between "block," singular, and "blocks," plural).

Second, Kathryn, Eric, and Gia did not produce constructions that were potentially analyzable as noun phrases as their first (or most productive) syntactic structures. Rather, the most productive structures they produced (after utterances with initial /ə/) were those which, in the adult model, express the basic grammatical relations: subject-object, subject-verb, and verb-object strings. Although the grammars of Kathryn and Gia specified a noun phrase constituent (with attributive adjectives in Kathryn's lexicon only), this structure was far less productive than others which occurred, and Eric did not produce noun phrases at all. Based on these two observation, children appear to learn the expressions "throw block" or "Baby (subject) block (object)" before the expressions "big block," "red block," or "blocks."

Finally, the results of this study indicated that (1) the status of the referent in the context in which an utterance occurs, and (2) the child's relation to the referent in terms of behavior are critically important as influences on language performance. There were four contextual variables which characterized the occurrence of early syntactic utterances: (1) existence of the referent within the context, (2) recurrence of the referent or addition to the referent after its previous existence, (3) action upon the referent, and (4) nonexistence of the referent in the context where its existence was somehow expected.

The manifestation of the referent in the contexts of speech events was most significant. Utterances most often referred to objects or events which the child was able to see, and functioned as comments or directions, where the referent was manifest or imminent in the context of the speech event, as opposed to reports of distant past or future events. All of the children used a relational term, "more" or "another," to signal another instance of the referent or recurrence of the referent after previous occurrence. The productivity of verb-object and subject-object strings reflected the tendency for the children to talk about objects being acted upon. And, finally, as might be expected given the foregoing observations, their first negative sentences signaled the nonexistence of the referent. On the simplest level, children appear to learn to perceive and to discriminate (and, ultimately, to communicate) (1) such aspects of a referent as its existence, recurrence, or nonexistence, and (2) such relational aspects of events as between agent, action, and object before, among other things, such features of objects as relative size, color, or other identifying attributes.

It might be said that children learn to identify particular syntactic structures with the behavior and context with which they are perceived and then progress to reproducing structures in similar, recurring contexts. To use a structure in a new situation, the child needs to be able to perceive critical aspects of the context of the situation. Thus, the sequence in which the child learns syntactic structures may be influenced as much by his ability to differentiate aspects of situational context and to recognize recurrent contexts as by such factors as frequency of exposure to structures or their relative complexity.

Programs for language therapy that present children with linguistic structure (for example, pivot grammar) without attention to content ignore the very nature of language. It appears that learning a linguistic code depends upon the child's learning to distinguish, understand, and express certain conceptual relations. It would follow that children with language disorders need to learn more than simply the permitted cooccurrence of different words in their efforts at the analysis and use of language.

REFERENCES

Bellugi, U., and R. Brown (eds.), *The Acquisition of Language*. Monograph No. 29, Chicago, Ill.: Society for Research in Child Development (1964).

Bloom, L., A comment on Lee's developmental sentence types: A method for comparing normal and deviant syntactic development, *J. Speech Hearing Dis.*, **32**, 294–296 (1967).

Bloom, L., *Language Development: Form and Function in Emerging Grammars*. Cambridge, Mass.: MIT Press (1970).

Braine, M. D. S., The ontogeny of English phrase structure: The first phase, *Language*, **39**, 1–13 (1963). [Reprinted in this volume.]

Brown, R., and U. Bellugi, Three processes in the child's acquisition of syntax, *Harv. Educ. Rev.*, **34**, 133–151 (1964).

Brown, R., and C. Fraser, The acquisition of syntax. In Charles N. Cofer and Barbara S. Musgrave (eds.), *Verbal Behavior and Learning*. New York: McGraw-Hill (1963).

Leopold, W. F., *Speech Development of a Bilingual Child*, Vol. III. Evanston, Ill.: Northwestern Univ. (1949).

McNeill, D., Developmental psycholinguistics. In Frank Smith and George A. Miller (eds.), *The Genesis of Language*. Cambridge, Mass.: MIT Press, pp. 15–84 (1966a).

McNeill, D., The capacity for language acquisition, *Volta Rev.*, reprint no. 852, pp. 5–21 (1966b).

McNeill, D., *The Acquisition of Language: The Study of Developmental Psycholinguistics*. New York: Harper (1970).

Miller, W., and S. Ervin, The development of grammar in child language. In Ursula Bellugi and Roger Brown (eds.), *The Acquisition of Language*. Monograph No. 29, Chicago, Ill.: Society for Research in Child Development (1964). [Reprinted in this volume.]

Piaget, J., *The Psychology of Intelligence*. Paterson, N. J.: Atherton (1960).

Schlesinger, I. M., Production of utterances and language acquisition. In D. I. Slobin (ed.), *The ontogenesis of grammar: A theoretical symposium*. New York: Academic Press, 1971, pp. 63–101.

Smith, F., and G. A. Miller (eds.), *The Genesis of Language*. Cambridge, Mass.: MIT Press (1966).

Zipf, G. K., *The Psychobiology of Language; An Introduction to Dynamic Philology*. Cambridge, Mass.: MIT Press (1965).

Correlations between the Syntactic Constructions of the Child and of the Adult

——*Jeffrey S. Gruber*

In this paper we shall investigate some of the very early utterances of a girl named Dory. We will present data consisting of complex utterances (those which consist of two or more decipherable words) occurring during the ten-week period between the ages of 1.24 and 1.42 years. Whether any complex utterances occurred before this period has not yet been ascertained.

The data are taken from the body of observations recorded on synchronized tape and film by my colleague at the Massachusetts Institute of Technology, Dr. Margaret Bullowa, with a minimum of interaction between the observers and the subject family.

Toward the end of the period investigated in this paper a change occurs in the utterance types of the child. An explanation for this development will be found in the nature of language itself. The child will be seen to be utilizing an innately possessed knowledge of the universal characteristics of language: such characteristics as are present in adult language as well as in the child's. Even though there is a change in the utterance types of the child, there is a continuity in the fact that the child always generates those characteristics of an utterance that are universally obligatory.

In Table 1 we present the corpus of complex utterances listed according to the observation in which they occurred. These lists do not include the possibly complex utterances which involved undecipherable sequences of sound.

All the productive utterances of week 1 through week 9 had a certain semantic similarity. To see this we must first eliminate all set phrases from the corpus, which, not being independent creations, should not be classified with simple, single words. Such set phrases occurred frequently. Many of them are due to the fact that Dory's mother performs a catechism with her daughter, carrying on a preset conversation about the family, friends, Santa Claus, or nursery tales. During these episodes Dory is expected to contribute a particular

This paper was presented at the Biennial Meeting of the Society for Research in Child Development, March 31, 1967, and is printed here with the permission of the author.

TABLE 1   CORPUS OF PRODUCTIVE COMPLEX UTTERANCES OF DORY FOR THE TEN-WEEK PERIOD 1.24 THROUGH 1.42 YEARS

WEEK 1—1.24 YRS.	WEEK 2—1.26 YRS.	WEEK 3—1.30 YRS.
me broken	see broke	mama want shoe
Dory spoon	mama pony	no my
see the book	want shoe	I no want
see book	spoon get	see baby
see powder	want have spoon	mama shoe
more vitamins	have spoon spoon spoon	here mama
vitamins more	see spoon	hi lamb
	see hot	I want up
	see flower	want rosie
	see pretty	want the baby

WEEK 6—1.34 YRS.	WEEK 9—1.40 YRS.
get spoon	I want teddy
see beads?	mama have me glass of water
Dory beads	thank you mama
see beads ə Dory	have the dish
see ə pretty	ə want bye bye
want beads	Dory come
want beads?	Dory car
I want beads	
see Cheerios	
want mama hand	
pepper see?	
salt see?	
coffee see?	
see salt	
wanna basket	
mama wanna basket	

WEEK 10—1.42 YRS.

PERFORMATIVES		REPORTATIVES	
me sock	Dory back	Kathleen coming	teddy all gone
Dory pin	Dory down	Leon sock	cookie all gone in tummy
see bracelet	see broke	shoe on floor	daddy crying
Dory sock	see baby	daddy doing	Santa Claus all gone
want mommie shoe	see kitty	shoe all gone	see the baby looking
mommie shoe	Dory kitty	Donnie out	Mother Hubbard all gone
Dory powder	see duck	powder all gone	Bo Peep all gone
Dory all done	see mama duck	teddy out	
Dory all gone		powder back	

answer or response to the conversation. It is readily apparent that the development in Dory's ability to perform in the catechism is separate from the development in her creative ability to string together linguistic elements independently and spontaneously. The big difference is that in creative language use Dory is truly representing thought by her speech, whereas in the catechism she produces a speech signal which, instead of representing a mental response, is itself the response to some event in the environment. Thus, for example, in week 2 we eliminated *get up there*, which is a repetition of what Dory's mother often said in the context of Dory's climbing up on the chair. Similarly, *here she comes* in week 6 was uttered as she dragged the waste basket from the corner. *Play with Jeannie* in week 9 is part of the catechism when such things as *outside* or *toys* are mentioned by the mother. Similarly it is easy to subtract other utterances from the corpus on the basis of behavioral context.

Now we can see the semantic unity among Dory's complex utterances for the first nine weeks of this period. We will claim that they are performative sentences only. To make clear what this means, one must clarify the linguistic distinction between talking about something and indicating something. In talking about something an object is described by some attribute. In indicating something, there is no description of the object named; the trivial implication that this object itself is being referred to in the act of communication is not itself what the utterance describes. For example, if one says, "The truck is big," or even, "I see the truck," one is attributing size and one's own vision to the truck, respectively. On the other hand, in addressing someone by saying, "I point out the truck to you," or, "I demand of you the truck," there is nothing being attributed to the truck. Such sentences are called performatives. A sentence in which an attribution is made will be called reportative. A performative sentence is a direct expression of what one is in fact doing by means of the utterance as well as at the time of the utterance. If one says, "I say to you that John is ill," one has in fact just said that John is ill. Performatives are often accompanied by behavior which has the same significance. "I indicate" is the same as pointing; "I demand" is the same as reaching for something.

We shall call the word used to refer to the thing talked about or indicated the *theme* of the utterance. The remaining word or words will be called the *complement*.

From the behavioral context it is abundantly clear that all of Dory's utterances for the first nine weeks of this period were performatives. For example, whenever *see* is uttered as the complement of some theme, Dory is either reaching for the object named by that theme, pointing to it, or showing it to her mother. This is amazingly consistent throughout the filmed and taped observations. Even when *see* is uttered without a theme Dory's activity is the same. Among the examples in the corpus we have *see the beads*, which was uttered as Dory held the string of beads over her head, *see hot* uttered as Dory reached out to touch the stove, and *see pretty* uttered as she pointed out her clothing. The complement *see* consistently has the performative meaning of "I indicate to you," and it is possible to claim that this word has no other meaning.

Other complements which are used to represent the same semantic content as *see*, i.e., "I indicate to you," are *mama, me, Dory,* and *here.*

The performative, "I demand," was expressed by the complements *me, my, Dory, more, want, get, have, I want, mama want, mama,* and *want mama.* From the context it was clear that the performative "I demand" was intended, and not the reportative statement expressed by the adult form, "I want." The difference between the two should be made clear. For the performative it is obligatorily the addressee that something is wanted of. This is not so for the reportative. Second, for the performative it is the communication itself which has the purpose of satisfying the desire. In the reportative adult form, "I want," it is not the act of communication itself which has this purpose, but, more specifically, it is the communicant who has this purpose, and the communication which then expresses this fact. Dory's bodily activity accompanying these performative utterances shows clearly that they too are for the purpose of satisfying the desire. Both the speech and the accompanying bodily activity represent the same communicative act. The speech act is for the child indistinguishable from the act of reaching for the subject.

A marked change occurs in the utterances of the last week of this period. Performatives are still produced, as shown in the first column for the corpus of week 10. But in addition there are utterances that cannot be simply performatives. These are shown in the second column. Here Dory is describing things in her environment. Her bodily activity does not communicate the same thing that her speech act does. The sentences are reportative; the complements here express attributions of the theme remote from the speech act itself. In *shoe all gone* Dory expresses the fact that her shoe has momentarily disappeared in her pant-leg. In *teddy out* she relates the fact that her teddy bear has just been removed from the box. Finally, following Dory's utterance *daddy crying,* her mother remarks, "That's the latest, everything's 'cry cry.'" Here Dory was reporting a fantasy or at any rate an event removed from the context of her speech act.

Let us look in particular at the two-word utterances composed of two nouns. We can interpret the utterances of this type as performative sentences during the first nine-week period so long as the complement noun is either *Dory* or *mama,* both of which are nouns implied in a performative speech act. Hence such constructions as *Dory shoe* or *mama shoe* are performatives. In fact, in each case Dory is demanding that her mother put her shoes on. However, in the tenth week we see other nouns than *Dory* and *mama* used in this way, e.g., *Leon sock.* Since *Leon* does not represent a category inherent in a performative, we cannot say the above is a performative. In some way sock is attributed to Leon here.

How can we account for this sequence of events from our understanding of the universal nature of language? Suppose it were the case that the child always expresses complete thoughts in his utterances. We would hold this to be true for utterances which were not merely conditioned responses such as occur in a catechism. By a complete thought we mean that all the categories that are universally obligatory in an utterance are generated. A noun, for example, would never represent just a noun but would holophrastically stand for a complete sentence, i.e., a complete underlying semantic representation.

Evidence has been brought forth by Ross (1970) showing that it is universally obligatory for every reportative sentence to be embedded in a performative sentence in deep structure which later is omitted from the overt utterance. Thus, "John is ill" has the same underlying form as "I say to you that John is ill." "Stand up" has roughly the same underlying form as "I demand that you stand up." We do not have time to present the evidence in favor of this hypothesis, but there is a considerable amount which has been gleaned from studies of the internal syntactic structure of English.

Given then that every utterance obligatorily includes one performative sentence, the simplest possible sentence would be one which is just a performative sentence and no more. In such a sentence the object of the performative would be a simple noun as in, "I indicate to you the shoe," instead of it being an embedded reportative sentence as in, "I indicate to you that the shoe is all gone." The latter type of sentence is obviously more complex. It appears that in the very early stages Dory produces only such simple performatives in which the object is just a simple noun. The stage reached at week 10 is that stage at which the object of the obligatorily generated performative may be an embedded sentence. The complement expressing the performative, as in adult speech, is usually omitted. But we notice that the performative complement can, in fact, be overt, as in *see the baby looking*. A limitation on the length of sentences probably prohibits performative complements like *see* and reportative complements like *looking* from occurring together very often.

It has been noticed that *want* is a very early verb for the child to use for sentence embedding, and it remains the only one for a very long period. This now becomes completely understandable inasmuch as *want* stands for the performative "I demand." If performatives are universally obligatory, as Ross holds, it represents a minimal degree of complexity for the child to generate *want* as an embedding verb. With respect to underlying forms, this degree of complexity is reached at week 10.

How can we explain the particular sets of words used to represent the performative "I demand"? This we can do on the basis that Dory represents one or more of the obligatory underlying semantic categories inherent in this performative. The subject of the performative obligatorily refers to the speaker; consequently we see *Dory, I, me,* and *my* being utilized. The indirect object is always the addressee, *mama. Want* is not a performative in adult language, but it involves many of the same categories as *demand*. In both *want* and *demand* the categories of *have* or *get* are included. *Want, get,* and *have* are utilized instead of *demand* because these are the words which Dory will have heard commonly and in which she will be most likely to infer the relevant categories. Similar comments are relevant for the word *see*.

The child, generating only simple performative-type sentences, will interpret the parents' speech as the same. That is, before the stage reached at week 10 the child will interpret the parents' speech as consisting of simple performatives regardless of what they in fact are. In particular, on hearing a declarative sentence from the parent, the child will believe that the parent is merely pointing out and naming some object. That is, for the child the parent is saying over and over again, "I indicate to you the *theme*," where *theme* is some noun referring to some object. It is as if the child were indeed learning to speak by means of a naming game that the parents play with him. As far as the child is concerned, this is in fact what is happening.

REFERENCE

Ross, J. R., On declarative sentences. In R. A. Jacobs and P. S. Rosenbaum (eds.), *Readings in English transformational grammar*. Waltham, Mass.: Ginn, 1970, pp. 222–272.

The First Sentences of Child and Chimpanzee[1]

——*Roger Brown*

The following paper, as indicated in the title, goes beyond the confines of our species to consider the psychological bases of language development. The age-old dream of King Solomon's ring—the ability to talk with animals—remains alive. Beatrice and Allen Gardner, at the University of Neveda, have succeeded in establishing more communication with a nonhuman animal than perhaps any other human-animal communication attempt in history. (For a more detailed description, see Gardner and Gardner [1971].) The question is, of course, how to relate the chimpanzee's skills with human linguistic competence. In exploring this question, Brown offers us a valuable review of early child language development at the same time. (For other discussions of the Gardner's study see Bronowski and Bellugi [1970] and the consequent exchange of letters in *Science*; McNeill [1970, pp. 54–55].) The Gardners' chimp learned deaf sign language—a communication system far more adapted to chimp physiology than human vocal speech. Ursula Bellugi and Edward Klima, in San Diego, are now studying the acquisition of sign language in deaf children. Their study will provide an important comparison point to the chimp development. The early stages of their work already suggest that human sign acquisition is much more like human vocal language acquisition than is chimp sign acquisition (personal communication from Ursula Bellugi).

Since the writing of Brown's paper, David Premack (1970, 1971) has

From *Psycholinguistics: Selected papers*, by Roger Brown. © 1970 by The Free Press, a Division of the Macmillan Company. Pages 203–231 reprinted by permission of the author and the publisher.

[1] Some of the research described in this paper was supported by PHS Grant HD-02908 from the National Institute of Child Health and Development.

publicized a very different attempt to teach something like human language to a chimpanzee. Premack's approach (at Santa Barbara) involves the manipulation of plastic symbols according to various rules of reference and combination. It is too early to fully evaluate his study. His chimp has learned a number of complex cognitive operations, but the debate as to the validity of the study as a language-learning analogy is going on full force.

Brown's paper is taken from a recent anthology of his writings, where it was published for the first time. The preamble to the paper was written by Brown for that volume, apparently some months after the paper had been written.
—D.I.S.

In 1968–69 several lines of thought about language development came together in an exciting way. Ursula Bellugi and I, in the 1964 paper called "Three Processes in the Acquisition of Syntax," which is included in this volume [Brown, 1970], had described one sort of common adult reponse to the telegraphic sentences of very young children, the kind of response called an "expansion." An expansion is essentially a reading of the child's semantic intention. Thus when Eve said, "Mommy lunch" her mother said, "That's right, Mommy is having her lunch." Dr. Bellugi and I did not commit ourselves as to the accuracy or "veridicality" of these readings. We were not sure whether children really intended, by their telegraphic sentences, what adults thought they intended, and we could not really see how to find out. Our focus was on the expansion as a potential tutorial mechanism. Whether or not children started out intending what adults attributed to them it seemed to us that expansions would cause them to do so in the end. In 1968 I. M. Schlesinger, working at Hebrew University in Jerusalem, and Lois Bloom, working at Columbia University, independently came to the conclusion that children really did intend certain aspects of the meanings attributed to them by adult expansions. They did not intend the meanings expressed in the expansions by grammatical morphemes, by inflections, articles, prepositions, and auxiliary verbs. There was nothing in the child's performance to suggest that they had these things in mind. What they did intend were certain fundamental semantic relations such as Agent-Action, Agent-Object, Action-Object, Possessor-Possessed, and so on. There was, in the child's speech, something to suggest that they intended these relations. This same "something," the aspect of child speech that justified the attribution to them of certain relational meanings, turns out to be missing from the linguistic performance of an important comparison case: the home-raised chimpanzee named Washoe.

Washoe, over a period of more than three years, has been learning the American Sign Language. She now produces many recognizable signs in circumstances that are semantically appropriate. What is more she produces sequences or strings of signs which seem very much like sentences. Does this mean that a chimpanzee has now been shown to have the capacity for linguistic syntax, a capacity we had long thought exclusively human? Perhaps it does. Still there is something missing; the very thing, curiously enough, that justifies the Bloom-Schlesinger semantic approach to the early speech of children.

In this paper the spotlight is on Washoe whose extraordinary feats naturally place her in the center ring. But there are also important events in the other rings. Bloom and Schlesinger are right, I think, and they have increased the power of the analyses we can make of child speech. They also bring to our attention some impressively general and conceivably universal aspects of child speech. As Table 8-2 indicates we begin to have enough analyses of children learning a variety of languages to see what is truly general in language development. And in the months since this paper was written the range has been expanded by dissertations written at Berkeley on the acquisition of Samoan, of Luo (spoken in Kenya) and of Tzeltal (spoken in a region of Chiapas, Mexico).[2]

The present paper, the most recently written of any in the book, has not previously been published. I should like gratefully to acknowledge the courtesy of Dr. R. Allen Gardner and Dr. Beatrice Gardner, who are raising Washoe. They have kindly shown me their films, sent me their diary summaries, and responded to questions I have asked them about this fascinating experiment in comparative psychology.

Once again, and for the the third time in this century, psychology has a home-raised chimpanzee who threatens to learn language. Washoe, named for Washoe county in Nevada, has been raised as a child by Allen and Beatrice Gardner of the University of Nevada since June of 1966 when she was slightly under one year old. At this writing the materials available consist of summaries of Washoe's Diary extending to the age of 36 months.

The first of the home-raised chimps was Gua, also a female, raised by the Winthrop Kelloggs nearly 40 years ago. Gua gave some evidence of understanding English utterances, she responded distinctively and appropriately to about 70, but Gua did not speak at all. Viki, the second chimp to be adopted by a human family and also a female, learned to make four sounds that where recognizable approximations to English words. Viki was given intensive training by her foster parents, Keith and Cathy Hayes, but the four word-like sounds seemed to mark the upper limit of her productive linguistic capacity.

Both Viki and Gua were asked to learn one particular form of language—speech—which is not the only form. The essential properties of language can be divorced from articulation. Meaning or "semanticity" and grammatical productivity appear not only in speech but in writing and print and in sign language. There is good reason to believe that the production of vowels and consonants and the control of prosodic features is, simply as a motor performance,

---

[2] [Editors' note: B. G. Blount, "Acquisition of language by Luo children." Unpublished doctoral dissertation, University of California, Berkeley, 1969. B. Stross, "Language acquisition by Tenejapa Tzeltal children." Unpublished doctoral dissertation, University of California, Berkeley, 1969.]

something to which chimpanzees are not well adapted. The chimpanzee articulatory apparatus is quite different from the human, and chimpanzees do not make many speech-like sounds either spontaneously or imitatively. It is possible, therefore, that Viki and Gua failed not because of an incapacity that is essentially linguistic but because of a motoric ineptitude that is only incidentally linguistic. The Gardners thought the basic experiment was worth trying again, but with a change that would eliminate the articulatory problem. They have undertaken to teach Washoe the American Sign Language, the language of the deaf in North America. What is required on the motoric level is manual dexterity, and that is something chimps have in abundance. They skillfully manipulate so many of man's inventions that one naturally wonders whether they can also move their fingers in the air—to symbolize ideas.

Why does anyone care? For the same reason, perhaps, that we care about space travel. It is lonely being the only language-using species in the universe. We want a chimp to talk so that we can say: "Hello, out there! What's it like being a chimpanzee?"

I have always been very credulous about life on other planets and talking animals, and so I have been often disappointed. Remembering the disappointments of Gua and Viki I was slow to take an interest in Washoe. From the beginning of their study the Gardners sent out periodic summaries in diary form to psychologists who might be expected to take an interest. I glanced over the first 4 of these and noticed that Washoe seemed to understand quite a large number of signs and that she was producing a few—in what appeared to be a meaningful way. This much Gua and Viki, between them, had also done, and it seemed likely that Washoe's linguistic progress would soon come to an end, but little advanced beyond that of her forerunners. Then, on the first page of the 5th summary, which covers the period when Washoe was estimated to be between 28 and 32 months old, I read the following: "Since late April, 1967, Washoe has used her signs—at that time there were six—in strings of two or more as well as singly. We have kept records of all occurrences of combinations in the period covered by the previous diary summaries, and found that Washoe used 29 different two-sign combinations and four different combinations of three signs."

It was rather as if the seismometer left on the moon had started to tap out "S-O-S." I got out the earlier diaries and studied them carefully and I read with the greatest interest the subsequent diary installments as they came along, and then the Gardners' article "Teaching Sign Language to a Chimpanzee" which appeared in *Science* in 1969. In the spring of 1969 the Gardners themselves paid us a visit at Harvard for two days, showing films of Washoe and discussing her achievements with a group here that studies the development of language in children. We were particularly interested in comparing Washoe's early linguistic development with that of three children whom we have followed for a number of years. In the literature these children are named: Adam, Eve, and Sarah.

From an evolutionary point of view the important thing about language is that it makes life experiences cumulative; across generations and, within one generation, among individuals. Everyone can know much more than he could possibly learn by direct experience. Knowledge and folly, skills and superstitions, all alike begin to accumulate and cultural evolution takes off at a rate that leaves biological evolution far behind. Among the various defining features of language there are two that are peculiarly important in making experience cumulative. They are semanticity or meaningfulness and productivity or openness.

Semanticity occurs in some degree in the natural communication systems of many kinds of animal society but productivity does not. Productivity is the capacity to generate novel messages for every sort of novel meaning. Languages have this property because they have grammars which are rules for the compositional expression of meaning, rules which create meanings from words and patterns. Signs in sequence suggest grammar, and so it was a momentous day when Washoe began to produce them. For grammar has heretofore been an exclusively human preserve.

WASHOE'S SIGNING PROGRESS

The signs of the American Sign Language (ASL) are described in Stokoe, Casterline, and Croneberg (1965) and a transformational grammar of the language has been written by McCall (1965).

There are two basic forms of ASL: finger-spelling and signing proper. In finger-spelling there is a distinct sign for each letter of the alphabet and the signer simply spells in the air. This system, like our alphabetic writing, is entirely dependent on knowledge of the spoken language. In signing proper, as opposed to finger-spelling, the configurations and movements produced refer directly to concepts. Some such signs are iconic, which is to say that the sign suggests its sense. The sign for *flower* in American Sign Language is created by holding the fingers of one hand extended and joined at the tips, like a closed tulip, and touching the tip first to one nostril and then another—as if sniffing a flower. That is a good icon. Many other signs are arbitrarily related to their references. Most deaf Americans use some combination of directly semantic signs and finger spelling. The Gardners attempted to teach Washoe only the directly semantic signs.

The Gardners are not deaf and did not know sign language at the start of their experiment. They learned it from books and from a teacher, but do not yet count themselves really fluent. They and their associates, when with Washoe, and someone is with her all day long, sign, as one would with a child, the names of actions and things; they sign questions and requests and they just chatter. In addition to providing this rich opportunity for incidental learning Washoe's human tutors have induced her to imitate signs and have used instrumental conditioning (with tickling as reward) to train her to sign appropriately for objects and pictures in books.

In the first seven months of the project Washoe learned to use four signs with some degree of appropriate semanticity. The *come-gimme* sign was directed at persons or animals and also at objects out of reach. The *more* sign, made by bringing the fingertips together overhead, seemed to ask for continuation or repetition of pleasurable activities and also to ask for second helpings of food. *Up* was used when Washoe wanted to be lifted and *sweet* was used at the end of a meal when dessert was in order. In the next seven months 9 more signs were added, and by the end of 22 months, when Washoe was about three years old, she seemed to control 34 signs.

In the spring of 1969 the Gardners showed a group of us at Harvard a film of Washoe looking at a picture book and making appropriate signs as a tutor pointed and signed "What's this?" On a first showing the performance was rather disappointing. The viewer is not entirely sure that he has seen the signs since there is so much action going on. However, this changes on a second viewing. The signs of sign language are not, at first, perceptual segregates for the uninitiated, but even a single viewing makes them very much more "visible." And, probably because so many of them are iconic, one very rapidly learns about 10–20 of them. I now do not doubt that Washoe produces the signs.

In the diary reports one can trace the semantic generalization of each sign and this generalization, much of it spontaneous, is quite astonishingly childlike. To appreciate the accomplishment it is necessary to recover a certain innocence in connection with some thoroughly familiar abstractions. Consider the notion connected with the English word *more* when it is used as a request. Washoe started out signalling *more* with the specific sense of more tickling. Far from

TABLE 8-1 SOME OF WASHOE'S SIGN SEQUENCES AS CLASSIFIED BY THE GARDNERS

A. Two Signs.
  1. Using "emphasizers" (*please, come-gimme, hurry, more*).
     Hurry open.
     More sweet.
     More tickle.
     Come-gimme drink.
  2. Using "specifiers."   3. Using names or pronouns.
     Go sweet (to be carried to fruitbushes).   *You drink.*
     Listen eat (at sound of supper bell).   *You eat.*
     Listen dog (at sound of barking).   *Roger come.*
B. Three or More Signs.
  1. Using "emphasizers."
     Gimme please food.
     Please tickle more.
     Hurry gimme toothbrush.
  2. Using "specifiers."   3. Using names or pronouns.
     Key open food.   *You me go-there in.*
     Open key clean.   *You out go.*
     Key open please blanket.   *Roger Washoe tickle.*

---

adhering to a particular context the sign rapidly generalized to hairbrushing and swinging and other processes involving Washoe which Washoe enjoyed. And then it generalized further to "second helpings" of dessert and soda pop and the like. And then to performances of another which only involved Washoe as a spectator—acrobatics and somersaults. Human children regularly use the word *more* as a request over just this same range. And when they start to make two-word sentences with *more* they use nouns to request additional helpings (e.g., *More milk, More grapefruit juice*), but also verbs to request that processes and exhibitions be repeated (e.g., *More write, More swing*).

The semantic accomplishments are remarkable, but it is the evidence of syntax that most concerns us. Table 8-1 sets out some of Washoe's strings or sentences; they are drawn from the Gardners' fifth and sixth summaries which appeared in 1968, and I have selected examples which, in English, look very much like sentences. The classification into combinations using "emphasizers," "specifiers," and "names or pronouns" is the Gardners' own. In Table 8-1 we have sign sequences which translate into English as *Hurry open, Go sweet, You eat, Open key clean, You me go-there in,* and so on. How do these multi-sign sequences compare with the first multi-word combinations produced by children learning American English and other languages?

THE AVAILABLE DATA ON CHILD SPEECH

The best index of grammatical development until the age of about three years is simply the mean (or average) length of the child's utterances. When speech begins, of course, all utterances are single words, and the mean-length-of-utterance (MLU) has the value 1.0. As soon as word combining begins the MLU rises above this value. For about 18–24 months almost all grammatical "advances" have the common effect of increasing the MLU. Because these advances tend to occur in the same order for all children learning American English (and perhaps more generally) when two children have the same MLU values the internal grammatical detail of their speech is also quite similar.

It is not the case that two children having the same MLU must be of the same chronological age. Children vary greatly in the rapidity with which they progress grammatically and, for that reason, chronological age is a poor index of linguistic level. Figure 1 on page 296 plots age against MLU for the three children we have studied. Utterance length was counted in morphemes rather than words so as to give credit for inflections like the -s of plurality, the -s of possession, the -ed for past tense, and the -ing of progressive aspect. As can be seen, the utterances of all three children grew steadily longer over this whole period. Eve advanced much more rapidly than Adam and Sarah.

The five straight lines marked with Roman numerals on the figure represent points we have arbitrarily selected for intensive analysis in preparing a five-stage description of linguistic progress in this period. At our first stage the MLU values for the three children ranged between 1.68 and 2.06. Many utterances were still single words; most were two or three words long; five words was the longest. Washoe seems to have been at about this point when she was 36 months old.

Adam, Eve, and Sarah at I, and Washoe at 27 months were not at the very beginning of syntax, and it is desirable to have child-speech data for earlier periods to compare with the earlier data for Washoe. There are, in the literature or in progress, longitudinal grammatical studies which include reports for developmental stages lying between an MLU of 1.0 and the level at which our children were first studied. Combining these reports with ours we have information on an initial period which is bounded by an MLU of 1.0, the threshold of syntax, and an MLU of 2.0, the level of the most advanced child in the set—Adam. For the present purpose we shall call this full interval "Stage I." It seems to correspond fairly exactly with the period for which the Gardners have provided data on Washoe: the age of 12 months through the age of 36 months.

The child-speech data include 18 analyses of 13 children which are fully comparable with one another because they are based on large samples of spontaneous speech, tape recorded in the home. These studies are listed in developmental order above the space in Table 8-2. Adam I, Eve I, and Sarah I belong to the set. So, too, do five analyses of the speech of three American children called Gia, Kathryn, and Eric, which appear in the 1968 doctoral dissertation of Lois Bloom. Then there are single analyses for each of three boys, Gregory, Andrew, and Steven, which were published by Martin Braine (1963) and single analyses for two little girls, Susan and Christy, published by Miller and Ervin (now Ervin-Tripp) in 1964. To this collection of studies of children learning American English, Melissa Bowerman, a doctoral candidate at Harvard, has recently added three analyses of two children learning a non-Indo-European language. The language is Finnish, and the children are Seppo and Rina. All of these studies concern Stage I speech; the Roman numerals appearing after the names of some of the children were assigned by the investigators in ordering their own analyses. The developmental order is based on the MLU except in five cases for which the MLU was not available. These five (Gregory, Andrew, Steven, Christy, and Susan) were placed in the order on the basis of another simple index.

Beyond the studies described above there is a large literature, mostly American, Russian, French, and German, reporting longitudinal studies of the diary type which are not fully comparable with one another nor with the 18 contemporary analyses we have described above. To represent this large literature and broaden the range of languages considered I have selected four studies: Werner Leopold's (1949) description of the first two years in the grammatical development of his daughter Hildegard who was learning English and German simultaneously; Antoine Gregoire's (1937) account of the first two years of his sons, Charles and Edmond, who were learning French; Dan Slobin's (1966) summary of the detailed account given by the Soviet linguist, A. N. Gvozdev, of the acquisition of Russian by his son, Zhenya; Yuen Ruen Chao's (1951) report on selected aspects of the grammar of his grandson Canta, when Canta, who was

TABLE 8-2 THE AVAILABLE DATA IN DEVELOPMENTAL ORDER

CHILD	MLU	AGE AT DATA	CHARACTER OF DATA	INVESTIGATOR(S)
Eric I	1.10	1;7	4 hours, tape recorded.	Bloom
Gia I	1.12	1;7	7 hours, tape recorded.	Bloom
Eric II	1.19	1;9	6 hours, tape recorded.	Bloom
Gregory		1;7.5–1;11.5	cumulative inventory.	Braine
Andrew		1;7.5–1;11.5	cumulative inventory.	Braine
Steven		1;11.5–2;0.5	12 play sessions, tape recorded.	Braine
Christy		2;0–2;3	taped weekly 45 minute sessions over 3 months.	Miller, Ervin
Susan		1;9–2;0	taped weekly 45 minute sessions over 3 months.	Miller, Ervin
Kath'yn I	1.32	1;9	$7\frac{1}{2}$ hours, tape recorded.	Bloom
Gia II	1.34	1;9	$7\frac{1}{2}$ hours, tape recorded.	Bloom
Eric III	1.42	1;10	$8\frac{1}{2}$ hours, tape recorded.	Bloom
Seppo	1.45	1;11	2 hours taped over 1 month.	Bowerman
Eve I	1.68	1;6	$3\frac{1}{2}$ hours taped over 6 weeks.	Brown
Sarah I	1.73	2;3	3 hours taped over 6 weeks.	Brown
Seppo II	1.77*	2;2	2 hours taped over 1 month.	Bowerman
Kathryn II	1.92	1;11	9 hours tape recorded.	Bloom
Rina I	1.95*	2;1	2 hours taped over 1 month.	Bowerman
Adam I	2.06	2;3	2 hours, tape recorded.	Brown
Hildegard		1;0–2;0	parental diary, selectively reported.	Leopold
Charles		1;0–2;0	parental diary, selectively reported.	Grégoire
Edmond		1;0–2;0	parental diary, selectively reported.	Grégoire
Zhenya		?	very selective, interpretative reports.	Gvozdev, Slobin
Canta		2;4	grandfather's diary, selectively reported.	Chao
Washce		1;0–3;0	foster parental diary, quite fully reported.	Gardners

* MLU is approximation within ±.10 due to special problems in calculating for Finnish.

learning Mandarin Chinese, was 28 months old. These studies are listed, below the space in Table 8-2, together with the comparison point we never expected to have, the Gardners' study of the first stages in the syntactic development of a chimpanzee, Washoe herself.

MAJOR MEANINGS IN STAGE I

Table 8-3 lists 10 kinds of structural meaning which, among them, characterize the majority of two-word sentences in Stage I. In the samples for which

TABLE 8-3   THE FIRST SENTENCES IN CHILD SPEECH

I. Operations of reference.	
Nominations:	*That* (or *It* or *There*) + *book, cat, clown, hot, big*, etc.
Notice:	*Hi* + *Mommy, cat, belt*, etc.
Recurrence:	*More* (or *'Nother*) + *milk, cereal, nut, read, swing, green*, etc.
Nonexistence:	*Allgone* (or *No-more*) + *rattle, juice, dog, green*, etc.
II. Relations.	
Attributive:	Ad + N (*Big train, Red book*, etc).
Possessive:	N + N (*Adam checker, Mommy lunch*, etc.)
Locative:	N + N (*Sweater chair, Book table*, etc.)
Locative:	V + N (*Walk street, Go store*, etc.)
Agent-Action:	N + V (*Adam put, Eve read*, etc.)
Agent-Object:	N + N (*Mommy sock, Mommy lunch*, etc.)
Action-Object:	V + N (*Put book, Hit ball*, etc.)

complete analysis is possible, those of Seppo, Rina, Adam, Eve, and Sarah the structural meanings account for about 75% of all multi-word utterances. The characterization by structural meaning is not all that there is to say about the first sentences, but it is the most important information for present purposes. In the contemporary study of child speech the earliest descriptions published were purely formal, and made little reference to meaning. In 1963 Colin Fraser and I described the first sentences as "telegraphic" in the sense that they are almost entirely composed of "contentive" words, of nouns, verbs, and adjectives; the little words or grammatical morphemes which are ordinarily omitted from telegrams are also omitted from early child speech. This is a purely descriptive generalization about surface form. As such it is correct and has been confirmed in all studies. The characterization of child speech as telegraphic does not provide for "productivity" or the construction of novel combinations. Martin Braine in 1963 characterized two-word child sentences in terms of a simple but productive grammar involving "Pivot" and "Open" classes. While Braine's description certainly fits his data it does not, as both Lois Bloom and Melissa Bowerman have recently shown, fit all children at I or even all children at the more primitive end of I.

The characterization of two-word sentences in terms of structural meanings was originated in contemporary work by I. M. Schlesinger of the Hebrew University in Jerusalem and by Lois Bloom, both writing in 1968. These researchers differ in the grammatical structures they employ, but they agree on one thing: telegraphic sentences looked at in full linguistic and non-linguistic context can be seen to express certain types of structural meanings. Parents of course have always been of this opinion, and they often will gloss a child's telegraphic utterance as a related English simple sentence. When Eve said "Mommy lunch" her mother said "That's right, Mommy is having her lunch." When Eve said "Fraser coffee" her mother said "Yes, that's Fraser's coffee." The Bloom-Schlesinger approach essentially assumes that such glosses, which the investigator can supply as readily as a parent, are accurate readings insofar as they interpret the child's words as expressing such relations as agent-object or possessor-possessed. They are not assumed to be accurate insofar as they attribute to the Stage I child knowledge of inflections, articles, and other grammatical morphemes for which there is no evidence in his speech. The arguments of Bloom and Schlesinger, as well as the results of our own continuing research, have convinced me that the early sentences are, in fact, expressions of certain structural meanings.

The classification of Table 8-3 is indebted to both Bloom and Schlesinger, but somewhat different from what either proposes. Set I, called "Operations of Reference," is made up of utterance-sets, such that each is defined by one or another constant term appearing in conjunction with various nouns, verbs, and adjectives. Nominative sentences are always used in the presence of a referent which is pointed at, or otherwise singled out for attention, and named. In connection with *hi*, Bloom has noticed that children do not use it as a greeting, do not, that is, use it just when someone hoves in view, but are, rather, likely to "light up" suddenly and say *hi* to someone who has been there all along; to someone, to some-animal, or to some-thing. Kathryn said *Hi, spoon*; Gregory, *Hi, plane*, and Adam, *How are you, belt*. These seem to be expressions of attention or notice. Recurrence of a referent (Bloom's category) includes the reappearance of something recently seen, a new instance of the same category, an additional quantity or "helping" of a substance, a new instance of a quality, and repetition of an action. Nonexistence (another of Bloom's categories) means that a referent which has been in the referent field or was expected to appear in it is not now to be seen.

In set II, called "Relations," we have no repeating words to define each class. Both initial and final words are varied, and what defines a set is a certain quite abstract semantic relation. The attributive might be said to take some person or thing (the noun) and "fill in" or "specify" the value of one of its attributes by naming it with an adjective. The possessive identifies, for a given thing, the person having special rights with regard to it. The children's possessive typically divides spaces and objects in the house among family members; it expresses a kind of primitive notion of territoriality and property. The locative (almost always without the preposition that is obligatory in adult speech) names a locus for a movable thing or a locus or terminus of an action. Agent-Action constructions take a verb and specify one of its arguments, the argument naming the (usually animate) initiator or performer of the action. Action-Object constructions name the other argument for two-argument or "transitive" verbs: the recipient or target of action. Agent-Object constructions seem, in context, to be sentences with verbs omitted. Thus *Mommy lunch* means *Mommy is having lunch*. The semantic relations, characterized above, are closely related to the grammatical relations called: modifier of a noun-phrase, subject of a sentence and object of a predicate. However, the grammatical relations are defined in purely formal terms, and while they may, in early child speech, be more or less perfectly coordinated with the semantic rules the two are not the same.

In the course of Stage I certain changes occur. At the lower, more primitive end, operations of reference tend to be more prominent than semantic relations. In the middle stretch operations of reference and two-term relations account for most multi-word utterances. At the end of Stage I, especially in the samples of Adam and Rina, there is a step up in complexity which is manifest in two ways. Several kinds of three-term relations become frequent: agent-action-object; agent-action-locative; agent-object-locative. At the same time one term, the nominal, in two-term relations, which is in the early period always a single noun, begins frequently to be elaborated into a two-word noun phrase. These noun phrases fill all of the positions originally occupied by single nouns. The noun phrases are, furthermore, all expressions of possession, recurrence, or attribution. In fact, then, the elaboration of the noun term is accomplished by filling noun positions with just those two-term operations and relations which are noun phrases and which have been long practised as independent utterances. It is quite wonderful to find that these first structural complications take just the same form in Finnish as they do in English. Finally, while I have omitted any discussion of negative, imperative, and interrogative operations from this discussion all are present in primitive form in Stage I.

The meanings expressed by the sentences of Stage I seem to be extensions of the kind of intelligence that has been called "sensory-motor" by the great developmental psychologist, Jean Piaget. Piaget's studies of the first two years of life (e.g. Piaget, 1937) convinced him that the infant does not at first conceive of objects and persons as permanently existing in a single space which also includes the self. Neither does he recognize that objects and persons are all potential "sources of causality" and potential recipients of force. In the first 18–24 months, in Piaget's view, the infant "constructs" the world of enduring objects and immediate space and time. The meanings of the first sentences pre-suppose the sensory-motor constructions, but they also go beyond them. The aim of sensory-motor intelligence is practical success, not truth; sensory-motor intelligence is *acted* not *thought*. The ability to create propositions which can be expressed in sentences must mature near the end of the sensory-motor period. If the meanings of the first sentences are an extension of sensory-motor intelligence then they are probably universal in mankind. Universal in mankind but not limited to mankind and not innate. Animals may operate with sensory-motor intelligence, and Piaget's work shows that it develops in the infant, over many months, out of his commerce with the animate and inanimate world.

COMPARISON OF WASHOE AND CHILD

How do Washoe's Sign Sequences (Table 8-1) compare with the sentences of Table 8-3? *More sweet* and *More tickle* look like expressions of Recurrence. *Go sweet* (to be carried to the fruit-bushes) seems to be an Action-Locative construction; *You eat* an Agent-Action construction; and *Gimme please food* an Action-Object construction. The sentences with *key* appear to express an Instrumental relation which also occasionally appears in Stage I child speech. Several of Washoe's three-term sequences look like instances of the three-term relations that appear at the end of Stage I for children; *Roger Washoe tickle* could be an Agent-Action-Object sentence and *You out go* an Agent-Action-Locative. In sum, the strings of Table 8-1 look very much the same as a sample of early child speech.

However, there is more to syntax than sequences or strings. The deeper question is whether Washoe was simply making signs distributed in time or whether the signs were *in construction*. What is the difference? As a first approximation, a sequence may simply name a series of ideas which succeed one another in time but do not combine cognitively, whereas a construction puts ideas into one or another structural relation.

In two superficial respects Washoe's combinations seem to be constructions and not simply sequences. Before one can make a grammatical analysis of child speech it must be segmented into utterances which mark off just those words that are "in construction" with one another. Segmentation proves to be very easily done, for the reason that children, when they begin to make combinations, already control several of the prosodic patterns that adults use to mark off sentences. One easily hears in child speech the "declarative" pattern, with high pitch and stress near the end and a final fall and fade, as well as the interrogative pattern that ends with a rising pitch. An adult who uses sign language also has devices for marking off sentences. Stokoe *et al.* (1965) say that in the declarative case the hands of the signer return to the position of repose from which they started when he began to sign. In the interrogative case the hands remain, for a perceptible period, in the position of the last sign or even move out toward the person being interrogated. When we talked with the Gardners we asked whether Washoe used such "terminal" or "juncture" signs. Not having been interested in this particular feature they were not quite sure, but since then Allen Gardner has written to me: "Once we started to look for it, it was very clear that Washoe's segmentation (and our own, of course) is very much the same as that described by Stokoe, *et al.* . . . . It is such a natural aspect of signing that we just were not aware that both Washoe and her friends were doing this all along. As in the case of speech contours it is so obvious that you don't notice it until you worry about it."

There is a second surface feature of Washoe's combinations which suggests that they are constructions rather than sequences. In child speech the very slow rise over time in utterance length seems to represent an increase of information-processing power. The fact that the child at I produces subject and object without any verb surely means that he operates under some kind of complexity limitation. Now it also is the case that Washoe's sequences gradually increase. Two signs are common before three and three precede four. Why should that be so if the sign combinations are not constructions? If they were only signs strung out in time and not interacting semantically and grammatically then one would think they might be of any length at all, and that there would be no reason for them to start short and become long.

The presence of terminal contours in child speech suggests that certain words are in construction but not what the constructions are; there are no contours to mark off the various relations and operations of Table 8-3. What is there in child speech to suggest that these structural meanings are being expressed and, specifically to the present point, is there anything not also found in Washoe's sign sequences? What there is in child speech, most generally, is the order of the words. The order, generally, is appropriate to the structural meaning suggested by the non-linguistic situation.

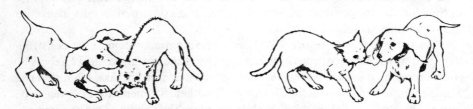

Figure 8-2. Pictures illustrating Agent-Object relations.

Consider the two drawings of Figure 8-2. An adult might say of the one on the left "A dog is biting a cat" and of the one on the right, "A cat is biting a dog." In both pictures just the same creatures and process are involved. The difference is that the arguments of the verb, the agent and object, are coordinated with different nouns in the two cases. It is the structure of the total situation that changes, and in English the changes are expressed by word order, by the order agent-action-object. What would a child of Stage I say in the two cases? Concerning the picture on the left he might say: *Dog bite* (agent-action); *Bite cat* (Action-object), or *Dog-cat* (agent-object). In effect, any two of the three terms in correct relational order. Of the picture on the right he might say: *Cat bite* (agent-action); *Bite dog*; or *Cat-dog*. The two sets of pairs are different; there is no overlap. It is this kind of discriminating response, discriminating with respect to the order of elements, that justifies the inference that the child distinguishes structural meanings. What should we say of a child who in connection with either picture simply produced all possible combinations and permutations of two content words: *Dog bite*; *Bite dog*; *Cat bite*; *Bite cat*; and *Cat dog*. We should say that there was no evidence that the structural meanings were understood. This, it turns out, is approximately what Washoe does.

The Gardners have kept careful records of all the occurrences of each combination of signs, and in their 5th and 6th diary summaries they report that the signs in a combination tend to occur in all possible orders. And that order often changes when there is no change in the non-linguistic circumstances. It appears, then, that we do not yet have evidence that Washoe's sequences are syntactic. Because syntax is not just sign-combination but is sign combination employed to express structural meanings. If Washoe does not intend structural meanings, if *Go sweet* and *Sweet go* are not action-object expressions, then what does she intend? What would her stream of ideas be like? It may be that it is a stream of conceptions having no relation beyond order in time. Having thought of "go" she next thinks of "sweet." Washoe's signs may be something like the *leitmotiven* in Richard Wagner's operas. Wagner, especially in the *Ring*, used short musical "motives" with a certain degree of semanticity, enough to enable musicologists to label them with names like *Valhalla, Curse of the Ring, Nibelungen gold, Renunciation of love*, and so on. In given passages the motives succeed one another, and the related ideas may be called to mind in the listener, but they do not enter into relations like agent-object and action-object. They do, of course, enter into musical relationship.

Not every child sentence presents contentives in the appropriate order. There are exceptions such as *Nose blow* (cited by Leopold) and *Balloon throw* (cited by Bloom) and *Apple eat* (cited by Miller and Ervin) and *Suitcase, go get it* (Adam I). Allen Gardner has written to me that he and Mrs. Gardner have not yet made a frequency comparison for the various orders in which each combination is used and, at this point, the possibility is quite open that Washoe has shown a "preference" for the orders that are correct for each relation. It is going to be interesting to learn the outcome of the Gardners' planned frequency comparisons. It must be said, however, that children show something much stronger than a statistical preference for correct order. In the full data of Table 8-2 violations of order are very uncommon; probably fewer than 100 violations in the thousands of utterances quoted. It is definitely not the case that all possible orders of a combination typically occur; they practically never do.

While word order comprises most of the evidence that the child intends structural meanings there is a certain amount of additional evidence. In 1963, Fraser, Bellugi and Brown conducted a test of grammatical comprehension using paired pictures for various constructions with 12 children between 37 and 43 months old. Figure 8-2 is, in fact, taken from that test and is used to inquire into comprehension of the agent and object functions in a sentence. Most of the items in the test are not concerned with the operations and relations of Table 8-3, but there were four test items, in all, concerning agent and object, and the three-year-olds in the experiment were correct on these 85 % of the time. The full report appears as the third selection in the present volume.

Of course, even the child of 37 months is well beyond Stage I, often by a year or more. However, in Britain in 1965, Lovell and Dixon administered the same comprehension test to 20 two-year-olds (average age: 2;6) as well as to older children. The two-year-olds showed a significant ability to decode the contrast.

Finally, we have the results of an action test conducted on one of our own children. Ursula Bellugi asked Adam, when he was 30–31 months old, to act out with toys whatever she said. And what she said involved agent-object-contrasts. For example: "Show me, 'the duck pushes the boat'" and, later on, "Show me, 'the boat pushes the duck.'" Adam responded correctly on 11 of 15 such trials, and this result further strengthens the conclusion that Stage I children have the semantic meanings described in Table 8-3.

While I am prepared to conclude that Washoe has not demonstrated that she intends the structural meanings of Table 8-3 I do not conclude that it has been demonstrated that she lacks these meanings. Appropriate word order can be used as evidence for the intention to express structural meanings, but the lack of such order does not establish the absence of such meanings. It does not do so because appropriate word order is not strictly *necessary* for purposes of communication for either the Stage I child or the Stage I chimpanzee. Let us look again at the pictures of Figure 8-2. If the child uses correct orders for the two pictures it is likely that he distinguishes the meanings. But, suppose we were parents in the presence of the action pictures on the left and the child used an inappropriate order: *Cat bite* or *Cat dog* or *Bite dog*. We should still understand him and would mentally make the switches to *Dog bite* and *Dog cat* and *Bite cat* which fit the situation. The structure being supplied by our perception of the situation we can receive the words in any order and understand them as the situation dictates. Even when we are unacquainted with the situation our knowledge of what is possible in the world enables us to set right some sentences such as *Nose blow* and *Balloon throw* and *Garbage empty*. It follows, therefore, that there is little or no communication pressure on either children or Washoe to use the right word order for the meanings they intend. In their world of very simple sentences, which are usually clarified by concurrent circumstances and which often have only one sensible reading in any case, they will be understood whether the order is right or not.

They will be understood, at least, until they begin to want to say things like *I tickle you* and *You tickle me* or *Mommy call Daddy* and *Daddy call Mommy* or *Car hit truck* and *Truck hit* car; and to say these outside of a clarifying action context. In terms of real-world possibilities the paired propositions are on the same footing. If the propositions do not refer to ongoing actions but to actions at another time, then the listener or viewer, if he is to understand the meassage correctly, must be given structural signals, of order or of some other kind, to indicate who or what is in each semantic role. In general, as sentences become more complex and more varied and become "displaced" in time from their references the need to mark attributives, possessors, locatives, agents, objects, and the like grows greater. The capacity for "displacement" is, like the properties of semanticity and productivity, universal in human languages and we notice now that experience cannot become truly cumulative until it is possible to report on events not concurrent with the act of communication.

My conclusions, therefore, is that the question of Washoe's syntactic capacity is still quite open. If she fails to mark structures distinctively when a real communication-necessity develops then we shall conclude that she lacks real syntactic capacity. If, on the other hand, when her sentences become complex and displaced in reference from the immediate context, Washoe begins to mark structure with whatever means is available to her in the sign language—why then. . . . Then, there is a man on the moon, after all.

REFERENCES

Bloom, Lois, Language development: Form and function in emerging grammars. Unpublished doctoral dissertation, Columbia University, 1968. [Published by M.I.T. Press, 1970.]

Bowerman, Melissa, Brief comparison of Finnish I and English I. Unpublished paper, Harvard University, 1969. [See M. F. Bowerman, Learning to talk: A cross-linguistic study of early syntactic development, with special reference to Finnish. Unpublished doctoral dissertation, Harvard University, 1970.]

Bowerman, Melissa, The pivot-open class distinction. Unpublished paper, Harvard University, 1969.

Braine, M. D. S., The ontogeny of English phrase structure: The first phrase, *Language*, 1963, **39**, 1–14. [Reprinted in this volume.]

Brown, R., and Ursula Bellugi, Three processes in the acquisition of syntax. *Harvard educational review*, 1964, **34**, 133–151.

Brown, R., and C. Fraser, The acquisition of syntax. In C. N. Cofer and Barbara S. Musgrave (eds.), *Verbal behavior and learning: Problems and processes.* New York: McGraw-Hill, 1963.

Chao, Y. R., The Cantian idiolect: An analysis of the Chinese spoken by a twenty-eight-months old child. In W. J. Fishel (ed.), *Semitic and Oriental Studies, University of California Publications in Semitic Philology*, XI. Berkeley and Los Angeles: University of California Press, 1951. [Reprinted in this volume.]

Fraser, C., Ursula Bellugi, and R. Brown, Control of grammar in imitation, comprehension and production. *J. verb. Learn. verb. Behav.* 1963, **2**, 121–135. [Reprinted in this volume.]

Gardner, R. A., and Beatrice T. Gardner, Teaching sign language to a chimpanzee. *Science*, 1969, **165**, 664–672.

Grégoire, A., *L'Apprentissage du langage; Les deux premières années.* Paris: Libraire E. Droz, 1937.

Hayes, K. J., and Catherine Hayes, The intellectual development of a home-raised chimpanzee. *Proceedings of the American philosophical society*, 1951, **95**, 105–109.

Kellogg, W. N., and Louise A. Kellogg, *The ape and the child*. New York: McGraw-Hill, 1933.

Leopold, W. F., *Speech development of a bilingual child; a linguist's record*, Vol. III, *Grammar and general problems in the first two years*. Evanston, Ill.: Northwestern University Press, 1949.

Lovell, K., and E. M. Dixon, The growth of the control of grammar in imitation, comprehension, and production, *Journal of child psychology and psychiatry*, **5**, 1965, 1–9.

McCall, Elizabeth A., A generative grammar of sign. Unpublished master's dissertation, University of Iowa, 1965.

Miller, W., and Susan Ervin, The development of grammar in child language. In Ursula Bellugi and R. Brown (eds.), *The acquisition of language. Mongr. Soc. Res. Child Developm.*, 1964, **29**, No. 1, 9–34. [Reprinted in this volume.]

Piaget, J., *The construction of reality in the child*. (Ist ed., 1937). New York: Basic Books, 1954.

Schlesinger, I. M., Production of utterances and language acquisition. In D. I. Slobin (ed.), *The ontogenesis of grammar: A theoretical symposium*. New York: Academic Press, 1971, pp. 63–101.

Slobin, D., Acquisition of Russian as a native language. In G. A. Miller and F. Smith (eds.), *The genesis of language*. Cambridge, Mass.: M.I.T. Press, 1966.

Stokoe, W. C., Dorothy Casterline, and C. G. Croneberg, *A dictionary of American sign language*. Washington, D.C.,: Gallaudet College Press, 1965.

Studies of Imitation and Comprehension[1]

As Ervin-Tripp has amply demonstrated in her paper reprinted above, the acquisition of language cannot be explained in terms of limitation. Yet imitation as a psycholinguistic phenomenon is of great interest in its own right, and, as Slobin and Welsh, and Smith show, below, elicited sentence imitation is a useful research tool in developmental psycholinguistics.

The first modern examination of sentence imitation was conducted by Brown and Fraser (1963). Working with children aged 25–35 months, they found that the mean length of imitated sentences was the same as that of the children's spontaneously produced sentences and had the same telegraphic character. This is similar to the findings of Ervin-Tripp, reported above, who also studied imitations in children of this age. The following study by Fraser, Bellugi, and

---

[1] Along with the three following papers (Fraser, Bellugi, and Brown; Slobin and Welsh; Smith), the papers by Ervin-Tripp (above) and Roeper (below) should be examined in relation to problems of imitation and comprehension of speech.

Brown, however, who worked with children aged 37–43 months, finds that children can imitate sentences which they cannot comprehend, and concludes that "imitation is a perceptual-motor skill not dependent on comprehension." This conclusion must be tempered by several considerations. What the older children retain in their imitations are the inflections and function words which are omitted in the speech and imitations of the younger children. If, in fact, the older children do not comprehend these functors, one can conclude that the age change in imitative capacity is based on an increase in immediate memory alone. The Fraser *et al.* comprehension test, however, is a stringent one and may underestimate the child's comprehension. The child must distinguish between two sentences which differ by a single feature and choose one of two pictures to go with the sentences (for example, *The boy draws* versus *The boys draw*). This task is confusing even to an adult. What is more likely is that the subjects of Fraser *et al.* had some control of many of the grammatical distinctions tested—but not fully stabilized control. This is what is suggested by Brown's later studies. When a new grammatical form emerges, it is often omitted, but is placed correctly when used (see Cazden; Brown, Cazden, and Bellugi; above). Thus, forms at the growing edge of competence may be recognized and imitated, but may not always be available for use in ongoing production and comprehension.

A study by Slobin (1968a) suggests that, in natural settings, children may be especially prone to imitate grammatical elements which are just barely comprehended. Using Brown's longitudinal data, Slobin examined the child's imitations of mother's expansions of his own speech. In such cases, children are very frequently able to add grammatical elements missing from their spontaneous speech (for example, Child: "Papa name Papa." Mother: "Papa's name is Papa, uh-hum." Child: "Papa name is Papa."). Smith's findings (below) suggest that when a child can comprehend most of an utterance, he will imitate that part beyond his comprehension, whereas sentences far beyond his competence will be ignored. Brown has found that many grammatical constructions appear first in spontaneous imitations of adult speech and only later as part of the child's own speech. Following Piaget's (1946) classic work on imitation, it seems that the child may imitate sentences which are just beyond his assimilative capacity. That is, imitation may be the external indication of an attempt to accommodate the child's linguistic schemata to new material. If this is the case, new or slightly complex events should be more imitated than familiar events. Ervin-Tripp's data, then, do not fully resolve the question as to whether imitation is "grammatically progressive," because we do not know what sorts of sentences were imitated by her children. Even if the grammatical form of imitations corresponds to the grammatical form of spontaneous speech, imitation could be grammatically progressive if it reflects the child's attempts to cope with difficult grammatical material. What we need to know, from Ervin-Tripp's data, is whether the *model sentences* which were spontaneously imitated tended to contain grammatical elements which were to appear in the child's spontaneous speech at the next level of development.

Studies of elicited imitation (Slobin and Welsh, Smith [below]; Menyuk [1963]) make it quite clear that imitation *does* work through comprehension. Smith and Menyuk found that ungrammatical sentences would be regularized in imitation, indicating that they had been understood. Slobin and Welsh found numerous sorts of recodings in imitation which demonstrated that their subject could understand sentences which exceeded her productive competence. For example, before the child could produce embedded relative clauses, she showed her comprehension of them in such imitations as the following: Adult: "The owl who eats candy runs fast." Child: "Owl eat a candy and he run fast." Similar evidence is presented by Roeper in his study of German children (below).

Thus one cannot conclude, with Fraser, Bellugi, and Brown, that "imitation is a perceptual-motor skill not dependent on comprehension." This is true only of some imitations. Children may rote imitate sentences without understanding—but within clearly definable limits of length and complexity. However, they also tend to reduce sentences in imitation to their level of ability—often revealing comprehension which goes beyond the evidence of their spontaneous speech. Furthermore, in natural settings, imitation itself may be an indication that the child is attempting to comprehend ongoing speech.

The following three papers also represent attempts to study the child's comprehension of speech—another important means for determining the child's linguistic competence. The Fraser, Bellugi, and Brown study represents a landmark beginning attempt at controlled study of comprehension, but it has been criticized for the artificiality and difficulty of its tasks (although such binary choice techniques have proven informative in a number of subsequent studies, such as Lovell and Dixon [1965] and Slobin [1966c]). Other studies have demonstrated the usefulness of having children carry out or act out instructions as an indication of their comprehension of various linguistic forms (see Amidon and Carey, 1971; Bem, 1970; C. Chomsky, 1968; E. Clark, 1971; Cromer, 1970; Donaldson and Balfour, 1968; Donaldson and Wales, 1970; Ferreiro and Sinclair, 1971; Huttenlocher, et al., 1968; Huttenlocher and Strauss, 1968; Kessel, 1970; Shipley et al., 1969; Sinclair-de-Zwart, 1967; Smith, this volume; Sokhin, 1959). Several studies have shown that much more can be learned of a child's competence if he is trained to perform in the experimental task and understands what is expected of him by the experimenter (Amidon and Carey, 1971; Bem, 1970; Shvachkin, 1954). Other methods of studying comprehension include response to questions (E. Clark, 1971; Ervin-Tripp, 1970); question conveyance (Bellugi, 1968); story retelling (Slobin, 1968b); matching sentence to picture (Slobin, 1966c). All of these studies underscore the importance of attending to the semantic and pragmatic functions of speech in relation to physical and social contexts.

Bever (1970a, 1971) has proposed a theory of language development based on successive emergence of various strategies for sentence interpretation. In this framework, comprehension is seen as a process rather than just as a reflection of the child's linguistic knowledge. (A similar approach is taken by Slobin [above] and Roeper [below].) For example (Bever, 1971), two-year-olds seem to use·a strategy of sentence interpretation that a noun-verb sequence means "actor-action." For example, given a toy horse and cow, two-year-olds can successfully act out the following sentences (in which the noun-verb sequences are italicized):

(1)   The *horse kisses* the cow.
(2)   It's the *horse kisses* the cow.
(3)   It's the cow the *horse kisses*.

But their performance is random on passive sentences such as:

(4)   The cow is kissed by the horse

in which there is no uninterrupted noun-verb sequence. Four-year-olds seem to use a strategy that the first noun is the actor, leading them astray on sentences like (3) and producing reversed interpretation of (4), but insuring good performance on sentences like (1) and (2). Thus comprehension does not uniformly improve with age as different strategies are brought to bear. (This approach has been recently applied by Amidon and Carey [1971] to the comprehension of conjoined sentences referring to temporally ordered events (*before, after, first, last,* and so on), in an impressive attempt to resolve the contradictions between several recent studies in this area [Bever, 1970b; E. Clark, 1971; Clark and Clark, 1968; Ferreiro and Sinclair, 1971; Smith and McMahon, 1970]. The issue is an important and interesting one to explore in detail, but too complex to summarize here.)   —D.I.S.

Control of Grammar in Imitation, Comprehension, and Production[1]

——*Colin Fraser, Ursula Bellugi, and Roger Brown*

"Most writers agree that the child understands the language of others considerably before he actually uses language himself." This sentence is from Dorothea McCarthy's comprehensive review (1954, p. 520) of research on the speech of children, and the sentence is certainly an accurate summary of what most writers have written. It is also an accurate summary of what parents believe that they have been observed. We will separate out several senses of the thesis,

From *Journal of Verbal Learning and Verbal Behavior*, 1963, 2, 121–135. Reprinted by permission of the authors and Academic Press, Inc.
[1] This research was supported by a grant from the National Science Foundation administered through the Center for Communication Sciences, Massachusetts Institute of Technology. The authors are grateful for the advice and assistance given by Dr. Jane Torrey (Connecticut College for Women), Mr. Joseph Mendelson (M.I.T.), and Mr. Sam Anderson (Harvard).

review the relevant evidence, and report some new data bearing on the understanding and production of grammatical features in speech.

The assertion that understanding precedes production can be taken to mean that *some* utterances are ordinarily understood before *any* utterances are produced. There is strong empirical support for this thesis if we are willing to accept the production of an appropriate response as evidence that an utterance has been understood. There are just two kinds of appropriate response that have been commonly reported for children. When an utterance makes reference the child sometimes identifies the referent; when an utterance is intended to be an imperative the child sometimes performs the designated action. Gesell and Thompson (1934), for instance, tested understanding of the questions: "Where is the cup?" "Where is the shoe?" "Where is the box?" by placing the child before a table on which rested a cup, a shoe, and a box and noting his identifying responses. Bühler and Hetzer (1935), in testing the child's understanding of such commands as "Get up" and "Lie down" and "Give that to me," required that the designated actions be performed. Appropriate responses of these two kinds are regularly obtained from normal children before any intelligible speech is heard. Indeed, Lenneberg (1962) has demonstrated linguistic comprehension of a high order in an 8-year-old child who is completely anarthric (speechless). In addition, the chimpanzee Gua, who was raised by the Kelloggs (1933), could, at the age of 9 months, make appropriate reaction to some 70 utterances though she never learned to speak at all. The Hayeses' chimpanzee, Viki, eventually approximated the sounds of several words but before she could do this she seemed to understand many utterances (Hayes, 1951).

The fact that some utterances usually seem to be understood before any recognizable utterances are produced is a generalization of little significance. The responses that suggest comprehension of an utterance include such very simple actions as orientation of the head, reaching, and grasping. It is not remarkable that some of these responses, those that are congenial to the child or animal, should come under the control of speech stimuli when the organism is not able to perform any of the culturally patterned articulatory movements that constitute speech. Any infant that can clap its hands can appear to its parents to understand "Pat-a-cake"; any animal that can run to its food dish can appear to its owner to understand "Come and get it." Certainly speech can operate as a signal for various nonverbal responses in many organisms that do not produce any speech.

The thesis that understanding precedes production is more interesting in a second form: Particular utterances or features of an utterance are ordinarily understood before the same utterances or features are produced. Our experiment is concerned with this version of the thesis in the case of particular features that are grammatical. Ervin and Miller, in their review of research on the development of language (1963) find that only a few studies have been made which bear, directly or indirectly, on the problem of the development of passive control of grammatical patterns. Neither these studies nor the ordinary observations made by parents provide evidence adequate to establish the thesis that passive control or understanding precedes productive use.

A monograph by Kahane, Kahane and Saporta (1958) illustrates one sort of evidence. Working from previously published materials on children learning French, English, or German, the authors find that the verbal categories of tense, voice, aspect, and agreement are understood before they are marked in speech. For example, one child is reported to have said "This mine" on a certain occasion and on another occasion "Glenna on bus." There is no verb in either utterance and no marking for tense. However, the parents of the child suggest that the first utterance really means "This *is* mine" and the second, "Glenna *was* on a bus." The Kahanes and Saporta take the parents' word for it and credit the child with understanding a distinction of tense that he is not yet marking. The authors do not go on to say that the child would understand distinctions of tense in the speech of another person but that is a reasonable extension of their position.

How do parents arrive at a gloss for a child's utterance such as "Glenna was on a bus" for "Glenna on bus?" Presumably there was situational support for the linguistic expansion. Perhaps the person named was at home when the child spoke but, on the previous day, had been on a bus. In these circumstances the parents would have said, "Glenna was on a bus" and what the parents would have said is what the child is presumed to have meant. The inference may be correct but it is not appropriate for determining whether understanding does or does not precede expression. When children first begin to combine words, these combinations are "telegraphic" (Brown and Fraser, 1963) and so grammatically incomplete. If whenever a child produces such an incomplete sentence he is to be credited with understanding the complete sentence that an adult would have produced in his circumstances, then the child's understanding must necessarily seem to be in advance of his production. To make an empirical test of the assertion that understanding precedes production one must look for evidence of understanding in the behavior of the child and not simply for the absence of linguistic expression from the child combined with an interpretation by his parents.

Parents, including linguists and psychologists, often see, in their own children, behavior that they take to be evidence of a grammatical understanding that surpasses production. A child, who never produces the kind of question that places the verb before the subject may nevertheless appropriately answer "Yes" (or "No") to such a question as "Are you hungry?" Before concluding that the child understands the significance of the verb-subject word order, however, one should try the effect of the single word "hungry" spoken with rising interrogative intonation or even without the intonation. A child who never produces a sentence containing both an indirect and a direct object may nevertheless respond appropriately to: "Bring your game to me." Again, however, one cannot tell whether the grammatical feature has been understood unless appropriate variations are tried. Would the child's response change if one were to say: "Bring me to your game"? Parents do not control experiments of this kind.

The set of sentences used by Gesell and Thompson in connection with a cup, a shoe, and a box is well designed to test understanding of the substantive words *cup*, *shoe*, and *box*. In the sentence frame "Where is the ———?" they permute the three nouns, and the response pattern reveals whether the variable element has been understood. These sentences do not test understanding of the interrogative pronoun *where* since this word is constant across all sentences. Most controlled tests of comprehension focus on the content words, especially on nouns and adjectives. However, there is an occasional exception in the literature that points the way to a test of grammatical comprehension. Gesell and Thompson, for example, have asked children to "Put the block *in* the cup" and have also asked them to "Put the block *over* the cup." By making a function word a variable they obtain evidence on the understanding of such words. No one seems to have compared this kind of evidence for the passive control of grammar in normal children with evidence of active or productive control in the same children, and we have done an experiment to fill the gap.

When we tried to think of tests of the productive control of grammar we found that production might mean any one of three things. (1) It could mean the spontaneous performance of grammatically contrasting utterances in the absence of any identifiable controlling stimuli. To find out whether particular productions of this kind had or had not occurred, an investigator would need to have the record of a child's total speech output and that is never possible. A systematic study of production must work with controlling stimuli of some kind, and here there are two possibilities: (2) The controlling stimuli could be model performances of the utterances under investigation, in which case *S*'s productions would be imitations; or (3) the controlling stimuli could be reference conditions appropriate to the emission of the utterances, in which case *S*'s performances would qualify as evidence of understanding, but the evidence would be appropriate speech rather than appropriate pointing. This third performance we will call *Production* and abbreviate as *P*; the performance that follows a model utterance we will call *Imitation* and abbreviate as *I*. The experiment we have done compares understanding or *Comprehension* (*C*) with production in the sense of *P* and also with production in the sense of *I*, but not with spontaneous production. Which kind of production it is that has been supposed to follow understanding, we cannot tell.

OPERATIONS FOR TESTING *Imitation, Comprehension,* AND *Production*

Consider now a concrete problem drawn from those we have devised to test *Comprehension, Imitation,* and *Production*. We begin with a pair of sentences: "The sheep is jumping" and "The sheep are jumping." These two sentences are identical except for the auxiliary verb, which is marked for a singular subject in the first sentence and for a plural subject in the second. Ordinarily in English the noun would also be marked (for example: "The dog is jumping" as opposed to "The dogs are jumping"), and so there would be redundancy in the

Figure 1. Pictures illustrating a grammatical contrast. Left, "The sheep is jumping"; right, "The sheep are jumping."

grammatical marking of number. We selected the irregular noun *sheep* so as to eliminate this redundancy and isolate a single grammatical variable.

For each of the two sentences there is an appropriate picture (see Fig. 1). In both pictures there are two sheep and a small hurdle. In one picture a single sheep jumps while the other looks on; in the other picture both sheep jump. It is necessary to have two sheep in both pictures so that a subject cannot simply match each sentence with its correct picture by noting whether the picture contains one sheep or more than one. This is necessary because the grammatical contrast presented does not encode the number of sheep present but the number of sheep performing a certain action.

There are three tasks: *I*, *C*, and *P*. For the *Comprehension* task (*C*) the *E* shows the two pictures and names them, but without revealing which name belongs to which picture. The *E* then speaks one of the sentences and asks *S* to point to the picture named. The *E* then speaks the other sentence and asks *S* to point once more. The *S* is not asked to speak at all. His appropriate response that can give evidence of comprehension is selective pointing.

In the Imitation procedure (*I*) no pictures are used. The *E* speaks two sentences that are grammatically equivalent to the two used in *C* (e.g., "The sheep is walking"; "The sheep are walking."). The *S* is then asked to imitate these, one at a time, following repetitions by *E*. Since we want to know whether *S* will imitate the features of the sentences that are crucial for correct pointing in the *C* procedure, we score, in the *I* task, only *S*'s retention of the contrasting *is* and *are*. His rendering of other parts of the utterance does not affect his score.

In the *Production* procedure (*P*) pictures are once again used—new pictures to match a pair of sentences grammatically equivalent to those used in the other tasks ("The sheep is eating"; "The sheep are eating"). The *S* is twice told the names of the two pictures but not which name goes with which picture. The *I* and *C* tasks by their very nature require *E* to speak the contrasting sentences twice each. The *P* task does not by its nature necessitate a repetition of the sentences, but we introduced this feature into the *P* procedure in order to equate, across tasks, S's exposure to each grammatical contrast. After repeating the names of the pictures E points to one picture at a time and asks S to name it. As with the I procedure we score only the grammatical contrast in S's rendition of the sentences, but to be scored correct for P the contrast has to be appropriately matched with the pictures.

HYPOTHESES

Imitation (I), Comprehension (C), and Production (P) will, in this paper, be called *procedures* or *tasks*. The experimental materials, we shall see, are made up of ten different grammatical contrasts, and these will be called *problems*. The contrast we have described, between the singular and the plural marked by *is* and *are*, is one such problem. Each of the ten problems was administered in all three tasks or procedures.

The rough prediction that comprehension will be superior to production can be somewhat refined if we think about the psychological operations that would seem to be required for the tasks I, C, and P. For all three tasks S must notice and retain the critical difference between the two sentences that make a pair. For the sample sentences we have been considering the contrast between *is* and *are* must be attended to and identified as a change that matters, as accidental variations of articulation and tone do not matter. A correct performance on all tasks depends upon common operations of perception, attention, and memory; the quality of these operations may depend on the nature of the sentence contrast, on its embeddedness, its familiarity, the number of redundant features, and the total length of the sentences. There is reason to expect, therefore, that the order of difficulty of the ten grammatical problems should be similar in all three tasks.

There is reason to expect that the three tasks across all ten problems will show consistent differential difficulty. To perform correctly on I it would seem that S must not only preceive the contrast between the two sentences but must also have sufficient motor control of speech to produce the difference. To perform correctly on C, the S must perceive the difference between the sentences and also the difference between the two pictures and know how the referential contrast is related to the grammatical contrast; he must have motor control of pointing but need not have motor control of the speech contrast. The P task requires all the operations of both I and C, save only the pointing that is required for C. P, then, would seem to be more complex than I since P entails more operations than I. P would seem to be more complex than C since it requires control of speech rather than pointing. If the likelihood of successful performance is inversely related to the number of psychological operations that must be performed in near simultaneity and to the complexity of these operations, then P should be more difficult than either I or C. In terms of the number of correct answers, then, we might expect $I > P$ and $C > P$. However, it is possible that the referential contrast offers situational support for the sentence contrast; without the pictures it may be difficult to pick up the difference in the sentences. This possibility would lead us to expect $P > I$ and $C > I$.

There are still other ways of thinking about the psychological operations underlying the three tasks. Perhaps imitation is not a purely perceptual-motor task; perhaps it usually works through the meaning system. Decroly (circa 1934), for instance, has argued that a child can only distinguish those words to which he gives a meaning, and since perceptual differentiation is necessary for imitation, imitation cannot succeed when understanding is absent. One might argue for the same prediction in a different way: perhaps in imitation, one ordinarily decodes a sentence, retains it as a meaning, and then encodes it for production. It may be difficult to retain sentences in any form other than as meanings. This argument, like Decroly's, predicts $C > I$.

There is another possibility. Speech is a much simpler system than reference, (Brown, 1958, pp. 202–216). Speech can be analyzed into a small number of distinctive features of both the acoustic and articulational levels. The total domain of a reference does not yield to any such simple systematic analysis. Consequently, we would expect control of the speech system to be more complete than control of the reference system, and that is the case since most adult speakers perfectly control speech but are far from knowing all the referential rules of their language. A sampling of referential problems of the kind used in our experiment would be likely to include some that children do not control, though these children may already control, perceptually and motorically, all the dis-

TABLE 1 POSSIBLE OUTCOMES AND REASONS FOR EXPECTING
EACH ONE

$I > C$	*Imitation* depends only on the perceptual-motor organization of speech, whereas *Comprehension* depends on reference, and reference is more complex than speech.
$C > I$	*Imitation* is not a purely perceptual-motor task but depends upon *Comprehension,* either for the perceptual differentiation of sentences or for their retention.
$I > P$	*Production* entails all the operations of *Imitation* and, in addition, depends upon knowledge of referential distinctions.
$P > I$	The presence of the pictures in *Production* facilitates the perceptual differentiation and retention of the sentences.
$C > P$	*Comprehension* and *Production* entail the same operations except that, whereas *Comprehension* calls for control of pointing, *Production* calls for control of speech and pointing is simpler than speech.
$P > C$	No reason why this should be so.

tinctive features of speech. If this were the case, then we should expect $I > C$.

There are three tasks. If we consider them in pairs and think only of the relation "more correct than" ($>$) then there are six possible outcomes. It is possible to think of a reason or a combination of reasons that will predict any of these except $P > C$. These two tasks are identical except that, where C requires selective pointing, P requires selective speech and it is difficult to conceive of speech as easier than pointing. It seems almost inevitable that $C > P$ and this prediction may be what some writers have meant when they said that comprehension precedes production. When the thesis is operationalized in this way an obviousness is exposed that goes undetected in vaguer formulations. However, if we understand the thesis to say that $C > I$ then it is not obvious since one can argue with at least equal conviction for $I > C$. The thesis does not predict the relative difficulty of I and P. The six possible relations of inequality for the tasks I, C, and P are listed in Table 1 opposite the reasons for expecting each one. The experiment was done to find out which of the possible outcomes would occur.

METHOD

The Imitation-Comprehension-Production (ICP) Test

The test involves 10 grammatical contrasts. A grammatical contrast is always created by the use of two utterances which are identical but for some grammatical feature. Subjects were required to process the grammatical distinctions in each of the three ways described above.

Examples of the 10 grammatical contrasts presented in the ICP Test are listed in Table 2 together with the criteria for scoring them. These 10 problems

TABLE 2   SAMPLE UTTERANCES (SET A) AND SCORING FOR
THE ICP TEST

Practice items

The girl with the big hat.	The boy with the blue belt.
The girl playing with the doll.	The bunny eating the carrot.
The cat with the brown face.	The dog with the black tail.
The boy playing with the truck.	The mouse eating the cracker.

1. Mass noun/Count noun.
   Utterances: Some mog/A dap.
   　　　　　　　Some pim/A ked.
   Scoring: *Some/A* + any nonsense syllables or appropriate English words.

2. Singular/Plural, marked by inflections.
   Utterances: The boy draws/The boys draw.
   　　　　　　　The kitten plays/The kittens play.
   Scoring: Noun without inflection and verb with -*s*/Noun with -*s* and verb without inflection.

3. Singular/Plural, marked by *is* and *are*.
   Utterances: The deer is running/The deer are running.
                The sheep is eating/The sheep are eating.
   Scoring: *Is/Are*

4. Present progressive tense/Past tense.
   Utterances: The paint is spilling/The paint spilled.
                The boy is jumping/The boy jumped.
   Scoring: *Is* and verb with *-ing*/No auxiliary and verb with *-d.*

5. Present progressive tense/Future tense.
   Utterances: The girl is drinking/The girl will drink.
                The baby is climbing/The baby will climb.
   Scoring: *Is* and verb with *-ing/Will* and verb without inflection.

6. Affirmative/Negative.
   Utterances: The girl is cooking/The girl is not cooking.
                The boy is sitting/The boy is not sitting.
   Scoring: Absence of *not*/Presence of *not*, + some assertion.

7. Singular/Plural, of 3rd-person possessive pronouns.
   Utterances: His wagon/Their wagon.
                Her dog/Their dog.
   Scoring: *His* or *her/Their.*

8. Subject/Object, in the active voice.
   Utterances: The train bumps the car/The car bumps the train.
                The mommy kisses the daddy/The daddy kisses the mommy.
   Scoring: $Noun_1$ + active form of verb + $noun_2$/$Noun_2$ + active form of verb + $noun_1$.

9. Subject/Object, in the passive voice.
   Utterances: The car is bumped by the train/The train is bumped by the car.
                The daddy is kissed by the mommy/The mommy is kissed by the daddy.
   Scoring: $Noun_1$ + verb + d + by + $noun_2$/$Noun_2$ + verb + d + by + $noun_1$.

10. Indirect object/Direct object.
    Utterances: The girl shows the cat the dog/The girl shows the dog the cat.
                 The boy brings the fish the bird/The boy brings the bird the fish.
    Scoring: Any verb + $noun_1$ + $noun_2$/Any verb + $noun_2$ + $noun_1$.

---

were selected because previous work (Brown and Fraser, 1963) had shown that complete productive mastery of the contrasts involved was not common in children before about 4 years and because pictorial representations of the differences of reference were possible.

We constructed six examples of each linguistic contrast, i.e., six pairs of utterances for each of the ten contrasts. The number of morphemes in the paired utterances necessarily varied from one grammatical contrast to another, but the six examples of any one contrast are of the same length. For all utterances, words familiar to young children are used: *cat*, *dog*, *mommy*, *daddy*, *boat*, *truck*, *fall*, *jump*, etc. The Mass noun/Count noun contrast utilizes nonsense syllables for the reason that the referential contrast between such real words as *some milk* (mass noun) and *a cup* (count noun) is clear on the lexical level. In such a case *S* would not need to know that when a noun in the singular can be preceded by *some* that the noun must be a mass noun, and that when a noun can be preceded by *a* the noun must be a count noun. However, when the utterances are "some tiss" and "a heg," only the grammar of mass nouns and count nouns can guide *S* to the selection of an extended substance as *tiss* and a bounded object as a *heg*. The 12 nonsense syllables required for the Mass noun/Count noun problems were rated by adults as relatively easy to pronounce (pronunciability ratings of less than 3.50 in Appendix E of Underwood and Schulz, 1960).

For each grammatical contrast there are two utterance-pairs for *I*, two for *C*, and two for *P*. Tasks *C* and *P* involve a contrast of reference and so there are pictures to illustrate the utterances assigned to these procedures. The Massachusetts Institute of Technology Illustration Service made brightly colored line drawings on 7 × 5 in. white cards. All details of the drawings were specified by the investigators following the general principle that the representations of paired utterances should be identical in every respect except the one coded by the grammatical contrast. The two pictures making a pair usually involve the same creatures and things and actions but differ in subject-object relations, in the apparent time of an action, or in the number of creatures performing an action.

In addition to the grammatical contrast items the ICP Test includes four practice items involving utterances that contrast in their substantive words, e.g., "The cat with the brown face" and "The dog with the black tail." The corresponding pictures are of the two different animals. With these items *E* instructed *S* in the three procedures: *I*, *C*, and *P*.

All of the pictures were mounted in loose-leafed photograph albums. The pictures were inserted between a sheet of backing material and a transparent cover; this proved to be a good way to preserve them from excited and sticky fingers. The pictures belonging to a contrasting pair were mounted side by side in such a way that there was no consistent relationship on any problem between the order in which a verbal contrast was given and the positions (left or right) of the pictures.

Subjects

From a pretest we learned that children 4 years of age or older performed correctly on *I*, *C*, and *P* with most of the problems. To insure that the performances should not generally be perfect we needed to work with children under 4 years and the pretest suggested that 3 years was the lowest age at which the test procedures would usually be possible. Accordingly, we worked with children whose ages ranged from 37 to 43 months, the mean being 40 months.

TABLE 3 ORDER OF TASKS AND PROBLEMS CORRECT FOR EACH SUBJECT

			ORDER OF TASKS[a]			PROBLEMS CORRECT			
SUBJECT	AGE	SEX	1ST	2ND	3RD	IMITATION	COMPRE-HENSION	PRODUCTION	TOTAL
E	3;5	F	C(A)	I	P(B)	18	15	12	45
C	3;6	F	I	P(A)	C(B)	17	17	10	44
L	3;7	F	P(B)	C(A)	I	18	14	6	38
F	3;1	F	C(B)	I	P(A)	17	11	8	36
G	3;5	M	C(A)	P(B)	I	17	9	6	32
K	3;3	M	P(A)	C(B)	I	13	11	4	28
D	3;5	F	I	P(B)	C(A)	15	9	3	27
B	3;5	M	I	C(B)	P(A)	13	8	3	24
J	3;6	M	P(B)	I	C(A)	10	10	2	22
I	3;2	M	P(A)	I	C(B)	12	3	2	17
H	3;3	F	C(B)	P(A)	I	7	8	1	16
A	3;1	M	I	C(A)	P(B)	9	6	0	15

[a] Letters in parentheses after C and P indicate use of Set A or Set B.

They were 12 monolingual English-speaking children, 6 boys and 6 girls, attending one or another of 4 Cambridge, Massachusetts, preschools. In order to obtain 12 children who completed the test it was necessary to attempt the test with 15 children, and so our sample selects in favor of the cooperative child.

Order of Tasks and Problems

We wanted to be certain that consistently correct responses should be possible only for *S*s having control of the grammatical contrasts presented. A *S* ought not to be able to infer correct responses from the positions of the pictures, the order of the problems, the order in which he was asked to respond to the parts of the contrast, or from any interrelationship among these variables. We also wanted our comparison of the quality of performance on *I*, *C*, and *P* to be free of practice effects. To make sure of these things we used counterbalanced and randomized orders.

Each child was to do a full set of problems with each of the three tasks. It was necessary to continue with a given task until the full set of problems was completed since a pretest demonstrated that changes back and forth among the tasks confused the *S*. Since the order in which a task was presented might affect the level of performance, each of the six possible task-orders was used with two children. The scheme can be seen in Table 3.

Of the six utterance pairs constructed for each grammatical contrast, two pairs were to be used in *I*, and for these pairs no pictures had been drawn. Pictures had been prepared for the remaining four pairs since these were to be used in *C* and *P*. While great care was taken to make equivalent all pairs that involved the same contrast, it seemed unwise always to use one set of utterances and pictures in *C* and the other set in *P*. Consequently, we divided the pictures and the utterances, matching them into sets A and B; the utterances of Set A appear in Table 2. For half of the *S*s *C* was done with Set A and *P* with Set B; for the other half of the *S*s the assignment of the sets was reversed. This scheme can be seen in Table 3.

Within a task each child received the individual problems in a different random order though the same random order was used across tasks for a given child. There was one departure from randomness in these orders: the Subject/Object contrasts in the active voice were always given last. The same pictures were used for this contrast and for that in the passive voice, and we wanted to make sure that the active-voice problems had no opportunity to affect performance on the passive-voice problems. In a revised edition of the ICP Test, which we now use, this minor inconsistency has been eliminated by adding enough pictures to provide different sets for the active-voice and passive-voice problems.

Each single problem involved two utterances and both utterances were pronounced twice by *E* on all tasks. The first pronunciation simply presented the contrast, and the order in which the paired utterances were spoken was randomly determined. For tasks *I* and *C* the posing of a problem necessitates a second pronunciation (e.g., "Show me: "The sheep are jumping.'") but, for task *P*, the problems can be posed without a second pronunciation (e.g., "What is the name of this picture?"). A second pronunciation was, however, included in the *P* task so as to equate exposure to sentences across tasks. The second pronunciation in the *P* task immediately followed the first and reversed the order of the utterances in the first. For problems 1, 7, 8, 9, and 10 in Table 2 the order in which the paired items were posed was randomly determined in all tasks. The remaining problems (2, 3, 4, 5, and 6) were always posed, in all tasks, in a fixed order. Each of these contrasts involves a simple affirmative sentence with a singular subject and a verb in a present tense. If this sentence were presented first we thought it possible that *S* might point correctly and then, ignoring the grammatical contrast in the second sentence, point correctly again by exclusion. To guard against such a possibility the crucial utterance in each of these contrasts was presented first and the simple base form second.

Procedure

All testing was done in the preschools in small rooms with only the child and two *E*s present. One *E*, who had previously visited the schools to become acquainted with the children, administered instructions and the test materials and encouraged and cajoled when necessary; the other *E* made a written record of the child's responses and operated a Wollensak T-1500 tape-recorder, which recorded the entire session.

Before performing any of the three tasks, the *S* was shown a colored picture-book and encouraged to talk about the pictures. This helped the child to overcome any reluctance to talk and provided a small sample of the child's spontaneous speech. To explain each of the three tasks (*I*, *C*, and *P*) and to test the *S*'s understanding of each task, *E* always began with the four practice items. To each *S* the *E* administered the tasks, the problems within a task, and the items within a problem in accordance with a predetermined schedule. The techniques of administration are described above as "Operations for Testing *Imitation, Comprehension*, and *Production*."

It was most expedient to continue testing a child in one session for as long as he proved cooperative and attentive. Three children succeeded in completing the entire performance in only one session each. Normally, however, two or three sessions on successive school days were necessary to take a child through all three tasks. With a few unavoidable exceptions it was possible to make breaks in performance coincide with breaks between tasks. After performing both halves of an item, *S*, whether or not he had answered correctly, was encouraged by *E* with some such remark as: "That's the way." Nonverbal rewards were not used. For the *I* task, in which there were no pictures to hold the child's attention, a "divided attention" technique was sometimes necessary. The *S* was allowed to hold some simple toy and *E* would administer an item whenever the child was not engrossed in the object.

RESULTS

Scoring

There were two records of each experimental session; one on tape and one written on the scene. The scorers took advantage of the information in both records. The criteria for scoring each problem appear in Table 2; a response was marked "correct" if it completely satisfied these criteria and was otherwise marked incorrect.[2] On the C task S sometimes pointed quickly, then reflected and corrected himself; the last definite pointing is the one we always scored. Two scorers independently scored all of the data (720 items). They agreed on 713 items or about 99% of the total. The seven disagreements, which were almost evenly distributed among the three tasks were resolved by discussion.

Quantitative Findings

Table 3 shows the age and sex of each S, the order in which each performed the three tasks, and the number of problems correct for each task and for all tasks combined. Even within the restricted age range represented, there was a correlation between age and total score: $\rho = 0.48$, p slightly above 0.05. The girls did somewhat better than the boys, but the difference was not significant.

Before comparing performances on the three tasks we must report several preliminary analyses. Six Ss performed task C with Set A of the materials and task P with Set B and six Ss did the reverse. A two-way analysis of variance, Groups by Tasks showed that neither the difference between the two groups ($F = .35$, $df = 1/30$) nor the interaction of Groups and Tasks ($F = .07$, $df = 2/30$) was significant. Therefore we will ignore in subsequent analyses the sets of materials used.

TABLE 4   MEAN TASK SCORES AND ORDER OF PERFORMING TASKS

	IMITATION	COMPRE-HENSION	PRODUCTION
As 1st Task	13.50	10.75	3.50
As 2nd Task	14.25	9.75	5.00
As 3rd Task	13.75	9.75	5.75

Table 4 shows the mean scores of Ss who did each of the tasks as the first task, the second task, or the third task. It is clear that order had no consistent effect on either I or C. On P, there was a slight tendency for Ss who performed P as their second task to do better than those who performed P first, and for

---

[2] We also devised and tested a more elaborate scoring system that distinguishes nine varieties of partially correct response. High scorer reliability was obtained for this system. However, since only 15% of the total responses fell into the nine additional categories, and since analyses using these categories yielded a pattern of results exactly like the pattern herein reported, we have simply called responses in these categories "incorrect."

those who did *P* last to score higher than those who did it second. However, it could not be demonstrated that this tendency was statistically significant. Three different analyses were performed: a two-way analysis of variance, Tasks by Order; a Kruskal-Wallis nonparametric analysis of variance covering *P* as the first, the second, and the third task, with *p* being multiplied by $\frac{1}{6}$ to take account of the fact that the order obtained is the one to be expected if practice on the other tasks facilitates performance on *P* (see Chassan, 1960); and a Randomization Test comparing *P* as first task with *P* as third task. In none of these did order produce a *p* of even 0.10. Therefore, we shall ignore in subsequent analyses the order on which tasks were performed.

Because all three tasks involve operations of perception, attention and memory, we predicted that the difficulty of the problems would be similar from task to task. In Table 5 the task scores for each problem appear. On any one problem the maximum possible score is 24 since there were always 2 items responded to by 12 *S*s. The Spearman rank correlations for the difficulty of

TABLE 5   TASK SCORES ON GRAMMATICAL PROBLEMS IN ORDER OF INCREASING TOTAL DIFFICULTY

Problem	Imitation	Compre- hension	Production	Total
Affirmative/ Negative	18	17	12	47
Sing./Pl., of 3rd- person poss. prons.	23	15	8	46
Subject/Object, in active voice	19	16	11	46
Pres. Prog. tense/ Future tense	20	16	6	42
Sing./Pl., marked by *is* and *are*	20	12	7	39
Pres. Prog. tense/ Past tense	17	13	6	36
Mass noun/ Count noun	12	13	1	26
Sing./Pl., marked by inflections	14	7	1	22
Subject/Object, in passive voice	12	7	2	21
Indirect Object/ Direct Object	11	5	3	19

problems from task to task are: $\rho_{IC} = 0.64$ $(p < 0.05)$; $\rho_{CP} = 0.72$ $(p < 0.05)$; $\rho_{IP} = 0.68$ $(p < 0.05)$.

In Table 1 we listed the six possible relations of inequality among the tasks, and now we can report which ones occurred. There might, of course, have been no significant inequalities among I, C, and P, but the Groups by Tasks analysis of variance reported above showed that there were significant differences among the tasks $(F = 16.05, df = 2/30, p < 0.01)$. We did t-tests between pairs of tasks $(IC, CP,$ and $IP)$ and found that all were significant with $p < 0.01$. The mean number of correct responses of Ss on I was 13.83; on C, 10.08; and on P, 4.75. In short $I > C > P$. In Table 3 it can be seen that this order holds with striking consistency for individual Ss. For all 12, $C > P$ and, for 9, $I > C$. In Table 5 it can be seen that the order held true for all but one of the grammatical problems; on that one (Mass noun/Count noun) C was higher than I by one point.

Guessing on the Tasks

On a very abstract level the three tasks, I, C, and P, make identical demands on S. In each task E provides two stimuli (s_1 and s_2) and requires two appropriately matched responses (r_1 and r_2). For I the stimuli are the two model utterances and the responses are S's pronunciations of the critical features of these two utterances in an order matching the order of the models. For C the two stimuli are again the two utterances, and the responses are pointing appropriately first to one picture and then to the other. For P the stimuli are provided by E pointing to the pictures, one at a time, and the responses are S's pronunciations of the critical features of the utterances corresponding to the pictures. The problem in all cases is to match r_1 to s_1, and r_2 to s_2.

For an adult S the first pointing in any item of the C task (e.g., "Show me: 'The sheep are jumping.'") would be a choice between two alternatives and the second pointing would be completely determined by the first. Consequently, for an adult S the probability (p) of guessing a correct answer on any item in the absence of grammatical knowledge would be 0.50. This is a substantial probability, and since there do not seem to be comparable opportunities for a chance success on I and P, where the responses are speech, it may seem that chance gives an advantage to the C scores.

However, our 3-year-old Ss did not handle the C task as adults would. On the practice materials, which involved familiar lexical distinctions, all the children did point first to one picture and then to the other, but this was because they were giving the correct answers.

On the grammar contrasts, too, when they saw the solution they pointed first to one picture and to the other. However, when they did not see the solution, they often pointed twice to the same picture, acting as if the second pointing were completely independent of the first. They sometimes pointed simultaneously at both pictures, and one S, on one occasion, gave an unscorable response. The probability of a chance success for these Ss was clearly less than 0.5. A case can be made for assuming it was 0.25 and a case can be made for assuming it was 0.11; neither case is perfectly satisfactory.

On the I and P tasks, too, there must have been some possibility of obtaining a chance success. The two relevant responses, r_1 and r_2, were twice produced by E just before S was asked to respond. If S randomly selected for production some number of words from those pronounced by E, then S would occasionally hit on the right combination to score a success. However, there is nothing to guide us in selecting an exact model for such a process. On the other hand, whenever S did produce first the one half of the grammatical contrast (r_1) and then the other half (r_2), the probability that these would occur in the correct order was 0.5, just as p was 0.5 when S pointed first to one picture (r_1) and then to the other (r_2). We have pulled out all the cases for each task in which both r_1 and r_2 were produced; the numbers appear in Table 6. Expansion of

TABLE 6   CASES IN WHICH THE TWO RELEVANT RESPONSES
(r_1 AND r_2) WERE PRODUCED

	IMITATION	COMPRE-HENSION	PRODUCTION
Total cases	167	168	68
Correct	166	121	57
Correct − incorrect	165	74	46

the binomial for $p = 0.5$ shows that the numbers correct are well above chance on all tasks. It is possible to argue that there are likely to be as many lucky guesses included in the correct responses as there are unlucky guesses which appear as incorrect responses. If one subtracts the number incorrect from the number correct to obtain an estimate of the number of successes not obtained by chance, the order $I > C > P$ is preserved and the differences are still all significant with $p = 0.02$ or less.

The comparison of cases in which both r_1 and r_2 were produced disregards the differential probabilities involved in producing, if one had no knowledge of the grammatical contrast involved, two relevant pointings as opposed to two relevant utterances. The probabilities would certainly favor pointing. Table 6 indicates that response production came nearer to guaranteeing success on P and on I than it did on C. However, some such difference would seem to be intrinsic to the tasks in question and so we conclude that insofar as the tasks can be made comparably difficult, the order of control for 3-year olds is $I > C > P$.

Qualitative Findings

For the student of language acquisition who seeks to discover the grammatical operations that are developmentally prior to attainment of the rules followed by adult speakers, the procedures of the ICP Test will be useful. The incorrect responses to several problems in the present test are sufficiently regular to suggest the nature of the underlying operations. We will describe a single example.

Consider the Subject/Object contrast in the passive voice. While young children probably do not often hear sentences in the passive voice they very frequently do hear all the individual morphemes involved; they hear *is*, *-ed*, and *by* if not *is chased by*. The *C* score for the passive-voice problems was only five correct. Evidently the sense of the passive construction cannot be guessed from a knowledge of its constituent elements. How do children process this construction when they do not correctly understand it?

Consider a sample pair of sentences: "The girl is pushed by the boy" and "The boy is pushed by the girl." When, for the *P* task, *E* pointed to the picture in which the girl was doing the pushing and asked for its name, *S* sometimes said: "The girl is pushed by the boy" and then, for the other picture, *S* spoke the other sentence. This is an incorrect response that perfectly preserves the form of the sentences but exactly reverses the correct pattern of application to the pictures. Five *S*s responded in this way, and 5 is a large number when we recall (Table 6) that there were only 11 such reversals on *P* in all the data. In addition these 5 reverse responses seemed to be made with high confidence. What incorrect rule would generate such a performance?

In active-voice sentences, subject and object appear in that order, whereas in passive-voice sentences the order is object and subject. Suppose that the 3-year-old processes each passive-voice sentence as though it were in the active-voice. "The girl is pushed by the boy" is not computed as: Object-Verb in the passive-Subject, but rather as: Subject-Verb in the active with odd appurtenances-Object. The odd appurtenances are *is*, *-ed*, and *by* which *S* may take to be signs of some uncommon tense like "will have pushed." Processing the sentence in this way would enable *S* to maintain the generality of the usual rule of English word order in which the subject precedes the object.

With the Subject/Object contrast in the passive voice we turned up a revealing pattern of evidence by accident. If an investigator wanted to use the ICP procedures to test hypotheses about particular aspects of grammatical operation, he could easily design problems that would be revealing by intention.

DISCUSSION

We predicted that the order of difficulty of the ten problems would be similar from task to task for the reason that all three tasks involve operations of perception, attention, and memory which should be affected by the nature of the sentences provided. The order of difficulty was indeed similar from task to task but there does not seem to be any single dimension of the contrasts that will account for the order. The contrast Singular/Plural marked by inflections may be harder than the contrast Singular/Plural marked by *is* and *are* because the bound morphemes are less well marked acoustically than are the free morphemes. The Subject/Object contrast may be easier in the active voice than in the passive voice because children hear fewer passive-voice sentences than active-voice sentences. Probably the order obtained for the problems is a complex resultant of many factors that increase difficulty including the perceptual obviousness of the contrast, the amount of redundancy in the contrast, the length of the total sentences, and the frequency with which the construction has been heard. It should be possible to investigate the importance of these variables with problems designed to that purpose.

Of the possible outcomes listed in Table 1, those that occurred are: $I > C$, $I > P$, and $C > P$. These occurrences reflect some credit on the ideas that led to their prediction and some discredit on the ideas that led to the prediction of their opposites. Because $I > C$ rather than $C > I$, it would seem that imitation is a perceptual-motor skill not dependent on comprehension. It would seem, in addition, that the highly systematic speech system is under more complete control at 3 years than is the less systematic and more complex referential system.

The conclusion that imitation is a perceptual-motor skill that does not work through the meaning system is supported by certain details in the data. Consider, for example, the Indirect object/Direct object contrast in such a pair as: "The woman gives the bunny the teddy" and "The woman gives the teddy the bunny." In five cases when Ss were given this problem, with appropriate pictures for the P task, they transformed the original sentences so as to express the indirect object with a prepositional phrase. They pointed correctly but instead of saying, "The woman gives the bunny the teddy" they said, "The woman gives the teddy to the bunny"; the latter construction is probably the more familiar of the two. If on the I task, these Ss had decoded the sentences into meanings, as they do on the P task, the same transformation ought to have occurred. It never did occur. On the I task S either correctly reproduced the originals or made errors that were not transformations. It seems reasonable to conclude that the imitation performance did not work through the meaning system.

Because $I > P$ occurred and $P > I$ did not, it would seem that increasing the number of psychological operations to be performed in near simultaneity increases the difficulty of the task. It would seem, in addition, that the presence of the referential contrast either does not have a facilitating effect on the perception and retention of the sentence contrast or else that the effect is less powerful than the one that results from increasing the number of operations. We have already concluded that imitation is a perceptual-motor performance and that speech is a simpler system than reference. It is consistent now to add that the sentences of the test could usually be differentiated and retained without the support of reference.

Because $C > P$ occurred and $P > C$ did not, it would seem that the motor control of speech is more complicated than the motor control of pointing.

We could not imagine that the contrary of this proposition would be true, and so this prediction was labelled obvious and the obvious worked out.

How stands the thesis that understanding precedes production in the development of child speech? The thesis is true if by production we mean task P, since C scores were higher than P scores. This outcome suggests that children learn a lot about the referential patterning, the stimulus control of grammatical forms, before they produce these forms. This learning which precedes the linguistic response may be a purely s-s registration of the correspondence between constructions produced by others and the circumstances of production, but, as our operation for testing comprehension shows, it need not be. Understanding could be s-r learning in which the r is some nonlinguistic response such as pointing. Production occurs when the appropriate linguistic response begins to appear, conforming to a stimulus pattern that may originally have been established in connection with nonlinguistic responses.

The thesis that understanding precedes production is false if by production we mean task I, since C scores were lower than I scores. It is very possible, however, that this latter outcome would reverse with still younger children. The longest sentences of the ICP Test were only eight morphemes long which means they were easily within the sentence-programming span of 3-year-old children. However, the much shorter span of children at about 2:6 should compel such younger children in the I task, to "reduce" the model sentences of the ICP Test. Brown and Fraser (1963) have shown that such reductions are accomplished by dropping the function words of the sentence, leaving a "telegraphic" string of nouns and verbs. The function words are the essential elements in which the sentences of the ICP Test contrast. Perhaps, then, 2-year-olds will omit these words in I and yet show by correct pointings on C that they can internally process more words than they can "print out." Such an outcome would suggest the existence of a longer span for internal sentence computation than for sentence production. We are now trying to adapt the ICP procedures to that least docile of subjects, the child between two and three.

SUMMARY

The familiar assertion that, in language development, understanding precedes production was tested for 10 grammatical contrasts with 12 3-year-old children. Understanding was operationalized as the correct identification of pictures named by contrasting sentences. Production was operationalized in two ways: (a) as the correct imitation of contrasting features in sentences without evidence of understanding; and (b) as the correct production of contrasting features in sentences applied appropriately to pictures. Production, in the second sense, proves to be less advanced than understanding in 3-year-old children. However, production in the sense of imitation proves to be more advanced than understanding in 3-year-olds.

REFERENCES

Brown, R., *Words and Things*. Glencoe, Illinois: Free Press, 1958.

Brown, R., and C. Fraser, The acquisition of syntax. In C. N. Cofer and Barbara Musgrave (eds.), *Verbal behavior and learning: Problems and processes*. New York: McGraw-Hill, 1963.

Bühler, C., and H. Hetzer, *Testing children's development from birth to school age*. New York: Farrar and Rinehart, 1935.

Chassan, J. B., On a test for order. *Biometrics*, 1960, **16**, 119–121.

Decroly, O., Comment l'enfant arrive à parler. *Cahiers de la centrale* (Centrale du P.P.S. de Belgique), circa 1934, **8**, 1–306.

Ervin, S. M., and W. Miller, Language development. In Child Psychology, *Yearb. nat. Soc. Stud. Educ.*, 1963.

Gesell, A., and H. Thompson, *Infant behavior*. New York: McGraw-Hill, 1934.

Hayes, C., *The ape in our house*. New York: Harper, 1951.

Kahane, H., R. Kahane, and S. Saporta, *Development of verbal categories in child language*. Bloomington, Indiana: Indiana Univer. Res. Ctr. Antthrop. Folklore, Ling., 1958.

Kellogg, W. N., and L. A. Kellogg, *The ape and the child*. New York: McGraw-Hill, 1933.

Lenneberg, E. H., Understanding language without ability to speak: A case report. *J. abnorm. soc. Psychol.*, 1962, **65**, 419–425.

McCarthy, D., Language development in children. In L. Carmichael (ed.), *Manual of child psychology*. New York: Wiley, 1954.

Underwood, B. J., and R. W. Schulz, *Meaningfulness and verbal learning*. Philadelphia: Lippincott, 1960.

Elicited Imitation as a Research Tool in Developmental Psycholinguistics[1]

——*Dan I. Slobin and Charles A. Welsh*

Imitation probably is not an important device in language acquisition, because the aspects of language which the child must acquire are not available to be imitated: he is exposed only to surface structures of sentences, but what he must acquire are deep structures and the transformational rules which relate

Presented to the Center for Research on Language and Language Behavior, University of Michigan, March 1967; circulated as Working Paper No. 10 (1968) of the Language-Behavior Research Laboratory, University of California, Berkeley. Also printed in *Language Training in early childhood education*, edited by C. S. Lauatelli, and published by the University of Illinois Press for the ERIC Clearinghouse on Early Childhood Education (1971, pp. 170–185). Printed here by permission of the authors and the University of Illinois Press.

[1] Many of the ideas suggested in this paper grew out of discussions with Barry A. Gordon, and many of the data were gathered and transcribed with the assistance of Susan Carter. To both we extend our thanks.

deep and surface structures. This argument has already been well developed by linguists and psycholinguists (e.g., papers in Smith and Miller, 1966), and we are not concerned in this paper with the role played by imitation in the natural situation of language acquisition. (This problem is discussed in Slobin, 1968.) Our present task is to determine what can be learned through the use of controlled, elicited imitations as a probe to discover the child's underlying linguistic competence. This is to say, we are concerned here with imitation as a device by which the investigator can learn about the child's language, and not as a device by which the child can learn about the adult's language.

The data examined here are part of a longitudinal study of linguistic development in one child. In keeping with the tradition of pseudonyms established by Brown and Bellugi's "Adam," "Eve," and "Sarah" (1964) and McNeill's "Izanami" (1966), we will refer to our subject as "Echo." She is a precocious first child of graduate student parents and has no siblings. This report is based on 1000 elicited imitations, collected between the ages of 2;3;2 and 2;5;3. (Ages are given in years, months, and weeks.) By *elicited* imitations we refer to the child's repetition of a model sentence presented in a context calling for imitation, as opposed to the child's spontaneous imitation of adult utterances.[2] The time segment examined here is part of a continuing study of Echo's linguistic and cognitive development.

Psycholinguistic literature presents the following general picture of sentence imitation by two-year-olds (e.g., Brown and Fraser, 1963): The child repeats stressed content words in proper order, with length and complexity of utterance not exceeding that of his spontaneous speech. That is, imitations have the same "telegraphic" character as the child's own utterances, in which many function words and inflections are missing. Our intensive study of elicited imitations shows that all of these general statements are in need of modification. In addition, the "classical" picture gives no explanation of why imitation should be of this nature. One is simply left with the notion that the child scans a sentence and picks up some of the stressed, familiar words, working from left to right. We do not yet have a clear understanding of why he picks out the words he does and the extent to which his knowledge of the language determines the way in which he recognizes, stores, and reproduces sentences in immediate repetition. We are beginning to understand aspects of this process a bit more clearly, and are in the process of building a model for sentence imitation—a model which will, we hope, also eventually reveal something about the way in which sentence recognition and comprehension takes place normally, in both children and adults.

The general picture presented in the literature seems to hold true, only if

---

[2] In the early stages of the investigation it was necessary to give the child explicit instructions to imitate (e.g., "Can you say . . ." or "Say . . ."). Such instruction soon became superfluous, as Echo apparently learned the subtle cues signalling a model sentence to be repeated. We are aware, however, of the problems posed by the fact that we have no way of assessing Echo's definition of the task or even if she always interprets the task in the same way.)

the model sentence is somewhat beyond the child's normal sentence processing span and is not anomalous. The following example corresponds well with this picture. (The model sentence, uttered by an adult, is given in capital letters; the child's imitation is given immediately below, in lower-case letters, followed by age in years, months, and weeks.)

(1) THE PENCIL IS GREEN
     pencil green (2;3;2)

Note that the child drops the article and copula as expected (though the article sometimes occurs in Echo's speech and imitations at this stage).

However, Echo also has much longer sentences in her free speech and at this same age can easily imitate another four-word sentence such as:

(2) TIGERS CAN DRINK MILK
     tiger can drink milk (2;3;3)

And she can even successfully imitate much longer sentences (although often omitting article and copula), such as:

(3) THE LITTLE BOY IS EATING SOME PINK ICE CREAM
     little boy eating some pink ice cream (2;3;2)

Number of words, or number of morphemes, is clearly not a relevant measure of how much of a sentence a child can imitate. At this age, in her free speech, she has sentences as complex as, "It'll get burned in there"; and sentences as long as, "This's Echo room, but then Daddy won't come in Echo room."

On the other hand, when she is somewhat older, and her grammar quite a bit more complex, she may drop out an entire embedded clause from a sentence which is not especially long in terms of morpheme count:

(4) MOZART WHO CRIED CAME TO MY PARTY
     Mozart came to my party (2;4;3)

(Mozart is a teddy bear.)

On the way toward discovering some of the determinants of Echo's imitations we came across several interesting side phenomena which deserve passing mention.

If items are omitted from imitation, it may be that they are simply not heard. It has been frequently noted that the words omitted by the child are those most difficult for a transcriber to pick up from tape recordings of adult speech. Perhaps, then, one can simply get a child to imitate a normally omitted item by saying it especially loudly and clearly. And, in fact, one can sometimes get Echo to imitate an omitted element simply by stressing it, as in (5). (Italic type indicates stress; "..." indicates pause.)

(5) THE PENCIL *IS* GREEN
     pencil ... *is* green (2;3;2)

(Note that hesitation pauses are important cues to sentence processing.) Stress in the model sentence can also lead to alteration, as well as insertion of new material:

(6) WE WERE HIDING
     we was hiding (2;3;2)
     WE WERE HIDING
     we was hiding
     WE *WERE* HIDING
     we *were* hiding

It is interesting that properly positioned stress is maintained in the imitations presented in (5) and (6). However, one cannot simply state as a rule that any stressed item will be imitated, and that position of stress will be maintained, because of examples such as:

(7) *THE* BOY IS EATING AND CRYING
     boy *eating* nuh crying (2;3;3)

Note, however, that stress is preserved in (7), although shifted to another position. The preservation of stress seems to be general, though its position is not always predictable. Even if all words are preserved, stress may still be shifted:

(8) *THERE* ARE THE RED BEADS
     there *are* the red beads (2;3;3)

The preservation of rhythmic and intonational aspects in imitation may be basic—and perhaps universal. (For example, Fitzgerald [1966], in a study of spontaneous imitations by two-year-old speakers of Gã—a tone language—found errors in segmental phonology to occur far more frequently than distortion of the tonal and rhythmic structures of the sentences imitated. In fact, 28 percent of segmental phonemes were incorrectly imitated, while only 2 percent of tonal phonemes were incorrectly imitated.)

We discovered, however, an important and intriguing exception to the generalization that rhythmic and intonational aspects of sentences tend to be retained in imitation. Echo consistently ignores repeated words in model sentences (9–11), unless the repeated word can be interpreted as an appropriate lexical item in the sentence (12).

(9)   MARK FELL FELL OFF THE HORSE
      Mark fell off a horse (2;3;2)
(10) I *CAN CAN CAN* EAT
      I can eat (2;3;2)
(11) I *NEED NEED* THE BALL
      I need the ball (2;3;2)
(12) I NEED THE BALL BALL
      I need the ball ball (2;3;2)

This was true at 2;3;2, and also when repeated a month later, at 2;4;3. Echo ignored doubling or tripling of words, even if they were nonsense words:

(13) KITTY WAS PERKING PERKING PERKING THE ICE CREAM
kitty was perking the ice cream (2;4;3)

A moment's consideration convinces one of the adaptive necessity of such a strategy in sentence recognition. A child could simply not arrive at a reasonable grammar of a language if he tried to account for stutterings and false starts in the speech of his parents. To ignore successively repeated words in a sentence may be a basic instruction in the child's language acquisition device.

Examples (10) and (11) show that even if repeated words are all stressed, they are not picked up as repeated. Word repetition can, however, be recorded as stress in repetition:

(14) WHERE WHERE IS KITTY?
where kitty? (2;3;2)
(15) MOZART FELL OFF OFF THE TABLE
Mozart fell *off* the table (2;3;2)

It may be significant that the only function of word reiteration in English—namely adverbial emphasis (e.g., "very, very good")—can also be realized by stress (e.g., "*very* good"). These two devices seem to bear a certain equivalence both in the adult system and in Echo's imitations.

Before proceeding to more central findings, allow us to briefly note one more suggestive phenomenon which we have turned up in our investigations. Often Echo will spontaneously produce a fairly long and complex utterance, and, if this utterance is offered as a model immediately after its production, it will be (more or less) successfully imitated. However, if the very same utterance is presented to the child ten minutes later—i.e., the child's own utterance—she will often fail to imitate it fully or correctly. For example:

(16) IF YOU FINISH YOUR EGGS ALL UP, DADDY, YOU CAN
HAVE YOUR COFFEE
after you finish your eggs all up then you can have your coffee, daddy
(2;5;1)

Ten minutes later:

you can have coffee, daddy, after

Half-hour later:

YOU CAN HAVE COFFEE, DADDY, AFTER YOU EAT YOUR
EGGS ALL UP
after you eat your eggs all up . . . eat your eggs all up

(The model sentences were offered by Echo's father. The sentence was still true on second presentation.) It would seem that the child has an "intention *to-say-so-and-so*"—to use William James' phrase—and has encoded that intention into linguistic form. If that linguistic form is presented for imitation while the intention is still operative, it can be fairly successfully imitated. Once the intention is gone, however, the utterance must be processed in linguistic terms alone—without its original intentional and contextual support. In the absence of such support, the task can strain the child's abilities and reveal a more limited competence than may actually be present in spontaneous speech. Thus whatever we discover in systematic probes of imitation must be taken as a *conservative* estimate of the child's linguistic competence.

These phenomena begin to point to a process which has occasionally been suggested in the literature—namely, that, in repeating a sentence, one must filter it through one's own productive system. To use Piaget's terminology, a sentence, when recognized, is assimilated to an internal schema, and, when reproduced, is constructed in terms of that schema. The question of interest, of course, is the extent to which such schemata correspond to the structures and principles of linguistic theory. We believe that our finding can begin to cast some light on that question.

Perhaps the most obvious examples of this sort of "assimilatory deformation," or "recoding in short-term memory," are cases in which one word is substituted for another, preserving meaning. This was the case in (6). Additional examples are:

(17) TOMORROW THERE WILL NOT BE A LONG LINE
      won't be a long line (2;4;3)
(18) THIS ONE IS THE GIANT, BUT THIS ONE IS LITTLE
      dis one little, annat one big (2;4;3)

This sort of rephrasing seems to be clear evidence that the child has retrieved the underlying meaning of the sentence and is encoding that meaning in a new form in imitation. This is a very basic point, and one that reappears again and again in various forms.

Example (18) shows another very interesting finding, in addition to the recodings of "giant" to "big," and "but" to "and." Note that the two propositions are inverted (with a change in conjunction). This is a very frequent finding in our data—and one that contradicts the generalization that order of elements is always preserved in imitation. If a sentence is a conjunction of two underlying propositions, and the child understands both propositions, she will very frequently give the second proposition first in her imitation. We find many examples of this sort of inversion of sentences—conjoined by "and"—a month earlier (19), (20), and more recently as well (21).

(19) THE RED BEADS ARE HERE AND THE BROWN BEADS ARE HERE
      brown beads are over here; red beads over there (2;3;3)
(20) THE RED BEADS AND BROWN BEADS ARE HERE
      brown beads here an' a red beads here (2;3;3)
(21) MOMMY ATE THE CANDY AND MOMMY ATE THE ICE CREAM
      mommy eat the ice cream and mommy eat a candy (2;5;3)

Note that Echo does not always give a literal repetition in these imitations, but that she has clearly retained the two propositions. In (19) she even gives them as separate sentences, not conjoined by "and."

The inversion of conjoined sentences clearly indicates that Echo comprehends the use of "and" as a sentence conjunction. In fact, she will sometimes introduce it herself:

> (22) THE CANDY IS MARPLE. THE SHOE IS MARPLE.
> . . . shoe marple an' a candy marple (2;3;3)

Not only does she comprehend the conjunction, but she must comprehend the structures of the two conjoined sentences as well. This is indicated in (22) (and elsewhere) by inverted imitation of conjoined sentences with nonsense words occupying certain slots. Even though she has omitted the copula in her imitation. she must have correctly analyzed its function in order to have repeated the model sentences as she did. (A nonsense word in copular position will be imitated.)

Inversion of conjoined sentences also reveals something of Echo's strategy in sentence imitation. The data suggest that she has retained the general syntactic form of the model sentence—in this case, two sentences conjoined by "and"—and what she is concerned with in output is to produce something of this general syntactic form. The exact content words and details of structure, however, are often lost, frequently resulting in the imposition of parallel construction, as in the imposition of "here" in the second part of (20).

This attempt to reproduce two parallel constructions can often take precedence over semantic content, as in:

> (23) THE BLUE SHOES AND BLUE PENCILS ARE HERE
> blue pencil are here and a blue pencil are here (2;3;3)

It looks as if Echo has filled up so much of her short-term memory with information about the syntactic structure of the model sentences that she has no more room for all the lexical items. She clearly knows, however, what sorts of items are needed. And so, when she comes to the second noun phrase, she fills it appropriately with a noun from the model sentence—"pencil"—but in so doing uses the same noun twice. This matter of finding words to fit an abstract syntactic frame—or *lexical* instantiation of the structure—is a very common occurrence, even when parallel constructions are given in the model sentence. For example:

> (24) SUE ATE THE CANDY AND MOMMY ATE THE ICE CREAM
> mommy ate the ice cream and mommy eat the ice cream (2;5;3)

(Another example of this phenomenon appears in the second imitation of example (30), where "bread and jam" is imitated as "jam and jam.")

Note that imposition of parallel constructions on conjoined sentences can occur with or without inversion. The imitations in (20) and (21) are examples of the two phenomena combined: Echo repeats the second sentence and then imposes some aspect of its structure and/or content on the first. If the two sentences are quite simple, however—as in the "X is here" type—she can sometimes impose parallel constructions without inverting:

(25) THE PENCIL AND SOME PAPER ARE HERE
      some pencil here and some paper here (2;3;3)

As a matter of fact, in the case of this simple sentence type, she can also perform the inverse operation of deleting and conjoining:

(26) HERE IS A BROWN BRUSH AND HERE IS A COMB
      here's a brown brush an' a comb (2;3;3)

She can even do this occasionally with conjoined subject-verb-object sentences—in the following example even pronominalizing the subject noun phrase and deleting all redundant elements from the second sentence, retaining only the object:

(27) DADDY IS GOING TO GET SOME COOKIES AND DADDY IS
      GOING TO GET SOME JUICE
      he gonna get some cookie and juice (2;3;3)

However, if the two conjoined sentences differ in structure, Echo has great difficulty in retaining both structures, indicating clearly that each syntactic structure takes up a certain amount of space in short-term memory. This is especially clearly revealed in hesitations, false starts, and imposition of parallel constructions, as in:

(28) MOZART GOT BURNED AND THE BIG SHOE IS HERE
      Mozart got burned an-duh . . . big shoe got burned (2;3;3)

(Echo used the form "got burned" productively in spontaneous speech at this time.) Sometimes this difficulty leads to repetition of the same sentence twice:

(29) THE BATMAN GOT BURNED AND THE BIG SHOE IS HERE
      big shoe is here and a big shoe is here (2;3;3)

Note that it is not predictable which of the two sentences Echo will start off with, but that she retains the notion that there must be two sentences, even if she repeats the same sentence twice. (This should not be taken as an absolute statement, however. Occasionally—when distracted, or tired, or for other, unknown reasons—Echo will repeat only one of two conjoined sentences. It is interesting that, in such cases, it is always the second of the two sentences which is repeated —reflecting the phenomenon noted above of frequent inversion in repetition of conjoined sentences.)

The imposition of parallel constructions suggests not only that syntactic structures are stored as abstract entities in short-term memory but that the child may establish a set for a given syntactic structure, thus "blinding" her to other structures. This suggests an experiment such as that performed by Mehler and Carey (1967) in which subjects, after hearing ten sentences of the type "They are recurring mistakes," found it more difficult to hear an eleventh of the type "They are describing events." Although we have not yet performed such an experiment with Echo, we have one bit of suggestive evidence for a similar establishment of a set for a given syntactic structure:

(30) THE BIRD ATE THE BREAD AND JAM
bird *ate* a jam (2;5;1)
THE BIRD ATE THE *BREAD* AND JAM
bird ate the *jam* and jam
THE BIRD ATE THE BREAD AND FLEW AWAY
bird ate . . . ate ate *ate*.
THE BIRD ATE THE JAM AND FLEW AWAY
bird ate the jam and flew away

The above examples give some hint of the rich data provided by imitations of conjoined sentences. About a month after we collected imitations of sentences such as those shown in (18–29), we noticed a very interesting phenomenon in Echo's imitations of conjoined sentences in which both sentences had the same noun phrase: she would pronominalize the second noun phrase, as in:

(31) THE PUSSY EATS BREAD AND THE PUSSY RUNS FAST
pussy eat bread and he run fast (2;4;3)

This suggests very strongly that she had mastered the transformation calling for pronominalization of repeated noun phrases in such structures and that she was using this transformation in producing an utterance based on the underlying structure she had retrieved from the model sentence. She would even introduce a pronoun for a second noun phrase if it was deleted in the model sentence:

(32) THE OWL EATS CANDY AND RUNS FAST
owl eat candy . . . owl eat the candy and . . . he run fast (2;4;3)

Her hesitations and false starts indicate she was working hard to produce an imitation matching her image of the model. The introduction of a pronoun for the second noun phrase suggests that her rules do not yet allow for the total deletion of a repeated noun phrase in this sort of structure (although note that she was able to do so a month earlier in the simple structure represented in example (27)).

At this age—2;4;3—she imitated sentences with embedded *who*-constructions in similar fashion, suggesting a comprehension which exceeded her productive competence, e.g.;

(33) MOZART WHO CRIED CAME TO MY PARTY
Mozart cried and he came to my party (2;4;3)

The parallel interpretation of conjoined sentences and of sentences with embedded *who*-constructions is especially clear in the following two examples, in which Echo's imitations of two different structures are virtually identical:

(34) THE OWL EATS CANDY AND THE OWL RUNS FAST
owl eat candy and he run fast (2;4;3)

(35) THE OWL WHO EATS CANDY RUNS FAST
      owl eat a candy and he run fast (2;4;3)

These examples suggest that *who* is ignored. It could be that Echo scans her memory of the model sentence looking for subject-verb-object (SVO) constructions; and, if a subject occurs twice, or if a second subject is lacking, she will use *he* in that position. In addition, her rules require that she join the two SVO constructions with *and*.

Further support for such an imitation device comes from numerous imitations such as the following:

(36) THE MAN WHO I SAW YESTERDAY GOT WET
      I saw the man and he got wet (2;4;3)

Note that word order in the first part of the sentence is not maintained. In her free speech, Echo uses *I* only in subject position, and so appropriately uses *I* as subject of sentences such as these. Thus it is not clear from such examples whether *who*-constructions of this sort are understood in adult fashion or whether a more simple rule of seeking SVO sequences is being applied. In sentences such as (33) and (35), *who* could simply have been ignored, and SVO still have been appropriately retrieved. Unfortunately, our data are scanty in this regard, but we have some suggestive evidence that this *who*-construction is beginning to be understood, and that it enters as a more compact way of pushing together in surface structure information which must be represented by two propositions—two "S's"—in deep structure. The clearest example is the following intriguing substitution in successive imitations of the same model sentence:

(37) THE MAN WHO I SAW YESTERDAY RUNS FAST
      I saw the man who run fast
      I saw the man and he run fast (2;4;3)

The notion that Echo may have been looking for SVO relations in the model sentences intrigued us, and so we constructed sentences in which it would be very difficult to retrieve the underlying structure if the necessary transformation rules were lacking. These were sentences in which the rate of information transmission in surface structure was very compact, due to various deletions, and in which embedded sentences were not introduced by cue words such as *who* or *that*. For example, two sentences can be simply conjoined by *and*: "The book hit the boy and the boy was crying." The first sentence can be embedded in the second in various ways, e.g., "The boy who the book hit was crying." In addition *who* can be deleted, giving: "The boy the book hit was crying." When Echo was 2;5;1 and 2;5;2 we administered systematically varied sets of sentences of these types. These structures were clearly beyond her competence and were generally treated as word lists, e.g.:

(38) THE BOY THE BOOK HIT WAS CRYING
      boy the book was crying (2;5;1)

Order was not necessarily preserved in these imitations, e.g.:

(39)   THE HOUSE THE BOY HIT WAS BIG
        boyhouse was big (2;5;1)

Occasionally reorderings looked as if Echo were searching for words with
which to instantiate an SVO relation, e.g.:

(40)   THE BOY THE CHAIR HIT WAS DIRTY
        boy hit the chair was dirty (2;5;2)

Such extractions of SVO relations seemed to occur only when they were semantically plausible in Echo's speech. She would never say "boy hit house" or "boy
hit marble"—perhaps because *hit*, for her, means "to strike with the palm of
the hand." She would, however, extract "boy hit chair" and "boy hit man"
from such sentences. It would seem that Echo's words bear both syntactic and
semantic markers, and that she will form SVO constructions when she can
identify not only two nouns and a verb but a constellation of nouns and verb
which can form a semantically acceptable relationship.

Echo frequently extracted SVO relations, in similar fashion, from scram-
bled sentences, e.g.:

(41)   THE MAN THE BOY THE BOOK HIT TORE WHO
        boytheman tore the book who (2;5;2)

There is, however, an important relation between sentence development
and memory span which should not be overlooked here. Echo will perfectly
imitate ungrammatical or anomalous sentences if they are short enough for her
to hold an auditory image in short-term memory. For example, as young as
2;3;2 she repeated all possible orders of the three words "John loves company."
The same, of course, is true of adult repetitions of deviant sentences. One must
only call on mechanisms of assimilatory deformation when the material—
because of its length or complexity, or both—exceeds short-term memory
capacity.

When sentences are short and simple enough, Echo makes amusing
attempts to assimilate new words into her existing grammatical schemata, thus
showing a fine sense of the role of context in providing clues for the lexical
categorization of unknown items. One of the most amusing examples is her
imitation of the following sentence, offered after one of the authors had read
what he considered a singularly poor paper on transformational grammar and
child language:

(42)   CHOMSKY AND VERITAS ARE CRYING
        Cynthia and Tasha . . . cry (2;5;3)

Cynthia and Tasha are friends of Echo. Clearly she has realized that the sentence calls for two proper nouns, and she has substituted two more familiar names which bear more phonological information than is available in short-term memory. This is especially evident in apparent search for unfamiliar words, as in:

> (43)   EX POST FACTO I SEE THE QUARTER
>   eptah . . . quarter I see ekso . . . ekso, ekso, ekso, ekso (2;5;3)

Examples (42) and (43) do not agree with the finding of Smith, Shipley, and Gleitman that children "tend not to listen to adult speech beginning with unfamiliar words" (Smith, 1966, p. 3). Not only did Echo attend to unfamiliar words appearing in sentence-initial position, but she frequently repeated them without difficulty, as in:

> (44)   CUI BONO IS THE QUARTER
>   cui bona a quarter (2;5;3)

This is a very sketchy summary of what one can discover from carefully examining about 1000 elicited imitations in one child over a period of less than three months. We hope to have demonstrated that the method is a fruitful one. It must be used, we believe, together with running collections and analysis of spontaneous speech. This very preliminary analysis has convinced us that sentence recognition and imitation are filtered through the individual's productive linguistic system. More specifically, we believe that we can tentatively offer the following generalizations:

Echo can spontaneously utter sentences which she cannot imitate. On the other hand, she can give *recoded* imitations of model sentences which exceed her productive capacities.

Emphasis can lead her to repeat words she would normally omit from imitation, but she generally ignores repeated words in imitating model sentences.

If she comprehends a sentence, she need not repeat it in the order given. Reordering can also take place as a result of imposing SVO constructions upon model sentences.

The process of sentence recognition includes retrieval of both form and content. Syntactic structures take up space in memory, and frequently content will be sacrificed to the retention of form in immediate, rote imitation. On the other hand, if content has been retrieved and stored, it may be encoded in the child's own syntax in imitation.

A fine-grained analysis of repeated imitations of systematically varied model sentences can reveal aspects of the child's theory of syntax, including transformational rules and the syntactic and semantic markers borne by lexical items.

REFERENCES

Brown, R., and U. Bellugi, Three processes in the child's acquisition of syntax, *Harvard. educ. Rev.*, 1964, **34**, 133–151.

Brown, R., and C. Fraser, The acquisition of syntax. In C. N. Cofer and B. S. Musgrave (eds.), *Verbal behavior and learning*. New York: McGraw-Hill, 1963, pp. 158–197.

Fitzgerald, L. K., Child language: An analysis of imitations by Gã children. Unpublished paper, Department of Anthropology, University of California, Berkeley, 1966.

McNeill, D., The creation of language by children. In J. Lyons and R. J. Wales (eds.), *Psycholinguistics papers*. Edinburgh: Edinburgh University Press, 1966, pp. 99–115. [Reprinted, in part, in this volume.]

Mehler, J., and P. Carey, The role of surface and base structure in the perception of sentences, *J. verb. Learn. verb. Behav.*, 1967, **6**, 335–338.

Slobin, D. I., Imitation and grammatical development in children. In N. S. Endler, L. R. Boulter, and H. Osser (eds.), *Contemporary issues in developmental psychology*. New York: Holt, Rinehart and Winston, 1968, pp. 437–443.

Smith, C. S., Two studies of the syntactic knowledge of young children. Paper presented at Linguistics Colloquium, MIT, 1966. [See C. S. Smith, An experimental approach to children's linguistic competence. In J. R. Hayes (ed.), *Cognition and the development of language*. New York: Wiley, 1970, pp. 109–135. (Reprinted in this volume.)]

Smith, F., and G. A. Miller, (eds.), *The genesis of language: A psycholinguistic approach*. Cambridge, Mass.: MIT Press, 1966.

An Experimental Approach to Children's Linguistic Competence[1]

—— *Carlota S. Smith*

Psycholinguistics is a field in which linguist and psychologist have collaborated in a rather unique way to study language behavior. The contribution of the linguist has been in the organization of linguistic material; the psychologist, in setting up and carrying out his studies, has sought to answer psychological questions about people's use of linguistic material. Generative grammar since the 1950s has provided much of the impetus for psycholinguistic work, partly because of its explicitness, but more significantly because of its abstract nature

From *Cognition and the development of language*, edited by John R. Hayes. New York: Wiley, 1970, pp. 109–135. Reprinted by permission of the author and the publisher.
[1] The experiments were part of a study of language acquisition, Grant #MH 07990, National Institutes of Health, administered by the Eastern Pennsylvania Psychiatric Institute.

and its essentially psychological orientation. The important distinction between competence and performance allows both linguist and psychologist to relate the often fragmentary utterances of natural speech to the coherent and complete description provided by a grammar. The structural descriptions of generative grammar not only provide organization, such as the hierarchical structure of sentences; they also suggest specific psychological inquiries because they attempt to represent what a speaker knows about his language. What is the nature of psychological inquiry? Most psycholinguists would probably accept the statement that they are studying the mechanisms that underline or form language behavior; specifically, they ask what processes are involved when a person understands or utters a sentence.

Language acquisition, as the study of children's language is usually called, is an area of psycholinguistics that has burgeoned with the others. In studying language acquisition, one focuses on the development of the human animal; one investigates the various stages enroute to adult speech and what is involved in the shift from one stage to the next; and one also seeks to shed light on some general questions of linguistic endowment and behavior.

In this chapter, I shall discuss some psycholinguistic work in the area of language acquisition; and in the course of the discussion, suggest a few general questions. In particular, I will be concerned, at different points, with the relation of generative (or any) grammar to psycholinguistic studies.

I would like first to mention two important problems that arise in investigating the linguistic competence of young children. It is generally agreed that performance, which is subject to nonlinguistic accidents of all kinds, does not reflect competence. The linguist or psychologist, in determining the competence of a native speaker, supplements records of spontaneous speech: he presents the speaker with systematically varied utterances and asks for direct linguistic judgments and paraphrases. One can't use these techniques with two- or three-year-olds; children are notoriously unable or unwilling to give direct linguistic judgments or paraphrases of their own speech or the speech of others. Thus the direct methods by which a linguist usually tests, extends, and limits his hypotheses, are useless. To study children's competence, we must develop indirect methods of obtaining linguistic judgments. This is a problem of methodology; the second problem is more far reaching.

There is a great difference between the utterances that a young child hears (which are presumably utterances of adult speech[2]), and the utterances that he produces. A description of children's linguistic competence should deal with this discrepancy, especially since their linguistic competence seems to greatly exceed their performance. Children appear to understand commands and simple speech before they speak at all; and children that speak telegraphically[3] appear to

---

[2] Although perhaps systematically simplified for the child's ears.
[3] This term was coined by Roger Brown to describe the early speech of children, in which function words do not occur.

understand fairly complicated adult utterances. We need, then, to ask the question, how much do children attend to and comprehend of adult speech? One reason that this problem has been so little studied is the difficulty of devising indirect approaches to it; but there are other, more serious, reasons for the lack of attention.

The study of comprehension, child and adult, is just beginning. In addressing ourselves to the question of children's comprehension, we must therefore concern ourselves with the nature of the basic processes as well as the acquisition of them. In studying comprehension, we take as fundamental the notion, clearly stated in discussions of generative grammar, that to understand a sentence one must know its structure. For grammarians, the word *structure* covers several aspects of a sentence: the surface structure, the deep structure, the derivation or transformational history, or all three of these. It is easy to confuse grammatical and psychological questions here. When we say that to understand a sentence, a person must know its structure, do we refer to a full structural description, in the technical sense? It has been suggested for instance, that the process of understanding a sentence involves the production of a full structural description (with heuristic short-cuts of Halle and Stevens 1964, Matthews 1962). But perhaps it would be more accurate to say that when one understands a sentence one *could* produce a full structural description, not that one does so—just as we sometimes say that knowing the meaning of a word involves knowing how and when to use it (but not actually using it in all possible ways). If this is a suggestive analogy, what it suggests is that the linguistic rules so powerful in generative grammar may not have the same importance for psychological studies.

There is no doubt about the psychological reality of linguistic units. This has been convincingly demonstrated in experiments by Miller (1956), Savin (1965), Fodor and Bever (1965), and others.[4]

I referred above to the role of linguistics within psycholinguistics; the organization of linguistic material into sentences, hierarchically ordered constituents, and the like, constitutes a major contribution of linguistics. When we adopt derivations as models for understanding, however, we are further extending the domain of linguistics; specifically, we are now looking for evidence of the psychological reality of linguistic rules. There may be a direct relation between a grammatical derivation of a sentence and a person's understanding or production of a sentence. If this is the case, then people behave more or less according to the rules stated in a generative grammar. But it is not clear that they do so. In fact, the more cautious grammarians have been careful to disavow the suggestion.

Consider briefly the early formulation of generative grammar as a model and a hypothesis for understanding.[5] The sentences of a language are reduced to

---

[4] Perhaps the first demonstration of this kind is Sapir's (1949) famous essay, "The Psychological Reality of Phonemes."

[5] In speaking of *understanding*, I do not mean to suggest a difference between the speaker and hearer of speech, but for brevity's sake will refer to only understanding.

a small number of simple sentences, and rules-transformations for combining and rearranging them. The result is a systematic statement that has great intuitive appeal because of its simplicity and elegance. Sentences have deep structure (the simple sentence(s) underlying them) and surface structure, the result of applying transformational rules. The two structures may be almost identical or quite different; what is understood is the deep structure of a sentence, perhaps with fixed emphasis and variations indicated by surface structure. A typical example of a type of sentence with different deep and surface structures is the passive.

But it is not *prima facie* evident that people do understand sentences with reference, somehow, to simple active declarative sentences. If they do so, then a passive, for instance, is understood as a variation of an active sentence, and is stored in immediate memory as a simplex sentence and an addendum of some kind. There have been some attempts to study this question by comparing the memory space taken up by passive and active sentences; the differences between the two types of structure is confounded with a difference in length. However, consider a comparison between an active sentence and a passive with deleted agent, such as:

(1)   John frightened Mary.
(2)   Mary was frightened.

If derivation is an important factor, we would expect the second of these sentences to take up more space in immediate memory, and perhaps to be more difficult to remember. Slobin (1968) has recently studied adults' and children's handling of these structures and found no evidence that they differ. And, as Fodor and Garrett (1966) point out, other recent experimental results do not point unequivocally to the interpretation that sentences are stored and understood as deep structures.

The passive with deleted agent is similar in derived structure to certain simplex sentences, such as:

(3)   Mary was frightened.
(4)   Mary was angry.

It seems unlikely that people understand these sentences in entirely different ways, one much more complicated than the other.

These comments do not apply to the type of generative grammar presented in Chomsky's *Aspects of the Theory of Syntax* (1965), (or to other, more recent proposals). The deep structures of *Aspects* are often very abstract; the deep structures in the type of grammar advocated by Lakoff (1966) and Ross (1967) for instance, are even more abstract. It is not clear what kind of grammatical rules would be involved if we attempted to work out a direct relation between these grammars and a psychological account of understanding.

Generative grammar has been oriented toward syntax, and so have most accounts of understanding. However, perhaps syntax has been overemphasized.

Consider the way language is used in the ordinary way; usually, as sentences are spoken or read—in context—there is little room for misunderstanding of a syntactic nature. Perhaps in understanding an utterance, one uses mainly semantic information, calling on syntactic information only when necessary. For instance, there is only one plausible way to interpret the triplet of words *John, broke, glass*: this means that there is only one plausible structure to impose on it and syntactic information is in a sense redundant. However, in some cases a triplet admits of more than one interpretation, e.g. *John, followed, Bill*; to understand this, one must draw on syntactic markers for subject and object; that is, one needs syntactic information. If understanding is approached from this point of view, we find that the grammatical derivation of a sentence is less important and the surface structure of a sentence is more important. It is interesting to note that the primacy of syntax is now being questioned on several counts (see for instance, McCawley, 1968).

The discussion provides an introductory framework for a description of some work in the field of language acquisition. In studying language acquisition, I have argued, one must study understanding; and the processes involved in understanding are themselves little understood. It is important, I think, to be clear about these still-open questions.

II

I would like now to describe and discuss two psycholinguistic experiments with young children; the experiments were conducted by Elizabeth Shipley, Lila Gleitman and myself. We were interested primarily in three areas: the linguistic input for a child; the mechanisms that the child uses in organizing linguistic input; and the structures that the child imposes on linguistic input.

RESPONSE EXPERIMENT

Description

Our subjects in the first experiment were children who were just learning to talk. The experiment was directed toward finding out what constitutes the *primary linguistic input* for children at this stage. What do children listen to? What do they understand of the speech addressed to them?—were the questions that we asked. We wanted to know whether the children were aware of the difference between their own speech and the speech of adults; this seemed a necessary prefatory question to the more general question of their linguistic competence. We were looking for evidence as to whether the children's competence differed from what one would suppose from their natural speech.

The phrase *primary linguistic input* should not be confused with *primary linguistic data*. The latter may be used in several ways. It sometimes refers to the linguistic environment of a child, that is, the utterances made in his presence; or to the utterances in his environment that a child attends to. But the phrase has also been used to refer to the structural information that a child is endowed with; and, again, to the early structures (whether or not different from adult structures) that the child imposes on what he hears. These different uses blur the distinction between what is heard and how it is structured. In dealing with the speech of children, one often wants to ask whether children impose "their own" or "adult" structures, so that it is important to keep this distinction clear. We were interested specifically in what the children attended to in utterances addressed to them.

The children we studied all spoke telegraphically, that is, their speech consisted almost exclusively of nouns and verbs. We expected that some of them would notice the difference between telegraphic and adult speech; for these children, we wanted to know how features of adult speech affected them. For instance, if the children listened mainly to the high-stress content words that occur in their own speech, then function words might make it difficult for them to find the content words. On the other hand, because of their familiarity, function words might facilitate the search.

In the experiment we presented children with systematically varied utterances, and looked for evidence that they noticed the differences. The utterances varied in structure: some were well-formed sentences, some were telegraphic, and some were minimal or holophrastic. Nonsense syllables were substituted for function words and for verbs in some of the experimental utterances. This variable, familiarity, was introduced to test how closely the children attended to the adult parts of adult speech.

Since we could not solicit direct judgments, the problem was to devise utterances that called for behavioral responses. We could then look for patterns in the behavioral responses that indicated whether the children discriminated between the utterances. Commands were the experimental utterances, and we were thus able to ask, in scoring responses, whether the children followed the commands. The commands all pertained to toys that were familiar to the children and visible during the experimental sessions. The children were asked to *pick up the doll*, *wind up the music box*, and the like, in eight different ways; they were free to respond to or ignore the commands. The stimulus types are given below. I will refer to particular stimulus types by the *italics* letters. Capital letters stand for nonsense syllables and lower-case letters stand for verbs, nouns, and function words. The stimulus type *Lyn* was included to test the importance of sheer length.

We faced many problems in presenting the commands to very young children. They have short attention spans, and their responses to relatively unknown adults and unfamiliar situations, are, at best, unpredictable. A fluid experimental situation was devised to allow for these difficulties. The sessions were held at the children's homes, and the mothers were enlisted to utter the experimental commands (the mothers were given practice so that all commands

FREE RESPONSE EXPERIMENTAL STIMULAE

STRUCTURE		
FAMILIARITY	CHILD-FORMS	WELL-FORMED
No nonsense syllables	*n:* Ball	*vfn:* Throw me the ball
	vn: Throw ball	
	Lvn: Please Jim, throw ball	
Nonsense syllables	*Xn:* Gor ball	*vZn:* Throw ronta ball
		Xfn: Gor me the ball
		XZn: Gor ronta ball

were uttered in a natural way). The stimulus toys were prominently displayed. Each session had the general form of an informal visit; the experimenter, an observer and the child's mother chatted with each other, and with the child, for about half an hour. Interspaced with the chat were the experimental utterances. After a stimulus was given, chat ceased (unless initiated by the child—absolute silence from the adults led, we found, to absolute silence from the child) for one and one-half minutes so that the behavioral and verbal responses of the child could be noted. The sessions were recorded on tape, and the experimenter and observer filled out standard question sheets for each stimulus.

Getting the child's attention proved to be another difficult problem; many children, especially the younger ones, were often so absorbed in their own activities as to be virtually unreachable. Yet we wanted to be sure that the child actually heard the stimuli. The mother was instructed to call a child's name, and then to give the experimental command only if she judged that she had the child's attention. There were many times, of course, when a child ignored his mother's call; she was, in these cases, to say something else and wait for another chance to deliver the stimulus. These experimental sessions, although incredibly time-consuming, were quite effective; the fluid situation made it possible for the children to ignore the adults and the stimulus toys for a time, and then return for more chat and more experimental utterances.

The subjects were 13 children, ranging in age from 18 months to 2 1/2 years, all of middle-class professional families. We had fairly extensive samples of their spontaneous speech from preliminary play sessions and the experimental sessions (excluding replies to experimental stimuli). The children were ranked for verbal maturity on the basis of these samples. We found that median utterance-length was an effective gauge of verbal maturity; this measure correlated highly with other measures, such as frequency of pronouns and verbs, and inflection. All the children spoke telegraphically, but one group of children was distinctly less mature than the other. For simplicity, I shall refer to the less mature as *younger* and the more mature as *older*; in general, the children's verbal maturity did correlate with age. The two groups of children differed significantly in their responses to the stimuli.

The children did not always respond to the stimulus commands, but there were clear patterns indicating that the experimental variables did significantly affect their responses;[6] in other words, the children did notice the differences between the commands. I will describe briefly the scoring and patterning of the responses and then comment on the implications of the patterns.

Behavioral and verbal responses were scored separately. There were two types of behavioral response that could be clearly distinguished—touches, when child touched the toy mentioned in a given stimulus, or looks, when he looked directly at the toy. Any interaction with a toy was scored as a touch, but we did not further distinguish these responses (in some cases the child followed a specific command, such as *bang on the workbench*, by banging; in other cases he simply touched the workbench; and in others, of course, he did neither). A touch was considered to be a more affirmative response than a look. Verbal responses were categorized as question, negative, repetition, and reply. Irrelevant verbalizations were not scored.

Responses

We ask first, which type of command the children tended to follow. The touch responses were interpreted as following the commands, and the familiar adult form *vfn* most frequently elicited touch responses. Stimuli eliciting the touch responses fell into three different (statistically) groups, on the basis of frequency of the responses.

TOUCH RESPONSES TO EXPERIMENTAL COMMANDS
(in order: stimuli that most frequently elicited touch responses are listed first)

vfn

vn n Lvn

vZn Xfn Xn XZn

A child was most likely to touch a stimulus toy if asked to do so in a familiar and adult way; notice also that he was more likely to follow telegraphic commands than to follow commands containing unfamiliar words (nonsense syllables). This pattern was significant for the group as a whole. There was, however, a very interesting correlation with verbal maturity. The older children most frequently followed well-formed and familiar commands; the youngest children most frequently followed familiar telegraphic commands (*vn* and *n*).

---

[6] All differences mentioned have been found to be statistically significant. See the papers mentioned in footnotes 7 and 8 for details.

A similar pattern emerges in a second composite category of responses. These responses indicated attention to the stimulus; they were looks, touches, and relevant verbalizations. As a group, the children attended most frequently to familiar adult commands, and least frequently to commands containing nonsense material. There is one interesting difference, however, between the touch responses and the attention responses. One stimulus that contained nonsense, vZn, elicited attention responses as frequently as did the familiar telegraphic stimuli:

ATTENTION RESPONSES TO EXPERIMENTAL COMMANDS

vfn
vn, n, Lvn, vZn
Xfn, Xn, XZn

vZn is the only stimulus type, of those containing nonsense syllables, that does not begin with nonsense. We note then that the children were least likely to follow, or to attend to, commands beginning with unfamiliar words.

Verbal responses were analyzed separately. Repetitions (responses containing all or part of the stimulus, and nothing else) were the only type of verbal responses affected by the experimental variables; the other responses were equally likely after all stimuli. Repetitions were dramatically affected by the familiarity variable. They were most frequent after commands containing nonsense syllables; that is, commands with nonsense tended to elicit repetitions. Repetitions were frequently followed by touch responses—having repeated a command, the children were likely to follow it (recall that all stimuli had the name of a familiar toy).

It seemed clear that repetition was an affirmative response. We interpreted the repetitions as efforts to make sense out of the unfamiliar words (nonsense syllables). In effect, the children were replaying the stimulus.

The older children, who are presumably more efficient listeners, tended to repeat only the nonsense syllables of the stimuli; the other children, perhaps unable to separate the familiar from the unfamiliar, tended to repeat some sense and nonsense. These spontaneous repetitions are not unlike those studied by Ervin (1964). Her remarks about repetition do not conflict with the result reported here. Ervin concluded that children's repetitions are not grammatically progressive; the children in our experiment were repeating, not unfamiliar structures, but lexical items. Perhaps at this early stage, repetition focuses mainly on lexical novelties.

There was a strong correlation between verbal maturity and frequency of repetition after nonsense-containing stimuli; the older a child, the more often he tended to repeat these stimuli. Actually, the youngest children did not tend to repeat stimuli that contained nonsense syllables; to these utterances they tended to make no response at all. It seems likely that the youngest children were not able to "find" the words they knew in sentences with nonsense, that is, totally unfamiliar words.

Discussion

This completes the rather sketchy description of our experiment. It is reported in detail elsewhere.[7] From these results we are able to make certain hypotheses about primary linguistic input for our subjects, and about their strategy or habits of listening.

The younger children focused on minimal utterances containing familiar words. These utterances elicited responses of attention and affirmation most frequently (from the younger children only). On the basis of our experimental data, we doubt that these children attend very much to the adult parts of adult speech. More generally then, we doubt that their primary linguistic input is as rich or as confusing as has sometimes been suggested. For whatever complex of linguistic, conceptual and perceptual reasons, children at this stage (approximately 18 months to 2 years) can apparently handle only the high-stress-content words that they utter themselves. Perhaps their listening is mainly an attempt to "find" words they know; too many other words, even familiar ones, may make it difficult to do this, and unfamiliar words may make it impossible.

How, then, do we explain children's affirmative behavioral responses to complicated commands from adults? For instance, a two-year-old may be told that he should get his coat to go outside, and may respond appropriately, that is, get the coat. But such responses do not necessarily mean that the children "understand" the entire adult utterances, that is, that they decode it linguistically. Rather, the child may hear a word he knows and understand from situational cues what behavior is expected of him. In other words, he may understand holophrastically. This view of the linguistic competence of young children is hardly a startling one—Vygotsky (1962), for instance, discusses children's presentential linguistic behavior in somewhat similar terms.

The linguistic competence of these children does not differ markedly from their performance, at least in the experiment I have described. The older children, on the other hand, show linguistic competence that is more advanced than their spontaneous speech. Adult speech had "demand quality" for them; they were more likely to respond affirmatively to it than to their own telegraphic speech. They listened closely to (at least some) adult speech, and attempted to decode it fully, as their responses to commands with nonsense indicate. But it is important to note that they did not attend to all of the simple adult speech addressed to

[7] E. Shipley, C. Smith, and L. Gleitman, "A study in the acquisition of syntax: free responses to verbal commands," *Language*, 1969, **45**, 322–342.

them in the experiment. The children's responses to stimuli containing nonsense indicates a systematic selectivity in their listening. Recall that one type of stimulus, *vZn*, elicited significantly more responses of attention than did other stimuli that contained nonsense; *vZn* is the only one of these stimuli that does not begin with nonsense.

Perhaps the primary linguistic input for these children consists mainly of utterances that begin with familiar words. This principle of listening would exclude from a child's attention a good many utterances, thus considerably simplifying his linguistic environment. When he hears an utterance beginning with unfamiliar words, he may ignore it as clearly impenetrable, even if it is addressed to him. Such a simplification makes slightly less improbable the amazing feat of learning to talk.

Our results do not give any information about how children organize, or structure, the material to which they attend—the linguistic input. However, the close attention that the older children paid to nonsense syllables (various responses of attention) suggests that, when an utterance is within certain limited bounds, they attempt to process all of it. In other words, we have demonstrated that the children attended to the function words of adult speech, but did not find out anything about the role of these words for the children. We do not know, for instance, whether they had any semantic value, or whether they somehow supported the high content nouns and verbs. Further research along these same lines might clear up questions of this kind. For instance, the function words might be varied with other function words, where the semantic import differed —*Throw me the ball* and *Throw him the ball*; they might be varied with familiar but inappropriate function words—*Throw to the ball, Throw of the ball*: and; they might be varied with content words—*Throw John the ball* (The stress pattern would change in this last sentence).

Actually, we do not have clear evidence that the verb played a semantic role at all. In most cases each toy had an activity appropriate to it and the verb used in the stimulus sentence asking for that activity (*Wind up the music box*; *Bang on the workbench*). However, since the children attended to the function words, and to the initial words of the stimuli which were either verbs or nonsense syllables, it seems probable that they did listen to the verbs. This might be tested with stimuli in which reasonable verbs were varied (*wind up* and *bring*, for instance) or by varying reasonable and unreasonable verbs (*wind up* or *step on* the music box).

An obvious limitation to this experimental technique is that the stimuli are all commands. We can be sure that children hear many commands; yet commands do not have the basic subject-verb-object order characteristic of English sentences. We would like to develop variations of the technique so that other types of utterances could be presented. We hope to work out games for young children in which statements as well as commands can be systematically varied, and in which we have clear behavioral responses to determine whether children discriminate between them.

III

REPETITION EXPERIMENT

Description

I turn now to a second experiment; this experiment involved older children and a different technique, but was directed toward essentially the same questions. We were interested in the children's linguistic competence, with emphasis on the linguistic input. Specifically, this experiment was designed to find out about structures that the children did not utter spontaneously. The technique was elicited repetition; children were presented with a variety of sentences, and simply asked to repeat them. From the children's successful and unsuccessful attempts, it was possible to infer a good deal about their ability to handle different structures.

The rationale behind this approach is this: we assume that in order to understand a sentence, one must be able to structure it. We set up a situation in which children are forced to structure sentences, and then compare their performance with sentences that they do and do not produce in spontaneous speech. Elicited repetition is such a situation if the stimuli are carefully chosen to strain the capacity of immediate memory. Repetition involves immediate memory, and it is well known that people can hold more material in immediate memory when they are able to structure it (Neisser, 1967; Savin 1968, Miller 1951). The experiment was conducted with three- and four-year-old children. The children repeated a variety of structures; some occurred in their natural speech and some did not.

We hoped to develop a profile of relative competence for the structures used; if successful, such profiles could be constructed for different developmental stages. A more general and more interesting goal was to discover what structural properties make sentences easy or difficult for three- to four-year-olds to repeat (and, presumably, to understand). Finally, we hoped to gain some insight, from the errors the children made, into the processes involved in their listening and structuring of language.

The situation in which a child repeats sentences after an experimenter is not, of course, a normal speech situation. Perhaps the most important difference is that there are no contextual cues in the experimental situation; the content of the stimulus sentences doesn't matter. (This may be one reason why the responses show as much attention to structure as they do.) However, to note that in normal situations context does matter does not invalidate experimental results. The point is that children *can* attend to particular structures, and perhaps a somewhat artificial situation is the best way to get them to do so.

Stimuli

The sentences that were presented varied in structure, and also in grammaticalness. The children heard grammatical and ungrammatical versions of each structural type. We expected the children to find it relatively difficult to repeat the ungrammatical sentences. We hoped that they would bring out some of the passive competence we were most interested in.

There were seven different structural types. They varied in transformational history, but none was maximally simple. Globally, the surface structures were the same; each had the surface form of a simplex with one complex area, that is, one in which one node or constituent had a somewhat complex internal structure.

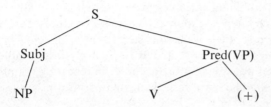

REPETITION EXPERIMENT STIMULI: STRUCTURAL TYPES

Adjective	They played with long yellow blocks.
Conjunction	Sam and Ronny built the sandbox.
Conjunction inversion	Not George but Danny came along.
Number	Two of the marbles rolled away.
Object complement	Mary wants to play the piano.
Relative clause	The lady who sneezes is sick.
Verb auxiliary	Daddy may have missed the train.

The adjectives occurred in all stimuli containing adjectival complexity. Adjective and conjunction complexity occurred in both subject and object noun phrases.

There were ungrammatical sentences of each structural type. These sentences had a grammatical error in the area of complexity. There were three types of errors:

Constant	Harry likes ride the horses.
Auxiliary	Harry wants to riding the horse.
Inflection	Two of the marble rolled away.

Length was held constant at six to eight syllables. We found in preliminary work that shorter sentences are usually repeated accurately by three and four year olds, and that longer sentences are usually repeated inaccurately. Simple familiar words were used in each sentence. The children heard several grammatical and ungrammatical instances of each structural type, but never the same sentence twice.

The subjects were 18 children, three to four years old, all from middle-class, professional families. We collected samples of natural speech for each child and, on the basis of samples, ranked the children according to verbal maturity. Median utterance length was again used as a measure. Although there were exceptions, generally the older children were more advanced in linguistic development. The children who ranked highest according to verbal maturity performed the best in the experiment, as one would expect—they repeated accurately most often, made few serious errors, and the like.

Results

Both of the experimental variables, structure and grammaticalness, significantly affected the children's responses. Certain structures were consistently easier for them to repeat; others were consistently more difficult. The two groups of structures were represented as A and B respectively in the table below. As expected, the children were much more accurate in repeating grammatical than ungrammatical stimuli. The main results, in summary form, are these:

REPETITION EXPERIMENT: RESPONSES[8]

	ACCURATE OR PERIPHERAL ERROR	SERIOUS ERROR	INADEQUATE RESPONSE
A Structures			
Grammatical stimuli	92%	5.4%	2.6%
Ungrammatical stimuli	60%	32%	8%
B Structures			
Grammatical stimuli	60%	26%	14%
Ungrammatical stimuli	33%	36%	31%

The responses were scored as accurate, inaccurate, or inadequate. Responses including less than 3 words of the stimulus, in proper order, were scored as inadequate, as were the occasional cases when the child refused to respond or asked the experimenter to repeat a sentence. Inaccurate responses were subdivided into groups containing serious and peripheral errors (such as a change of number from singular to plural, or a change of tense from past to present). For overall scoring, the peripheral errors were grouped with accurate responses; this grouping did not change the general pictures of the data.

The A and B structures emerged solely on the basis of the children's responses. They also differ on other grounds for these children; A structures occurred in our records of their spontaneous speech, and B structures did not.

[8] The experiment is reported in detail in C. Smith (1969), "A study of the syntactic knowledge of young children," ed. T. Bever and W. Weksel, *Studies in Psycholinguistics*, in press.

A STRUCTURES

Conjunction	(Sam and Harry built the house.)
Complement	(Susie likes to ride in the bus.)
Number	(Two of the marbles rolled away.)

B STRUCTURES

Adjective	(The little green frog jumped out.)
Relative	(The boy who was running fell down.)
Verbal Auxiliary	(Daddy may have missed the train.)
Conjunction Inversion	(Not Jane, but Mary, spilled the milk.)

Discussion

I will consider first the question of the children's ability to structure different types of sentences, or, in other words, which structures were within, and which beyond, their competence? The response to grammatical stimuli show that A structures were much easier for them to repeat than B structures; for an answer to the question of whether they knew more about the structures of A sentences, let us consider in some detail responses to ungrammatical stimuli.

The ungrammatical sentences were difficult for the children to repeat accurately, but they usually attempted to repeat them, and usually made mistakes in doing so. One type of mistake occurred with striking regularity—the children tended to respond to an ungrammatical sentence with a grammatical version of the same sentence. For instance:

(5) (Stimulus) Mine old green coat has holes.
     (Response) My old green coat has holes.

I will refer to responses of this kind as *normalizations*. They were frequent, especially with A stimuli. There was an interesting correlation between normalizations and accurate repetitions of grammatical stimuli: if a child tended to accurately repeat grammatical sentences (of a given structure), he tended to normalize ungrammatical sentences.

A normalization indicates that a child has recognized the structure of the stimulus sentence—that is, that he has successfully disentangled the structure from the error. Such responses indicate, at the least, that the children were organizing the stimuli as sentences, rather than as sequences of words. And the correlation between effect of grammaticalness and normalizations shows that the A sentences were easier for the children to recognize in ungrammatical form than were the B sentences.[9]

Since it was relatively easy for the children to repeat grammatical A

[9] The question of whether or not the children actually heard the grammatical errors may legitimately be raised—our data indicates that they did hear the errors.

sentences, we must ask what the extra burden on the faculties is, in an ungrammatical A sentence. The answer is obvious—the grammatical error. Consider the repetition of a sentence in terms of a scheme of the repetition process.

SCHEME FOR REPETITION PROCESS

Input → Storage → Output
(Identification)   (Reproduction)

In terms of this familiar scheme, repetition involves three stages. At each stage, an ungrammatical sentence presents more material than does a grammatical sentence. At the stage of identification, the child must disentangle the structure and the grammatical error—we can think of the error as a kind of footnote to the structure. He must store both structure and footnote, which is more cumbersome than the storage of structure alone; he must reproduce both, which must at the least involve an extra operation. And since the children respond with normalizations to A stimuli, we infer that the difficulty comes with storage, or production, rather than with identification.

The children's responses to ungrammatical stimuli suggest strongly, then, that they do impose structure on the A sentences, and that the structure does not differ from adult structure.

The B structures are more problematic and more interesting; recall that the A structures occur in the children's spontaneous speech, but the B structures do not. Since the responses to each type differ, the B structures must be considered separately. Of the four types, sentences with verbal auxiliaries were probably most beyond the competence of the children. They were rarely repeated accurately, when presented in grammatical form; they were rarely normalized or repeated accurately when presented in ungrammatical form. Notionally, of course, the verbal auxiliaries are complicated and relatively adult, so that this result is not surprising. A second type of B structure was sentences with two prenominal adjectives. The children's responses suggested that the density of the adjectives caused difficulty, but not the adjective structure (they frequently left out one of the two adjectives). We might say, then, that the adjective sentences were difficult for mechanical rather than grammatical reasons; the recursion overloaded the children's capacities in some way.

The other B structures, conjunction inversion and relative clauses, elicited uneven responses. There were accurate responses, but they did not occur with the frequency and regularity and normalizations of responses to A stimuli. Still, children certainly recognized the structures some of the time. Perhaps with these structures we have cases of sentences that the children understand but do not use—sentences that are within their competence, but not to be found in their natural speech. Relative clauses and conjunctions such as *not . . . but* occur rarely in the speech of three to four year olds. The children's responses indicate that they have some control of these structures, although not as much as they have in the A structures.[10]

A profile of relative competence for all seven sentence types would show three different levels of competence: group 1 structures the children know best, which elicit accurate repetitions of grammatical sentences and normalizations of ungrammatical sentences; group 2 structures the children know least, which elicit accurate repetitions of grammatical sentences and a few normalizations; and group 3 structures of which the children have uneven control, which sometimes elicit grammatical repetitions and sometimes elicit normalizations. Group 1 sentences occur in the children's natural speech; these are structures the children both comprehend and produce. The children neither comprehend nor produce group 2 sentences, we hypothesize, since they do not occur in natural speech and the repetition data does not indicate that the children know their structure. Group 3 sentences are within the competence of the children, according to the repetition data, even though the children do not produce them spontaneously. It is this last group, of course, that the analyst of children's speech has difficulty in discovering. With a suitable range of structural type as stimuli, one could use repetition to assemble quite complete profiles of linguistic competence for different stages of development.

I consider now the more general question of the linguistic input for our subjects. It seems likely that children have some kind of listening strategy that limits linguistic input; that they do not attempt to process or structure everything that they hear. The profile of linguistic competence gives some notion of which utterances the children were able to structure, of a variety addressed to them. To discover something of the strategy they used in listening, we shall look at what happened when the children did not correctly structure what they heard—that is, did not correctly repeat or normalize the stimulus sentences.

There was a tendency to simplify the complex area of a sentence, in responses which were neither accurate repetitions nor normalizations. If the children did not successfully identify a structure—grammatical or ungrammatical—they tended to ignore the complex aspects of the structure altogether in their responses. For example, a typical pair of complex stimulus and simplified response:

(6) (Stimulus)   The boy who was running fell down.
     (Response)   The boy fell down.

To discuss this matter further, it is necessary to explain the scoring of inaccurate responses (these contained at least three words of the stimulus sentence, in the order in which they occurred). Inaccurate responses that did not contain a peripheral error were scored as structure-preserving or structure violating; these categories pertained only to the complex part of the sentence.

---

[10] Slobin has pointed out that children sometimes utter sentences that they do not comprehend. The additions presumably are not understood with the familiar material, and may simply sound pleasantly adult.

In structure-preserving responses, the children usually omitted some material but retained some that was structurally important, such as:

(7) (Stimulus)   The old gray wolf chased rabbits.
     (Response)   The old wolf chased rabbits.
(8) (Stimulus)   The lady should have gone home.
     (Response)   The lady should gone home.
(9) (Stimulus)   The boy who was running fell down.
     (Response)   The boy running fell down.

Structure-violating responses indicated by omission that the children did not "understand" the stimulus sentence; that is, that they were unable to impose the correct adult structure on it. If a response simply omitted the complex part of a constituent, it was scored as structure-violating. For instance:

(10) (Stimulus)   The old gray wolf chased rabbits.
      (Response)   The old gray chased rabbits.
(11) (Stimulus)   The boy who was running fell down.
      (Response)   The boy who was fell down.

There are several interesting aspects to this classification. The first is that we were able to make it at all, that is, that children's responses fell only into these categories. Quite a different classification, including errors in various parts of the sentence, might have been required. But the errors were almost uniformly located in the complex parts of the sentence. The children did not leave out the complex constituent altogether, nor did they repeat the complex part of a sentence but omit the rest. They might also have made disorderly errors, garbling crucial words, for instance, but in fact they did not make such errors.

Structure-violating responses occurred almost entirely after B stimuli. (This is consonant with our finding that children may have difficulty reproducing ungrammatical A stimuli, but are able to identify them easily). Of the structure-violating responses, some *reduced* the stimulus to a simplex sentence (as in 10) and some *confused* the complex constituent of the stimulus (as in 11). There were twice as many reduced responses as confused responses.

The children tended to pick out simple structures from complex structures, then, when too complex a sentence was presented to them. We might say that they imposed their own structure on the sentence, that is, a structure that they know. As a result, part of the sentence is ignored. Two other examples of reduced responses may make the phenomenon clearer:

(12) (Stimulus)   Mommy could have lost her purse.
      (Response)   Mommy lost her purse.
(13) (Stimulus)   Not Jane, but Betty, called you.
      (Response)   Betty called you.

It seems likely that such responses are due to identification or decoding failures. The children structured only the simplest part of the sentences; they omitted the complex parts, perhaps not hearing them clearly. Generalizing, we can say that children tend to omit, or even not to hear, material that they cannot handle. This may sound rather mysterious; how can children know what material they will not be able to handle? It becomes less so when we realize that adjectives, relative clauses, verbal auxiliaries, and the like receive less stress than the head noun of a noun phrase or the main verb of a verb phrase. Intonation may provide cues to the important and familiar parts of sentences. In attending to these, the children may simply ignore the unfamiliar and more difficult parts.

The responses of these three and four year olds suggest that the listening of children may be selective; if children tend to notice what they do know, they may in consequence eliminate what they don't know. In the response experiment discussed earlier, we found also evidence of the selective listening of children.

The results we obtained in the repetition experiment indicate that the linguistic competence of three to four year olds is greater than their spontaneous speech indicates. The A stimuli exemplified structures that the children produce and understand; some of the B stimuli exemplified structures that the children probably understand, but do not produce. We inferred that the children had only a limited ability to handle sentences with relative clauses and with conjunction inversion. They were not always successful in repeating grammatical stimuli of these types; ungrammatical versions tended to elicit reductions rather than normalizations. The children apparently tended not to recognize these structures with the additional factor of the grammatical error to cope with.

I have pointed out that children frequently responded to B stimuli with reductions. In these responses the children may be said to have imposed a structure on what they heard; as McNeill (1966b) puts it, they seem to have been "looking for" simple structures (and finding them). In another vocabulary, the children decoded the stimuli according to their own ability to structure sentences.

I turn finally to the problem of characterizing the structures that were easy and difficult for the children to repeat. We seek a structural property that differentiates the two groups of structures; in other words, we would like to know whether the various easy structures were similar in some way, and the various difficult structures similar in some way. Knowledge of such a property might enable us to predict, on structural grounds, the order in which grammatical structures are acquired. Such knowledge might also help us to separate three factors in linguistic development that have so far been inextricably tangled; these factors I will call the mechanical, the grammatical, and the notional.[11] Let us consider briefly the different types of stimulus sentences.

The stimuli had similar surface structures, but they differed in deep structure and transformational history. There were two expanded simplex sentences; the other structures had two or three simplex sentences, and involved the application of different transformations. The sentences can be compared in

---

[11] It is appropriate to separate the grammatical and notional, at least tentatively, since a child may understand a notion but not understand a particular grammatical expression of that notion.

several ways according to the number of simplex sentences involved, the number of transformations required to generate them, or the type of transformation involved. I give below a classification made according to the number of simplex sentences in each structure.

One Expanded Simplex Sentence
    Number
    Verbal Auxiliary
Two Simplex Sentences
    Complement Embedding
    Relative Clause Embedding
    Conjunction
    Conjunction and Inversion
Three Simplex Sentences
    Adjective Embedding

As we expected, sentences with longer transformational histories were relatively difficult for the children to repeat. But this criterion of complexity does not explain any of our results. It does not explain, for instance, why sentences with relative clauses fell into one category (B stimuli) and sentences with complements fell into another (A stimuli); both are derived from two simplex sentences, and both involve embedding transformations.[12]

It is necessary to consider the surface structures of the stimulus sentences, to explain our results rather than their derivation. This is hardly surprising. The children's task was, in a sense, to impose a structure on the sentences they heard. In emphasizing surface structure, we suggest that sentences differ in how easy they are to hear; some sentences may be more transparent, more accessible to the imposition of structure, than others. Consider the surface structure properties of the relative clause sentences (difficult) and the object complement sentences, for instance. The relative classes were all interposed between the subject and main verb of the sentence, whereas the object complement followed the main verb and did not disrupt the main structural elements of the sentence. Such a difference might well make the latter type of sentence easier to repeat than the former. This example suggests location of complexity as a factor in surface structure; location may be important but was not in fact, the decisive factor in separating the easy and difficult in our data.

We differentiate between A and B surface structures in terms of a property I will call *compression*. Compression refers to the way semantic information occurs in a sentence. When sentences have low compression, semantic information is distributed fairly evenly through the sentence; when sentences have high compression, semantic information is bunched together, or compressed, at the noun-phrase or verb-phrase level. In terms of tree structure, highly compressed sentences have NP or VP nodes dominating several information-carrying ele-

---

[12] There are differences between the embedding transformations that produce relative clauses and object complements.

ments; in less compressed sentences, NP or VP nodes dominate relatively few information-carrying elements. For example, the sentence below has low compression. The information-carrying elements are underlined.

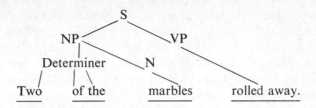

This sentence has high compression.

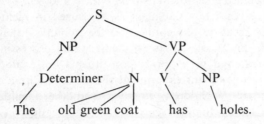

The A structures have relatively low compression, and the children found them easy to repeat. The B structures have relatively high compression, and the children found them difficult to repeat.

Latencies of the children's responses were measured (timed from the end of the stimulus to the beginning of the response). In general, responses to B stimuli took longer than responses to A stimuli. This was especially true for the younger children. Perhaps the children's faculties are overburdened if much information is compressed into a single noun phrase or verb.

The effect of compression suggests a hypothesis about children's acquisition of structure, namely, that degree of compression may be a factor in the order in which structures are acquired. Structures of relatively low compression may be learned earlier than structures of relatively high compression. In transformational terms, this would mean that transformations resulting in surface structures of high compression may be learned relatively late.

The effect of compression is confounded with other aspects of surface structure in the examples given here. Structure, location, length, and discontinuity (as in the relative clause of a subject noun phrase) undoubtedly interact with compression, and there may be additional factors as well. Compression appears to be dominant for the task of repetition but we are, after all, interested in repetition because of its relevance to understanding; perhaps under other circumstances the factor of compression would be less important. If the notion of compression is to have more than a rough usefulness, the different factors of surface structure must be carefully identified and disentangled. The notion of compression has certain problems of categorization that must be solved; it is easy to compute compression for some sentences, but problematic for others. Roughly, the categorization problems resolve to this: we do not know whether all words of English fit neatly into two categories, those of high or low information carriers (content and function words, in the traditional formulation); nor do we know whether various combinations of words are equivalent in compression (for instance, do two low-information words have the same compression as one high-information word?). These are rather clear problems that will, I hope, be investigated in the near future. With this caveat, I would like now to discuss some implications of the notions of compression.

Our subjects' ability to deal with sentences was affected by how compressed the sentences were—that is, by the amount of semantic information in the noun phrase and verb phrase constituents. *Noun phrase* and *verb phrase* are abstractions that partly explain how language is organized in memory and understanding. We may recall in this connection the "chunks" that George Miller (1956) discusses in his classic paper on memory and processing limitations in adults. Noun phrase and verb phrase constituents are analogous to Miller's chunks, and the results of our experiment show that children can handle only chunks of limited size. As children's linguistic and other faculties develop, they are able to handle larger chunks—sentences with higher degrees of compression.

Limitations on the memory and processing abilities of children account for the bound of compression, apparently; therefore, we may call it a mechanical constraint rather than a grammatical or notional one (although further investigation may show interaction between grammatical structure and compression). Extralinguistic constraints such as this are often referred to in the literature on language acquisition. But usually discussion of their specific nature is inextricably linked to a particular account of understanding, namely, a close generative model. Thus it has been suggested that children are able to perform only a limited number of transformational operations and, therefore, are unable to handle sentences that have complex derivations. Assumed is the doubtful explanation that people generate sentences much as a grammar does. Unless we accept this doubtful viewpoint, the discussion of specific constraints on numbers of transformational operations has no value.

We need not commit ourselves to a particular account of understanding before we study it. Our finding of the importance of compression shows, for instance, that certain extralinguistic constraints may be isolated more or less independently of such matters. On the other hand, we expect that the discovery of such constraints may affect the focus of studies of understanding. In the present experiment it is noteworthy that compression is a property of surface structure, not of deep structure or derivational complexity.

Mechanical constraints may limit a child's linguistic competence in more than one way. Notional, grammatical and mechanical faculties do not necessarily develop at the same rate; although a child may understand a particular notion, and its expression, extralinguistic factors may prevent him from using it linguistically.[13] I do not mean that only extralinguistic factors, such as memory constraints, keep children from talking with full adult competence. But it does seem possible that in some circumstances mechanical constraints may keep a child from using his full linguistic capabilities. For instance, certain structures may be relatively inaccessible for mechanical reasons; a child may not understand an expression in a highly compressed sentence that he would understand if it were presented in a sentence with less compression. This suggests another reason for disentangling mechanical from other factors, insofar as possible; otherwise, we may systematically mistake a child's linguistic capabilities.

Children may be able to handle grammatical expressions thought to be beyond them—if they are broken into small units that the children can process. Consider, for instance, the passive. Brown has demonstrated that young children do not "understand" passive sentences, that is, they do not correctly identify actor and acted-upon. But this is odd, for it seems likely that children understand the *notion* expressed by the passive. For instance, we would expect them to understand a passive with deleted agent such as *Mary was hurt*. It would be interesting to repeat Brown's experiment, presenting children with two sentences and then asking them to identify the actor and acted-upon. Suppose, for instance, stimuli such as this was presented: *Mary was hurt*; *Mary was hurt by the boy*; or *Mary was hurt and she was hurt by the boy*. Perhaps the simple structure of the first sentence, and the separated words in the second, would allow enough mental time for a young child to process all the material. It seems likely that children fail to comprehend passive sentences because they are too compressed, and not because of notional gaps or ignorance of linguistic signals.

CONCLUSION

Surface structure was the most important factor determining whether a sentence was easy for the children to repeat accurately, and, we assume, to understand. This perhaps unexpected result suggests a general point—that surface structure deserves more attention than it has heretofore received, both in speculative and experimental approaches to the problem of understanding. It is often noticed that certain recursions (self-embedding, for instance) are difficult to understand because they make stringent demands on immediate memory. But other aspects of surface structure that are more subtle or difficult to isolate have been little studied. An important first step will be to clarify somewhat the relation between linguistic and extralinguistic factors in surface structure. This would make it possible to investigate notional and linguistic development on the one hand, and the development of the memory and computation abilities that I have called "mechanical" on the other.[14]

[13] McNeill apparently has a similar idea in mind when he refers to children's knowledge of basic grammatical relations before they can indicate that they have this knowledge.
[14] It seems unlikely that these factors can be entirely separated.

There are probably two senses in which the importance of surface structure has been underestimated. First, as I have argued above, mechanical factors may make certain sentences more or less accessible to analysis and understanding. But second, surface structure, rather than derivation, may be the vehicle for understanding. In terms of generative grammar, what I am saying is that the structures that result from the applications of grammatical rules may be the proper focus of study: the question for psycholinguistics is, how do people impose an interpretation on surface structure? It is relevant here to recall an insight of Zellig Harris (1964). Harris has pointed out that most English sentences, however complex in their derivation and internal structure, have the global structure of simplex sentences. Harris was not concerned with a psycholinguistic account of understanding; but I suggest, as an extrapolation, that global structure may be of primary importance for understanding.

One might speculate that, to understand a sentence, a person must know its global structure. There are other rearrangement transformations, besides the notorious passive, that do not result in the typical global structure of English. Perhaps it is necessary, for understanding, to recover a certain global structure for sentences such as these: *It surprised me that he came, It was a book that John lost,* and *Modern music he does not like.*

I do not propose that we abandon entirely the notion that, in understanding, people recover underlying sentences; but it might be fruitful to consider how much recovery is necessary, rather than how much recovery is possible.

In this presentation and discussion of two experiments I have tried to suggest an approach to some important problems in the field of language acquisition and of psycholinguistics in general. Experimental studies of linguistic behavior, in which utterances can be systematically varied, are required for serious study of linguistic competence. Also required, I think, is a conscious attempt to keep separate grammatical and psychological explanations of linguistic behavior. The structural descriptions of generative grammar may represent what people know about sentences, rather than what they do in understanding and producing them.

REFERENCES

Brown, R., and U. Bellugi, Three processes in the child's acquisition of syntax. In E. Lenneberg (ed.), *New directions in the study of language.* Cambridge, Mass.: M.I.T. Press, 1964.

Brown, R., and C. Fraser, The acquisition of syntax. In U. Bellugi and R. Brown (eds.), The acquisition of language. *Monogr. Soc. Res. Child Developm.,* 1964, **29**, (1).

Chomsky, N., *Aspects of the theory of syntax.* Cambridge, Mass.: M.I.T. Press, 1965.

Ervin, S., Imitation and structural change in children's language. In E. Lenneberg (ed.), *New directions in the study of language.* Cambridge, Mass.: M.I.T. Press, 1964. [Reprinted in this volume.]

Fodor, J., and T. Bever, The psychological reality of linguistic segments. *J. verb. Learn. verb. Behav.*, 1965, **4**, 414–421.

Fodor, J., and M. Garrett, Some reflections on competence and performance. In J. Lyons and R. J. Wales (eds.), *Psycholinguistics papers.* Edinburgh: University of Edinburgh Press, 1966.

Halle, M., and K. N. Stevens, Speech recognition: A model and a program for research. In J. A. Fodor and J. J. Katz (eds.), *The structure of language.* Englewood Cliffs, N.J.,: Prentice-Hall, 1964.

Harris, Z., Co-occurrence and transformation in linguistic structure. In J. A. Fodor and J. J. Katz (eds.), *The structure of language.* Englewood Cliffs, N.J.: Prentice-Hall, 1964.

Lakoff, G., Deep and surface grammar. Unpublished paper, 1966.

McCawley, J., The annotated respective. Unpublished paper, 1968.

McNeill, D., Developmental psycholinguistics. In F. Smith and G. A. Miller (eds.), *The genesis of language.* Cambridge, Mass.: M.I.T. Press, 1966. (a)

McNeill, D., The creation of language. In J. Lyons and R. J. Wales (eds.), *Psycholinguistics papers.* Edinburgh: University of Edinburgh Press, 1966. (b)

Matthews, G. H., Analysis by synthesis of natural languages. *Proceedings of the International Congress on Machine Translation and Applied Language Analysis.* London: H.M.S.O., 1962.

Miller, G. A., The magical number seven, plus or minus two. *Psychol. Rev.*, 1956, **63**, 81–97.

Miller, G. A., and S. Isard, Some perceptual consequences of linguistic rules. *J. verb. Learn. verb. Behav.*, 1963, **2**, 217–228.

Miller, G. A., and J. Selfridge, Verbal context and the recall of meaningful material. *Amer. J. Psychol.*, 1951, **63**, 176–185.

Neisser, U., *Cognitive psychology.* New York: Appleton-Century-Crofts, 1967.

Ross, J., Auxiliaries as main verbs. Unpublished paper, 1967.

Sapir, E., The psychological reality of the phoneme. In D. Mandelbaum (ed.), *Selected writings of Edward Sapir.* Berkeley/Los Angeles: University of California Press, 1949.

Savin, H., and E. Perchonock, Grammatical structure and the immediate recall of English sentences. *J. verb. Learn. verb. Behav.*, 1965, **4**, 348–353.

Shipley, E., C. S. Smith, and L. Gleitman, A study in the acquisition of language: Free responses to commands. *Language*, 1969, **45**, 322–342.

Slobin, D. I., Recall of full and truncated passive sentences in connected discourse. *J. verb. Learn. verb. Behav.*, 1968, **7**, 876–881.

Smith, C. S., A study of the syntactic knowledge of young children. In T. G. Bever and W. Weksel (eds.), *The structure and psychology of language.* New York: Holt, Rinehart and Winston, in press.

Thorne, J., On hearing sentences. In J. Lyons and R. J. Wales (eds.), *Psycholinguistic papers.* Edinburgh: Edinburgh University Press, 1966.

Vygotsky, L. S., *Thought and language.* Cambridge, Mass.: M.I.T. Press. 1962.

FRENCH •

First Stages of Sentence Formation in Children's Speech

—— *Paul Guillaume*

The history of different languages shows not only that words change their meanings but also that new grammatical devices evolve; this suggests that we could go back to a primitive state prior to grammar. In fact, though, a complete lack of morphological differentiation does not occur. When we see a new expression appear to fill a particular function, it is always at the expense of terms differentiated in another way. The language often contains an expression for that function already, so the new one supplants the old.

The facts that we cannot examine in the history of languages are available to us in the child. It is true that imitation of a language already formed is the principle of acquisition, but such assimilation cannot be entirely passive; it probably goes through a number of stages essential to the acquistion of any complex language. The same psychological mechanisms (for instance, the one which underlies analogical formations) probably play a part in languages being maintained and in their being acquired by individuals. Lastly, the problem of the development of the child's language is interesting in its own right, independently of any conclusions that could be drawn from primitive languages.

The procedure for this study is as objective as possible. It is a question of finding objective criteria for stages of language development, based both on understanding of the speech of others and on the child's spontaneous speech.

Comprehension will be defined by the child's reactions. Language is essentially a means for one man to act upon another; every expression has an imperative value; it is an invitation to react, to pay attention, or to recognize. Later on, when the aptitude for dialogue develops, it constitutes an invitation to respond with speech to the enquiries of the interlocutor. In assessing the replies, actions, or further speech, one has to take account of the material meaning of the words and of their functions (word order, inflections, particular grammatical devices). Difficulties arise from the inseparable nature of the form and content. The grammatical tools are bound to the meaningful words, and the sentence heard is part of an intuitive situation, so much so that the whole may accidentally provoke correct replies, without each speech element having been understood in its own particular function. The points when the response is correct where the situation and the meaningful words alone are not adequate to prompt a correct

Les débuts de la phrase dans le langage de l'enfant. *Journal de Psychologie*, 1927, **24**, 1–25. Translated from French by Eve V. Clark and reprinted by permission of Presses Universitaires de France.

response, and when new combinations of familiar words, conforming to the linguistic rules, are immediately given an interpretation, have to be noted.

One cannot extrapolate directly from language that is understood to spoken language. In order to explain the child's speech, it is not enough to allow for reversible associations which would be established between "ideas" and "words." The two functions are never that closely linked. The latter (words) lag behind the former. Those who more or less know a foreign language or dialect can often understand it but not speak it; one's native speech, likewise, in vocabulary and form, shows differences between speaking and understanding. This is because speech proceeds directly from imitation, while everything that is understood is not necessarily imitated. Speech is not only an invitation to act or to perceive; it also, under certain circumstances, invites repetition. The child repeats the word at the same time as he performs the action; the word is associated with games accompanied by words. The moment at which utterances become independent of the external verbal model must be examined, not only because the utterance has been directly inspired by the situation but rather because the child has become capable of constructing a whole new utterance with familiar words according to the rules of the language.

Such distinctions are sometimes very minute; however, continuous observation of a few children who can be followed for several years and whose progress can be noted continually provides a certain safeguard. It is this method that we have followed, and supplemented, in some instances, by notes taken of the conversations of children between two and five years old in a kindergarten.

WORDS IN THE SPOKEN LANGUAGE AND IN THE WRITTEN LANGUAGE

It is a commonplace, nowadays, to say that in the child's speech the sentence—understood or uttered—is anterior to the words, or rather that there are neither real words nor real sentences. Later, an "awareness of words" will develop. But when? Certain facts lead us to believe that this occurs at a very late stage and does not appear until the start of scholastic education. Therein lies a misunderstanding about language which must first be cleared up.

The writing of half-literate people does not, it is said, show any awareness of individual words. I have collected a small set of letters documenting this. The letters represent different levels of education in the writers. In the letters there are three types of alterations made, all arising from the same cause: *segmentation*, *liaisons*, and *confusions of homonyms*.

In the liaisons, several words are treated as a single one: *aidi* (ai dit — I have said), *esque* (est-ce que = is it . . .), *cecerai* (ce serait = that would be), *semy* (s'est mis = placed himself), *set* (c'est = it is). In the segmentations, one word is split up: *a bitant* (habitant = inhabitant), *trou vais* (trouvais = found, 1 sg.), *tom bra* (tombera = will fall, 3 sg.), *a ses* (assez = enough), *sin cerre* (sincère = sincere), *en core* (encore = more, again), and so on. Sometimes the two occur together: *ja prend* (j'apprends = I am learning), *dé colle* (d'école = of school), and so on.

Liaisons and segmentations do not occur randomly; they often tend to wrongly isolate familiar words,[1] and above all, those words for which the writer knows the *graphic form*. He will write *sans* (= without, for *s'en* = of it, them), *sais* (= know, 1 sg., for *c'est* = it is), *long* (= long, for l'on = impersonal 3 per. pronoun). Segmentation lends itself better to these false perceptions; at least one of the isolated members is a small familiar word, article, pronoun, preposition, and so on. Examples: *de mande* (demande = ask, 3 sg.), *par le* (parle = speak, 3 sg.), *au temp* (autant = as much), *vous loire* (vouloir = to want), *et tant* (étant = being), *pret sans* (présent = present), *a vons* (avons = have, 1 pl.), *sous mis* (soumis = submitted, past part.). No doubt the preposition *sous* (= under) explains *sous mis*; the pronoun *vous* (= you) appears in *vous loire*; the adjective *pret* (= ready) provides the *t* of *pret sans*; the *p* of *au temp* (see above) comes from the word *temps* (= time, weather). If there is any doubt about the role of graphic memory in the segmentation of the sentence, we need only consider the very numerous examples in which letters or groups of letters visibly representing our pronouns, articles, or elided conjunctions are carefully separated from the rest of the word by an apostrophe. Note that such elements are seen as individual segments only in the written, not the spoken, forms. For example: *l'es* (les = pl. def. art.), *l'eur* (leur = their), *l'ettre* (lettre = letter), *qu'and* (quand = when), *auqu'un* (aucun = anyone), *qu'ar* (car = for), *l'orsque* (lorsque = since), *d'ont* (dont = whose), *d'éjà* (déjà = already), *m'a* (ma = my, fem. sg.), *c'est* (cette = this, fem. sg.), and so on.

This tendency is further demonstrated in the confusion of homonyms which is frequent even in the writing of those who do not use incorrect liaisons and segmentations. In the examples below, it can be seen that the word substituted retains its spelling; but one may write indifferently *ses* (= his), *ces* (= those), *est* (= is), *et* (= and); *non* (= no), *nom* (= name); *étais* (= was, 1 sg.), *été* (= been, past part., or = summer); *voie* (= way), *voix* (= voice); *prix* (= prize), *pris* (= taken, past, part., or prie = pray), *vent* (= wind), *vend* (= sell); *vie* (= life), *vit* (= saw, 3 sg.); *mes* (= my, pl.), *mais* (= but); *peu* (= little), *peut* (= can, 3 sg.); *ci* (= here), *si* (= if); *maire* (= mayor), *mère* (= mother); *paire* (= pair), *père* (= father); *crin* (= hair), *craint* (= fear, 3 sg.); *dont* (= whose), *donc* (= therefore), and so on.

In interpreting such facts as these, we must keep in mind that the people who write so badly do, however, speak their language fluently; their speech is not a simple mosaic of ready-made utterances applicable to each situation; they know how to *construct* sentences according to the rules of the language with the vocabulary at their disposal. The very way in which words are combined bears

---

[1] See A. Lalande, La conscience des mots dans le langage, *Journal de Psychologie*, 1905 (January issue).

witness, in a sense, to their individuality and their differentiation. No one supposes that the person who writes *l'ettre* (for *lettre*) cannot say: *J'ai écrit une lettre* (= I have written a letter), *des lettres* (= some letters), *j'ai envoyé ma lettre* (= I have sent my letter), *j'ai reçu votre lettre* (= I got your letter); *lettre* behaves as a single indivisible word in the spoken language (jusr like *car*, *déjà*, and so on; see above). If someone writes *sans* instead of *s'en*, that does not prevent him from saying *Je m'en vais* (= I am going away), *tu t'en vas* (= you are going away), *il s'en va* (= he is going away), and so on. Despite the arbitrary graphic liaisons and segmentations, the spoken sentence obeys rules which provide it with well-defined points of articulation. The utterance is constructed from real elements which the speaker knows how to manipulate. Thus the grammatical differentiation of words does exist in a way in the spoken language even though the graphic forms of a substantive may be confused with those of a verb, that of a possessive pronoun with that of a demonstrative pronoun, that of a participle with that of an infinitive, and so on. The man who writes (without distinguishing them): *Il faut les donner* (infinitive) or *les donnais* (1 sg. imperfect) will say, correctly, *Il faut finir, il faut rendre* (infinitives); wherever the forms are differentiated by the sound, he knows perfectly well how to use the one and the other in any sentence construction.

The expression "awareness of words," therefore, has no exact descriptive value and can only give rise to misunderstandings. The individuality and differentiation of words depend on different layers of habits, and these terms take on a new meaning on each new occasion when one goes from the spoken to the written language, and from the latter to a logical and explicit grammatical analysis. In the educated adult, these functions have become closely welded; he passes easily from the one to the other. The written form becomes symbolic of the whole; however, it is superimposed fairly arbitrarily on the spoken form. It may be surprising that the graphic division of the sentence into words does not result from a simple graphic transposition of the words from the spoken sentence, the one being molded on the other or deduced from the other. But there is no perfect correspondence between the two systems of articulations in all their details (for example, the inflections of words could logically be separated from the stem). In fact, we have seen that the graphic segmentation above all reveals the influence of the written model rather than directly reflecting the organization imminent in discourse.

THE SENTENCE UNDERSTOOD, BUT UNDIFFERENTIATED

In order to give an account of the origin of the organization of discourse, we have to return to the first two years of childhood. Here we have a child of eight or nine months who already understands a series of sentences that signal familiar games: *Bats la mauvaise tête!* (= smack naughty head), to tap oneself on the head; *Envoie un baiser* (= blow a kiss), *Fais ami! ami!* (= make friends), to shake hands; *Danse l'espagnole! Danse la française!* (= dance the Spanish way! dance the French way!), indicating two poses with different hand positions; *Fais blablab* (= do blab), to make one's lips vibrate against a finger; and so on. Perhaps it is the general form of the intonation pattern that is known rather than its elements. However, one could believe that all the sounds do not have the same value, that certain words stand out, that others are only subsidiary filling, embellishments, passing comments. One is never obliged to speak to a child with rigorously uniform and concise utterances. He hears variants, but also essential words bearing stress which are sometimes repeated. This does not hamper the child much, for he also begins to recognize the same sentences spoken by other people despite differences of voice pitch. It is quite possible, then, that certain words acquire a precocious individuality.

On the other hand, it is impossible to class these words into grammatical categories. This seems to be true even of the names of people (papa, mama, Marie, Suzanne). They are named at the time of certain actions; the names are imperatives, signals; one has to turn toward that person, look at him, smile at him, blow him a kiss, lean over to be picked up in his arms. There is no need to separate the name of the person and that of the action in this signal of complex experiences. The same goes for the personal name of the child. To ask at what point a child understands his name is to ask a strange question: one would have to describe in detail the succession of reactions which the name evokes. First, it is a commonplace summons: it is the attitude, the look of whoever says it that makes the child feel that it has something to do with him. It is a synonym of words like: *Attention!* (= here!), *Regarde par ici!* (= look over here!). It is the signal for interesting experiences, for an action in which he is to participate. It is an interjection, and imperative, as well as a name. The same reflections apply to the names of things: the attributes of the objects are inseparable from the actions related to them which make them interesting.

What characterizes the period of the first sentences that are understood is the sporadic success of tests. If I say to P. (12.8),[2] "Donne à papa" (= give to papa), referring to a candy he has in his hand, he gives it to me. If I say to him, "Donne à maman" (= give to mama), he gives it to me again. I repeat my order. He puts it in his mouth. Thus there is nondifferentiation of or lack of attention to the special form of the utterance, a habit of guessing on the basis of the whole situation rather than according to an exact, analytic perception of the content of the sentence. The child replies randomly to every sort of question (Qui? = who, Quoi? = what, Comment? = how). He counts more on intuition than on language to make distinctions. He must be compared to the child who begins to read and continually tries to guess instead of carefully sounding out the word. When there are several ways of understanding something, there is always a special laziness over the least familiar method. There is no doubt that at this stage, the least familiar thing is language. Even a correct understanding reveals

---

[2] The first number refers to the months, the second to the days of the child's age.

more about the relations between each word and the intuitive situation than about the structure of the sentence. From 9.17 on, P. seemed to understand sentences like "Calinette à papa! Calinette à maman!" (= give papa a kiss, give mama a kiss): he put his hand on the cheek of the person named even if the latter made no gesture; but the sentence had to be repeated emphatically. The first time he was ready to perform, but hesitated over the person: it was at this point that I repeated "À maman! À maman!" (= to mama, to mama). This utterance was juxtaposed in some way to the first one rather than subordinated to it. The second part is interpreted by its occurrence in the concrete situation created by the first, and not by its function as a member of the sentence. According to a linguist who has thoroughly studied the origins of the sentence.[3] the words here are *predicates of the situation*; in reality, there are as many meaningful sentences as there are words. If the whole has a psychological unity, since it is a question of aspects of the same action, that unity is not yet that of a grammatical organism obeying the rules of a particular language; the whole has no more the structure of a French sentence than of a foreign sentence, of a sabir or of a creole, of a telegram or of an announcement. Even these comparisons are inadequate, because, for us, words are still separated into parts of speech; they appear as members of possible sentences; they are called complements not only because of their material meaning but because of their ever-present formal value.

THE UNDIFFERENTIATED WORD SENTENCE

Spoken language confirms the absence of differentiation between words. We know that the child's imitation is a simplification. The same reasons that reduce a word to one syllable and even to one vowel underlie the condensation of our sentences to one word in the child (the easiest one to pronounce, the best known, the one that is stressed). A bit later on, the child adds to his utterances those sounds which correspond to the subordinate words. The progress which replaces *A plus* (= no more) with *Je n'en ai plus* (= I haven't any more) is of the same order as that which transforms *colat* into *chocolat* (= chocolate), and *ti* into *parti* (= gone). But alongside the phonetic aspect, there is both a semantic and a grammatical aspect: these are what we are interested in.

The first words are used in a variety of contexts which makes their definition difficult. *Papa* (P. at 12 months) is said in the presence of an object belonging to me, when the child picks up some paper, a card, my pen, when he goes into my empty study, when he wants to write, to come close to me, to see me, when he recognizes me after an absence. He says *Maman* when he wants to suckle, to be picked up in someone's arms (even when addressing me), to attract the attention of his mother to an object he is displaying or to his physiological needs. *Nénin* is used to ask for the breast, but also to ask for a cookie. If one wanted to

[3] Wegener, *Grundfragen des Sprachlebens*, 1885.

interpret this as a kind of verb meaning *À manger* (= to eat), it would be difficult to explain his saying it when pointing to the red button of a garment, the point of a bare elbow, an eye in a portrait, the face of his mother in a photograph. *Tata* is said when he wants to sit on the pot or urinate, or when he has done so; when he sees a stain on the tablecloth, on an apron; when he puts a pencil, a copper ball, a piece of fruit, or a potato into his mouth; when he sees the dish-water, coffee grounds, someone he dislikes. *Blablab* means the action of vibrating one's lips against a finger, then the mouth, especially that of a child in a portrait, then every portrait, every drawing, the picture postcards that I sent when I was away, every manuscript or printed page, a paper or a book, but then it means the act of "reading" or the wish to read: almost all these meanings co-existed at age 11.15. For the same period, here is a list of words used in isolation; I have indicated the probable meanings, according to the context of use: these demonstrate the equivocal nature of the word, its fluctuations between a nominal and a verbal meaning. Almost all the words are related to familiar games: *Bo* (= brush or = to brush), *Ba* (= broom or = to sweep), *Pain* (= give bread or = eat bread,) *Bain* (= bath or to bathe), *Ke* (= key or = put the key in or take it out of the lock), *Papou* (= soup, = good soup, or = eat soup), *Papo* (= hat or = put on a hat), *Tit-tat* (= tic-toc, = watch, or = listen to a watch close to one's ear), *Mba* (= kiss), *Ba* (= box or = play with a box). One no more finds real adjectives than one does real substantives or verbs. The child repeats after us *Bon! Beau!* (= good! = pretty!) and ends up by saying them in the same situations. At first, these were exhortations or encouragements: "It's good" to make him eat up his soup; "It's pretty" to call his attention to something, and so on. *Bon* (= good) therefore also means *Eat!* or *the soup*. This is very true, for when he began spontaneously combining words much later he would ask for more soup, saying *Encore bon!* (= more good) and would refuse more saying: *Pas encore bon!* (= no more good).

We know that, according to Stern,[4] the development of the vocabulary has three stages: substance, action, quality or relation, in the sense that each phase sees a preponderant development of one category of words: substantives, verbs, adjectives, and prepositions. Thus, in the second phase, in one of the children studied by Stern, the number of verbs went from 4 to 21, while that of the nouns went from 23 to 73: the first class grows more quickly than the second. But what is the principle of the division into categories? Notice, first of all, that there is a residual category, that of the interjection, which, at the same time, grows from 17 to 28 words. Moreover, one glance at the contents of the groups shows that it is not a question of the categories to which the models imitated by the child would belong in our grammar. It is rather the value that the words take on in the child's language at that period. But the principle is a fine-drawn one and somewhat arbitrary in its application. Thus, for example: *ände* (Hände = hands) placed with the substantives, seemed only to be used at that period in relation to

[4] C. Stern and W. Stern, *Die Kindersprache*, 1907.

an action (being taken into one's arms). The distinction between interjections and verbs is undefinable: if *ei-schei* (ein, zwei = one, two, meaning "run") and *pieke-pieke* (a game) are verbs, why are *baba* (= to go for a walk), *Kikä* (= hide-and-seek), *tsch-tsch* (another game), *op! op!* (playing with a ball), *ei-ei* (game with a doll), *bitte bitte* (= please, please, to ask for something), *alle!* (= gone, finished) all interjections? From one count to another, interjections go into the category of verbs because their form rather than their meaning has changed, and the impression that one is left with of a rapid increase in the number of verbs is rather artificial. Stern himself noticed that the first meanings "show fluctuations which seem to defy all attempts at classification into ordinary categories" [p. 164]. He also says, "The distinction made above between interjections and substantives is only valid as far as external consideration of the grammatical form goes; from the psychological point of view, the separation has no basis. The verbal units of the child do not belong to any word class because they are not words but sentences." What then is external consideration of the grammatical form if not a consideration—a premature one—of what these words become later on? Grammatical categories cannot be defined save by functional facts; the relation between the word and the concrete situations, and the other words of the sentence. The examination of a child's vocabulary or of a collection of isolated word sentences never allows one to make these distinctions.

PSUEDOSENTENCES

When does the time come to begin calling a series of words uttered by the child a sentence? Two sets of facts have to be distinguished here: on the one hand, direct reproductions of ready-made sentences which cannot possibly be personal combinations of truly independent words: for example, *A pu* (il n'y en a plus = there isn't any more). *A bu* (ça brule = that's burning), *A peur* (j'ai peur = I'm frightened), *A ba* (a boire = to drink), *Ta y est* (ça y est = there you are), *Ptite pepée* (petite poupée = tiny dolly), *Donne à main* (donne la main = give [me] your hand), and so on; on the other hand, personal formations consisting of several word-sentences juxtaposed, the whole presenting no grammatical unity.

In practice, the two cases are fairly easy to distinguish; in the first, the intonation pattern is unbroken; in the second, the words are separated by pauses, and each word is stressed separately (we will separate the different elements by dashes corresponding to the naturally discontinuous nature of the utterance). Here are some examples of the second case. We suggested to the child that he feed from someone else; he replies *Apu-Maman!* (non, c'est maman que je veux = no, I want mama) (12.19). He insists on being allowed to suckle, then suddenly remembers that I oppose it (he was about to be weaned): *Nenin! Nenin! Papa?* (15.8). Seeing a baby cry, he asks for it to be given something to drink: *Nini peur bobo nénin* (regarde ce bébé! Il pleure! Il a mal! Il faut lui donner a boire = Look at the baby. He's crying. He's hurt. Give him something to drink) (17 months). Frightened when he sees that a gun is going to be fired, he says: *A peur A peur A pu Bobo* (J'ai peur, ne tire pas, ça fait mal = I'm frightened, don't fire, it hurts.) (15.8). Having had a fight with a little girl, he tells us: *A mord A peur Bobo Annette* (je l'ai mordue elle pleure, elle a mal, Jeannette = I bit her, she's crying, it's sore, Jeannette) (16.28).

Each vocal gesture spills out spontaneously from successive adaptations to a complex situation: let us not forget that it is always a question of mental interaction, whether the child wants to make the people around him intervene, interest them in what he feels, or whether they are seeking his confessions, his judgments, his explanations. Besides, each word is merely the incomplete echo of a sentence suggested to the child on another occasion in a similar situation. These groups of words must also be "translated" as a series of sentences. There is a rapprochement between the way the child expresses himself and the spontaneously used procedure to make him understand a sentence by breaking it up and by repeating it. Just as the child understands our sentences as a series of juxtaposed predicates of the concrete situation, so he speaks using word sentences which are directly linked to aspects of the situation. However, it is still too soon to look for grammatical links.

Lacking a grammar, do these series possess any syntax? Does the order of elements obey any rule? If there is one, it is quickly effaced by the extensive influence of imitation. But the problem is not very different from that of the syntax of groups formed by juxtaposition, no longer word sentences, but true short sentences. We can study it in either type of example. Theoretically, the order of the terms reflects the train of thought; it goes from the interesting, essential point to the secondary aspects. After the first word, the following ones emphasize, specify, explain, reply to unspoken questions. From this come the antitheses like the one in the example above (*A pu maman!* = no mama), or in the juxtaposition of three real sentences: *Nenin caca! Maman nenin! Papa bobo!* (je ne veux plus de ce sein—je veux celui de maman—mais papa gronderait = I don't want any more of this breast—I want mama's—but papa will complain) (15.24). The first part is a reaction to the suggestion made to him, the second indicates his personal wish, and then the thought of the consequence strikes him. Sometimes his thought leads from facts observed to a practical attitude, as when he threatens the doctor whom he blames for his mother's illness (20.4): *Docteur misère à maman caillou! baton!* (= Doctor—hurt mama—stone!—stick!). As in such sequences as: *Sou—sière* (sou—epicière = penny—grocer, that is, give me a penny so I can go to the store) (16.28); the second word is in apposition, explaining the main word. The same word may occur in different positions, with different nuances of meaning: *Net—cop—Nini* (une amande—coupe-la—pour moi = an almond—cut it—for *me*) (18.2). *Nini—verre—à boire* (pour moi aussi! —dans un verre, comme les grandes personnes—à boire = for me too!—in a glass like the grown-ups—drink). In a story, the order of thought may be that of the events themselves, but it can also be the result of going from an interesting effect back to the cause. He tells of a small punishment: *Tape—bobo* (= smack —naughty) (13.27). On another occasion, he tells of falling down, saying, *Bobo—tête—coup* (= sore—head—hit) (18.18). In the first instance, it was a question of remembering something; in the second, it was a recent occurrence— he still feels the pain, while the accident itself is secondary. It is curious to see how the child interprets a complicated order that he is told to pass on: "Va dire à papa de venir chasser les mouches pour que tu puisses dormir, quand tu auras mangé à ta soupe" (= go tell papa to come and get rid of the flies so that you can sleep when you have finished your soup). The child translates: *Papa!— Soupe—Peït* [his name]—*Némir—Tape—Moute* (= papa—soup—Peït—sleep— smack—fly) (18.27). Sometimes he retains the order of the events, sometimes he goes from the result to the cause. The child would never spontaneously try to express such a complicated sequence; however, he could produce a long chain of actions, each one being the cause of the next, if he had some personal aim. Thus L. (14.15) coming to look for her mother: (*Maman, ici* (= mama, here. She pulls her over to an armchair), *Assis!* (assieds-toi = sit down), *Oper* (= pick me up), *Dédé* (= I want to sit in your lap), *À teter* (= let me suck). Each word is separated from the one following it by the action required of her mother. Concrete thought is foresighted and must go from the result to the means of achieving it in order to produce the actions in the desired order. Language, though, is still only a series of isolated reactions to aspects of the situation, insofar as the latter is changed by the performance of the actions. While concrete thought anticipates the future and can organize it, language remains a function of the present. There are no sentences, but an inorganic series of predicates of the situation.

THE FIRST SENTENCES—PEOPLE'S NAMES

Let us look for them first in comprehension of speech. At the beginning of his second year, the child appears to understand sentences like: "Brush papa . . ., mama . . ., Marie, . . ., your little brother (a doll)." A familiar game consisted of doing *coui-coui* (pinching one's nose), *dida-dida* (pulling one's ear), *bla-blab* (vibration produced by intermittently opening and shutting one's mouth with one's hand), and so on. These words are associated with the name of someone present (Do coui-coui to papa, to Mr. L., and so on), and the child plays the game. He adapts his action immediately to a series of people, and the new combination of words is understood straight away. A word like "papa" is here no longer a sentence but a member of a sentence. At first, such utterances had to be stressed word by word, so that the effect of the second is influenced by the intuitive situation already modified by the first one. No doubt progress consists of reducing the immediate effect of the first words perceived to an activity preparatory to the ultimate response, left in suspense until the completion of the sentence by the awaited "complements."

What are the first words affected by this progress? I have been struck by the role played by *people's names* in the sentences understood by children I have been able to observe. Their function in the sentence varies besides; they are subjects, direct or indirect complements, and so on. The word with which they are associated is still undifferentiated, signifying the total experience. At the same time, this seemed far less clear to me in the case of other combinations of familiar words. We have seen that P. (12.13) brushes the hair of one person or another when asked, and even does so to a doll (something he had not seen done). Then I said to him: "Brush the hat." (He knows the word "hat" in the sense that he knows how to find the object and put it on his head when asked, "Where is the hat? Put on your hat.") He does not understand the sentence. He lets go of the brush and picks up the hat, wants to put it on his head. If I repeat my order, he returns to the brush and wants to polish my shoes. Each of these two words tends to set off habitual reactions. The action proper is not performed. Notice that a construction of this type is always involved to some extent in the comprehension of sentences: if the child has never seen the prescribed action, the sentence he understands constrains his imagination to make the object appear in a new light whereby it can reasonably undergo the action expressed by the verb. If the action is one familiar to him, the form of the sentence suggests to him a function for the object which may not be the one he thinks of spontaneously. But, at the time of my observations, "hat" is not the name of an object. It suggests a certain experience with the hat, too specialized and too exact for it to be combined with his experience of the brush. On the other hand, at this same point, the names of *people* call forth a variety of actions without themselves specifying any one function: the child's thought is completed by the context. These are nouns that have really been differentiated.

The child's spontaneous speech confirms this development a little later on. He may still hesitate when the name is vocative. However, the link between the words becomes real when, instead of serving to attract someone's attention to some fact, the vocative becomes an invitation to participate in an action named by the other word, for example, in *Ici, Pepette* (= come here, Pepette) (L. 13.13). The relation is even closer in the following examples: *Adé papa, adé maman* (P. wants to put a die into his father's and mother's hands) (14.25); *A bo Baby* (= I brush Baby) (15.10); *Maman bobo* (= Mama sore; his mother has a sore on her lip) (15.17); *Ai a main a var* (= Mr. F., I want to hold his hand, see him) (the person named was not present); *Ahmed toutoute* (= Ahmed plays the trumpet); *Papa kir* (papa écrit = papa is writing) (16.24); *Sauveur caou* (Sauveur caillou = Saviour pebble; the Saviour, I'll throw him a pebble) (17.2). There are other examples cited above (*maman nénin, papa bobo,* and so on.) The beginning of the eighteenth month definitely establishes this stage: this type of sentence becomes very frequent; at the same time, there is a tendency to reply to all sorts of questions, at random, with the name of a person. In the following month these combinations frequently expressed attribute or possession: *Taté papa* (café papa = coffee papa; must give coffee to papa); *A pour à Nini* (poudre à Nini = powder for Nini; put some powder on Nini); *Nini donner de l'eau*

(= Nini give water); *Nini à bout* (Nini à bouche = in Nini's mouth); *Pantalon à papa, soupe à P.—Chocolat à bouche à papa* (= papa's trousers, P.'s soup—chocolate in papa's mouth) (19.22). His own name recurs continually in small sentences: *Chaise à P.* (= P.'s chair), *Donner à P.* (= give to P.), *P. travaille* (= P. is working), *P. veut les mettre* (= P. wants to do them), *P. il sait* (= P. he knows), *P. il fait* (= P. he does), *P. il pleure* (= P. he's crying), *P. est malade* (= P. is ill), *P. il veut* (= P. he wants it), *P. est la* (= P. is there) (20 months). In his sister's speech, we find the same development of the sentence: *Viens ici, Foufou* (= come here, Foufou; the name is one used for her brother) (12.19), *Fait dédé* [dodo] *Foufou* (= is sleeping, Foufou), *Il a bobo, Foufou* (= he's hurt, Foufou) (14 months), *Foufou le néné* (F. est allé promener = F. has gone for a walk), *Foufou le pam* (F. est tombé = F. has fallen down), *Néné papa* (papa va promener = papa's going for a walk), *Le papo le papa* (le chapeau de papa = papa's hat), *Le bobo le maman* (maman a bobo = mama's hurt), *A bobo a maman Danane* (D. a bobo comme maman = D. is hurt like mama) (14.15). Notice that there are two names of people in the last sentence combined with a common attribute.[5]

In this type of sentence, the word associated with the person's name is difficult to characterize from the grammatical point of view. It is still undifferentiated, and—which comes down to the same thing—the function of the person's name remains indeterminate. If we wish to see one of the words as a verb, the proper name could sometimes be the subject (*Papa kir* = papa is writing), sometimes the complement (*Sauveur caou* = a pebble for Saviour). The idea of a verb is just as well conveyed by a substantive (*Adé papa* = die [dice] papa). When the name is the child's own, it can just as well be the subject as the direct or indirect object.

THE LANGUAGE OF "WANTING"

Besides personal names, another element in free combinations appears fairly precociously in sentences: this is the expression of wants, that is, the verbal expression of negative reactions (refusal of attentions, of objects, aversion to certain actions or treatments) and of positive reactions of wanting something (an object, an action, its continuation or renewal). These words fairly quickly come to represent attitudes with respect to a verbal suggestion—assent or dissent—to an awaited event—observation of the absence or presence of an object or fact. The language of "wanting" thus takes on an intellectual value. The words are borrowed from a variety of categories in the imitated

---

[5] All the work on the first stages of sentence formation mentions a large number of combinations of people's names (or sometimes of individual personified objects) with another word. In the table where Stern listed the first sentences uttered by fourteen German, English, French and Polish children, we find no less than twenty-eight such out of a total of forty samples.

language, such as *A plus* (= I don't want any more, or = there isn't any more). *Pas*, *A pas*, *Non*[6] (= not, = no), to which must be added *Caca* (= dirty), an expression of aversion which is as expressive of wants as of emotion. The object of these negations goes at first unexpressed. They are word sentences, predicates of intuitive situations; but already the variety of unexpressed objects or facts to which these negations apply prepares for their appearance in two-word combinations at the next stage. In the combinations, the object of the negations does not yet have any definite grammatical form. *Pas momo* (= not sleep) (P. 14 months) can be interpreted either as "I don't want to sleep" or "I don't want the bed." Here are some other examples of these negations: *A pu papo* (= I don't want this hat) (P. 12.19), *A peu a pu* (= I don't want it to rain any more) (P. 14 months), *Pas beau* (= not nice; referring to a dog), *Pas bon* (= not good; referring to an orange), (13.18), *Nénin caca* (= I don't want to suckle) (15.26).

From the twentieth month on, negation accompanies a large number of what might be called verbs: *A po pas* (je ne peux pas = I can't), *Sais pas* (= don't know) (20.4), *A pas vu* (= didn't see), *A trouve pas* (= don't find) (21. 16). In another child's speech *A pas la mémé* (= not mama; refusing to let her brother climb on her mother's knee) (12.19). *A pas tété!* (= *ibidem*) (14 months).

We might be tempted to contrast affirmation with negation. But adherence to a desire or belief does not generally have to be expressed by a word; one simply obeys the suggestion. On the other hand, it is essential to defend oneself against someone else's wishes. *Oui* (= yes) does not appear in L.'s speech until 14 months (still very rare), nor in P.'s until 20 months. It remains an independent interjection. On the other hand, the child does have to demand the renewal or the continuation of certain actions; later on, the same words will be used to note the repetition of a fact or multiple examples of an object. *Encore* (= again, or = more) exists as a word sentence for P. at 14.3 (to ask again for a caress, a game to explain that he has not finished an action, to get some object back again: bread, cake, a banana, and so on.) Sometimes he even uses it to ask for something for the first time. The diversity of complements soon gives rise to sentences expressing the complement: *Nénin encore* (= more good) (15.26). At 18.27, I notice that this word is the one that most frequently appears in his own two-word combinations with no pause between the words: *Encore bon* (= more food; asking for more soup), *Encore feuille* (= more leaf; pointing at leaves on a tree, one by one), *Encore des jujubes* (= more jujubes), *Encore une guenane* (= more pomegranate), and so on (20.17). The same evolution is found in utterances that are emotive rather than intellectual. They are first used absolutely in a variety of concrete cases, then later with complements expressed. Thus, P. says: *Peur* (= 'fraid) or *A peur* (= I'm afraid) when a strange woman picks him up (14.25), when in a dark room, when he is stung by an insect (14.30),

---

[6] We do not have any examples of *non* (= no) used in combinations. German children, though, often use *nein* (= no) instead of *nicht* (= not) in such cases.

when spoken to severely, when he hears a gunshot (15.5), when he is carried in a basket, when he nearly falls down (15.9), when he has been scolded, and so on. Later he says *A peur bebetes* (= 'fraid of bugs) in speaking of the ants he has just seen (they were not in sight at that instant). Similarly, *Bobo* (= sore, hurt), which expresses hurt and fear at the same time in a large variety of instances, comes to be used in a sentence: *A pour bobo* (= the powder hurts) (16.4).

Thus we have seen the distinction of two sorts of words as autonomous word sentences: on the one hand, people's names, and on the other, expressions of "wanting." These two now occur freely in combination with nouns that are undifferentiated in relation to a total experience. But these two word classes are like opposite poles in the language. People especially are the objects of individual, concrete, stable perception and thought. They are also beings separate from the speaker, from his interests and his functions. They seem to exist "in and by themselves." Lastly, the words referring to them are easily detached from those referring to the experience as a whole, and become "names." On the other side, words expressing wants or desires are first of all *identical* to the speaker's feelings about his experiences; they are the verbal counterparts to his reactions, which are so little detached from him that they cannot at first be adequately characterized. The structure of the sentence expresses the dissociation of the primitive expression into one part that is represented or thought and into one part that is lived or acted.

THE NAME OF THE OBJECT

There is no great difference, particularly for the child, between things, animals, and people. He personifies and animates things; he goes easily from the combinations studied previously to sentences such as: *Sien, tape* (chien tape = dog, smack; that is, I smacked the dog) or L. (12.19) who watches water trickling from a gutter (which is generally called *dada*) and says: *Pipi dada* (= pee-pee gutter).

The names of things do not, strictly speaking, constitute a grammatical category: for us, the category of substantives has ended up including semantic equivalents of all words (names of qualities, actions, states, relations) and by finding the grammatical modes and constructions appropriate for each one. But the child's first substantives after the names of people are indeed names of *things* in a very narrow sense, as is shown in the vocabularies for the first half of the second year: they consist of the nouns for food, for objects connected with the games and needs of the child, above all manipulative objects, appropriate to his size and usage. We often notice very wide generic terms preceding specific names: for example, P. (13.27) uses *ato* (which seems to come from "marteau" = hammer) and until 14.22 uses it for the following: buttonhook, hand mirror, comb, handbag, a casserole, hairpin, wooden spade, key, gun, box, belt, wallet, ruler, puttees, bowl, safety pin, night light, coffee grinder, plate, and spoon.

This master word never refers to people, animals, or food: it is equivalent to *machin* (= gadget) or *chose* (= thing).

It has often been said that there is a decisive point at which the child discovers "that everything has a name." Miss Sullivan, Helen Keller's teacher, has left us a dramatic account of this "discovery" (in a six-year-old child who develops suddenly), and psychologists have assumed that it also occurs, though much earlier, in the normal child. I have no idea where to situate this sudden revelation: the development of the names of things, in the period when this can be observed, proceeds at a steady pace. At 12.10, P. uses 6 names of objects; at 13.27, 11; at 14.3, 19; at 15.30, 26; at 16 months, 38; at 17.12, 53; at 18.6, 68; at 18.27, 79; at 19.22, 96; at 20.17, 118; at 21.15, 168 (this is counting the new words added to the existing ones without supplanting them). Questions about the names of things, whose appearance ought to coincide with the decisive moment, do not appear any more suddenly: *Ceca?* (qu'est-ce que c'est que cela = what is that) is repeated once in imitation at 16.28 and is at first rare; it is only at 22 months that it becomes a mania. It is not until the age of two years that the initially very rare inverse question appears: hearing someone say a new word, the child inquires about the object: *Que c'est ça 'a l'hopital'?* (= what is "at the hospital"). Is it not that the real series of analogical effects have been condensed into a sudden "discovery" generalization for the sake of a convenient explanation?

All these names appear at first as isolated word sentences. They are used to refer to diverse thought functions. Either they denote objects of some wish (the child demands them, announces that he wants to act upon them), or they serve for localization (the part of the body which hurts, the place he is going to), or else they designate the recognition of the object, they acknowledge its presence. The latter form seems to be important in building up the function of the noun. Generally, the object becomes independent of the action relating to it less easily than the person does. It appears in its relation to the "me," in the role which actual need or usage gives it. But later on, naming things becomes a great game for the child (for example, when he is shown pictures); this game is no longer subordinated to immediate use: it is the object and not its function which is foremost. It is recognized and named disinterestedly, ignoring all uses. The name tends, therefore, to take on a meaning independent of any action or relation in which the object would be the goal.

It is only in the sentence containing causal words that it truly gains this value. To avoid repetitions, the examples will be given with reference to the verbs, since their differentiation and that of the noun go hand in hand. The physiognomy, though, of the name is complete only when the distinction between individual and generic names has been made. This is not a primitive concept: it implies an opposition between the individual object and an ungiven whole to which it is compared. The young child lives too much in the present to be capable of this mental complexity. A group of functional facts allow us to follow this development. First, as a semantic index, notice the use of the same word for similar objects which are, however, too different to be confused: P. (13.27) uses *papo* for his hair, different women's hats, a military cap, and so on. The word *autre* (= other), understood at age 12.3, when it is applied to one of two objects forming a pair (breast, hand, foot, ear), is said, as a word sentence, to designate the other breast (14.24), the other slipper, the other ball (14.30), another identical cake (15.10), another variety of cake seen in the same box (15.12), another person (15.17), other lines (16.8), and so on. In a neighboring meaning, we see the word *encore* (= more) sometimes associated with the partitive *(des)*: *Encore une grenade, l'autre* (= another pomegranate, the other one), *Encore des jujubes* (= more candies) (20.17). The definite article becomes regular in the singular and plural at about 21.6. It had been preceded by the use of demonstratives: *celle-la* (= that one), *pas celle-là* (= not that one) and so on, applied to objects of the same type. The possessives *mon, ton* (= my, = your) appear at 21 months. In another child, I noted *mon* (= my, masc.), *le mien* (= mine, masc.), at 21 months, and *ton* (= your, masc.), *ta* (= your, fem.), *le tien* (= yours, masc.) at 23 months. The word *tous* (= all, masc. pl.) follows the enumeration of objects at 22.26. The indefinite pronoun *en* (object pron.) and article *un* (= a, an) at 23.10: *Tu en as?* (= have you got some), *Je voulais un petit oua-oua* (= I wanted a little doggie), *Je l'as un* (= I have it one) and finally the opposition between *même* (= same) and *autre* (= other) at 23.15. She asks of a character pictured several times in a book: *Que ce que c'est, l'autre? C'est le même* (= what is it, the other? It's the same). Therefore, the character of the common noun becomes clearer as the child masters various ways of expressing linguistically the notion of type.

THE VERB

The word sentences are often reproductions of our verbs. Here are some examples, in addition to those we have already cited: *Habir* (habiller = dress; ask to be dressed), *Por, Assis* (porter = carry; assis, asseoir = sit; asking to be carried or to be sat down), *Nener* (promener = walk, go for a walk), *Nemir* (dormir = sleep; "I want to sleep" or "I am sleeping"), *Our* (ouvrir = open; "I want to open it" or "open it for me"), *Lever* (= get up; asking to get out of bed), *Descendre* (= get down—from his chair), *Cour* (courir = run), *Tebe* (tomber = fall; expressing fear of falling), *Laver, Rézé* (= wash; arroser = water), *Monter* or *Monte* (monter = climb—on a chair, into bed, up a tree), *Donne, sonne* (sonner = ring; on hearing a bell), *Coule* (couler = flow; seeing water in a drain), *Grate, Travaille* (gratter = scrape; travailler = work; "I'm working"), *Jeter* (= throw; "I want to throw"), *Prendre* (= take, "I want to take, be taken"), *Boutonne, Pique* (= spotty; = bitten, by an insect; statement of fact), *Balance, Arrange* (balancer = swing; arranger = arrange; statements of fact), *Caché, Cassé* (= hidden; = broken; statement of fact), and so on. All these examples occur between 16.26 and 20.4. The model imitated is sometimes in the personal mode (*Habir, Por, Our, Cour* come from *habille, porte, ouvre, court*), sometimes in the imperative or the infinitive (*Assis*, *Nemir*, *Laver*, *Descendre*). Occasionally two forms are found: *Our* (ouvre) and *Ouvrir* (infinitive), *Casse* and *Cassé* (past part.) or *Casser* (infinitive). However, it would be a big mistake to see in this the beginnings of verb conjugation. The child imitates a sentence he has heard: if he is on his chair and someone says to him: "Do you want to get down?" he will say *Descendre* (= get down) in such a context. (The frequency of the infinitive forms can be explained by the imitation of sentences introduced by *vouloir* = want to, *pouvoir* = be able to, *aller* = go, and so on. [these verbs are all followed by an infinitive construction in French] or by the prepositions *à*, *de pour*, also followed [in French] by an infinitive.) He says *Our* because he is imitating "Ouvre!" (= open!) or "Tu veux qu'on ouvre?" (= do you want it opened?). A little later on, in exactly the same circumstances, he will say *Ouvrir* because he is imitating "Tu veux ouvrir?" (= do you want to open it?), "Il fait ouvrir?" (= do you have to open it?)

To a certain extent, the form of the word is accidental. Naturally—it is the rule for all imitation—each new use tends to supplant the preceding one in evoking the verb form, which does not necessarily preserve the exact value that it had in its original use. Too much emphasis, therefore, should not be placed on these forms. The determination of person, tense, and mode are fortuitous; the child does not know how to use them to express the various nuances. But there is more to it: these forms are not even verbs, if what is called a verb is the word which in the total experience refers especially to aspect, action, or state; these forms still refer to the experience as a whole. The child will use a verb form and a nonverb form indifferently with *exactly the same meaning*. P. (18.2) says *Cour* or *Zouzoute* (courir = run; joujou = toy), *Nemir* or *Tasiet* (dormir = sleep; la sieste = rest), *Descendre* or *Par terre* (= get down; = on the ground), *À boire* or *De l'eau* (= drink; = water), *Tise* or *Dodo* (coucher = to sleep; = bed, sleep), *Por* or *A bas* (être porté = be carried; au bras = in arm(s)). Action is not truly isolated in language until both the agent and the object of the action have been differentiated.

However, before the sentence made up of several words appears, there is already a preparatory stage for the function of the verb when the word sentence is applied to different contexts whose common feature is essentially the action, while actors, objects, and situations vary. Every utterance has an individual origin; certain verbs are only used by the child, for a time, in connection with an undesignated person (himself), sometimes the subject, sometimes the direct or indirect object of the action. *Habir* (16.26) applies to *his* being dressed, *Némir* to *his* going to sleep, *Néné* to his going for a walk; *Lever* means "I want to get out of bed," *Descendre*: "I want to get down from my chair." Some pseudoverbs apply only to a particular object, for example: *Our* (ouvrir = open) to a door. But later on, the word becomes attached to the acton: the subject, object, and context begin to vary. Thus, he says spontaneously: *Habir* (= dress) to suggest that I put on my slippers that he has brought me (the actual incorrectness of the expression [in French] indicates that it his personal generalization)

(17.12). *Our* (= open) is applied not only to my door but to a piece of fruit, to a box, to a pea pod; one could claim that these too are imitations of the use of this word by other people, but that cannot be the case when he says *Our* (17.18) to ask for his shoes to be untied. *Tébé* is used when he is afraid of falling down, but also when I tip the chair I am sitting on. We have emphasized elsewhere[7] the roles of imitation and of assimilation of other people and of the child in the genesis of the verb.

Finally, the dissociation of the action, of the person, and of the object becomes evident in the language in the sentence of two or more words that contains a verb. The verb is combined with the name of a person, most often with that of the child himself. For example: *Donne à P.* (= give to P.), *P.* [veut, va] *les mettre* (= P. [wants to, is going to] put them), *P. il fait* (= P. he does), *P. il sait* (= P. he knows), *P. il peut pas* (= P. he can't), *P. il casse* (= P. he breaks) (20.4), *Monter à papa* (= climb up to papa) (20.11), *P. a mangé* (= P. has eaten) (20.17), *P. il pleure* (= P. he's crying), *P. est malade* (= P.'s ill), *P. a besoin* (= P. needs), *Papa fait la musique* (= papa is playing music), *P. a vu, a pas vu* (= P. has seen, hasn't seen), *Morte maman* (= mama is dead), *Morte Marie* (= Marie is dead) (21.6).

Even more often, the verb is associated with the name of a thing, for example: [Je] *tape* les *mouches* (= [I] swat [the] flies), [Je] *mange la soupe* (= [I] eat soup) (17.18), *Ote sie* (= take off shoe) (17.18), *Donne le contenu, donne la pelote* (= give the contents, = give the ball), [J'] *amasse de la terre* (= I'm piling up earth), *Fermée la fenêtre* (= shut, the window), *Cocottes mouillees, froid* (= birdies wet, cold), *Quitte la peau* (= take off the peel), *Donne la lettre* (= give the letter), *Donne de l'eau* (= give water), *Va chercher les chaussons* (= go and look for the shoes), *Fais voir la bande* (= show me the plaster), *Tourne la tête* (= turn your head), *Lève la tête* (= raise your head), *Cassées les jambes* (= broken, the legs), *Donne la main* (= give me your hand), *Partons à la maison* (= let's go back to the house) (20.4). Lastly, in the same period, we find a few combinations of three meaningful words, for example, *Donne chocolat a P.* (= give P. chocolate) (20.4). *Va chercher les chaussons a Papa* (= go and look for papa's shoes), *Donne la montre a P.* (= give P. the watch), *P.* [va] *chercher* [le] *Docteur* (= P. [is going to] look for [the] doctor) (21.16). At this stage, the personal construction of the verb with an object complement becomes so common that the child extends it to intransitive verbs: [Je] *travaille les cailloux* (= [I] am working the pebbles) (22 months). The anomaly of this utterance is a mark of his personal construction. He also speaks of *Taper les citrons* (= to hit the lemons, instead of "abattre les citrons" = knock down the lemons) (22 months). The two members of the sentence are both able to enter into combinations where each has its own function: the two have been differentiated.

The structure of the sentence is also defined by the word order. It is no longer a question of two or several word sentences juxtaposed, representing two

---

[7] *L'imitation chez l'enfant*. Paris: Alcan, 1923, p. 155.

instants of thought. The construction is required by the rules of the language; it no longer undergoes the capricious variations of the train of thought. Sometimes when the words come out in successive bursts, there is a tendency to reconstruct them afterwards in the normal order. One should not be deceived by some inversions. If P. says, *Fermée la fenêtre* (= shut the window), it is because he is imitating "elle est fermée, la fenêtre" (= it is shut, the window). If he says *Chercher Docteur* (= look for doctor), one has to understand "P. va chercher..." or "... veut chercher . . ." (= P. is going to look for . . ., or = wants to look for), and so on. The infinitives with an imperative meaning, preceding their complements, are elliptical reproductions of subordinate statements introduced by verbs like *vouloir* (= to want, wish) or by prepositions. The German child, under the same circumstances, will place the complement before the infinitive (*Flasche trinken* = drink water), and, for the same reasons, conforming to the rules of German, will also place the past participle at the end (Flasche trunken = water drunk), as well as the separable verb particles, frequently the only thing expressed (see Stern).

The development which separated a particular symbol for people from the undifferentiated word sentence has continued by isolating the symbol for objects. People and things correspond, in the total environment, to what is most distant from the subject, to what is most independent of his emotional and active life, although things are less likely than people to become autonomous beings and are rather more likely to be instruments of his needs and the passive objects of his actions. At the other pole of experience, the attitude of the subject, living rather than thinking, is isolated by the verbal aspect. The verb which in its turn becomes individualized, in a sense, prolongs the language of "wanting." The parallelism is clear if one considers the primitive forms. Whether the verbal forms from the word sentences or from the true sentences are taken into account, between the ages of 17 and 22 months in one of our children, about three quarters of the forms are imperative in meaning and only one quarter indicative. Words like *Encore* (= more) and *Donne* (= give) are scarcely separated by any nuance of meaning, and both take the same sort of complement. At the moment, the verb is above all an expression of "wanting" which tends to specify the modalities of the action required. Just as the terms of "wanting," positive or negative, become expressions of intellectual attitudes on the part of the subject with regard to the thought of others and of himself, so the verb rapidly comes to describe an action instead of requiring or announcing it: the indicative develops side by side with the imperative. Finally, to understand the evolution of expression of thought in a language like ours [French] consists of an arbitrary segmentation of experience as a whole, that is, both subjective and objective, in a way that corresponds to certain abstractions. The system, elaborated by the need to express more and more complex ideas by means of analogy which extends the categories, is difficult to assimilate in its present form. In order to master abstractions, one has to find images and symbols for them in something concrete. At the same time, a practical or emotional interest must correspond to this dissociation of reality. The human being, attitudes toward varied experiences, the objects and actions within experiences—these are the sum of the perspectives and interests of the child at the age which we have described. It is the expression of these aspects that he is assimilating into his language. This anthropocentricity is the key to the system of abstractions in the language, probably because therein lies its origin: the structure of the sentence and the functions of its members cease to seem artificial if one considers that language was first used to speak of man, and later of the whole of nature, in terms made for man.

GERMAN •

Theoretical Implications of Word Order, Topicalization and Inflections in German Language Acquisition

——*Thomas Roeper*

Chomsky's theory of transformational grammar enables us, as we shall see, to describe the syntactic deviations from adult German produced by the forty-five children in our experiment. This theory entails the claim that every child possesses a "language acquisition device" or a set of heuristics which permit him to infer the structure of the speech he hears. In short, he knows innately some of the crucial characteristics of language—or within what bounds they fall—even before he begins to decipher what adults say. All languages, consequently, are alike in the kinds of transformations they allow and in their organization of rule schema.

The "heuristics" involved, as yet unknown, probably cause all children— no matter what language they learn—to pass through the same series of stages. Each stage comprises a set of hypotheses about the adult grammar to be learned. In addition, a different factor, ease of performance (limits on memory, and so on) may lead children to favor certain structures over those used by adults. In the discussion below we shall offer evidence of the existence of some of these structures, and shall infer what a few of the associated hypotheses might be. We concentrate on puzzles that may be "universal" aspects of language acquisition.

METHODS

The subjects for our experiment were 45 children from the town of Lübeck in Northern Germany. Almost all of them were either four or five, though a few were older and a few younger. They were, consequently, in the latter stages of language acquisition. We used a group of 60 short sentences, composed of

Published here for the first time, by permission of the author. (Originally written in 1969; footnotes revised March 1971).

familiar words and involving as wide a variety of structures as possible.[1] Using these sentences, we administered correlated tests of *imitation*, in which each child repeated sentences, and *comprehension*, in which each child performed what the sentence said. A set of dolls and toys (animals, people, cars, and so on) were used in the comprehension tests. It was impossible to manipulate the dolls correctly unless the syntactic relation between the words in the sentences was understood. In the sections that follow we discuss those results that seemed fruitful or that suggest further research.

A THEORETICAL OBSERVATION

Transformations show the relation between structures. For instance, in English a deletion transformation relates *you eat tomatoes* to *eat tomatoes*. Or an object-preposing transformation shows the relationship between the object in *John liked something* and *what did John like*. Ultimately all the structures in a given language can be derived from one initial abstract structure.[2] This structure is similar but not identical across languages. English seems to have the underlying (abstract) structure Subject-Verb-Object (SVO), while Japanese probably has the structure Subject-Object-Verb (SOV); that is, the same elements in a different order. At some point a child must settle upon one base structure as the simplest underlying structure from which other structures can most easily be derived. Thus far there has been little discussion of underlying structures in the literature on language acquisition. Though problematic, the question is important for the following reason: it is in principle impossible to know what transformational relations a child controls until we know the order of constituents he bases his transformations upon.

All underlying orders share at least these universals: (a) the grammatical relations (subject of verb, object of verb) (b) the imposition of linear order on constituents (word order). In terms of a child this means that he must have an innate disposition toward the recognition of word order. Broadly speaking, there are three ways a child might come to know the correct order for his language:

[1] Most of this evidence was gathered in the summer of 1968 (supported by an NDEA Summer Fellowship through Harvard University).

My mother, Annemarie Roeper, administered the experiment. She also invented many of the test sentences and inspired the children and me with her spirit of discovery. Very helpful advice, guidance, and good discussion came from W. A. O'Neil and David McNeill. For vital assistance I would like to thank Frau Schild, Frau Ristenpark, and most of all, the children in the Rudolf Groht Kinderheim, Lübeck, West Germany.

Footnotes refer, when not specified, to additional data gathered while supported by a Harvard Traveling Fellowship 1969–1970. I have tried to indicate in the footnotes where subsequent work has strengthened hypotheses or offered new perspectives. The full treatment of each subject below—and questions of stress phonology—appear in my Ph.D. disssertation, Harvard University (in preparation).
[2] N. Chomsky, 1965, p. 124 ff.

A. There is a fixed innate constituent order. Languages deviate only by transformation from this order.

B. There is no fixed constituent order, but there is a very specific method to determine the correct order. For example, the child by trial and error tests the permutations of subject/verb/object, and so on.

C. There is no fixed word order, and a rather abstract method of inference is involved in the determination of the underlying order. Consequently, there is a fixed subset of possible orders available to the child.

These hypotheses describe a triangle of extremes and the true processes may involve all three. Hypothesis A may hold true for the relations between certain parts of a sentence; for instance, subjects almost always precede objects (though this may not be universal). Similarly, as we shall see below, this may hold true for the position of the indirect object. Hypothesis B may be true inasmuch as children sometimes impose a false order on sentences (see Slobin, below). Hypothesis C may be partially true, since children learn language more quickly than one could if one relied exclusively upon a trial and error routine.[3]

WORD ORDER IN GERMAN

German is a crucial language for such questions because, like Russian, it has, seemingly, "free word order," with full paradigms of inflections. To the casual observer, the inflections seem to be the only reliable guides to grammatical relations.

Chomsky maintains, nonetheless,[4] that the major structures (such as questions, relative clauses) must all be derived from a single underlying phrase-marker of ordered constituents. Other permutations of constituents are merely "stylistic" variants. Nevertheless, the child, unless informed by some innate premonitions, has no means at the outset to differentiate the stylistic variations from the nonstylistic changes in structure.

In his survey of Russian research Slobin (1966) has found evidence that supports the view that word order is important at an early stage in the acquisition of any language. Russian children, he says, seem to use subject/object/verb though the statistically predominant adult form is subject/verb/object.[5] We hypothesized, therefore, that at those points in German where one could obey either word order or inflections that the children would obey word order, though adults would obey inflections.

[3] Emonds (1970) has made a far-reaching distinction between structure-preserving transformations, which operate in subordinate clauses, and root (or structure-destroying) transformations, which operate in matrix clauses. He takes crucial evidence from German. His work may provide the child with a strategy for the discovery of deep structures: focus on subordinate clauses where order is preserved. This hypothetical strategy is consistent with the evidence cited in footnote 9.

[4] N. Chomsky, 1965, pp. 126–127.

[5] D. Slobin, 1966; M. Bowerman, 1970.

ORDERING OF INDIRECT OBJECT AND DIRECT OBJECT

We asked the children to repeat:

(1) Gib das Haus dem Auto.
(Give the house to the car.)

or to perform:

(2) Gib das Schweinchen dem Affen.
(Give the piglet to the monkey)

Both this form, verb/direct object/indirect object, and the more frequent form, verb/indirect object/direct object, are acceptable because the inflections on the articles indicate what is what. Eleven of 30 children switched articles in their imitation, placing the indirect object before the direct object: *Gib dem Haus das Auto*. Likewise, in the comprehension test 16 of 44 gave the monkey to the piglet. If we questioned the children about what they had done, their answers confirmed our view that they had relied upon word order rather than inflections. We concluded, therefore, that even older children may favor word order as a guide to grammatical relations.

It is interesting to note that most of these children were not ignorant of inflectional differences. Though aware of them, it seems, they required that inflection agree with word order. From the point of view of an adult grammar, of course, agreement is an unnecessary requirement. For the children, however, it may play a natural role in acquisition. This line of reasoning would explain why some of the children balked when we asked them to repeat (1), and simply said "I can not." They detected a conflict in their criteria for the identification of grammatical relations.

FIXED WORD ORDER HYPOTHESIS

These particular cases of allegiance to word order are consistent with a stronger hypothesis; namely, that humans are innately predisposed to have the indirect object precede the direct object. A surprisingly high number of languages exhibit this characteristic.[6]

There are two points in grammatical theory at which such an hypothesis could be proposed: (1) as a restriction on the underlying order of constituents upon which transformations are defined, and (2) as an *output* constraint. Such a

[6] O. Jespersen, 1964.

J. Mehling (1970) has argued convincingly that the basic tendency is to place the direct object next to the verb. If we assume SOV underlying order in German, then the putative universal fits the facts. English, in her view, is still shifting from an SOV to an SVO language; to put the direct object near the verb it is necessary to employ dative movement: *Give me a penny → Give a penny to me*. Use of this transformation has gradually increased in English.

constraint limits the configurations which transformationally derived structures may assume. Perlmutter[7] suggests that an output constraint is the only way to account for the fact that indirect objects always precede direct objects in Spanish. However, the second alternative does not apply to German, in which either order is permitted in the derived structure.

POSITION OF THE VERB IN GERMAN

If we do not assume that the underlying order of constituents is fixed for all languages, then we must suppose that a child has some means to infer the correct —the simplest—underlying base for operations. It is quite possible that general cognitive abilities to infer abstract structures are involved; as we shall see, the problem is not trivial in German.

English is rather clearly a subject/verb/object language (SVO). Consider:

(3) a. John hit Jane.
     b. John, who hit Jane, likes chocolate.

In both (a) and (b) the verb follows the subject. In (b) the verb follows the subject "who" in the embedded clause and the verb "likes" follows the subject of the matrix sentence (which is *John who hit Jane*). In German, however, there is a conflict in such cases:

(4) a. Hanns liebt Maria.
     (Hanns loves Maria.)

     b. Hanns, der Wurst *isst*, liebt Maria.
     (Hanns, who Wurst eats, loves Maria.)

In (a) the verb appears after the subject, while in the embedded sentence of (b) the verb occurs after the subject and object (SOV). Either of these word orders could serve as the underlying order, but not both. One form must be the transform of the other. For a wide variety of reasons (for example, participles in perfected sentences occur in final position), Bierwish has chosen verb-final order.[8] Yet, once again, such a decision need not be obvious to a child, who, in principle, could adopt either order. Moreover, since the child encounters many more simple declarative sentences (Hanns loves Maria, SVO) in his early years, and

[7] D. Perlmutter, 1968.
[8] Evidence has been mounting in favor of SOV order for German. See Emonds (1970), Mehling (1970), Bresnan (forthcoming); all present clear evidence in behalf of this view. Ross (1967a) argues otherwise, but his view is persuasively refuted by Mehling, I think. Other arguments from generative semantics, on a more abstract level, could cause a revision but not a rejection of the formulations presented here. For those who may still dissent, our evidence (especially the evidence in footnote 9) should be considered one more argument in favor of SOV structure in German.

since he uses primarily declaratives himself during this period, it seems likely that he might at first make the wrong choice, verb-medial (SVO) order.[9]

Accordingly, we provided the children with sentences where they might demonstrate their preference for the wrong order:

(5) Er liebt das Haus das an der Ecke *steht*.
(He loves the house that on the corner *stands*.)

Sie weiss warum er nicht froh *ist*.
(She knows why he not happy *is*.)

Er freut sich dass es schön ist.
(He is happy that it pretty *is*.)

Thirty-nine of 41 children repeated these sentences correctly, although they are fairly long. Only two children did what we had expected; they imposed SVO order on all of the dependent clauses:

A. "Er liebt dass das Haus welche *steht* an der Ecke"
(He loves that that house which *stands* on the corner.)
"Die weiss der *ist* nicht froh."
(She knows he *is* not happy.)

B. "Er liebt das Haus *steht* an der Ecke."
(He loves the house *stands* on the corner.)
"Er weisst warum *ist* er nicht froh."
(He knows why *is* he not happy.)

Since most of the children observed the verb-final structure, we concluded: (a) the evidence is compatible with the verb-final hypothesis, and (b) the evidence is not decisive; there may have been an earlier period during which verb-medial order was overtly relied upon by all children.[10]

RULE GENERALITY

We were able to give further scrutiny to SVO and SOV structures through a question on the comprehension test. The question required that the child shift the verb. Similar sentences were used with American children at Harvard.[11]

[9] There is striking evidence now that German children acquire verb-final (SOV) structure very early. Park (1970) reports on three two-year-old children who all consistently placed the object before the verb at the two-word stage (totals: 82 [obj-verb]/20 [verb-obj]), unlike American children and unlike the normal declarative sentences of their parents. In the three-word stage, when the first transformations may appear, there were still SOV utterances more than 50 percent of the time (23/41 instances). Bowerman's report of occasional SOV structure in Finnish (1970), which she (perhaps mistakenly attributes to "free word-order," is marginal by comparison. The evidence from German may be explainable by the strategy proposed in footnote 3.

[10] This conjecture is less likely in the light of footnote 9. It could be true for a stage in language comprehension prior to production.

[11] C. Cazden, 1967; P. Menyuk, 1969.

(6) Ask Daddy what *he can* make with that.
   Children: "What *you can* make with that."
   (Adult: What *can you* make with that.)

The children, aged five and six, failed to perform the subject-verb inversion (you can → can you). This failure occurred most consistently with negatives (can't). The American children seemed either to premise their replies on the model sentence or to use a simple structure of the form question word + normal sentence; that is, to place a question word (what) before a normal sentence (You can make something). We expected that German children of the same age and younger would do the same. That is, we expected them either to imitate the model (a) or to use the Q-word + S structure (b):

(7) Frag die Mutter warum sie nicht *schläft*.
   (Ask the Mother why she not *sleeps*.)
   a. Expected reply: Warum du nicht schläfst.
      (Why you not *sleep*.)
   b. Expected reply: Warum du schläfst nicht.
      (Why you sleep not.)
   c. Correct adult reply: Warum schläfst du nicht.
      (Why sleep you not.)

But not one child produced a sentence of the structure Q-word + S (b). One child followed the model, changing only *she* to *you* (a). Twenty-seven children produced the correct adult form (c).[12] This was a surprising result; if anything, the task looked more difficult in German than in English.

The explanation lies in the rules of verb placement in the two languages. In English one inverts the subject and the auxiliary of the verb only in questions (and a few adverbial phrases): Q-subj-aux-verb → Q-aux-subj-verb. In German, where the verb appears at the end in the underlying form, both declarative and question sentences involve permutations of the verb:

(8) $X - Y - Verb → X - Verb - Y$
   where X = noun, adverb, question word, imperative
            Y = object, negative, adverb, or anything else

This means that the transformational relation under discussion is the same for a declarative sentence *Peter geht weg* (Peter goes away) and a question sentence *Wo geht Peter* (Where goes Peter). The rule says that the verb is placed in second position no matter whether the first element is a subject-noun, wh-word, adverb, or imperative morpheme. In other words, the categories to which this rule applies are broad, hence the rule has far greater applicability and far greater generality than the corresponding rule in English.

Possessing greater "generality" and "applicability" does not mean (necessarily) that the structures created by the rule occur more frequently in

---

[12] The same results were obtained with many more children.

everyday speech. It means that the rule is defined in abstract terms. There is no obvious reason why rules of this sort should be easier to acquire than more specific rules. Evidently, however, this rule is acquired more easily than a similar but more restricted rule of English. From this the following hypothesis, which may be too strong, emerges: a child acquires those rules first which have a minimally specified structural description (for example, uses X rather than *noun*, where X includes *noun*, *adverb*, *question*, and so on). That is, the acquisition device tends to register syntactic relations at this level of abstraction.[13] Of course, the evidence submitted here is fragmentary; the importance of rule generality in language acquisition deserves further attention.

"FORWARD" AND "BACKWARD" OPERATIONS

We turn now to some data which also pertain to the abstract character of certain rules. When sentences are conjoined, often one or more of them is reduced:

(9)   John ate steak and Bill ate beef
       John ate steak and Bill beef.

One can, apparently, delete the second verb if it is identical to the first. The operation looks very simple: a surface structure rule deletes identical words in parallel sentences. The children seemed to have mastered sentences of this kind in the imitation exercises (22 children);

(10)   Die Mutter macht nicht die Tür, aber die Fenster *auf*.
       (The mother opened not the door, but the windows *up*)

       Reply: "Die Mutter macht nicht die Tür *auf*, aber die Fenster."
                (The mother opened not the door *up*, but the window.)

In their reply the second sentence is left a skeleton; only the object "Fenster" remains. Another sentence, however, which seemed similar in kind, elicited a different response:

(11)   Nicht der Vater, aber der Junge macht die Tür zu.
       (Not the father, but the boy made the door shut.)

       Reply: Nicht der Vater macht die Tür zu, aber der Junge macht die Tür zu.
                (Not the father made the door shut, but the boy made the door shut.)

Instead of maximum reduction we have full expansion, giving two complete sentences (2 children).[14] A number of other children found this sentence difficult and replied incoherently (seven children). Why would a child reject a structure

---

[13] A good deal of human learning seems to involve the opposite method of inference: a small distinction is noticed which is gradually generalized over a broad domain.

[14] The reply, in sheer length, is surprising. If the child's reply is less complex for him than the model sentence, then we have more clear evidence that other factors may contribute more decisively to *complexity* than sentence length does.

(11) which he himself had just used (10)? The structures must differ in some respect. If we digress for a moment the difference can be recognized. In German and English, (a) below transforms into (b) but not (c). That is, forward reduction is permitted, but not backward reduction:

(12) a. John likes Sue, and Bill likes Mary
b. John likes Sue, and Bill Mary.
c. *John Sue, and Bill likes Mary.

In other languages, such as Japanese, (c) is possible but not (b). However, both German and English permit backward reduction if the two sentences differ only in the subject, not the object (Not John, but Bill closed the door.) Although permitted, this kind of sentence proves difficult for the German children. Therefore, we conclude, German children acquire backward reduction—a restricted operation—after they acquire forward reduction, a more general operation. Presumably, the reverse is true in Japanese, where backward reduction has few or no restrictions.

Even deeper principles of organization may be involved. Languages in which *forward* reduction is preferred or more "acceptable" seem to share other characteristics—though many unsettled issues are involved. All these languages have rules of rightward permutation (that is, *the woman (who wears mink) came in → the woman came in who wears mink*.)[15]

In sum, we have suggested that the generality of rules is an important factor in their acquisition. Moreover, a child may face some abstract choices that predetermine the character of many of the particular rules he must learn. This choice may decide, for instance, the "directionality" of language: left-or-right and forward-or-backward. Associated with this decision are other properties: (a) the direction of permutations, and (b) the direction of conjoined sentence reduction. Although there are many theoretical questions that are still unanswered, still there are clear possibilities for further psycholinguistic research. For instance, do forward reduction and rightward permutation emerge at once?

EMBEDDING AND BRANCHING STRUCTURES

We asked our subjects to repeat a sentence that contained a center-embedded relative clause:

(13) Das Auto das er hat, fährt gut.
(The car that he has runs well.)

Eight of the 22 children able to reproduce this sentence inserted the demonstrative pronoun *das* after the relative clause:

(14) Das Auto das er hat, *das* fährt gut.
(The car that he has, *it* runs well.)

Thus they changed a structure of the form [a [b b] a] to a topic-comment structure of the form [a [b b] [c c]. That is, they went from $_a$[das auto $_b$[das er hat]$_b$

---

[15] J. R. Ross, 1967*b*.

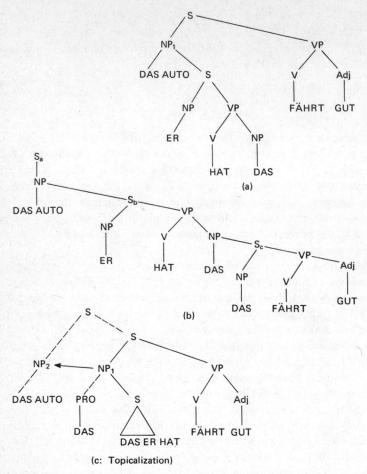

Figure 1.

fährt gut]ₐ to ₐ[das auto [_b das er hat]_b [_c das fährt gut]_c (see Figure 1.) In other words, they imposed a right-branching structure on what had been a center-embedded sentence.[16] Their response conforms to the fact that for both children

---

[16] More children have performed the same operation with similar sentences. In an unevenly divided group of 40 children, 56 percent of three-year-olds, 48 percent of four-year-olds, and 16 percent of five-year-olds added a pronoun. Menyuk (1969) reports that 87 percent of English kindergartners extrapose S's while first-graders use embedded clauses freely.

There were numerous instances of topicalization where less than a sentence was involved:

> Die Farbe der Tasche meiner Jacke ist rot.
> (The color of the pocket of my coat is red)
> Reply: "Die Farbe meiner Jacke, *die* ist rot."

> Die Füsse der Mutter tun weh.
> (The feet of the mother hurt.)
> Reply: "Die Füsse, die tun weh."

and adults right-branching sentences are easier to produce and comprehend than center-embedded ones.

If such sentences are perceptibly more difficult for adults, they may be prohibitively difficult for children. Therefore, for children, a kind of grammatical redundancy (extra pronoun) may be a requisite for performance, *sine qua non*. It is interesting to note that topic-comment structures are apparently characteristic of very early stages of acquisition (for instance, "car it broken").[17] Although this structure disappears in time, it may reappear, so it seems, to meet a subtle performance barrier.

Let us examine the *topicalization* operation.[18] The operation copies a node NP_1 at the left of the sentence, giving NP_2: NP_1 is then pronominalized into *das*. This copying transformation preserves the information that a part of the structure (das fährt gut) is still a sentence (see Figure 1).

Cursory examination of surface structure would lead one to suppose that the topic (a) in the structure $_a$[das Auto [$_b$ das er hat]$_b$ [$_c$ das fährt gut]$_c$ bore the same relationship to (b) as it does to (c). However, if we topicalize both S_1 [er hat das Auto] and S_2 [das Auto fährt gut] we produce $_1$[das Auto $_2$[das Auto [er hat das] [das fährt gut]. If we pronominalize *das Auto$_2$*, we get *das Auto das er hat das, das fahrt gut* (or *the car which he has it, it runs well*). Since these sentences are ungrammatical, there must be a different operation for the creation of (b) (*das er hat*). This other operation is the familiar *relativization*. The crucial difference between the two operations is that *relativization* involves permutation (or *chopping*) while *topicalization* is a *copying* transformation, in which nothing is moved. Ross shows that *copying* transformations are subject to fewer constraints than movement transformations. It may well be that the distinction between copying and permutation transformations is an important one, which, furthermore, may appear early in the period of language learning.[19]

The application of both *relativization* and *topicalization* means that the head noun of (b) relates to the matrix NP (*das Auto*) as a relative clause, while the head noun of (c) relates to the matrix as a comment to topic. If this difference is significant, then we should look for evidence that the difference between them is psychologically real. Some clear evidence of this kind appeared. Many of the children substituted *was*, a relative pronoun, for *das* (like *which* for *that*). *Das* is the demonstrative pronoun which may or may not serve as a relative.

(15)   Das Auto, *was* er had, *das$_2$* fährt gut.

None of the children ever substituted *was* for the *das$_2$*. That is, none of them mistook the topic-comment relation for a subject-relative relation. In general, the introduction of *was* occurred frequently in all test sentences where we had used *das* as a relative pronoun (10 children). In conclusion, the children showed a

---

[17] J. Gruber, 1967. The topic-comment structure is still used as an emphatic in adult speech: *That car he's got, it's great*. It also occurs frequently in the black dialect. It may also be explainable in terms of general memory processes.

[18] J. R. Ross, 1967a.

[19] This kind of *copying* transformation may play a far more important role in an acquisition device than it does in the adult grammar.

consistent preference for the unambiguous relative, except where it would violate psychological reality; namely, where the relation was topic-comment.

SENTENCE-INITIAL INDIRECT OBJECT

One of the sentences in the repetition test elicited the following curious response:

(16) a. Test: Die Füsse der Mutter tun weh.
                   (The feet of the mother hurt.)

      b. Reply: Der Mutter die Füsse tun weh.
                   (To the mother the feet hurt.)

The inflection -r is identical for the indirect object (dative) and the possessive (genitive). It is not surprising that the children might consider the genitive article to be a dative article. However, it is surprising that they would not place the indirect object near the verb, since it is supposedly a part of the verb phrase in the underlying order. There is a permutation transformation in Bierwisch's account that transfers any noun to a sentence initial position. Nonetheless, the existence of such a transformation does not explain the preference for this structure by one third (8) of the children.

Three possible explanations come to mind:

A. This indirect object is actually a topic in a topic-comment structure.

B. All indirect objects should not be attached to the verb phrase but should occur in sentence-initial position in a topic-comment structure.

C. A combination of both of these. The child assumes that sentence-initial nouns are topics, but gradually learns that they bear a transformational relation to the indirect object associated with the verb phrase.

The third explanation seems most probable. However, there are other pertinent factors too complex to discuss here. There is some slight evidence in behalf of hypothesis C. Many children did not seem to control the inflections whatsoever. Some of them used exclusively nominative inflections. Some seemed to differentiate only inflected and uninflected. Two children shifted *Mutter* to the sentence-initial position but did not add inflections:

(17) Die Mutter die Füsse tun weh.

Presumably when they acquire inflections they will discover the relation of such head nouns to the indirect object (though this discovery is not necessarily contingent upon the control of inflections). If they regard the relation as topic-comment until that time, then we have identified one erroneous structure into which the children have found themselves temporarily led.

CONCLUSION

We have tried to illustrate the kinds of issues that may be at stake when a child begins to perceive the relation between one structure and another. He draws deep and far-reaching conclusions about his language. One decision—if it is correct—may give him insight into many other transformational relations in the language. Or, put differently, one decision may govern a number of similar transformations. Much of what we have done needs corroboration from work in other languages and from work with younger children who make, probably, these crucial decisions.

REFERENCES

Bierwisch, M. (1963), *Grammatik des deutschen Verbs*. (Ost) Berlin: Akademie-Verlag.

Bowerman, M. F. (1970), Learning to talk: A cross-linguistic study of early syntactic development with special reference to Finnish. Unpublished doctoral dissertation, Harvard University.

Bresnan, J. (1970), On sentence stress and syntactic transformations. *Language* (forthcoming).

Brown, R., and U. Bellugi (eds.) (1964), The acquisition of language, *Monogr. Soc. Res. Child. Developm.*, 1964, **29** (1).

Cazden, C. (1967), Implications of the competence-performance distinction. Unpublished paper, Harvard University.

Chomsky, N. (1965), *Aspects of the theory of syntax*. Cambridge, Mass.: M.I.T. Press.

Emonds, J. (1970), Constraints on transformations. Unpublished doctoral dissertation, M.I.T.

Fodor, J. (1966), How to learn to talk: Some simple ways. In F. Smith and G. A. Miller (eds.), *The genesis of language*. Cambridge, Mass.: M.I.T. Press.

Gruber, J. (1967), Topicalization in child language. *Foundations of Language*, 3:37–65.

Jespersen, O. (1964), *Elements of English grammar*. University of Alabama Press.

McNeill, D. (1968), The development of language. Draft of chapter. [Published in P. H. Mussen (ed.), *Carmichael's manual of child psychology*, 3d ed., Vol. 1. New York: Wiley, 1970.]

Menyuk, P. (1969), *Sentences children use*. Cambridge, Mass.: M.I.T. Press.

Park, T-Z (1970), The acquisition of German syntax. Unpublished paper, Psychologisches Institut, University of Münster, Germany.

Perlmutter, D. (1968), Deep and surface structure constraints. Unpublished doctoral dissertation, M.I.T.

Roeper, T. (1971), A child's mental structures: Theoretical issues in language acquisition with evidence from German. Doctoral dissertation, Harvard University (in preparation).

Ross, J. A. (1967a), Constraints on variables in syntax. Unpublished doctoral dissertation, M.I.T.

Ross, J. A. (1967b), Gapping and the order of constituents. [To be published in M. Bierwisch and K. Heidolph (eds.), *Progress in linguistics*. The Hague: Mouton.]

Slobin, D. I. (1966), The acquisition of Russian as a native language. In F. Smith and G. A. Miller (eds.), *The genesis of language*. Cambridge, Mass.: M.I.T. Press.

JAPANESE •

The Creation of Language by Children

——*David McNeill*

THE BASIC GRAMMATICAL RELATIONS

The basic grammatical relations are the concepts of subject and predicate of a sentence; main verb and object of a verb phrase; and modifier and head of a noun phrase. They are defined in linguistic theory as configurations of the base structure of sentences (Katz and Postal, 1964;[1] Chomsky, 1965). The subject of a sentence, for example, is the NP directly dominated by S in the base structure. The predicate of a sentence is the VP directly dominated by S (or, alternatively, dominated by Pred P—the difference will be ignored here, but see Chomsky, 1965, for discussion). The object of a verb phrase is the NP directly dominated by VP, whereas the main verb of a verb phrase is the V directly dominated by VP. Although not mentioned in the reference cited, the modifier of a noun phrase will be taken to be some kind of determiner directly dominated by NP, whereas the head of a noun phrase will be defined as the N directly dominated by NP. These definitions appear to be universal, which is to say that all languages appear to possess the configurations necessary to apply them, and so the definitions themselves are entered in linguistic theory. They may be written as follows, in a formulation that will become convenient later on:

Subject of	NP, S
Predicate of	VP, S
Main verb of	V, VP
Object of	NP, VP
Modifier of	D, NP
Head of	N, NP

[1] [References are given at the end of the paper following this one.—Ed.]

The configurations to which these definitions apply are located in the base structure of sentences, not the surface structure, because of sentences like *John is easy to please* and *John is eager to please*, where the surface structures are the same, yet the word *John* stands in two different grammatical relations—object in the first, subject in the second. Thus, the definitions are "abstract" in the sense used here.

The hypothesis given above—that abstract features mentioned in linguistic theory will appear in children's earliest grammatical productions—requires that the basic grammatical relations will be honoured in very early speech collected from children. One source of support for this hypothesis comes from a child exposed to English, a little boy called Adam by Brown and Bellugi (1964).

At the time his speech was first recorded, Adam appeared to have three grammatical classes—verbs, nouns, and pivots. The evidence for distinguishing these classes was distributional. This is to say that English verbs had privileges of occurrence in Adam's speech different from those of English nouns. Adam's pivot class had a third privilege of occurrence, but it was grammatically heterogeneous from the point of view of English.

A little arithmetic shows that with three grammatical classes, N, V, and P, there are $(3)^2 = 9$ different possible sentence-types two words long, and $(3)^3 = 27$ different possible sentence-types three words long. If a child were combining words at random, all (or nearly all) these nine and twenty-seven different combinations should occur. However, not every combination is a manifestation of one or another basic grammatical relation. Only four of the nine two-word possibilities correspond to one or more of these relations, the remaining five being inadmissible from this point of view. An admissible combination would be $N + V$ (e.g., *Adam run*), corresponding to the subject-predicate relation. An inadmissible combination would be $P + P$ (e.g., *my that*). Among the three-word combinations, only eight manifest one or another basic grammatical relation, the remaining nineteen being inadmissible. An example of an admissible combination is $V + N + N$ (e.g., *change Adam diaper*), corresponding to the verb-object relation, whereas an inadmissible combination would be $V + V + N$ (e.g., *come eat pablum*).

Examples of every admissible combination were contained in the first three samples of Adam's speech that Brown and Bellugi collected. In itself, this result is not surprising. Altogether, some eight hours' recording were involved, and some 400 utterances from Adam. If the child were placing words together on some principle that allowed most of the possible combinations, those corresponding to the basic grammatical relations would be expected on grounds of the large sample size. However, all 400 of Adam's sentences were of the admissible type. There were no others. Thus, although *change Adam diaper* might have occurred, *come eat pablum* did not; for details, see McNeill (1966a).

That this should be the outcome is certainly not obvious, *a priori*. In fact, one might have supposed that the result would have been different. Superficially, adult speech contains many examples of inadmissible sequences of Adam's grammatical classes. For example, the sentence-type represented by *come and eat your pablum* is common enough. To judge from some of Braine's (1963a) experiments with artificial languages, people find it difficult to avoid acquiring patterns to which they are exposed, even when told that the patterns do not exemplify what they are to acquire. If we assume that the same sensitivity holds true of young children, then some explanation must be offered for the fact that Adam did not produce sentences like *come eat pablum* after hearing examples like *come and eat your pablum* in parental speech. The explanation that suggests itself is that Adam was attempting to use only those sentence patterns that express the basic grammatical relations. An adult sentence like *come and eat your pablum* did not serve as a model utterance because it does not directly manifest these relations, being instead a rather complex construction involving several transformations not yet part of the child's grammatical competence. In short, Adam may have been actively searching for ways to express the basic grammatical relations in his speech. As a result, his own earliest grammatical constructions were limited to direct expressions of these relations.

Thus, there is indication that children's earliest speech contains abstract linguistic features, in this case, the basic grammatical relations. The same conclusion is reached from an examination of the early speech of children acquiring Japanese.

I have recently begun collecting samples of speech from two children who live in Tokyo. Each child is visited twice monthly, in her home, where everything said to and by the child is tape recorded. Both girls are (at the present time: February 1966) approximately two years of age. Neither is especially gifted at Japanese; and from one exactly seventeen word-combinations have been recorded during the past three months. The second child, however, produces large quantities of patterned speech, and the evidence described below comes from her. In the interest of maintaining the tradition begun by Brown, she will be called Izanami, after the goddess of Japanese mythology who helped create the world.

In certain respects, Japanese is particularly revealing for the study of language acquisition. It contrasts with English in several ways, of which one is especially relevant to the question now under consideration. Japanese is a postpositional rather than a prepositional language. Very roughly, postpositions are comparable to prepositions in English (although not all English prepositions can be translated into Japanese postpositions, and conversely). Among the postpositions that have no English equivalent are two that obligatorily mark, in the surface structure of Japanese sentences, the grammatical subject of the sentence.

The two subject markers are *wa* and *ga*. Although both follow the subject NP of a sentence, they are not identical, and receive different analyses in a transformational grammar of Japanese (Kuroda, 1965). The differences between *wa* and *ga* will first be introduced by a few examples, then, following Kuroda, they will be characterized somewhat more systematically:

A man-ga is standing on the corner
The man-wa is standing on the corner
Man-wa is mortal

In answer to the question, "which man is sick?", one would reply

That man-ga is sick

whereas in answer to the question, "who is sick?", one could reply

That man-wa is sick

A person, naming some object, would say

This-wa is a digital computer,

whereas hearing someone refer to the vending machine in the corner as a computer, one could correct him by saying

This-ga is a digital computer.

The distributional similarity of *wa* and *ga* is as close in Japanese as in these English examples, so that what is presented to a child in parental speech will not distinguish them. However, as the examples indicate, *wa* and *ga* play very different grammatical roles. Subjects of sentences that state general truths, subjects that have attributes given to them by the predicate, subjects that function like the logical premises of judgments, and words like *this* and *that* when they are used in definitions, all take *wa*. Quite often, *wa* can be translated into English with the expression "as for . . . ." Thus, the examples given above can all be rendered:

As for that man, he is standing on the corner
As for man, he is mortal
As for that man, he is sick
As for this, it is a digital computer

In each case, an attribute—standing on the corner, mortality, computerhood—is judged applicable to the subject of the sentence. Kuroda calls this usage "predicational judgment." So much for *wa*.

The postposition *ga* differs from *wa* in two ways. That is to say, *ga* has two distinct senses, both different from *wa*. In one sense, *ga* is used in simple description. Instead of the predicate of the sentence being a property judged applicable to the subject, the subject and predicate stand in some roughly equal relation to one another. They are merely linked (see Weinreich, 1963, for a discussion of this relation). The connection is always felt to be momentary, as in *a man is standing on the street corner.* Typically, the subject of the sentence is a specific, yet indefinite noun, as in the example just cited. One does not attribute a property to an arbitrary member of the category, *man*. One merely observes what he is doing at the moment. The descriptive sense of *ga* reflects such momentary linkage.

The second use of *ga* excludes possibilities from a known set of alternatives. In this sense of *ga*, information is conveyed not only about the subject of the sentence, but also about the members of the set of alternatives not mentioned in the sentence. Thus, to use one of Kuroda's examples, if three people, John, Bill, and Tom are lying side by side in three beds and a doctor arrives asking, "Who is sick?", the answer *John-ga is sick* means not only that John is ill but, in addition, that Bill and Tom are well. Heavy stress often conveys this meaning in English—*Jóhn is sick*. The corresponding sentence with *wa* conveys information about John alone. If the reply is *John-wa is sick*, meaning "as for John, he is sick," nothing is learned about the state of health of Bill or Tom. The vaporous quality of much Japanese philosophy may exist because of this postposition, *wa*.

To turn now to the acquisition of Japanese: the proposal made before, and supported by the evidence of Adam's speech, strongly suggests that the postpositions *wa* and *ga* will appear early in Izanami's speech. This is because the subjects of adult sentences are consistently marked by *wa* and *ga*, which, in turn, relate to the base structure through fairly simple transformations. If Izanami is attempting to express the grammatical relation of subject in her sentences, she would have a basis for discovering and then using these transformations. If, on the other hand, she is not attempting to express the relation of subject, there would be no basis for her to formulate the transformation, so *wa* and *ga* should not appear.

What of the distinction between *wa* and *ga*? Izanami's mother uses *wa* twice as often as she uses *ga*. Presumably, this would favour acquisition of *wa*. Moreover, *wa* is involved whenever the mother introduces new vocabulary, describes permanent states and general truths, or attributes properties to objects. Some examples addressed to Izanami are *this-wa is a tape recorder* (pointing to it), *grandmother-wa lives in Kyoto*, and *papa-wa is big*. We can be certain that such sentences from Izanami's mother are understood, inasmuch as they are the principal means of introducing new vocabulary and information to the child, and there is no doubt that Izanami acquires both. Moreover, all these sentences involve a concrete object as the designated subject of the sentence (*this* accompanied by ostensive definition, *grandmother*, *papa*), as opposed to the *ga*-marked subject of a sentence, which is always an arbitrary member of a general category. For all these reasons, therefore, we might expect *wa* to appear.

The mother uses *ga* both in simple descriptions of transitory states and in the exclusion of alternatives from a known set. Some examples of the former are *you-ga sit well* (as Izanami manages not to topple over while sitting Japanese-style on the floor), and *yes, a bird-ga is on the fence*; whereas some examples of the latter are *which-ga do you want?* and *your other friends-ga want to play with you*. It is not clear what to expect Izanami to do with the descriptive *ga*. On the assumption, often made, that children develop grammatical relations by the labelling of enduring physical relations in the real world (e.g., the names of objects, or the relation of agent to action, as in the fact that people walk, children cry, houses stand, etc.), one would not expect *ga* to be acquired early. *Ga* is never used when these conditions prevail; *wa* is the required postposition. On the other hand, assuming that this kind of relation with the physical world is irrelevant to the acquisition of syntax, one would expect *ga* to appear as well as *wa*. The exclusive use of *ga*, because it requires a child to hold alternatives in mind and to exclude all but one, ought not to be acquired early.

The facts are as follows. Izanami uses only one of these postpositions, and it is *ga*. In eight hours of recorded speech, there were approximately 100 occurrences of *ga* and six occurrences of *wa*. All occurrences of *wa*, save one, were with the same word. Moreover, about one-quarter of the occurrences of *ga* were of the exclusive type, as in *this one-ga I like* and *the airplane-ga I prefer*.

In short, Izanami sharply distinguishes *wa* from *ga*, despite their distributional similarities in parental speech, selecting the descriptive use of *ga* as the principal concept to be encoded. It is clear from this fact alone that she is not working solely from the surface clues available to her, since on this basis *wa* and *ga* are virtually indistinguishable. *Ga* is included almost whenever called for in her speech, whereas *wa* is almost never supplied when required. *Ga* is never used in contexts calling for *wa*. Evidently, Izanami knows the transformation that introduces *ga*.

Izanami's sentences at the present stage of development are mostly two, three, and four morphemes long—which means that she is still in the earliest phase of producing patterned speech. Hence, there is strong support here for the proposal that children attempt to express the abstract relation "subject of" in their most primitive grammatical efforts, which confirms what we have already seen in the speech of Adam.

The child's use of *ga* and her exclusion of *wa* clarifies the cognitive implications of the effort to express the grammatical relation of subject. The conceptual correlate of this relation is the linkage of subject and predicate as in momentary description. It is not the discovery of enduring relations between specific agents and actions in the physical world, nor the kind of relation involved in the application of names to objects. Izanami belies this hypothesis. Indeed, on Izanami's evidence, naming appears to be completely separate from grammatical development, since appellation in Japanese requires *wa*, which Izanami invariably omits, although naming of objects is common in her speech. If the development of appellation led to developments in grammar, Izanami's postposition would have to be *wa*.

The conceptual content of *wa* thus appears to lie outside a child's attempt to express the subject relation. It is important to note in this connection that Kuroda came to the same conclusion on completely independent grounds. The postposition *wa*, although it marks the subject of a sentence and never co-exists with *ga*, nonetheless represents an essentially different concept that is added to the notion of grammatical subject. Accordingly, the situations that call for *wa* do not represent to a child the basic grammatical relation of subject (if by this, we now mean momentary description), even though it is a grammatical subject that should be marked. Hence, Izanami omits *ga* and ignores *wa*. This would seem to be very strong evidence of a child's impositions of conceptual constraints on to the speech he produces.

There remains the problem of Izanami's use of the exclusive *ga*. It appears to indicate that she can hold in mind several alternatives at once, select one of the set, and simultaneously exclude the rest. Presumably, children are not able to perform mental gymnastics of this order until they reach the age of seven or eight (Bruner and Olver, 1966), so its appearance in Izanami at the age of two occasions some surprise. It is possible, of course, that the linguistic evidence should be interpreted at face value. However, there is an alternative explanation. According to at least one Japanese informant (Nobuko B. McNeill), *ga* in its nondescriptive use not only encodes exclusion but also subjective certainty. Apparently one can easily tell the self-confident from the timorous in Japanese debates by noting who uses *ga* and who uses *wa*. The *ga*-sayers are the self-confident ones. The Japanese Milktoast prefers *wa*. All Izanami's uses of *ga* in its non-descriptive sense were statements of preference—*this one-ga I like, airplanes-ga I prefer*, and so on. If we can assume that a two-year-old knows what she likes, perhaps the apparently exclusive use of *ga* would be explained. Unfortunately, this account is *ad hoc* because there is no general reason to expect children to express subjective certainty through grammatical means.

In addition to the findings already cited from children acquiring Japanese and English, Slobin (1966) has presented evidence that children acquiring Russian also attempt to express abstract grammatical features in their earliest speech. Unlike adult Russian, where inflections carry information about the grammatical relations in sentences and word order is highly flexible, the earliest sentences of Russian children lack inflections and are composed in rigid order. This phenomenon can be explained if one assumes that Russian children attempt to express abstract structures but lack transformation rules of introducing inflections. Indeed, rigid word order is precisely what would be expected on the hypothesis that children include abstract features in their early speech, but must add to this inborn structure the particular transformations employed in their native language. As Slobin (1965) writes: "The most economical representation of an inflected language like Russian would order the language in the underlying representation. Inflections could then be added to the characteristic positions of parts of speech, and an additional rule or rules would then re-order this string."

The basis on which a child chooses to build sentence order may depend on what he believes to be the local manifestation of the basic grammatical relations. For the Russian child described by Slobin, sentences were produced in the order subject-object-verb, whereas the statistically predominant order in parental speech was subject-verb-object. There are several ways in which such a difference could arise. In general, the attempt to express the basic grammatical relations means producing sentences with an underlying structure of the type conventionally represented by labelled brackets or tree diagrams. The attempt to express the basic grammatical relations does not, however, determine the order in which constituents will appear (and, indeed, this is one of the idiosyncratic aspects of language). Linguistic theory can offer no guidance to a child at this point, so order must be discovered from parental speech. In the case of the Russian child described by Slobin, it is possible that occasional appearances of SOV sentences in parental speech led him to conclude that SOV is the preferred order in Russian. But deviant orders can arise in other ways as well. Consider, for example, the English sentence fragment, *hit the ball*. In fact, it is a verb phrase, manifesting the verb-object relation. However, to a child who expects the basic grammatical relations to hold in parental speech but does not yet know the order of constituents in English, the fragment *hit the ball* is ambiguous. Depending on a child's interpretation of the meaning of the fragment, it can be taken to manifest either the verb-object relation or the subject-predicate relation. If he thinks the fragment means "the ball hit something," then he must analyze it as corresponding to the relation of subject-predicate. Such a child would be expected to produce sentences backwards for a time. As a matter of fact, reversal of constituents occurs in the early speech of children. One of Braine's (1963b) subjects, for example, produced sentences like *allgone shoe, allgone lettuce*, which are inversions of the corresponding sentences in adult English (*the shoe is allgone, the lettuce is allgone*). It is possible that the Russian child's SOV order also arose from such initial "ambiguities" in parental speech.

We have seen three indications that children include abstract linguistic features in their early speech. In every case, the abstract feature appears to have been one or another basic grammatical relation. Since the evidence comes from children acquiring three very different languages, it appears that children do identical things in the face of radically different conditions of learning. The proposal that linguistic theory represents children's capacity for language accordingly gains empirical support.

Other abstract features that appear early in children's speech can be briefly mentioned, also. In particular, the forms underlying negation (Bellugi, 1964; summarized in McNeill, 1966a) and interrogation (Bellugi, 1965) appear early and can be taken as evidence in favour of the proposal.* In general, one would expect that the capacity for language acquisition is very rich, governing many (if not all) abstract aspects of language. Future observations of children developing linguistic competence will provide opportunities to evaluate this expectation.

* [An analysis of the development of negation in Japanese is presented in this volume: "What does a child mean when he says 'no'?", by David and Nobuko McNeill. Bellugi's work on negation and interrogation is reported in this volume in the paper by Klima and Bellugi, "Syntactic regularities in the speech of children."—Ed.]

The following analysis of *wa* and *ga* in terms of intrinsic and extrinsic predication has been provided more recently by McNeill. —Ed.

Intrinsic and Extrinsic Predication

It is in the acquisition of Japanese that a division between what we shall call extrinsic and intrinsic predicates is most clearly seen.[1] Japanese, like many languages, uses postpositions. Two of these particles, *wa* and *ga*, mark the surface subjects of sentences. While *wa* and *ga* have superficially similar distributions, their implications for the underlying structure are very different: *wa* is for intrinsic predicates and *ga* for extrinsic. Intrinsic predicates, those calling for *wa*, state a property the speaker feels to inhere in the subject. No unusual ontological insight is required. Habitual activities, for example, are regarded as intrinsic—*daddy-wa works in an office*. So is attribution—*government architecture-wa is grotesque*, membership in a hierarchy—*the collie-wa is a dog*, definition—*that-wa is a collie*, and the assertion of truisms—*all men-wa are mortal*. Sentences with *ga* have predicates that state properties the speaker feels to be extrinsic to the subject. They often form a momentary description—*there is a dog-ga in the yard* (when this is not customary)—but this is not an invariant rule. As with an intrinsic predicate the information contained in an extrinsic predicate is asserted about the subject, but unlike an intrinsic predicate the connection is thought to be adventitious.

How are *wa* and *ga* acquired? At first neither postposition appears in the speech of children. At 28 months (with the children studied by McNeill, 1966b) *ga* begins to be used, though not frequently. When used, it is used appropriately, with extrinsic predicates. About six months later *wa* appears and it too is used appropriately, with intrinsic predicates. Thus, extrinsic predicates appear to develop before intrinsic predicates. However, this is only half the story, and the second half reverses the interpretation of the first. It is possible for a native speaker of Japanese to classify utterances containing neither *wa* or *ga* according to the postposition required. McNeill (1968) found that approximately 90 percent of the sentences in his records were sufficiently clear to be so classified. The results of this procedure are clear: Children's early sentences contain twice as many intrinsic predicates as extrinsic predicates. Although *ga* is the postposition most often included in early child speech, *wa* is the postposition most often omitted.

We have what appears to be a contradiction. On the evidence of the postposition first acquired extrinsic predicates are dominant, whereas on the evidence

From *The acquisition of language: A study of developmental psycholinguistics*, by David McNeill. New York: Harper & Row, Publishers, 1970, pp. 30–32. Reprinted with the permission of the author and the publisher.
[1]Lee and Ando (n.d.) refer to this distinction as "designative" and "predicative," respectively.

provided by direct judgments of children's sentences intrinsic predicates are dominant. The contradiction is resolved when we observe the effect of the two predicates on the subject NPs of sentences. If we look at whether a child utters a predicate alone or a predicate with a subject, we find that subjects are usually *included* with extrinsic predicates and *excluded* with intrinsic predicates. *Wa* cannot appear without a superficial NP so it appears after *ga* even though there are twice as many contexts calling for it.

Exactly this same tendency appears in the speech of English-speaking children. English-speaking children present a situation comparable to young Japanese children (in that they also use neither *wa* or *ga!*) and a native (but bilingual) speaker of Japanese can classify their sentences according to which postposition they "require." American children use twice as many intrinsic and extrinsic predicates as do Japanese children and also include subjects with extrinsic predicates and exclude them with intrinsic predicates (McNeill, 1968). In Table 4 are examples of the two types of predicates from four children, two English-speaking and two Japanese speaking.

We can now see why children omit mentioning themselves as the subjects of sentences. The predicates of such sentences are intrinsic to young children, perhaps because infantile egocentrism (Piaget, 1926) makes everything a child says of himself seem inherently true.

TABLE 4 INTRINSIC AND EXTRINSIC PREDICATION IN THE SPEECH OF JAPANESE AND AMERICAN CHILDREN

Eve

	(extrinsic)	Mommy sit bottom
		Fraser read Lassie
	(intrinsic)	on Wednesday (the stock answer to "When's Cromer coming?")
		on my head (said of a hairband)

Adam

	(extrinsic)	Bunny rabbit running
		Cromer right dere
	(intrinsic)	pretty, Mommy?
		go dere, Mommy? (said of a puzzle piece)

Izanami

	(extrinsic)	Reiko said "no"
		tape goes round and round
	(intrinsic)	the same (said of two dresses)
		office (said of her father)

Murasaki

	(extrinsic)	the lion's mommy is seated
		a giraffe is eating grass
	(intrinsic)	can't eat the rind (said of an orange)
		delicious (said of a cracker)

The first grammatical relation to appear in the holophrastic period is presumably the assertion of properties. Greenfield (1968), for example, noted *hot* at 13 months. It is possible that these first relational utterances are intrinsic predicates, which assert permanent properties of objects, and not extrinsic predicates, which describe situations. The example of *hot* used with a *cold* coffee cup supports such an interpretation. Contrary to the belief of some philosophers (e.g., Quine, 1960), children may begin talking with general terms. And contrary to the beliefs of nearly everyone, they may not begin by describing things.

REFERENCES

Bellugi, Ursula, The emergence of inflections and negation systems in the speech of two children. Paper presented at New England Psychological Association, 1964.

Bellugi, Ursula, The development of interrogative structures in children's speech. In K. Riegel (ed.), *The development of language functions*. University of Michigan Language Development Program, Report No. 8, 1965, 103–138.

Braine, M. D. S., On learning the grammatical order of words, *Psychological Review*, 1963, **70**, 323–348. (a)

Braine, M. D. S., The ontogeny of English phrase structure: The first phase. *Language*, 1963, **39**, 1–13. (b) [Reprinted in this volume.]

Brown, R., and Ursula Bellugi, Three processes in the child's acquisition of syntax. In E. H. Lenneberg (ed.), *New directions in the study of language*. Cambridge, Mass.: M.I.T. Press, 1964.

Bruner, J. S., and Rose Olver (eds.), *Studies of cognitive growth*. New York: Wiley, 1966.

Chomsky, N., *Aspects of the theory of syntax*. Cambridge, Mass.: M.I.T. Press, 1965.

Greenfield, Patricia, M., Development of the holophrase. Unpublished paper, Harvard University, Center for Cognitive Studies, 1968.

Katz, J. J., and P. M. Postal, *An integrated theory of linguistic description*. Cambridge, Mass.: M.I.T. Press. 1964.

Kuroda, S. Y., Generative grammatical studies in Japanese. Doctoral dissertation, M.I.T., 1965.

Lee, Laura, L., and Kyoko Ando, Language acquisition and language disorder in Japanese. Unpublished paper, Northwestern University, n.d.

McNeill, D., Developmental psycholinguistics. In F. Smith and G. A. Miller (eds.), *The genesis of language: A psycholinguistic approach*. Cambridge, Mass.: M.I.T. Press, 1966, pp. 15–84. (a)

McNeill, D., The creation of language by children. In J. Lyons and R. Wales (eds.), *Psycholinguistics papers*. Edinburgh: Edinburgh University Press, 1966, pp. 99–114. (b)

McNeill, D., Two problems for cognitive psychologists. Problem 1: Predication. Center for Cognitive Studies Colloquium, Harvard University, 1968.

Piaget, J., *The language and thought of the child.* New York: Harcourt, Brace, 1926.

Quine, W. V., *Word and object.* Cambridge, Mass.: M.I.T. Press, 1960.

Slobin, D. I., Grammatical development in Russian-speaking children. In K. Riegel (ed.), *The development of language functions.* University of Michigan Language Development Program, Report No. 8, 1965.

Slobin, D. I., The acquisition of Russian as a native language. In F. Smith and G. A. Miller (eds.), *The genesis of language: A psycholinguistic approach.* Cambridge, Mass.: M.I.T. Press, 1966, pp. 129–148.

Weinreich, U., On the semantic structure of language. In J. Greenberg (ed.), *Universals of language.* Cambridge, Mass.: M.I.T. Press, 1963, pp. 114–171.

RUSSIAN •

General Course of Development in the Child of the Grammatical Structure of the Russian Language (According to A. N. Gvozdev)

————*D. B. El'konin*

Perhaps the most monumental child language diary is that of the Soviet linguist Aleksandr N. Gvozdev (pronounced GVOZDyeff), briefly summarized here in part by the distinguished Soviet psychologist D. B. El'konin. (Other partial summaries in English can be found in Slobin [1965, 1966b].) Gvozdev kept a diary of the speech of his son, Zhenya, almost daily for the first few years of the child's life, and recorded his language extensively until the age of nine (1921–1929). Sadly, the published diary is dedicated "to the bright memory of my son Zhenya, who perished on the front in the Great Fatherland War" (World War II).

The diary was recorded in a phonetic notation, either during the child's speech or shortly thereafter. Gvozdev's books (1948, 1949) present the huge corpus in several cross-cutting topical arrangements, with continuing intensive and insightful analysis of the material—both phonological and grammatical. He characterizes his task in terms of discovering the child's developing linguistic competence. He is clearly interested in discovering the child's generative systems, although it appears that he rarely intervened to test his son's comprehension or production by systematic elicitation procedures. This is the one major weakness in what is the most exhaustive picture yet published of language development in a single child.

A brief guide to problems of Russian grammar can be found on page 268.

—D.I.S.

Excerpted from D. B. El'konin, *Razvitiye rechi v doshkol'nom vozraste.* Moscow: Akademiya Pedagogicheskikh Nauk RSFSR, 1958, pp. 34–61. The chapter is El'konin's summary of Gvozdev (1949). Translated from Russian by Dan I. Slobin.

FROM 1;0 TO 1;10[1]

One-word sentence

Combination of two word roots in one sentence. Emergence at the end of this period of three- and four-word sentences consisting of formless words.

FROM 1;10 TO 2;0

A. Sentence Types

From an external point of view, a significant increase in sentence length is observed. While in the previous period combinations of subject and object of action (with omission of designation of action) or of designation of action and object (with omission of subject) were characteristic indicators of the fact that the child was not able to combine more than two words, in this period three-word sentences have become commonplace. There are also four- and five-word sentences, especially after 1;11.

On the basis of interrelationships of words in sentences it is clear that sentences are not disordered conglomerations, but, on the contrary, the mass of sentences presents quite an orderly picture. The following types of subordination are found: (1) nominative case + verb in agreement with nominative; (2) verb + governed noun of the following types: (2a) object (full or particular), (2b) place (location or direction of action), (2c) recipient of action; (3) verb + adjoining infinitive; (4) verb + adjoining adverb, (5) noun + genitive case governed by noun (found at end of period, and rarely).

Thus in this period there is a significant development of preverbal subordination. Prenominal subordination (except for agreement between verb and name) is absent. There are no particles serving syntactic functions.

B. Parts of Speech

The most important fact, due to which this period acquires great significance, is the beginning of division of words into morphological elements. In reviewing the acquisition of individual categories, isolated instances of analogous word formations—the most indicative evidence of morphological segmentability of words—may seem insufficiently convincing, but the fact that such instances appear successively in all categories considered is indubitable evidence for a transition from word roots to words consisting of meaningful elements. And this takes place at about the age of two years, after only one year of linguistic development!

In comparison with the preceding period, in the course of which sentences increased only by means of juxtaposition of discrete word elements, in the present period there is a twofold development of the sentence: on the one hand, sentence

---

[1] [Editor's note: Ages are given in years and months, separated by a semicolon].

length increases to three and four words (synthetic growth of sentences), and, on the other, individual words used in sentences become complex meaningful units (and not simple word roots) made up of meaningful units (morphemes). This can be referred to as the analytic development of sentences. As a result of this twofold development, a typical three-word sentence of this period can consist of six meaningful units.

The acquisition of word forms is expressed in the appearance in nouns of singular and plural; nominative, accusative, and genitive cases; and diminutive suffixes; and in the appearance in verbs of present and past tense, imperative, and infinitive.

This period is distinguished from the following one by the absence of forms of agreement between verbs and nouns, the absence of adjectives and particles, and also by the fact that a significant number of words are still encountered as word roots, not yet segmented into morphological elements. This period is characterized by the presence of expanded sentences and the absence of complex sentences.

FROM 2;0 TO 2;2

A. Sentence Types

This period marks the emergence and formation of complex conjunction-less sentences with various semantic relations between constituent sentences. Mononuclear sentences develop—both impersonal and indefinite-personal. Personal sentences have a nonverbal predicate expressed by a noun or by either the full or short form of the adjective.

Verbal government is strengthened and considerably broadened. There are many instances of the use of grammatical cases (already noted in the previous period) and, in addition, cases take on a number of new meanings: object toward which action is directed (dative case), instrument, subject of action, comitativeness (instrumental case), designation of objects with numeral quantifiers, and adverbs (genitive case).

Agreement has not yet been mastered. Thus there are only isolated cases of agreement between adjectives and pronouns. As before, there are no conjunctions and no prepositions.

B. Parts of Speech

In the area of development of grammatical forms this period is characterized by the strengthening of morphological segmentation of words (which began in the previous period) and by the acquisition of a number of new forms. New cases appear in nouns (dative, intrumental). The future tense of the verb is formed (simple and complex). The categories of person and number are acquired, as well as the category of reflexiveness. The first adjectives appear (still lacking agreement with nouns). The functions of adverbs are broadened and the first particles appear.

FROM 2;2 TO 2;4

A. Sentence Types

The greatest step forward in this period is the development of the complex sentence: conjunctionless sentences become more frequent and varied, and, what is most important, *complex conjoined sentences appear. Conjunctions appear with coordinate parts of the sentence.*

There are no significant changes in the structure of simple sentences: there is a beginning, albeit weak, of dependence of adjectives in agreement and governing nouns upon the noun; sentence government is broadened (although prepositions are still frequently omitted); several new forms of connection appear (personal verb dependent upon another verb.)

B. Parts of Speech

Significant changes are seen in this period in regard to the development of grammatical forms. A number of categories are acquired—for example: in animate nouns the accusative case begins to be isolated and the genitive case begins to be acquired for adverbs of quantity; the use of verbal forms in an impersonal sense is broadened; conjunctions and prepositions begin to appear; the use of adjectives gradually expands.

There are no significant changes in the acquisition of the category of gender: confusion of gender in all parts of speech is very clearly evident.

"The characteristic feature of the period under study," Gvozdev points out, "is the child's free use of the morphological elements of the language, as demonstrated by the abundance of varied constructions on the basis of analogy: this is evidence of great success in regard to the segmentation of words into meaningful elements, especially since the isolation of roots, suffixes, and endings is carried out with exceptional accuracy. At the same time, there is a clear tendency to replace infrequent forms by autonomous constructions on the model of more frequently used forms. In these substitutions it is evident that one ending drives out others and become predominant; typically all, or almost all, formations based on analogy have one such ending. Thus, in the accusative case such an ending is *-u*; in the instrumental *-om* is used; in the verbs there are widespread formations with the suffix *-i*. Among the verbs there are widespread formations of the present tense and the imperative on the basis of the past tense, and, contrariwise, there are infinitives and past tense forms based on the present tense. All of this points to an intimate connection among all verbal forms and to a tendency to construct such forms from a single basis" (Gvozdev, 1949, Part 1, pp. 110–111).

FROM 2;4 TO 2;6

A. Sentence Types

In this period there is a significant *proliferation and consolidation of conjunctionless and conjoined sentences.*

In simple sentences there is an increase in prepositional constructions, with rare omission of prepositions. (The use of prepositions has become the rule.) Adjectives, which were extremely rare earlier, occur in great numbers. The number of links of dependent words has increased. Thus, verbs can take three dependent words, and three ordered links of dependent words occur (for example verb + infinitive + accusative case + adjective in agreement).

There is an increase in the use of impersonal sentences of various types, as well as personal sentences with constituent predicates—generally without copula, although the first cases of use of the copula are observed.

B. Parts of Speech

In this period the most noticeable changes are in the use of prepositions: they are no longer omitted, but are used in significant numbers.

The use of adjectives has considerably broadened, but their agreement with nouns is not yet mastered. There is some advance in gender agreement, both in adjectives and verbs in the past tense: the number of cases of lack of agreement has decreased. Many forms based on analogy are used, as in the previous period.

With the disappearance of the circumlocution of self-reference in the third person, the acquisition of the category of person is completed.

FROM 2;6 TO 2;8

A. Sentence Types

In this period there is an increase in the frequency of complex sentences, especially conjoined complex sentences.

The use of conjunctions is more frequent with coordinate parts of the sentence: the first uses are noted of generalizing words with coordinate parts of the sentence.

There is a new expansion in the use of compound predicates, and, along with this, use of the copula (first noted in the previous period).

B. Parts of Speech

In this period there is further expansion of the functions of cases and the phonetic variants of endings.

The number of prepositional constructions increases and new prepositions enter.

There is a slight expansion in the use of adjectives, with a clear tendency to replace short forms by long ones. Gender agreement of adjectives and past tense verbs with nouns is not yet mastered, but examples of correct agreement continue to accumulate. In use of the past tense it is clear that gender agreement is acquired earlier in the presence of noun subjects than pronoun subjects.

There is a significant expansion in the use of both verb and noun suffixes (with the appearance of suffixes for the formation of nouns from verbs and adjectives).

The first passive past tense participles appear. The use of the comparative among nouns has been strengthened.

FROM 2;8 TO 2;10

A. Sentence Types

The use of complex sentences continues to grow during this period. Conjunctionless sentences are used very frequently, are correctly structured grammatically, and express a variety of semantic relations between the component sentences.

The use of complex sentences with conjunctions increases. New conjunctions appear, in particular those expressing logical relations of goal and condition: *chtoby* [in order that] and *yesli* [if]. There is more frequent reporting of the speech of others—both directly and indirectly. In compound predicates the use of the copula has become established. The use of impersonal sentences is expanded, along with increased complexity and diversity in their structure.

B. Parts of Speech

There are no major changes in grammatical forms during this period. Two conjunctions designating logical relations appear (*chtoby*, *yesli*). There is some increase in use of prepositional constructions, especially for the designation of indirect relations.

As in the previous period numerals control case use (the nominative case is still frequently found in these combinations), and the accusative is used with animate nouns (still frequently the same as the nominative).

The child has still failed to master gender agreement for adjectives and past tense verbs (with the exception of instances of self-reference).

Formations based on analogy are used to a significant extent.

FROM 2;10 TO 3;0

A. Sentence Types

The greatest change in this period is the significant expansion of complex sentences with conjunctions. As opposed to the previous period, in which conjunctionless sentences were in the overwhelming majority, *conjoined sentences are now frequently used*. While sentences with various conjunctions were found very rarely in earlier periods, in the present period they occur in quite large numbers. Most frequent are sentences with the conjunctions *kogda* [when] and *chtoby* [in order that]. Sentences with the conjunctions *kotoryy* [which, who(m)] and *kakoy* [what] appear. Sentences with *kotoryy* have a number of idiosyncratic features in comparison with adult speech.

The first cases are noted of complex sentences with primary- and secondary-part subordinates.

B. Parts of Speech

The functions of noun cases have increased: nominative in apposition; cases governed by the prepositions *cherez* [over, across, through] and *dlya* [for]; accusative without preposition for temporal reference.

Special aspects of noun government have still not been mastered: the accusative for animate nouns and the genitive for numerals.

The acquisition of gender agreement for adjectives has been completed. Gender is always used correctly in the full form of the adjective. Simultaneously, acquisition of gender agreement with past tense verbs is also accomplished: the gender of the past tense verb always agrees with that of the nominal subject. Gender confusion in the past tense is observed only with the personal pronoun *ya* [I], while gender agreement is always correct with the pronoun *ty* [you, familiar].

Almost no oblique cases are found in adjectives. The conditional appears in the verb, at last.

There are attempts to use the plural polite form in addressing a single individual.

FROM 3;0 TO 3;3[2]

A. Sentence Types

The number of complex conjoined sentences continues to increase. New conjunctions appear: *chto* [what], *koli* [if], *kuda* [whither], *skol'ko* [how many). As before, there are difficulties in forming sentences with the conjunction *kotoryy*, especially in regard to word order.

B. Parts of Speech

The semantic functions of cases continue to expand. In particular, there is an ever more detailed expression of spatial aspects of actions: first instances appear of the prepositions *do* [up to, as far as], *pod* [under], and *po* [along].

Special cases of government are mastered: (1) accusative identical to genitive for animate nouns and (2) numeral government of genitive singular and plural.

Adjectives always agree correctly in gender. (The acquisition of agreement had already been accomplished in the previous period.) Agreement with the past tense verb is also correct; the earlier confusion when using the pronoun *ya* [I] is no longer observed.

[2] Gvozdev notes: "In light of the fact that the grammatical system is basically acquired by age three, the course of development will continue to be traced only for those categories which have not yet been completely mastered, making special note of all instances which deviate from the norms of the Russian language. As a result, the general review sections will be significantly shortened. Since the tempo of acquisition has begun to slow down, reviews will be made by three-month periods" (1949, Part 1, pp. 181–182).

The conditional, first noted in the previous period, continues to be used. As before, formations based on analogy are widely used.

FROM 3;3 TO 3;6

A. Sentence Types

Several new question words appear: *skol'ko* [how many], *otchego* [why], *chey* [whose], *chto li* [maybe]. Oblique cases of pronouns appear: *kto* [who], *chto* [what], *u kogo* [by whom, whose], *iz chego* [from what], *chem* [with what, by means of what], *v chem* [in what]. The disjunctive *ili* [or] also appears. There is further consolidation of the previously acquired complex sentences with conjunctions, with continuing use of the conjoining words *kto* and *kakoy*.

B. Parts of Speech

Semantic functions of noun cases and case constructions continue to develop: cases with the new prepositions *ob* [about], *vmesto* [instead of], *posle* [after]; replacement of nominative predicate by instrumental.

There is an increased use of adjectives instead of one noun governing another: *Leninogo papy* [Lena (adj.) papa] instead of *papy Leny* [papa of Lena]; *stolbinaya ten'* [post (adj.) shade] instead of *ten' ot stolba* [shade from (the) post]. There is a clear tendency to replace possessive adjectives with short endings by adjectives with full endings.

The use of the conditional with verbs has become commonplace. There is widespread formation of new verbs from other parts of speech, and formation of new verbs to express aspectual nuances. As before, formations on the basis of analogy are widespread.

FROM 3;6 TO 3;9

A. Sentence Types

There is some expansion in the use of complex sentences (conjunctions *ved'* [after all], *vse-taki* [however, nevertheless]). There are a few instances of detachment, especially of participles. The instrumental predicate has still not been mastered.

B. Parts of Speech

There are almost no changes in the use of parts of speech. Animate nouns continue to take some accusatives which coincide with the nominative.

As in the previous period, there are many specially constructed adjectives.

Analogy formations are widespread in the various parts of speech. Most striking is the expansion of verb creations in various forms.

FROM 3;9 TO 4;0[3]

Parts of Speech

There are no significant changes in parts of speech.

There are still instances of accusatives for animate nouns which coincide with the nominative. The genitive plural is used with the numbers three and four.

The particle *pust'* is observed in the imperative, although this particle is more characteristic of literary speech.

Original word creation is widely practiced in the areas of nouns, adjectives, and verbs. Some noun formations are non-suffixal.

FROM 4;0 TO 4;4

"In light of the fact," Gvozdev notes, "that the acquisition of the grammatical structure has already achieved significant successes *and the basic grammatical categories have been established*, further progress in four-month periods is frequently minimal; therefore continued summaries of the results of such progress will not be reported. *What remains to be mastered are primarily various details of the morphological expression of grammatical categories*" (Italics added) (1941, Part 1, p. 221).

On the basis of detailed study of the formation of the grammatical structure of Russian, Gvozdev indicates the following developmental periods:

First period—from 1;3 to 1;10. This is the period of sentences made up of amorphous word roots which are used in a single, unchanged form in all instances. This period is clearly divided into two stages: (a) the one-word sentence stage (1;3–1;8) and (b) the multi-word sentence stage, consisting mainly of two-word sentences (1;8–1;10).

Second period—from 1;10 to 3;0. This is the period of acquisition of the grammatical structure of the sentence, associated with the formation of grammatical categories and their external expression. The period is characterized by the rapid growth of various types of simple and complex sentences, in which sentence parts receive syntactic expression.

This period embraces three stages: (a) formation of initial forms (1;10–2;1), (b) use of the Russian inflectional system for the expression of syntactic relations (2;1–2;3), (c) acquisition of subsidiary words for the expression of syntactic relations (2;3–3;0).

Gvozdev notes that this period "is sharply set off from the first period, but is not separated from the following period by sharply marked boundaries" (1949, Part 2, p. 190).

Third period—from 3;0 to 7;0. This is the period of acquisition of the Russian morphological system, characterized by the acquisition of types of

[3] There are no new sentence types in this period.

declension and conjugation. In this period the child sorts out synonymous morphological elements, previously confused with one another, into separate types of declension and conjugation. At the same time he generally masters all of the individual special features of the forms.

Characterizing the results of the acquisition of the grammatical structure of Russian, which the child accomplishes in about eight years, Gvozdev writes: "The level of mastery of the native language achieved by school age is very high. At this age the child has already mastered the entire complex system of grammar, including the most subtle rules of syntax and morphology of the Russian language, and also has a firm and error-free command of the multitude of special cases. Thus, the Russian language which he has acquired is truly native to him. And, in this language, the child receives a perfect tool of communication and thought" (1949, Part 2, p. 189).

Thus between the ages of two and seven, the child carries out a gigantic task in his mastery of all the basic forms of his native language. In this regard, it is especially interesting to attend to the formation of those forms of speech which comprise the fundamentals of connected discourse. These forms include, above all, complex conjoined sentences and the great variety of case forms for the expression of object relations. Complex sentences with components joined by conjunctions are first noted by Gvozdev in the period 2;4–2;6. There is intensive development of such sentences from this point onward. The gradual appearance of conjunctions in complex sentences is presented in Table 1. The table shows that, of 39 conjunctions and conjunctive words used by the child in complex sentences, 15 are used before the age of three; another 13 are added between ages three and four; and another 11 between four and six. Thus, the majority of conjunctions and conjunctive words (28 out of 39) begin to be used in speech before age four.

The use of case forms is first noted at the very end of the second year of life. In the course of the entire third year the acquisition of various case forms continues at an especially intense rate. The order of acquisition of case forms can be seen in Table 2. The table shows that by age three the child has mastered all of the basic case forms—both prepositional and nonprepositional. Of 47 case forms used in the entire period from two to seven, by age three 39 forms are already in use; in the period between 3;0 and 3;6 another eight forms enter. After 3;6 no new case forms are acquired. The acquisition of forms of complex sentences with conjunctions and the acquisition of the various case forms—both prepositional and nonprepositional—comprise the foundation for intensive development of connected discourse.

Various attempts have been made in the psychological literature to account for the rapid acquisition of grammatical forms in preschool age. K. Bühler, in his day, advanced the proposition that the basis of this process of acquisition lies in the supposed *discovery* of the inflectional nature of the language which is made by the child. After this discovery the child supposedly begins to understand the

TABLE 1   USE OF CONJUNCTIONS IN COMPLEX SENTENCES (AFTER GVOZDEV)[a]

AGE PERIOD	CONJUNCTIONS AND CONJUNCTIVE WORDS
2;4–2;6	Complex sentences with constituents joined by conjunctions are rare; there are only isolated cases of sentences with the following conjunctions: *a* [and/but], *i* [and], *a to* [or else], *potomu chto* [because], *kogda . . . kogda* [sometimes], *znachit* (quasi-conjunction) [so, well then]
2;6–2;8	Conjunctions: *I* [and], *A* [and/but] (1—with omission of negation, 2—with negation in the same sentence part, 3—after a pause), *A TO* [or else], *KOGDA* [when], *KAK* [how], *TOL'KO* [only], *ZNACHIT* [so, well then]
2;8–2;10	Conjunctions: *i, a, a to, kogda, kak, POTOMU CHTO* [because], *GDE* [where], *CHTOBY* [so that], *tol'ko, yesli* [if]
2;10–3;0	Conjunctions: *i, a, a to, kogda, kak, chtoby, ZATO* [in return]. Conjunctive words: *GDE* [where], *KOTORYY* [which, who(m)], *KAKOY* [what]
3;0–3;3	Conjunctions: *i, a to, kogda, kak, chtoby, YESLI* [if], *potomu chto, CHTO* [that, what], *KOLI* [if] Conjunctive words: *gde, KUDA* [whither], *SKOL'KO* [how much/many], *kotoryy*
3;3–3;6	Conjunctions: *i, DA* (coordinative) [and], *a, a to, kogda, KAK* (temporal or expressive) [how], *chto, chtoby, YESLI* (assent or conditional) [if], *koli, potomu chto* Conjunctive words: *kuda, gde, KTO* [who], *kotoryy, kakoy*
3;6–3;9	Conjunctions: *i, DA* [but], *a, a to, kogda, KAK* (temporal reference to previous action; comparative) [when, as], *CHTOBY* (goal reference; reference to request or desire expressed in main sentence) [so that], *yesli, chto, potomu chto* Conjunctive words: *gde, V CHEM* [in which], *skol'ko, kto, KOTORYY* [which, who(m)] (1—at beginning of sentence, with corresponding noun in subordinate phrase; 2—usage in accordance with norms of the literary language)
3;9–4;0	Conjunctions: *i, A* [and/but] (without negation and with negation in the second part of the opposition), *a to, kogda, KAK* [how, when, since] (used expressively and to signify manner of action in the presence of the adverb *tak* [such] in the main sentence), *chtoby, yesli, chto, potomu chto, KHOTYA* [although]. Conjunctive words: *gde, CHTO* [that, what] (in various cases), *kakoy*

[a] The table presents conjunctions whose use was observed during the given age period. The first observed use of a conjunction is given in capital letters.

TABLE 1—*continued*

AGE PERIOD	CONJUNCTIONS AND CONJUNCTIVE WORDS
4;0–4;4	Conjunctions: *I* [and] (indicating drawing of conclusion), *a, kogda, kak, chtoby, yesli, potomu chto, VED'* [after all], *VSE-TAKI* [anyway], *khotya, ILI* [or] (in both subordinating and disjunctive functions), *CHEM* [than] Conjunctive words: *CHTO* (in the causal sense of "why"), *skol'ko, kotoryy*
4;4–4;8	Conjunctions: *I* (concessive), *a, kogda, KAK* [when, as] (temporal or comparative senses), *chtoby, yesli, potomu chto, OTTOGO CHTO* [because (of)], *khotya, CHEM* [than] (comparative), *CHTO* [what] (indicating effect or consequence) Conjunctive words: *chto, gde, kto, ZACHEM* [what for, why], *skol'ko, kotoryy, kakoy*
4;8–5;0	Conjunctions: *i, a, a to, kogda, kak, yesli, koli, khotya* Conjunctive words: *chto, kto, POCHEMU* [why], *kotoryy*
5;0–5;6	Conjunctions: *a to, kogda, kak, chtoby, yesli, potomu chto, chto* Conjunctive words: *kto, OTCHEGO* [why], *kotoryy*
5;6–6;0	Conjunctions: *a, kogda, kak, yesli, chtoby, chto* Conjunctive words: *kto, gde, kotoryy*

basic principles of inflected languages—namely, that relations can be expressed by means of phonetic changes in morphological parts of words. This notion cannot be accepted. Bühler excessively intellectualizes the process of the child's cognizance of language. If the child does, in fact, make such a discovery, it would have to crown the process of acquisition, thus resulting from the course of development and hardly lying at the foundation of such development.

A number of psychologists, linguists, and educators have mentioned a supposed "feeling for language" inherent in the child between the ages of two and five or six, making it possible for him to master all of the most difficult aspects of language. This position was taken in the prerevolutionary Russian literature by Ushinskiy (1948). In the Soviet literature, the noted child language expert and children's writer K. Chukovskiy does not tire of repeating that in the period from two to five the child possesses an extraordinary feeling for language, and that this feeling, along with the child's mental work in language processing, forms the basis of the intensive ongoing process of language acquisition. At the same time, Chukovskiy correctly emphasizes the active character of the acquisition process and comes out against the theory of mechanical and passive acquisition of the native language. Chukovskiy writes: "Without such a heightened sensitivity for phonetics and morphology, a bare imitative instinct would be completely powerless and could not transform dumb infants into native speakers. Of course, one cannot ignore the fact that in all cases—without a single

TABLE 2 ORDER OF FORMATION OF CASE FORMS (AFTER GVOZDEV)

Age Period	Case Forms
1;10–2;0	Accusative of object Accusative with locative preposition (preposition is omitted in speech) Partitive genitive Nominative
2;0–2;2	Dative of person Dative with preposition indicating recipient of action (preposition is omitted in speech) Instrumental of means of action Instrumental with comitative preposition (preposition is omitted) Instrumental of goal (with preposition *za*, which is omitted) Prepositional case for locative designation
2;2–2;4	Genitive with locative preposition (with use of preposition *u* [near])
2;4–2;6	Accutative with locative preposition (with use of prepositions *v* [into] and *na* [onto]) Genitive with locative preposition (with use of prepositions *u* [near] and *iz, ot,* and *s* [indicating direction away from source]) Dative with preposition *k* to designate recipient of action Instrumental with preposition *s* to designate "together with" Instrumental of goal with preposition *za* Prepositional case for locative designation with *v* [in] and *na* [on]
2;6–2;8	Accusative with preposition *pod* [under] as directional locative Genitive for object of negated verb Genitive with preposition *u* to indicate possession Genitive with preposition *bez* [without] to indicate absence or lack of something Dative without preposition to indicate benefactor of action Instrumental without preposition to indicate material used to carry out action Instrumental without preposition to indicate object of action Instrumental to indicate cause or source of phenomenon Instrumental with preposition *pod* for locative designation
2;8–2;10	Accusative with prepositions *pro* and *ob* [about] to indicate topic of speech Genitive with preposition *iz* [from] for locative designation Genitive with preposition *ot* [from] for locative designation Genitive with preposition *u* [near] for locative designation Genitive with preposition *posle* [after] for temporal designation Instrumental without preposition for designation of time of action
2;10–3;0	Accusative without preposition and with adjective for temporal designation

TABLE 2—*continued*

AGE PERIOD	CASE FORMS
	Accusative with preposition *za* [by] to indicate touching part of an object [for example, *za konchik brat'* 'to pick up by the tip'] Accusative with preposition *cherez* [across, through] to indicate an object or a space completely traversed Genitive with preposition *u* to indicate the person or object possessing something. Genitive with preposition *iz* [of] to indicate material of which something is made Genitive with preposition *dlya* [for] to indicate person or object benefiting from action Instrumental without preposition to indicate subject in the passive
3;0–3;3	Accusative with non-locative senses of *na* [for example, *kupit' na den'gi* 'to buy for money'] Genitive with preposition *do* [up to] to indicate motion up to a fixed point Dative with preposition *po* [along] to indicate motion along a surface
3;3–3;6	Accusative with preposition *pro* in the sense of "for" [*dlya*] Genitive with preposition *ot* [from] to designate cause [for example, *ot dozhd'ya* 'from the rain'] Genitive with preposition *vmesto* [instead of] Dative with preposition *po* [out of] to designate cause [for example, *po gluposti* 'out of foolishness']
3;6–3;9	Nothing new appears. Further development consists of mastery of precise case forms.

exception—mastery of one's native tongue is the result of the mutual work of the child and those who surround him. But all attempts by adults would be totally fruitless if young children did not have a refined feeling for the structures and sounds of words" (1956, p. 68). The merit of Chukovskiy's position is not only that he opposes mechanistic theories and emphasizes the active character of the acquisition process, but also that he has collected a huge (albeit uncoordinated) mass of data on children's word creation.

Gvozdev also notes the special linguistic gifts of preschool age children. Thus he writes: "Being guided by meaning, the child freely creates forms on the basis of meaningful elements. Even greater originality is demanded in the construction of new words, since in these instances new meanings are created; this requires versatile powers of observation and the ability to discriminate objects and events on the basis of their characteristic attributes. The keenness of children's observations and the artistic vividness of many childish words are well known. Words created by children are truly very close to the verbal creativity demonstrated by literary artists. Thus we are dealing here with true creativity, substantiating the linguistic giftedness of children" (1949, Part 2, p. 187).

One cannot agree with the frequent attempts by Chukovskiy and Gvozdev to draw together children's word creation and literary word creation. But the fact that preschool age is a period of heightened sensitivity to linguistic phenomena is well established. Independent word creation is a process demonstrating the child's acquisition of the system of suffixes of the native language. This process of acquisition has its own logic. In Gvozdev's research the question of word formation is examined in considerable detail. Table 3 shows the order of

TABLE 3   ORDER OF ACQUISITION OF NOUN SUFFIXES USED FOR WORD FORMATION (AFTER GVOZDEV)[a]

AGE PERIOD	MEANING OF NOUN SUFFIX	PHONETIC SHAPE OF SUFFIX
1;0–2;0	Word roots. No word formation	
2;0–2;2	Diminutive and affectionate suffixes, first appearing at the end of the previous period[b]	-chk-, -ochk-, -k-, -chik-, -ik-, -ok-, -ichk-
	Diminutive and affectionate suffixes with the range of phonetic forms found most frequently in the preceding period as well (new phonetic variants are noted)	-nk-, -ishk-
	Pejorative suffix	-k-
2;2–2;4	Diminutive and affectionate suffixes	-k-, -ok-, -ik-, -chk-, -chik-, -ts-, -yshk-, -ish-
	Pejorative suffixes	-yshk , -ishk-
2;4–2;6	Diminutive and affectionate suffixes	-k-, -ok-, -yshk-, -chk-, -ochik-, -chik-, -ts-, -nk-, -ushk-
	Pejorative suffix	-ishk-
	Suffix for designation of object on the basis of its action; used to form a noun from a past-tense verb root (one instance noted)	-il-

[a] The table includes all cases of word formation noted in each period.
[b] "It should be noted that not one case of analogic formation was noted with these suffixes; but there is a large number of forms with a given root (with a diminutive suffix and without one), among them many cases clearly indicating appropriate use of the suffix together with an affectionate intonation. Thus it can be concluded that the categories of diminutive and affectionate have been mastered" (Gvozdev, 1949, Part 1, p. 50).

TABLE 3—*continued*

AGE PERIOD	MEANING OF NOUN SUFFIX	PHONETIC SHAPE OF SUFFIX
2;6–2;8	Diminutive and affectionate suffixes	*-k-, -chk-, -ochk-, -shk-, -oshk-, -ik-, -yen'k-, -unchik-*
	Pejorative suffix	*-k-*
	Augmentative suffix	*-ishch-*
	Suffix for designating object on the basis of its action	*-k-*
	Suffix for qualitative designation of object	*-ashk-*
2;8–2;10	Diminutive suffixes	*-unchik-, -nk-, -ochk-, -yshek-*
	Suffix for designating object on the basis of its action	*-ishk-*
2;10–3;0	Mastery remains at the preceding level: diminutive and affectionate suffixes are used	
3;0–3;3	Diminutive suffix	*-ul'chik-*
	Suffix for designating objects of feminine gender	*-its-*
3;3–3;6	Diminutive suffixes (Govzdev notes a special facility in the formation of new diminutives for animal young)	*-ik-, -its-*
	Suffixes designating actor	*-shchik-, -nik-*
	Suffix of abstract action	*-yy-*
3;6–3;9	Suffix designating actor	*-yets-*
	Suffix designating feminine gender	*-its*
	Suffix for abstract concepts	*-yen'-*
3;9–4;0	Diminutive suffix	*-ushk-*
	Suffix designating animal young	*-yenysh*
	Augmentative suffixes	*-in-, -ishch-*
	Suffixes designating actor (Gvozdev notes the formation of nouns without suffixes: *a*—from verbs, *b*—from nouns with diminutive suffix)	*-shchik-, -tel'*
4;0–4;4	Formation based on adjective, using suffix designating actor	*-yets*
	Suffix designating feminine gender	*-ikh-*
4;4–4;8	Suffixes designating feminine individuals	*-its-, -ovk-*
	Diminutive and affectionate suffixes	*-ochek-, -yechk-*

TABLE 3—*continued*

AGE PERIOD	MEANING OF NOUN SUFFIX	PHONETIC SHAPE OF SUFFIX
4;4–4;8	Suffix designating animal young	*-yat-*
	Suffix designating separate individuals	*-ink-*
	Suffix designating collectivity	*-yenchik*
	Suffix designating object on basis of action	*-k-*
	(Gvozdev notes an instance of a complex word with a conjoining vowel)	
4;8–5;0	Suffix designating actor	*-shchik*
	Diminutive suffix also used to designate separate individuals	*-ink-*
	Suffix designating object on basis of action	*-k-*
	Abstract suffix	*-ot-*
	(Gvozdev notes formations without suffixes to designate large objects)	
5;0–5;6	(Gvozdev notes verb-based noun formations without suffixes	
	Suffixes designating actor	*-ar', -un*
	Suffix designating actor and feminine gender	*-un'-*
	Diminutive suffix also used to designate separate individuals	*-ink-*
	Augmentative suffix	*-in-*
	Suffix designating animal young	*-at-*
	Suffixes designating various objects	*-nik, -ok, -k*
5;6–6;0	Diminutive suffixes	*-its, -ochk-*
	Affectionate suffix	*-ashk-*
	Augmentative suffix	*-ishch-*
	Suffixes designating actor	*-shchik, -nik*
	Suffix designating feminine gender	*-un'-*
	Suffixes designating animal young	*-yenchik, -yat-*
	Abstract suffix	*-yeni*
	(Gvozdev notes formation of a complex word with conjoining *o*)	
6;0–6;6	Diminutive suffixes	*-ichk, -ochk, -its-, -ok, -ik, -ushk-*
	Augmentative suffix	*-in-*
	Diminutive suffix also used to designate individuality	*-ink-*
	Suffixes designating animal young	*-onok, yenok*

TABLE 3—*continued*

AGE PERIOD	MEANING OF NOUN SUFFIX	PHONETIC SHAPE OF SUFFIX
6;0–6;6	Suffixes designating actor	*-ukh-, -kh, -k, -tel', -ach, -yets*
	Suffix designating feminine gender	*-ikh-*
	Suffix designating feminine actor	*-un'-*
	Suffixes designating objects	*-nk, -shk-*
	Suffix designating object on basis of action	*-k*
	Suffix designating abstract action	*-yen'*
	(Gvozdev notes suffixless nouns formed from: *a*—verb, *b*—diminutive noun, *c*—noun with negation; and also formation of complex words)	
6;6–7;0	Diminutive and affectionate suffix	*-ik*
	Diminutive suffix	*-ichk, -its-, -ok-, -ochk-, -yechk-, -ts-*
	Diminutive suffix with negative nuance	*-ishk-*
	Diminutive suffixes also designating individuality	*-ink-, -inochk-*
	Suffix designating animal young	*-onok*
	Suffixes designating animal young in the plural	*-at-, -yat-*
	Augmentative suffixes	*-in-, -ishch-, -ye, -ukh*
	Suffixes designating actor	*-nik, -yets, -ak, -ar', -kh, -ukh*
	Suffix designating individual exceptionally endowed with a given quality	*-il-*
	Suffixes designating feminine gender	*-its-, -ikh-, -yn-*
	Suffixes designating object on basis of action	*-uchk-, -yak-, -b-*
	Suffixes designating object	*-ok, -k-*
	Suffix designating geographic name of country, region, and so on	*-i*
	Abstract suffixes	*-ost', -ot-*
	Suffix designating object located beneath another object, with the preposition *pod* [under]	*-y*
	(Gvozdev notes suffixless formations from: *a*—verb, *b*—noun with suffix *-k-*, partially losing diminutive meaning for designation of large objects. Also noted are complex nouns with conjoining vowels and formation of nouns with the prefixes *pere-* [trans-], *pro-*, *vz-*)	

acquisition of productive noun suffixes. The table shows that by age three the only suffixes to have been acquired are diminutive, affectionate, pejorative, and augmentative. There are only isolated instances of suffixes designating objects according to action and quality. The acquisition of all the remaining suffixes is carried out after age three and extends through the entire preschool period.

In this regard it should be noted that the development of word formation occurs at a later age than the acquisition of those morphological elements used to express the various syntactic relations. This points to the relatively greater difficulty of acquiring the means of word formation.

At the same time, however, Gvozdev notes the great ease with which his son Zhenya could create new diminutives, with appropriate suffixes, at the age of 3;5. Gvozdev describes a special sort of game he played with his son. Zhenya said to his father: "I'm a *mishul'chik* [little bear] and you're a *medved'* [bear]." Father: "And if I'm a *lev* [lion], then what are you?" Zhenya: "*Livunchik* [little lion]." The game continued as follows: The father would ask a question and Zhenya would answer. Zhenya gave the following word formations to his father's questions: *tigr — tigrichek malen'kiy* [tiger (dim.) little]; *slon — ya byl slonishka* [elephant (dim.)]; *krokodil — ya krokodil'chik* [crododile (dim.)]; *olen' — a ya olenchik* [deer (dim.)]; *loshad' — zherebrenochek malen'kiy* [horse — colt (dim.) little]; *korova — ya byla by telka, ya byl by malen'kaya korovka* [cow — calf (dim.), little cow (dim.)]; *volk — mishul'chik* [wolf — bear (dim.)]; *svin'ya — porosenochek* [pig (dim.)]; *sobaka — ya byl by malen'kaya sobachka* [little dog (dim.)]; *zebra — ya byl by malen'kiy izeberchik* [little zebra (dim.)]; *los' — losik malen'kiy* [elk (dim.) little]; *lisa — lisinchik malen'kiy* [fox (dim.) little]; *kenguru — kengurunchik malen'kiy* [kangeroo (dim.) little]; *zhirafa — zhivarchik* [sic.] [giraffe (dim.)]; *krolik — krolichik* [rabbit (dim.)]; *zmeya — zmiya* [snake (dim.)]; *tarakan — tarakanchik* [cockroach (dim.)]; *mukha — tozhe mukha* [fly (not dim.)]; *zhuk — ya byl by komar* [beetle — I'd be a gnat].

These facts point to the considerable ease with which the child was able to make use of the appropriate suffixes of word formation. . . . [El'konin goes on to summarize the research of Bogoyavlenskiy, translated in full in this volume.—Ed.]

REFERENCES

Gvozdev, A. N., *Formirovaniye u rebenka grammaticheskogo stroya russkogo yazyka,* two parts. Moscow: Akad. Pedag. Nauk RSFSR, 1949. [Reprinted in A. N. Gvozdev, *Voprosy izucheniya detskoy rechi.* Moscow: Akad. Pedag. Nauk RSFSR, 1961, pp. 150–471.]

Chukovskiy, K., *Ot dvukh do pyati,* 11th ed. Moscow: Gos. Izdat. Detskoy Lit. Min. Prosveshcheniya RSFSR, 1956. [English translation: K. Chukovsky, *From two to five,* translated and edited by Miriam Morton. Berkeley/Los Angeles: University of California, Press, 1966.]

Ushinskiy, K. D., *Sobr. soch,* Vol. 2. Moscow: Akad. Pedag. Nauk RSFSR, 1948.

SEMANTICS

Although many of the preceding papers raise questions of semantics, the following three devote central attention to this problem.[1] Eve Clark concerns herself with the functions of alternative descriptions of temporal events. In a more recent study (1971) she has attempted to show that children learn temporal conjunctions in terms of semantic features—binary features of meaning analogous to the distinctive features of phonology (see Bierwisch, 1970) (for example, *before* = + Time, − Simultaneous, + Prior; *after* = + Time, − Simultaneous, − Prior). Her husband, Herbert Clark (1970), has made a similar argument in regard to children's learning of polar adjectives and comparatives. McNeill and McNeill (below) also make use of binary semantic features in their analysis of Japanese negation. The semantic feature approach is currently controversial in linguistics and psycholinguistics, and Amidon and Carey (1971) have provided a provocative counter argument to the Clarks in a recent series of experiments (see the discussion on sentence interpretation strategies, p. 464). Herbert Clark (1970), however, has succeeded in resolving some puzzling questions of semantic development in terms of semantic features. His discussion stems from the puzzling finding by Donaldson and Balfour (1968) that, at a certain stage, children seem to interpret *less* as if it meant *more*. Reviewing a large body of research, Clark argues that children first learn that both members of a pair of polar adjectives refer to the general dimension (for example, both *less* and *more* mean *some*, that is, 'having extent'). Then they learn that there is a dimension, identifying both terms with the positive pole (*less* = *more*). Finally they learn that the dimension is polar. The same sort of analysis is used by Eve Clark (1971) in regard to the development of *before* and *after*. The Clarks' hypothesis needs much more support, but it represents an important direction of thinking in the study of semantic development.

The paper by Antinucci and Parisi presents a highly promising direction, based on current work in generative semantics (see Fillmore and Langendoen, 1971; Lakoff, 1970; McCawley, 1970; Ross, 1970). The central concern here is not so much with the semantic features of individual lexical items as with the semantic configurations underlying sentences. Their approach and analyses are presented in numerous working papers in Italian from the Istituto di Psicologia, CNR, Rome (along with Cristiano Castelfranchi, and others), and in an earlier English paper (Parisi and Antinucci, 1970).

The paper by McNeill and McNeill is another aspect of their study of

[1] See pp. 171–172 for a discussion of the role of semantics in analysis of child language development.

584

Japanese acquisition (see McNeill [above]; McNeill, Yukawa, and McNeill [1971]). The course of semantic development of negation in Japanese outlined in their paper is very similar to Lois Bloom's analysis of the development of negation in English, and comparisons have been made elsewhere (Bloom, 1970; McNeill, 1970). McNeill and Bloom, in their books, also compare their accounts of the development of negation with that of Klima and Bellugi (above).

—D.I.S.

ENGLISH •

How Children Describe Time and Order[1, 2]

——Eve V. Clark

Recent research into language development has been concerned with the formal syntax of the child's language, and many studies have concentrated on trying to write transformational generative grammars to account for utterances produced by the child at different stages (Berko, 1958; Menyuk, 1963; Bellugi and Brown, 1964; Brown and Bellugi, 1964; Bever, Fodor, and Weksel, 1965; Klima and Bellugi, 1966; McNeill, 1966). Inevitably, too great a concentration on syntax leads one to ignore the role other factors play in the development of language. The approach I shall suggest in this paper is complementary to these formalized grammars in that it stresses the function of language. By function, I mean the pragmatic and semantic reasons for a child's choice of one syntactic form over another in a particular situation. For example, he might say, describing two events in time, *He opened the door and he came in, or He came in after he opened the door,* or, alternatively, *After he opened the door, he came in.* These are three different ways of describing the temporal order of the same two events. In the present paper, I will first suggest that there are functional reasons for the development of the child's choice of these description types, and then examine data from $3\frac{1}{2}$–4-year-old children for confirmation of this point of view.

To begin with, I shall look at three principles which interact to determine which one of the several possible descriptions of two serial events an adult will choose in a particular context. These three principles also affect the child's use of the different description types. They do not, however, predict any order of

[1] This paper is based on part of my Ph.D. dissertation, submitted to the University of Edinburgh (Department of Linguistics) in 1969. I wish to thank the members of the S.S.R.C. Cognition Project, University of Edinburgh, and in particular Margaret Donaldson and R. J. Wales. I also wish to thank Sandra L. Bem, H. H. Clark, and W. C. Watt for their criticisms and comments during the preparation of the manuscript. Printed by permission of the author.
[2] Throughout this paper, I shall use the term "coordinate" to describe those sentences with clauses conjoined by *and, and then,* or *and so.*

acquisition until we take into account the function of each of the different descriptions in English. The three principles will be discussed under the headings order of mention, derivational simplicity, and choice of theme.

ORDER OF MENTION

The first principle is that order of mention, the order in which two events are described by a speaker, is "simpler" when it coincides with chronological order, that is, the order in which the events are perceived to have happened. In English, order of mention may or may not coincide with chronological order. First, if the speaker uses only single clauses, the only way that he can recount a succession of events is by keeping to the chronological order of their occurrence:

> (1)   He opened the door. He came in. He went over to the table. He picked up a book. He sat down.

The same applies if the speaker uses coordinate clauses to describe a succession of events:

> (2)   He opened the door and he came in.

Event 1 must be described before event 2. But events may be mentioned out of chronological order if the speaker uses an appropriate temporal conjunction between the clauses. For example, we can speak of the result before mentioning the cause:

> (3)   He took a taxi because he missed the bus.

The coordinate clause construction (2) is therefore simpler than (3) by the principle of order of mention.

There is psychological evidence which supports this principle by showing that people prefer to use a linguistic description of events in which order of mention corresponds to chronological order. Clark and Clark (1968), in a memory experiment, found that subjects remembered best the meaning of those sentences in which order of mention coincided with chronological order. In addition, the subjects often made errors by interpreting order of mention to mean chronological order when they had forgotten the appropriate conjunction. Thus the sentences in which temporal order was best remembered were:

> (4)   He came in *and* he shut the door.
> (5)   *After* he came in, he shut the door.
> (6)   He came in *before* he shut the door.

rather than the alternative descriptions:

(7) He shut the door *but first* he came in.
(8) He shut the door *after* he came in.
(9) *Before* he shut the door, he came in.

Groethuysen (1935–1936) also found that adults would recount the events of the preceding day in the order in which they occurred, that is, in chronological order. Fraisse (1963) has pointed out how difficult it is for adults to repeat a sequence of digits or letters just heard in any other order than the one in which they were perceived. Children also, unquestioningly, repeat any such list in the order given. Also, in an experiment in which pairs of sentences that described a series of two events were compared, Katz and Brent (1968) found that both adults and children (grades 1 and 6) tended to prefer those sentences in which the order of mention coincided with the chronological order of the events. Finally, the preference for chronological order in the order of mention could also partly explain why children make the mistakes they do in certain sentence-completion tasks (Piaget, 1926; 1928). When they are asked to complete the sentence "The man fell off his bicycle because . . . ," they assume that the first event mentioned *is* the first event, and therefore expect to talk about the *second* of two events in their completion of the sentence. Thus they would say "The man fell off his bicycle because *he broke his arm*," ignoring the meaning of the conjunction which would tell them that the event mentioned in the first half of the sentence is in fact the second event in time.

DERIVATIONAL SIMPLICITY

The second principle is that of derivational simplicity. This notion of simplicity applies only to the so-called complex sentences, that is, those with a main and a subordinate clause:

(10) They arrived after the play had begun.
(11) He was late because the road was closed.
(12) When Tom got in, he opened all the windows.

Simplicity here refers to the number of steps (transformations) in the derivation of a sentence from its deep structure. Derivational simplicity is seen in the case where the only difference between two sentences with identical meaning and with almost identical surface structure is the clause order, that is:

(13) He got up from his chair when he saw the door open.
(14) When he saw the door open, he got up from his chair.

The principle of derivational simplicity is that the first of these sentences, (13), is transformationally simpler because the second, (14), has undergone an

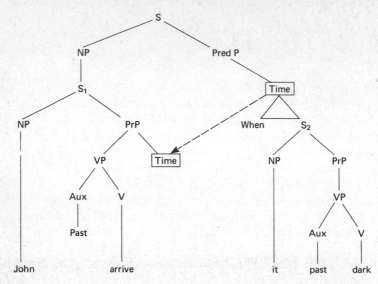

Figure 1.

additional transformation which has preposed the subordinate clause into first position in the sentence.

Linguistically, the source of the subordinate clause can be shown to be an adverbial or adjunct constituent of the predicate phrase. For example, *He arrived when it was dark* has a high-level constituent structure like that of *He arrived then* (see Lees, 1961; a similar analysis is found in Smith, 1964, and in Doherty and Schwartz, 1967). The subordinate clause is derived from a node in the phrase-marker to the right of the matrix sentence into which it is subsequently embedded (see Figure 1). Figure 1 is essentially taken from Chomsky (1965), but I have revised it in the light of evidence discussed by Lakoff and Ross (1966). In this derivation, the subordinate clause is first attached to the predicate phrase of the main clause by an embedding transformation (see dotted line in Figure 1); it is only after this that it may be preposed into first position.

Additional evidence for this derivation of the subordinate clause comes from one explanation of the pronominalization and proverbalization rules within the sentence in English. Consider the following examples:

(15)   John came in when he finished cutting wood.
(16)   When John finished cutting wood, he came in.
(17)   When he finished cutting wood, John came in.
(18)   He came in when John finished cutting wood.

In (15), (16), and (17), *John* and *he* may refer to the same person. However, in (18) *John* and *he* must refer to different people. To exclude (18), then, as an instance of intrasentence pronominalization, we may assume that pronominal reference can only be anaphoric—that is, referring to someone or something which has already been mentioned—and at the same time that this pronominalization can take place either before or after the preposing transformation, as, for instance, in (16) and (17). The restrictions on (18), with anaphora, are explicable only if the subordinate clause is derived from a high-level constituent to the right of the main clause. Proverbalization works in the same way:

(19)   He jumped over the fence after he decided to do so.
(20)   After he decided to do so, he jumped over the fence.
(21)   After he decided to jump over the fence, he did so.
(22)   He did so after he decided to jump over the fence.

As with pronominalization above, the proverbalization (*do so*) in (22) may not refer to *jump over the fence*. There are other problems which arise in connection with anaphoric reference, but these problems are not related to the derivation of the subordinate clause as such (see the discussion in Lakoff, 1968). Given these facts supporting the derivation of the subordinate clause from a constituent to the right of the main clause in deep structure, we can conclude that the simpler form of sentence with a subordinate clause is the one with the subordinate clause second, that is, to the right of the main verb. A later transformation can then prepose the subordinate clause, as in (12), (14), and so on.

Derivational simplicity is independent of the chronological order of mention because the subordinate temporal clauses can describe either the first or the second event, for example:

(23)   He ran round the garden *after* he got out of the pool.
(24)   He went swimming *before* he ran round the garden.

However, for the majority of temporal conjunctions, (*when, if, since, after,* and so on), the subordinate clause describes the first event:

(25)   He came home *when he was ready*.
(26)   He will pick up the mail *if Tom fetches him*.
(27)   They came in *because they got cold*.
(28)   He read the book *after he heard about the reviews*.

In (25)–(28), the simpler derivational form does not allow chronological order of mention. Event 2 in each instance is described before event 1. In English, though, there are two subordinating conjunctions which do make the chronological order of mention and the derivationally simpler form correspond, *before* and *until*:

(29)   He ran across the road *before he picked up the ball*.
(30)   He banged on the door *until he was let in.*

Although the "simpler" sentence with a subordinate clause is derived to the right of the main clause, this does not mean that all subordinate temporal clauses will occur in second position in surface structure, particularly when other "performance" considerations intervene. The fact that the derivationally simpler form of sentence has the subordinate clause second, though, does have developmental consequences.

CHOICE OF THEME

This is the choice made by every speaker when he decides what he is going to talk about. Any communication in English is organized in *theme* and *rheme*. The theme is the first member of the sentence and is the "subject" of the utterance. The rheme comprises the information given about the theme.

There are certain general properties of themes. In English, the theme is generally the (animate) subject to the sentence, but it may also be the object of the verb in passive sentences (Svartvik, 1956). In Wh- questions, the theme is the interrogative word, and in clauses beginning with "link" words (adjuncts) like *therefore, so, however, then*, the adjunct is the theme. Theme is not only a within-sentence choice, but also one that acts across sentences; the rheme of one sentence is often repeated as the theme of the following one. Such sequences in language provide a natural link between different utterances. Compare:

> (31)   I saw a man. The man was mending a box.
> (32)   I saw a man. The box was being mended by the man.

The first of these sequences is more "natural" than the second where there is no rhematic-thematic continuity between the two successive utterances.

Theme has mainly been discussed in terms of its occurrence within the clause (Firbas, 1959; Halliday, 1967a; 1967b). However, I shall extend this notion and claim that, within the utterance, the theme of a sentence can be a whole clause rather than one word or phrase. This is substantiated by the fact that many (subordinate) clauses can be deleted almost entirely, leaving a word or phrase as theme:

> (33)   *After I had lunch*, I saw Joan.
> (34)   *After lunch*, I saw Joan.
> (35)   I ate lunch. *Then* I saw Joan.

In (34) the theme of the sentence is an adverbial phrase, *after lunch*, but this is derived from the clause *after I had lunch* (33). Thus the whole clause, when preposed, can act as the theme. In (35) the theme of the second sentence, *then*, takes the place of the first sentence; this example again shows the relation between clause and adjunct as theme. The underlined words are thematic.

Theme can be chosen independently of both chronological order and derivational simplicity. If the speaker chooses the first event as theme, he is forced to use the simpler order of mention. With this constraint, he may select a simple coordinate sentence,

> (36)   He closed the door and he went out.

a derivationally simple subordinate construction,

> (37)   He closed the door before he went out.

or a derivationally complex one,

(38)   After he closed the door, he went out.

But if he chooses the second event as theme, he must use a sentence with the more complex order of mention. Here he may select an adversative coordinate sentence,

(39)   He went out but first he closed the door.

a derivationally simple construction,

(40)   He went out after he closed the door.

or a derivationally complex one,

(41)   Before he went out, he closed the door.

We should keep in mind, however, that conjunctions like *before* are uncommon in English; (37) and (41) are used only in limited contexts. Furthermore, adversative or contrary-to-expectation constructions like (39) are very rarely used by young children, and are understood only with difficulty by older children (Minkus and Stern, 1923; Piaget, 1926). This suggests that the speaker's choices are actually limited to (36) and (38) for simpler order of mention and to (40) for complex order of mention.

One last point should be made about the difference between the coordinating and the subordinating constructions. Let us take the instance in which the choice of theme makes the order of mention for both constructions the same as the chronological order:

(42)   I saw George and I went home.
(43)   After I saw George, I went home.

The relation between the two events described in (43) is far closer than in (42); I shall call this relation the *contingency* relation between events. In (43), my going home is contingent on, or follows from, my seeing George. With a coordinate conjunction between the two clauses, though, there is no such relation between the two events. Contingency between events is found where one event (described in the main clause) is dependent on the other event (in the subordinate clause); in coordinate clauses, both events have an equal status, therefore one cannot be said to be dependent on the other. Thus, where the choice lies between the coordinate and the subordinate constructions in describing events in chronological order, presence or absence of contingency between the two events as they are perceived by the speaker will determine which description type is used. The existence of this type of contingency is presumably one criterion adult speakers use for deciding between (42) and (43).

The effect of theme on how people normally generate descriptions has been shown experimentally by Prentice (1967). In her study, a subject was cued with either the word for the *actor* or for the *object* in a situation. Next, the situation itself, portrayed in a slide, was presented to the subject. The subject was then asked to describe the picture he had been shown. Her data, as might have been expected, show that when the subject was cued with the *actor*, he generated a majority of active sentences containing the word order *actor-object*, while, given the *object* as a cue, he more often used the word order *object-actor* and generated a large number of passive sentences. Tannenbaum and Williams (1968) found similar results in a study where the subject's attention was first focused on either the *subject* or the *object* of a situation which was then presented pictorially. Each picture was marked with an A or a P indicating that the subject was to describe it with an active or passive sentence. The latencies for generating an active or passive description were then observed. Passives always took longer than actives even when the focus was the *object*; however, the passive took less time to generate when the focus was the *object* than when it was the *subject*. (See also Turner and Rommetveit, 1968, who did a similar experiment.)

Theme, then, is largely dependent on the context, whether this consists of cuing or focusing beforehand, as in the two studies just discussed, whether the context is what has occurred previously in a conversation, or whether it is the physical situation—objects and other people—which surrounds the speaker. The recognition of theme, and its place at the beginning of the sentence, is probably one of the factors which precedes the learning of various linguistic structures, including, of course, descriptions of successions of events.

HYPOTHESIS

The hypothesis that I have derived from these three principles predicts the following stages of development:

1. The child uses short sentences, describing the events in chronological order.
2. He uses coordinate clauses, still describing the events in chronological order.
3. He recognizes, at some time prior to (4), that the order theme-rheme is the usual (unmarked or simpler) one in English.
4. He develops an alternative to the coordinate clause construction for when he is describing events out of chronological order. This involves a main clause followed by a subordinate clause. At first, the conjunction may be omitted.
5. After the conjunctions are freely used in (4), the contingency relation between the events is recognized, much as the unmarked theme was in (3).
6. The subordinate clause is used in first position so that the order of mention again corresponds to chronological order, as in (1) and (2).

This hypothetical sequence is derived from the three principles—and their assignments of simplicity—but not directly so. In addition, we must consider the functions of the description types. First, consider an adult trying to choose among *He ate and he left*, *He left after he ate*, and *After he ate, he left*. For the adult, *He ate and he left* is simplest: it has the simpler order of mention and no derivational complexity. But there is no way of differentiating the simplicity of the other two. *He left after he ate* is simpler derivationally, whereas *After he ate, he left* is simpler in order of mention. We have no *a priori* reason for deciding whether derivational simplicity takes precedence over order of mention, or *vice versa*. We cannot decide which principle is most important psychologically in determining difficulty in adult speech.

In children, though, we have functional reasons for differentiating all three description types, for we must answer the question, Why does a particular form develop at all? In the child, as in the adult, *He ate and he left* is simplest. This develops to indicate two related events occurring in succession; the principle operating here is order of mention. With this perfectly adequate way of describing two events, why should the child develop either of the other two forms? The first reason is that he comes to recognize what theme is and finds occasion to talk about the second event, rather than the first. He needs an alternative order of mention, one that is not chronological. So he acquires the use of *He left after he ate*, for that allows him to speak of the second event as theme. In using this form, however, he learns that it also implies a contingency relation. Later, when he wants to imply contingency while still speaking of events in their chronological order, he acquires the third description type, *After he ate, he left*. Thus, for functional reasons, the child develops *He ate and he left* first, *He left after he ate* second, and *After he ate, he left* last. This, in brief, is the argument for the hypothesis I have presented. I will now consider the reasons for each stage in detail.

In stage (1) when the child begins to describe a succession of two events in time, he does it by using very short sentences, one sentence per event; these sentences follow the chronological order of the events in the order of mention. This assumption is based on the child's limited memory span, his linguistic knowledge, and his utterance length in the early stages of language acquisition. At stage (2), he begins to coordinate clauses, joining two or more of his utterances by *and*, *then*, or *so*: "He opened the door and he came in." He still talks about events in the order in which they occurred.

Somewhere in the first stage, he begins to realize that the theme of an utterance is always the thing that is mentioned first. Gruber (1967) has discussed the unordered "topic-comment" construction (from which theme-rheme develops in the speech of one $2-2\frac{1}{2}$-year-old-child. The child used both topic-comment and comment-topic freely: *fire truck there*; *all broken wheel* (1967, 49, 50). The utterances given in his data, though, never refer to more than one event. Once the child recognizes that topic-comment, which later develops into theme-rheme, is the usual order for the English sentence, he will look for an alternative construction when he wishes to talk about the second of two events. The second event is mentioned first as theme and is followed by the first event. He must choose the construction with the subordinate clause second. At first, subordinating conjunctions may be omitted (Bloch, 1921), that is, *You're not going in my box—you'll get stuck* (A. G., in present data). In such cases, the intonation patterns usually differentiate these forms from the simple short sentences. The primitive subordinate clauses are preceded by a main clause which does not have sentence-final (falling) intonation, while each clause in the chronological series does have sentence-final intonation and is thus a complete sentence in itself: "He came in. He closed the door. He sat down." Subordinating conjunctions begin to appear around 2½–3 years (Bloch, 1921; Woodcock, 1934).

At stage (4) when the child begins to use the construction with the subordinate clause second, he has an alternative to the coordinate clause construction. He can now make either the first or the second of two events the theme of his utterance: "He picked up the book and sat down" or "He sat down when he'd picked up the book." These two constructions are functional alternatives in describing time sequences, and this contrast provides the motivation for the child's learning to use subordinate clauses at all. If there were no need to speak of events other than in the order in which they occurred, there would also be no reason to have any construction with the temporal subordinate clause second in the language at all.

The question that now arises is why, in that case, is there a sentence-type with the subordinate clause preposed? Isn't this a redundant structure given the presence of the coordinate clause construction where the theme is also the first event? Compare "He opened the door and came in" and "After he opened the door, he came in." The coordinate sentence is less specific in describing the relation between the two events, whereas the subordinate clause (*after*) is very specific and contrasts with *when, as, since, while,* and so on. The contingency relation of *when, since, after,* and so on, cannot be expressed by a coordinate clause construction. Earlier there is no need for a thematic *equivalent* to the coordinate clause construction, but there is a functional need for a thematic *alternative* to the coordinate construction. The child does not need to develop the construction with a subordinate clause first until he wishes to describe more specific temporal relations than the one indicated by *and* or *and then*.

The three stages which would provide the most tangible evidence for the developmental sequence I have proposed are (2), (4), and (6). Therefore I have examined construction types with coordinate clauses, subordinate clause second, and subordinate clause first, as they appear in the data of children describing events in time. The criterion for coordinate clauses was that the two clauses be joined by *and, and then, then,* or *so.* Coordinate predicates in which the subject of the second clause has been deleted were also counted in this group, that is, "He jumped over the box and fell down." The criterion for subordinate clauses was that they be introduced by one of the following temporal conjunctions: *after, before, when, while, till (until), since, if, unless, because.*

SUBJECTS AND DATA

The subjects were 15 children, 9 boys and 6 girls, attending an Edinburgh nursery school run by the SSRC Cognition Project. All the children selected to attend the school came from the same socioeconomic background (lower to lower-middle class). Their Stanford-binet Intelligence test scores at entry ranged from 92 to 127. At entry, to the school, all the children were within a few months of $3\frac{1}{2}$ years. Five of them began school in February 1967; one began in March and the other nine began toward the end of April after the school holidays for Easter.

The children spent three hours at the school every weekday morning. During a typical morning, the children would spend an hour or so in freeplay, with two or three adults in attendance. Then, after a mild break, someone would read them a story and ask them about their activities. They then played outside if the weather was fine, or took part in communal songs and games for the rest of the morning. During the morning, some children might be taken out individually for testing on various cognitive tasks being investigated by members of the Cognition Project.

The data consisted of the children's spontaneous speech recorded during free play and conversation at story time. It was recorded with a portable, battery-run, Sony tape recorder, and the transcriptions were supplemented by fairly detailed notes of both the utterances and the context, that is, referents of the utterance, unusual intonation patterns, and the people the child was addressing or answering. Speech was recorded for varying intervals, often five to ten minutes at a time, sometimes less, depending on the child's activities, the noise level, and his desire to talk.

For convenience, the data are divided up into four sets, each covering a period of three to four weeks. There are two periods in the first term (five children in the first, six in the second) and two during the second term (fifteen children in each). The first set of data collected from each child will be referred to as I, the second as II, and so on. Some children will have only I and II on their protocols, while others may have as many as four. For those children with four sets, there was a gap of a month between II and III; similarly, for the one child with three sets, there was a gap of a month between I and II. Otherwise the periods were consecutive.

RESULTS AND DISCUSSION

The occurrence of the following three syntactic forms were noted in each protocol:

a. coordinate (temporal) sentences, A
b. subordinate temporal clauses in second position, B
c. subordinate temporal clauses in first position, C.

Table 1 lists their occurrence for each subject and for each set of data. Each protocol is "named" by the child's initials.

If there is a developmental progression in the appearance of constructions A, B, and C, there are a number of possible forms that this progression could take. For example, the progression could go from A to B to C ($A < B < C$), or vice versa, $C < B < A$. On the other hand, the development could go from the simultaneous appearance of any two of the above constructions to the other one,

TABLE 1   SYNTACTIC CONSTRUCTIONS PRESENT IN THE CHILDREN'S SPEECH[a]

PROTOCOLS	I	II	III	IV
S. R.	ϕ	A, B	A, B	A, B
A. G.	A, B	A, B	A, B	A, B
W. J.	A, B	B	A, B	A, C
B. L.	A	A	A, B, C	A, B
N. W.	A, B	A, B, C	A, B, C	A, B, C
L. C.	A	A, B	A, B, C	
B. F.	A	A, B		
C. W.	A, B	A, B		
M. F.	A, B, C	A, B		
G. S.	A	A		
C. L.	A, B	A, B		
L. I.	A, B, C	A, B		
B. H	ϕ	ϕ		
N. A.	A, B	A, B, C		
M. C.	A, B, C	A, B		

[a] A—coordinate clause construction; B—subordinate clause in second position; C—subordinate clause in first position; ϕ—none of these three constructions present.

for example, (A, C) < B, or conversely from any one to the other two, for example, B < (A, C). Or only one or two of the three might develop at all. The possible developmental progressions are shown in Table 2. Opposite each category are noted the protocols which illustrate that particular progression. For example, let us take W. J.'s protocol: in I, he has A and B; in II, B alone; in III, A and B again; and in IV, A and C. This protocol goes into the category (A, B) < C, since A and B occur at the same time, and both occur before C.

The progression in the development of the syntactic forms A, B, and C predicted that the sequence should go from A, the coordinate clause construction, to B, the construction with the subordinate clause second, to C, with the subordinate in first position. For the hypothesis to be verified, there are three specific predictions to be confirmed: (1) A, coordinate clause construction, will precede B, subordinate clause second; (2) A will precede C, subordinate clause first; and (3) B will precede C.

Each of these predictions is fully supported by the data. In particular, prediction (1), that A appears earlier than B, is supported by four of the protocols (B. L., L. C., B. F., G. S.) and is refuted by none of them. The small number of protocols supporting this prediction was due to the fact that most of the children had already acquired both forms A and B by the time data were collected. Prediction (2), that A appears before C, is supported by 11 protocols, and, again, refuted by none. The 11 protocols are first L. C., W. J., N. W., N. A., and B. L.,

TABLE 2   POSSIBLE DEVELOPMENTAL PROGRESSIONS IN THE
DESCRIPTION OF TEMPORAL SEQUENCES

POSSIBLE PROGRESSIONS	PROTOCOLS	TOTAL
A < B < C	L. C.	1
A < C < B		
B < A < C		
C < A < B		
C < B < A		
B < C < A		
(A, B) < C	W. J., N. W., N. A.	3
A < (B, C)	B. L.	1
(A, C) < B		
B < (A, C)		
C < (A, B)		
A < B	B. F.	1
A < C		
B < C		
C < A		
B < A		
C < B		
(A, B, C)	L. I., M. C., M. F.	3
(A, B)	S. R., A. G., C. W., C. L.	4
(A, C)		
(B, C)		
A	G. S.	1
B		
C		
φ	B. H.	1

in which A did precede C. In addition, all the protocols in which C has not yet appeared, but where A is present, also support this prediction, that is, S. R., A. G., C. W., C. L., B. F., and G. S. The last prediction, (3), that B precedes C, is borne out by nine of the protocols and likewise refuted by none of them. Four of the protocols (L. C., W. J., N. W., and N. A.) showed that C appeared later than B, and five implicitly support the prediction (S. R., A. G., C. W., C. L., and B. F.), since C has not yet appeared there at all. Subjects M. F., L. I., B. H., and M. C. neither support nor refute any of these predictions.

Additional, but less extensive, data were collected from all the children during the following school year (September 1967 to June 1968). There is little interest in the children who had already acquired all three constructions by June 1967, the last set of data in their protocols (see Table 2). Five of the seven remaining children, however, did acquire the constructions they were lacking. A. G., C. W., and C. L. went from (A, B) to (A, B, C) within the next six to twelve months. B. H., who had not used any of these constructions prior to

June 1967, acquired all three in the order A < B < C in the next eight months, and **G. S.** went from A to (A, B). Only two children showed no change (S. R. and B. F.), continuing to use only (A, B). Thus the five children who did show development provide further confirmatory evidence for the hypothesis proposed here.

Table 3 supplements Table 1 by tallying the occurrences of each construction, coordinate clauses, subordinate clauses second, and subordinate clauses first. The number of occurrences of each construction, A, B, and C, was compared with the total number of utterances in the data for that period and with the number of children using each construction. There is, predictably, an increase in the proportion of these constructions used over time to the total sample of spech collected. In periods I and II, the three constructions make up approximately 4 percent of the total utterances, while in periods III and IV, they make up 8 percent of the total. Only those instances in which a conjunction was used were counted.

There were, however, several instances in each period of data of sentences with an implicit subordinate clause second. The child's intonation seemed to indicate that the conjunction has been omitted, for example: *You're not going to go in my box—you'll get stuck*, or *We can both go in together—there's enough room*. This kind of omission seems to occur most often in subordinate clauses where *because* would be supplied by adults. A similar thing happens with the coordinate conjunction *so*. Although here there is no intonational evidence, it is clear from the context that the second event in time is a consequence of the first, for example, *It's too hot for you just now, I'll put it in the little oven to cool it off* (regardless of the strange function attributed to the oven). It might be noted that adults, too, often omit these conjunctions. The addition of these "conjunction-omitted" forms (or at least those recognized as such) to the numbers in Table 3 would not significantly alter the ratio of temporal descriptions to total speech in any one period.

There was a fairly high correlation between average utterance length for the last period of data collected and the number of construction types used by each child. Opposite each child's average utterance length for the last period, it was noted whether he used no temporal constructions (ϕ), one (A), two (A, B), or all three (A, B, C). The correlation coefficient between utterance length and number of construction types used (0, 1, 2, or 3) was .64.

Although this correlation is fairly high, it is not perfect. Utterance length does not seem to be directly connected with the development of different syntactic structures, but it does appear to be highly correlated with the child's linguistic development in the early stages (Smith, 1935; Anderson, 1947; Davis, 1937). It is possible that there is only an indirect relation between increasing utterance length and increasing derivational complexity (see Brown and Hanlon, 1970) in spite of the close relation between utterance length and the presence-absence of specific items such as the auxiliary in negatives and questions (Klima and Bellugi, 1966). This indirect relation could explain the absence of

TABLE 3 FREQUENCY OF CONSTRUCTIONS A, B, AND C IN DATA FOR
EACH PERIOD, I–IV

PERIOD	NUMBER OF UTTERANCES			TOTAL UTTERANCES	NUMBER OF CHILDREN			TOTAL CHILDREN
	A	B	C		A	B	C	
I	65	33	5	4272	13	9	3	15
II	44	29	3	1673	13	12	2	15
III	21	15	8	473	6	6	3	6
IV	13	9	3	309	5	4	2	5

TABLE 4   AVERAGE LENGTH OF UTTERANCES IN MORPHEMES

PROTOCOL	I	II	III	IV	INCREASE OVER TIME STUDIED
a) S. R.	4.54	5.05	5.35	6.10	1.56
A. G.	4.20	4.38	5.56	5.48	1.28
W. J.	4.77	4.80	5.30	6.37	1.60
B. L.	3.86	4.42	4.93	5.00	1.14
N. W.	5.35	5.25	6.26	7.45	2.10
L. C.	3.70	4.68	4.70		1.00
b) B. F.	5.06	4.90			− 0.16
C. W.	4.80	4.92			0.12
M.F.	4.46	6.17			1.71
G. S.	3.91	3.97			0.06
C. L.	4.56	5.17			0.61
L. I.	5.60	6.04			0.44
B. H.	4.18	4.60			0.42
N. A.	6.12	6.67			0.55
M. C.	5.35	6.36			1.01

coordinate and subordinate temporal clause constructions in B. H.'s protocol, and also, for example, why S. R., in the last period of recording (IV), has an average utterance length of 6.10 morphemes as opposed to L. C.'s 4.80 morphemes when, at the same time, L. C. produced all three constructions (Table 1) and S. R. produced only two of the three.

Having looked at the general statistical features of the data, I now wish to illustrate each of the stages proposed in the hypothesis with examples from the protocols. These examples are meant to be representative of the data as a whole.

At stage (1) we expect to find short sentences describing events in chronological order. Although there are not very many examples in these data, this is clearly the first stage and has been reported in other studies of younger children (Bloch, 1924; Guillaume, 1927; Stern and Stern, 1928; Leopold, 1949). The context in which the present group of children used these short sentences was the monologue accompanying particular tasks such as building with blocks or making jigsaw puzzles. These commentaries were necessarily in chronological order, and they are clearly one of the sources of chronologically ordered descriptions. For example, S. R. doing a puzzle: *Does it go there? This bit goes there. This bit goes there. Where does this one go?* and so on, until he finished the puzzle. Similarly, B. L., first asking me to build a tower for him, said: *Build my building? Please. That one* (pointing to block). *Just a bit more there. Here. That one* (indicating where he wanted the blocks). Later on, speaking to another child, he comments on the blocks: *That's go there. That one can go there? Those go up. Go there. And this goes up too. Watch that fall.* (The occupation for the day was building towers up till they fell.) Another child, who used a mixture of short sentences and coordinate clauses, talking about a visit to the sea and his swimming, said: *I went too far and I couldn't get back again. I paddled to Egypt. I saw a sip* (ship). *And I was clever and paddled to Mummy.* This utterance is divorced from its physical context, unlike the commentaries above, since N. A. is saying what he recalls and not commenting on a sequence of actions before his eyes.

There is evidence at this and later stages that children are aware of the temporal order of two events. Playing on the boxes, A. G. one morning called out: *I'll fall off and jump*, but immediately corrected himself, *I'll jump and I'll fall.* Later the same day, *I want to get on there* (onto the box). *I'll jump. I'll fall.*—No, you won't.— *I will, I will fall. I can't stand up.* It was very clear from the context that A. G. was perfectly well aware of the sequence involved in jumping and falling while on the boxes. This would account for the correction he made in his earlier utterance.

Although *and* is used before this stage by the child, it is always with the meaning *and* "&." The ampersand (&) implies an unordered sequence, so that "Y & X" is exactly equivalent to "X & Y." The second meaning of *and* "and subsequently" is derived from its use in conjoining simple sentences which describe events in chronological order. At first the child merely uses *and* "&" to join the short sentences describing events in order, but as the child is constrained to keep the chronological order in his order of mention (as long as he wishes to indicate sequence), *and* takes on the meaning of "and subsequently" in such contexts. At the same time, the order of mention constraint rules out the possibility that *and* could instead take on the meaning of "and previously" which is the other alternative.

Hence, at stage (2), the succession of events in time is usually clearly stated in coordinate clause constructions. The children made commentaries, recounted past actions, and occasionally referred to immediate future sequences. S. R.'s *I wonder if I can hold this on my head and get down* (speaking about a toy he was trying to balance as he climbed off the box), and A. G.'s *I want to look at them* (some visitors) *and come back in* are two utterances typical of this type. L. I.'s protocol contains several examples in which the chronological succession is further stressed by the use of temporal adverbs: *I'll finish SOON and somebody else can have them* (referring to the shapes used to cut out Play-doh), and, to Mrs. B.: *FIRST you'll have your coffee and THEN we'll go outside* (to the playground).

Although attention to theme is apparent in very many of the children's utterances, it is so closely bound to the physical context, the nursery school, that it is difficult to demonstrate convincingly to anyone unfamiliar with the details of that context. I have therefore selected a number of examples to illustrate stage (3) which are rather dependent on the linguistic context, what various people were talking about, than directly on the physical setting. That children *do* attend to context is shown by their use of pronominalization, by which they refer to someone or something mentioned in a previous utterance. For example, Mrs. B. — Has anyone seen William this week? — *I saw HIM a few days ago.* — Is he feeling better? — *HE said no but I said yes* (N. W.). Similarly, during a slight altercation B. L. and S. R. had the following exchange: *Knocked they books down. Steven'll pick THEM up.* — *No, I'll not. You knocked some of THEM down so you'll pick THEM up* (Pronominal referents are capitalized.)

There are many examples in the children's speech which show that they also choose theme from context. In these cases, the rheme of the preceding utterance is taken up as the theme of the following one; this process may directly influence the choice of construction, that is, a subordinate clause second rather than a coordinate clause construction. The relation between the rheme of one sentence and the theme of the next is demonstrated in the following passage. In it, A. G. takes his initial theme from the physical context: he is holding up a biscuit which he refers to deictically, *That's a biscuit I got from my Granny. I goed to see HER. SHE's in the ward. SHE's sick.* (She was in hospital.) The pronoun in the rheme of his second sentence (*her*) becomes the theme (*she*) in the following ones.

Another example: one morning N. W. was screaming rather loudly; Mrs. B. — Don't scream, Nicola. — *Why not? They're screaming when the ball goes* (a game being played by some others). In this instance, it is N. W.'s choice of "they're screaming" as her theme that makes her use a subordinate clause second. Her utterance would have sounded rather odd had she used a coordinate clause construction instead, for example, "Why not? The ball goes and they scream," as there would be no direct link between Mrs. B's remonstrance and N. W.'s protest.

There are a number of other examples in which choice of theme decides whether a subordinate clause is used in second place, at stage (4). One morning when several of the children were playing with the "car" (a pile of blocks, one of which has a steering wheel attached to it), and B. L. was taking the part of the policeman but not using the right signals, S. R. jumped up, saying: *No, this is what a policeman looks like when a car stops* (holding up his hand appropriately). Another time, A. G., trying to prevent M. F. from touching the piano while he was playing, called to Mrs. B.: *He's to wait till I've finished.* Another day when L. I. asked for some Play-doh shapes to play with, C. W. answered: *You can have one of my ones after I've finished.* An interesting example which shows both the adjunct position (at the end of the clause) and the rheme of one sentence taken as the theme of the following two-clause sentence is L. I.'s *We've never been out today, but we'll go out when Mrs. Bruce comes back.* The adjunct in the first clause is *today*; *been out* is the rheme which becomes the theme in the second of the three clauses. The occurrence of the subordinate clause in second position here is clearly governed by the thematic choice.

In support of stage (6) I will quote a few examples of subordinate clauses occurring in first position. W. J., who was constructing a garage from Lego (small plastic bricks), pointed and explained: *When the train stops, this is where it goes.* N. W. used this construction on several occasions, for example, *If wee Brian's naughty to me, I'll smack him,* and another time, using a coordinate clause construction as well: *My mummy's got two baths in the house and when I was a little baby, I used to go in the bath and I still go in the bath.* On the same topic, which preoccupied all the children one week, M. C.: *When I was a baby, I got washed in a basin.* An interesting sentence was used by L. C.: *Before I went home for tea, I buyed something for teatime.* This particular construction was very unusual, and was the only example in all the protocols of a conjuction attached to the second event and placed first. Such sentences are marked (complex) in two respects: order of mention and derivational complexity. As mentioned above, in English there are only two conjunctions, *before* and *until,* which produce this doubly marked form when the subordinate clause is preposed.

Finally, it is very important to notice that the prior stages in the development of temporal descriptions are not merely supplanted by new forms as the child's linguistic knowledge increases. In fact, the different stages hypothesized here are all to be found in adult speech. For instance, stage (1) frequently appears when a radio commentator describes a football game or a race: he resorts to short chronologically ordered sentences. A novelist may do the same thing to give an impression of suspense. Clearly the function of stage (1) may be slightly different in adult speech, but it is still present. The other syntactic forms discussed in these data, of course, are also present in adult speech: coordinate sentences (stage 2), sentences with the subordinate clause second (stage 4), and those with the subordinate clause first (stage 6).

CONCLUSIONS

The stand I have taken in discussing these data is based on a functional attitude toward language. How can X be said in English? Why is there more than one way of stating X? What functions do these different ways of saying X fulfill? I will give another illustration to make this clearer, using the active and passive voices in English. Let us take an active affirmative sentence:

    (i)   The car hit the boy,

and the corresponding passive affirmative:

    (ii)   The boy was hit by the car.

In English, these two sentences are functional alternatives, just as the coordinate clause construction and the construction with the subordinate clause second are in describing time sequences. When the theme is the agent (answering the question, What did the car do?), the active affirmation sentence is used. When the theme is the recipient of the action (What happened to the boy?), the passive affirmative is used. Besides these pragmatic considerations, though, there are sometimes syntactic ones: for instance, there is a tendency in English to make the grammatical subject animate (Clark, 1965; see Svartvik, 1966, for further discussion). Now we can answer the question, What different functions do the active and passive voices fulfill? They allow the speaker to *focus* on the agent or on the recipient of the action. The voice used will depend on the speaker's focus or choice of theme.

Similarly, the three principles account for many of the pragmatic considerations in describing time sequences, and therefore help explain the developmental sequence in children's acquisition of temporal descriptions. To sum up, of the three principles, choice of theme basically makes the speaker use one syntactic construction rather than another. Developmentally, it directly affects the order in which a child will learn to use certain syntactic structures. The two other principles are equally important; psychologically, there is a strong preference for mentioning events in chronological order unless there is some (pragmatic) reason not to, and linguistically, there is a preference for using the subordinate clause in second position (the unmarked—simpler—form of the two).

In the present study, the function of each type of temporal description allows one to predict a particular developmental sequnce in language acquisition. The predictions confirmed here could not have been made solely on the basis of writing a transformational generative grammar for each child; something more than the syntax has to be taken into account. This is not to say that the syntactically oriented studies are not necessary, for they do provide a source for what the child says at different stages. The present approach, though, may answer why these stages in language development occur in a particular order and also reveal the pragmatic criteria that can be used in predicting the order of appearance of particular structures.

To sum up, the present study demonstrates that acquisition of language can be in part explained by function. Function was determined in this case by the properties of discourse, the external context, and certain psychological phenomena. Given the present results, it seems that this approach to language acquisition might be further extended. A consideration of the functions of different linguistic notions, such as modality or causation, within the language as a whole, could lead to more insightful research in language acquisition and development.

REFERENCES

Anderson, J. E., An evaluation of various indices of linguistic development. *Child Development*, 1937, **8**, 62–68.

Bellugi, U., and R. Brown. (eds.), *The acquisition of language. Monographs of the Society for Research in Child Development*, 1964, **29**.

Berko, J., The child's learning of English morphology. *Word*, 1958, **14**, 150–177.

Bever, T. G., J. A. Fodor, and W. Weksel. The acquisition of syntax: A critique of contextual generalization. *Psychological Review*, 1965, **72**, 467–482.

Bloch, O., Les premiers stades du langage de l'enfant. *Journal de Psychologie*, 1921, **18**, 693–712.

Bloch, O., La phrase dans le langage de l'enfant. *Journal de Psychologie*, 1924, **21**, 18–43.

Brown, R., and U. Bellugi. Three processes in the child's acquisition of syntax. In Lenneberg, E. H. (ed.), *New directions in the study of language*. Cambridge, Mass.: M.I.T. Press, 1964.

Brown, R., and C. Hanlon. Derivational complexity and order of acquisition in child speech. In J. R. Hayes (ed.), *Cognition and the development of language*. New York: Wiley, 1970, pp. 11–53.

Chomsky, N., *Aspects of the theory of syntax*. Cambridge, Mass.: M.I.T. Press, 1965.

Clark, H. H., Some structural properties of simple active and passive sentences. *Journal of Verbal Learning and Verbal Behavior*, 1965, **4**, 365–370.

Clark, H. H., and E. V. Clark, Semantic distinctions and memory for complex sentences. *Quarterly Journal of Experimental Psychology*, 1968, **20**, 129–138.

Davis, E. A., Mean sentence length compared with long and short sentences as a reliable measure of language development. *Child Development*, 1937, **8**, 69–79.

Doherty, P., and A. Schwartz, The syntax of the compared adjective in English, *Language*, 1968, **43**, 903–936.

Firbas, J., Thoughts on the communicative function of the verb in English, German and Czech. *Brno Studies in English*, 1959, **1**, 39–68.

Fraisse, P., *The Psychology of time*. New York: Harper & Row, 1963.

Grégoire, A., *L'apprentissage du langage*. Liège-Paris: Droz, 1937, 1947.

Groethuysen, B., De quelques aspects du temps. *Recherches Philosophiques*, 1935–1936, **5**, 139–195.

Gruber, J. S., Topicalization in child language. *Foundations of Language*, 1967, **3**, 37–65.

Guillaume, P., Les débuts de la phrase dans le langage de l'enfant. *Journal de Psychologie*, 1927, **24**, 1–25. [Translation printed in this volume.]

Halliday, M. A. K., *Some aspects of the thematic organization of the English clause*. The RAND Corporation (Memorandum RM-5224-PR), Santa Monica, 1967. (a)

Halliday, M. A. K., Notes on transitivity and theme in English, part II, *Journal of Linguistics*, 1967, 3, 199–244. (b)

Katz, E. W., and S. B. Brent, Understanding connectives. *Journal of Verbal Learning and Verbal Behavior*, 1968, **7**, 501–509.

Klima, E. S., and U. Bellugi, Syntactic regularities in the speech of children. In J. Lyons and R. J. Wales (eds.), *Psycholinguistics papers*. Edinburgh University Press, 1966. [Reprinted in this volume.]

Lakoff, G. Pronouns and reference. 1968 Linguistics Department and the Computation Laboratory, Harvard University mimeo.

Lakoff, G., and J. R. Ross, Criterion for verb phrase constituency. *Mathematical Linguistics and Automatic Translation*, NSF-17, 1966.

Lees, R. B., Grammatical analysis of the English comparative construction. *Word*, 1961, **17**, 171–185.

Leopold, W. F., *Speech development of a bilingual child*. Evanston: Northwestern University Press, 1949.

McNeill, D., Developmental psycholinguistics. In F. Smith and G. A. Miller (eds.), *The genesis of language*. Cambridge, Mass.: M.I.T. Press, 1966.

Menyuk, P., Syntactic structures in the language of children. *Child Development*, 1963, **34**, 407–422.

Minkus, W., and W. Stern, Die Bindewort Ergänzung. *XIX Beiheft angewandte Psychologie*, 2d edition, Leipzig, 1923, 37–73.

Piaget, J., *Language and thought of the child*. London: Routledge and Kegan Paul, 1926.

Piaget, J., *Judgment and reasoning in the child*. London: Routledge and Kegan Paul, 1928.

Prentice, J. L., Effects of cuing actor vs. cuing object on word order in sentence generation. *Studies in Language and Language Behavior*, Progress Report IV, University of Michigan, 1967, 474–479.

Smith, C. S., A class of complex modifiers. *Language*, 1961, **37**, 342–365.

Smith, M. E., A study of some factors influencing the development of the sentence in pre-school children. *Journal of Genetic Psychology*, 1935, **46**, 182–212.

Stern, W., and C. Stern, *Die Kindersprache*. Leipzig: Barth, 1928.

Svartivik, J., *On voice in the English verb*. The Hague: Mouton, 1966.

Tannenbaum, P. H., and F. Williams, Generation of active and passive sentences as a function of subject or object focus. *Journal of Verbal Learning and Verbal Behavior*, 1968, **7**, 246–250.

Turner, E. A., and R. Rommetveit, The effects of focus of attention on storing and retrieving of active and passive voice sentences. *Journal of Verbal Learning and Verbal Behavior*, 1968, **7**, 243–248.

Woodcock, L. P., When children first say why-because-if. *Cooperating School Pamphlets*, Bureau of Educational Experiments, N. Y., 1934, **7**.

ITALIAN •

Early Language Acquisition: A Model and Some Data[1]

——*Francesco Antinucci and Domenico Parisi*

1. This paper describes the first results of a research still in progress on the early stages of language acquisition. It is an observational and longitudinal study that uses the same methodology introduced by Brown and his collaborators (Brown and Fraser, 1963; Brown and Bellugi, 1964). Periodic recordings (two-hour sessions every two weeks) of the spontaneous linguistic production of a little girl called Claudia are made and later transcribed and analyzed. In addition to the child's sentences, everything that is said to her by her parents or by the experimenters is also recorded and transcribed, and accurate and detailed notes are taken of the situations in which the verbal interchanges take place.

Claudia is a normal, healthy little girl whose father has a Ph.D in engineering; her mother is an elementary teacher, but during the period of the experiment she was not teaching and spent all her time with Claudia. The child was 1;3 years old when the research was started. She is now 3 years old. The analyses reported here, however, are based on the period between 1;3 and 1;7.

2. The model of linguistic competence we have applied in analyzing this child's language is of the generative semantics type. This section will be devoted to illustrating the general form of such a model. However, we should like to make it clear that we shall neither illustrate the model in detail nor present evidence to support it. The reader interested in these questions is referred to a number of other publications (Parisi and Antinucci, 1970; Parisi, in press).

According to this model, the grammar of a language specifies the set of well-formed semantic representations and provides the means for mapping these representations onto surface structures. Semantic representations are configurations of semantic units. Each semantic unit is formally represented as an n-place predicate. Configurations are obtained by substituting predicates as arguments.

These configurations are taken to represent both the meaning of sentences and of single lexical items. Semantic representations of sentences and lexical items differ in that sentences are associated with "closed" configurations and lexical items with "open" configurations. A "closed" configuration has no

Printed by permission of the authors.
[1] A modified version of this paper was read at the Fourth Annual Meeting of the Società di Linguistica Italiana, Rome, May 1970. The help of Paola Tieri and Virginia Volterra in the data collection and analysis is gratefully acknowledged. The authors are affiliated with the Istituto di Psicologia, CNR, Rome, Italy.

free arguments, since all of its arguments have been filled in with semantic material, in a way similar to McCawley's NP descriptions (McCawley, 1970). An "open" configuration has at least one open slot.

The process of mapping semantic representations of sentences onto surface structures is achieved by two components of the grammar: lexicon and syntax. The lexicon is a list of entries associating open semantic configurations with words or morphemes. Syntax is a set of transformational rules. The joint operation of these two mechanisms determines the surface structure of sentences.

3. The notion of semantic representation of sentences is essential in the above model. When we try to apply the model to the development of linguistic competence in children, obviously special emphasis will be placed on the attempt to extract and describe the meaning of each sentence in the child's language, that is, its underlying semantic configuration. The aim of our research is to study the first appearance and the development of such semantic configurations and of the mapping system which gives both a syntactic and a lexical form to the semantic material underlying a sentence.

How can we get at the meanings of the sentences and lexical items used by Claudia? There are various factors which can help us. The first and perhaps the most important is a careful and detailed observation of the extralinguistic context in which sentences and lexical items occur, and of the intentions manifested by the child. In this task the mother's interpretations were very helpful and we often used them. We obtained a second type of evidence by observing how the child understood the sentences said to her. This understanding can be ascertained by watching the child's verbal and motor responses to questions and requests from adults. A third form of evidence as regards the meaning of single lexical items can be obtained from their combinatory properties with other lexical items.

During the period under examination from 1;3 to 1;7, the mean sentence length in Claudia's speech increases from 1.3 to 1.6 morphemes. In this period we found sentences formed by one or two or even three morphemes. What is the surface structure of these sentences? In current research this problem has been mainly approached through a distributional analysis of the child's utterances, which has led to the setting up of the so-called "pivot grammars." But such an analysis is as unsatisfactory and unrevealing in the study of child language as it has proved to be in the study of adult language. As we mentioned above, we see the surface structure of a sentences as the result of a mapping from the underlying semantic configuration. Therefore, the above question can be answered only through a reconstruction of the semantic configurations underlying the child's utterances.

In any semantic configurations of sentences there is a particular sub-configuration which forms the sentence's predication (P), usually a finite verb. The semantic structure of P automatically determines the number of NPs which are the complements of P. The lexical representation of a verb is a configuration of semantic units with one or more unfilled variables, which will eventually be filled in by additional semantic material corresponding to the verb's NP complements. For instance, the meaning of the Italian verb *dare* (give) is represented in the lexicon as

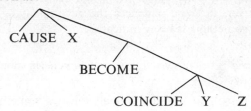

CAUSE   X

BECOME

COINCIDE   Y   Z

A simple sentence with *dare* will have three complements, that is, three NPs which will be substituted for X, Y, and Z in such a structure. In other words, a sentence must consist of a predication plus a certain number of NPs, this number being determined by the semantic nature of P.

If we now observe Claudia's two- or three-word sentences, we clearly see that many of these sentences have exactly this structure: a predication plus one or more NPs. (Many other sentences do not have this structure. We shall not consider these nor one-word sentences for the moment. We will take them into account later on.) Let us look at some of these sentences. One series includes the predication *etto* (here is) followed by different NPs:

Etto a² papis Here is pencil	(Here is the pencil)
Etto a paia Here is ball	(Here is the ball)
Etto Papà Here is daddy	(Here is daddy)
Etto u Mamma Here is mommy	(Here is mommy)

Claudia's *etto* is a one-place verb whose function is to indicate the object or person that the following NP designates. Its meaning is likely to include the semantic component DEIXIS$_x$ only and to be very similar in meaning to the adult words *ecco* (here is) and *questo* (this).

Another deictic verb of the same type is *itto*:

Itto a paia Seen ball	(Did you see the ball)
Itto a papis Seen pencil	(Did you see the pencil)
Itto nai Seen keys	(Did you see the keys)

² This *a* does not seem to be an independent meaningful morpheme at this stage of development. Hence we consider it as nonexistent.

But the analysis of the *itto* sentences raises an interesting question. *Itto* is usually accompanied by an NP which designates the object or person indicated; however, in some sentences the accompanying NP designates the *person to whom* something is being indicated.

For instance, in

> *Itto a mamma*   (Did you see, mommy)
> Seen mommy

mamma is the person to whom Claudia indicates something, not the actual object. This never occurs with *etto*. This leads us to think that *itto* differs from *etto* by being a two-place deictic verb: one of its arguments is the indicated object and the other is the person to whom the object is indicated. In order to account for the *itto* sentences, we will have to assume a semantic configuration in which *itto* appears as a predicate with two NPs. Claudia expresses only the predicate and one of the two NPs. Therefore, we have a semantic structure which is not completely brought to the surface.

This is even clearer when we consider the sentences in which the verbs *da* (give) and *tazie* (thank) occur. These verbs seem to be synonymous at this stage: Claudia uses them when someone gives something to another person or when someone receives something from another person:

> (a) *Tazie a Mamma*   (Giving something to her mother)
>   Thank mommy
> (b) *Tazie a Mamma*   (Receiving something from her mother)
>   Thank mommy
> (c) *Tazie a Claudia*   (Asking something from her mother)
>   Thank Claudia
> (d) *Tazie a pietta*   (Receiving a spade from her mother)
>   Thank spade
> (e) *Tata da*   (Giving a doll)
>   Doll give
> (f) *Dai pallone*   (Asking for a ball)
>   Give ball
> (g) *Dai a Mamma*   (Asking something from her mother)
>   Give mommy
> (h) *Mamma da*   (Giving something to her mother)
>   Mommy give

How can we account for the fact that so many different meanings can be assigned to sentences which have a practically identical surface structure: the verb *da* or *tazie* plus an NP? We assume that the semantic configuration underlying all the above sentences is the following:

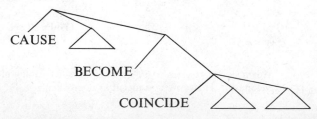

This configuration includes the semantic components of *da* or *tazie* (corresponding to the adult verb *dare* [give]) plus the semantic material, indicated by triangles, expressed by the three NPs which are the arguments of the verb.

For each of the sentences (a)–(h), we will therefore have the following configurations, which for brevity's sake are expressed in English:

(a') Claudia gives Y to mother.
(b') Mother gives Y to Claudia.
(c') Mother gives Y to Claudia.
(d') Mother gives the spade to Claudia.
(e') Claudia gives the doll to Z.
(f') Mother gives the ball to Claudia.
(g') Mother gives Y to Claudia.
(h') Claudia gives Y to mother.[3]

Let is suppose the child has a limited capacity of lexicalization, so that she has to obey the rule: "lexicalize the predication and any *one* of its NPs." (This rule also holds for the *itto* sentences.) This would explain how such semantic configurations are mapped onto the surface structures. Forced by the above rule to lexicalize only one NP in addition to the predication, Claudia omits one or the other of the NPs contained in the semantic structure.

What justifications are there for assigning the sentences a semantic structure which is so different from the surface structure? A first and most important proof is the meaning that must be assigned to a sentence by observing the situation and Claudia's actions and intentions when pronouncing the sentence. When she says *da*, it is difficult to suppose that she does not know who must give, what must be given, and who must receive, as in that case we should be supposing that she does not execute the mental operations—which we call semantic components—corresponding to all these elements.

A second proof is that *da* or *tazie* occur with *all three* NPs of the semantic structure, even if only one NP is present in each particular sentence. This we have seen in sentences (a)–(h) and will be confirmed below.

Our hypothesis appears to receive further support if we take into consideration the three-word sentences with the verb *da*. These sentences appear at a later stage than the sentences already considered, and they manifest an obvious expansion of the lexicalization span. We now have the simultaneous lexicalization of two NPs, in addition to the predication:

Da a nonna bototto   (Grandma gives me cookie)
Give grandma cookie
Acesco a dai a palla   (Francesco gives me ball)
Francesco give ball
A da Mamma ciata   (Mother gives me orange juice)
Give mommy orange juice

[3] A complete semantic representation would show the specific semantic material used by Claudia on each particular occasion and would include no unfilled variables.

Up to now we have been considering two- and three-word sentences. Now we can extend our analysis to cover one-word sentences and sentences with no overt predication. We have the following sentences with *da* as verb:

Da	(Giving something to her mother)
Give	
Iacca	(Asking her mother for some water)
Water	
A me	(Asking Francesco for something)
To me	
Mamma iacca	(Asking her mother for some water)
Mommy water	
A me mimmi	(Asking for candies)
To me candies	

The first three are one-word sentences (traditionally called holophrases); only the predication (*da*) or only Y (*iacca*) or only Z (*a me*) of their underlying semantic structure is lexicalized. The fourth and fifth sentences are two-word sentences where the predication is omitted and two of the three underlying NPs are lexicalized: either X (*Mamma*) and Y (*iacca*), or Y (*mimmi*) and Z (*a me*).

Consequently we will have to reformulate the lexicalization rule by abolishing the privilege previously accorded to the predication: "lexicalize one (or two or three, according to the lexicalization span) of the elements in the semantic structure, be they the predication or its NPs." The choice of which element(s) to lexicalize is considered arbitrary at this point, but no doubt criteria can be discovered.

A similar extension can be made for the verbs *etto* and *itto*. We have the following one-word sentences with a deictic predication:

A bau	(Showing a dog)
Dog	
A papis	(Showing a pencil)
Pencil	
A paia	(Showing a ball)
Ball	
Itto	(Showing something to someone)
Seen	

where either the predication (first three sentences) or its NP (fourth sentence) are omitted. In

Mamma a paia	(Showing the ball to her mother)
Mommy ball	
Mamma acici	(Showing the bird to her mother)
Mommy bird	
Papà tati	(Showing the researchers to her father)
Daddy people	

the two NPs of *itto* are lexicalized, but the verb itself is omitted.

So far we have seen three verbs, *etto*, *itto*, *da*, or *tazie*, but our analysis can be extended to all the other verbs and therefore to all of Claudia's sentences, the only difficulty being the incomplete lexical analysis of certain verbs. Let us look at two more verbs: *api* (open) and *tottò* (spank):

Api	(Asking someone to open something)
Open	
E l'api letta	(Asking someone to open a little box)
Open box	
Pallone l'ape	(Asking someone to take off some rings
Ball open	around a deflated balloon)

Api is a two-place verb whose meaning can be roughly represented by the following configuration:

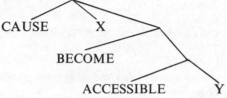

In the first sentence above, both arguments are omitted. In the following two sentences X is omitted but Y is present.

Tottò	(Someone spanks someone else)
Spank	
Tottò mamma	(Mommy spanks me)
Spank mommy	
Tottò Piocchio	(I spank Pinocchio)
Spank Pinocchio	

Tottò is also a two-place verb. In the first sentence both arguments are omitted; in the second sentence one argument is omitted; and in the third sentence the other argument is omitted.

Further proof to support our analysis of Claudia's sentences can be obtained from the verbal interchanges between Claudia and the people around her, usually her mother. In these interchanges we see coming to the surface the postulated elements which otherwise Claudia would not lexicalize. Here are two examples with *etto* and *itto*:

(1) CLAUDIA: *Pupa*
              Doll
     MOTHER: *Dov'è la pupa?* (Where's the doll?)
     CLAUDIA: *Etto*
              Here is
(2) CLAUDIA: *Itto*
              Seen
     MOTHER: *Ho visto, amore che cosa?* (What have I seen, dear?)
     CLAUDIA: *A ianne*
              Spinning top

In (1) Claudia at first lexicalizes the argument only (*pupa*), then under the stimulus of the mother's question, also the verb (*etto*) appears. In (2) the two events occur in reverse order.

(3) MOTHER: *Ma l'aranciata la dai alla bambola o a Claudia?* (Are you going to give the orange juice to the doll or to Claudia?)
CLAUDIA: *Tazie*
Give
MOTHER: *A chi, alla bombola o a Claudia?* (Who to, to the doll or to Claudia?)
CLAUDIA: *Tazie a Claudia*
Give Claudia

(4) MOTHER: *Come si chiama questa?* (What's this called?)
CLAUDIA: *Bamboa*
Doll
MOTHER: *Cosa le dai alla bambola?* (What are you giving your doll?)
CLAUDIA: *Totto*
Cookie

(5) MOTHER: *E nonna cosa ti dà* (And what does grandma give you?)
CLAUDIA: *Bototto*
Cookie
MOTHER: *Il biscotto ti da la nonna?* (Grandma will give you a cookie?)
CLAUDIA: *Da a nonna bototto*
Grandma give cookie

Let us see some more interchanges. This is with the verb *oio* (want):

(6) CLAUDIA: *Papà nanà*
Daddy swing
FATHER: *Che vuoi?* (What do you want?)
CLAUDIA: *Papà oio nanà*
Daddy want swing

(7) MOTHER: *Che cosa fa adesso la televisione?* (Is the television on?) (Note the T.V. is off)
CLAUDIA: *A nanna*
Sleep
MOTHER: *Fa la nanna* (It's sleeping)
CLAUDIA: *Cione a nanna*
Television sleep

(8) MOTHER: *Che cosa vuoi mangiare? La pastasciutta?* (What do you want to eat? Noodles?)
CLAUDIA: *No*
No
MOTHER: *Non vuoi mangiarla?* (Don't you want to eat it?)
CLAUDIA: *Mangia a mamma*
Eat mommy
MOTHER: *La mangia la mamma?* (Mommy eats it?)
CLAUDIA: *A mamma pastaciutta*
Mommy noodles

4. Let us now go back to the sentences with *da* or *tazie*, that is, to sentences (a)–(h). We assumed the semantic structures (a')–(h') as underlying those sentences. Now such structures are obviously not adequate to represent the meanings of sentences (a)–(h). For instance, we assumed two identical semantic structures for the two sentences

    (b) *Tazie a mamma*
    (c) *Tazia a Claudia*

but these two sentences have quite different functions. In (b) Claudia *describes* the fact that the mother is giving her something, whereas in (c) she *asks* her mother to give her something.

A more complete analysis requires that a richer semantic structure be assigned to these sentences. The problem is not limited to the above two sentences. Additional examples in which Claudia is asking for something are:

Api	(Asking someone to open something)
Open	
Papà, e dicchi	(Daddy, put a disk on)
Daddy disks	
Pupa a nanna	(The doll must go to sleep)
Doll sleep	

Examples in which Claudia is describing something are:

Etto a paia	(Here is the ball)
Here's ball	
Ianne a pu	(The spinning top has stopped turning)
Spinning top all gone	
Tai	(Pointing to a pair of spectacles)
Glasses	

In fact, all of Claudia's sentences do have some function or other. Let us assume that for the sentences in our corpus these functions are only two: "describing" and "requesting." Can we include this new fact in our model in a consistent way? Austin (1962) has introduced the concept of a performative verb, that is, a verb which when used in the first person singular of the indicative present is an act and not the description of an act, as nonperformative verbs are. If I say *I promise*, I am promising just by uttering these words, whereas if I say *I eat*, I am not eating but only describing my act of eating. *To Promise* is a performative verb; *to eat* is not.

However, when I say *I eat*, I am describing that I eat; in other words, behind this sentence there is a performative verb, albeit an abstract, not lexicalized, performative verb. More precisely, underlying all declarative sentences there is a semantic structure which corresponds more or less to the meaning of the English verbs *to declare, to say, to state* (Ross, 1970).

What we called the functions of the sentences in Claudia's speech are these performative semantic structures, which can be lexicalized or not. A performative structure does not add anything to the sentence it introduces, it only indicates how the sentences is to be taken, its function. If I say *I promise to come*, I am saying that I will come and that this is to be taken as a promise. If I say *Come!* what I am saying is that *You come* has to be taken as a request. If I say *John eats*, I am indicating that *John eats* is to be taken as a description or information.

Gruber (this volume) has already argued that children's sentences include performative structures. We only have to translate this in terms of our model and to apply it in a systematic way to our data.

We assume that only two functions need be postulated for Claudia's sentences, that is, "describing" and "requesting." We represent these functions as specific semantic configurations which dominate the semantic configuration representing the meaning of each particular sentence.

"Describing" is the following configuration:

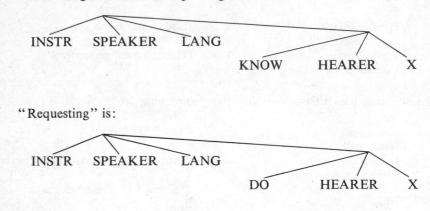

"Requesting" is:

The semantic components in these configurations are: $INSTR_{xyw}$, $SPEAKER_x$, $LANG_x$, $KNOW_{xy}$, DO_{xy}, and $HEARER_x$. $INSTR_{xyw}$ stands for "X use Y in order to Z." Therefore a sentence has a "describing" function when "the speaker uses language in order that the hearer knows X." It has a "requesting" function when "the speaker uses language in order that the hearer does X." We are not saying that all the above components are completely differentiated in Claudia's semantic competence. It may be, for instance, that Claudia always uses INSTR with SPEAKER and LANG as its first and second arguments, respectively, and that only at a later stage does she learn that these arguments can be filled in with different semantic material. But we claim that most of Claudia's sentences express either the "describing" or the "requesting" semantic configuration.

We can now give a more complete representation of the semantic structure of sentences (b) and (c):

For (b) we have:

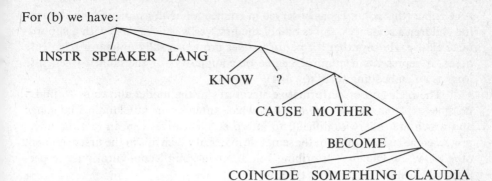

For (c) we have

As can be seen, in the (b) configuration the first argument of KNOW is filled with a question mark. This indicates that we are not certain whether the person to whom Claudia wants to describe the situation is her mother or Claudia herself. We often find that Claudia's sentences with a "describing" function seem to have the purpose of describing a situation or naming things for Claudia's benefit and nobody else's.

We have a parallel case for the sentences with a "requesting" function. For instance, *Pupa a nanna* (doll sleep) is a request, but it is not clear whether this request is addressed to someone else or to Claudia herself. If the latter is the case, we have what is usually called the expression of an intention.

It is of interest to observe that there is at least one case in which the "requesting" configuration is lexicalized by Claudia. This occurs in the sentences with the verb *oio* (want):

Oio pipì	(I want to do wee-wee)
Want wee-wee	
Oio nanà	(I want to go on the swing)
Want swing	
Oio palla	(I want the ball)
Want ball	

As Gruber (this volume) has observed in connection with *want* in English-speaking children's sentences, this is one of the first verbs children use with a subordinate clause. He says that "if performatives are universally obligatory, as Ross holds, it represents a minimal degree of complexity for the child to generate *want* as an embedding verb" (p. 444).

The inclusion of performative structures in the model allows us to find a possible explanation for the vocatives which often occur in Claudia's language and which are otherwise difficult to interpret.[4] Vocatives can, in fact, be interpreted as the lexicalization of the semantic material which fills in the first argument of KNOW or DO in "describing" and "requesting" configurations, respectively. As instance of the first type, we have:

Mamma ianne	(Claudia tells her mother that the spin-
Mommy spinning top	ning top is turning)
Mamma piitto	(Claudia shows her mother her navel)
Mommy belly button	
Papà a tati	(Claudia tells her father that the re-
Daddy people	searchers are present)

and of the second type:

Papà dicchi	(Claudia asks her father to play some
Daddy disks	disks)
Mamma a papis	(Claudia asks her mother to draw)
Mommy pencil	
Mamma iacca	(Claudia asks her mother for water)
Mommy water	

5. We have been arguing that in the period of time under consideration Claudia's sentences have an underlying semantic structure which includes (a) a predication with its necessary NP-complements and (b) a performative superstructure. No change occurs in this period in the general nature of the semantic configurations that Claudia lexicalizes. A quantitative change does occur, however, in the lexicalization process itself, in that Claudia is able to lexicalize an increasing number of elements which are present in the underlying configurations. This is reflected in the increase of the mean length of her sentences.

It is interesting to observe that no element is present in Claudia's sentences which does not belong to the sentence nucleus, that is, predication plus NP-complements. It is only at a later stage that additional structure is added to Claudia's configurations and begins to emerge in her sentences. Data we are now processing seem to show that this additional structure takes the form of adverbials, that is, predications which take the sentence nucleus as one of their arguments.

---

[4] In his purely distributional analysis of child language, Braine (1963) deliberately excludes the vocatives from the data.

REFERENCES

Austin, J. L., *How to do things with words*. Oxford: Oxford University Press, 1962.

Braine, M. D. S., The ontogeny of English phrase structure, *Language*, 1963, **34**, 1–13. [Reprinted in this volume.]

Brown, R. W., and U. Bellugi. Three processes in the child's acquisition of syntax. In E. H. Lenneberg (ed.), *New directions in the study of language*. Cambridge, Mass.: M.I.T. Press, 1964.

Brown, R. W., and C. Fraser. The acquisition of syntax. In C. N. Cofer and B. S. Musgrave (eds.), *Verbal behavior and learning*: New York: McGraw-Hill, 1963.

Gruber, J. S., Correlations between the syntactic constructions of the child and of the adult. This volume, pp. 440–445.

McCawley, J. D., Where do noun phrases come from? In R. A. Jacobs and P. S. Rosenbaum (eds.), *Readings in English transformational grammar*. Waltham, Mass.: Ginn, 1970.

Parisi, D., *Il linguaggio come processo cognitivo*. Torino: Boringhieri, in press.

Parisi, D., and F. Antinucci, Lexical competence. In G. B. Flores d'Arcais and W. J. M. Levelt (eds.), *Advances in psycholinguistics*. Amsterdam: North-Holland, 1970.

Ross, J. R., On declarative sentences. In R. A. Jacobs and P. S. Rosenbaum (eds.), *Readings in English transformational grammar*. Waltham, Mass.: Ginn, 1970.

JAPANESE •

What Does a Child Mean When He Says "No"?[1]

—— *David McNeill and Nobuko B. McNeill*

The emergence of negation in English is a portrait of a child's resolution of complexity. Very roughly, negation in English requires two transformations—one to remove an underlying negative element from where it is located in the deep structure of a sentence, and the other to introduce an auxiliary verb (*do* or *can*) to support this element in the surface structure (Klima, 1964). This sketch omits most significant matters, but it reveals an important part of what a child must acquire in order to negate in the English manner.

From *Proceedings of the Conference on Language and Language Behavior*, edited by E. M. Zale. New York: Appleton-Century-Crofts, 1968, pp. 51–62. Reprinted by permission of the authors and the publisher.
[1] This report is a slightly revised version of the paper presented by the major author, David McNeill, at the Conference on Language and Language Behavior. It is based on research supported by a contract with the Office of Education, U.S. Department of Health, Education and Welfare, under provisions of P.L. 85–531, Cooperative Research, and Title VI, P.L. 85–864, as amended.

One hypothesis about language acquisition is that it rests on a set of specific cognitive capacities. These may be innate and may be described by the so-called theory of grammar, or linguistic theory (Chomsky, 1965; Katz, 1966; McNeill, 1968). The suggestion is that the universal form of language reflects children's capacity for language—language has the form described by the theory of grammar because of the innate capacities of children to acquire language. Children's capacities everywhere in the world impose the same features on language, which, therefore, appear as linguistic universals.

An advantage of this view is that it accounts for the existence of linguistic abstractions, features in adult grammar that are *never* included in the overt forms of speech. Such features, of course, cannot be presented to children; yet, they exist as a part of adult linguistic knowledge. On the capacity hypothesis, such abstractions are held to be linguistic universals, deriving from children's capacity for language, and they are *made* abstract through the acquisition of transformations.

An example of a linguistic abstraction, never presented as an overt form of speech, is the location of NEG at the beginning of the deep structure of English sentences. On the capacity hypothesis, this abstraction is *possible* because the location of NEG on the boundary of a sentence reflects an aspect of children's capacity for language. This principle would be, roughly, that every proposition can be denied by attaching to it a minus sign.

In this light, it is interesting that Bellugi (1964) finds the earliest negative sentences from children to be NEG + S and S + NEG—i.e., sentences in which a negative element (usually *no* or *not*) is placed outside an otherwise affirmative sentence. Examples are *no drop mitten*, and *wear mitten no*. This form of negation persists until a child shows independent evidence of having the two transformations mentioned above, at which time it completely disappears—having now presumably become abstract (McNeill, 1966). The same is true of the primitive negation of children learning Russian (Slobin, 1966) and French (our records).

THE SYNTAX OF NEGATION IN JAPANESE

We mention these findings with children exposed to English and other languages in order to compare them to the development of negation in Japanese. Syntactically, negation in Japanese is rather simple. Except for order, the relevant part of the deep structure is identical to the deep structure of English sentences:

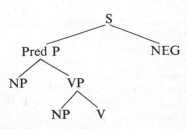

In Japanese, however, there are *no* order-changing transformations involved in carrying the negative aspect of this structure to the surface. The surface structure of a negative Japanese sentence is also *NP NP V NEG*. On the capacity hypothesis, therefore, the development of negation in Japanese should be likewise simple. Indeed, on the capacity hypothesis, Japanese children should not be *able* to make syntactic errors.

We thus take it to be consistent with the English findings and the capacity hypothesis that neither of the two children we have been following has *ever* uttered a grammatically-deviant negative. Their negative sentences are identical to some of the negatives that Bellugi described, i.e., S + NEG, and this is entirely correct in Japanese.

Syntactically, the development of negation thus poses no problem in Japanese. The language does not require more from children than is already available in their general capacity for negation. In Japanese, the problem is of a different sort.

THE SEMANTICS OF NEGATION IN JAPANESE

Although syntactically simple, negation in Japanese is *semantically* complex. In contrast to English, for example, the language provides several distinct forms; it is here that one can gain some insight into the process of development.

There are four common forms of negation in Japanese: *nai* (aux), *nai* (adj), *iya*, and *iiya*. *Nai* (aux) is the form introduced into the phrase-marker given above. It is attached both to verbs, as indicated, and to adjectives. *Nai* (adj), like all adjectives in Japanese, has verbal force, so that one can say, for example, *peace-nai*, meaning *there is no peace*. *Iya* stands alone, and means, roughly, *I do not want*. *Iiya* also stands alone and means that what was just said is wrong *and* something else is right. There are other forms than these four, but they are restricted to special situations—formal speech, for example.

These four forms—*nai* (aux), *nai* (adj), *iya*, and *iiya*—embody three dimensions of meaning. *Nai* (adj) is used in such sentences as "there's not an apple here," said after someone has asked about a place where there is no apple. The use of *nai* (adj), therefore, depends on the *non-existence of objects and events*.

Nai (aux) is used in such a sentence as "that's not an apple," said after someone else, pointing to a pear, said, "that's an apple." The use of *nai* (aux), therefore, depends on the *falsity of statements*.

Iya is used in such sentences as "no, I don't want an apple." *Iya* by itself conveys the idea of "I don't want," and its use, therefore, depends on *internal desire*, or the lack of it.

Iiya is used in such sentences as "No, I didn't have an apple, I had a pear." Contrastive stress can convey this idea in English: "No, I didn't have an *apple*, I had a *pear*." The import of *iiya* is that one alternative (already mentioned or somehow in mind) is false and another is true. We will call this type of negation *entailment*, since, in this case, the negation of one statement entails the truth of another.

The four kinds of negative in Japanese thus involve three dimensions, or contrasts: *Entailment-Non-entailment*, *External-Internal*, and *Existence-Truth* (the last to be understood as indicating the *condition* of negation—the *existence* or lack of it, of some *thing*, versus the *truth*, or lack of it, of some *sentence*).

One can organize the dimensions of negation into a cube, always a mark of progress in this area, and locate the four negative terms in Japanese at the appropriate corners (see Fig. 1).

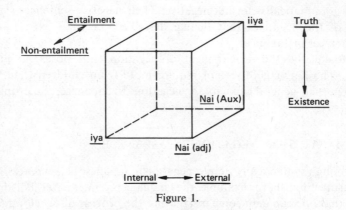

Figure 1.

Alternatively, one can define the terms of negation in Japanese by means of feature matrices:

	NAI (*adj*)	NAI (*aux*)	IYA	IIYA
Existence	+	−	+	−
Entailment	−	−	−	+
External	+	+	−	+

According to these matrices, *iya* and *iiya* are diametrically-opposite kinds of negation, and the two kinds of *nai* are identical, except that one depends on the non-existence of objects and the other on the falsity of sentences. Both implications accord with native intuition.

The matrices also help explain what always strikes English speakers as a bit of oriental exotica, when they first learn how Japanese affirm or deny negative questions. If someone asks, in English, "Is there no pear?" and you wish to give an affirmative answer, the correct response is "no, there is no pear," or some more idiomatic variant. In Japanese, however it is the reverse. If one wishes to give an affirmative answer, the reply should be, "Yes there is no pear." A similar reversal exists for denial. In English it is "yes, there is a pear," but in Japanese it is "no, there is a pear."

The difference is that "yes" and "no" in Japanese are (− Existence), whereas "yes" and "no" in English are (+ Existence). Thus, the Japanese "yes" refers to the truth-value of the sentence, whereas the English "yes" refers to the existence of the pear. Similarly for "no" in the two languages: in Japanese it signifies a false statement, whereas, in English it signifies non-existence.

The cube indicates that there are four other negatives possible but not used in Japanese. One, for example, would be a negative that denies the *truth of statements* on the grounds of *internal desire*, but which does *not entail* a true alternative. It would be a negative for existentialists: What you don't desire is false, but nothing in particular is thereby true. This is despair.

These three dimensions can be found in English negation also, but English is ambiguous with respect to them. The English "no" is (+ Existence) when discussing the physical environment, but it becomes (− Existence) in other contexts: for example, "three plus two is six," "*no*." And when one says, "No, anything but *that*!," presumably the left side of the cube is evoked. But English does not have separate terms sorted out in the analytic Japanese manner. When a child says, for example, *no dirty* in English, he is at least four-ways, and possibly eight-ways, ambiguous.

Japanese, since it distinguishes among words along the three dimensions of negation, makes it possible to trace the order in which the dimensions emerge. We have looked for patterns of confusion—which negatives replace others—and from these patterns have attempted to infer the sequence of development. In effect, we have asked, how is the cube built up? Or, equivalently, in what order are the rows of the feature matrix added?

THE DEVELOPMENT OF NEGATION IN JAPANESE

We have worked with tape-recordings of the speech of two Japanese children. Both children are girls and both live in Tokyo. To date, there is some seven months' accumulation of speech. One of these children presents very little data, and what she does present so far eludes our understanding. The other child, whom we call Izanami, will be described here.

At 27 months, the youngest age at which we have recordings, three of the four negative forms occur. These are *nai* (adj.), *nai* (aux), and *iya*. *Iya* is always used alone. *Nai* (adj) is used alone and after nouns, and both are correct syntactic contexts in Japanese. *Nai* (aux) is used with just one verb—*shira-nai*—meaning "I don't know."

Of the two forms abundantly present at 27 months, *nai* (adj) is always used when called for, as far as this can be judged from context. That is, whenever non-existence is referred to, Izanami uses *nai* (adj). *Iya*, however, is often replaced by *nai* (adj). For instance, if Izanami's mother said, "Let's give you some," Izanami would sometimes apparently reply, "There's no giving," instead of "I don't want." *Nai* (adj) intruded thus into as many as 40 per cent of the contexts appropriate for *iya*. *Iya*, on the other hand, never intruded into contexts appropriate to *nai* (adj).

This pattern of confusion would arise if Izanami did not yet know *any* of the dimensions involved in negation, but reacted instead only to non-existence. Then *nai* (adj) would be used whenever called for, and *iya* (being in her vocabulary) would oscillate with *nai* (adj) in contexts calling for an expression of personal desire, but not involving non-existence. Let us assume then that Izanami began with the registration of simple non-existence as the occasion for negation. In effect, she began with the *nai* (adj) *termini* of each of the three dimensions, but did not yet have the dimensions themselves. She built from *Existence, Non-entailment*, and *External*. We have called this *Stage 1*.

About two months later, two things happened to *iya*. First, it began to appear in contexts calling for *nai* (aux). For example, if Izanami's mother said (falsely), "This is an apple," pointing to a pear, Izanami would reply with *iya*, apparently meaning "I don't want it." This is only apparently odd. We will re-return to it shortly. The second development with *iya* is that it began to appear in contexts calling for *iiya*.

The last intrusion, *iya* in place of *iiya*, is totally inexplicable on the feature analysis. These terms share no features—they are at opposite corners of the cube —and so should never be confused, so long as at least one dimension has been acquired. Moreover, *iya* has been present in Izanami's vocabulary since the beginning, but it appears in contexts calling for *iiya* only now, after two months. We are fairly certain, therefore, that the intrusion is the result of a new development.

Let us suppose that it is not *iya* but really *iiya* that appears in contexts calling for *iiya*. Vowel-vowel sequences are common in Japanese, but Izanami has none at this time. Since *iya* and *iiya* can be distinguished only through a difference in vowel length, it is at least possible that Izanami intends to say *iiya*, even though she actually says *iya*. In support of this interpretation is one further fact. From the beginning, *nai* (adj) has appeared in contexts calling for *iiya*, but the intrusion *ends* at this same time—again, indicating that Izanami has acquired *iiya*. If we accept the interpretation that Izanami says *iya* when she intends to say *iiya*, we can conclude that Izanami has added the *Existence-Truth*, or the *Entailment-Non-entailment* dimensions, or both.

Of the two, the evidence favors *Existence-Truth*. Recall that contexts calling for *nai* (aux) begin taking *iya* about this time. Instead of saying, "It's not an apple," Izanami apparently says, "I don't want an apple." However, if it is really *iiya* appearing in place of *nai* (aux)—so that she is saying, "It's not an apple (but something else)"—we then know that Izanami has acquired the *Existence-Truth* contrast only. It could not have been *Entailment-Non-entailment* because *iiya* and *nai* (aux) are distinct on this feature—one being *Entailment*, the other being *Non-entailment*. They could not be confused, if this dimension had been acquired. However, they are alike on *Existence-Truth*, both being marked for *Truth*, and so *could* be confused if Izanami had acquired this dimension alone.

Thus, the first dimension to emerge is *Existence-Truth*, and its appearance marks *Stage 2*, at which time Izanami's knowledge of negation presumably is as follows:

	NAI (*adj*)	NAI (*aux*)	IYA	IIYA
1. No contrasts				
2. Existence	+	−	+	−

Stage 3 took place two months later. The replacement of *iya* by *nai* (adj), which has been present from the beginning, stops altogether. Izanami no longer apparently says, "There isn't an apple," when she should say, "I don't want an apple." The new development must signify acquisition of the *External-Internal* dimension, as well as the virtually certain appearance of *iya* (as opposed to the truncated *iiya*). No other possibility exists, given our semantic analysis, since *External-Internal* is the only dimension on which *iya* and *nai* (adj) contrast. There is no problem here of distinguishing *iya* and *iiya*, of course, since the observation involves the pronunciation (or lack of it) of *nai*. For the same reason, no assumptions are made about the meaning of *iya* when Izanami uses it, but only about the existence of *iya*-contexts.

Thus, Izanami has two dimensions by Stage 3, and *iiya* and *nai* (aux) are synonyms:

	NAI (*adj*)	NAI (*aux*)	IYA	IIYA
1. No contrasts				
2. Existence	+	− ·	+	−
3. External	+	+	−	+

About a month later, Izanami apparently acquired the *Entailment-Non-entailment* dimension. The evidence is that she distinguished *nai* (aux) from *iiya*, and so eliminated the remaining confusion: *(i)iya* no longer appeared in *nai* (aux) contexts. Thus, Izanami developed the entire system of negation in Japanese in some five months' time.

At the moment that Entailment-Non-entailment emerged, an interesting further development occurred. A new word, *chigau*, appeared, and did so in considerable numbers. It has been completely absent from Izanami's speech before this time.

Chigau is not a negative. It is variously translated as "different," "wrong," or "disagree"—and so is different from such words as "no," "not," or "no-but." Syntactically, it is a verb.

However, Izanami uses *chigau* in none of the senses just given. For her, *chigau* is an omnibus negative, used in completely diverse contexts. It appears in situations calling for *iiya* and *iya*—even though *iiya* and *iya* share no features of negation at all—and possibly appears also in contexts appropriate to *nai* (adj) and *nai* (aux), although we have not observed this. If we assume that Izanami's use of *chigau* has not demolished the system of negation just developed—as, indeed, it apparently has not, since she continues to use the four terms of negation as well—we must conclude that *chigau* has negative import but is marked on none of the dimensions of negation. Thus, it appears in contexts calling for Truth as well as Existence, External as well as Internal, and Entailment as well as Non-entailment. In fact, Izanami's use of *chigau* resembles most closely the use of *un-uh* in English: "Do you want some?" "Un-uh"; "Did you have a pear?" "Un-uh, I had an apple"; "Springfield is the capital of Massachusetts." "Un-uh"; "Does she have a wart on her nose?" "Un-uh." *Un-uh*, too, represents omnibus negation.

How are we to account for the sudden appearance of an omnibus negative? It seems most plausible to suppose that Izanami's use of *chigau* reflects the *concept* of negation, as opposed to the particular forms of denial (*iya, nai* (adj), etc.), or the particular dimensions of negation. As such, *chigau* adds the idea of general denial, as an abstract possibility, and so liberates negation from the semantic constraints represented in the three contrasts of Truth-Existence, External-Internal, and Entailment-Non-entailment.

However, the interesting fact is not so much that Izanami eventually developed a form of omnibus negation, but that she did so *after* having developed the various special forms of negation. For Izanami's parents use *chigau* in the omnibus sense, too. *Chigau*, as a kind of featureless denial, has been presented to Izanami as a model throughout the five-month period we have studied (and doubtlessly before), yet Izanami resisted developing *chigau* precisely until she had acquired the last of the three contrasts of negation. On this evidence, generic negation is not primitive, as often claimed. It is, instead, a late development, constructed from, and possibly summarizing, the three features of negation discussed above. It is these features that are preliminary. If anything in Izanami's history of negation reflects some aspect of children's capacity for negation, it is the features of negation and not the general concept of denial.

We can summarize our findings, and answer the question, "What does a child mean when he says 'no'?" by setting down the following five points:

1. At first, Izanami had no features of negation at all. At this point "no" meant something did not exist, and nothing more. Subsequent development consisted of forming contrasts with the ends of the dimensions represented in *nai* (adj); that is, with Existence, External, and Non-entailment.

2. The first such contrast to emerge was between Existence and Truth. In addition to marking the existence and non-existence of events and objects, Izanami came to mark the correctness and incorrectness of statements. By Stage 2, "no" had come to mean false, as well as not here, creating an order of development that appears to be quite natural. Izanami judged relations about language only after she had judged other relations about the external world.

3. The next contrast to emerge was between External and Internal. Besides registering the non-existence of events, Izanami began to mark her desires concerning events. By Stage 3, "no" meant disapproval or rejection, as well as false and not here. Another direction of development, therefore, was from outside to inside, and this, too, seems to be in a natural order. Note that Izanami had the idea of linguistically registering the truth of statements before she had the idea of linguistically registering her inner states in relation to outer ones.

4. The last contrast to emerge was Entailment-Non-entailment. With this dimension, "no" also came to mean "no but," which requires an ability to organize statements into mutually exclusive pairs. Because Entailment-Non-entailment requires a child to hold in mind two propositions at once, it would naturally follow either of the other two contrasts, both of which involve judgments about single propositions or events.

5. The last step was the formation of an abstract concept of negation—the equivalent of *un-uh*. If *chigau* is a construction, its appearance last is also natural.

It is possible that these same steps, insofar as they follow a natural order, are also taken by English-speaking children. As pointed out above, the three dimensions of Japanese negation are used in English as well. Hopefully, future work will discover some way to investigate this possibility.

REFERENCES

Bellugi, Ursula, The emergence of inflections and negation systems in the speech of two children. Paper presented at *New England Psychological Association*, 1964. [See Klima and Bellugi, this volume, p. 333.]

Chomsky, N., *Aspects of the theory of syntax*. Cambridge, Mass.: M.I.T. Press, 1966.

Katz, J. J., *The philosophy of language*. New York: Harper & Row, 1966.

Klima, E. S., Negation in English. In J. A. Fodor and J. J. Katz (eds.), *The structure of language*. Englewood Cliffs, N.J.: Prentice-Hall, 1964.

McNeill, D., Developmental psycholinguistics. In F. Smith and G. A. Miller (eds.), *The genesis of language: A psycholinguistic approach*. Cambridge, Mass.: M.I.T. Press, 1966.

McNeill, D., On theories of language acquisition. In T. Dixon and D. Horton (eds.), *Verbal-behavior theory and its relation to S-R theory*. Englewood Cliffs, N.J.: Prentice-Hall, 1968.

Slobin, D. I., The acquisition of Russian as a native language. In F. Smith and G. A. Miller (eds.), *The genesis of language: A psycholinguistic approach*. Cambridge: M.I.T. Press, 1966.

BIBLIOGRAPHY

Ament, W., *Die Entwicklung von Sprechen und Denken beim Kinde.* Leipzig: Ernst Wunderlich, 1899.

Amidon, A., and P. Carey. Why can't five-year-olds understand *before* and *after*? Submitted to *J. verb. Learn. verb. Behav.*, 1971.

Anisfeld, M., J. Barlow, and C. M. Frail, Distinctive features in the pluralization rules of English speakers. *Language and Speech*, 1968, **11**, 31–37.

Anisfeld, M., and M. Gordon, On the psychophonological structure of English inflectional rules. *J. verb. Learn. verb. Behav.*, 1968, **7**, 973–979.

Antinucci, F., and D. Parisi, Primi resultati di uno studio sullo sviluppo linguistico infantile. *Atti del IV Convegno della Società di Linguistica Italiana.* Rome: Bulzoni, in press.

Argoff, H. D., Forthcoming doctoral dissertation on the acquisition of Finnish. Univer. Calif., Berkeley.

Asch, S. E., and H. Nerlove, The development of double function terms in children: An exploratory investigation. In B. Kaplan and S. Wapner (eds.), *Perspectives in psychological theory: Essays in honor of Heinz Werner.* New York: International Universities Press, 1960. Pp. 47–60.

Austin, J. L., *How to do things with words.* Cambridge, Mass.: Harvard Univer. Press, 1962.

Balassa, J., A gyermek nyelvének fejlödése. *Nyelvtudományi Közlemények*, 1893, **23**, 60–73, 129–144.

Bar-Adon, A., Primary syntactic structures in Hebrew child language. In A. Bar-Adon and W. F. Leopold (eds.), *Child language: A book of readings.* Englewood Cliffs, N.J.: Prentice-Hall, 1971. Pp. 433–472.

Bellugi, U., The acquisition of negation. Unpubl. doct. dissert., Harvard Univ., 1967.

Bellugi, U., Linguistic mechanisms underlying child speech. In H. Zale (ed.), *Proceedings of the Conference on Language and Language Behavior.* New York: Appleton-Century-Crofts, 1968.

Bellugi, U., and R. Brown (eds.), The acquisition of language. *Monogr. Soc. Res. Child Developm.*, 1964, **29** (1).

Bem, S. L., The role of comprehension in children's problem solving. *Developmental Psychol.*, 1970, **2**, 351–358.

Berko, J., The child's learning of English morphology. *Word*, 1958, **14**, 150–177.

Bever, T. G., The cognitive basis for linguistic structures. In J. R. Hayes (ed.), *Cognition and the development of language.* New York: Wiley, 1970. Pp. 279–362. (a)

Bever, T. G., The comprehension and memory of sentences with temporal relations. In G. B. Flores d'Arcais and W. J. M. Levelt (eds.), *Advances in psycholinguistics.* Amsterdam: North-Holland, 1970. Pp. 284–291. (b)

Bever, T. G., The influence of speech performance on linguistic structure. In

G. B. Flores d'Arcais and W. J. M. Levelt (eds.), *Advances in psycholinguistics.* Amsterdam: North-Holland, 1970. Pp. 4–30. (c)

Bever, T. G. The integrated study of language behavior. In J. Morton (ed.), *Biological and social factors in language learning.* London: Logos Press, 1971.

Bever, T. G., J. A. Fodor, and W. Weksel, On the acquisition of grammar: A critique of "contextual generalization." *Psychol. Rev.*, 1965, **72**, 467–482. (a)

Bever, T. G., J. A. Fodor, and W. Weksel, Is linguistics empirical? *Psychol. Rev.*, 1965, **72**, 493–500. (b)

Bever, T. G., and D. T. Langendoen, A dynamic model of the evolution of language. *Ling. Inquiry*, 1971, **4**, 433–464.

Bierwisch, M., Semantics. In J. Lyons (ed.), *New horizons in linguistics.* Baltimore: Penguin, 1970. Pp. 166–184.

Blagoveshchenskiy, V., Detskaya rech'. *Russ. filol. vestnik.* 1886, **16**.

Bloch, O., Notes sur le langage d'un enfant. *Mémoires Soc. Ling. Paris*, 1913, **18**, 39–59.

Bloch, O., Les premiers stades du langage de l'enfant. *J. Psychol. norm. pathol.*, 1921, **18**, 693–712.

Bloch, O., La phrase dans le langage d'un enfant. *J. Psychol. norm. pathol.*, 1924, **21**, 18–43.

Bloom, L. M., *Language development: Form and function in emerging grammars.* Cambridge, Mass.: M.I.T. Press, 1970.

Blount, B. G., Acquisition of language by Luo children. Unpubl. doct. dissert., Univer. Calif., Berkeley, 1969. [Working Paper No. 19 (1969), Language-Behavior Res. Lab., Univer. Calif., Berkeley.]

Blount, B. G., The pre-linguistic system of Luo children. *Anthrop. Ling.*, 1970, **12**, 326–342.

Blount, B. G., Socialization and pre-linguistic development among the Luo of Kenya. *Southwest. J. Anthrop.*, 1971, **27**, 41–50.

Blumenthal, A. L., *Language and psychology: Historical aspects of psycholinguistics.* New York: Wiley, 1970.

Bogoyavlenskiy, D. N., *Psikhologiya usvoyeniya orfografii.* Moscow: Akad. Pedag. Nauk RSFSR, 1957. [English translation of pp. 261–271: The acquisition of Russian inflections. Reprinted in this volume.]

Bolin, I., and M. Bolin, De två första årens språkutveckling hos en svensk flicka. *Svenskt arkiv för pedagogik*, 1916, **4**, 159–223.

Bolin, I., and M. Bolin, Psykologiska och språkliga iakttagelser rörande en svensk flicka. *Svenskt arkiv för pedagogik*, 1920, **8**, 1–55.

Bolinger, D. L., *Aspects of language.* New York: Harcourt Brace Jovanovich, 1968.

Borgström, C. H., Språkanalyse som barnelek. *Norsk tidsskrift for sprogvidenskap*, 1954, **17**, 484–485. [English translation: Language analysis as a child's game. Reprinted in this volume.]

Bowerman, M. F., Learning to talk: A cross-linguistic study of early syntactic development, with special reference to Finnish. Unpubl. doct. dissert., Harvard Univer., 1970. [Cambridge Univer. Press, in press.]

Boyanus, S. C., *Russian pronunciation and Russian phonetic reader*, 2 vols. Cambridge, Mass.: Harvard Univer. Press, 1955.

Braine, M. D. S., On learning the grammatical order of words. *Psychol. Rev.*, 1963, **70**, 323–348. (a)

Braine, M. D. S., The ontogeny of English phrase structure: The first phase. *Language*, 1963, **39**, 1–13. (b) [Reprinted in this volume.]

Braine, M. D. S., On the basis of phrase structure: A reply to Bever, Fodor, and Weksel. *Psychol. Rev.*, 1965, **72**, 483–492.

Braine, M. D. S., On two types of models of the internalization of grammars. In D. I. Slobin (ed.), *The ontogenesis of grammar: A theoretical symposium*. New York: Academic Press, 1971. Pp. 153–186. (a)

Braine, M. D. S., The acquisition of language in infant and child. In C. Reed (ed.), *The learning of language*. New York: Appleton-Century-Crofts, 1971. Pp. 153–186. (b)

Brogan, P. A., The nesting constraint in child language. Unpubl. paper in series "Language, Society, and the Child," Language-Behavior Res. Lab., Univer. Calif., Berkeley, 1968.

Bronowski, J., and U. Bellugi, Language, name, and concept. *Science*, 1970, **168**, 669–673.

Bronstein, A., *The pronunciation of American English*. New York: Appleton-Century-Crofts, 1960.

Brown, R., Linguistic determinism and the part of speech. *J. abnorm. soc. Psychol.*, 1957, **55**, 1–5.

Brown, R., *Social psychology*. New York: Free Press, 1965.

Brown, R., The development of Wh questions in child speech. *J. verb. Learn. verb. Behav.*, 1968, **7**, 279–290.

Brown, R., *Psycholinguistics: Selected papers*. New York: Free Press, 1970.

Brown, R., *A first language*. Cambridge, Mass.: Harvard Univer. Press, in press. (Chap. I: Semantic and grammatical relations; Chap. II: Grammatical morphemes and the modulation of meaning.)

Brown, R., and U. Bellugi, Three processes in the child's acquisition of syntax. *Harvard educ. Rev.*, 1964, **34**, 133–151. [Also in E. H. Lenneberg (ed.), *New directions in the study of language*. Cambridge, Mass.: M.I.T. Press, 1964. Pp. 131–162.]

Brown, R., C. Cazden, and U. Bellugi. The child's grammar from I to III. In J. P. Hill (ed.), *Minnesota Symposia on Child Psychology*, Vol. 2. Minneapolis: Univer. Minn. Press, 1968. Pp. 28–73. [Reprinted in this volume.]

Brown, R., and C. Fraser. The acquisition of syntax. In C. N. Cofer and B. S. Musgrave (eds.), *Verbal behavior and learning: Problems and processes*. New York: McGraw-Hill, 1963. Pp. 158–197. [Also in U. Bellugi and R. Brown (eds.), The acquisition of language. *Monogr. Soc. Res. Child Developm.*, 1964, **29** (1), 43–79.]

Brown, R., and C. Hanlon. Derivational complexity and order of acquisition in child speech. In J. R. Hayes (ed.), *Cognition and the development of language*. New York: Wiley, 1970. Pp. 11–53.

Bryant, B., and M. Anisfeld, Feedback versus no-feedback in testing children's knowledge of English pluralization rules. *J. exp. Child Psychol.*, 1969, **8**, 250–255.

Burling, R., Language development of a Garo- and English-speaking child. *Word*, 1959, **15**, 45–68. [Reprinted in this volume.]

Chao, Y. R., *Mandarin primer*. London: Cambridge Univer. Press, 1948.

Chao, Y. R., The Cantian idolect: An analysis of the Chinese spoken by a twenty-eight-months-old child. *Univer. Calif. Publ. Semitic Philol.*, 1951, **11**, 27–44. [Reprinted in this volume.]

Cheng, C. C., *Mandarin phonology*. Unpubl. doct. dissert., Univer. Ill., 1968.

Chomsky, C., *The acquisition of syntax in children from 5 to 10*. Cambridge, Mass.: M.I.T. Press, 1968.

Chomsky, N., *Syntactic structures*. The Hague: Mouton, 1957.

Chomsky, N., *Aspects of the theory of syntax*. Cambridge, Mass.: M.I.T. Press, 1965.

Chomsky, N., *Cartesian linguistics*. New York: Harper & Row, 1966.

Chomsky, N., *Language and mind*. New York: Harcourt Brace Jovanovich, 1968.

Chomsky, N., and M. Halle, *Sound patterns of English*. New York: Harper & Row, 1968.

Christian, J. M., Developing bilingualism in a two-year-old Gujarati-English learning child. Mimeo, Univer. Alabama, Dept. Anthrop. and Sociol., 1971. (a)

Christian, J. M., Style and dialect selection in Hindi-Bhojpuri learning children. Mimeo, Univer. Alabama, Dept. Anthrop. and Sociol., 1971. (b)

Clark, E., How young children describe events in time. In G. B. Flores d'Arcais and W. J. M. Levelt (eds.), *Advances in psycholinguistics*. Amsterdam: North-Holland, 1970. Pp. 275–284.

Clark, E. V., On the acquisition of the meaning of *before* and *after*. *J. verb. Learn. verb. Behav.*, 1971, **10**, 266–275.

Clark, H. H., The primitive nature of children's relational concepts. In J. R. Hayes (ed.), *Cognition and the development of language*. New York: Wiley, 1970. Pp. 269–278.

Clark, H. H., and E. V. Clark, Semantic distinctions and memory for complex sentences. *Quart. J. exp. Psychol.*, 1968, **20**, 129–138.

Cohen, M., Sur les langages successifs de l'enfant. *Mélanges Vendryes*. Paris, 1925. Pp. 109–127.

Cohen, M., Observations sur les dernières persistances du langage enfantin. *J. Psychol. pers. pathol.*, 1933, **30**, 390–399.

Cohen, M. (ed.), *Études sur le langage de l'enfant*. Paris: Scarabée, 1962.

Cromer, R. F., The development of temporal reference during the acquisition of language. Unpubl. doct. dissert., Harvard Univer., 1968.

Cromer, R. F., 'Children are nice to understand': Surface structure clues for the recovery of a deep structure. *Brit. J. Psychol.*, 1970, **61**, 397–408.

d'Arcais, G. B. F., and W. J. M. Levelt (eds.), *Advances in psycholinguistics*. Amsterdam: North-Holland, 1970.

de Boysson-Bardies, B., and J. Mehler, Psycholinguistique, message et codage verbal. I: L'acquisition du langage. *L'année psychologique*, 1969, **69**, 561–598.

Delattre, P., A comparison of syllable length conditioning among languages. *Int. Rev. appl. Ling.*, 1966, **4**, 183–198.

Denev, D., *Mislene i yezik v govornoto razvitiye na detzata.* Sofia: Nauka i izkustvo, 1969.

Deže, L., and P. Vlahović, Teorijsko-metodološka pitanja izučavanja sintakse dečjeg govora. *Prilozi proučavanju jezika* (Novi Sad), in press.

Dezső, L., A gyermeknyelv mondattani vizsgálatának elméletimodszertani kérdései. *Általános Nyelvészeti Tanulmányok*, 1970, **7**, 77–99.

Dingwall, W. O., and G. Tuniks, Government and concord in Russian: A study in developmental psycholinguistics. In B. Kachru, R. B. Lees, Y. Malkiel, and S. Saporta (eds.), *Papers in linguistics in honor of Henry and Renée Kahane.* Urbana: Univer. Ill. Press, in press.

Dinneen, F. P., *An introduction to general linguistics.* New York: Holt, Rinehart and Winston, 1967.

Donaldson, M., and G. Balfour, Less is more: A study of language comprehension in children. *Brit. J. Psychol.*, 1968, **59**, 461–471.

Donaldson, M., and R. J. Wales, On the acquisition of some relational terms. In J. R. Hayes (ed.), *Cognition and the development of language.* New York: Wiley, 1970. Pp. 235–268.

Drach, K., et al., The structure of linguistic input to children. Language-Behavior Res. Lab., Univer. Calif., Berkeley, Working Paper No. 14, 1969.

Drachman, G., and A. Malikouti-Drachman, Studies in the acquisition of Greek as a native language: I. Some preliminary findings on phonology. Paper read at Winter Mtg., Ling. Soc. Amer., 1971.

El'konin, D. B., *Razvitiye rechi v doshkol'nom vozraste.* Moscow: Akad. Pedag. Nauk RSFSR, 1958. [English translation of pp. 34–61: General course of development in the child of the grammatical structure of the Russian language (according to A. N. Gvozdev). Printed in this volume.]

Endrei, G., Adalékok a gyermeknyelv fejlödéséhez. *A Gyermek*, 1913, **7** (8–9).

Engel, W. von R., *Il prelinguaggio infantile.* Brescia: Paideia, 1964.

Ervin-Tripp, S. M., Summer workshops in sociolinguistics: Research on children's acquisition of communicative competence. *Items*, 1969, **23**, 22–26.

Ervin-Tripp, S., Discourse agreement: How children answer questions. In J. R. Hayes (ed.), *Cognition and the development of language.* New York: Wiley, 1970. Pp. 79–107. (a)

Ervin-Tripp, S., Structure and process in language acquisition. In J. E. Alatis (ed.), *Report of the Twenty-First Annual Round Table Meeting on Linguistics and Language Studies.* Washington, D.C.: Georgetown Univer. Press, 1970. Pp. 312–344. (b)

Ervin-Tripp, S., An overview of theories of grammatical development. In D. I. Slobin (ed.), *The ontogenesis of grammar: A theoretical symposium.* New York: Academic Press, 1971. Pp. 189–212.

Ervin-Tripp, S. M., Forthcoming book on child language development. New York: Holt, Rinehart and Winston.

Ervin-Tripp, S. M., and D. I. Slobin, Psycholinguistics. *Annu. Rev. Psychol.*, 1966, **17**, 435–474.

Feofanov, M. P., Ob upotreblenii predlogov v detskoy rechi. *Vopr. psikhol.*, 1958, **4** (3), 111–124.

Feofanov, M. P., *Usvoyeniye uchashchimisya pis'mennoy rechi.* Moscow: Akad. Pedag. Nauk RSFSR, 1962.

Ferguson, C. A., Contrastive analysis and language development. *Monograph Series on Language and Linguistics*, No. 21. Washington, D.C.: Georgetown Univer. Press, 1968.

Ferreiro, E., *Les relations temporelles dans le langage de l'enfant.* Geneva: Droz, 1971.

Ferreiro, E., and H. Sinclair, Temporal relationships in language. *Internatl. J. Psychol.*, 1971, **6**, 39–47.

Fillmore, C. J., The case for case. In E. Bach and R. T. Harms (eds.), *Universals in linguistic theory.* New York: Holt, Rinehart and Winston, 1968. Pp. 1–90.

Fillmore, C. J., and D. T. Langendoen, *Studies in linguistic semantics.* New York: Holt, Rinehart and Winston, 1971.

Fodor, J. A., and M. Garrett, Some syntactical determinants of sentential complexity. *Percept. & Psychophys.*, 1967, **2**, 289–296.

Fodor, J. A., M. Garrett, and T. G. Bever, Some syntactic determinants of sentential complexity, II: Verb structure. *Percept. & Psychophys.*, 1968, **3**, 453–461.

Fraser, C., U. Bellugi, and R. Brown, Control of grammar in imitation, comprehension, and production. *J. verb. Learn. verb. Behav.*, 1963, **2**, 121–135. [Reprinted in this volume.]

Frontali, G., Lo sviluppo del linguaggio articolato nel bambino. *Vox Romanica*, 1943–44, **7**, 214–243.

Furth, H. G., *Piaget and knowledge: Theoretical foundations.* Englewood Cliffs, N.J.: Prentice-Hall, 1969.

Gardner, B. T., and R. A. Gardner, Two-way communication with an infant chimpanzee. In A. Schrier and F. Stollnitz (eds.), *Behavior in nonhuman primates.* New York: Academic Press, 1971. Pp. 117–184.

Garman, M. A., P. D. Griffiths, and R. Wales, Murut (Lun Bawang) prepositions and noun-particles in children's speech. *Sarawak Museum Journal*, 1970, **20**, 1–24.

Geodakyan, I. M., and V. G. Kurginyan, Psikholingvisticheskiy analiz dnevnik-ovykh zapisey. *Materialy tret'yego Vsesoyuznogo simpoziuma po psikholing-vistike (Moskva, iyun' 1970 g.).* Moscow: Akademiya nauk Soyuza SSR, Institut yazykoznaniya, 1970. Pp. 119–120.

Gheorgov, I. A. Die ersten Anfänge des sprachlichen Ausdrucks für das Selbst-bewusstsein bei Kindern. *Arch. ges. Psychol.*, 1905, **5**, 329–404. [Also in E. Meumann (ed.), *Sammlung von Abhandlungen zur psychologischen Pädagogik.* Band 2, Heft 1. Leipzig, 1905.]

Gheorgov, I. A., Pripos k"m gramatichniya razvoy na detzkiya govor. *Godishnik Sofiyskiya Univer.* Sofia, 1906.

Gheorgov, I. A., *Ein Beitrag zur grammatischen Entwicklung der Kindersprache.*

Leipzig: Engelmann, 1908. [Also in *Arch. ges. Psychol.*, 1908, **11**, 242–432.]

Gili y Gaya, S., *Funciones gramaticales en el habla enfantil*. Publicaciones pedagógicas, Serie II, No. XXIV. Rio Piedras: Universidad de Puerto Rico, 1960.

Gimson, A. C., *An introduction to the pronunciation of English*. London: Edward Arnold, 1962.

Gleason, H. A., Jr., *An introduction to descriptive linguistics*, rev. ed. New York: Holt, Rinehart and Winston, 1961.

Grégoire, A., *L'apprentissage du langage*. Vol. 1, *Les deux premières années*. Vol. 2, *La troisième année et les années suivantes*. Paris: Droz, 1937; Paris/ Liège: Droz, 1947.

Greenberg, J. H., Order of affixing: A study in general linguistics. In J. H. Greenberg, *Essays in linguistics*. Chicago: Univer. Chicago Press, 1957. Pp. 86–94.

Greenberg, J. H., Language universals. In T. A. Sebeok (ed.), *Current trends in linguistics*, Vol. 3. The Hague: Mouton, 1966. Pp. 61–112. [Also published separately by Mouton: Series Minor, Nr. LIX, 1966.]

Grimm, H., Strukturanalytische Untersuchung der Kindersprache. Dissert., Dept. Psychol., Univer. Heidelberg, 1971.

Grossman, P. F., and R. J. Scholes, The role of grammaticality and intonation in imitations of word strings by Hebrew speaking children. *Communication Sciences Lab. Quart. Prog. Rept.* (Univer. Fla.), 1971, **9** (1), 21–32.

Gruber, J. S., Topicalization in child language. *Foundations of Lang.*, 1967, **3**, 37–65.

Guillaume, P., Les débuts de la phrase dans le langage de l'enfant. *J. Psychol. norm. pathol.*, 1927, **24**, 1–25. (a) [English translation: The first stages of sentence-formation in children's speech. Printed in this volume.]

Guillaume, P., Le développement des éléments formels dans le langage de l'enfant. *J. Psychol. norm. pathol.*, 1927, **24**, 203–229. (b) [English translation: The development of formal elements in the child's speech. Printed in this volume.]

Gvozdev, A. N., *Usvoyeniye rebenkom zvukovoy storony russkogo yazyka*. Moscow: Akad. Pedag. Nauk RSFSR, 1948. [Reprinted in A. N. Gvozdev, *Voprosy izucheniya detskoy rechi*. Moscow: Akad. Pedag. Nauk RSFSR, 1961. Pp. 49–148.]

Gvozdev, A. N., *Formirovaniye u rebenka grammaticheskogo stroya russkogo yazyka*, 2 parts. Moscow: Akad. Pedag. Nauk RSFSR, 1949. [Reprinted in A. N. Gvozdev, *Voprosy izucheniya detskoy rechi*. Moscow: Akad. Pedag. Nauk RSFSR, 1961. Pp. 149–467.]

Haden, E. F., Accent expiratoire. *Studies in Ling.*, 1962, **16** (1), 23–39.

Hakes, D. T., and H. S. Cairns, Sentence comprehension and relative pronouns. *Percept. & Psychophys.*, 1970, **8**, 5–8.

Halle, M., *The sound pattern of Russian*. The Hague: Mouton, 1959.

Harms, R. *An introduction to phonological theory*. Englewood Cliffs, N.J.: Prentice-Hall, 1968.

Hartman, L. M., The segmental phonemes of the Peiping dialect. *Language*, 1944, **20**, 28–42.

Hatch, E., Four experimental studies in syntax of young children. Tech. Rept. 11, Southwest Regional Lab. for Educational Res. & Developm., Inglewood, Calif., 1969.

Hayes, J. R. (ed.), *Cognition and the development of language*. New York: Wiley, 1970.

Heffner, R. M. S., *General phonetics*. Madison: Univer. Wisc. Press, 1960.

Hockett, C. F., Peiping phonology. *J. Amer. Oriental Soc.*, 1947, **67**, 253–267.

Hockett, C. F., *A manual of phonology.* (*Internatl. J. Amer. Ling. Memoir. II.*) Baltimore: Waverly Press, 1955.

Hoyer, A., and G. Hoyer, Über die Lallsprache eines Kindes. *Z. angew. Psychol.*, 1924, **24**, 263–384.

Huth, A., Die Nebensätze in der Kindersprache. *Z. pädag. Psychol. u. exp. Pädag.*, 1919, **20**, 163–183.

Huttenlocher, J., K. Eisenberg, and S. Strauss, Comprehension: Relation between perceived actor and logical subject. *J. verb. Learn. verb. Behav.*, 1968, **7**, 527–530.

Huttenlocher, J., and S. Strauss, Comprehension and a statement's relation to the situation it describes. *J. verb. Learn. verb. Behav.*, 1968, **7**, 300–304.

Imedadze, N. V., K psikhologicheskoy prirode rannego dvuyazychiya. *Vopr. psikhol.*, 1960, **6** (1), 60–68.

Jacobs, R., and P. S. Rosenbaum, *English transformational grammar*. Waltham, Mass.: Blaisdell (Ginn), 1968.

Jacobs, R., and P. S. Rosenbaum (eds.), *Readings in English transformational grammar*. Waltham, Mass.: Ginn, 1970.

Jakobson, R., *Child language, aphasia and phonological universals*. The Hague: Mouton, 1968. [English translation of *Kindersprache, Aphasie und allgemeine Lautgesetze*. Uppsala: Almqvist & Wiksell, 1941.]

Jakobson, R., and M. Halle, *Fundamentals of language*. The Hague: Mouton, 1956.

Jakobson, R., and J. Lotz, Notes on the French phonemic pattern. *Word*, 1949, **5**, 151–158.

Jespersen, O., *Nutidssprog hos börn og voxne*. Copenhagen/*Christiana*: Gyldendal, 1916. (2d rev. ed.: *Børnesprog: En bog for forældre*. Copenhagen/*Christiana*: Gyldendal, 1923). [English translation in *Language: Its nature, development, and origin*. London: Allen/New York: Holt, 1922. Pp. 101–188.]

Kaczmarek, L., *Kształtowanie się mowy dziecka*. Poznan: Towarzystwo Przyjaciół Nauk, 1953.

Kaper, W., *Kindersprachforschung mit Hilfe des Kindes: Einige Erscheinungen der kindlichen Spracherwerbung erläutert im Lichte des vom Kinde gezeigten Interesses für Sprachliches*. Groningen: J. B. Wolters, 1959.

Kaplan, E. L., The role of intonation in the acquisition of language. Unpubl. doct. dissert., Cornell Univer., 1969.

Karpova, S. N., Osoznaniye slovesnogo sostava rechi rebenkom doshkol'nogo vozrasta. *Vopr. psikhol.*, 1955, **1** (4), 43–55. [Abstracted in D. I. Slobin, Abstracts of Soviet studies of child language. In F. Smith and G. A. Miller (eds.), *The genesis of language: A psycholinguistic approach.* Cambridge, Mass.: M.I.T. Press, 1966. Pp. 370–371.]

Karpova, S. N., *Osoznaniye slovesnogo sostava rechi doshkol'nikami.* Moscow: Izd-vo Mosk. Univer., 1967.

Katz, J. J., *The philosophy of language.* New York: Harper & Row, 1966.

Kelemen, J., A gyermeknyelvi mondatszók. *A Mondatszók a Magyar Nyelvben*, 1970. Pp. 94–100.

Kenyeres, E., A gyermek első szavai és a szófajok föllépése. Budapest, 1926. (A *Kisdednevelés* kiadása.)

Kenyeres, E., Les premiers mots de l'enfant et l'apparition des espècies de mots dans son langage. *Arch. Psychol.*, 1927, **20**, 191–218.

Kernan, K., The acquisition of language by Samoan children. Unpubl. doct. dissert., Univer. Calif., Berkeley, 1969. [Working Paper No. 21 (1969), Language-Behavior Res. Lab., Univer. Calif., Berkeley.]

Kernan, K. T., Semantic relations and the child's acquisition of language *Anthrop. Ling.*, 1970, **12**, 171–187.

Kernan, K. T., and B. G. Blount, The acquisition of Spanish grammar by Mexican children. *Anthrop. Ling.*, 1966, **8** (9), 1–14.

Kessel, F. S., The role of syntax in children's comprehension from ages six to twelve. *Mongr. Soc. Res. Child Developm.*, 1970, **35** (6).

Kingdon, R., *Groundwork of English stress.* London: Longmans Green, 1958.

Kiparsky, P., Linguistic universals and language change. In E. Bach and R. T. Harms (eds.), *Universals in linguistic theory.* New York: Holt, Rinehart and Winston, 1968. Pp. 171–204.

Kiparsky, P., Historical linguistics. In J. Lyons (ed.), *New horizons in linguistics.* Baltimore: Penguin, 1970. Pp. 302–315.

Klima, E. S., Negation in English. In J. J. Fodor and J. A. Katz (eds.), *The structure of language: Readings in the philosophy of language.* Englewood Cliffs, N.J.: Prentice-Hall, 1964. Pp. 246–323.

Klima, E. S., and U. Bellugi, Syntactic regularities in the speech of children. In J. Lyons and R. J. Wales (eds.), *Psycholinguistics papers.* Edinburgh: Edinburgh Univer. Press, 1966. Pp. 183–208.

Kolarič, R., Slovenski otroški govor. *Godišnjak Filizofskog fakulteta u Novom Sadu*, 1959. (Novi Sad, Yugoslavia).

Kospartova, M., Osobenosti na detzkiya govor. *B"lgarski yezik*, 1969, **19**, 532–545.

Kuniya, Y., Development of language in early childhood. *Psychologia*, 1969, **12**, 166–174.

Ladefoged, P., *A phonetic study of West African languages.* London: Cambridge Univer. Press, 1964.

Lakoff, G., Linguistics and natural logic. *Studies in Generative Semantics*, No. 1. Phonetics Lab., Univer. Mich., Ann Arbor, 1970.

Langacker, R. W., *Language and its structure: Some fundamental concepts.* New York: Harcourt Brace Jovanovich, 1968.

Leont'yev, A. A., *Slovo v rechevoy deyatel'nosti.* Moscow: Nauka, 1965.

Leont'yev, A. A., *Psikholingvisticheskiye edinitzy i porozhdeniye rechevogo vyskazyvaniya.* Moscow: Nauka, 1969.

Leopold, W. F., *Speech development of a bilingual child: A linguist's record.* Vol. 1, *Vocabulary growth in the first two years.* Vol. 2, *Sound-learning in the first two years.* Vol. 3, *Grammar and general problems in the first two years.* Vol. 4, *Diary from age 2.* Evanston, Ill.: Northwestern Univer. Press, 1939, 1947, 1949a, 1949b.

Lewis, M. M., *Infant speech: A study of the beginnings of language.* London: Kegan Paul/New York: Harcourt Brace, 1936. [2d ed. 1951].

Lewis, M. N., The beginnings of reference to past and future in a child's speech. *Brit. J. educ. Psychol.*, 1937, **6**, 39–56.

Lieberman, P., *Intonation, perception, and language.* Cambridge, Mass.: M.I.T. Press, 1967.

Lightner, T. M., Segmental phonology of modern standard Russian. Unpubl. doct. dissert., M.I.T., 1965.

Lindblom, B., Temporal organization of syllable production. *Speech Transmission Lab. Quart. Progress & Status Rept.* (Stockholm, Royal Inst. Technol.), 1968, **2** (3), 1–5.

Lindner, G., Beobachtungen und Bemerkungen über die Entwickelung der Sprache des Kindes. *Kosmos*, 1882, **6**, 321–342, 430–441.

Lindner, G., Zum Studium der Kindersprache. *Kosmos*, 1885, **9**, 161–173, 241–259.

Lindner, G., *Aus dem Naturgarten der Kindersprache: Ein Beitrag zur kindlichen Sprach- und Geistesentwickelung in den ersten vier Lebensjahren.* Leipzig: Grieben, 1898.

Lindner, G., Neuere Forschungen und Anschauungen über die Sprache des Kindes. *Z. pädag. Psychol. Pathol. Hygiene*, 1906, **7**, 337–392.

Lovell, K., and E. M. Dixon, The growth of the control of grammar in imitation, comprehension, and production. *J. Child Psychol. & Psychiat.*, 1965, **5**, 1–9.

Lynip, A. W., The use of magnetic devices in the collection and analysis of the preverbal utterances of an infant. *Genetic Psychol. Monogr.*, 1951, **44**, 221-262.

Lyons, J., *Introduction to theoretical linguistics.* London and New York: Cambridge Univer. Press, 1968.

Lyons, J. (ed.), *New horizons in linguistics.* Baltimore: Penguin, 1970.

MacWhinney, B., Forthcoming doctoral dissertation on the acquisition of Hungarian. Univer. Calif., Berkeley.

Mallitzkaya, M. K., K metodike ispol'zovaniya kartinok dlya razvitiya ponimaniya rechi u detey v kontze pervogo i na vtorom godu zhizni. *Vopr. psikhol.*, 1960, **6** (3), 122–126.

Manova-Tomova, V., *Emotzii i govor u malkoto dete.* Sofia: Narodna Prosveta, 1969.

Markova, A. K., Ovladeniya slogovym sostavom slova v rannem vozraste. *Vopr. psikhol.*, 1969, **15** (5), 118–126. [Eng. transl.: Mastery of the syllabic composition of words at an early age. *Soviet Psychol.*, 1971, **9**, 235–249.]

Martin, S. E., Problems of hierarchy and indeterminacy in Mandarin phonology. *Bull. Inst. Hist. & Philol.* (Academia Sinica), 1958, **29**, 209–229. (Taipei, Taiwan.)

McNeill, D., The creation of language by children. In J. Lyons and R. J. Wales (eds.), *Psycholinguistics papers*. Edinburgh: Edinburgh Univer. Press, 1966. Pp. 99–114. (a) [Partly reprinted in this volume.]

McNeill, D., Developmental psycholinguistics. In F. Smith and G. A. Miller (eds.), *The genesis of language: A psycholinguistic approach*. Cambridge, Mass.: M.I.T. Press, 1966. Pp. 15–84. (b)

McNeill, D., *The acquisition of language: The study of developmental psycholinguistics*. New York: Harper & Row, 1970. [Coincides in large part with chapter of same title in P. H. Mussen (ed.), *Carmichael's manual of child psychology*, 3d. ed., Vol. 1. New York: Wiley, 1970, Pp. 1061–1161.]

McNeill, D., and N. B. McNeill, What does a child mean when he says "no"? In E. Zale (ed.), *Proceedings of the Conference on Language and Language Behavior*. New York: Appleton-Century-Crofts, 1968. Pp. 51–62. [Reprinted in this volume.]

McNeill, D., R. Yukawa, and N. B. McNeill, The acquisition of direct and indirect objects in Japanese. *Child Developm.*, 1971, **42**, 237–249.

Meggyes, K., *Egy kétéves gyermek nyelvi rendszere*, Nyelvtudományi Ertekezések 73. Budapest: Akadémiai Kiadó, 1971.

Menyuk, P., A preliminary evaluation of grammatical capacity in children. *J. verb. Learn. verb. Behav.*, 1963, **2**, 429–439.

Menyuk, P., *Sentences children use*. Cambridge, Mass.: M.I.T. Press, 1969.

Menyuk, P., *The acquisition and development of language*. Englewood Cliffs, N.J.: Prentice-Hall, 1971.

Menyuk, P., and S. Anderson, Children's identification and reproduction of the speech sounds /w/, /r/, and /l/. *J. Speech & Hearing Res.*, 1969, **12**, 39–52.

Messer, S., Implicit phonology in children. *J. verb. Learn. verb. Behav.*, 1967, **6**, 600–613.

Mikes, M., Acquisition des catégoires grammaticales dans le langage de l'enfant. *Enfance*, 1967, **20**, 289–298.

Mikes, M., Mondattani univerzálék a gyermeknyelvben. *A Hungarológiai Intézet Tudományos Közleményei* (Novi Sad-Újvidék), 1971, **8**.

Mikes, M., and L. Matijevics, Jegyzetek az alső mondatok szültéséről a gyermeknyelvben. *Magyar Nyelv.*, 1971, **3**.

Mikeš, M., and P. Vlahović, Razvoj gramatičkih kategorija u dečjem govoru. *Prilozi proučavanju jezika, II*. Novi Sad, Yugoslavia, 1966.

Miller, W. R., The acquisition of formal features of language. *Amer. J. Orthopsychiat.*, 1963, **34**, 862–867.

Miller, W. R., The acquisition of grammatical rules by children. Paper read at meeting of Linguistic Society of America, New York, 1964. (a) [Printed in this volume.]

Miller, W. R., Patterns of grammatical development in child language. *Proceedings of the Ninth International Congress of Linguists, Cambridge, Mass., 1962*. The Hague: Mouton, 1964. Pp. 511–518. (b)

Miller, W. R., and S. M. Ervin, The development of grammar in child language. In U. Bellugi and R. Brown (eds.), The acquisition of language. *Monogr. Soc. Res. Child Developm.*, 1964, **29** (1), 9–33. [Reprinted in this volume.]

Miller, W. R., and S. M. Ervin-Tripp. *Development of grammar in child language*. New York: Holt, Rinehart and Winston, forthcoming.

Mowrer, O., *Learning theory and the symbolic process*. New York: Wiley, 1960.

Mukhina, V. S., *Bliznetzy*. Moscow: Prosveshcheniye, 1969.

Murai, J., *Gengo kinō no keisei to hattatsu*. Tokyo: Kazamashobo, 1970.

Murato, K., *Yoji no gengo hattatsu*. Tokyo: Baifukan, 1968.

Mussen, P. H. (ed.), *Carmichael's manual of child psychology*, 3d ed., 2 vols. New York: Wiley, 1970.

Nakazima, S., A comparative study of the speech developments of Japanese and American English in childhood (Part Three)—The reorganization process of babbling articulation mechanisms. *Studia phonologica*, 1969–70, **5**, 20–36.

Nazarov, A. N., Poryadok slov v pis'mennoy rechi uchashchikhsya. *Izv. Akad. Pedag. Nauk RSFSR*, 1954, **136**, 221–256.

Ohwaki, Y., Die ersten zwei Jahre der Sprachentwicklung des japanischen Kindes: Ein Beitrag zur Psychologie der Kindersprache. *Tohoku psychol. Folia*, 1933, **1**, 71–110.

Okubo, A., *Yoji gengo no hattatsu*. Tokyo: Tokyodo, 1967.

Olds, H. F., An experimental study of syntactical factors influencing children's comprehension of certain complex relationships. Rept. No. 4, Harvard Center for Res. & Developm. on Educational Differences, 1968.

Oller, D. K., The effect of position-in-utterance and word length on speech segment duration. Unpubl. paper, Depts. of Psychol. and Ling., Univer. Texas, 1971.

Olmsted, D. L., A theory of the child's learning phonology. *Language*, 1966, **42**, 531–535.

Omar, M. K., The acquisition of Egyptian Arabic as a native language. Unpubl. doct. dissert., Georgetown Univer., 1970. [To be published by Mouton.]

Pačesová, J., *The development of vocabulary in the child*. Brno: Univer. J. E. Purkyně, 1968.

Parisi, D., *Il linguaggio come processo cognitivo*. Torino: Boringhieri, in press.

Parisi, D., and F. Antinucci, Lexical competence. In G. B. Flores d'Arcais and W. J. M. Levelt (eds.), *Advances in psycholinguistics*. Amsterdam: North-Holland, 1970. Pp. 197–210.

Park, Tschang-Zin, Language acquisition in a Korean child. Working Paper, Psychologisches Institut, Univer. Münster, Germany, 1969.

Park, Tschang-Zin, The acquisition of German syntax. Working Paper, Psychologisches Institut, Univer. Münster, Germany, 1970.

Pavlova, A. D., *Dnevnik materi*. Moscow, 1924.

Pavlovitch, M., *Le langage enfantin: Acquisition du serbe et du français par un enfant serbe*. Paris: Champion, 1920.

Pfanhauser, S. B., Rozwój mowy dziecka. *Prace filol.*, 1930, **15**, 273–356.

Piaget, J., *La formation du symbole chez l'enfant: Imitation, jeu et rève, image et représentation*. Neuchâtel: Delachaux et Niestlé, 1946. [English translation: *Play, dreams and imitation in childhood*. New York: Norton, 1951.]

Piaget, J., *Six psychological studies*. New York: Vintage Books, 1967.

Piaget, J., Piaget's theory. In P. H. Mussen (ed.), *Carmichael's manual of child psychology*, 3d ed., Vol. 1. New York: Wiley, 1970. Pp. 703–732.

Pichevin, C., L'acquisition de la compétence entre 2 et 4 ans: Problèmes de recherche. *Psychol. Française*, 1968, **13**, 175–196.

Pike, E. G., Controlled infant intonation. *Language Learning*, 1949, **2**, 21–24.

Politzer, R., *Teaching French*, 2d ed. New York: Blaisdell, 1965.

Popova, M. I., Grammaticheskiye elementy yazyka v rechi detey preddoshkol'nogo vozrasta. *Vopr. psikhol.*, 1958, **4** (3), 106–117. [English translation: Grammatical elements of language in the speech of pre-preschool children. Printed in this volume.]

Premack, D., A functional analysis of language. *J. exp. Anal. Behav.*, 1970, **14**, 107–125.

Premack, D., Language in chimpanzee? *Science*, 1971, **172**, 808–822.

Průcha, J., K teorii osvojováná jazyka u dětí předškolního a školního věku. *Pedagogika*, 1971, **21**, 529–539.

Radulović, L., Forthcoming doctoral dissertation on the acquisition of Serbo-Croatian. Univer. Calif., Berkeley.

Rasmussen, V., *Barnets sjælige udvikling in de første fire aar*. Copenhagen/Christiana: Gyldendal, 1913. [English translation: *Child psychology*, Vol. 1. London: Gyldendal, 1920/New York: Knopf, 1923.]

Rasmussen, V., *Et barns dagbog*. Copenhagen/Christiana: Gyldendal, 1922.

Ravem, R., Language acquisition in a second language environment. *Internatl. Rev. appl. Ling.*, 1968, **6**, 175–185.

Ravem, R., The development of wh-questions in first and second language learners. *Occasional Papers*, No. 8, Language Centre, University of Essex, Colchester, 1970.

Roeper, T., Theoretical implications of word order, topicalization, and inflections in German language acquisition. Printed in this volume (1972). (a)

Roeper, T., Approaches to acquisition theory, with data from German children. Unpubl. doct. dissert., Harvard Univer., 1972. (b)

Rosenbaum, P. S., *The grammar of English predicate complement constructions*. Cambridge, Mass.: M.I.T. Press, 1967.

Ross, J. R., On declarative sentences. In R. A. Jacobs and P. S. Rosenbaum (eds.), *Readings in English transformational grammar*. Waltham, Mass.: Ginn, 1970. Pp. 222–272.

Rozengart–Pupko, G. L., *Rech' i razvitiye vospriyatiya v rannem vozraste.* Moscow: Izd-vo Akad. Med. Nauk SSSR, 1948.

Rūķe-Draviņa, V., Zur Entstehung der Flexion in der Kindersprache: Ein Beitrag auf der Grundlage des lettischen Sprachmaterials. *Internatl. J. Slavic Ling. & Poetics*, 1959, **1/2**, 201–222. [English translation: On the emergence of inflection in child language: A contribution based on Latvian speech data. Printed in this volume.]

Rūķe-Draviņa, V., *Zur Sprachentwicklung bei Kleinkindern: Beitrag auf der Grundlage lettischen Sprachmaterials. 1. Syntax.* Lund: Slaviska Institutionen vid Lunds Universitet, 1963.

Sanches, M., Features in the acquisition of Japanese grammar. Unpub. doct. dissert., Stanford Univer., 1968.

Sanches, M., Language acquisition and language change: Japanese numeral classifiers. Paper read at Annu. Mtg., Amer. Anthrop. Assoc., San Diego, Calif., 1970.

Schane, S. A., *French phonology and morphology.* Cambridge, Mass.: M.I.T. Press, 1968.

Schlesinger, H. S., and K. P. Meadow, *Deafness and mental health: A developmental approach.* San Francisco: Langley Porter Neuropsychiatric Institute, 1971.

Schlesinger, I. M., Production of utterances and language acquisition. In D. I. Slobin (ed.), *The ontogenesis of grammar: A theoretical symposium.* New York: Academic Press, 1971. Pp. 63–101.

Scholes, R. J., *Phonotactic grammaticality.* The Hague: Mouton, 1966.

Scholes, R. J., and P. F. Grossman, Utterance imitation by Hebrew-speaking children. In *Studies presented to Archibald A. Hill*, forthcoming.

Scupin, E., and G. Scupin, *Bubis erste Kindheit: Ein Tagebuch.* Leipzig: Grieben, 1907.

Sedláčková, E., *Development of the acoustic pattern of the voice and speech in the newborn and infant.* Prague: Academia Nakladatelství Ceskoslovenské Akademie Věd (Řada Matematických a Přírodních Věd, Ročnik 77—Sešit 10), 1967.

Shipley, E., C. S. Smith, and L. Gleitman, A study in the acquisition of language: Free response to commands. *Language*, 1969, **45**, 322–342.

Shugar, G. W., Personal communication re study of Polish acquisition, January 31, 1971.

Shvachkin, N. Kh. Psikhologicheskiy analiz rannikh suzhdeniy rebenka. *Izv. Akad. Pedag. Nauk RSFSR*, 1954, **54**, 111–135.

Simonyi, Z., Két gyermek nyelvéről. *Magyar Nyelvŏr*, 1906, **35**, 317–323.

Sinclair-de-Zwart, H., *Acquisition du langage et développement de la pensée.* Paris: Dunod, 1967.

Sinclair-de-Zwart, H., Developmental psycholinguistics. In D. Elkind and J. H. Flavell (eds.), *Studies in cognitive development: Essays in honor of Jean Piaget.* New York: Oxford Univer. Press, 1969. Pp. 315–336.

Skorupka, S., Obserwacje nad językiem dziecka. *Sprawozdania z posiedzeń*

Komisji Językowej Towarzystwa Naukowego Warszawskiego, Vol. 3. Warsaw, 1949.

Slama-Cazacu, T., *Relaţiile dintre gîndire şi limbaj în ontogeneză* (3–7 *ani*). Bucharest: Ed. Acad. R.P.R., 1957.

Slama-Cazacu, T., Aspecte ale relaţiilor dintre gîndire şi limbaj in însuşirea structurii gramaticale de către copiii ante-preşcolari (2–3 ani). *Rev. Psihol.*, 1960, **6** (2), 43–63.

Slama-Cazacu, T., The oblique cases in the evolution of child language. *Revue de Linguistique*, 1962, **7** (1), 71–85.

Slama-Cazacu, T., *Introducere în psiholingvistică*. Bucharest: Ed. Ştiinţifică, 1968.

Slama-Cazacu, T., Studiile europene asupra limbajului copilului (1920–1968). IV: Bibliografie. *Studii şi cercetăre lingvistice*, 1968, **20**, 479–508.

Slobin, D. I., Grammatical development in Russian-speaking children. In K. Riegel (ed.), *The development of language functions*. Ann Arbor, Mich.: Univer. Mich. Lang. Developm. Program, Rept. No. 8, 1965. Pp. 93–101. [Reprinted in A. Bar-Adon and W. F. Leopold (eds.), *Child language: A book of readings*. Englewood Cliffs, N. J.: Prentice-Hall, 1971. Pp. 344–348.]

Slobin, D. I., Abstracts of Soviet studies of child language. In F. Smith and G. A. Miller (eds.), *The genesis of language: A psycholinguistic approach*. Cambridge, Mass.: M.I.T. Press, 1966. Pp. 361–386. (a)

Slobin, D. I., The acquisition of Russian as a native language. In F. Smith and G. A. Miller (eds.), *The genesis of language: A psycholinguistic approach*. Cambridge, Mass.: M.I.T. Press, 1966. Pp. 129–148. (b)

Slobin, D. I., Grammatical transformations and sentence comprehension in childhood and adulthood. *J. verb. Learn. verb. Behav.*, 1966, **5**, 219–227. (c)

Slobin, D. I., Soviet psycholinguistics. In N. O'Connor (ed.), *Present-day Russian psychology: A symposium by seven authors*. Oxford: Pergamon, 1966. Pp. 109–151. (d)

Slobin, D. I. (ed.), *A field manual for cross-cultural study of the acquisition of communicative competence*. Berkeley, Calif.: Univer. Calif. ASUC Bookstore, 1967.

Slobin, D. I., Imitation and grammatical development in children. In N. S. Endler, L. R. Boulter, and H. Osser (eds.), *Contemporary issues in developmental psychology*. New York: Holt, Rinehart and Winston, 1968. Pp. 437–443. (a)

Slobin, D. I., Recall of full and truncated passive sentences in connected discourse. *J. verb. Learn. verb. Behav.*, 1968, **7**, 876–881. (b)

Slobin, D. I., Early grammatical development in several languages, with special attention to Soviet research. Working Paper No. 11, Language-Behavior Res. Lab., Univer. Calif., Berkeley, 1968. (c)

Slobin, D. I., Questions of language development in cross-cultural perspective. In K. Drach *et al.*, The structure of linguistic input to children. Working Paper No. 14, Language-Behavior Res. Lab., Univer. Calif., Berkeley, 1969. (a)

Slobin, D. I. (ed.), Special issue on Soviet psycholinguistics. *Soviet Psychol.*, 1969, **7**, (3). (b)

Slobin, D. I., Universals of grammatical development in children. In G. B. Flores d'Arcais and W. J. M. Levelt (eds.), *Advances in psycholinguistics.* Amsterdam: North-Holland, 1970. Pp. 174–186.

Slobin, D. I., On the learning of morphological rules: A reply to Palermo and Eberhart. In D. I. Slobin (ed.), *The ontogenesis of grammar: A theoretical symposium.* New York: Academic Press, 1971. Pp. 215–223. (a)

Slobin, D. I. (ed.), *The ontogenesis of grammar: A theoretical symposium.* New York: Academic Press, 1971. (b)

Slobin, D. I., *Psycholinguistics.* Glenview, Ill.: Scott, Foresman, 1971. (c)

Slobin, D. I., *Leopold's bibliography of child language*, revised and augmented edition. Bloomington, Ind.: Ind. Univer. Press, 1972.

Slobin, D. I., and C. A. Welsh, Elicited imitation as a research tool in developmental psycholinguistics. Printed in this volume.

Smith, C. S., An experimental approach to children's linguistic competence. In J. R. Hayes (ed.), *Cognition and the development of language.* New York: Wiley, 1970. Pp. 109–135. [Reprinted in this volume.]

Smith, F., and G. A. Miller, *The genesis of language: A psycholinguistic approach.* Cambridge, Mass.: M.I.T. Press, 1966.

Smith, K. H., and M. D. S. Braine, Miniature languages and the problem of language acquisition. In T. G. Bever and W. Weksel (eds.), *The structure and psychology of language.* New York: Holt, Rinehart and Winston, in press.

Smith, K. H., and L. E. McMahon, Understanding order information in sentences. In G. B. Flores d'Arcais and W. J. M. Levelt (eds.), *Advances in psycholinguistics.* Amsterdam: North-Holland, 1970. Pp. 253–274.

Smoczyński, P., *Przyswajanie przez dziecko podstaw systemu językowego.* Lodz: Łódzkie Towarzystwo Naukowe, Wydział 1, 1955, (No. 19).

Snyder, A. D., Notes on the talk of a two-and-a-half-year-old boy. *Pedag. Seminary*, 1914, **21**, 412–424.

Söderbergh, R., *Reading in early childhood: A linguistic study of a Swedish preschool child's gradual acquisition of reading ability.* Stockholm: Almqvist & Wiksell, 1971.

Sokhin, F. A., O formirovanii yazykovykh obobshcheniy v protsesse rechevogo razvitiya. *Vopr. psikhol.*, 1959, **5** (5), 112–123.

Solberg, M., Doct. dissert. on Quechuan acquisition, Cornell Univer., 1971.

Solov'yeva, O. I., *Metodika razvitiye rechi i obucheniya rodnomu yazyku v detskom sadu.* Moscow: Uchpedgiz, 1960.

Spolsky, B. [Study of spoken Navaho of six-year-old children.] Noted in *Computers and the Humanities*, 1970, **5**, 110–101.

Staats, A. W., Linguistic-mentalistic theory versus an explanatory S-R learning theory of language development. In D. I. Slobin (ed.), *The ontogenesis of grammar: A theoretical symposium.* New York: Academic Press, 1971. Pp. 103–150.

Stern, C., and W. Stern, *Die Kindersprache: Eine psychologische und sprach-theoretische Untersuchung.* Leipzig: Barth, 1907. (4th, rev. ed., 1928).

Stross, B., Language acquisition by Tenejapa Tzeltal children. Unpubl. doct. dissert., Univer. Calif., Berkeley, 1969. [Working Paper No. 21 (1969), Language-Behavior Res. Lab., Univer, Calif., Berkeley.]

Stross, B., Elicited imitations in the study of Tenejapa Tzeltal language acquisition. *Anthrop. Ling.*, 1970, **12**, 319–325.

Szuman, S. (ed.), *O rozwoju języka i myślenia dziecka.* Warsaw: Państwowe Wydawnictwo Naukowe, 1968.

Talmy, L., Semantic-componentry and Samoan acquisition. Working Paper No. 35, Language-Behavior Res. Lab., Univer. Calif., Berkeley, 1970.

Tarnóczy, T., Resonance data concerning nasals, laterals and trills. *Word*, 1948, **4**, 71–77.

Templin, M., *Certain language skills in children.* Univer. Minn. Inst. Child Welfare Monogr., No. 26, 1957.

Tischler, H., Schreien, Lallen und erstes Sprechen in der Entwicklung des Säuglings. *Z. Psychol.*, 1957, **160**, 210–263.

Troubetzkoy, N. S., *Principes de phonologie.* Paris: 1949. [French translation of *Grundzüge der Phonologie.* Prague, 1939.]

Turner, E. A., and R. Rommetveit, The acquisition of sentence voice and reversibility. *Child Developm.*, 1967, **38**, 649–660.

Tutundzhyan, O. M., Issledovatel'skaya rabota po detskoy i pedagogicheskoy psikhologii v Armenii. *Vopr. psikhol.*, 1971, **17**, (3), 132–137. [Eng. transl.: Investigations of educational and child psychology in Armenia. *Soviet Psychol.*, 1971–72, **10**, 113–127.]

Ushakova, T. N., O prichinakh detskogo slovotvorchestva. *Vopr. psikhol.*, 1970, **16** (6), 114–127. [Eng. transl.: Causes of children's word invention (A psychophysiological model of the genesis of the syntactically structured verbal utterance). *Soviet Psychol.*, 1971–72, **10**, 155–177.]

Velten, H. V., The growth of phonemic and lexical patterns in infant language. *Language*, 1943, **19**, 281–292.

Vihman, M. M., On the acquisition of Estonian. *Papers and Reports on Child Language Development* (Committee on Ling., Stanford Univer.), 1971, No. 3, 51–94.

Voegelin, C. F., and F. M. Voegelin, Index to languages of the world. *Anthrop. Ling.*, 1966, **8**, (6–7).

Vygotsky, L. S., *Thought and language.* Cambridge, Mass./New York: M.I.T. Press and Wiley, 1962. [English translation of *Myshleniye i rech'.* Moscow: Sotzekgiz, 1934.]

Ward, D., *Russian pronunciation.* New York: Hafner, 1958.

Watt, W. C., On two hypotheses concerning psycholinguistics. In J. R. Hayes (ed.), *Cognition and the development of language.* New York: Wiley, 1970. Pp. 137–220.

Wawrowska, W., Badania psychologiczne nad rozwojem mowy dziecka (od 1,0–2,3 lat). *Prace psychol.* (Warsaw), 1938, **1**.

Weir, R. H., *Language in the crib*. The Hague: Mouton, 1962.

Weir, R. H., Questions on the learning of phonology. In F. Smith and G. A. Miller (eds.), *The genesis of language: A psycholinguistic approach*. Cambridge, Mass.: M.I.T. Press, 1966, Pp. 153–168.

Werner, H., and B. Kaplan, *Symbol formation*. New York: Wiley, 1963.

Werner, H., and E. Kaplan, The acquisition of word meanings: A developmental study. *Monogr. Soc. Res. Child Developm.*, 1952, **15** (1).

Zakharova, A. V., Usvoyeniye doshkol'nikami padezhnykh form. *Dokl. Akad. Pedag. Nauk RSFSR*, 1958, **2** (3), 81–84. [English translation: Acquisition of forms of grammatical case by preschool children. Printed in this volume.]

Zarębina, M. *Kształtowanie się systemu językowego dziecka*. Wrocław-Warszawa-Kraków, 1965.

Zlatoustova, L. V., [Duration of vowel and consonant sounds of the Russian language.] *Uch. zap. Kazan'skogo Gos. Univer. im. V. I. Ul'yanova-Lenina*, 1954, **114** (6), 99–123. [Cited in Oller, 1971. See L. V. Zlatoustova, *Foneticheskaya struktura slova v potoke rechi*. Kazan', 1962.]